GREEN BUTTERFLIES

A LIFE STORY of PTSD, CHRONIC PAIN, DEPRESSION, ANXIETY, ISOLATION

... and TRANSFORMATION

STEVE DiGROSSI

Printed in the United States of America

Cover Concept and Design by Steve DiGrossi

Edit by Jody Mabry

ACKNOWLEDGEMENTS

A very special thank you to my editor, Jody Mabry, for taking my voice — my words — and ever so gently polishing my grammatical errors. For adding a few stop signs along my road of run-on sentences! For formatting the interior layout for publication and going above and beyond professionally and personally with this project. I've met an exceptional person in Jody through this process that I am proud to call a new friend.

JD for motivating me to finally write this story.

My aunts, uncles, cousins, and few close friends who are my true "family". The people who will always have my back. Who have supported me through my most recent, deepest darkness and worst of pain; the loss of my beloved mother to cancer in June of 2015, several months after completing the first draft of this book.

Grazie to my father for finally, after ninety years on this planet, seeing — and admitting — the truth. Too often, we don't know what we've got until it's gone, or see the light until it blinds us. It's better late than never, dad.

A huge thank you to Christine for being my "little sister" and the daughter my mother always deserved.

A super-special "woof" to my boy, Max, for being the shadow that never left my side. For sticking to me like glue during my darkest hours. For teaching me to appreciate and enjoy the simple things in life. For helping me to smile through my pain.

Finally, and most importantly, from the core of my heavy heart, I thank my dear mother, Olivia ("Lee"), for always being the light in my life and the life in my soul. For showing me what love is and what honor means. Without your love, encouragement, and words of wisdom throughout my life, I wouldn't be here today and able to fulfill my life's meaning of helping others, beginning with this very book. I am eternally with you as you are with me. I love you always and forever, mom. SYOTOS.

DEDICATION

This book is dedicated to the memory of my beloved mother, Olivia.

AUTHOR'S NOTE

Out of respect for their privacy, I have changed or omitted the names of people who appear on the following pages.

In staying true to myself, I neither pull punches nor do I sugarcoat the reality of my life. It is the truth as I've lived it. It has been a far cry from pretty. Light-years from easy. It is a journey I often refer to as pure evil.

However, as I scratch the surface of that journey and offer the reader — my audience — a glimpse into my world through the pages of this story, always know:

> *"There is light at the end of even the blackest of tunnels.*
> *Defy the darkness.*
> *Push forward.*
> *Never surrender."*

— *Steve DiGrossi*

PREFACE

4 Green Butterflies is the eye-opening life story of *Steve DiGrossi* and his 45-year war with PTSD, chronic pain, depression, anxiety, isolation, and — ultimately and rather remarkably — his enlightening transformation.

Steve is a streetwise and college-educated, exercise and martial arts-addicted son of a New England mobster. He lived every minute of every day, his entire life, at the mercy of these disorders. This story chronicles Steve's life, beginning with his cultural background from the early days of his grandparents and parents, and continues through 45 years of an unrelenting living hell, concluding just prior to Christmas 2014. It was then that he underwent a miraculous transformation coupled with the most earth-shattering, crushing news and emotional electrocution Steve has ever had to endure.

Traumatized from childhood by alcoholism and addiction within his dysfunctional family, bullied throughout boyhood, and betrayed time and again as an adult, Steve pushed on to become a state trooper. All the while, he battled the daily demons of PTSD, depression, anxiety, and isolation. These struggles began at the age of five, and would continue, uninterrupted, for the next 45 years.

Steve would soon be physically disabled in the line of duty and immediately prior to moving to a federal position with the Drug Enforcement Administration (DEA) — a dream since childhood, draped on the hope of saving others (and the emotionally-battered child inside of him) from the perils and casualties of drug addiction.

A life-altering spinal injury snuffed out his only medication — his addiction to training — his only outlet, his only means of escape from the emotional imprisonment of these horrendous disorders. He was left with the never-ending emotional pain and devastation of the past, multiplied many times over by this point, but now, for the past 18 years, living with endless, excruciating, physical pain and mobility issues.

This is a life that went from bad to worse, each and every year of his pitch-black, completely unbalanced, godforsaken existence — a dark cloud forever hovering above, never a blink of sunshine. His mother — the only warmth and love in that perpetual, frigid darkness; the only positive force and light that had ever seeped through the perennial gloom that smothered all of his days. She was the sole source of strength pulling him back from the ledge over the many decades of ceaseless torment and hopelessness.

Finally, after 40-plus years of unremitting, torturous pain and despair, a transformation begins; a loosening of the noose, a partial release from the death-grip of these disorders. Like a phoenix rising from the ashes, clarity and meaning in his life is at long last found and being fulfilled by doing his part. Through his story, Steve is reaching out to as many people as he can. People who suffer with these disorders — and those who love them. He hopes to connect with, and help prevent each person from going through the depths of hell he has endured, without reprieve, for over four decades; that diabolical darkness that is each and every one of these disorders.

However, with never so much as a minuscule possibility of a lull in a life plagued by pain, suffering, despair, and consistent bad luck, there would be no peace now either. Within months of his resurrection, Steve's beloved mother is diagnosed with terminal cancer. Above all else he's endured in his life, this news — his mother's mortality — shook him the hardest and most violently. His mother has been the lone anchor in that savage sea of mayhem that has been his world. His anchor in that bitterly cold, deep and dark sea of disorders was now slowly being raised and taken from him.

As he'd lost his ability to train — his medication — many years earlier, he was now faced with losing the linchpin that kept that final seam intact and from bursting throughout his entire life. He must now draw upon all that he's learned from over four decades of crawling through the bowels of hell and the past year of his recovery and transformation, accept and prepare for the final, furthermost depth of that infernal abyss he had been banished to since the age of five.

My mission, post-publishing this book, is to establish and bring support groups for those suffering with emotional disorders such as PTSD and depression, as well as chronic physical pain, to the forefront. My ultimate goal is to do for those suffering with PTSD, depression, and anxiety what Bill Wilson and Dr. Bob Smith did for alcoholics beginning in 1935 with Alcoholics Anonymous (AA). As support groups and meetings for recovering alcoholics offer necessary and life-saving support in that area of recovery, I know firsthand the importance and need for these very type of support groups for those of us suffering from these debilitating emotional disorders.

I envision this book being a required read in every college intro to psychology class. It's that important in the world of emotional disorders. I have no doubt that once published, many of you who suffer with these disorders — ranging from regular folk just like me to influential politicians, celebrities, and business people — will get on board with the book and my goal of establishing readily available and life-saving AA-like support groups across the country.

This story is the first of several books to come, and the first step in bringing those of us suffering, together, to help ourselves and one another, just as AA does for alcoholics.

4 Green Butterflies is a true-life story and springboard that can, and will, change and save lives. It is the beginning of my life's meaning.

Steve DiGrossi

INTRODUCTION

The major regrets in my life — all of which I had no control over — are a direct result of childhood PTSD (Post Traumatic Stress Disorder), adult PTSD, clinical depression, chronic pain, anxiety, and the isolation and crippling emotional collapse that spawned from these disorders.

I have been at the mercy of severe and incapacitating disorders that took control of nearly every aspect of my life beginning at the age of five. I have endured a 40-plus year war with PTSD, severe depression, and paralyzing generalized and social anxiety which directly led to my avoiding everything possible — including the most important people in my life. These disorders prevented me from being at family get-togethers, social events and, ultimately, from achieving many of my goals and dreams.

PTSD extracted the child from my childhood and became even more dominant in my later teen years. By the time I was in my twenties, I was suffering with immobilizing major depression and isolating myself from everyone and everything — becoming progressively distant with each passing year. I was experiencing frequent and intense anxiety and panic attacks, dreadful outbreaks of sweating while in social settings, my heart feeling like it would burst from my chest — that cold, dark cloud constantly hovering above me, with incessant feelings of gloom and doom.

I lost faith in everything I once believed in. I was becoming increasingly irritable and angry with each passing day. I would re-experience events and feelings of the past that I could not escape. I couldn't find an ounce of joy or happiness anywhere in my life and began to isolate myself more and more, avoiding all contact at all costs; subconsciously creating distance in order to survive.

Isolation equated to self-preservation throughout my life. My refuge was, ironically, both my sanctuary and my prison.

The only thing that kept my keel half even was my focus on health and training — weight training and martial arts. This was my positive addiction, my one and only drug. It was my outlet, my escape, and my savior. Training became the armor that protected me from the reality of my life.

To this day, I have never so much as tasted alcohol, nor have I taken drugs — ever! After all, my childhood PTSD was in large part a direct result of my brother's alcohol and drug addiction. I saw what it did to my mother and the evil of that enslavement. The effects of these two diseases are calamitous and far-reaching.

My training was what allowed me to get through each day of my life. It lasted from when I began focusing on exercise and martial arts at the age of 12 until a combination of completely life-altering and physically debilitating accidents beginning a couple decades later. For some 20-plus years I trained each day of my life.

Routinely, I worked out two to three times a day. I logged hours upon hours of training every day, with martial arts, boxing, weight training, running, and everything else in between. Each day was dedicated to the discipline that shielded me from insanity.

This was the sole link to my mental stability and the only reason I was able to function at all. These disorders prevented me from "firing on all cylinders" and kept me far from functioning at 100% of my capacity.

My training enabled the endorphin kick necessary to temporarily (mostly measured in hours) correct the chemical imbalances of the brain responsible for pain and depression caused by the disorders which incapacitated me emotionally.

Constant, and intense training would carry me from hour-to-hour, sometimes day-to-day, but was no match in eradicating these fully constraining disorders. These conditions and the resulting isolation sidelined my life and disconnected me from everything that meant anything to me, including my family — specifically my aunts, uncles, and cousins.

When I say my family (aunts, uncles, and cousins), I am referring mostly to my mother's brothers, sisters, in-laws, nieces and nephews and their children, whom I've never met as a result of these disorders. My father was an only child.

These are wonderful, kind, and loving people who mean the world to me. I had no idea how to reach out to any of them to either seek help or try and explain my feelings, the pain, and the darkness that was my life. I truly didn't understand my emotions at the time either. However, I did know there was something very wrong. I didn't feel right emotionally and it was getting worse with time.

People around me — including family and friends — saw perhaps a cocky and bold kid with a tough exterior. I put on a good game face my entire life in order to survive. I was not the person on the inside that I would have you believe from my exterior. Behind that mask — that persona — I was falling apart. I was lost and confused. I lacked confidence and self-esteem. I felt worthless. I was drowning in a sea of sadness, fear, and doubt; weighted down and pulled under by persistent pain and anger. My life was completely void of balance, harmony, and peace of mind. I was becoming more and more entangled in a web of despair.

I had no one to talk to. No one knew the turmoil, trauma, and the emotionally crippling pain and fear I had endured from the age of five, witnessing an alcohol and drug addicted brother, day in and day out, for too many years of my childhood. He was ripping my family apart and tearing my mother's heart from her chest. I watched, time and again, my mother screaming and crying because she didn't want her addict son to die. Instead, for years, I was traumatized while listening to the arguing, the crying, the screaming, witnessing the drug rages, and explosive, violent behavior of an addict and all the repercussions that come from living with an addict.

I would hide in my room most times — curled up behind the door, or deep under the covers of my bed — and shake with fear. I remember times when I would grab onto my mother's leg and squeeze as tight as I could. I didn't want to let go.

I was terrified and didn't want to lose the one person I knew loved and cared for me in this world — my mother. I didn't want to see her this way. I didn't want to hear her screaming and crying. It was absolute chaos.

No one knew what this was doing to me — not even my mother — and the trauma would result in childhood PTSD that would emotionally impair me more and more as time went on and incidents were remembered and relived, some over and over and over again.

I had a father who was neglectful and ineffectual as both a husband and a parent. I would come to understand much later in life that *his* behavior was not intentional nor malicious. It was what nature and nurture had made him, resulting in very limited capacities in many areas. This, in addition to my father's alcoholism, contributed heavily to my childhood PTSD and the disorders which destroyed much of my life.

My mother was devastated from all angles, and in a maternal battle — alone — to save her oldest son from dying. I would endure this madness — also alone — for too many of my childhood years. No one ever realizing what this was doing — or did, to me.

🦋 🦋 🦋 🦋

My mother's oldest son, whose life she saved, has never, to this day, some 40-plus years later, said, "thank you" or "sorry," for his mother's sacrifices, pain, the river of tears she has cried, or the piece of her heart he has forever mangled. He never thanked her for the massive amount of money paid to attorneys, bail, treatments and rehabs, his racked-up bills and debts, caring for his daughter (her granddaughter) who was born to two addicts. He never apologized for trying to kill me (literally), her youngest son, or for the toll his addiction had taken on his mother's own life. There has been no expression of gratitude ever shown. Always an attitude of entitlement.

🦋 🦋 🦋 🦋

I'm sure some of my aunts and uncles, among others, knew there was a problem with my brother. My mother did her best to hide the truth of the matter, which is a common, codependent behavioral pattern within the dysfunctional family of an alcoholic and/or addict. I'm also sure no one had any idea what the extent of his addiction was, what I was going through, and what would result from my having to witness and endure this madness for so many years of my childhood. It all happened in the very home where I had the right to feel safe and protected, where I had the right to create joyful childhood memories.

It is said that life is not measured by the number of breaths we take, but by the moments that take our breath away. Those moments in my life have not been happy moments, but they certainly took my breath away, time and again. Many of those memories play over and over on the reel of my mind tormenting every fiber of my being.

This trauma would follow me into my 30's, paralyzing me emotionally and keeping me in isolation, distancing me from all and everything that meant anything to me. I missed scores of weddings, parties, and get-togethers I had been invited to over the years. I never showed at these cherished, celebratory events. My soul was crushed and bleeding from the weight of these disorders, their grip preventing me from living my life and sharing it with friends and family. I lost out on close friendships with good people, quality relationships, and strong family ties with those that meant the world to me, all due to these disorders and their control of my life. I don't think anyone had any idea

— in the slightest — what was going on in my life. I do believe most thought I was becoming antisocial, never realizing the life-changing disorders I was living with and the severity of those disorders.

If someone doesn't understand — truly understand — what PTSD and severe depression is, and what it does to a human being, along with its byproducts such as crippling anxiety and panic attacks, which I have suffered with since the age of five, that person cannot understand in the least what the first thirty years of my life had been like. In actuality, it is impossible for anyone to fully comprehend the control, detrimental effects, and overall devastation these disorders have on someone's life unless you have walked in the same shoes and lived with any of these disorders.

I was then involved in a line of duty accident as a state trooper in my 30's — and another very serious accident some years later. That was the beginning of the end for me. My cervical, lumbar, sacral, and coccyx sections of my spine were completely decimated. Now, in addition to the past 30 years of emotional suffering and torture, I had to endure what would become the worst blow to my life in every aspect imaginable; a spinal injury that would physically incapacitate me and leave me with chronic and crippling pain every minute of every day. Day in, and day out, year after miserable year, the pain and condition progressively worsening in every possible way.

I lost everything; my health (what was remaining of it), my career, goals and dreams, and any hope I may have been hanging onto by a thread. My belief in God — whom I would curse daily for years on end for afflicting me with endless emotional and physical torture, for not protecting me, for abandoning me, for allowing everything to be mercilessly snatched away from me. It was now *all* gone, replaced by chronic physical pain every minute of every day without fail. The constant fear of being totally paralyzed from any further jolt or impact to my spine. The inability to concentrate and focus, the inability to sleep, and the never-ending anger, anxiety, and isolation. Most importantly, I had now lost my only "drug," my only "medication," my only means to escape the emotional imprisonment of the past several decades. I had now lost 95% of my ability to train. My spine was too far gone to so much as lean the wrong way. There are days when I cannot stand. Days when I cannot sit. Days when I cannot move at all. I no longer had the one positive addiction — my outlet — that enabled me to cope and move on from day to day, year to year, my entire life.

Training was my needle. My bottle. My pill. It was my escape route, and was now gone. My lifeline severed.

I lost my first engine during my childhood. Now, my second and last engine, had been wiped out. I began a free fall plunge into the abyss, eventually shattering into a million pieces upon hitting its bottom in the furthest regions of an unfathomable hell.

Numerous orthopedic doctors and spine surgeons had informed me that the damage to my spine was some of the most extensive and complicated they had seen. Most couldn't believe I was able to stand and to walk. A strong, well-developed core from years of dedicated, and intense training assists in my ability to stand and walk on most days. However, whether standing, sitting, walking, and often laying, the pain is incessant and excruciating. The pain, along with mobility issues, continues to spread and worsen with each passing year.

Each spine specialist had conveyed to me the very real possibility of paralysis. There isn't much that is more frightening and anxiety producing than knowing you may very well be paralyzed, and it can happen at any time. Let alone to someone whose life revolved around training. That training was my only link to sanity in many ways.

I was told for years by many doctors and psychiatrists that I would not survive the major depression and chronic pain if I didn't begin to take medication.

Having lived through, and having been scarred deeply by the horrors of addiction, I've had a very strong aversion to any type of drug — whether prescription or illicit, as well as alcohol since childhood. That repulsion has always kept me from medicating and the real possibility of becoming reliant on and under the control of any drug, regardless of my pain and condition. Somehow, and for some reason, I am still here. I am still breathing, still alive, still fighting, and still resisting the conventional and often habit-forming comfort of medication. I have no charge over this phobic repugnance towards even the meds with possible restorative benefits. I often find myself wondering how much — if anything — this has contributed to my losses over the years, ever aware of the toll that has been taken from decades of undeviating and horrific emotional and physical pain. I am always walking a very fine line between lucidity and madness; walking alone, *always* alone. forever in the shadows. I exist in complete blackness with no one to lean on or prop me up. There is no one around who understands — truly understands these disorders and my life as it has been for some 40-plus years. My emotional and physical pain is a constant reminder of all that I've lost, knowing that those who see me without being confined to a wheelchair, without being reliant on sucking oxygen from a hose, or feeding through a tube don't understand — can't possibly understand — I am suffering from very severe and devastating conditions that have torn my life to shreds for decades. In many respects, far beyond the disorders and disabilities of those you can actually see and easily identify.

I have never dealt well with death. The passing — or sickness — of those I love and care for is out-and-out anguished misery of yet another heart-crushing dimension.

Personally, I don't fear death. I've actually welcomed it most days of my existence. I have feared life. Eternal rest was a welcome alternative to the endless pain and suffering that was the only guarantee of my tomorrows. Day after day since the age of five, each new sunrise brought back only the perpetual darkness to my world. Never so much as a speck of rejuvenating light was allowed to enter for nearly 45 years. It has been a life shrouded by complete, unrelenting murk and imbalance.

I was 12-years-old when I first experienced the death of a loved one. My grandfather had passed. I remember my uncle *Lucio* calling my house to relay the news to my mother. I remember my mother breaking down and crying... deeply, painfully. I remember wrapping my arms around her to console her.

We cried together. We were there for each other. She is the only person in my life that has ever been there for me. There is no one in this life that means more to me than my mother. There never will be. Many times in my life when I felt I had enough of the pain and suffering, *heart* kept me breathing for the sake of my mother. She had been through unimaginable pain and sorrow in her life, I would never do anything that would hurt her — ever.

My mother dedicated her life to her family. She gave her heart, soul, and peace of mind in the interest of her three children and three grandchildren. Her oldest son and daughter, as well as her grandchildren (the grandchildren are not "children". They are

adults in their 30's and 40's and fully accountable for their actions and behavior) have disrespected, dishonored, and betrayed her.

These vile, cold-hearted, dregs of humanity shattered her heart to pieces and pushed an 83-year-old woman to the brink of a nervous breakdown.

These thoroughly despicable, "immediate" family members are yet another part of my life's curse — another handicap that has made my life that much more painful and miserable.

They are the antithesis of everything I believe in, everything I stand for, everything family is and should always be: undying loyalty, respect, honor, and trust; the very foundation of family and friendship. I would slit my own wrists before I betrayed a friend or family.

These are truly heartless, completely self-centered vultures. Many years, birthdays, and holidays have come and gone without a card, not a call, not a visit to their parents or grandparents from any of these ungrateful, blood-sucking parasites.

Of all the emotional and physical pain and loss I have weathered in my life, it pales in comparison to the pain I feel for my mother and the rage and deep-seated animosity I have felt towards these vermin for what they've done to my mother.

My mother is an angel. The most kind, giving, loving, selfless person you could ever meet. Anyone who knows her will tell you the same. She is also the strongest person I have ever known. I can't imagine how it must feel to give birth to children to whom you gave your heart and soul — who you lived for — who, in return, have treated you worse than a rabid dog. How it must feel when your only daughter, who lives 20 minutes away, doesn't call to say "hi" or "I love you," never stops by to kiss her mother's cheek and see if there is anything she can do for her now 87-year-old mother — as her mother did for her, her entire life.

I can't imagine how it must feel when your only daughter is probably the greatest disappointment of your life, your only granddaughter being a very close second.

How it must feel to realize your children and grandchildren — who you basically raised and gave as much love and nurturing to as your own children — your very own blood, are Satan incarnate.

Their treatment of their mother, their grandmother, is malevolent, immoral, and of the greatest of sins. The vile behavior and conduct towards her is disgraceful. It is inexcusable, unconscionable, and unforgivable.

I have disowned each of them for what they have done to my mother. In my eyes, each is a poisonous, stomach-turning, breathing mass of cancer. Having this swine as my immediate family is a greater curse than having lived the past 40-plus years of never-ending pain, suffering, and loss.

.... And that is how I once felt — and badly hurt — not so very long ago. It was an acid eroding me from within for far too many years. That intense hatred eating away at my soul every minute of every day. Destroying only my peace of mind. No one else's.

It took many years of psychotherapy and the cathartic process of writing my story to purge my soul of the deepest of angers and hatred in me.

That blistering rage and detestation has since been exorcised but I will never — can never — consider someone of this caliber friend or family, and have respect and love in my heart for this type of person.

I remember my father sitting at the table when that call came in. He never once said a word. No consolation. Nothing. He didn't even get up from the table.

The inability to express — to actually *feel* — compassion and empathy are just a couple of many of my father's impaired traits. It was one more ingredient — another part of the equation — fueling a firestorm of dysfunction within my immediate family.

On occasion, a glimmer of emotion would appear, but only as a result of my father's romancing the bottle. His drinking to drown his sorrows and to cope has, unfortunately, become worse at his present age of 89.

Alcoholism is a disease inherent on my father's side of the family. I had lived with, and suffered considerably, from the effects of this disease throughout my entire childhood — and to this very day.

I remember my grandfather's wake. The first, and last, wake I would ever attend. I remember running out of the funeral home crying, shaking, and terrified. This was barbaric. I loved this man and he's lying in a coffin; dead. What is the purpose of showing a loved one — dead — in a coffin? Why would anyone want to have their last memory of someone they love — dead — in a coffin? I vowed to never be part of this primitive ritual ever again.

I was in my 40's when my aunt *Adela* (Nov 22, 2007), uncle *Giorgio* (Jan 05, 2006), and uncle *Nico* (Feb 13, 2010) passed. I vividly remember each of the calls to me from my mother. She was completely crushed. Her love for her family is the glue that kept this woman together through all the gut-wrenching turmoil in her life. I grieved long and hard — as always, by myself — no one to talk to, and no way to express what I was feeling to anyone. I lamented not only because these people I loved so deeply were now gone, but because I never had the chance to tell them how much I truly loved and admired them. I never had the chance to tell them my story and the reasons I seemed to vanish from the family — from the face of the earth — over the past thirty years. Never being able to share with them the *truth* of my *childhood* and what those years of never-ending traumatic experiences had done to me. The *truth* of my *life* and the disorders that have crippled me emotionally and, many days, physically, and how these disorders and a physical disability controlled my every move to complete isolation and emotional imprisonment.

To my aunt, uncles, and grandparents that have since passed, you were the warmth and color in my childhood world of frigid blackness. You are now the lustrous and vitalizing stars of this healing midnight odyssey that influence and guide me.

My greatest regret is the decades of isolation I've endured as a result of these disorders which kept me from the most important, loved people in my life. Not being able to share with my family — my aunts, uncles, cousins, and a few very dear friends — what has gone on and what has gone wrong in my life for over four decades, and the very reasons why I seemed to evanesce into thin air.

I would tell them that not one day ever went by that I didn't think of them and wish I had been with them and part of my *family*, that I love them always, and miss them desperately. The few happy memories I have of this life were with my mother, grandparents, aunts, uncles, and cousins. Those few and far between soothing impressions of long ago are as precious to me as a cool spring is to the heart of a parched desert.

What I've had to endure in this lifetime I wouldn't wish on the worst of those who walk among us. It is evil; pure evil. And that God my mother has such strong belief and faith in — I have cursed *that* God in all ways, every day, for the many decades of my misery. *That* God I was taught at an early age may close one door, but will always open another. I had been sentenced to solitary confinement — emotional imprisonment with no doors and without sunshine — just a cold, hard reality of never-ending, chronic emotional and physical pain, and suffering my entire life.

I grew up believing in God — trusting in God — that we all have a special talent, some specific *meaning* in life. Could it be that some of us were put here to simply suffer? To do nothing but carry the cross day in and day out, for whatever reason, for whatever duration we can tolerate the crucifixion?

PTSD, chronic pain, depression, and anxiety all lead to isolation. Isolation saps the soul and weakens the mind. It has guided my life to within two steps of insanity. The complexity of this battle is mind-boggling and overbearing. The perfect storm of emotional paralysis and a physical disability that stunted my life, and halted my being.

The sooner these disorders are identified and addressed — support being a major key in battling and controlling these conditions — the better the chance to live a more fulfilling, less interned life. The longer and deeper one sinks into these disorders, the darker it becomes and the harder it is to climb out and find a blink of light.

I hope that my story — a life that has been plagued by never-ending physical and emotional pain and suffering for over four decades, without reprieve — can somehow inspire others who may be suffering with a physical disability and/or the disabling symptoms of any emotional disorder. You are not alone. You are not unique in your pain and suffering. There are all too many of us affected by these disorders, an overwhelming majority of which brought forth by traumatic events in our lives that we did not ask for. Most suffering terribly — alone — in darkness, draped by the stigma that overshadows our anguish.

For as long as I can remember I have lived with shame and embarrassment due to these disorders. This is just one factor that keeps those of us suffering with these disorders in the shadows and in darkness; hurting alone. Often hiding behind a mask — a public facade — concealing a living hell.

It took a lifetime for me to clearly understand that there is nothing to be ashamed of. No one at the mercy of these disorders chooses the trauma that scars their soul and unrelentingly haunts them to the core. These disorders cannot be willed away. It has been extremely grueling and near-impossible coping with and bearing the agony and grief created by these disorders, day in and day out over a lifetime.

Through this life journey of pain and despair it seemed, more often than not, that each arduous step I took forward always produced two lightning-quick steps backward. Suffering on a daily basis with PTSD, chronic pain, depression, anxiety and other disorders that torment your every thought leaves a person completely beaten down, broken, and despondent.

You believe — you come to know — that if it wasn't for bad luck, you'd have no luck at all. You believe you've been dealt the worst possible hand in this game of life. These disorders are all-consuming. They begin to eat you from the inside out.

More days than I care to remember I wanted to just give up and throw in the towel. I wanted to grip the extended hand of insanity and be led through that final step. At last, be done with it. Once and for all be at peace.

It would take everything I had, and then some, to continue forward — through what always seemed a losing battle against bone-crushing waves of pain and a sweeping tide of despair — to make it through the day. It is an exhausting and agonizing struggle to keep breathing when you are slowly drowning. Most times I was able to resurface and gain some composure not for myself but for the sake of my mother. Sometimes, in life, when you can't do for yourself, you must do for someone else. For me, that someone else was *always* my mother, and meant my surviving one more day.

In every part of this nightmarish journey, I crawled forward and always uphill, through the darkness, as others seemed to effortlessly walk in well-lit corridors in the direction of their life's meaning. As in a bad dream, I was in motion but made no headway. Arms stretched before me and blinded by chronic pain and depression, I kept searching for the door God was supposed to open as so many other doors, time and again, slammed shut before I could get both knees to the threshold.

This journey through the bowels of hell has lead me to a "*window*," a "*platform*" through which I can rant about a life that has been taken over and consumed by disorders that too many of us suffer with. Again, most of us alone, in silence. Through this window I can share my deepest secrets of a life of pain and suffering.

The story of my lifelong battle with PTSD, chronic, crippling pain, major depression, anxiety, and panic attacks. My experiences in life with bullying and betrayal and how this cut deep into my already bleeding soul.

I hope to shed light onto these unforgiving disorders. I want to touch the souls and open the eyes and hearts of those who may now, through my story, be able to recognize the characteristics and identify the signs and symptoms of these disorders. I want them to be in a position to help a loved one, a friend, a co-worker, another human being in need by offering support, encouragement, and unconditional love.

Through my story, I hope to provide inspiration and consolation for the many among us who suffer immeasurable pain and despair without remission.

If I can reach just one person who is suffering and let them know they are not alone. They are not unhinged or worthless. They are not weak, as their pain and suffering is very real. Their pain and suffering is no fault of their own. They did not choose the trauma which triggered the disorders that now cloak their lives and have completely smothered their spirit. If I can help just one person who is suffering in the clutches of any physical disability and/or emotional disorder — or provide insight to someone who may be able and willing to support and help that person — then my life of pain and loss may not have been entirely in vain. It would be a sliver of meaning finally found and fulfilled.

There is no greater gift that I can be given than being able to help another person from, or from going to the diabolical darkness that is each and every one of these disorders and has been my prison for over four decades.

I have been in a very bad place for a very long time. I have felt most days of my life that I have been appointed a sadistic life sentence of solitary confinement with no possibility of parole. I've lived an existence of emotional imprisonment where the illusory, impenetrable walls are much more restricting than their physical counterparts and close in on you much quicker; always feeling trapped, suffocating, awaiting slaughter. With each passing year, falling apart at the seams and feeling each stitch as it begins to burst. Always two steps from insanity.

I have been dealt some very shitty cards in this game of life. I can count on one hand the times I have felt true joy and happiness over the years. The times I have smiled. My world feeling like a very cruel joke, a curse in many ways. The odds truly stacked against me. My life's scale forever tilted by sheer darkness.

I wouldn't wish upon my worst of enemies, even for one day, the relentless pain and suffering I have endured during this lifetime. I have said it before, and I will say it again and again: this journey has been evil. Pure evil.

Aside from *that* God I was raised to believe in, few, if any, including my beloved mother, know but the very tip of the iceberg that is my story; perpetual darkness and complete imbalance — a life of persistent emotional and physical pain. A world of uninterrupted, utter desolation.

I was motivated to write this story with the encouragement of an insightful and understanding Licensed Clinical Social Worker (LCSW) who has helped me to put many pieces of my life's puzzle together and has rekindled my flickering will to find the light at the end of that seemingly interminable and darkest of tunnels.

While I have walked hand in hand with despair for most of my life, I have found comfort and a long-lost sense of peace in my soul through this process. My story, a candle on the sill of this window. A pinch of possibility illuminated.

The sharing of my story — this introduction section and the forthcoming pages — is not only for the purpose of soul purging catharsis, but also, and most importantly:

1. To offer solace and hope to those whose existence has been turned upside-down as a direct result of any emotional disorder and/or physical disability.

2. To offer firsthand insight to those not living with these disorders, but who may know someone exhibiting the signs and symptoms. With a new awareness and ability to recognize the signs and symptoms of these disorders and conditions, a friend

or loved one can intervene with an offering of trusting, compassionate support. That understanding, concern, and intervention could be the very difference between life and an existence of emotional imprisonment... or death.

My life has been a ceaseless emotional war since childhood. Now, for nearly 20 of the past years, it has also been a daily physical war. I truly don't know which is worse — the everyday emotional or physical battle — but having to endure two wars of this nature simultaneously — having had both engines taken out — I have felt is simply the cruelest of tortures. It is a curse if ever there was one. That is, unless and until my lifelong, unrelenting agony can help others to overcome, or prevent, the forceful, mind-warping grip of hellacious disorders such as PTSD and depression.

It has been my experience throughout this journey that the undenying common denominator of most all addiction is unbearable emotional and/or physical pain. More often than not, the trauma that caused that emotional and/or physical pain is being repressed. That pain, often buried deep inside, leads to depression and addiction.

Depression is perhaps the most serious and misunderstood of all disorders. It is the commonality of an awful lot of addiction, destruction, and death.

I believe that support — from individuals and groups of individuals who walk in the same shoes — is essential in understanding, coping with, and getting through PTSD, depression, anxiety, and chronic physical pain.

The time has come to bring those of us suffering with these emotional disorders, as well as chronic physical pain, together, in a readily available and safe environment — a system paralleling that of AA — to help and save ourselves as well as others suffering with the same disorders.

1

I came into this world during the summer of 1964. My mother was 37-years-old and my father was 39-years-old at the time of my birth. I had a brother 13 years my senior and a sister 16 years ahead of me.

My mother didn't want another child at this time in her life. I was the proverbial *mistake* — and from the very beginning, and throughout most of my life, I would carry that oppressive feeling around like a 100-pound sack bound across my shoulders.

That impression of myself was brought on mostly as a result of my dysfunctional family environment, with the exception of my mother, and the immediate family members within that infrastructure.

I may have been *unplanned*, but my mother and I would become — from an early age, and remain consistently over the next five decades — the only light in each others' lives. Each of us was the others strength, love, hope, and reason to continue forward.

My mother suffered a brief bout of postpartum depression (PPD) after my birth. Strangely enough, many of the symptoms of PPD were the very symptoms of PTSD I suffered with beginning at the age of five, bearing the weight of for the next 40-plus years; the sadness, hopelessness, low self-esteem, guilt, shame, feelings of being overwhelmed, sleep disturbances, emptiness, social withdrawal, becoming easily frustrated, spells of anger, increased anxiety, panic attacks, and isolation.

From that very early age, and apart from the disorders that would take control of, and destroy nearly every aspect of my life, I knew in my heart and felt in my bones that something wasn't right within my immediate family. There was something vital missing. It would take the next 40-plus years of immeasurable, unfluctuating, and extraordinary pain and suffering — and the past two years of an enlightening therapy and recovery process — to fill in that blank. To finally put that concluding piece of this scourged life's puzzle into place.

My birth year was a time in the United States when the average cost of a new car was $3,500.00. The price of gas for that car was just .30 cents a gallon!

The Beatles were the greatest thing since sliced bread. They rose to prominence in the U.S. this year, were dominating the music charts and becoming the most popular musical group in the world. They were an emerging threat to the real King's reign — the most popular and, in my opinion, the greatest entertainer the world would ever see — Elvis Presley. Elvis would also become my musical idol in the years ahead. I admired the man and was in awe of the performer.

I believe — I sensed at a very early age — he was an exceptional human being and an extraordinary man with a unique, very big, loving heart. My idol would be taken down in his prime by depression and isolation which led him, like many being feasted on by these disorders, to drug addiction which, in turn, took his life.

His deep love for, and strong bond with, his mother paralleled my relationship with my own mother. Losing his mother and the divorce from his first wife, Priscilla, years later was devastating to him, and I believe a major factor and trigger that spiraled him into a deep depression.

I was 13-years-old when Elvis died. I didn't know the man, but I did know his pain and suffering. I felt and lived it firsthand every day of my life beginning at the tender age of five.

I cried when my idol died. Little did I know, I was slowly being dismantled and consumed throughout my childhood — and would continue to be tormented and torn to shreds throughout my entire adult life — by one of the very disorders which took from this world the greatest entertainer that ever lived.

Motown and its artists were making beautiful music as well as history in 1964. The Motown Sound would become a comfort to my soul in years to come. Along with songwriting — a deep-seated, life-long passion — that heavenly Motown Sound was one of only a few brief escapes from the emotional imprisonment that would become my life.

One of my favorite TV shows as a child, *The Munster's*, debuted this year.

The landmark Civil Rights Act of 1964 is passed by Congress.

One of the greatest boxers of all time, Cassius Clay, wins the heavyweight championship of the world and changes his name to Muhammad Ali.

One of my childhood idols, Bruce Lee, is first introduced to the martial arts community at the Long Beach International Karate Championships in August of 1964.

Several other of my childhood idols, including tournament fighters Chuck Norris, Benny "The Jet" Urquidez, and Bill "Superfoot" Wallace, would earn their stripes at this karate tournament in the years that followed.

America's official military involvement in the Vietnam War would begin within a year of my birth and last for the next ten years. The Vietnam War would have a peculiar, twofold impact on my life in years to come.

My father's grandparents immigrated to the United States from Calabria, Italy. My father's mother, *grandma M*, was born in the U.S.

My father never knew his biological father. His father abandoned him and grandma M when my father was a child. My father never spoke of his father but made it clear he hated him, and he never wanted to see him, know of him, or speak of him. It was a traumatic experience in my father's childhood and life, no doubt.

My father was an only child. He was raised by my grandmother and influenced in life by the streets, which he grew up on, in the North End section of the city of Providence, Rhode Island.

The North End was a predominantly Italian neighborhood and one of the three main Italian neighborhoods where the New England Mafia set up shop.

My father's role models during his lifetime were his uncles and his mentor, *Vito R*, who was a father figure to him and a made-member of the Genovese crime family of New York.

For decades, and unbeknownst to many — especially in law enforcement — Vito was the low-key power pulling the strings behind the curtain of the New England Mafia.

My father never graduated from high school. He hardly ever attended school, actually. His education came strictly from the streets. He had a side trade, but was a connected guy and that was his life. He spent most of his time away from his biological family. He was married to the life and the lifestyle of another world.

I never saw much of my father when I was a child and throughout my younger teenage years. When I did, there was a physical presence but, sadly, nothing more.

I recall too many times during my childhood — and to this day — when my father was intoxicated. Most of the time it broke my heart. In addition to the pain it caused me, I always found it to be very embarrassing. A shame I've carried with me from as far back as I can remember. Drinking was an integral part — alcohol the norm — of the underworld lifestyle he led.

Alcoholism is one disease that had a devastating effect on my life. It was a major contributing factor which destroyed my emotional well-being. The effects of this disease are partially responsible for stealing the "normal" from my entire childhood and adult life — and I've never myself consumed an alcoholic beverage. Ironic, isn't it? Just another part of the curse that kept me feeling that this life had been unfair from the get-go.

Grandma M was a kind woman with a very quiet demeanor.

I remember, as a child, taking the bus with her into the city to have Chinese food every now and again. She would always sit, very calmly, never more than a word or two the entire trip or while enjoying her Chinese food with a cup of tea.

At home, it was a sure bet to see grandma M sipping a cup of tea while nibbling on some Italian pastries. Two of what appeared to me to be a couple joys in her life were those Italian pastries and tea. Chinese food may have been a close second.

She was mostly alone as I remember and insisted on working until the day she began to get senile in her 70's. Grandma M was a housekeeper for a large business in the city. She would usually work a few hours in the evening cleaning the offices. She took the city bus most times to work. That's how she wanted it.

My father always picking her up from her work in the evening. As a child, I would occasionally take the ride to pick her up.

One day, her employer called my father and let him know that grandma M was forgetting where she was, experiencing confusion and disorientation. This is how it began. It got worse in the months and years that followed, to the point grandma M wasn't able to bathe, eat, or dress herself. Just thinking of this I can't help but to choke-up. To this day, it pains me very deeply.

She worked her entire life and not because she needed the money. She didn't. My father took care of her financially. I believe — I'm pretty sure — she was addicted to work as I was addicted in my life to training and health, my father and his uncles to alcohol, and my brother to alcohol and drugs. Addiction was in our genes I guess. Working was her escape. Her peace of mind.

In retrospect, I believe my grandmother was a very lonely woman who suffered with depression. This is my sole opinion based on having lived with this disorder every day of my life since the age of five.

She mostly kept to herself, isolating in much the same way I have done for several decades now. No one really to talk to. Even when others are around, who could possibly understand how you feel, and what you are feeling? What you are experiencing and battling with emotionally? The loneliness, anxiety, panic attacks, despair, and sadness. The sheer darkness that blankets your life, that few can see.

Aside from a niece who would pick her up once every week or two to go to lunch or shop at the mall where she enjoyed just walking around, grandma M mostly kept to herself and was usually alone. She stayed in her apartment most times, never asking for anything from anyone.

She would eat with us often — especially with Sunday dinners — but still never really engaged in conversation. She was very quiet and withdrawn most times.

My mother and father would bring her food, Italian pastries, the newspaper, etc. and invite her to go out or come up for dinner most evenings. I would always go downstairs to her apartment to see her, talk a bit, or see if she needed anything from the store. She was a woman of few words, really. Her eyes said it all.

She would always give me money when I shoveled the snow in the yard, went to the store for her, or just because. I didn't want it. She insisted.

Looking back, it was a very sad situation — not unlike the situation of depression and isolation I have endured my entire life. As is common with depression, a person may isolate even when others are around. We were an arm's length away at all times. Even though her family was within steps of her, I believe she was lonely, she was very sad, very much depressed and isolated. Depression often leads to isolation, and isolation leads to dementia in many elderly people.

When she reached the beginning stage of dementia, my father took care of her in her apartment within our home for several months. My father would bathe her feet and cut her toenails in the beginning.

As the dementia progressed, grandma M was no longer able to bathe herself and my parents had a caregiver come to the home daily to bathe and care for her.

Grandma M had now lost control of her bowels and my father would have to fit her with adult diapers and change those diapers several times a day, sponge-cleaning her in the process, until the caregiver arrived to bathe her.

As the dementia further progressed, grandma M started losing her balance and falling. I recall coming home from school one day and finding her on the floor, unable to get up. I picked her up and got her to her chair, tears rolling down my face. I vividly remember how heavy she seemed and she was a small woman of less than 5' tall, maybe 100 lbs. tops.

I couldn't believe this could be happening to my grandmother.

The incident is one that torments me to this day. That look on my grandmother's face as she was laying on the floor. Her arms flailing helplessly, unable to speak, and unable to get up. She was deteriorating before my eyes.

My parents would find her in this situation a couple more times before my father spoke with her doctor regarding the falls and this phase of dementia.

He was told it was time to admit grandma M to a nursing home before she was seriously injured in a fall. Having to admit grandma M into a nursing home broke my heart. However, it was necessary and in the best interest of my grandmother.

To me, watching a loved one slowly deteriorate is a worse fate than having a loved one pass. Her mind was gone and the body followed very slowly and painfully behind.

I know my grandmother was the most important person in my father's life. Much the same as my mother is in my life.

My greatest fear in this lifetime is my mother having to endure this very situation or the chronic pain or immobility of any disease or condition.

Grandma M was admitted to a nursing home where she basically languished for some five years and then passed, finally, at peace. She was at a severe stage of dementia for about five years before she passed. She didn't recognize anyone, including my father when he went to visit.

I was 16 when dementia began to consume her. A piece of me died inside when she began losing her mind. She died years before she entered that nursing home, possibly years before that as depression and isolation sucks any remaining oxygen from your lungs and leaves you but an empty shell.

I couldn't visit her in that nursing home. Just as I cannot and will not go to a wake or funeral. These are things my mind and heart could never handle. Call it what you will, but my anguish for those I love who have passed, or are still here in pain, suffering, or dying is multiplied many times over compared to the average person.

Grandma M passed away on her birthday, Dec 26th, 1985 — the day she turned 86-years-old. I was 21.

I still feel the pain and sadness today as I did some three decades ago.

I wish I had known then what I know now about depression. I would have never let her out of my sight. I would have done whatever it took to make her smile and laugh.

Being around and interacting with others — socialization — especially those who genuinely love and care for you, and the best medicine of all, laughter, is a must to get through another day of the devastating effects and deeper depths of PTSD and depression. It's a necessity to break the cycle.

It takes those around you that are not suffering with these disorders to pick up on the telltale signs and act in the best interest of the loved one or friend.

I think of grandma M often. I love and miss her very much. If there is a heaven — a God — then I know she is safe and at peace, having a cup of tea with a cannoli and enjoying a conversation. Smiling and laughing... Finally.

My mother's parents immigrated to the United States from Pico, Italy. They would have three children before my grandmother — *grandma G* — died of a blood infection at the age of 29; my mother's oldest brother, Lucio, and a younger brother, Nico. My mother was the middle child at this time and three-years-old when her mother died. A traumatic experience for anyone, let alone a little girl of three-years-old losing her mother.

My grandfather would remarry within a few years and have five more children: my mother's brothers Giorgio, *Giulio*, and *Antonio*, and her sisters *Paola* and *Marcella*.

My mother's family lived in the Federal Hill section in the city of Providence. This was also a predominantly Italian neighborhood and another of the three main neighborhoods where the New England Mafia was well established, Federal Hill being the New England Mafia's headquarters.

Unlike my father's side of the family, my mother's family was poor — but extremely rich in the love they shared as a family and for one another.

My grandfather began working in the U.S. as a coal bagger to support his family. He was from a family of farmers in Italy and, later in life, would return to his roots and spend as much time as possible tending his gardens. He was never so happy as the time he spent in those gardens. Planting and then picking all those fresh fruits and vegetables was his passion.

I remember, as a child, spending time with him both in Rhode Island and at my uncle Nico's home in Florida. We played a few variations of the old Italian hand game, Morra. I remember how worn his fingers were from the unremitting, back-breaking manual labor that was his first job in the U.S. and necessary to care and provide for his family — his life and joy. Those fingers may have been worn but they were steady and very gentle as we'd stroll through the gardens and grapevines, picking fresh vegetables, fruit, and those sweet-smelling, heavenly red and purplish black grapes for his homemade wine.

I vividly remember Pop relaxing and enjoying a glass of homemade red wine along with his tobacco pipe during these later years. I can still smell that aromatic red wine and the distinct scent of his pipe to this very day. It's one of the few childhood memories that bring joy to my heart and a smile to my face.

He was a peaceful and gentle, warm and kind man whom I loved very much. I felt love in his touch, in his kiss on my cheek and forehead, in the tone of his voice and emanating from those beautiful Italian words. I always saw love — my grandfather's gentle and tender soul — within his eyes.

Of all the never-ending pain and suffering I have endured during this lifetime — growing up in an extremely dysfunctional environment with alcoholism and addiction snuffing out my childhood and all the loss, heartache, and despair within my life that would follow — I like to believe that I have my grandfather's genes and some of the traits that made him the man he was and the man I admired.

His was a time when *family* meant something, when the bond between family members was unbreakable. Not a word had to be spoken. The love and respect for each other was always evident and undeniable. It is to this day within my mother's family.

My mother has always said, "*You can feel if love is genuine through the hug.*"

She always felt that love with her brothers, sisters, in-laws, nieces and nephews — my aunts, uncles, and cousins. It is a very special family and family bond.

Childhood PTSD and the disorders that spawned from this condition robbed me of that special family bond. It is one of the greatest regrets of my life — and one of which I had no control.

My mother would always say of my grandfather, "*He loved everything and everyone. He loved all animals, all people.*" As difficult as life may have been for pop, he was blessed with a happy soul and a beautiful, loving family. He was a very humble, grateful man.

Pop passed in 1977 and was laid out on my mother's birthday, February 2nd, of all days. He was 87-years-old. I was 12.

Pop's death was my first experience with losing a loved one. It was extremely shocking and extraordinarily difficult back then — the suffering and/or death of a loved one is no less painful and anxiety producing today. In some respects, it has become much more agonizing.

I know Pop was very proud of my mother. I know my grandma G would have been very proud of the woman and mother she became.

My mother overcame many obstacles and hardships in her life. Many that would have broken and destroyed most. Many more than I could ever have overcome. There's the plain to see trauma, pain, and sorrows, and then there's the immediate family agony and heartbreak she's had to endure — and those secrets that can only be taken to the grave. She truly is a remarkable woman. An angel on this earth and in my life. The only light that has ever pierced the darkness that has been my world.

My grandmother, *grandma C*, was born in the U.S. and spoke both English and Italian. My grandfather, on the other hand, never spoke a word of English. The entire family spoke to him in Italian.

Grandma C was 15 years my grandfather's junior. She was a sweet woman who had a rather short temper with pop. I recall — more often than not — her getting very feisty with him. When she got upset, she would start yelling at Pop in Italian. Pop would just smile. He was always happy. Not an angry bone in his body.

Grandma C suffered with diabetes and, at one point as a result of this disease, had one of her legs removed from the knee down.

Grandma C passed in February of 1992.

The passing of loved ones over the years has definitely contributed to the depth of my depression.

I didn't see much of grandma C the years leading up to her

passing. I was now well into full-blown depression, isolating more than ever, and trying desperately to hold it together and move on with my life.

I love and miss them both very much and wish I had been able to spend more time and bond deeper with each of them. It wasn't meant to be, as it seemed too often over the course of my life, most good things just weren't.

I grew up in the Eagle Park and North End sections of the city of Providence. The same Italian neighborhoods where my father grew up. I lived in a multi-family house until I was three-years-old. Grandma M, some of my father's aunts, uncles, and cousins lived above us. That's how most Italian families lived in the day — multi-family homes with relatives in each of the units.

Most of my father's side of the family had passed either before I was born or during my very early childhood. I wish I had memories of that side of my family, but I don't remember any of them.

I do recall the stories I've been told over the years — how I was loved and watched over by my family during my infancy and through the first years of my life. The immediate family, the bond, and the values would slowly begin a downhill descent from that point on.

I also spent a fair amount of time with my sister during these very early years. She would babysit me, take me with her on walks or wherever she might be going. Families and the times were so much different back then. Those were definitely the glory days.

The generations of my mother and father and my grandparents were all about family and strong family bonds — respect, honor, and loyalty within family and among friends. Regardless of any disorders, diseases, or dysfunctionality within a family, there is never a reason — never any excuse — to disrespect, dishonor, or betray your family, or anyone, ever, under any circumstances.

There's a growing decay that has eaten into and destroyed the moral fiber and core values that made not only families, but our country unbreakable. I have seen this deterioration within my own immediate family. I have also witnessed it firsthand and all too often over the last couple of decades and generations within our country. In my opinion, it's a decadence akin to the beginning of the fall of the Roman Empire all over again.

🦋 🦋 🦋 🦋

When I was three-years-old, my father built a single-family home on a lot he owned directly behind the multi-family home we lived in. My sister, 19 at the time, would have her own room until she married at 24 and moved out. My brother, 16 at the time, would share a room with me for several years and later move into my sister's room.

My father had the basement completely finished into a full in-law apartment for grandma M — complete with a separate entrance, full kitchen, living room/TV room, bedroom, bathroom, and a large portion of the lower level would become a "family room" where the entire family could gather to watch TV and converse together.

In later years, when I was 16 — when grandma M had to be admitted to a nursing home — I would get to convert that area into a full home gym. It was complete with a dozen pieces of various heavy duty gym equipment, punching bags, and a couple thousand pounds of weights. It was my haven. My escape. My closest, furthest getaway where I spent most of my days and nights of free time training and listening to music while doing so, Motown and R&B when alone. It soothed my soul which ached continuously, unbeknownst to anyone.

I always felt grandma M's presence with me downstairs. The sadness I remember seeing in her eyes. The loneliness I know she felt troubles me to this day.

🦋 🦋 🦋 🦋

Depression destroys more lives in this country than any other disorder we know of. My hope is that people begin to understand what it is — what it looks like — and how to intervene and help break the cycle before the disorder flourishes, seizes and destroys, or takes, the lives of those we love.

🦋 🦋 🦋 🦋

My parents had met through a mutual friend. My mother was 19 and my father was 21 when they married.

My father's life and place of business was the streets. For him, there was no need for school and he didn't like it anyway. He dropped out of school very early, never graduating.

My mother dropped out of high school in the 11th grade to support herself and to take on more of a mother figure role to all seven of her siblings.

My mother was attracted to my father's lifestyle and the money when they met. You could say she married for the wrong reasons and paid dearly for it in more ways than one. There was never any affection or real love shown between my parents —or with my father towards his children. I've never seen a hug, a kiss, heard a, "How was your day?" nor a loving conversation between my parents. As far back as I can remember, there has been only anger, bitterness, and tension, and it was usually quite apparent to everyone who was around them within our family. It was always a very uncomfortable situation for me and most others throughout my childhood, and to this very day. It was the kind of atmosphere that not many could stand to be around for very long. It was a very disturbing undercurrent of negative energy to say the least.

Things were actually better — much more peaceful — between my parents during all the years my father was hardly home and any time they did spend together was mostly out and about.

Mom was treated like royalty by other wise guy friends and associates. There were the lavish parties, front row seats at high end Vegas shows, meeting celebrities from Telly Savalas and Dean Martin to Frankie Valli and Frank Sinatra. There were extravagant gifts, dinners, and vacations.

Knowing and being in the company of top mobsters, entertainers, politicians, and other very powerful people was a turn-on for any woman. Life was good in that way. There was money, connections, and good times. However, there was no immediate family structure in my home.

My father was physically around every now and again, and provided financially for his family, but there was no emotional connection or support with his children or wife. Call it nature, nurture, a combination of the two, or whatever, but my father was very limited in his capacities outside of financially providing for his family. My immediate family was dysfunction at its finest. Look up "dysfunctional family" in the dictionary and you'll see our family portrait!

My mother was always my rock. Most males have that connection with their father. I didn't. My bond, love, and affection for my mother would grow with each passing year and, to this day, she is my best friend, my confidant, my strength, and my light. I have never in my lifetime felt more love and compassion from another human being. She is my inspiration. She is the one treasure in my life and, aside from a heart that refuses to quit or be beaten, she is the sole reason I am still alive and able to write this story.

Unlike the majority of New England mob guys, my father had some very strong, powerful connections and friendships beyond the New England area. He had firsthand knowledge and access to the kind of things seen only in movies, or read about in books.

My father was well-liked and respected on the streets. He was easy-going and rather laid-back. He was never a greedy, money-hungry guy. If he was, and with his connections and the opportunities presented him during his lifetime, he would have been worth a small fortune. He is not. He was content and without much ambition for more and more as most others in this lifestyle.

I remember times during my childhood when I would go with him to a store he owned with the then Capo of the North End, *Marcello R.* I would sit on the stoop in front of the store, cars coming by, the drivers beeping and waving. Men coming and going from the corner and the store. Lots of handshaking, cheek kissing, whispers in the ear, and hand gesturing. Lots of envelopes being passed.

Many of the wise guys would pinch my cheek or pat me on the head and often give me money. By the time I was ten, I had a bigger bankroll than most adults. Nice deal for a kid! I would anxiously wait for certain guys to drive by or come to the store. Like any kid, we have our favorite characters. I would overhear things being discussed that would make a wire tapper's jaw drop. I have seen and heard things throughout my life that can only be taken to the grave. Keeping your mouth shut is a way of life growing up as I did. There was absolutely nothing worse than a "rat" in my culture; someone who runs his mouth, spills secrets, and can't be trusted. There was a code of honor; a code of silence. It was embedded in the culture. It certainly was back in the day. The times, values, and generations have definitely changed since then.

2

I first walked through the gates of hell at the age of five. And with each passing year, I crossed into a deeper and darker abyss.

My childhood began with a front row seat to the horror that is alcoholism and addiction.

Alcoholism was inherent on my father's side of the family. So was the denial.

My brother was an alcoholic and an addict throughout my childhood and into my adulthood. I had to endure this, as a child, in my own home, from the age of five until 13. It would continue from afar for many years thereafter.

I also recall on too many occasions throughout my childhood, adult years, and to this day when my father was inebriated. My father's lifestyle went hand in hand with alcohol consumption and abuse.

I recall his vehicle accidents, rage, crying, passing out on the floor, and so much more.

I was eight-years-old the first time I saw my dad completely pass out from being drunk. He collapsed to the floor in the hallway of our home. I thought he was dead. It scared the crap out of me. I remember screaming, "*We have to call an ambulance!*"

No one else seemed as worried as I was. They knew the reason he passed out. He didn't have a heart attack and he wasn't dead.

I remember my brother — of all people — tapping him on the face, saying, "*Dad, wake up, wake up.*"

My father's alcoholism was another major contributing factor which kick-started my PTSD, anxiety, and depression.

I came into this world with a couple strikes against me before I even made it to the plate.

It is said, and I *do* believe, that "life is not measured by the number of breathes you take, but by the moments that take your breath away." The majority of my "moments" in life — especially during my childhood — were devastating. I don't have too many fond memories, smiles and joy to reflect upon.

Sure, there were some good times very early on, but those times were always outweighed and overshadowed by the trauma in my life — the PTSD, depression, and anxiety resulting from this trauma.

As a child, I learned how to hide in plain sight. I couldn't let anyone know that I was different, that I was suffering deeply with emotional pain. I wanted to fit in and be like the other kids, but I wasn't. I had been concealing my pain and suffering from everyone around me from this very early age and for the next 40 years — each decade worsening with one traumatic event after another wreaking havoc upon my mind and body, devastating my soul, and isolating me from everything and everyone I cared for and cared about. Until I began writing this story, I had never bared my soul and lifelong pain in such detail.

My first scarring childhood memories are from 1969 when I was five-years-old. I recall my mother screaming and crying. Her oldest son, 18 at the time, was an addict in a rage.

Distressing incidents and tormenting memories such as this have played over and over in my mind throughout my life. These are the majority of my memories from childhood — the beginning of my PTSD, depression, and anxiety.

This is also the time frame when the Woodstock Festival took place — summer of 1969. Woodstock being synonymous with the counterculture movement of the 1960's — hippies, music, free love, drugs and drug experimentation. It was a pivotal moment in popular music history as well as the history of our country. My brother was no doubt caught up in this movement.

The childhood memories I have — many of which had been repressed for years, some for decades — are mostly unpleasant and disheartening. The incidents that took place within my home and immediate family were traumatic and pretty much the same type of scenario throughout all the years of my childhood and adolescence.

Often when I hear glass breaking, loud arguing, screaming, crying, doors banging, sirens, I have an instantaneous regression back to that small child huddled in fear in his room, helpless and afraid. Not afraid for himself, but for his mother. Helpless as he had to endure watching his mother suffer year after year, battling to save her addict son from dying.

Most times when I see someone who is drunk or high on drugs, whether on TV or on the street, it takes me back to my childhood and I re-experience the uncomfortable emotions I felt having to suffer through the alcohol and drug addiction of my brother, year in and year out. What I had to put up with through all my early years — my entire youth — due to the addiction of my brother, no person, especially a child, should have to endure.

My father's alcoholism was petty compared to my brother's addictions. However, it was no less damaging to my mind and scarring to my soul.

I began Kindergarten in 1969 at the age of five. This was my first ever culture shock. My elementary school — K through 5 — was a short distance from my home. In the beginning, I would get a ride to school but soon started walking to and from most days. Sometimes with other kids from the neighborhood, but mostly alone.

I vividly remember my first day of kindergarten and the fear of leaving my mother. What would happen if I was not there with her? Would she be okay? Would she be there when I got home?

Kindergarten wasn't too bad in the beginning as the traumatic experiences taking place at home had only recently begun. You could say that Kindergarten was the only normal period of social interaction I had with others in my life. I was still not completely jaded by trauma or fully under the control of PTSD. I actually remember enjoying the company of other kids and the teachers; playing, smiling, and laughing.

However, this short-lived normal childhood would begin to change very quickly. As time went on and I progressed from one grade to the next, so did the turmoil and trauma at home as well as from other areas of my life.

I distinctly recall how my feelings towards being around others started to change. I began feeling different than the kids around me. I just didn't fit in for some reason. It was nearly impossible to play with other kids — in the playground, at recess, or gym time — and actually enjoy it. I would always be worried about my mother and what was going on at home. I just didn't feel the happiness and joy the other kids were experiencing. This feeling of sadness, fear, and constant worrying would grow worse as the months and years progressed.

It was around this time in 1970 that I began traveling to Florida annually with my parents. This was mostly during school's winter break, although some of our Florida trips were before and after the break. Sometimes my mother would talk to the school principal and my teachers to get permission (and the extra school work that would be due when I returned) to keep me out of school a couple weeks longer than the winter break period.

I enjoyed the winter trips and that southbound drive down I-95 heading for the sunshine, beach, and invigorating warm weather.

My mother made it her duty to make sure I was studying and doing school work during those long car drives. My mother — a very religious, strong-faithed Catholic — insisted I also learn my prayers during these long drives to and from Florida. I did. It made her happy. That's all that really mattered to me since childhood and to this day.

I began saying my nightly prayers every evening before bed from around the age of six, without fail, never missing one night, sometimes praying several times a day. I would pray faithfully for the next 25 years. I had a very strong faith and belief that was instilled in me by my mother.

However, as the years went by I began feeling completely alone. The Lord wasn't hearing any of my prayers. In fact, year after year, everything kept getting worse in my life. I began to feel cursed. I felt that the God I believed in — the God I prayed to devotedly — wasn't there for me.

Why did I have to suffer every minute of every day of my life, in every way possible? Why couldn't I fit in and be happy like the other kids?

As a kid, I couldn't wait to start seeing the "Pedro says" and "South of the Border" signs along I-95 — and finally getting to that landmark border!

I remember stopping once at the border. It was like pulling teeth to get my father to do anything with the family or with me. We took a few pictures and we were off.

We would stay at various hotels in south Florida until my father purchased a home there some years later. My fondest memories from the 1970's were at the Waikiki in Miami.

My father's lifestyle continued in Florida during that annual vacation just as it did when we were home in Rhode Island. Many of his friends were there. Connected and made guys from all over the country would gather in South Florida during the winter months.

My father loved Florida. My mother never liked the heat, humidity, or Florida very much. I thought it was an awesome place, especially since I loved warm, sunny days and the beach. I always felt a sense of peace whenever around the ocean, from childhood until this day. As a kid, I spent a lot of time on the beach during those vacations — pretty much alone — collecting shells, building sand castles, and popping man of war jellyfish with a stick.

I always had that sense of peace here that I never had back home.

My mother was always within an arm's distance. There were no other kids around unless we went to my uncle Nico's house. My cousins *Deana* and *Lino*, a few years older than me, lived there with my aunt *Ria* and uncle Nico.

My grandfather spent a lot of time in Florida with my uncle Nico. I always enjoyed being around Pop. I looked forward to going to my uncle Nico's home as a kid.

Our return trips back to Rhode Island were mostly uneventful and hurried, as usual. We did stop a few times on the way back to buy fireworks in the Carolina's. 4th of July was always a huge deal in the neighborhoods back home.

I remember stopping at Disney World in Orlando, Florida, during their grand opening, October of 1971. Wow! This place was unreal! Unfortunately, I never got the chance to be a kid and to enjoy it. My father was never excited about these kinds of things. He wanted to get to Florida, or back to Rhode Island — like yesterday.

I remember getting a book of tickets for the rides. As my luck would have it, something happened to the electric within the park and many of the rides came to a stop. Needless to say, we didn't stick around long after that.

I still have the three full books (two adult, one child) of ride tickets from Disney's Oct 1971 grand opening. Another reminder of the childhood that never was.

My brother and his girlfriend, *Laura*, had a child in 1971. My niece, *Strega*.

He was 19 and Laura was a year younger. I had just turned seven-years-old.

My brother, with the financial help of my parents, would try and do the right thing by his daughter, which included getting married at 19-years-old and getting an apartment for himself, his new wife, and his newborn daughter. He did, in our North End Neighborhood.

Needless to say, this would not change his behavior pattern and lifestyle. There was now violence in his new home and family situation.

He would move back in with us within a year, continuing with his addiction and lifestyle — and my having to endure another six years of this insanity in my home.

My niece and her mother, who was a neighborhood girl battling demons of her own, would live in the neighborhood with her parents for some time.

My parents were always there for, and cared for, their new granddaughter financially, physically, and emotionally. Strega was always with us. My mother basically raised her as if her own daughter. Strega's mother at the time was pretty much a female version of my brother. So, in all reality, my niece was looked out for by my parents and Laura's parents.

She was well cared for and showered with family love and attention from my parents, Laura's parents, myself, aunts, uncles, cousins, and everyone else in our family. She was family and was shown and taught right from wrong, family values and the like.

I would become a father figure to her in later years — even receiving Father's day cards and *thank you* notes for my always being there for her.

Her mother would call me whenever she thought Strega might be hanging with the wrong crowd or up to no good. I always looked out for her.

When I was ten-years-old, my parents set my brother up with a place in Florida. He would leave his wife and 3-year-old daughter behind. However, his wife would soon follow him there. Their problems continued, just from a distance.

My brother would come back home within a few months. I would have to, once again, continue to endure the pure madness within my home for a few more years.

There are literally hundreds of traumatic incidents and events that occurred during my childhood, from both inside and outside of my home. I would need to write a separate book focusing specifically on these incidents in order to even begin to cover the wide array of trauma I've seen and lived through.

There are a few incidents, however, that have always stood out in the forefront of my mind that I will share here. While there are many violent, heart-stopping incidents that have occurred during my childhood and beyond that make these experiences look rather lame, the few that follow, for some reason, I remember quite vividly. Each haunting me at higher levels;

I was 11-years-old. My father was notified by neighborhood guys that my brother was in a particular bar one evening, drunk and/or under the influence of drugs, and causing trouble. My father went there to get him out before he was arrested (again).

They got into my father's car and were followed to our home by two state police cruisers, with two troopers per cruiser.

When my father and brother arrived home, four troopers got out of the two cruisers, some words were exchanged, and the four troopers began to beat both my father and brother with batons.

Neither my father, nor my brother resisted but were struck multiple times about the head and body causing large gashes on their heads and faces, requiring dozens of stitches to close the wounds.

I witnessed this brutality through the front door of my home, screaming and crying, while my mother, hysterical herself, held me back so I couldn't go outside to their rescue.

This incident was just one of many in my life that had scarred me emotionally in more ways than one.

Go figure... I would, in years to come, dedicate my life to protecting and serving — law enforcement — and the pursuit of justice.

This wasn't the first case of injustice and police brutality I had witnessed in my life — either as a civilian or a state trooper. It wouldn't be the last.

🦋 🦋 🦋 🦋

Injustice has become all too common in our country. I grew up believing in God, in good triumphing over evil, and in our justice system.

Unfortunately, what I have found to be true is that the one wearing the badge and the one with the title of Judge, Senator, Mayor, Captain, or the like before his or her name isn't held to the same standard of accountability as the rest of us regular folk.

I've seen and lived through more injustice and corruption in my life — both as a streetwise kid and young man and as a state trooper — than I care to remember. It has spread like wildfire in our country and it seems the privileged and those supposedly on "the right side of the law" very seldom pay for their crimes.

Instead, in today's society, they are rewarded for their wrongdoing. Many seem to get promotions, TV shows, book deals, and another run at political office as their punishment. The injustice is truly disgusting and only getting worse with each passing decade.

🦋 🦋 🦋 🦋

I actually looked up to my brother in my early years — alcoholic and drug addict, or not. He was my older brother, I loved him, and I would do what I had to do to protect him.

Another incident I vividly remember as a child — this one where I would have killed for my brother;

The doorbell rang at my home one afternoon. There were two very large neighborhood guys, both over 6' and 200 lbs., standing at the front door. One of them, *Dozer*, I knew. The other, *Noog*, asked for my brother. I was the only one home at the time. I knew something bad was up once again.

Ten minutes later, a neighborhood kid came to my house and told me that two guys were chasing my brother through the park. I remember the emotion that came over me; I had to kill these guys before they killed my brother.

I was all of 12-years-old.

I grabbed a .308 rifle that was in the closet of the house, stormed out the door and, with the other kid in tow, ran towards the park. I ran around that entire park with a rifle in my hands looking for these guys so I could help my brother. I wasn't going to allow these two gorillas to hurt him.

I didn't see my brother or the two goons anywhere. In retrospect, luckily for me *and* for those two apes.

I was quickly approached by an older neighborhood guy who calmed me down, took the rifle, and brought me (and the rifle) back home.

One of the guys who came to my house looking for my brother, Noog, was just recently released from prison and was known as a tough guy, but a classless punk, also involved in drugs. He was accompanied by his cousin, Dozer, a neighborhood guy and runner with my father's crew.

Dozer (both guys, actually) should have known better. You don't go to my father's house looking for his son, regardless of the reason. He was dealt with and apologized. His reasoning was that he wanted to be able to control his cousin's actions and not let things get out of control.

He was told he may now have to partake in the repercussions coming to his cousin for disrespecting my father by going to his house in that manner. He begged up and down to let him handle it peacefully and there would be no more trouble or disrespect.

My father was a street guy but was, in my opinion, too easy-going and peaceful in his demeanor for that life. Any other guy in his position and that lifestyle would have, at the very least, seriously hurt the degenerate, low-life, disrespectful punk cousin, Noog.

I know, for a fact, others would have killed him.

That was *the life* and the way of life on the streets back then. There are rules and regulations in society and in every organization whether it is the military or organized crime. There are consequences for breaking and/or disregarding those rules. This is known and accepted by everyone who enters into and is associated with these organizations, these families, this lifestyle and way of life.

You do the crime, you do the time if you're caught, or whatever the penalty may be for your actions.

I was a firm believer growing up — as I am to this day — that every adult is fully accountable for his or her actions. Accountability cannot be ignored or overlooked in any organization or society or that structure will crumble.

As time went by, I grew tired of my brother's lack of discipline and the fact that there were no consequences for his actions.

Another scarring incident when I was 13-years-old that still flashes in my mind much too often;

My brother was in a rage, looking for money. He had always gone to my grandma M for money — she never refused. My father had enough of his taking advantage of his grandmother. He also knew that my brother had been stealing money from grandma M.

🦋 🦋 🦋 🦋

I started working and making a buck when I was eight-years-old. I would shovel snow all winter and help a friend with a paper route.

Some days I'd make over $100 depending on how much snow had fallen. I Made $400 in one day during the Blizzard of 1978!

My brother would think nothing of stealing the money I broke my back to earn. He would find my hiding places and help himself. My brother had been stealing from all of us — and everyone else within arm's reach — for many years to fuel his addiction.

He stole $500 from my father once and left him an IOU

note! If that was my adult son, he'd still be limping — if walking at all — from the broken legs he'd have gotten for stealing from his father.

🦋 🦋 🦋 🦋

My brother was arguing with my parents when he forcefully opened, and violently slammed, the side door to the house so hard it shattered the window glass and left a huge hole in the wood paneling behind it.

This was my turning point. The day I had finally had enough. I looked at my parents and said, "*This has to end. When are you going to do something about this? When are you going to make him responsible for his actions?*"

My father's response, "*What do you want me to kill him?*"

I remember responding, very angrily, "*That might not be a bad idea.*"

My parents, stunned by my comment, just looked at me. I certainly didn't mean it, but had had enough. eight years of this never-ending, torturous, disrespectful bullshit! Something had to be done. How about some tough love?! Throw his ass out if he is unwilling to help himself get well.

I felt like the adult now and that I was dealing with children — all three of them — and I was all of 13-years-old.

My father, and those of his lifestyle back in the day, were firmly against and forbid dealing in drugs or dealing with anyone who took any kind of drugs. If my brother had been part of the life, he no doubt would have been killed. An addict can't be trusted. An addict is a liability and the responsibility of the immediate family. That would have been my father's responsibility. I've overheard many conversations about this between my father and those of his life.

My mother went through hell, and then some, with my brother for many, many years. He mangled her heart and left a piece of it permanently damaged.

At the end of the day, she may never have recovered if he was killed. Any way you slice it, this was her son and she was an Italian mother-bear through thick and thin, and to the very end.

My brother moved to California when I was 14. His addiction and the problems and suffering he caused my mother would continue from afar for the next six years.

My parents kept enabling him by repeatedly bailing him out of jail, paying for his attorneys, and sending him money. The codependent behavioral pattern continued full steam ahead.

My sister married and moved out of our home in 1972. She was 24. I was eight. She married her high school sweetheart, *Biagio,* when he returned from Vietnam.

He came back home a different person she would find out post marriage.

Biagio was an intelligent guy. A very talented artist and a professional photographer.

Biagio became very controlling when he came back from Nam. He would tell my sister what to do, what to wear, where she could go. He became verbally and emotionally abusive to my sister. She started living like a prisoner in her own home and he was the warden.

Like much of my life to this point, I would witness and have to endure more abuse when with my sister at her home on Federal Hill. Biagio would be very strict with me whenever I was at their home.

I recall occasions when he would have me stand in a corner facing the wall as punishment for whatever he felt was worthy of his disciplining. He would forbid me to speak. I was a child and had been living day in and day out through the trauma within my home. I didn't need two years of additional grief from this end. I found him to be very troubled, very strange upon his return from Nam. I didn't like him much when he came back. Think it's safe to say, Vietnam had its way with Biagio's mind. The effects of which my sister would now have to endure.

I could see at my young age that my sister was under his control and afraid of him. I would also be witness to many of his verbal assaults on my sister in their home. He would yell and swear at her, sometimes at me.

My parents were unaware of what was going on under my sister's roof.

He acted a bit differently — more in control of his emotions — when at my house and around my family, but it seemed he would snap and slip every now and again and get angry and mean. I recall Biagio trying to discipline me once in my parent's home. He spoke very angrily towards me.

My mother put him in his place — made him understand very quickly that he wasn't to speak to me that way *or* discipline me... Ever. It wasn't his place to do so.

I think, at this point, my mother could see there was something wrong with Biagio and their marriage as my sister was never happy. My sister was probably afraid to speak to my mother or father about the problems she was having at home. Then again, none of us ever spoke to each other about our problems or feelings. Needless to say, she was out of there and divorced two years post that marriage. Ironically, Biagio would have a significant and positive impact on my life some eight years down the road.

My sister re-married in 1976. She was 28, I was 12. She had been dating her new husband, *Rob*, for about one year prior to marrying.

I remember my sister taking me out with them on different occasions. For lunch, to the park with his kids, to the movies. I liked Rob and his kids. My mother liked them, too. His kids were always very respectful to my parents and everyone else within the family.

Rob was a police officer and a military veteran at the time they met. Like my sister, he was previously married. He had six children from his first marriage, none of whom ever lived with my sister and Rob. My father wasn't crazy about the arrangement, or the fact that Rob wasn't 100% Italian. However, my father would later pull strings to get Rob promoted to sergeant within the police dept. and quash some bad blood between Rob and the then police chief. However, problems with the police dept. would linger.

My mother and father were close friends with Rob's chief. It is a fact, without my mother's speaking with the chief regarding her now son-in-law, and my father's help, that promotion never would have happened.

Shortly after Rob's promotion to sergeant, my parents were at a function with the chief. My mother thanked him for his help in seeing the promotion through. The chief's reply to my mother, verbatim, "*I did it for you, Olivia.*"

Rob had an older brother, *Bosco*, that my father knew from the streets. He was a streetwise guy and hustler who knew and mingled with some of my father's younger associates.

Bosco was nearly 20 years my father's junior — a different generation — but they liked and respected each other. My mother also became very fond of Bosco and his wife.

I remember the first time I met Bosco. The resemblance to my musical Idol, Elvis Presley, was remarkable. Needless to say, I recall functions during the day when the ladies would swoon over him. I always liked him — he was a straight-forward, street guy.

My sister and Rob would have their 1st child, my nephew, *Stronzo*, in 1978. Their 2nd child, my nephew, *Carlo*, three years later in 1981.

Both Stronzo and Carlo spent much of their childhood with, and being influenced by myself, my mother, father, aunts, uncles, cousins and our way of life. Our Italian culture.

As the years went by, outside influences would pull them — as well as my niece — in different directions, splintering generational customs within our family.

The important Sunday dinners, Thanksgivings, Christmas and Christmas Eves, birthday celebrations, respect within and for the family, parents and grandparents were no longer paramount in their minds and lives.

Times and generations were changing for the worse and the strong family bonds, values, and customs that kept the family firmly held together were disappearing rapidly in our immediate family. True colors — souls — were being clearly revealed.

3

When I was in the 4th grade, one of my teachers was concerned that something was going on with me — bothering me and influencing a particular behavior. I was almost 10-years-old and this was the first and only time in my life that anyone recognized (even remotely) that something seemed out of place — just not right — in my life.

My mother was notified and would go to the school for a meeting with some of my teachers. They noted that I was finishing my classroom work far ahead of everyone else, and my work excelled beyond my 4th grade curriculum. They said that I was getting very bored in the classrooms and would drift off daydreaming; not paying attention. I was not engaging in classroom activities beyond what was required. I had seemed pre-occupied, worried, or sad.

They had hit the nail on the head. However, they were unaware of the trouble and trauma within my home. We didn't discuss those types of things — our family matters — with anyone. That is the way it was. That is how I grew up.

If I had known enough to speak to a teacher or counselor and explain what I was going through — what I was feeling inside — and get some professional help, it may have spared me the life of pain and emotional imprisonment that was ahead of me.

I had been given some written tests and, along with the teachers' observations, it was determined that I was a grade ahead of my classmates. That may have been half of the problem but certainly not the part that truly needed to be addressed. The teachers wanted to move me up a grade, but my mother wanted me to stay in classes with peers my own age. I agreed. Suffering anxiety already, unknown to anyone else, I was frightened to death just thinking of moving up a grade with "those older kids" and not knowing anyone in my classes.

The school's administration suggested an advance type of learning program — with a mentor — for the remainder of the school year. My mother agreed. The mentor was a master's degree student at Providence College. His name was *Peter G.*

Peter would come to my elementary school once a week and I would study different things a bit more advanced than what was currently being taught in my 4th grade classes.

We would walk back to Providence College sometimes where he would show me around the school. We'd go into the classes as they were being taught so I could see what it was like. I remember him showing me his last name on a map in one of the classrooms. He shared the same last name with a city within one of our Midwest states. We'd also play some basketball and go to the school's gym. It was my first introduction to a gym and weight-training equipment. I thought it was awesome!

He also came to dinner at my home once. He wasn't Italian and was in awe of my mother's home-cooked Italian food. He kept complimenting my mother on how incredibly delicious it was.

He was a really nice guy. It was the first time an adult male had shown any interest or concern and spent any quality time with me. The entire experience left a positive, lasting impression on me.

I was 10-years-old, 5th grade, when bullying began.

I was always a small kid. Just about everyone else was bigger than me. I'm a physically small adult, topping out at 5' 5 ½ " and never above a very fit 150 lbs.

Bullying would be a part of my daily life and trauma from the 5th grade through the 8th grade.

The North End Neighborhoods began to crumble when "outsiders" started moving in as the old-timers were passing on and families that called the neighborhoods home for generations began to move away. The neighborhoods were no longer predominantly connected by and comprised of the immigrant families that had lived there for generations. Many of these families came from countries such as Italy, Ireland, and England. Prior to this *outsider-invasion*, everyone knew each other. The neighborhoods were safe and everyone looked out for one another. Back then, no one even locked the doors.

It all started changing in the late 60's.

One sign was when the peddlers were no longer selling their fresh fruit, vegetables, and fish on the streets of the neighborhoods... And those were the days!

I remember one of the elderly guys from the neighborhood, *Nick* — one of the original old-timers — who walked with a cane. He would take his daily walk by my yard, calling out to me, "*Great arm, Lefty.*" I was around five-years-old and loved to throw a ball against an abutting concrete wall in my yard. I was left-handed, of course.

I wish I had been born earlier to fully enjoy the close-knit, family oriented neighborhoods and lifestyle of the day. The way of life and the customs were all but gone come the mid to late 1970's. Even the Mob's physical presence in the neighborhoods would soon begin to fade.

It started first in the Eagle Park area. My elementary school was in this area. I spent most of my time hanging out and riding bicycles in Eagle Park until around 12-years-old when I began hanging around with a different crew and spending time around Charles St. in the North End.

These outsiders didn't share the same values as I grew up with, they weren't of our culture. There was no respect from children for adults or the elderly. Graffiti was beginning to deface the neighborhood buildings and parks. It was common now to see young kids drinking alcohol and smoking pot in the neighborhood parks.

The bullying started with a couple big, outsider kids who recently moved into Eagle Park. These kids were drinking alcohol and smoking pot in the 5th grade!

It was the usual bullying tactics; constant teasing, name calling, throwing things at me, threats. I was already in the ferocious grip of PTSD, deep into a depression, and suffering with anxiety. This was something I didn't need. It was another round of torment that would inflict a bit more emotional pain upon me and rip my life and world apart just a little more.

I didn't have a clue what was going on with me — the emotional torment — was childhood PTSD. I did know there was definitely something wrong emotionally because I was never like other kids. I couldn't find happiness or joy in anything other kids were doing. I never enjoyed playing with other kids, and never seemed to smile or laugh. I was always worried about my mom at home and everything else under the sun. I didn't need any more trauma in my life but the misery always seemed to find and torture me from all angles.

I endured bullying for several years.

I remember telling my cousin *Bruno* about one of the bigger kids bullying me. My cousin was a couple years older than me and like a big brother. He was the big brother I never had. This was my aunt Adela and uncle Lucio's son. He came over one day and insisted on tracking down one of these kids. My cousin Bruno was about the same size, maybe slightly bigger than this bully. But, as with any coward facing someone his own size or bigger, the kid was literally shaking when my cousin approached him. Bruno had him drop to his knees and apologize. The kid — the coward — pretty much crapped his pants. He was like putty in Bruno's hands. Cousin Bruno smacked him in the head a few times — nothing serious, just enough to get the point across — and told him to never bother me again, and off we went.

I have only seen my cousin Bruno twice in the past thirty years. I did, however, email him as I wanted him to be the first in my family — along with my mother and closest friend, Honey D — to read the introduction to this book and know of my intentions to write this story as well as shed light on the disorders that have enveloped me my entire life and kept me from my family, friends, and life in general.

After reading the introduction, Bruno wrote back and, among a more detailed response, said, "I always knew there was something wrong, Cuz. I just couldn't put my finger on it.

I wish I had known and could have helped."

Me, too, Cuz. Me, too.

Another incident of bullying that happened in my neighborhood involved a life-long neighborhood kid, *AZ*, who lived at the end of my street. This was rare. This sort of thing usually didn't happen among families who knew each other for generations. Our families knew each other well.

I was 10-years-old. He was 15-years-old. He was a wild, cocky kid. Every time he saw me, he wanted to wrestle. Crazy! I was just a kid and half his size — literally. I would ignore him but he would occasionally knock me down on the grass and *practice* his moves. Picking on — bullying — someone half his size.

One day he knocked me to the ground and jumped on me full force, breaking my left collar bone. That was excruciatingly painful, but not half as painful as the trauma I had been dealing with day in and day out now for years from both inside and, now, outside of my home.

My parents were furious. He and his parents apologized and tried to make it appear an innocent accident. I knew better and so did he. He kept away from me from then on.

When 5th grade finished, it was time to move on to elementary school — grades 6 through 8. The school was about a half mile east of my house, on Charles St. in the North End.

This was my second culture shock so far in my life — going to a school with such older and bigger kids.

Kids were now coming from many different surrounding neighborhoods within the city and there were lots of different nationalities, personalities, shapes and sizes of kids. Instances of bullying would continue through the 8th grade.

Some kids would constantly tease me, calling me "Blinkie." I would blink continuously. It was a nervous tic and a byproduct of my childhood PTSD and anxiety.

Anxiety also caused me to get up two to three times in the middle of each and every night to urinate. This began when I was six-years-old. I never wet the bed, thankfully. However, I never slept much, either.

My mother noticed this trend and we brought it to the attention of my pediatrician. I remember his response as if it was yesterday; "*You're better off peeing a lot than not going at all.*"

This was the beginning of the bad luck I would have my entire life with most doctors who either knew nothing about the profession they were licensed to practice or just didn't give a shit.

Though I have barely slept more than three hours each night since my line of duty accident nearly two decades ago, within an hour or so of *finally* falling asleep, I still get up and go to the bathroom to urinate. My entire life, I've never experienced a peaceful sleep — and never a deep sleep of more than two to three hours.

In high school, the byproduct of my childhood PTSD and anxiety would be stress-related, very painful, Frankenstein-like sties on the lids of my eyes, along with severe head and facial sweating and heart palpitations that have stayed with me to this day.

Anxiety is one disorder that kept me pretty much isolated most of my life and robbed me of that very life. I have suffered with this disorder for over 40 years.

Over the years, there have been many instances of severe anxiety and panic attacks lasting days on end, without sleep, that nearly took my life.

Consistent anxiety is a worse fate than death.

Anxiety is the single most unpleasant and devastating emotional state a person can experience, bar none. It is pure evil. The Devil's preferred method of torture.

There was a large, African-American kid in one of my classes in the 6th grade. Black, white, yellow, or whatever, a person's skin color or sexual preference never mattered to me at any point in my life. I've never had a prejudice bone in my body. I knew all too well what it was like to be discriminated against, bullied, the short shit, different than the others, the misfit, being the odd man out, on the outside looking in. I have always judged people by the content of their soul, not the color of their skin or their sexual orientation. It was a routine thing for this big punk to pick on me every day. Name calling and all the rest. The usual bullying tactics. I would just ignore it and wish he would just go away and leave me alone. But these type of problems during my childhood never did. My internal pain was now accompanied by an anger that began to fester.

One day he decided to flick me in the face with his hand while I was seated in a classroom. It brought out that anger in me that was otherwise repressed. I'm not sure what took hold of me, but I stood up and slammed my pen into the side of his neck. He screamed and cried, blood and ink covering his neck.

We were both sent to the principal's office. Our parents were called.

There was a justifiable reason for my actions that day that was not addressed. I'm not sure if anyone really knew or understood what bullying was back in the mid-1970's. Neither of us was suspended. He made a few comments the next few days, but never bullied or touched me again.

Bullies don't expect you to stand up for yourself and, when you do, however you do, they cower. Their true colors are shown. The colors of a coward are yellow. A streak that runs up each and every one of their backs.

I remember catechism classes beginning at our church when I was in the 6th grade. I was already well into feeling horrible, having anxiety attacks, and trying to isolate at this early stage of my life. I guess I was very good at hiding my pain and suffering as no one ever picked up on my PTSD and the symptoms of which were slowly destroying me emotionally. Needless to say, I didn't want to go to catechism classes. It was bad enough, I had severe anxiety going to school every day.

My mother insisted I make my first communion.

She spoke with one of the priests at our North End Catholic church and worked out a one on one study program with him. Once I had enough hours of the classroom teachings, I could make my first communion. I did, and this made my mother very happy. As I got older, and my depression and anxiety progressed — my faith waning — I pulled away from the church, too. I never did make my confirmation.

My mother never asked me to do anything for her. She never asked anyone for anything, actually. She did insist I learn my prayers at an early age and she really wanted me to learn to play piano. Later in life, she was adamant that I pass the entrance exam for, attend, and graduate from Classical High School and that I go to, and finish college. I did both. Each for my mother.

Aside from that, she would always tell me her one prayer was for me to be happy. The one thing, to date, I could not do for her — or myself. Maybe her God wasn't listening to her prayers either.

Happiness, which I believe to be the most important aspect of a complete life, has always eluded me. It has been devoured, chewed up and spit out, by the disorders which imprisoned me my entire life.

We had a grand piano in our living room. My mother had it painted green. Same color as our house. Green was her favorite color. When I was 10-years-old, my mother asked me to give piano lessons a try. I agreed. I can think of nothing, since childhood, and to this very day, that I wouldn't do that my mother asked of me.

She hired a private piano teacher to come to our house to teach me piano.

I have a deep-seated passion for music and song from early childhood and to this day. I love the craft of songwriting and think highly of musicians. Musicians are a different breed — the coolest breed! However, I really didn't *feel* the piano. Once again, I got bored with it, and the instructor knew it. After a few months, he told my mother that he could see I was not interested in playing the piano, perhaps another instrument would hold my attention. No one ever asked me, nor did I say anything, but I would have loved to learn to play guitar.

Guess it's never too late but the disorders that have controlled my life for decades stole any desire, ambition, and drive from me long ago. PTSD, depression, and anxiety make it difficult to put one foot in front of the other, let alone take on and complete most projects.

There was this Puerto Rican kid who moved into the Eagle Park Neighborhood in the mid-70's, at the time when the neighborhoods began deteriorating. This kid was trouble with two legs. A complete nut-bag and terror. He always carried a knife with him and made sure everyone knew it.

His bullying began the summer before the 6th grade. I had just turned 11-years-old. He was a few years older than me and this kid was built with muscles everywhere! I'd never seen someone around my age with actual muscles.

Most of the kids in my age-range were afraid of him. I didn't want anything to do with him either. Honestly, the kid was scary looking! The kind of person that makes the hair on the back of your neck stand up.

He never wore a shirt during summer. He had scars all over his face and body. Only God knows what happened to him during his childhood. He bullied everyone, including the bullies! He mostly spoke — yelled — in Spanish and no one knew what he was saying.

He would always try and knock me off my bike. When he did, he would take my bike and ride around on it until he decided it was time to give it back. Sometimes leaving it far away from the park area where I'd have to walk to reclaim it.

One day, after a year or so of his constant bullying — I was 12 at this time — he started screaming at me in Spanish. I had no idea what he was saying. Then, out of nowhere, he attacked me and got me into a headlock. This was the first time a bully actually physically attacked and hit me.

I surprised myself as I reacted immediately and swept him to the ground, got out of his headlock, and got him into a rear naked choke hold.

I didn't know exactly what this move or hold was called back then, but, strangely enough, as I grew older and was forced into fights — always being the smaller kid — I almost always seemed to go for and get my opponent in this hold. It became my signature move as time and life moved forward. It was similar to a lion going for the neck of its prey, only I was usually the prey turning the tables. I could have killed him, literally, and he knew it. I kept just enough pressure on his neck so he couldn't move. He was screaming a different tune now and flailing like a fish out of water. All the time I was worried about that knife he always carried. I didn't want to hurt him so I told him I was going to let him go and get up. I knew that if he pulled that knife, I would have to run like hell. When he got up, he tried like all bullies to save face, but he knew I had his number. This was the first time I made my opponent — in this case a bully — tap-out. It wouldn't be the last.

I figured for sure he was going to pull that knife and charge me.

However, I stood my ground. Surprisingly — luckily — he didn't. I'm pretty certain if I had been his size or bigger, he would have used that knife.

I took a lot of abuse from bullies, but did not like anyone hitting or physically attacking me.

Years of bullying created an anger within that was starting to rear its ugly head. I would not allow someone to physically attack me without retaliation.

I never had much confidence or belief in myself from this early age and throughout my life, but I was usually more skilled than the next kid. Especially my skills in fighting.

Like most, I've had my share of losing. I've been in fights in my lifetime where I didn't shine as I did in others. Especially some of my battles during my younger years up through my mid-teens. You've got to lose every now and again to know how to win. Fighting, whether on the street or in the ring, is a learning process like everything else in life. The more you do it — the more you practice at something — the better you will get at it. The way I grew up, where I came from and what I went through during my childhood and later years, you either learned to fight and stand up for yourself or you were taken advantage of and treated like trash.

As crazy as this may sound to someone who may have grown up in a totally different, less hostile environment, that's the way it was. The way of the streets.

Fighting was a way of life, of survival.

40-plus years later, days and nights of constant, crippling pain and unable to so much as move some days, I still unconsciously size-up guys wherever I am and go through a strategy in my head to submit — to defeat — the person if it came to that. Yes, I know, it sounds a bit crazy. However, that way of life — the way of emotional and physical survival — is ingrained so very deeply in my mind. You can take the boy out of the streets but can never take the streets out of the boy. Any way you slice it, it has been an education that has earned me a particular skillset that all the classroom teachings and money in this world couldn't buy. You have to live it to truly comprehend it.

Being a physically small kid and adult, most who I fought during my day were almost always taller and larger than me. I was often outweighed by an easy 50 pounds, on average.

I had to learn to close the distance, among other strategies, from

an early age, to fairly gain the upper hand and survive being beaten —
in every sense of the word.

I've had some good days and fights and some bad days and fights.
Through experience comes knowledge, and there lies the power. I
didn't fully gain that knowledge of my abilities until my late twenties.
Through intense discipline and training, I became one with myself. My
mind and body became one. *Heart* is what allowed a mind being
ravaged by PTSD and depression to meld as one with my body. This
knowledge and awakening would have happened much sooner in my
life but for the constant struggle — the war — I had with these
disorders, which were ripping my life apart. I have been fighting
multiple battles my entire life. I've lost some battles along the way. I
haven't lost this war yet, nor do I intend to.

I am who I am. I would rather die than give up or be beaten.
You'd have to kill me before I quit in any type of fight. I grew up with
heart. That's something you either have or you don't. It can't be bought
and it can't be taught. Heart is what kept me alive during my childhood
and through the life of hell, the 40-plus years of torture I had to
endure. *Heart* is what keeps me alive today.

I was a huge martial arts fan from early childhood and would
carefully watch and try and master the many moves of my idols: Bruce
Lee, Chuck Norris, Benny "The Jet" Urquidez, and Bill "Superfoot"
Wallace.

I would begin training in boxing and karate at the age of 12.

I had so much pent up hurt and anger that I poured this negative
energy into my outlets — my training being my primary "addiction"
and "medicine" at this time.

I was always smaller than the others, but always quicker and
usually stronger. Most of the fights I got into in my life — and there
were way too many — had my opponent tapping-out as I overpowered
with speed, strength, and technique, wrapping my opponent into a
submission hold that usually involved a choke or compression lock.
Some say you can't tap-out in a street fight. That is up to the one in
control of the submission hold. I've heard the words "*I quit,*" "*Enough,*"
"*I'm done,*" and similar, in many street fights throughout my life where I
had my opponent in a submission hold. I've always prided myself on
being honorable, fair, and a man of my word. If someone tapped-out, I
gave him the benefit of the doubt that he was man enough to know
he'd been beaten, and it was over. That was usually the case. However,

not everyone I submitted and gave a break to — let get back to his feet — was as honorable.

I realized throughout my childhood and adulthood that I was different than most in nearly all ways — the way I thought, the way I felt, the way I suffered, the way I carried myself and functioned, my values.

It's very difficult in life — especially for a child — when you are so much different than those around you. As a kid, you just want to fit in. I just so happened to be cut from a different cloth and the disorders that ruled my world didn't help matters either.

I've never been one to pat myself on the back — I've never had any confidence to begin with — but I had a lot of natural, physical ability in sports and fighting. It was innate. When I started training in a certain sport or focused on a certain goal, it was that much more evident. Whatever I did in athletics and sports or focused on, I put 200% into — complete dedication and discipline — and excelled.

Strangely enough, due to the disorders which emotionally imprisoned me, I was never firing on all cylinders. I'll mention this often throughout this story. I've always wondered just how far I could have gone if I had been normal from childhood.

I always went to the extreme — bikes, martial arts, powerlifting, or work. This was my only way of escaping the emotional pain. Part of the addictive nature in my genes. Perhaps I had some obsessive-compulsive disorder (OCD) as well. If there had been a positive male role model in my life to look up to, who paid attention to me and encouraged my talent when I was young, I probably could have learned to believe in myself and could have become a very successful athlete, professional martial arts fighter, motorcycle racer, songwriter, or so much more. All of my talent was wasted because I never believed in myself and there was never anyone in my life who encouraged me and made me believe in myself. I know my mother tried later in my life when she began to realize the severity and depth of my sorrow and despair. My mother would always tell me, "*I believe in you. Believe in yourself.*"

The damage had already been done.

There was a North End Neighborhood bully, *Chooch*, who tormented me for a few years through middle school — 6th through 8th grade range. This took place mostly in the Charles St. area of the neighborhood. I had left the Eagle Park Neighborhood behind around

6th grade and spent most of my time in the Charles St. area — at the Boys Club, or riding bikes and dirt bikes with some neighborhood kids.

Chooch's bullying was so bad I had contemplated at the tender age of 12 lying in wait and beating him severely with a baseball bat. I knew how it felt to be hit with a bat. I wanted him to know too.

When I was 10-years-old, I was hit across the face, full-force, with a baseball bat by another kid during a street pick-up ball game in the neighborhood. There were more than a few nut cases where I came from. I Lost half of my front tooth and received multiple stitches in my lip. I have a bond on my left front tooth to this day along with one of many scars to go with it.

Chooch was a couple years older and much bigger than me. His method of bullying was to constantly threaten me. A few times he grabbed my shirt below the neck with two hands, made verbal threats and bullied this way.

I caught up with Chooch a few years later on the East Side. In high school, my friends and I — and just about every other group and click from surrounding high schools — would gather and socialize on the East Side; Thayer St. in the Brown University area and the river area, which abuts and runs along the Seekonk River/Narragansett Bay, parallel to Blackstone Blvd. I was bigger now, more muscular, and had been training consistently in martial arts, boxing, and weight training. I was gaining a reputation at this time for my ability in martial arts and my strength for my size.

At the request of friends, I would occasionally demonstrate my skills — be it speed, power, or accuracy — by knocking objects off their heads or out of their hands with spinning back kicks, among other tricks with kicks. My flexibility and muscle control—my ability to hold kicks vertically — were also on display. I had the flexibility of an Olympic gymnast by this time — Russian and vertical splits and all.

I was holding my side kicks nearly perfectly vertical, as one of my idol's, Bill "Superfoot" Wallace, did so effortlessly and amazingly.

Bill Wallace's style — his speed and accuracy, incredible flexibility, and overall fluent control — was the primary hook that attracted me to martial arts. Bill Wallace was *the* major influence, followed closely by Bruce Lee, which began my addiction to training. I wanted to be just like these guys, just like my martial arts idols.

By my late teens, I was bench pressing 315 lbs., squatting 495 lbs., and routinely repping-out strictly with over 1,000 lbs. on the leg press

— at a 150 lb. body weight, drug-free, body fat percentage always in the single digits.

Steroids were becoming popular around this time and many my age and in the years to come were juicing — taking steroids. I felt about steroids the same way I felt about alcohol and other drugs — it wasn't for me and I'd have nothing to do with it. Pound for pound, I was out-lifting guys twice my size and most of the juicers.

When I ran into Chooch on the East Side, I was 16, he was 18. I saw him walking up the sidewalk with some neighborhood kids I grew up with. He didn't see me, but a couple other kids he was with did. I approached him and blocked him from walking past me. Everyone there knew what I was thinking. I wanted to beat him to a bloody pulp. However, I had never — and would never — hit someone first in a fight. It wasn't my style.

Another neighborhood kid, *Big Dog (BD)*, who he was with, begged me not to beat him. He asked me to do him that favor. I always liked BD. Unfortunately, like most from the neighborhood during my childhood, he took a left in life and went south — the way of most. BD said Chooch was trying to beat a drug addiction and get clean.

I didn't hit him, but I did grab him by the shirt, just below the neck, with two hands — just as he did to me for several years of his bullying — and pushed him against the side of a building, looked deep into his eyes and said, "*Remember me, asshole?*"

He was shaking like the coward he had been his entire life and pleaded to give him a break and not to hit him. He had no idea I would never hit him unless he made a move or swung first. Not only could I never hit someone first in a fight, I couldn't hit someone this frightened and useless. However, deep down inside I was hoping — maybe praying — he would swing or make that move.

Of all the bullies who tormented me as a child and cut so deeply into my soul, I had a very strong aversion for this particular punk. He probably should have gotten what he had coming to him. Anyone else in my shoes at that time most likely would have hurt him pretty badly. Maybe the one thing I inherited from my father was that too easy-going and peaceful demeanor as it applied to the streets and that life.

I told BD I spared beating the scumbag as a favor to him.

He shook my hand and thanked me.

We went our separate ways.

4

I began riding bicycles around the age of six. I loved it! no training wheels for me! I became comfortable and skillful around eight-years-old.

It was my first addiction, my first medication, my first means of escape at this time from the everyday trauma that was my life.

I spent as many hours as possible riding bikes and outside of my home — practicing tricks, taking the bikes apart, and making new ones. I was doing things on a bike in a few years that was unheard of back in the early 1970's; some of the things they began doing in the X-Games BMX competition decades down the road. I was hitting dirt jumps and man-made ramps with the "Superman" move, jumping over other bikes and people, doing stoppies before anyone knew what a stoppie was. I could ride wheelies around the block, and do figure eight's forever without coming down once. The bike became an extension of my body. We were one. Whatever I did, whatever I focused on, whatever my medicine was at the time, I put 200% into it and then some. I poured my heart and soul into it in an effort to escape the trauma that was consuming me. And it got me through one more day. Always excelling at my addiction because it was necessary to function. Necessary to survive.

As with the training and martial arts I would soon become addicted too. Each filled the void in my life and offered me the boost I needed to cope and move forward. Absorbed in my addictions was the only time I ever felt good in my own skin. It cleared my head of the emotional pain. It kept my mind from the horror that was my life. It kept the demons at bay.

A Good childhood friend of mine, *Beets*, lived on the same street. We grew up together from an early age of four or five. I didn't know then what was going on in his life, but, in looking back, I can see clearly that Beets was suffering the same childhood PTSD as I was. His father was an alcoholic and, I believe, there was some violence in his home between his mom and dad.

Somewhere around the first grade, Beets and I were playing in his yard. He stole one of my toys and wouldn't give it back. When I insisted he give it back, he reached under a pedal car, retrieved a hammer, and hit me over the head with it.

I remember all the blood pouring down my face. I was terrified.

Crying, I climbed over the fence from his yard and ran up the street back to my house. My mother and aunt V took me to the hospital where I received seven stitches in my head. This was the first of an awful lot of stitches I'd receive to my head and on my face during my lifetime. These stitches were also the scariest, being the first.

We were kids, the same age, same size. Our families were close and, after a couple weeks, Beets and I were close again too.

Beets and I both learned to swim at the Wanskuck, North End Boys Club. Method back then — just throw you in the deep end and you learn pretty quickly how to swim. I certainly did after taking in a couple mouthfuls of chlorinated pool water!

Luckily, I swallowed that chlorinated pool water before someone dropped a grenade of a turd in the pool! One of the club lifeguards saw a log floating and yelled, "Everyone out of the pool now!" All the kids who could get out on their own did so quickly. The rest who were treading water in the deep end were pulled out with extension poles. Needless to say, the club's monitors were a bit angry. They drilled everyone to find out who did it. I guess they thought it was intentional. No one ever admitted who couldn't hold it and used the pool as an outhouse. Or, perhaps, being thrown into the deep end scared the shit out of someone — literally.

It was both disgusting and funny at the same time. The event for some reason kept a shady smirk on Beets' face for the next month. He was certainly a hoot and a half.

He was a bit more serious when we'd go to the Providence Civic Center to watch an older neighborhood kid, *JD*, compete in karate tournaments. JD was a member of the Rhode Island Thunderbolts karate team. This was the mid-1970's and I would soon begin my own training at Pesare's Kenpo Karate in the North End. I was already a big fan of martial arts and it would quickly become my new outlet, medicine, and addiction. It was my way of life and survival.

Before that outlet became my savior, bicycle riding was my medicine and escape. Beets and I would ride bikes together mostly every day. He was pretty good too! It was his addiction, as it was mine. I clearly see that in retrospect. A lot of friendly competition between us. Two addictive, over-the-top and going to extremes, competitive personalities between us. Each doing his best to submerge a painful, bleeding soul.

Beets would soon become addicted to motocross racing. Later

becoming a professional motocrosser. Unfortunately, he would break his neck in a race and that would pretty much end his pro career as he knew it.

I remember visiting him several times while he wore the halo that was screwed into his skull. I couldn't imagine at that time having to endure something of that nature. Little did I know, I would have been better off breaking my neck, back, or both and completely healing as Beet's spine did, than sustaining the extensive, severe spinal damage and persistent physical pain that I did in the years to come.

Few things in life are worse than chronic, excruciating, and debilitating physical pain that progressively worsens, day after day, year after year, with a constant fear of paralysis hanging over your head.

Beets would later find long-distance cycling as a replacement and his new outlet.

He also stayed within the motocross circuit in some capacity — spending as much time as possible doing what made him feel good.

I remember going to watch Beets race back in the day. He was a damn good motocross racer. Crazy good! He put his heart and soul into it and then some. I can relate. It was necessary for survival. Like me, Beets never drank or took drugs — he saw what it did within his own family and took a right where most in this situation take a left and go down the same path as family member(s). He weight-trained a lot, too, as I did, beginning in our early teens.

I saw Beets throughout my childhood and up through my twenties every now and again.

I remember discussing depression with him on one occasion when I was back in Rhode Island a few years after my line of duty accident and well into a major depression. Dealing with hellish physical and emotional pain every minute of every day. I was in my mid-30's at this time. I had never really discussed this with anyone before, but knew he had faced a serious spinal injury that took a toll on him for a period of time. He knew exactly what I was talking about and going through. He told me to keep in touch and let him know if I needed anything or wanted to talk.

Like everyone in my life, that meant anything to me, I pulled away and isolated. You become so frozen, so crippled emotionally that you have not an ounce of ambition and drive to do anything at all for yourself, or to reach out and communicate with anyone, regardless of their importance in your life. This is one of the effects of PTSD and major depression. If there is no one there on a daily basis for support and to take you by the hand, pull you back from the hell that is your life, and walk with you in a positive, clear direction, it is almost impossible to move forward.

Fortunately for Beets, his injuries healed, his emotional and physical pain subsided, and he didn't sink into a deep and lasting depression as I did. He did have others — support — around him to pick him up and push him forward. So, he didn't isolate from the world as I did.

Beets was, like me, very close with his mother. His mother being his biggest fan, as my mother was mine. I know he moved on later in life, married, and had a child. It was good to hear that he found happiness and had loving support in his life. I think of him often.

My father would buy me my first minibike when I was 10-years-old. The little 50cc kind with no gears!

In looking back, I guess you could say my parents spoiled me with material things. Though, the one thing I really needed — attention, support, and encouragement from my father, or another adult male role model was never there.

Perhaps my mother subconsciously believed that the material things could somehow take the place of that father figure and male role model that was missing in my life. I am living proof that it did not. It cannot.

I was addicted immediately to minibike riding. Motorcycles would soon take the place of bicycles as a primary outlet. I would go on to ride many dirt bikes back in the day — from Honda XR-75's to Suzuki RM 125's.

Back in the 70's, there was still a lot of undeveloped land even in the inner city. We had several areas of multiple acres of dirt and hills where we could ride dirt bikes. There were acres of dirt behind, and surrounding the Voc-Tech; Rhode Island Vocational Technical High School, which would later become the Rhode Island School for the Deaf. There was a really cool dirt race track in the Canada Pond area abutting HWY 146, stretching from the North End/Boys Club area up to North Providence. There was great dirt riding behind the cemetery on Smithfield Ave., along the railroad tracks running parallel with I-95 from Providence into Pawtucket.

No one could believe how fast and hard I would hit the dirt jumps there. One day — I was thirteen at the time — a bunch of neighborhood kids came there to watch what everyone had been talking about. I was riding an XR-75 at the time.

Being the center of attention, my adrenaline was flowing and I definitely wasn't thinking clearly. I hit a six-foot jump at around 40 mph — faster than ever before — I overshot the landing and wound up coming down in soft, deep beach sand. The bike hit and stuck, throwing me at 40-plus mph head-first into the soft dirt. I wasn't wearing a helmet or any other gear. The bike then flipped, tumbled, and landed on top of my right leg, pinning me while the exhaust pipe burned deeply into my right calf. I couldn't move an inch. With dirt in my face and mouth, I began screaming for someone to help me get the bike's hot exhaust off my burning calf.

Of the dozen or so kids there to witness my disaster that day, only one neighborhood kid, *Squeaky*, ran immediately to help me.

Many of the neighborhood kids were burnouts by this time — drinking, smoking pot, skipping school, and stealing everything that wasn't nailed down. They had no compassion or concern whatsoever.

Squeaky pulled the bike off of me. After getting the bike to start again, I drove home to tend to my burned calf. It was extremely painful, especially trying to clean it out and keep it clean for the next week. I have a large scar there to always remind me of my early Evel Knievel days!

Dirt bikes would soon give way to one of the few real loves of my life — one of the few true joys of my life: riding sport bikes. They've been called rice rockets and crotch rockets. I've had, and enjoyed, them all; 600's up to my last bike, and favorite of them all, a Honda 1000 RR.

At 18-years-old, I found that peace in my soul taking long motorcycle rides down endless, winding farm roads, to the beach or wherever. It didn't matter, I was in the zone. My mind was clear and my soul was happy when riding. The motorcycle was an extension of my body — we were one — much the same as the bicycles in my earlier years.

I never rode my sport bikes without a helmet and usually had heavy-duty street riding gear on. As with all outlets in my life, I would always go to extremes. Balls to the wall, so to speak. Always pushing myself to the limits, always pushing the envelope.

I quickly excelled as a street rider, skillfully carving corners at hair-raising speeds, my knees gently caressing the pavement beneath me. It made my crippled soul feel alive. It cleared my mind of all the pain and murkiness and kept me focused on the day and the days ahead.

With every roll of the throttle, with every bodily movement, with each mile passing in blissful slow motion, the sunshine and the warm, summer wind canvased and painted my soul with pure joy. For a brief time, my mind and soul were free. Unencumbered by the grip of these horrendous disorders that otherwise consumed and controlled my every thought, my every action. I was in another world — it was a beautiful thing to truly be free.

As Bob Seger wrote and sung so eloquently in his song, "Like a Rock,"

> *"My hands were steady, my eyes were clear and bright... I felt like a million... I felt like number one."*

Seems the closer my dance with death, the more I felt alive. On reflection, should I have fallen at these speeds and maneuvers, it wouldn't have been pretty and, most likely, would have been fatal.

Even this joy, this love, would come to a sudden halt with my spinal injury.

Everything that ever served as my medicine, my outlet — my escape from the pain and darkness that was my life — in time would be taken away from me. One by one, I would lose my entire sanity-saving arsenal.

I would be left with no medication — no way to quell the pain — but rather to suffer emotionally and physically day in and day out for decades.

I've asked myself throughout the many years, "How can I continue to believe in that God I was raised to believe in? In a Higher Power who would allow bad things to happen, over and over again, to good people?" I see it every day, all around me. Evil triumphing over good. "Where are the blessings from these bad situations?"

I have never wanted to feel like, or consider myself, a victim. It is a very hefty, oppressive, self-defeating feeling to carry around for any amount of time, let alone a lifetime. One — another shackle — that can only keep you forever enslaved. On the flip side, it has been over four decades — over 40 consistent years — in which I have not lived, but have taken air into my lungs and merely existed for the sole purpose of suffering emotionally and physically. Enduring loss after loss of everything meaningful, everything needed in my life to cope and function. I have never felt more betrayed in my life than I have felt by that God I grew up believing in.

Can God's blessings finally come by way of my shedding light onto these unforgiving, damning disorders and making a difference in — perhaps saving — someone else's life?

🦋 🦋 🦋 🦋

In June of 2013, I was one of millions who watched — without blinking — an astonishing feat broadcast live around the world; Nick Wallenda's 1,500' high, 22-minute-high wire walk across a 2" wide steel cable over the Grand Canyon. He had no tether or safety net. What he did have was his balancing pole. It was his balancing pole that allowed him to maintain that incredible steadiness. Without that balancing pole, it wouldn't have been possible. He would have fallen 1,500' to his death.

My life has been void of true emotional stability since very early childhood. Perpetual darkness and complete imbalance has ruled my world. My life's scale forever and fully tilted by blackness, my mind and soul hanging on for dear life.

My training has been my primary balancing pole my entire life. It allowed me to reset not only the chemical imbalance of the brain responsible for depression, but that emotional balance needed in life in order to stand and function. The disorders I suffered with and that controlled my life kept me dangling — between insanity and lucidity — on that wire of life.

My training — my emotional balancing pole — however, kept me stable while walking the high wire.

My training — like Nick Wallenda's physical balancing pole — kept me from falling off this high wire and plummeting to the bottom. I, too, had no tether or safety net. There was no one there to catch me should I fall. I was isolated. I was alone on that wire as Nick Wallenda was during his breathtaking high wire walk across the Grand Canyon.

My entire life, only my training — my emotional balancing pole — was capable of keeping my mind lucid, my footing steady, and moving me forward. Keeping me from spiraling downward into absolute darkness, infinite chaos, and being pulverized on impact. It kept me from falling to my death.

We all need a means — an outlet — to assist us in balancing our lives.

For nearly 20 years now, I continue to ask myself, "What, if anything, has that Higher Power I believed so strongly in and prayed so faithfully to most of my life replaced my balancing pole with?"

Meaning and clear purpose being around the corner — the next page ...

5

When I was a kid, I loved the Italian feasts that would come to the neighborhoods every year. In addition to that wonderful daily aroma of fresh Italian bread and pizza coming from the family owned Italian bakeries and pizzerias in the neighborhood, the smell of the Italian sausage and peppers would mask the entire neighborhood for the duration of the feasts. A heartwarming and wonderful smell it was — and still is!

The atmosphere was exciting and impossible to ignore if you were a kid. Even a kid whose life was slowly being controlled into hell by PTSD, depression, and anxiety.

I remember my first introduction to a feast. It was a beautiful and most memorable summer night in Rhode Island, during the early 1970's. I was helping my uncle *Fausto* and aunt Paola at their food stand at the St. Mary's Feast in Cranston, Rhode Island. My cousin, *Pina*, was working too.

I was collecting money and handing out Italian sausage and pepper sandwiches, doughboys and slices of pizza. Wow, those dollar bills and quarters just kept coming and coming! The Italian sausage and peppers, pizza, and doughboys flying out of the food stand and gobbled up!

My uncle Fausto gave me a stack of quarters a mile high at the end of the feast for helping out. Cool beans, I thought!

The Italian food and pastries at the feasts were incredible back in the day. Oh, the memories I have every time I smell Italian sausage and peppers! The feeling — the mood — was very special at the feasts in the early days, more so being with family and sharing the experience.

As a child, I always looked forward to playing the carnival-type games and, the best part of the feast, the fireworks! Those were the days! Though they were few and far between, those were the only normal days of my life. Some of the very few happy moments and cherished memories from my childhood.

North End feasts were easy to get to as they were within walking distance. However, if a feast was in my aunt *Angela* and uncle Giorgio's Federal Hill Neighborhood, my mother would drive me over to go with my cousins. The feast on the Hill was the granddaddy of them all! It was always an awesome time. Being with and hanging out with my cousins at the feast made it that much more enjoyable. Everything, actually, was that much better anytime and anywhere I happened to be with my cousins when we were kids.

I distinctly remember on one occasion when a feast was coming to a neighborhood some distance from mine. I asked my mother to take me. I had never asked my father to do anything, as I knew he wouldn't enjoy it and would rather spare myself the disappointment. My mother insisted my father take me. That was a first (and last). He moaned and groaned and finally we got into the car and drove off in the direction of the feast. We drove some time and he complained he couldn't find it. I noticed the bright and colorful festival lights off in the distance and pointed this out. I remember my father being aggravated and saying, *"They're just about to close, we'll come back another time."*

I realized at that early age of ten that I would never have a traditional father/son relationship with my dad. He wasn't capable of it. Be it his own childhood and upbringing without a father, trauma in his own life, alcoholism, being married to *the life* or whatever, I just accepted it. As other disappointments set in during my childhood and later life, I started to believe that perhaps it was me. Maybe I was to blame. Maybe I was no good. Maybe I was defective and not worthy of a normal childhood and family life. How could anyone be this unlucky unless they deserved it? The emotional pain and despair would only continue to worsen with each passing day.

As a kid, I spent a lot of time with my mother. There was no male role model in my life to spend quality time with. Most of my morality and character traits were influenced by my mother. That is a blessing as far as I'm concerned and one of the few things in my life that I'm proud of.

My mother was always a shopper and bargain hunter. During my early childhood, I was more often than not with my mother shopping. If we didn't go to one of my aunt's houses, we were usually — for some portion of the day — shopping.

My mother would food shop like she was feeding an army! My father, who was a physically small man of 5'5" and 160+ lbs., actually ate enough for a small army!

The man could just eat and eat and then eat some more! I've yet to meet anyone who derives such extraordinary joy from eating as does my father.

My mother delights in — and does to this day — shopping for clothes, shoes, and handbags. Doesn't every woman? Never extravagant or spending more than she could afford. I know shopping was her way of taking her mind off the dysfunction and chaos within her own family — it soothed her soul. It allowed her mind to escape the pain, suffering, and disappointment within her own life for a short time. We all have some activity, some outlet that is our medicine — that helps maintain our sanity. What we do to feel good about ourselves and clear our minds and souls of stress and pain. Shopping was — and still is in her late 80's — my mother's outlet.

It rubbed off on me as a child and later in life I would acquire one of my mother's fetishes — shoes.

I had a thing for shoes, particularly, sneakers throughout my life. At one time I had accumulated well over one hundred pair of sneakers and shoes. Many I had never worn! I would eventually donate most to charity.

To this day, if I happen upon a good sale and could save a significant amount of money on a purchase, I still get a little excited. Thanks, Mom!

As long as you aren't hurting anyone — or yourself — we all deserve and *need* an outlet; an escape.

My mother never drank alcohol. However, her bad habit — one that can cause severe health issues and death — is cigarettes. Cigarette smoking has been the only negative addiction of my mother's for some 65 years. My mother began smoking at the age of twenty-two and has been smoking, consistently, for some 65 years! The trauma she has endured and the stress she has been under most of her life and, presently, day to day having to live with, and deal with, my father and the pain of being betrayed and disrespected by her own children and grandchildren has kept her addiction alive. It's an outlet — albeit, a negative one — that calms her nerves.

These old-timers didn't believe in divorce. If anyone should have been divorced, it was my parents — and a long, long time ago. They have absolutely nothing in common. There is no — and never has been — love, respect, or communication between them. It has been this way since my childhood and to this very day. A very sad, very stressful situation for my mother and everyone who had to be — and still has to be — around and witness to such uneasiness and heartache.

I could never be at peace and enjoy the company of, and conversation, with my mother in my father's presence. The tension with both of them in the same room creates a very stifling atmosphere.

I honestly have no idea how my mother has maintained her sanity with what she has had to deal with in her life; my father at the top of that list, her wicked immediate family a very close second.

My father is on a whole different wavelength than most. He is a *rara avis*. He cannot be explained. He has to be experienced.

Later in life, Mom would really enjoy playing the slot machines at the casinos that popped up in Connecticut and Rhode Island.

However, she was in slot heaven when she came to visit me a couple times in Las Vegas. Her joy when being in the various casinos — enjoying those one-armed bandits — was contagious. Regardless of my constant pain, depression, and anxiety, it warmed my heart knowing she was enjoying herself so much. Her mind and soul was at ease when on those slots. Proceeds from all those machines built the city of Las Vegas many times over!

🦋 🦋 🦋 🦋

It's hard to believe how some things the government considers morally unacceptable and has deemed "illegal," in time miraculously becomes morally acceptable and perfectly legal. Once the government gets their piece of the money-pie that is — similar to prohibition in the U.S. during the 1920's. Just repeal one amendment and ratify another to get the money pouring into the government coffers. Money corrupts. Governments and the men and women who run them are no exception.

Marijuana is now being legalized in some states. The government is taxing it at over 20%! Maybe the future of our country will see legal crack and heroin houses too. The power and influence of dead white men on little green pieces of paper is simply incredible!

🦋 🦋 🦋 🦋

My mother never spent more than she could afford at the casinos. She would set her limit and be done when she reached that limit, whether that was in five minutes or five hours. She never borrowed money or took money out of her bank account to keep shopping or to play the slots. She would never take money from the home budget and neglect paying bills or buying food.

She was very responsible and deserved whatever joy she could afford to buy herself. She earned that right one-thousand times over.

I remember one instance shopping with my mother in an A&P grocery story in our neighborhood. I was five-years-old. I wanted a candy bar and my mother said no. I decided to put it in my pocket and, as we were in the parking lot, I took it out and began to eat it. My mother looked at me, smacked me in the head, and marched me right back into the A&P where she asked for the manager. She told him I had just stolen one of his candy bars. The manager politely scolded me and gave me a quick lesson in morality. My mother's lesson when we got home was much longer and much more severe. Morality lesson number one, lived and learned that very day.

Whether shopping for food or clothing with my mother, I had my share as a child. It was a daily routine. I would get bored rather fast at the department stores as Mom — usually with aunt *Mimi* or another aunt or friend — would shop trance-like for hours. To amuse myself and keep from going nutty, I would hide in the clothes racks and would jump out and scare the ladies as they looked through the racks of clothes. I thought it was pretty funny scaring them. Most of the ladies did, too, and would laugh after catching their breath. No harm, no foul.

However, there was an instance with one lady who started swearing at me very loudly. My mother heard the commotion, came over, they had a few words and the woman began swearing at my mother. My mother walked away. All was over. Not by a long shot! I was furious that this lady was yelling at my mother and was very rude and cocky after we both apologized. I decided to hide in a rack further up the aisle.

When she came by, I stuck her big toe with a pin I had found on the floor. Needless to say, the shit hit the fan. But my six-year-old "justice" had been served! With another morality lesson and punishment from Mom forthcoming!

I once found $60 outside the front door of a shoe store my mom was shopping in. She took me and the money back into the store to see if anyone had lost it. Not telling them how much was found, of course. No one came forward to claim the money. My mom let me keep the $60 and we bought a new bike with it.

From that day forward, every time I went shopping with my mother, I kept my head down and searched and searched for the next jackpot!

My mother enjoyed flea markets back in the mid to late 1970's. They were actually pretty cool back in the day. One place I didn't mind going shopping with my mother. She would actually set up sometimes and sell some of her personal items and other odds and ends.

I liked looking around at all the different things — especially the old stuff — being offered for sale. I would find some great vintage collectibles, comic books, marbles, cards, parts for my bikes, etc. It was during this time I'd been bitten by the vintage collecting bug. I always loved the days of old and the items from those times.

I remember going with my mother often on weekends to the flea market located at Jolly Cholly's Funland in North Attleboro, Massachusetts. I would also spend some time in the amusement park there. Usually alone but for once or twice when a neighborhood friend would come along with us for the day. I enjoyed playing the pinball machines — in the pinball arcade — more than anything.

My favorite ride was the bumper cars. However, I was never able to ride them as there was a height requirement and I wasn't tall enough.

I was always thinner and shorter than most of the other kids my age. I remember getting to the flea market some mornings before the amusement park opened. I would sneak in there and try desperately to lower that darn wooden height requirement sign that was posted on the fence leading to the bumper cars. No luck. I would have to wait a few more years before I was tall enough to ride the bumper cars.

I've noticed throughout my life a high priority — a prerequisite — for many has been a height requirement. From dating to the not so distant past of law enforcement; if you weren't a certain height (many agencies required a minimum height of 5'9"), you couldn't apply and wouldn't be hired by the particular police department. Seems everyone likes their men tall. I was smacked on the butt by the short stick when I was born. I had no luck in this area, either!

6

My aunt Mimi was a staple within our family. She was always with us at our home and came with us most everywhere when I was a child. She would come with us often when we went to visit my aunts and uncles. She would be at most family functions.

She was one of a kind. A delightful, warm, and loving woman. aunt Mimi was always happy and always had a smile on her face. She was a joy to be around.

Mom and aunt Mimi were very close. They had a truly special relationship. A lot of love and respect between them.

Aunt Mimi was the wife of my father's uncle, *Vito*, whom I never met — he passed away before I was born. Aunt Mimi lived in the neighborhood, right up the street from us. She would walk down to our house often, spending the whole day and night with my mother and the rest of the family. She liked to walk and always insisted on walking down to our house, which was about a quarter mile from her house. She didn't drive and never had a driver's license. Mom would pick her up if it was raining, the weather was bad, or if we had a storm coming up. Aunt Mimi was terrified of thunder and was afraid to be alone during storms.

Aunt Mimi died the summer of 1982. Right after my high school graduation. She was 86. I had just turned 18.

Aunt Mimi was in excellent shape and sharp as a tack for an 86-year-old woman. She didn't look her age, either.

She was crossing the street to pick up a morning paper and was hit by a car. She died immediately. The driver said he was blinded by the sun and didn't see aunt Mimi crossing the street.

I remember when my mother broke the news to me. I was crushed. Once again, losing someone I loved so much took its toll on me. I remember laying down on my bed and just sobbing for hours. My mother took it very hard as well.

The only thing that kept me from drowning in sorrow and anger was my outlet — training — and the fact that I knew she died quickly and didn't suffer, that she would never be afflicted by any other diseases or become senile and suffer with dementia like grandma M did. That is the worst of fates.

I have a favorite picture of aunt Mimi standing by the pool at my aunt *Farfalla* and uncle Giulio's house. I find it difficult to look at the picture. But it's one of those few pictures and memories that brings me back to a time and place when I felt a bit of childhood happiness with my family — my real family.

We would go to aunt Farfalla and uncle Giulio's often. I would swim in the pool when I was a kid and hang around with my cousins *Lia, Ciana,* and *Arachidi*. Spending time with my mother, aunts, uncles, and cousins were some of the only times of my childhood — my life actually — when I was happy for a short while. The only joyful memories of childhood are from these family times.

I could never put into words just how much I miss and love my aunts, uncles, and cousins. Each one of them is special to me — and beautiful in their own unique way.

I spent time with all my aunts, uncles, and cousins when I was a kid:

My aunt Farfalla and uncle Giulio and their children, my cousins, Lia, Ciana, and Arachidi.

My aunt Adela and uncle Lucio and their children, my cousins *Gabby, Kara,* and Bruno.

My aunt Paola and uncle Fausto and their children, my cousins *BB, Vio,* and Pina.

My aunt Marcella and her children, cousins *Bessa* and *Damo.*

My aunt Angela and uncle Giorgio and their children, my cousins *Gio, Rico, Ettore, Silio,* and *Rena.*

I remember as a child having to climb all those stairs at both my aunt Angela's Federal Hill multi-family house and my aunt Marcella's Mount Pleasant multi-family house and front yard. With my little legs and all those big stairs, it felt like it took a week to get to the front door!

My uncle Antonio and aunt *Gee* and their children, my cousins *Tony, Della,* and *CeeCee.*

My uncle Antonio bought a house in Florida the same time as my uncle Nico in the early 1970's. He lived on the same street, three houses down from my uncle Nico and aunt Ria and their children, my cousins Deana and Lino. I spent a lot of time with them when in Florida, especially when Pop was there with uncle Nico.

I have wonderful, early childhood memories of going to the beaches in Rhode Island during the summers; 2nd (Sachuest Town Beach) and 3rd beaches in Middletown and 1st beach in Newport.

Sand Hill Cove, Galilee, Scarborough, and Narragansett beaches. My favorite destination of all was always the beach. Spending time by the ocean and being with family was the best!

I remember some fun times with my aunts and cousins at Spring Lake Beach in Burrillville, Rhode Island, during my childhood, too. It wasn't the ocean I loved so much, but, being with family, the lake was cool enough! I hold the joyous memories from these times close in my heart. It keeps my spirit alive and that blood that flows through my veins from turning to rust.

As a child, I would often go to the beaches — and everywhere else — with my mother and her best friend, aunt *Bianca*. She was always with us during my very early childhood.

I remember aunt Bianca buying me an awesome red pedal car for my birthday when I was 4-years-old. I would ride it up and down the driveway all day long!

She would take me everywhere as a child and buy me all kinds of things.

I also remember the flask that was always in her hand and her car. I asked what the flask was once. Aunt Bianca said it was her medicine. It seems throughout my life, many of the people I loved were drowning their pain and sorrows in that particular medicine. That medicine destroys the lives of more human beings — and those around them — than just about any other "medicine" civilization has ever known.

Aunt Bianca was an ex-girlfriend of my uncle Nico. I would hear the story often as I got older. She never stopped loving him, even after both had married and moved on. She spoke of him and her love for him to my mother right up through her illness, the cancer that took my aunt's life in March of 2002. She was a beautiful soul and like a sister to my mother. She is loved and missed immensely. I keep her memory and the love I felt for her — as with all those I have loved and lost; my aunts, uncles, Pop, grandmothers, and friends — alive and always in my soul.

I would also go to the beach and everywhere else as a child with my mother and her good friend, aunt *Vicki*. I remember once driving with aunt Vicki and my mother to the beach. A kid threw a rock at and hit aunt Vicki's car. Aunt V chased the kid with the car as he ran down the street. She soon jumped out of the car and chased him through a yard calling him every profanity-laced name I'd never heard! My ears are still ringing from that wonderful but oh-so-vulgar verbal beating the kid took! She didn't play around, that's for sure!

Then there were those special times during childhood spent with family at Rocky Point Amusement Park on the Narragansett Bay side and shoreline of Warwick Neck in Warwick, Rhode Island. The chowder was the best around! I also enjoyed Crescent Park on the shores of Narragansett Bay in Riverside, Rhode Island. The carousel there was something to see in the day and something I'll never forget!

The times spent at the Castle Theatre on Chalkstone Ave. in Providence watching movies with my mother, aunts, and cousins was always a good time. I remember my mother and aunt Paola turning red with embarrassment during a back-seat kissing scene in one of the movies we went to see. My cousin Pina and I never blinked!

My two favorite movies when I was a kid were *Jaws* and *Planet of the Apes.*

I remember going to see *Jaws* with my cousin *Dee*, my aunt *Bella's* oldest daughter. I have a deep-seated love for being in and around the ocean. However, after seeing this movie, I wouldn't go near the ocean for the next five years!

Planet of the Apes was frightening as a child and left me with my mouth hanging open. Could this be possible I thought? I was only 4-years-old or so when the movie *Planet of the Apes* debuted. It is the one and only movie throughout my life that just scared the pants off me! I had nightmares for the next year!

Up the street from the Castle on Chalkstone Ave. in the Mt Pleasant area was one of my favorite bakeries, Deluise Bakery. Some of the best-ever Italian pastries around.

Their homemade whipped cream that they topped off the pies with was simply the best anywhere! One of the few bakeries I can't wait to visit whenever I am in Rhode Island.

Then there's Sweet Berry Farm in Middletown, Rhode Island. A post-and-beam farmer's market sitting on 100 acres in beautiful Middletown, Rhode Island, just down the street from my favorite spot of all, Sachuest National Wildlife Refuge, and my alma mater, Salve Regina. Pick your own here — from the summer's in-season, fresh fruits, vegetable, and flowers to a winter's pick Christmas tree! The bakery is staffed by chefs who create some absolutely incredible, most delectable sweets. One of my favorite places in all of Rhode Island.

I remember going to my uncle Fausto's A&W drive-in restaurant as a child. The kind with the carhop waitresses that bring your food out to your car. You would have to blink your headlights to get service. These type of drive-in restaurants were prevalent in the 1950's. I always wished I had grown up in the 1950's. The times were so much more family oriented. The values and customs honored and strong. Those were the days! Drive-in restaurants and carhops were showcased in movies such as *American Graffiti* and TV shows like *Happy Days*. It was the early 1970's, but a taste of yesteryear! You could drive up, blink your headlights for service, place your order with the carhop, and then be served right in the parking lot. Eat your burger and drink your cola while gazing up at the stars in the summer sky! Uncle Fausto's A&W had that awesome, freshly made — right on the premises — root beer in the frosty mugs and the best doughboys and clam cakes in Rhode Island!

I remember My uncle Giorgio and uncle Giulio's winemaking. I never drank, but to this day, every time I smell wine, I think of my uncle Giorgio, uncle Giulio, and my pop, who simply loved a glass of homemade red wine. Uncle Giulio also made a killer pizza!

Of all my cousins, I spent a bit more time hanging out with my cousin Bruno when I was a kid. He was the big brother I never had. Mom would take me over to aunt Adela and uncle Lucio's house to spend time with him. Bruno and I, along with some of his friends every now and again, would go fishing, boating, swimming, play games, go to the mall or the movies.

It was always a great time being over at aunt Adela's house or anywhere she was present. She was the life of any party — of the family. A natural comedienne; very funny, always happy, always joking around, always making everyone laugh.

I remember one instance (of dozens) in particular. I was 12-years-old. My mother had just purchased a very heavy wrought iron chair for the front porch. I remember my mother telling aunt Adela about it over the phone; how beautiful it was and how it fit so perfectly on the porch.

The next day, as I was looking out the window, I saw my aunt Adela pull up to the front of the house. She saw me in the window and raised her finger to her lips, signaling me to stay quiet and play dumb. I knew she was up to something that was going to be very funny. She came up to the porch and proceeded to try and pick up the iron chair my mother had just purchased the day before. It was very heavy but aunt Adela, hunched over and struggling with all her might, dragged it to her car and actually got it into the car. She then came back and rang the bell. My mother came from downstairs and after a few minutes of chit chat, aunt Adela asked Mom where the chair was. She wanted to see it. Mom said, "*On the front porch, you didn't see it on the way in?*"

"*No*" replied aunt Adela, and both went outside to the porch.

My mother's jaw dropped and she began by saying, "*I can't believe it. Someone stole the chair. That thing was very heavy, I don't know how they picked it up. It took two of us to carry that chair.*"

Aunt Adela let my mother bust for a few more minutes. Then they went to aunt Adela's car so she could show my mother the chair she bought earlier in the day at a local flea market! Another practical joke by aunt Adela; that was her trademark of happiness and joy within our family.

You've never seen an Italian feast and such an incredible spread of food as my aunt Adela did in the day. Tables of home cooked and delectable Italian cuisine and pastries. You wouldn't see this amount of food at a wedding! My mother's cooking and spreads were a close second, but aunt Adela's took the cake! She did this for any and all occasions. However, holidays were a sight to see and behold. She was non-stop, always.

I could never get across in words how much I miss her and how much pain and regret I carry with me for the decades of isolation that kept me from aunt Adela and the rest of my family. The Isolation and the loss it caused in my life has been a much worse fate than death itself.

The holidays — Thanksgiving and Christmas time — were always a very special time during my childhood and within my family; immediate family, aunts, uncles, cousins, and close family friends. Whenever I think of Christmas, one special memory I have is of one of my mother's dearest, lifelong friends, *Mina D*. Mina was another old schooler with class, morals, dignity, and a big, loving heart. She was also an incredible cook and baker. She still is at 88-years-old as of this writing!

She would make one of the most incredible fruit cakes I have ever tasted. Fruit cakes have a funky reputation as being a tacky gift and terrible food — a bad rap all-around. However, until you taste Mina D's fruit cake, you've never had a quality, simply lip-smacking delicious fruit cake. If Mina would have taken this recipe and fruit cake to the next level, she could have been the "Mrs. Fields" of fruit cakes. Mina would special bake me one every Christmas, beginning when I was a child. She, along with her daughter, *Dora*, a good friend of my sister's growing up, would spend a lot of time with our family, especially during the holidays.

Those were truly magical days and times.

I have found the past couple decades of emotional imprisonment and isolation much more difficult during the holiday season. My depression and anxiety are multiplied many times over as I reminisce of the beautiful time it truly was during my early childhood and before these disorders took a firm hold of my life and turned it upside-down.

I remember spending time with my cousins Gio, Rico, Ettore, Silio, and Rena when I was a kid. We would hang around at my aunt Angela and uncle Georgio's home on Federal Hill, watch TV or play games. We'd go to feasts on the Hill and in surrounding areas, play in the park across from their house, and go to events at the Civic Center, located right down the street in the city. I always enjoyed the time with them. It took my mind off of the pain and despair that was slowly but surely eating me alive.

My aunt Angela has the biggest of hearts. She is a very warm, sincere person. She is all about family and family values. This is my mother's sister-in-law, but, as with aunt Adela and aunt Farfalla, there has always been a special bond and love as if blood sisters.

🦋 🦋 🦋 🦋

Aunt Angela was truly disgusted — and made it known — by the betrayal and vile treatment my mother would be subjected to by her own children and grandchildren in her later years. My mother told me that aunt Angela actually cried over this.

My aunt Angela would always check up on my mother and let her know she was there for her, for anything, anytime — as did the rest of her family; brothers, sisters, in-laws. Something — true love, respect, and genuine concern — my mother's own son, daughter, and grandchildren never once in their lives showed their own mother, or grandmother.

🦋 🦋 🦋 🦋

I remember aunt Angela freshly baking these incredible chocolate-

chocolate chip cupcakes with a cream cheese center. I loved these when I was a kid. She would always let me know when she made them and would always get some to me if I couldn't make it over.

There were some really great times with my aunts, uncles, and cousins when I was a kid. I wish someone had known what I was going through during these times. I did one hell of a job hiding in plain sight, that is for sure.

I joined a Boy Scout troop headquartered at Holy Ghost Church on Federal Hill when I was a kid. My cousins Gio and Rico were already Boy Scouts with this troop.

The only way I could go to Camp Yawgoog for a week with my cousins was to be a member of the Boy Scouts. So, I did just that. I became a Boy Scout and went to camp with my cousins Gio and Rico.

We spent a full week at camp Yawgoog. It was totally awesome! There were actually male role models at camp. Adults spending time with you and teaching you things. Encouraging you to try and to succeed at a task — and complimenting you on your accomplishments.

There was a rifle range, archery, obstacle courses, boating, all kinds of activities; a million things to do. There was a trading post too. You could buy some really cool things there. I bought my mother a piece of scrimshaw at the trading post and had it inscribed, "*I Love You, Mom.*" I had been thinking of her every day, hoping everything was okay at home while trying desperately to enjoy this rare occasion.

We hiked the many trails in the woods. We slept in sleeping bags and in tents all week, under the enormous pine trees. Pretty cool! I think of that week at camp every time I smell fresh pine. It brings back a very rare, wonderful memory of childhood.

One day I couldn't find my cousin Rico. I went to his tent and he was there, very sad, with a black eye. One of the kids in our troop punched him in the face. It made my blood boil. Cousin Rico was a quiet kid and the sweetest, kindest, most likeable kid you would ever want to meet. The furthest you could get from a punk and the closest you could get to a saint of a kid. When cousin Gio — Rico's older brother — found out that day, he was furious. Both cousin Gio and the kid that punched Rico in the face were a couple years older — and much bigger — than me and Rico. Cousin Gio tracked the kid down and found him in his tent. I remember camp chaperones actually letting cousin Gio enter the tent and dole out a beating on the kid while everyone else was made to stay outside. I could hear the wrestling and some groaning going on within the tent. After a few minutes, cousin Gio came out and it was over. That's family. That's justice. That was the Boy Scouts, Federal Hill style!

The dining hall had lots of great food and desserts. I looked forward to seeing what was on the menu each day in the hall. One afternoon, there just so happened to be trouble on that menu. There was this kid in the hall who would pick up with and continue the stress in my life when I thought I was free-and-clear of trauma for a week. He was in our troop and a real trouble maker with everyone. He had a reputation of being a tough kid in his neighborhood. Most kids were afraid of him. I wasn't. I would ignore him and not react to his tactics. Guess it bothered him.

During lunch this one afternoon he approached me, rattled off a few derogatory comments and then proceeded to push me. No reason other than he was a punk and bully. Without fail, trouble always seemed to find me. This was the first time in my life a bully was actually my size. He was a small kid — smaller than most everyone else — just like me. I closed in and grabbed him as soon as his hands landed on my chest, swept his feet, and took him to the ground. I got him into a headlock and tightly twisted his head, cranking his neck. All the other kids standing around and watching this punk get what he had coming to him. He couldn't move and I knew he was in pain. He squirmed a bit and cursed an awful lot and after about 20 seconds, he said, "*All right, all right.*" To me, that was a tap-out. I let him go, he got up, still screaming and cursing at me, and attacked me again! This time, I hit him with a left hook as he came at me and dropped him to the ground. By this time, camp supervisors and our troop's chaperones were at the scene and got between us. He continued to threaten me and everyone else around. This kid was a little off his rocker to say the least. Tough? Not really. A few loose screws? For sure!

This was one of the very few times in my life when I actually fought someone who wasn't larger than me. The reason there are weight classes in professional fighting is that that is the only fair fight method. My entire life — being smaller than everyone else — I always had to make it my business to close the distance and get my opponent to the ground where I had the advantage most times. Luckily, my instincts usually did just that.

I received a couple of merit badge's during my summer week at camp. One for rifle shooting proficiency and one for swimming ability.

None for fighting! I became the camp's definition of an "expert swimmer" by swimming a certain number of laps continuously which equaled one mile, staying under water and also staying afloat for a certain amount of time. The swimming instructor would call me *Paisano* every time he saw me. He was Italian, too. He said I was a great swimmer.

As a result of my accomplishments in swimming, I was able to take the canoe, by myself, across the pond to the island. This was awesome! The tranquility and sense of peace I felt in my soul was an eye-opening and very rare experience in my life.

When I left the camp, I had earned my first rank. I was now a tenderfoot within the Boy Scouts. Unfortunately, as my PTSD, depression, and anxiety were ever-present and progressing, I would pull away from everything, including the Boy Scouts.

Most importantly, I met some really nice kids during this time who could have been — should have been — lifelong friends.

Back in the North End, I won the Pinball Wizard Championship at the Boys Club. I was 12-years-old, 7th grade at this time. I loved playing pinball! It was another escape and took my mind far away from all the turmoil at home, the bullying going on all around me, and everything else that seemed to find, and torment me.

There was a neighborhood guy who opened a pinball arcade a block down from the Boys Club during the summer of 1976. I spent a fair amount of time playing pinball in there as well. I remember one day my mother sent my father looking for me as I hadn't been home the entire day and it was getting late. My father came to the pinball arcade. He was also drunk. He was driving a car I loved; a powder blue, 1976 Olds Cutlass Supreme. I would learn to drive with this car a few years down the road. He parked in the driveway and came in the arcade to get me. When pulling out of the driveway, he smashed the whole side of the car on a fence post. Needless to say, it was very embarrassing. I wanted to just crawl under a rock and disappear. For a while, I was razzed by all the neighborhood kids who were there to witness my father's drunken escapade.

Around this same time — 7th grade — I played on one of the local business-sponsored basketball teams one season at the Boys Club. Most of the kids I was hanging around with were playing on teams. A couple kids asked me to join their team as they needed another player.

As tough as it was due to my depression and anxiety, I joined the team. I had been playing — practicing shooting and dribbling — for a couple years prior at one of the local parks. I was pretty good for a short, left-handed kid!

When the games took place at the Boys Club, I noticed that many of the other kids had parents and family there cheering them on. Same at the karate school where I would soon train. I mentioned this once to my mother as it bothered me no one ever came to watch me play basketball or train in karate school. My mother told my father he should show up like a father does. I remember my father making an appearance at a basketball game and a karate class once — and only once — with some wise guy friends. They stayed all of 15 minutes.

The simple truth is I've pretty much been on my own from a very early age. I basically raised myself in many respects from childhood. My mother did the very best she could with what she had to work with.

There was only so much oxygen in the room, so to speak, and my brother and his addictions consumed most, if not all, of it during my childhood. No one knew the pain and darkness I existed in; perhaps believing I was just fine because I "looked" okay. My mother never knew what was going on beneath the surface. She never knew about the constant emotional trauma from multiple areas of my life — inside and outside of my home — or the resulting disorders taking control of that life. Her world was being torn to shreds, her sanity on the line, just as mine was. She was alone, as I was. No one to talk to. No one to turn to. My father provided financially but, aside from that, was good for absolutely nothing else but the additional heartache and stress he caused my mother.

There was never an adult male role model around to watch over me, guide me, encourage me, or help me with any problems I had. My mother was there — always — but, as far as my childhood PTSD and what I was going through emotionally during this time, along with the bullying, she had no idea. I told no one my feelings, my pain, my fears, or thoughts, and no one ever asked. I had to figure out, from childhood, and by myself, how to deal with, and overcome any and all problems that I had, including the emotional pain, suffering, and despair that was eating me alive.

I remember once when I was 12-years-old, my mother, brother, and father were in the kitchen talking about a neighborhood kid who was growing up without a father and no direction. I chimed in and said,

"No one has ever been there for me. I've been raising myself. What's the difference?" My father said nothing. My mother responded, *"Do you really feel that way?"* My brother laughed and said, patronizingly, *"You raised yourself?"* I replied, *"I sure have been. Who has been there?"* He laughed again as if it was a joke. My feelings and pain meant nothing.

Granted, there was a roof over my head, food on the table, and clothes on my back, but I most certainly did raise myself in many respects. Sometimes I wonder how I actually made it without winding up dead or becoming addicted to alcohol or drugs like everyone else around me.

As a child and teenager growing up, I had an awful lot of freedom with not much supervision, if any at all. The love for my mother and between us kept me always on the straight and narrow. Always thinking for myself, knowing what it would do to her if I took that left and went south.

My world had no structure, no balance, and no guidance. There was not one respectable, adult male role model in my life.

I'm sure my life could have turned out much worse in many ways. Perhaps how it did turn out was the lesser of the evils, and, for that, along with one of my life's very few blessings — my mother — I have always been grateful.

7

I was first hooked on martial arts at the tender age of seven by way of the 1971 movie, *Billy Jack*, starring Tom Laughlin.

Billy Jack was a hapkido master and Green Beret Vietnam war vet. Billy Jack is the hero in the movie who defends a group of students and children who are part of a hippie-themed freedom school and are abused and humiliated — bullied — by one of the main villain characters, Mr. Posner, and his gang of thugs.

The scene below is an excerpt from the movie and the one scene that piqued my interest and passion for martial arts. Billy Jack is speaking to Mr. Posner, and is surrounded by Posner's thugs:

Mr. Posner: *"You really think those Green Beret karate tricks are gonna help you against all these boys?"*

Billy Jack: *"Well, it doesn't look to me like I really have any choice now, does it?"*

Mr. Posner: (laughing) *"That's right, you don't."*

Billy Jack: *"You know what I think I'm gonna do then? Just for the hell of it?"*

Mr. Posner: *"Tell me."*

Billy Jack: *"I'm gonna take this right foot, and I'm gonna whop you on that side of your face...* (points to Posner's right cheek) *...and you wanna know something? There's not a damn thing you're gonna be able to do about it."*

Mr. Posner: *"Really?"*

Billy Jack: *"Really."* (kicks Posner's right cheek, sending him to the ground).

At seven-years-old, I was simply amazed how Billy Jack could take his right foot and kick the guy's right cheek! How was that possible? I was hooked!

I would soon be watching, one after another, over and over again, one of my childhood Idol's — Bruce Lee and the martial arts movies *Fist of Fury*, *Way of the Dragon*, *Enter the Dragon*, *The Game of Death*.

I would also watch any and every TV show and movie that spotlighted my martial arts idols Bruce Lee, Bill "Superfoot" Wallace, Chuck Norris, and Benny "The Jet" Urquidez. I would study and master many of their moves. These guys were my heroes!

I actually began *training* — exercising daily — at the age of nine.

I would get up early no matter where I had to go or be, and begin training before I did anything else. I would practice the moves of my martial arts heroes every morning, without fail. As the years progressed, this routine would soon expand to include other exercises and stretches.

I would begin doing hundreds upon hundreds of push-ups and sit-ups combined with stretching and flexibility exercises each and every morning beginning at nine-years-old and to this very day.

The first-thing morning routine has always been approximately one hour of this type of exercise — stretching and meditation. It is — and always has been — my morning medicine; my morning cup of coffee, so to speak. I've never had a cup of coffee. I don't know what it tastes like but it sure smells good!

I have spent the first hour of each morning of my life — for the past 40 years — dedicated (addicted) to training, stretching, and meditating. I can count on one hand the days I've had to miss this morning routine over the past 40 years. I may have had to miss the later morning, afternoon, or evening intense training sessions — weight training, boxing, sparring, running — but the morning routine was an absolute necessity to begin the day then as it is now.

I have pushed myself through this morning routine even through the lowest points of my life — times when I was near-crippled physically or hadn't slept for days. It would take a total collapse of my mind and/or body in order for me to miss this morning routine — and that has happened.

I may have lost my ability to do 95% of what I used to do in regards to an extensive training regimen, but I have improvised, tweaked, and altered my routines in order to continue to do what I can still do regardless of my spinal injury. Quite often it makes my physical pain worse and sometimes it literally incapacitates me, but it temporarily clears my mind and allows my soul to exhale with joy.

Discipline, dedication, addiction — however it may be viewed, training has always been my medicine. I will continue to push on and forward doing whatever exercises and training I can until the day I am no longer breathing.

I started formally training in karate at 12-years-old. I began at George Pesare's Kenpo Karate in the North End, across from the park where all the neighborhood hung out. Hopkins Square was at the corner of Charles St. and Branch Ave. and St. Ann's Plaza was at the corner of Branch Ave. and Hawkins St. This area comprised The Park — the main area where the Charles St. Neighborhood kids and guys hung around.

I encountered bullying even in the karate school when I began. Another bully to add to the list. He was older than me, bigger than me, and had been training for a couple years. He was a classless neighborhood kid who knew nothing about the core of martial arts. He lacked discipline, respect, and restraint. Another one I caught up with in years to come. Once I grew a bit, became more confident in my abilities and fighting, and had a reputation to go with it, his attitude suddenly changed. Few things in life are lower than a coward.

Pesare's Kenpo Karate training was grueling and like no other. We would train and fight with no gear. Meaning, you would fight with no gloves, no head-gear. It was raw fists and kicks to the face and body. If you want to be tough, you learn to fight and take a punch and kick without any head or body gear.

Some of the older guys in the school would literally lick the blood off their faces and bodies. It — the school and George himself — was hardcore to say the least.

I was very unorthodox in my training and fighting style. Even *this* school's demanding and raw training system couldn't hold my attention.

I would go on to train religiously, with my own training system and style — just like my childhood Idol, Bruce Lee — combining various martial arts styles, boxing, and weight-training.

I would train every day of my life until a line of duty accident in my early 30's resulted in a severe and debilitating spinal injury that would be the beginning of the end of my training and my medication as I had known it for decades.

I realized when I began training that it was always hard to breathe. I learned I had a deviated septum from early childhood. A bone continually grew larger within my left nasal passage and the blockage within that passage greater. My father had this same problem. He did at one point have surgery to remove a portion of the bone, but it grew back very quickly and he was back to square one. I inherited this condition, as well as Degenerative Disc Disease (DDD) and Scoliosis from my father.

🦋 🦋 🦋 🦋

My father was hospitalized when he was in his late 30's as he could not walk and was in excruciating pain as a result of his Scoliosis. His doctor recommended five weeks of hospitalized traction. He complied. He had to learn to walk again after getting out of the hospital and being in traction 24/7 for five weeks. It did alleviate most of his pain and mobility problems. However, he still suffers with occasional back pain (and arthritis) to this day, in his late 80's.

🦋 🦋 🦋 🦋

For decades, I have only been able to breathe through my right nasal passage. I learned as a child to function with just a 50% oxygen flow coming into my lungs from that one nasal passage. There is near-complete blockage within the left nasal passage. Most times, it is completely blocked, making it even more difficult to breathe — especially when I would train intensely.

I'm also allergic to just about everything that grows and then some; trees, plants, pollen, dust, etc. Sinus infections were common throughout my childhood and adulthood.

As I got older, I grew accustomed to the 50% maximum air intake. Add the deviated septum blockage and sinus problems to my allergies which began during my childhood, and this would routinely clog up the only free nasal passage. This would cause me to breathe out of my mouth a lot during childhood.

Frequent nosebleeds were also very common during my childhood. My nose would just start bleeding at anytime, anywhere. This would happen in school and just about everywhere else. Blood pouring down my face while breathing out of my mouth was pretty embarrassing as a kid. Routine nosebleeds would continue into my late 30's.

Complete nasal blockage routinely happens to this day when I lay down to try and sleep. Since my line of duty accident, sleep is all but non-existent. I haven't slept more than three hours straight in nearly two decades as of this writing, and that's a good night. No sooner than I lay horizontally, I can't breathe any longer through my nostrils. Nasal strips have been a must for the past 15 years in order to get some oxygen flow through at least the one unblocked nasal passage while laying down. I actually had to sleep in a recliner chair for a few years post my line of duty accident. I was unable to put any type of pressure at all on the cervical portion of my spine, making lying horizontally to sleep nearly impossible.

Between constant physical and emotional pain, anxiety, and the inability to breathe, I have been sleep deprived for years.

It has always been difficult for me to breathe. However, when you add anxiety to the mix, this disorder's common feelings of suffocation and claustrophobia are multiplied many times over.

Few things in life are more terrifying than a severe anxiety or panic attack coupled with the inability to breathe through your nostrils.

It was around this time in my life — 11-years-old — I was having an awful lot of trouble breathing, nosebleeds and anxiety were constant, bullying in full-swing, and, of course, I started to become attracted to girls — what timing! Could I have been more of a mess?

Tina R. was my first crush at 11-years-old. I was in the 6th grade. I was pretty intimidated by her outspokenness as well as her appearance. I thought she was the cutest girl I'd ever seen! She was also the toughest girl in my age-range in the neighborhood!

She used to call me *Mousey*. Said I looked like a mouse but she liked me. Go figure!

It took a couple of years for me to get up enough nerve but she would become my first kiss at age 13.

It was a hot summer's night in July of 1977 at the Ascham St. Park, located behind Carcieri's Italian Market on Charles St. in the North End. I remember it like yesterday. I was actually very scared. I had no confidence then, either, but was beginning to develop my *mask* — that tough, impenetrable exterior that would protect me from the rest of the world. Its primary purpose was to hide my pain, suffering, despair, and feelings of worthlessness from everyone around me. Conceal the disorders — PTSD, anxiety, depression — that controlled and devastated my life. Shroud the bleeding soul I carried like a ton of bricks behind that mask.

I was training now and had my minibike — my outlets, my

medicines, my escape from the pain that was feasting on my mind and soul.

Tina would constantly tease me. She'd tell me that I liked her and wanted to kiss her, but didn't know how. She couldn't have been more accurate with both observations. I finally worked up some nerve and met her in the dugout of the field.

It's truly incredible how fast time goes by. Almost 40 years gone with a blink of an eye. I often wonder if I had lived a normal life — a balanced, happy, emotionally and physically pain-free life — If I'd be twice as old by now? Does time go by even faster when you are happy, your mind occupied with positivity and optimism, your soul filled with meaning, love, and joy?

Casper L. was a North End Neighborhood kid and bully. Another kid who would constantly bully everyone. He was a couple years older than me. He wasn't as bad to me as other bullies I had to deal with in my life. Mostly bullying words and chest puffing here and there. Everyone else, he would hit, take to the ground, and play with like a rag doll.

One day, right in the Boys Club — I was 13-years-old — he decided to go beyond the bullying words and chest puffing and started throwing punches at me.

I moved around and he kept missing. He got frustrated and came at me full force, getting me into a headlock.

It was a very similar situation as had happened with the Puerto Rican kid in Eagle Park a couple years earlier. I swept him down to the ground and put him into what would become my signature move; a neck choke. He couldn't move, and, in trying to save face, actually said these very words, verbatim, "*All right, I think you learned your lesson, now let go.*" He was definitely one sandwich short of a picnic!

He tried to keep face when I let him up but, once again, I could see it in the eyes, he knew I had his number. Should I decide to fight back, he may very well lose complete face when he is beaten by the bullied one.

Casper would talk crap every now and then, but knew not to touch me again. He was a very troubled neighborhood kid who would go on to a life of crime like many of the others from the area.

Strange as it sounds, I liked Casper. We'd talk every now and again and, in between his tough-guy act, I could see through his own mask and somehow knew and felt his pain and the reasons he acted as he did.

Unfortunately, Casper's mask did him more harm than good growing up. It didn't protect him but got him killed. A few years down the road, he would have his head blown off by a shotgun blast after breaking into a house where the owner was inside and ready to defend his home at all costs.

Such a waste of life. Casper was, like many from the neighborhood, a lost soul. With some help and guidance, he could have been a productive member of society rather than another criminal statistic and number hanging off a toe at the morgue.

I met one of my best friends, *Rocco F.*, the summer of 1978 at the Boys Club. I had just turned 14. We became good friends from that very day and hung out through high school and the beginning of college. We met in a peculiar way. A bunch of punks were planning on jumping him outside of the Boys Club. They didn't like the way he looked and acted. Basically, he didn't pay any attention to them. Their egos didn't like that. I didn't know him at the time, but I was all about being fair. Right from wrong. Honor and respect. He was with his older brother, *Donnie*, playing basketball in the club's gym. I approached him and told him to watch his back, a few kids were up to no good and he was the target. He asked me which kids were plotting. I told him I couldn't go there, but to just watch his back when he left.

Rocco was a take-no-crap type of kid. Not a trouble-maker in the least and not a hang-around kid either. He went to St. Ann's School on Branch Ave., across from the Boys Club, through the 8th grade. He was the kind of kid who did his homework first, then went to play basketball at the Boys Club. He didn't hang around in the neighborhood, or with any of the neighborhood kids. He came from a good home where he was close to his parents, brother, and sister. His father was a straight-forward, legitimate guy. Rocco was heavily influenced by his father. No dysfunction in his family like most everyone else from the neighborhood.

As he left the Boys Club with his brother, he noticed a bunch of kids watching him. He went up to the group and asked, "*Who has the problem with me?*" No one said a thing. He went over to the biggest of the kids — who was the primary instigator — and told him if he had a problem they could take care of it right now. Again, no one said anything. Typical of punks and cowards — they cower when someone actually stands up to them.

I ran into him and his brother up the street as they were walking home. He approached me, thanked me, asked me my name. We struck up a conversation and realized we were both going to Classical High School come that fall. We became very good friends from that day on and for the next eight or so years.

We lost touch in our early 20's, when PTSD, depression, and anxiety really started to take control of my life, pushing me further and further into isolation, away from friends, family, and life itself.

He went on to college from high school, as I did. He then went directly into law school from college, eventually becoming a very successful attorney.

Rocco died in November of 2009 — in his mid-40's — of a massive heart attack. I got a call from my mother the same night it happened. My heart sunk and tears filled my eyes when she broke the news to me.

Like everyone who was important in my life, he never knew my story, why I disappeared, never returned calls, never kept in touch, never showed at any of our high school reunions.

I always thought I'd have the chance to explain my life to him someday. Reveal the tortured soul behind the mask.

RIP, my friend.

As I left the crumbling Eagle Park area behind come 7th Grade, I spent most of the next two years hanging around with a different crew. Riding bikes, mini-bikes, hanging around at the Boys Club and in the parks in the Charles St. area through the 8th grade. This was mainly Hopkins Square and St. Ann's Plaza (Charles St. Park), Ascham Park, Metcalf Park into the field behind Esek Hopkins Middle School.

There was an incident while hanging around with some friends in Charles St. Park. I was 13-years-old, 8th grade; an African-American kid crossed the imaginary line on the south side of Branch Ave. over into Hopkins Square. I remember several neighborhood kids — older than me at the time — approached the kid and words were exchanged. Before you knew it, the African-American kid was being beaten pretty badly by three neighborhood kids. This made me sick. What came next shocks me to this day. Another neighborhood kid went over to the one-sided beat-down and hit this kid across the head with a baseball bat.

I grew up on the streets and have seen just about everything in my day. Still, at 13-years-old, I couldn't believe this. I have no problem if two people want to fight for whatever reason — as long as it's fair. But jumping this kid because he walked onto "sacred" turf is ridiculous. Hitting this kid across the head with a bat for crossing onto that hallowed territory — for being in an area off-limits to all but those who live there — is insane!

I make no claims to sainthood. I have, however, throughout my years, always lived my life by a code; discipline, honor, respect, undying loyalty, and fairness to all — always. Always treat others how you would like to be treated. If you've sincerely earned and deserve a beat-down or something more severe, I've never had a problem with that. That's all some people understand and respond to — especially on the streets. If this person had just raped someone's sister, or molested their child, or perhaps broke into a grandmother's home, beat and robbed her, I would have joined in and helped to dole out just punishment.

In certain instances, I am all for street justice as opposed to the "injustice system" where all too often the judges, politicians, LEO's (Law Enforcement Officers), and the wealthy, among others, are not held to the same standards and punishments as the rest of society — and get away scot-free.

I remember a rescue squad coming to take the kid away. I don't know how severe his injuries were or whether he sustained permanent injuries. I remember thinking that this kid had a mother, a family that loved him, and he did absolutely nothing to deserve what had happened to him. To me, it was obvious that his movement was unintentional and he was not being disrespectful to anyone.

This was just another brutal, unjust incident I would witness — both handed-out by civilians and law enforcement — during my childhood and later life.

I have witnessed things in my life that actually made this incident look like child's-play. For obvious reasons, there are many experiences and incidents I have firsthand knowledge of and have witnessed in my life that cannot be discussed or written about. Where I come from, that kind of knowledge can only be taken to the grave.

I could never understand how someone could dislike — or truly hate — someone else based solely on the color of the person's skin. I was pretty much alone among the neighborhood kids with my unprejudiced beliefs but it was always well known with anyone I was around or who knew me. I stood up for what I believed in as a child and to this day. If it was wrong or cowardly, I'd have nothing to do with it.

My mother would always tell me the story of my grandfather's good friend back in his early days — the 1930's. My grandfather would take his friend from work home with him for a glass of wine and some simple Italian food. The man was African-American and was a good friend of my grandfather's. My grandfather loved everyone. Pop didn't speak English and his friend didn't speak Italian. However, they understood, respected, accepted, and loved each other as friends and enjoyed each other's company. This is how we should all conduct ourselves and live our lives. This world would be a much more civil, loving place if we did.

I realized around this time in my life that my soft spot in this world would be injustice and outright disrespect. I had a serious problem with it. However, if this applied to animals or the elderly — the center of that soft spot — and took place in my presence, it was going to get real ugly, real fast. All bets are off, the gloves come off, and all is now fair and justified in my mind when dealing with someone who has disrespected, abused, or hurt an animal or an elderly person.

Few things create such an anger in me. Few things pain my heart so deeply. I've been in fights throughout my childhood and adult life standing up for and defending both animals and the elderly. Mistreatment or assault of either wasn't going to happen on my watch. I've witnessed kids outright disrespecting the elderly by throwing things at them, swearing at them, belittling them, threatening them. I've seen adults taking advantage of and trying to get over on the elderly. Some their very own parents and grandparents. I've seen a lot of elderly abuse in the city during my bussing years to and from high school.

Morality in our country has slowly gone down the shitter with each new generation. It truly is disgraceful and embarrassing that those of our country — our culture — are becoming so disrespectful, self-centered, and apathetic.

I have never let disrespecting the elderly go if I witnessed it. I couldn't. I always got involved and, if it led to a physical confrontation, so be it. I have no problem being judge and jury in a situation such as this. The person would get what they had coming.

In every elderly person, I've always seen my Pop, my grandmothers, my aunt Mimi, and other elders from my family that are no longer with me.

I've seen kids as well as adults mistreating and torturing dogs, cats, birds, and other animals.

I once saw a guy at the beach hit a seagull with a wooden oar and kill it. I'll skip the details, but my blood boiled and the piece of garbage got what he had coming to him when he threatened to do to me what he had just done to the seagull.

Like my grandfather, I have a deep-seated love for all animals. Animals have always put a smile on my face — and there have been very few of those in my life. I always found joy and happiness in my soul when around animals. I've felt a sense of peace like no other. I'm that guy who pulls over to the side of the road to pick up the turtle slowly crossing in front of oncoming traffic, moving it to safety before it gets run over by a car. The same guy that remembers each time — and there have been many — he has seen an animal in distress, hit by a car, or killed, and the deep sorrow and pain I felt as a result of that.

One thing that will always stand out in my mind about this time in my life was the Blizzard of 1978. It was late morning, February 06, 1978. I remember watching from a window of one of my classes in middle school this very heavy, quickly falling snow just blasting down and blowing in all directions. All the kids were excited. Most of the teachers seemed to be panicking and for good reason. Before you knew it, this storm took a turn for the worse and everyone realized that this was far from your average snow storm.

School was dismissed and everyone began trying to make their way home. It got so bad, so quickly, that many kids and faculty were stuck in various schools around the state for days. My middle school was on Charles St. in the North End. I was only a few blocks from my house.

However, it was still tough making progress in the heavy snow. I couldn't see two feet in front of me, walking was very difficult, and I wasn't dressed for a blizzard.

Walking home, I was witnessing car accident after car accident, cars getting stuck, and lots of people just plain panicking. I helped a few people along the way. We'd get the car moving and it would just get stuck again or slide into something.

I remember walking over the HWY. 146 bridge and seeing cars piling up and coming to a stop. They were stranded and would be buried there, as well as I-95 and every other major road and highway, for days on end.

It snowed continuously and heavily for two days straight. At times, coming down at three inches per hour! Accumulating three to five feet of snow in various parts of Rhode Island. Drifts reported to 27-feet high!

The entire city stood still for about a week. I remember looking around, thinking this might be what the end of the world would look like. There was nothing but multiple feet of snow covering everything. Cars were abandoned on the highways and local roads; literally buried beneath mountains of snow.

Sadly, there were many lives lost during this blizzard. Many who had to remain in their cars that evening lost their lives from carbon monoxide poisoning when the snow piled up over the tail pipes of the cars.

I remember finally getting home. What was usually a 20-minute walk took nearly two hours trekking through this stuff! I was completely soaked and freezing.

My mother was never so glad to see me!

I remember having to jump out one of the windows the next day to get out of the house and start shoveling us out. The snow drifts were well over 20-feet and covering all sides of the house right up onto, and over the roof! It was impossible to open the doors. I had never seen anything like this. It was incredible! I shoveled us out continuously for the next several days.

In addition to clearing the snow from our home, I made hundreds of dollars that week shoveling snow from yards around the neighborhoods. I never asked anyone for a certain amount of money to shovel them out and I would never take money from the elderly who needed help shoveling out. I left it to the others to pay me what they thought it was worth. Most were very thankful and generous with this storm. The accumulation and impact was like no other. It was certainly something to see and live through. A most memorable experience.

8

I started going my separate way towards the end of the 8th grade. It was time to leave the North End and the many who were falling victim to alcohol, drugs, and the thug life far behind.

I had already taken and passed the written entrance exam required to attend Classical High School — highly regarded as one of the top public college-prep high schools in the country at this time. My mother had always been very impressed by classical's widely held top-notch reputation. My attending and graduating from Classical was another wish of my mother's which I gladly fulfilled for her.

When I moved on to Classical in 1978, the only things I truly missed that I left behind in the North End were The Baron Cologne, disco, and French Star jeans from Chess King. These were the staples of the day and my North End Neighborhood.

My brother moved to California when I was 14-years-old. I had just started high school. He would not be physically present in our home for the next six years. However, his addiction, problems, and the heartbreak for my mother would continue from afar.

My aunt *Bella*, uncle *Rio*, and cousin *Tia* moved back to Rhode Island from California around this time — the beginning of my freshman year in high school. Aunt Bella is my father's first cousin. My grandma M and aunt Bella's mother, *Lorna*, were sisters.

Aunt Lorna also came back to Rhode Island from California. Aunt Bella and her immediate family wanted aunt Lorna to be in Rhode Island as she was starting to get senile and would probably need to be admitted to a nursing home shortly.

Aunt Lorna was in Rhode Island very briefly before she was admitted to the same nursing home as grandma M. They were on different floors of the nursing home, each suffering with dementia. My father would take grandma M by wheelchair to visit her sister, Lorna. they didn't so much as recognize each other.

🦋 🦋 🦋 🦋

I've said it before and can't say it enough: we all deserve the right to die with dignity, when and how we choose. Competent patients do have a right to refuse life-support. They also have a right to create a directive stating if, or when, life support should be withdrawn or withheld should their condition at the time prevent them from making that decision. I'm no expert, but it seems these rights of the patient apply only to "end-of-life," or "life-support" care as it relates to the body being compromised. Cases in which the patient is suffering a debilitating illness which severely damages the body but leaves the mind intact.

Every person — every patient — should have the right to self-determination. If they are unable to determine for themselves and suffering, unable to function on their own, with no chance of recovery — whether the body or the mind is completely compromised — the family should be able to determine whether their loved one is ready to pass in peace and with dignity.

Many may remember Dr. Jack Kevorkian. He also believed this. He was the infamous euthanasia activist commonly — disgracefully — referred to as "Dr. Death". He was a strong advocate of the terminally ill patient's right to die by way of physician-assisted suicide. He was convicted of second degree murder and imprisoned for eight years for his direct role in a case of voluntary euthanasia.

When you lose your mind to dementia or Alzheimer's, you are terminally ill as far as I'm concerned. Your mind is dead, your body following behind very slowly — and very painfully for those who love the person. Having to watch the suffering of a loved one who is terminally ill and deteriorating before your eyes is what is truly inhumane, not the right of this person to die by physician-assisted suicide or voluntary euthanasia.

We do it every day for our beloved four-legged companions — man's best friend — when they are in this predicament. My boy, Max, is a beautiful and loving nine-year-old (at the time of this writing) yellow Labrador retriever. We've been together since the day he turned eight-weeks-old. He is the son I never had. He is family. I love him like I would my own flesh-and-blood son. Unless you have a pet and that bond, it is difficult to understand the genuine, unconditional love between man and dog. I am not the strongest person when it comes to someone I love being sick, suffering, or dying. However, I can say with certainty, however difficult it may be, I will never allow my boy to suffer if there is no hope of his recovering — if he is terminally ill or cannot function in a capacity conducive to a happy, pain-free life.

The humane thing to do is to lovingly euthanize to end the

suffering and allow the soul to move on to a place of pure peace.
There is no reason we as human beings should have to suffer when
terminally ill — be it the body, mind, or both.

There are currently, as of this writing, only three states
within the U.S. that have Death with Dignity Laws and allow
terminally ill patients the right to pass with dignity and hasten
their death without suffering.

It seems only when the government finds a way to make
money off physician-assisted suicide or voluntary euthanasia —
like has been done with alcohol, gambling, and marijuana — it
will no longer be inhumane and a crime, or so difficult to have
these laws passed in each and every state within the USA.

We should all have the right to pass from this world in
peace, with dignity.

🦋 🦋 🦋 🦋

My aunt Bella is a special woman. I love her very much. I
remember her always telling me that she loved me. And I know she
did, I felt the love.

When I was younger, aside from my mother, I didn't hear "*I love*
you" — or feel it — very often. She is a warm, genuine, caring person.

Aunt Bella, Rio, and cousin Tia (who is a couple years younger
than me) would spend time with us while they lived in Rhode Island.

Cousin Tia would in time marry my buddy *ChiChi's* older brother,
Rosco C. They would soon have two children and move back to
California, along with aunt Bella and uncle Rio.

High school began and I had moved on and away from most of
the neighborhood kids. Some of us from childhood who turned right,
down the straight and narrow, remained in contact. A couple of
neighborhood kids, brothers *DB* and *Zeppi*, though we went to
different high schools, stayed in contact and hung out through the high
school years and beyond. Zeppi and I still keep in contact. He was a
few years younger and like a little brother to me growing up. He is a
good soul and a friend to this day. We share a lot of the old school
values. Zeppi was always good-natured and happy. Always had a smile
on his face. Strange, we've known each other for over 35 years and he
has no idea what has gone on and what has gone wrong in my world.
No one does. That mask I wore my entire life did its job and enabled

my survival. My positive addictions — my outlets and my medications — suppressed my pain and allowed me to function and appear normal. This kept everyone around me from knowing — from seeing — my constant struggle and suffering.

What I'd left behind in the North End wasn't for me, and everyone I came up with knew my feelings. No one I hung out with beginning in high school and beyond ever did drugs, smoked pot, or cigarettes. Most, with the exception of myself, drank socially at parties and clubs. I was dead-set against drinking, smoking pot, and taking drugs.

Most, I guess, follow in the footsteps of alcohol and drug addiction. I went the exact opposite way. I never smoked anything or drank alcohol in my life. I never took drugs of any kind, with the exception of occasional, short-term, prescription medication, antibiotics, and OTC's such as Ibuprofen and Aleve.

Over the years, I've watched many kids I knew during childhood become alcoholics and addicts. Some kids I grew up with overdosed, some wound up in and out of jail, others were banged up pretty good, and a few were killed. I believe that many of them — if not all — were dealing with very similar trauma in their childhood and lives as I was in mine. The only difference being, they went one way to quell the pain and I somehow went another.

I was now city-bussing across town to high school and hanging out with a different crew, Rocco F. being one of them. All of whom in their lifetimes became successful, productive members of society. A bunch of real nice, classy guys. Most were from the neighborhood, families not connected but legitimate, honorable, hard-working people.

Not one of my friends had even the slightest idea what I was going through during my childhood, adolescence, and adulthood. They have no idea to this day.

PTSD, depression, anxiety, and isolation have kept me from contacting and communicating with some truly wonderful people that I would have been proud to call lifelong friends. These disorders ruined any and every relationship that did, or could have meant something in my life.

Most of us — especially children and adolescents — who suffer with these disorders usually don't know exactly what the problem is, but feel emotionally different than everyone else. We are seldom, if ever, truly happy. We just can't function properly — normally — as others around us do. We may have feelings of hopelessness, constant worry, doubt, fear, anxiety, anger. Some of us may begin overeating — using food as an outlet to drown the pain — and gain weight. While others may under eat and lose weight. Some may begin pulling away from everything and everyone that meant something to them in life.

Addiction to alcohol and/or drugs is all too common when suffering with these emotional disorders.

I wish I had known — and had been able — to either reach out to a school counselor, family member, priest, a friend, or an LCSW to discuss my feelings, my pain and troubles. Or, that someone caught on and knew enough about the manifestation of these disorders to try and reach me, help me, pull me back from the endless murk — the hell that I was spiraling into.

Taking that city bus across town to high school was a shocker and an eye opener at 14-years-old. All the different types of kids from all over, especially within the city, waiting for and on buses to take them to the various schools and back to their neighborhoods.

I mingled with all kinds, and being streetwise I connected with and understood most everyone, all while my mask concealed my own pain and suffering, despair, and feelings of worthlessness from the rest of the world. I fought that battle daily by way of intense training. It kept my keel even and allowed me to function *normally* each day. It allowed me to blend in.

9th grade was the third and, to that date, the most major of culture shocks.

Being a high school freshman in and of itself was very stressful. That first year of high school markedly compounded my existing anxiety. I immediately began developing stress-related sties on the lids of my eyes. My anxiety was now dreadful times ten, causing severe sweating, especially from the head and face, and coming-through-the-chest, heart palpitations. My PTSD and depression in full swing.

I would have to speak with most teachers throughout high school and college regarding my fear of public speaking. Being in the spotlight — in front of the class — was not going to happen. No one was going to see me shaking, sweating, suffering; my soul bleeding.

There were many oral presentations required in my high school as well as my four years of college. I was unable to do oral presentations or anything that put me at the center of attention, in front of the class or a group of people.

I found, as with every other profession in life, there are good and bad teachers; compassionate and supportive teachers and the out-of-touch and insensitive teachers who possessed no tact whatsoever. Some were there for the right reasons while others should not have been there at all. They knew nothing about teaching. Nothing about understanding, reaching, or touching their students.

They knew nothing of listening to and communicating with their students. Either way, it didn't matter. I wasn't about to make a complete fool of myself and let everyone see the sweat pouring from my body, my hands and legs shaking, or, possibly — probably — passing out.

I wore a mask and body armor my entire life for a reason; to keep these disorders and their symptoms, as well as my pain and suffering concealed, in order to be able to function and survive.

Some teachers allowed me to do written papers in place of oral presentations. Some wouldn't allow any compromise so I took the failing grade. With a couple of these "teachers," it would have been more than a pleasure, to be quite frank, to stick my foot where the sun didn't shine. Live and learn — and learn I did. Mostly how not to ever be an insensitive asshole. Some of the more indelible life lessons I've learned were in high school and from the rigid, unsympathetic "teachers".

In certain classes, students would be called, daily, to the blackboard or in front of the class to work out problems. Any time I was called upon to get up and get in front of the class I'd just say I wasn't prepared and take the hit — the demerit for the day.

I did just enough school work to get me by and keep from falling below the required GPA. I was dealing with so much depression, anxiety, and anger, I would have crawled under a rock and stayed there if I could.

A newfound popularity in high school made it even more difficult to stay out of focus — out of that spotlight. Strange as it was, I went from an unknown, picked-on and bullied, odd-man-out, to "popular" in high school and college and up through my early 20's, at which time I completely vanished into a devastating isolation.

My high school years were a mix of calamitous internal pain and suffering and this newfound popularity that was certainly a joy compared to the previous decade of bullying and being on the outside looking in. You would think I would have less stress and anxiety being popular. No chance. Concealing my pain and suffering behind my mask was added stress and anxiety. My body armor weighed very heavy on me in many ways but was an absolute necessity.

Though I began to develop this shield and armor about a year earlier in the eighth grade, I now had to tweak my protective covering as the environment was much more intense and the stakes at their highest. My new and improved "*hard-ass mask*" and "*nothing can hurt me, tough-as-nails persona*" began as I entered my freshman year in high school and would last for the next 35 years before I would begin to peel off my protective covering by way of intense psychotherapy and writing this story.

I noticed a lot of bullying going on throughout high school. Classical may have been one of the top public college-prep high schools in the country, but it had its share of characters — mostly upperclassmen — and their brand of harassment like every other high school. Always physically smaller than the rest, trouble came my way on more than a few occasions throughout my life and mostly the first couple years of high school. I would always try and avoid trouble but sometimes that was not possible. I took no crap at this time in my life as I did for too many years prior. All the years of trauma and bullying I had endured created a very real, very intense anger inside of me that was forever brewing and more than likely apparent in the mask I now wore.

I don't deny that as I got older I had a short fuse — a temper that got very hot, very quickly. All the pain coming to the surface whenever certain buttons were pushed. If you played the music at this time in my life, we were gonna dance. Experience had taught me that not too many cowards and punks know how to actually move to the music.

My mask may have looked like the Devil at times, I'm sure. However, my soul was always heavily weighed down by horrendous disorders and bleeding profusely from the years of pain and suffering, hopelessness and sorrow. My mask on, the tough exterior in position, and the somewhat cocky and confident attitude in place forming an invisible shield, a body armor for the sole purpose of protecting the fragile and bleeding soul that laid beneath it. It was a matter of survival. It was my way of keeping everyone an arm's length away. From getting too close for comfort. Who would attempt to penetrate such a rocklike exterior? My pain and suffering — my truth, my reality — would be safe from all around me.

For the sake of some clarity, I would offer this analogy with regards to the mask I have worn for some thirty-five years and the reason it has been necessary;

If a man is a homosexual but remains in the closet his entire life, he is concealing his truth behind a mask. He is hiding a fact, a part of himself that embarrasses him, that he feels makes him weak, less worthy than others in the majority, the *norm* so to speak. He is not like everyone else. Most people want to fit-in, be "normal" and like the majority. Many homosexual men — and I have friends and family members who are homosexual and I love them dearly — will marry and even have children to conceal that truth. The wife or husband has no idea what lies behind that mask. It is very difficult and extremely stressful to live a life believing you must hide your truth in order to survive.

I never knew just how severe my emotional imprisonment was during my life, if it had a name, what it was called, or what caused it. I only knew that the emotional pain and suffering I felt was very real and interfered with, and destroyed, any *normal* that should have been my life.

I wasn't like everyone else. Where I came from, men don't cry, they don't hurt, they don't feel emotional pain or experience depression "like women". They don't have anxiety and panic attacks and they don't talk about these things, either. How I came up, emotional pain and suffering — these very disorders — are a sign of weakness. It is not possible to reveal the truth being concealed behind a mask when you feel you will be persecuted, chewed up and spit out — whether by family, friends, or society in general. You keep the secret, the pain and suffering, the shame behind that mask. It is a matter of self-preservation.

Through therapy, my recovery process, and learning my truth — the reasons behind my pain, suffering, and emotional collapse, what exactly caused it, and what exactly it was that had a death-grip on me for decades — I was able to slowly begin to come out, begin to take off that mask and reveal the truth of my soul — the pain, suffering, and despair — and the vicious disorders that have controlled my entire life into isolation.

Through recovery, we begin to understand and accept who we are and what we are and that there is nothing to be ashamed of. We are not hiding evil behind that mask. We are protecting our souls and ourselves from what we feel will be frowned upon by those around us. We are avoiding being persecuted while enabling our very survival.

Reputation and what others think of you — how you are perceived — has always been of utmost importance to all the guys I knew growing up. You live and die by reputation. This reminds me of an instance when I was in my mid-20's, working in retail security while finishing up my last two years of college; I ran into my cousin Silio and his sister, my cousin Rena, one day while working at the department store.

Both Silio and Rena were a few years younger than me. I had spent more time with my cousins during my younger years. I had been rather reclusive and isolating the past five years or so while I was on my college hiatus and deep into my songwriting and up until this present time. I hadn't seen them too much over the past years. However, I had always been close with my cousins. We were family and there for each other regardless. I remember Rena saying to Silio that day, "*Go ahead, tell cousin Steve what you want to do.*"

Silio then looked directly at me and said, "*Cuz, you can't laugh at me.*"

I told him I wouldn't laugh at him regardless of what he said. He hesitated a bit and I could see the stress and nervousness building on his face. After a few very uncomfortable minutes, he said in a rather low whisper, "*I want to work with hair.*"

I said, "*You mean you want to be a barber and cut hair for a living?*"

"*Yeah, I like cutting hair, it's what I want to do,*" he replied.

"*So, what's the problem? Sounds like you found something that makes you happy and can call a career. I think it's a great idea,*" I responded.

He said, with a smile, "*Thanks, cuz. I just don't want everyone to laugh at me, think I'm weird or something.*"

I knew what he meant and how he felt. I had lived it and hid it my entire life. No one was ever aware of my pain and suffering. The bleeding and tortured soul behind the mask. And, as was the case my entire life, these disorders and my emotional state perfectly camouflaged behind that mask and progressively worsened with each passing year.

I told him to always follow his heart. As long as he isn't hurting anyone else in the process, he deserves to do in life whatever makes him happy, whatever he believes in. Whether that is cutting hair or selling flowers out of the back of his car, it doesn't matter.

His fear was showing those around him that he loved doing something he believed others would consider "less than manly". This is the mentality of our upbringing. Fortunately, this wasn't a serious dilemma sprinkled with shame that required a mask but rather just coming to grips with and accepting that he genuinely enjoyed a profession where many males were branded as homosexuals.

Silio was a macho and masculine, heterosexual guy. However, how we grew up, being that our reputations were so important, we were always aware of and concerned with how others perceived us.

It was a very stressful, and nerve-racking way to live if you actually had to wear a mask to hide a truth that you believed would otherwise be your reputation's demise and leave you outcast, in a category of *weak* or perhaps worse.

Speaking of reputation and what most of our culture might consider less than a masculine pastime, I began writing poetry and dabbling in songwriting my freshman year in high school. It was a way to express on paper my innermost feelings of suffering, pain, and despair. I could never share these emotions with anyone, it would reveal too much. I needed that mask and shield to remain intact and in place to survive.

My poetry and songs were my reality. Pain exhaled onto paper. It spoke of a life of suffering, despair, loss, anger, dreams, and being different. No one, outside of mostly professionals in the music industry, would ever view or critique my poems or songs.

They were too personal and revealed too much of the bleeding soul, the real person beneath that mask. If I was able to reveal that pain and suffering — that weakness I believed many would consider it — I wouldn't need a perennial poker face.

My own mother would never see my work — my songs — until I slowly began stripping the mask and shield from my being and began writing this book some 35 years post my freshman year, when the writing all began.

Writing poetry and songs was one outlet that kept me connected to who I really was — the real person falling apart behind the disguise. Writing was always painful, but cathartic. It kept me grounded. It somehow kept a bit of hope pulsating within.

I never attended a day of gym class in high school. Ironic, as I exercised and trained each day — hours upon hours — and, more than likely, was in better shape than anyone in the entire high school. I had a note from my doctor that I couldn't participate due to very bad allergies and difficulty breathing. That was half the problem, the other half was severe anxiety.

If I could find a way to stay out of the spotlight, I would do it to survive.

The note was only for that first year, but I was never added to the gym class roster. No teachers in the gym department even knew I existed!

This was perfect for me; I had a whole hour-plus each day in school with no spotlight on me and was temporarily off the radar. I would find a quiet spot somewhere where I could be alone and connect with my inner-self by writing some poetry or songs.

I met one of my best friends, *Jimmy G*, freshman year in high school. We were pretty inseparable throughout high school. We hung out through the first two years of college too. However, not nearly as much, as I was in college in Newport, Rhode Island and he was in college in Boston, Massachusetts. Post sophomore year in college was also the time I began falling into a very deep, devilishly dark depression and isolating from everyone and everything.

Jimmy was a really great kid. He was respectful to all and a down-to-earth, good-hearted person. He wasn't a fighter or into fighting or martial arts. He did do a lot of weight training with me through the years. He wasn't a street kid. Not very street-wise. Didn't hang around the corners or knock around any of the neighborhoods.

He lived a few miles outside of my neck of the woods. His father owned a local business with the main office in the North End. He came from a respected, legitimate family. A real nice home-life with wonderful parents, a sister, and brother.

No signs of dysfunction there. A very similar family life to that of my friend, Rocco. It was really great to see the kind of loving relationship Jimmy had with his father. The kind I longed for my entire life.

We learned to drive about the same time — the summer of 1980; our birthdays a few days apart. After two years of city-bussing to school, we would alternate junior and senior year driving to school between a few of us.

We were involved in our first car accident together. It was summer 1980. We had both just turned 16 and had only been driving a few months.

My parents had bought me a car for my 16th birthday. I may have been spoiled and showered with material things but what I really needed in my life was nowhere to be found — and all the material things and money in the world couldn't provide it.

I was driving, Jimmy in the passenger's seat, and another friend, *Dave S*, in the back seat. We were coming from Federal Hill traveling east on Atwells Ave. going into the city of Providence. As we approached the intersection of the I-95 southbound exit to Atwells Ave. and were passing beneath the recently completed gateway arch over Atwells Ave., we all noticed the newly placed LaPigna (pinecone) sculpture hanging from the center of the arch. Within seconds of looking at the pinecone, my car was hit from the driver's front left quarter up through the driver's door section by a semi-tractor. The semi rolled over my car and crushed the entire front and the entire left front quarter panel of the car through the driver's door.

I was pinned and trapped beneath the dashboard. Jimmy wound up with a fractured nose from his impact with the windshield. He also had multiple cuts and bruises. Dave was banged around pretty good and sustained multiple cuts and bruises but suffered no serious injuries.

Firefighter's that responded to the accident had to extract me using the jaws-of-life as my side of the car — inside and outside — was completely crushed and flattened like a pancake.

I don't remember much as I was semi-conscious from the time of impact. However, I was told at the hospital by one of the police officers doing the accident report that a fireman at the scene said the left front pillar (the metal bar between the driver side window and the windshield) saved my life. If not for that metal bar, the semi's tires would have crushed me alive as the truck ran over my car.

I have thought of that accident often over the many years. Half of me always wished I had died that day. The other half is grateful that I lived — regardless of the deepening pain and suffering that was to come--for the sake of my mother.

The doctors at the hospital couldn't believe that I only had minor injuries and a concussion with no major breaks or damage internally. The doctors said that if I wasn't in such good shape and so muscular, especially my chest area, I would have at the very least broken all of my ribs and my sternum as the impact threw me into the steering wheel, which broke off when my chest slammed into it (not many wore seatbelts in 1980).

At the very second the accident happened, a few of my father's friends just so happened to be passing by the scene. They noticed it was my car involved in the accident and came over to see what happened. They immediately went to notify my father who was less than a half mile away at one of his friend's clubs on Federal Hill. They told my father what happened and that there were a couple witnesses at the scene who might give statements to that effect. The witnesses at the scene had told my father's friends that they thought I went through the red light. As soon as my father got to the scene, the couple witnesses that were there noted that they didn't actually see the accident and left before the police arrived.

The police report showed that the driver of the semi-tractor was traveling at over 50 mph — twice the off-ramp speed limit — when he struck my car and proceeded over it, crushing it in the process. There was also marijuana found in his truck.

I do remember seeing that the traffic signal was green as we were approaching it. At that time, when we looked at the arch's pinecone, we were, literally, only a couple hundred feet from the intersection and traveling at around 25 mph. I honestly can't say for sure if it was green, yellow or red upon impact.

Jimmy later said he couldn't see the light as we were literally under it but he saw the semi screaming off the I-95 southbound exit ramp to Atwells Ave. and yelled to me to watch out. It was too late.

I was banged up pretty bad but nothing serious. All three of us spent a few hours in the hospital and were released. It could have been much worse. It could have been fatal for one or all of us.

My father was actually by my side through the whole thing. He arrived on the scene before the police, fire department, and paramedics. He said he couldn't believe what he was seeing — and the fact that I was still in the car, buried beneath the crushed dashboard. He said he was talking to me, asking me if I could hear him and if I was okay. He said I was mumbling, so he knew I was alive. He was worried but felt a sense of relief once I was extracted in one piece from the mangled mass of metal, was conscious, talking, and the paramedics gave him the thumbs up.

As the years progressed in high school, there was lots of testosterone flowing and plenty of male conflict. Fighting began and was commonplace. There were very few fights within the school itself as this high school would not tolerate such nonsense. Students had to maintain a certain conduct and grade point average or you were booted out. Most conflict occurred off school grounds and within surrounding neighborhoods, as well as at parties and the clubs during weekend nights.

I have been involved in dozens of street fights over the years. I never once sucker punched anyone or hit someone first. If someone had a problem with me, I would always take a couple steps back and tell them to play the music. If they charged me, swung at me, pushed me, it was on. All that pain I carried inside from childhood kept a fire — a rage — burning inside of me always. I had a lot of pent-up anger and when, and if, someone pushed my buttons, that anger and pain came out and it wasn't pretty.

I have been sucker punched several times during my life. That is always a cowardly thing to do for anyone who considers himself a man. I remember one incident in particular that burns me to this day; I was in my 20's. I was sucker punched from behind by a guy nearly twice my size. He was an easy 6' and 200+ lbs. I was 5' 5 ½ " tall and all of 150 lbs.

Being a physically small guy, I was always the target of a coward. This piece of shit walked up to me in a parking lot as I was leaving a store. He reeked of alcohol.

I didn't like the way he looked, the way he was acting, and wanted nothing to do with this person. He mumbled a couple things and then, for some reason, extended his hand as if to introduce himself to me. I figured he would try and use the old handshake hold and cross with the other fist to sucker punch me. To avoid this, I told him to get lost and kept my distance. I never had any patience with those that were drinking and acting the fool. He walked away from me and quickly came up behind me as I was getting into my car. He hit me from behind and across the jaw with a punch that was most likely intensified by a weighted object in his hand. This was the first time in my life I had been knocked out. I came to within seconds of hitting the ground as I remember feeling the multiple kicks I took to the face while I was semi-conscious and laying there.

Needless to say, I dropped my guard by turning my back to him and not paying attention. I paid for my mistake with multiple stitches to the face, a concussion, and equilibrium problems to this day.

A coward is in the same league in my book as a rat, a child molester, a rapist, and those who prey on and abuse the elderly and animals. They have no soul. They have no manhood. They are the scum of the earth.

I remember on several occasions running into my brother-in-law's son, *Vinny*, at my high school. He didn't attend my high school but was dating an upperclassman at the time. He was a few years older than me. Nice kid. Bigger, streetwise, take-no-shit type of kid. He was always very respectful to my parents. My parents speak highly of him, his wife, and their son to this day.

I saw Vinny one day in the hallway of the school. He was looking around rather intently. He walked over to me and we talked a bit. He asked me if I knew a particular kid in the high school. I did. The kid, *DJ*, was in one of my classes. He was a punk and bully. Vinny was looking for him because DJ was bothering his girlfriend. Strangely enough, I remember feeling a bit sorry for DJ. It wasn't going to be pretty for him when Vinny finally caught up to him.

In the interim, I had my own problem with DJ. This punk was now tormenting and bullying my cousin Rico.

Rico wasn't a fighter but a sweet, kind kid who kept to himself and never bothered anyone. He wouldn't think of hurting a fly. That's the kind of peaceful innocence a coward looks to prey on.

Rico asked me to talk to DJ because this kid kept bothering him. I pulled DJ to the side one day and told him to lay off bullying my cousin or he'd have a serious problem with me. DJ tried to push through me while I was speaking to him and wound up on the ground, in an empty classroom, squirming like the coward he was. That was the last day he ever bothered my cousin.

Unfortunately, bullies are in every school, private and public, every work environment, every part of society. What these bullies all need is a good old-fashioned, street-justice ass-kicking. Knock some teeth out, break a jaw or an arm. It's the only way to get through to this type of person. It works every time.

Growing up as I did, you make your bones on the street. People learn really quick what you're made of. A reputation is born one way or another. I was always a straight-forward, fair kid. I didn't have a prejudice bone in my body.

I was like my grandfather — I liked everyone, gave everyone a chance to prove themselves, treated everyone fairly as I wanted to be treated. You may not have known it looking at me, as I always had my guard up — the shield and armor in place — and that stern looking mask on to protect myself. I could never back up or back down from anyone or anything. For me, it was a matter of pride, of which I had a difficult time my entire life swallowing. I'd rather die than be a coward in any sense of the word.

Fighter or not, fair or not, mask or not, where I came from, no one admitted to having the kind of feelings I was dealing with. No one talked about this kind of thing. It was actually frowned upon and my kind of pain and suffering would usually be viewed as a sign of weakness — especially among street guys. Only women were allowed to feel that kind of emotional pain and suffering. Bullshit! Real men suffer, real men deal with emotional pain, real men are afflicted with these overpowering disorders, and real men cry.

Self-praise isn't my thing, but I have lived this hell for over four decades and consider myself as close to an expert as one can be regarding these disorders and the havoc they wreak on a person's mind and body. In too many instances these disorders — as well as physical pain — are the sole basis for addiction, suicide, and death.

Most guys I have known throughout my life — some who would just as soon kill you as look at you — couldn't walk in my shoes for four days, let alone four decades. It takes an exceptionally strong mind to cope and live with these disorders and the destruction they impose on your life. Few people know these disorders as intimately as I do. While I am the last person on earth to pat himself on the back, again, I have lived this torment — this evil — through an entire lifetime and know firsthand what the truth and facts of these disorders are and what they do to a person and his or her life.

Unlike most psychiatrists, therapists, and others who may study these disorders and those affected by them, I've not only been to hell, but I have crawled on my hands and knees in the deepest and darkest regions of that inferno for some 40-plus years, without reprieve, and lived to tell about it. I have 3rd degree burns — and the knowledge that comes of that — enshrouding my entire being and scorched upon my mind for as long as I have air in my lungs. I know every nook and cranny within that sadistic, misery-laced maze of insanity like the back of my hand.

I learned through decades of hands-on experience and several years of therapy and a recovery process that support was one of the — if not *the* — most vital necessities in battling and overcoming the shackles of PTSD, depression, and anxiety that had bound me into emotional imprisonment and isolation, spiraling me down to the deepest depths of that hell I've existed in my entire life.

The toughest road is the one I've walked alone.

I started coming into my own — feeling a bit more confident with my training and its' ability to get me over the humps and through the days — around 17, as I was getting ready for my senior year of high school.

You'd never have known looking at me or talking to me, but I had zero confidence in myself in every other area of life outside of training.

I was completely consumed by emotional pain and despair. My training was the only reason I was able to function at all. It was the crutch that kept me upright and moving.

Many times throughout my life, others saw — whatever it may have been — something in me that I could never see. Whether that be talent in some area or appeal in another.

Senior year, I lost out by only a few votes for "best looking" in our senior yearbook. Go figure! Me — little Mousey — as runner up for best looking guy senior year of high school. At least I lost out to one of my closest friends, Rocco F!

My life certainly did a one-eighty popularity-wise in high school. There were more than a few girls in high school who actually liked me. Little did they know, I had no belief in myself whatsoever but played it off rather well. Outside of high school, I met girls at parties, clubs, and when out with friends. Not one ever saw the doubt and despair behind the pretense. There were many I could have had deep, meaningful friendships with and possibly more if not for the disorders which controlled my every move.

There was nothing I wanted more than to confide in someone — particularly a girlfriend — who I trusted would stand by me and help me from the hell I was living.

The things I truly cherished and needed most of all my entire life — support, strong relationships, tight bonds with people I cared for — were the things that these disorders prevented, making it impossible for me to take down that wall.

These disorders custom-fit me with chains that bound me into emotional imprisonment. Eventually, in the years to come, this lead to full-blown isolation.

It was strange being popular in high school — girls wanted to date me, hang out with me, be around me. The short kid with the mask! Perhaps it was that very mask, that "bad boy" image portrayed that some were attracted to. Regardless, I enjoyed being around girls more than guys. Dating or just spending time hanging out was great. My soul was more at ease around females. It is to this day. However, I could never totally be myself and that always bothered me and, eventually, lead to even more pain, suffering, and isolation in hiding my truth — the bleeding, tormented soul behind that facade — when I felt I needed to reveal it to build a meaningful relationship.

There were lots of parties throughout high school where most everyone would be drinking, except for me. Everyone knew I didn't drink or do drugs. I was often the designated driver. I was always sober and never strayed from that path.

I was also well into a major depression and suffering with severe anxiety. I had too many scarring, horrible memories that I couldn't clear from my mind.

Being around alcohol and intoxicated people certainly didn't help any but this was the norm in high school and college back then, as it probably still is today.

My training kept my keel even and allowed me to function normally day to day in most every capacity, including keeping my cool and going with the flow at these alcohol-laden parties. My mask and shield — that tough, somewhat cocky persona, and hard, impenetrable exterior — was like the razor-sharp quills on a porcupine and kept others from coming too close, from seeing my inner pain and suffering.

That armor, along with my training, was much more appealing — and effective — for me during my life than drowning the pain with alcohol as many who may have been in my very shoes emotionally seemed to be doing at these parties.

Later in life, as the numbing and euphoric effects of my training began to wane, through complete isolation I was able to keep safe distances.

It was difficult being in any type of relationship. My mind was always worried about others finding out about my being different — the disorders destroying me emotionally. This was *my* secret. That secret kept walls up throughout my life. I allowed no one the opportunity to penetrate that barrier.

Even with the boost from my training, I always felt completely out of place, uncomfortable in my own skin, at all times, always. The mask and armor I had developed was the hardened exterior that kept my bleeding soul protected.

I couldn't let down my guard with anyone — friends, girlfriends, teachers, family — or I would be exposed and doomed as I believed. So, with that wall — my shield — always up and my mask and body armor exuding a take no prisoners, tougher-than-nails persona, I may not have been as easy to get along with as others as my teen years progressed. This would be the case throughout my life. Most of the others weren't battling with PTSD, depression, and anxiety or the extreme dysfunctionality and trauma within their family and lives. They had no idea what an emotional disaster my life really was.

Bottom line, I had no idea what *normal* was in a relationship or most any other aspect of life. I had no template to follow and no male adult role model to teach me or for me to try and emulate. I had a difficult time getting close with anyone. Close enough to let my guard down and be "me". Only way to survive was to keep the wall up, the mask always on, and I became that tough, somewhat cocky kid who took no shit. Little did anyone ever know, I was just the opposite, hiding behind a persona in order to preserve my sanity and survive.

In looking back, I can now see that a trail of burned bridges and a mile of scars from the stitches were the result of that pain, suffering, and anger forever brewing below the surface due to the disorders that controlled my life into a living hell.

Through my masked persona, *"I was a Rock, I was an Island,"* as the one and only Paul Simon wrote in his masterpiece song of 1965, "I am a Rock". The song reflects the mood and feelings of the songwriter at that point in his life. Through time and life's experiences, our mood and feelings change as we learn, heal, and grow.

For someone who lived day in and day out with PTSD, depression, anxiety, and isolation, the lyrics to this song speak volumes to me.

This is a song that, to me, so perfectly manifests the mind-set and symptoms of emotional pain and suffering, depression and isolation, and the need for both an *outlet* and a *mask* to protect oneself — *to survive.*

Below is the last verse to the song which captures the sentiment in a nutshell:

I have my books
And my poetry to protect me;
I am shielded in my armor
Hiding in my room, safe within my womb
I touch no one and no one touches me
I am a rock
I am an island

And a rock feels no pain
And an island never cries.

Music has been a major part of my life since childhood. A sanity-saving tool in many ways. It was my sole support system. It took the place of what I — what each one of us suffering with these disorders — needed most desperately in my godforsaken world of darkness, pain, and despair; understanding, trusting, compassionate people and support.

Music and song is an all-inclusive instrument which allowed me to connect with, and express my deepest feelings whether creating it or simply identifying and healing with it.

As the O'Jay's sang in their mid-1970's hit song, "I Love Music" written by the incredibly talented and prolific R&B/soul songwriting team of Kenneth Gamble and Leon Huff;

Music is the healing force of the world
It's understood by every man, woman, boy and girl.

Music most certainly is the universal language. It transcends boundaries and brings people together, physically and emotionally. It touches each of us in our hearts and souls. It moves us like nothing else. We can all interpret the song as we wish — it can have different meanings to different people — and make it our own, having that special meaning to each of us while touching all of us. Music can make you happy or it can make you sad. Emotions that each of us know intimately and deal with daily, throughout our lives. Either way, we can all relate to these two very powerful emotions and share them together

— bringing us together — through music, through the art of the song.

Music is the universal outlet and medicine that everyone can feel a part of. Music says the things we need to hear, it gives us hope, it keeps our dreams alive. It validates our feelings. It lets us know we're not alone and that others think like we do, they feel pain and happiness like we do.

Music unites people like nothing else. It is magical. It is a never-ending sunrise.

Music inspires. It motivates. It heals.

Music has been the only companion with whom I could always be "me".

Music is one of the very few loves and outlets that have helped me to cope, and survive my demons, and daily battles throughout my life. It is the only medicine of those very few that still remains intact all these decades later.

Music liberated my soul but my heart continued to long for — and does to this day — an everlasting intimacy that neither rhythm, nor rhyme could possibly yield.

I met my high school sweetheart and first serious (lasting more than a few months) girlfriend, *Lisa L*, the end of my sophomore year of high school. She attended my high school through her sophomore year and then transferred to another school. We began dating and were together through my junior and senior year and the very beginning of my first year of college, though we were not as close any longer and beginning to go our separate ways as a couple at that time.

She came from a wonderful family and had the perfect family life. Lots of love, affection, and respect between her and her parents, younger, and older brother. It was a beautiful, non-dysfunctional family that I felt at home with when around them — and that was pretty often for a couple of years.

They treated me like family and I truly enjoyed spending time with them. However, no one ever knew what I was going through. My mask and my addiction to training was doing what it was supposed to do; concealing the tormented soul that ached horribly and without fail.

There were lots of functions within her family that I attended though I was petrified. I was pretty good at hiding the overwhelming emotional pain and suffering I had forever brewing inside, and from anyone seeing or knowing about it.

However, there were times, even after intensely training prior to social functions or larger gatherings, my anxiety would cause severe outbreaks of head and facial sweating, my heart pounding so hard and fast I don't know how I ever kept from passing out. I found myself in bathrooms an awful lot when this happened, wiping the dripping sweat from my face and head, catching my breath, and trying desperately to slow my heart-rate, calm down, and get some of the anxiety under control. It was noticed on some occasions. I passed it off as my having had a very hard workout earlier in the day, my blood pressure being elevated as a result, along with dehydration. Everyone knew I was very heavy into training and proper nutrition. Still, regardless of what others may or may not have believed, I was always extremely uncomfortable with sweat pouring off of me and the constant feelings of hysteria I had from the anxiety.

My entire life, I always figured most people would think I was a drug addict or going through some kind of withdrawal like the DT's — *delirium tremens*. The symptoms of anxiety are very close to the symptoms of withdrawal. Imagine, me of all people, a drug addict or going through withdrawal! Yet, what other people were thinking always weighed heavy on my mind.

It didn't matter where I was most times, panic and anxiety attacks could — would and still do — just happen; standing in line at the bank, grocery shopping, out to dinner, working, in class, or anywhere else. Sometimes there was a trigger, other times not. It was always embarrassing and I'd do what I needed to do to get out of that situation as quickly as possible.

The only time and place I was ever truly comfortable was training and in a gym. I was at ease and was always sweating anyway. So, I fit right in! I didn't have to run away to regain some composure. Probably why as a kid I always loved Halloween. I had a real mask that night and no one could see me sweating or shaking. I actually fit in — I didn't stand out — and was "like everyone else" that one night of the year.

Lisa and I would skip the junior prom at both her high school and mine, but would attend my high school's senior prom. I may have been popular during this time in my life but I would still rather forego any social gatherings if at all possible. Mask or not, popular or not, I was always extremely uncomfortable in my own skin and always knew what was ahead of me at any social gatherings or get-togethers. The anxiety, sweating, shaking, heart palpitations. I would do whatever was necessary to skip the event(s) if at all possible.

As I got older, I began skipping and avoiding just about everything that had to do with social gatherings. I became more and more isolated in order to keep my disorders under wraps. Isolation became necessary to maintain my sanity and survive, especially later in life when the euphoric effects of my training began to wane.

After the first year of dating, I actually spent more time with Lisa's family than I did with her — skiing, fishing, cookouts, boating, and other events. These are some of the very few wonderful memories and special times of my middle and late adolescent years. I would always think to myself; this is how a *normal* family acts and treats one another. In retrospect, it is probably everything I ever hoped for in a functional, loving family atmosphere. I guess I tried to feel what "normal" was really like for some years. It was the life I never had. Seeing the love and affection between Lisa's dad and her younger brother, *Rosco*, was amazing. Her dad would always hug and kiss Rosco, telling him how much he loved him. My heart was both happy for him and a bit envious of him. Rosco — the entire family — was blessed and very fortunate.

Even as Lisa and I began drifting apart once college started for me, her family and I still kept in touch and got together now and then to go skiing.

I'd run into Rosco and Lisa's older brother, *Orzo*, every now and again at the gym or at a local store. I kept in touch with *Mr. and Mrs. L* by way of birthday and Christmas cards for the next 10-plus years — right up until I became a state trooper and my life quickly went from bad to the absolute worst with my line of duty accident.

I loved each of them very much. I always felt the same in return.

I think of them all quite often. They are beautiful, loving, very special people.

Unbeknownst to them, and to myself at the time, I learned an awful lot about what *normal* really was from this family. I was fortunate to have spent several quality years with them.

Like everyone else that mattered in my life, no one in this family knew what I had gone through and what I was living with daily — in my soul, in my mind — the crippling PTSD, depression, anxiety, and despair.

My best friend, Jimmy G, started dating *Sandi B*, during our senior year. Sandi was an underclassman and a good friend of my girlfriend,

Lisa. All four of us would hang out together throughout this last year (for three of us) of high school.

Problems arose as Sandi began telling my girlfriend how she was using Jimmy because he came from money. She continually bragged that she had him wrapped around her finger. She would call him derogatory names, degrade him, and admit one of the only reasons she bothered seeing him was to hang out with and be around me and my girlfriend.

Many of these comments were also made in my presence. I found her attitude and comments deplorable. Worst part about the whole thing, she made it clear to me that she liked me — in a very physical way. Most guys would not have thought twice about it as she was a very attractive, sexy girl.

However, I wasn't most guys and my life has always revolved around honor, trust, loyalty, and respect. These virtues are the most important aspects of any relationship in my world. I would never — under any circumstances — betray, lie to, or disrespect a friend or family. Anyone for that matter.

I decided (It was actually Christmas Eve) after a few months of this eating away at me to have a heart-to-heart talk with my best friend. I told him it was difficult for me to tell him this but I felt obligated because we were best friends and I didn't want to see him used, disrespected, and badly hurt. I told him what I knew to be true, what I heard with my own ears and had seen with my own eyes.

He told me he didn't believe anything I had just told him. I asked him if he really believed I would lie to him. He said he didn't, but just couldn't believe what I was telling him.

I learned that night that in addition to money, women are the greatest weakness of most men.

A few years down the road, I actually wrote this song inspired by this very experience:

"Women & Money"

V1

...(Intro 2 bars music)[1-2]
Got the women to the left[3] (1 bar music[4])
Got the money to the right[5] (1 bar music[6])
Both can start a fire[7]
That burns you day and night[8]

CL1

> She can move a mountain[1]
> He makes all the rules[2]
> Both have got you by the balls[3]
> And there's nothin' you can do[4]

Chorus

> Women and money
> Bring[1] you to your knees[2]
> Once you're bitten
> You[3] can't break free[4]
> Women and money
> Both[5] quick to the kill[6]
> If one don't getcha'
> Then[7] the other will[8]

V2

> ...(2 bars music)[1-2]
> Got desire wrapped in pink[3] (1 bar music[4])
> Got the power packed in green[5] (1 bar music[6])
> Both a sweet addiction[7]
> From which you can't come clean[8]

> ... CL 2 ...
> ... CH 2 ...

Bridge:

> She's got what you need[1]
> Like water and the air we breathe[2]
> No doubt about it ...no[3]
> Can't live without it[4]
> He's one hell of a guy[5]
> Without him you can't survive[6]
> No doubt about it ...no[7]
> Can't live without it[8]

> ... CL 3 ...
> ... CH 3 ...

© Steve DiGrossi

Most men have a difficult time with common sense and thinking clearly with the head on their shoulders when it comes to a woman.

I have been called brutally honest my entire life. I don't believe in sugarcoating anything. No one has ever had to wonder if I was being up front with them whether in business or friendship. I am honest and straightforward to a fault and it usually winds up, in my case anyway, that most people can't handle the truth and would rather have the sugarcoated version than what truly is — reality.

We were young — senior year in high school, 17-years-old — and I was highly offended. I actually wound up losing respect for my best friend for being so naive and feeble minded, and basically — most importantly to me — pretty much calling me a liar.

Once I lost respect for someone, I found it near-impossible to continue a worthwhile, positive relationship. We did continue to hang out for the next couple years, though our friendship was definitely strained.

I was also plummeting into a very deep depression and isolation during this time and losing contact with most everyone and everything in my life.

Jimmy would marry another girl some years down the road. I think of him often. I hope to reconnect at some point and share my story with him.

I had worked various jobs throughout high school and college. City summer jobs while in high school, ranging from errand and office work with the State of Rhode Island Division of Motor Vehicles to digging holes and painting bridges with the State of Rhode Island Park and Bridge Maintenance Department. They were tough jobs to get in the summer without a connection. My father helped to get me a few along the way.

Other jobs I worked were in general and retail security, a major wholesale club, instructor for a driver training academy and licensed real estate agent among others.

I always hustled to make a buck on the side. Whether buying a single antique and collectible or purchasing entire collections, inventories, or estates for resale. I would break my back and bend my mind to make a dollar, but I loved it.

I had no bad habits and saved most of my money, reinvesting over the years in different ventures from vintage collectibles to real estate. I didn't spend money on alcohol or drugs, weekend partying, gambling or the like. I was very responsible with money. It's a good thing, as I would have been living under a bridge after my line of duty accident and resulting disability.

I had enough money at 16 to buy my own car. However, the summer post my sophomore year, my parents bought me that first car for my birthday — a 1979 Pontiac Trans-Am. It was my favorite of all cars at the time. I was ecstatic and beyond thankful.

The word *spoiled* came up often now when some family and friends were speaking of me. If they only knew the truth — the living hell that was my reality.

The fact that money can't buy happiness and peace of mind and material things can't take the place of a father figure and a normal, supportive family atmosphere — one that is full of hugs, encouragement, and genuine love. While it was far from a normal and supportive family, if it wasn't for my mother, I'd have been completely without those hugs, encouragement, and genuine love during my lifetime.

Though I had my own hard-earned money and purchased just about everything I wanted, my mother, of course, would buy clothes (among other things) for me throughout high school and would always ask me if I needed any money or wanted anything at all. I didn't. I wanted her to take care of herself — that's all I ever wanted. Still, she was always slipping money into my pocket and buying me things anyway. She's done this my entire life — and to this day! She was always thinking of me and everyone else before herself. Always.

I was able to save a lot of money while living at home. Only thing I spent a substantial amount of my money on when in high school was equipment for my home gym. My parents helped with college tuition, in addition to the loans I applied for and received. When I finished college in 1991, at some point over the next several years, I payed off my only debt — my student loans. I was now debt-free. I have never to this day had any outstanding debts. If I charge on a credit card, the amount owed is paid in full with the next billing cycle. I have never had an outstanding balance on a credit card in 30 years. They've never gotten one cent of interest from me. I'm probably not their favorite type of customer!

I also ran errands for my father beginning in high school and took care of some business for him when he was in Florida for a few months during most winters.

My father would tell me often, "*You could have been a boss in another time. If you came up during my day or were born in your brother's place, you would have been a boss. It's all over now. Times have changed for the worst.*"

I would hear these very words and this sentiment throughout my adult life.

The "life" and the "customs" began to quickly deteriorate come the 1970's. The code of honor and the code of silence was the glue that held this way of life together. It was slowly losing its hold and the way of life with it. The newer generations of wise guys were now violating long-held customs and rules that were in place to keep that way of life strong, impenetrable, and alive.

When someone got pinched now, ratting was common to save themselves from lengthy to life prison sentences. Especially drug-related pinches. Drug dealing was out of the question — strictly forbidden — with the old-timers in the life. It was bad business and the old school bosses knew what would happen if they had a hand in it, if it became part of the racket — and they were right. The old-timers were passing on and those that remained were ailing. The life was fracturing. New generations and most bosses had little in common with the old school bosses of the 1920's up through the 1950's and most of the 1960's. Things were no longer as they were for decades. You couldn't trust anyone and many in the life were getting paranoid.

I don't disagree with my father that I could have been a boss in the life in his day. I was cut from the same cloth as the old school regime. I was a dinosaur in "the new world". Honor, respect, loyalty, and discipline such as mine were near-extinct. If I was to become involved in the life during my time, I would be looking over my shoulder constantly as I came up. I no doubt would have been killed or had to kill continuously to survive. This new breed of wise guy didn't think and believe as I did. I was *squola vecchia*, old school. *Very* old school. My character traits and beliefs are deeply and forever rooted 'till the day I die.

It hasn't been easy for me from childhood to present. I've been different than most on many levels, but it's who I am and who I'll be 'till the very end.

My father would tell me throughout my high school years and into my adulthood, "*Those days are gone. You're streetwise, book smart, you're sharp. You have personality and no bad habits. Go to law school. Become a lawyer, a politician.*"

I know what my father meant. Many of his friends — connected and made guys — had sons and family members who were politicians and attorneys. It was the way to go, so to speak. He saw both of these professions as having a license to steal with a *get out of jail free card* to go with it. I know of many attorneys, law enforcement officials, judges, and politicians that were in the pockets of the mob. Many that wouldn't be in their positions this very day if not for made and connected guys such as my father. They were very similar in their criminal ways. Only difference, they were college educated, had a fancy title before their name, and were getting away with criminal activity like no one else — especially mob guys — could ever get away with.

I saw most politicians as wolves in sheep's clothing. Most being pathological liars. Bending rules, breaking laws, conflicts of interest, dirty backroom deals, backstabbing, broken promises, greedy and stealing in every way possible — and getting away with it. That wasn't for me. I have always been a man of honor. If I say I'm going to do something — If I give you my word — rest assured, it will be done. My word is my bond. I don't go back on promises — ever! I say what I mean and mean what I say.

I see an old school mob boss back in the day as more honorable than these thieves — including corrupt judges and law enforcement officials — that take office, lie through their teeth time and again, and rob the people blind.

Granted, there is good and bad in all professions. I've known some very decent, hard-working, law-abiding, sincere politicians. However, they are few and far between. Politics is a very dirty business in my opinion. If you're not corrupt when you get in, odds are you will be very soon.

I would hear my father say often throughout my life, "*A greedy person is worse than a rat.*" I agree that both are in the same category of slime ball. Greed is rampant among those we elect to office. Greed has brought on many wars throughout history and has destroyed much and many along the way. Our country once had at least a few honorable, strong leaders and politicians back in the day. A time when men were men. When your word meant something and carried weight. When leaders cared for the people more than the dollars. Today, what do you see in many of our country's leaders and politicians? It's a joke, but too painful to laugh. A sign of the times today is criminal behavior and immorality among these privileged politicians being rewarded. Few things are more sickening than having to watch and listen to a hypocrite. Watching some of these politicians on TV — especially the bull-crap, mud-slinging, cut-throat commercials come election time — makes me nauseous; smiling faces and lie upon lie to get the vote, get the power, screw the people, and line their pockets. It's all about money and power, and enough is never enough.

Money may be the root of all evil, but in and of itself there is nothing evil about money. We all need it to survive in this world. However, that evil is birthed by an enlarged ego layered with a very thick coating of greed.

Today, in most instances, what the people are forced to elect to office is the lesser of the evils. This breed, in my opinion, is slowly destroying everything our country once was and stood for. Our government is *totally* broken and out of control. It's disgraceful. It's disgusting.

I love my country. As a state trooper, I took an oath to protect and serve. I put my life on the line and lost the better half of it in pursuit of that endeavor. I would have gone further in my dedication to country — my ultimate goal as a DEA agent fighting against another deadly form of evil that is slowly weakening and eating away at our country. It wasn't meant to be.

My grandparents immigrated to this country in order to create a better life and opportunities for themselves and their family. Honest, hard-working people who left their country of birth for a country that could offer them *life*. And it did.

They had to overcome many obstacles in order to raise their families and find success in their new, beloved home; The United States of America. Their Italian roots — and that of their children and grandchildren — firmly merged with their American pride and love of this great country.

What continues to happen in my backyard is destroying our culture — our country. For me, it is no different or less painful than watching someone I care for slowly ruining his or her life through substance abuse.

I had a lot of acquaintances throughout high school and my life.

My father once told me, "*When you're lying on your deathbed and you look back at your life, if you can truly say you had one friend — one true friend —*

you were the luckiest guy in the world."

Friendship — true friendship — is very rare in life. Especially how I grew up, where I came from, and the life I've lived. True friends are there through thick and thin, to the very end. Unconditionally.

Jimmy and Rocco could have been those true friends in my life. I loved and respected them for the genuinely good, decent human beings they were.

Each had great family lives with a loving family atmosphere. No dysfunction, no trauma in their families or lives. They had goals and plans. They had male role models in their corners supporting them, encouraging them, lending a hand and guiding them. They were able to smile and enjoy life as well as their accomplishments along the way. They didn't have to wear a mask or shield their souls to survive. They had no walls up. They were never "on guard". They had nothing to hide. Nothing to be ashamed of.

Subconsciously, I think I wished I could be like that. Be like them. Be normal. But that wasn't possible. In retrospect, I believe I lived a bit vicariously for a short while through a couple friends I admired and had a lot of respect and love for.

I was never able to express my feelings or what I was going through, always hiding behind that mask and tough exterior my entire life in order to function and survive. Always trying to outrun my shadow. Leave that tortured and crushed soul behind.

It took me nearly 45 years to realize that isn't possible.

I think of Jimmy and Rocco often. I missed out on some very special, real, and true friendships with some truly remarkable people throughout my life. All due to these disorders which viciously extracted the lifeblood from my body and controlled me into a life sentence of suffering and isolation.

My mother had a hysterectomy during my senior year of high school. I was 17. I remember the fear I had knowing she was in the hospital and would undergo an operation. My anxiety level was peaked for months leading up to this and for some time during her recovery.

I recall going to visit her with my friend, Jimmy, immediately after the operation. Jimmy took her flowers which put a big smile on her face.

I felt — I hoped — that she was out of the woods. However, the hospital setting and atmosphere — seeing her laying in that bed hooked up to hoses and other medical equipment — kept me petrified for weeks to come.

My mother also had several cysts removed from her breasts during her lifetime — during my childhood.

She has suffered consistently with debilitating migraine headaches since she was a little girl. I remember as a child and throughout my life my mother barely being able to stand due to these migraines. She would often have to go lay down in a dark, quiet room until the pain and pressure subsided or passed.

She has suffered tremendously her entire life with colitis. I remember from childhood whenever she'd be at a family function or out to dinner, she would never eat; always fearful of the imminent diarrhea. On the flip side of the colitis, she has severe bowel problems. She often gets constipated and backed-up. This has caused and still causes life-threatening problems for my mother. Her colon has torn, plus a hernia, and severe hemorrhoids that exacerbates the situation.

I understand her very heavy, consistent cigarette smoking for some 65 years. She is anxiety-ridden and has always been under extreme pressure from all angles of life. Most recently she has had some problems with her lungs and was diagnosed with the preliminary stages of chronic obstructive pulmonary disease (COPD). My grandfather and my mother's brother, Nico, both died from emphysema. My uncle Nico was attached to an oxygen tank the last years of his life. The emphysema that took the lives of my grandfather and uncle Nico is a horrendous disease. One of the main causes of this disease is long term exposure to tobacco smoke. Knowing all of this, my mother's addiction to cigarette smoking has never diminished. I understand addiction very well — I have lived it for over 40 years. We do what we do — our addiction — to quell the constant pain and despair in our lives and to maintain, as we believe, our immediate sanity at that time.

My mother had come home from the hospital and while she was sore and tired for some time, she recovered completely.

She wanted desperately to have a party for my upcoming high school graduation and 18th birthday. I was against this for the obvious reasons. However, she wanted to get family and friends together and celebrate the dual occasion.

There wasn't much in life that ever brought me joy except being able to make my mother happy and see a smile on her face. So, a party it would be. My only request was that we didn't have it anywhere but our house. I wanted to be in a comfortable environment where I had more control over my anxiety.

It turned out to be one of the last family get-togethers I would be part of as my PTSD, depression, and anxiety would continue to escalate through the coming months and years and the resulting isolation became the norm that allowed me to keep my pain and suffering hidden.

Senior year in high school, my mother contacted Biagio, my sister's ex-husband. We hadn't seen him in some eight years. My mother asked for his help in pointing me in the right direction with regards to college. She knew he was an intelligent guy who had completed many years of advance study in college — attending Brown University and Rhode Island School of Design — and would be able to help out.

She called him and explained the situation. He mentioned that he was currently teaching at Salve Regina College (became *University* in 1991). We (my mother and I) made an appointment to meet him at Salve the following week for lunch, a tour, and introduction to some of the staff.

I told him my intentions were to be a special agent with the DEA (Drug Enforcement Administration). He told me that Salve Regina had a top-notch Administration of Justice department with very knowledgeable and accomplished instructors and professors in that department. Many of which were current and retired FBI and other law enforcement agencies.

Salve is a private, catholic college with relatively smaller classes and teacher to student ratio. It's more one-on-one and personal than larger colleges and universities. You get to know the instructors, professors, and students personally unlike a larger university where you can become a number. That was probably the only part that scared me somewhat. It was a small school with smaller classes. I wouldn't be able to disappear and become that number — stay out of the spotlight. Aside from that, it all sounded like a good fit for what I was looking for.

It was also an incredible and beautiful 80-acre campus, mostly on the Atlantic Ocean, in one of Newport, Rhode Island's historic districts. What was not to like about it?!

Inside though, I was trembling with fear. My anxiety in full-swing.

Nevertheless, I did all the application paperwork over the next month or so and was accepted into the upcoming freshman class of fall 1982.

9

I would be attending Salve Regina College. Here comes the 4th culture shock of my life.

The time leading up to my freshman year in college was another of those extremely anxiety producing chapters of my life. However, when I arrived, I actually settled in relatively quicker than I thought I would.

I would be living on campus my freshman year. I was assigned to Carey Mansion, which is ranked as the fifth largest of the Newport mansions after The Breakers, Ochre Court, Belcourt Castle and Rough Point.

I had made arrangements with Biagio to meet him in Newport the day I — all freshmen — would be moving in. My mother, father, and I drove down and met him for lunch. Biagio was still wiry with an explosive personality and short fuse. Paradoxically, a cerebral guy with a penchant for confrontation. He nearly came to blows with a guy in the parking lot of the restaurant because this guy slightly dinged my car while opening his car door. He became very angry and chewed this guy a new a-hole. I told him to take a deep breath, I was already very stressed, there was no damage, and it was no big deal. He noted I had an expensive sports car and the guy should be more careful and considerate. He went on about how some people are discourteous, just don't give a shit, and need a wake-up call. I couldn't have agreed more but this wasn't the time or place.

We went into the restaurant and ate, talked a bit, and then he took us over to Carey Mansion to move me in.

From the moment we pulled up to and I looked at this mansion — where I would actually be living my freshman year of college — I had a strange feeling like never before. A feeling that made me sick to my stomach. It is a very sinister looking structure. As I walked into the mansion, I felt an immediate chill, a distressing aura of trepidation. The interior was concrete and steel and very cold. There was no warmth to be found inside or anywhere in the vicinity of this mansion. Not unlike that of a prison or asylum. It seemed even the sun refused to shine through its inhospitable, steel windows. A foreboding sign of what lay inside.

If the wicked disorders that had taken control of my life and were slowly destroying me emotionally had a face — a home--it would look very similar to Carey Mansion. The inside of this mansion was my depression personified.

There is a reason this mansion was used in the late 1960's gothic soap opera TV series, *Dark Shadows*. The series used the exterior as their Collinwood Mansion, where the vampire Barnabus Collins lived — in his coffin!

I was unaware upon my arrival of the mansion's history. The show, along with the TV version of the mansion, was host to werewolves, witches, warlocks, zombies, and everything else synonymous with horror and evil.

In a 2011 episode of the TV show, *Ghost Hunters*, The Atlantic Paranormal Society claimed to have found ample evidence that Carey Mansion itself was haunted. Believe me, it was!

Needless to say, I didn't even unpack. I had Biagio take me over to the Director of Campus Life so I could move out before I even moved in!

There were no other rooms available at this time for a freshman other than Carey Mansion. The director made a few calls and found a couple upper-classmen, *PJ* and *BC*, in Conley Hall, that had an extra bed in their room and welcomed me to live with them my first year.

This was more like it. Conley Hall had a warm feeling — a feeling of *life* inside and outside of the building.

I moved in, got to know my roommates, The dorm's RA (Resident Assistant) and everyone else living in Conley Hall. Conley had a decent kitchen, TV room, and pool room. I would spend a fair amount of time playing pool at Conley Hall my freshman year.

Freshmen were discouraged from having cars on campus. Basically, you could have a car but you weren't allowed to park the car at your dorm freshman year. Go figure! I kept my car on campus and with me freshman year. I would park it on the street at night and walk back to my dorm so I didn't violate any rules. Having my car at my disposal was an absolute necessity in order to get to the gym, which was located some miles from the school, in Middletown, Rhode Island. Nothing was going to keep me from the gym and my medication.

My girlfriend at the time, Lisa, came down to see me the first few weeks. I would also go back home on weekends. However, Lisa and I had started going our separate ways come my freshman year. Our relationship was pretty much over at this point. We saw each other on and off over this year, but we had both begun moving on in different directions.

My friend Jimmy would come down every now and again when he had some time in between his classes in Boston. We'd even do some training together in Newport (and back in Rhode Island) through freshman year.

My buddy Rocco would come down with some other guys to our campus parties and Newport clubs freshman and sophomore years. We'd hang out like the old days of high school.

I'd go down to Rocco's college — University of Rhode Island (URI) — every now and again, too, to hang out with him and a few other guys I knew who were attending URI.

Everything would change for the worse once my sophomore year was over.

I found one of the best things about college was the freedom. I wasn't required to be in school from 8:00 a.m. to 2:30 p.m. Monday through Friday. I chose my classes, instructors, and times. I wasn't required to show up for classes in college.

However, at Salve, it was a bit stricter than larger colleges and universities. Most instructors didn't allow you to miss too many classes. Still, it was a major relief from high school. If I was having bad anxiety that day, I didn't have to go to class and there were no teachers breathing down my neck looking for a doctor's note for missing their class. Even so, with what I was going through emotionally, I did just enough to get by my freshman and sophomore years. I was always distracted and slowly being consumed by the emotional disorders that tormented me every minute of every day.

My newfound popularity carried over from high school into my freshman and sophomore years of college. Even after high school's popularity, it was still a very strange feeling going from bullied and odd-man-out to popular, where people like you and want to be around you.

In college, it now, for some reason, felt like "rags to riches". Maybe like it would feel to hit the lottery. I was a street kid rubbing elbows with classmates from all over the U.S. as well as many other countries around the world.

Some of these kids came from prominent and very affluent families. Some of their parents were renowned doctors, lawyers, politicians, businesspeople, CEOs of major companies, and celebrities too. I met kids from Africa and other continents and countries who were members of royal families. It was a far cry from the streets of the

North End. I was meeting so many different types of kids from all walks of life and learning so much about other cultures. I had an opportunity to make some very special, quality friendships during my college years. It began that way, but, as always, with my mask and armor in place, the wall up and forever on guard to protect myself from anyone seeing — knowing — the real person suffering desperately beneath my protective ensemble, I never let anyone get too close. I was always hanging on for dear life from an emotional ledge, my fingertips slowly giving way to gravity, forcing me back into isolation.

Several new college friends would come up to Providence every now and again to train with me or hang out. We'd mostly hang out on campus and in the city of Newport and Middletown during the school years. We'd keep in touch over the summer. First time in my life part of me felt a bit of "normal", if that was even possible. To quote a line from Cody Jarrett (James Cagney) in the 1949 classic film *White Heat*, "*Made it, Ma! Top of the World!*" Part of me certainly felt as if I was at the top of the world. Especially with regards to my mother's hopes and wishes. The other part of me was still extremely uncomfortable in my own skin. Still experiencing persistent anxiety and panic attacks, severe depression, and constant feelings of hopelessness and worthlessness. My life progressively worsening with each passing year regardless of any movements forward or accomplishments.

Top of the world and still lost in a vortex of multiple, fully constraining disorders that were slowly destroying my life.

I knew where I was and what it took to get there. Each day an intense struggle to survive and move forward. I also knew I was not going to be able to live this dream, this taste of "normal", this "rags to riches" story. The disorders that controlled my every move would not allow any sunshine to enter my darkness, any yin to compliment my yang, any positive balance to my life's scale, any normalcy to surround me for too long.

Normal would have been living on campus the entire four years of college and completing my B.A. four years from when I walked through the doors of Salve.

Normal would have been enjoying a once in a lifetime opportunity and experience — college — while making life-long friends and great memories. The best times of my life should have been my college years. Like Cody Jarrett, top of the world, but it could only blow up in my face. Another significant loss I can never regain or relive.

I never had a clue in life how to be normal. To be like everyone else. Nothing about me was normal and I knew it.

My normal was this group of disorders controlling my every move, keeping my anxiety levels elevated at all times, always feeling pain and sadness, lost and without hope, keeping me in isolation, and pretty much walking dead. All the while behind a public facade, a mask concealing a bleeding and ravaged, tortured soul.

These disorders stole from me everything that was ever important in my life, each and every step of the way.

My college years would have been — very well should have been — a glorious, special time in my life but for the death grip of my constant inner pain and suffering.

Fighting during my college years was not as common as it was during my high school years. However, whenever you have lots of guys and testosterone in one place — whether it be a college setting or a club — with alcohol and females, there is going to be some male conflict. Not to mention, there are always bullies wherever you may go in life. As had been the case my entire childhood and throughout my life, a bully — a coward — always looks to pick on the smallest, or what he considers the weakest, target. So, as was common in my life, I had my share of fights, mostly off campus, with those who believed my being physically smaller was to their advantage. The music played every now and again and usually ended abruptly for the bully.

Trauma routinely followed me wherever I might go in life. One such instance happened within the first couple months of living on campus, at Conley Hall.

I had met and got along with everyone living within my residence hall and beyond. There were about 40 guys living in Conley Hall my freshman year. One of the kids I had befriended, *Red*, told me of his story growing up poor in a large family and how his dad worked his butt off to send him to Salve. The family didn't have a lot of money and he wanted to make something of his life, give back to his dad and family. I had a lot of respect for him regarding his attitude and intentions, and told him so. He seemed like a decent kid with morals, values, manners, and respect.

However, after about a month or so of being on campus, he began drinking and smoking an awful lot of marijuana with his roommate, who was a shady, sneaky, low-life type of kid. Growing up as I did, a kid like this roommate would have been beaten to a pulp and ostracized from the neighborhood. Just as a rat or child molester would be.

I kept the peace, but didn't like this roommate from day one. Not many, including the RA, liked the roommate.

Red's personality started to change as he drank and smoked pot more often.

One day as he was leaving the residence hall, he looked into the pool room, called out my name and yelled, *"Fuck you,"* while sticking his middle finger up at me. I was a bit shocked, a bit aggravated, and a whole lot of angry. He kept walking and left the hall.

I waited for Red to come back to the dorm that night so I could confront him about the outright disrespect. When he finally came back to the dorm, I had cooled down a bit as many hours had passed. As he was walking up the stairs to his room, I approached him at the intermediate landing area.

It wasn't an aggressive, provoking manner, but I took a firm stance and told him we needed to speak about his disrespecting me earlier in the day.

Red was a big kid, 6' and over 200 lbs. I asked him, rather politely all things considered, why he would disrespect me that way, especially since we both got along just fine. Red was under the influence of something that night and probably was earlier in the day too. Instead of apologizing, he looked down at me and said, *"Fuck you."* At the same time as he was speaking these words, he took his left middle finger and stuck it in my face. I smacked his hand out of my face with my right hand and hit him with a left hook to the side of his jaw and, as he began to fall, I grabbed him Muay Thai style behind his neck with both hands, pulled his head quickly downward and at the same time forcefully raised and slammed my left knee into his face. He dropped to the ground. His roommate then jumped down a flight of stairs onto my back. I flung him off and, as I turned around to grab him, the wussy ran like a bat out of hell back up the stairs. As I chased him up those stairs he bee-lined into his room and locked the door. He emerged a minute or so later, after the RA and everyone else in the dorm was on the scene, holding a bat at the doorway to his room. I begged the RA to let this coward come at me with the bat or let us go outside to see what this low-life had for his manhood. The RA took the bat and told him to go back into his room. He had me and Red go with him to his room to discuss what had just happened. I explained and Red, his face bleeding and beginning to swell, agreed that he instigated the fight.

Red's father came down to our dorm a few days later and spoke with the RA. He wanted to meet and talk with me. I had no problem with that. I met with him and the RA. The father was a very nice, soft-spoken, polite man. Everything Red said he was. He asked me if the feud was over. He said he didn't want his son to get hurt.

I explained to him that I never had a problem with Red, I actually like him and we got along just fine. I told him he must have been having a bad day as he (Red) initiated the fight. I wasn't about to tell him his son had become a big fan of alcohol and marijuana, most likely influenced by his conniving, punk roommate.

I gave his dad my word that I had no further problem with or anger towards Red as long as Red was willing to drop it and didn't continue to disrespect me and get in my face like that again. The dad assured me he would not and thanked me for being so polite and understanding.

I sure hope that Red was just going through a college phase and straightened out and made his father proud in the years to come. His dad was an awesome guy and deserved as much. The kind of dad any kid would be proud to call his father.

It was very difficult freshman year living on campus and suffering with these disorders. There were always people around me — in the dorm, my room, classes, cafeteria. Twenty-four hours a day I had to have my guard up. My depression and anxiety in full swing. I knew I would not be able to continue living on campus.

There was no escape from the spotlight and I needed space — privacy — to unwind and relax, take that mask off, and just breathe.

There was nowhere to hide, so I ran. I ran to where I have always felt comfortable and at ease; alone with nature and by the ocean.

I spent time along Ocean Drive in Newport sitting on rocks — the jetty — shooting out into the ocean, walking First Beach (Easton's Beach) in Newport, Rhode Island, and Second Beach (Sachuest Town Beach) and Third Beach in Middletown, Rhode Island.

However, my soul was home and I was always most comfortable at Sachuest Point National Wildlife Refuge in Middletown, Rhode

Island — connected with Second Beach (Sachuest Town Beach) shoreline. The refuge is a 242-acre peninsula between the Sakonnet River and Rhode Island Sound. The refuge is bound by the Sakonnet River to the north and east, The Atlantic Ocean to the south, and the Sachuest Bay to the west. There are approximately 2.5 miles of nature trails that is paradise found to me.

One of the first poems I ever wrote was at 15-years-old and was conceived here at Sachuest. It is titled *Friend of Nature* and speaks to the aesthetics of this heavenly place and how it soothes my soul and puts my mind at ease.

This little piece of paradise is where I studied for many of my college exams during my four years at Salve. It is also the place that inspired me to compose many songs throughout the years.

Located in the south easternmost part of the town of Middletown, Rhode Island, it is a four-mile-drive east, and located directly across the bay from Salve Regina. I would sit on the southernmost rocks extending out into the bay and just stare at the beauty in all directions. Salve Regina's Ochre Court within view, a mere couple of miles across the bay, setting just feet west of the Newport Cliff Walk.

On any given day you can gaze at rabbit, owl, duck, falcon, deer, hundreds of species of bird, and a host of beautiful, colorful butterfly and other creatures both on land and in the surrounding bay.

It has always been my number one destination when riding motorcycles in Rhode Island. Many summers I would find myself there several times a week as long as the weather permitted. Nothing throughout my life has felt as peaceful and heavenly to me as riding my motorcycle on a warm and sunny, summer's day to Sachuest, sitting amid the natural beauty of land and ocean and all of its creatures, and just take in the wonder of it all and enjoy the peace and escape it allowed my soul.

Whenever I am able to get back to Rhode Island, this is my first destination after visiting my parents. A piece of my soul eternally floats above this heaven on earth. It is a very, very special place to me.

Below is one of the first poems I ever wrote. I was 15-years-old and, while it follows no formal poetic structure, it felt good to just exhale the feelings onto paper.

It is — and has always remained — a first draft. I never attempted to re-write it. I left it as it was the day I wrote it some 35 years ago as a freshman in high school. It reveals my soul — my struggle — at that time. It was inspired by my first visit to Sachuest Point in 1979. I felt a special connection with this little piece of heaven the moment it came into view and I first stepped onto its protected ground.

This poem has always been very special to me as it was raw (emotion) and it was my "first". It was my first poem and my first attempt at revealing my pain and an *outlet* that tranquilized my discomfort:

"FRIEND of NATURE"

Standing alone
Coiled in despair
Dazed by the beauty
Lost with a stare

The serenity of the night
The cool of the breeze
The mystic starred sky
The force of the sea

Drawn to the water
Enchanted by above
Only to find
My peace of mind

Feelings of life
Flow through like a stream
Here I shall be
Where my soul is free

Sit tranquil and flow
Embark on my dreams
Escape from the zoo
And all of its' schemes

The aesthetics of nature
Always I'll crave
My hopes reappear
My spirit will rave

I remember speaking on a couple different occasions with one of my instructors, *Father M*, regarding a presentation coming up in a class that he was teaching — my fear of public speaking and oral presentations. We also had conversations about music and my values, what was important to me in life. Fr. M was, prior to becoming an instructor at Salve, a professional musician in Ireland. Rather successful too. His calling was in the priesthood and teaching, and he followed his heart and gave up a very lucrative music career to do so. I admired the man. He gave me some good advice with regards to things we had discussed. He was a very wise, caring man. He told me once, post a long, deep conversation, verbatim, "*Never compromise who you are, Steve.*" I never have. Regardless of these disorders which have ripped my life to shreds for decades, I have always maintained my beliefs and values and stayed true to who I am — that man behind the mask, the bleeding soul beneath the armor.

I decided I needed to commute to Salve my sophomore year. The school is approximately 30 miles southeast of the city of Providence. I would still be attending full time but would schedule all my classes for two or three days per week. It was much less stressful not having to be in the spotlight 24/7 while living on campus. I didn't have to keep my guard up around the clock, every day and night. I could now deal--as always, alone, in private — with my ever-worsening depression and anxiety attacks without prying eyes always occupying my immediate space.

10

I met the girl of my dreams, *Kay*, the very beginning of my sophomore year at Salve. She was an incoming freshman.

It was a beautiful, sunny and crisp fall day in 1983. I was leaving O'Hare Academic Center, which sits in the middle of Salve Regina's campus. This was the main classroom building which overlooked the Atlantic Ocean and was located nearly smack dab in the middle of the world famous Newport Cliff Walk. I walked out the front doors, up the outside stairs, and we caught and locked eyes as she was walking down the stairs towards O'Hare. She was the most beautiful girl I'd ever laid eyes on! We both turned around a second time to look again. She smiled. I was awestricken.

To this day, I have never seen a woman that could recreate that moment and take my breath away.

I knew a lot of kids in the school by my sophomore year. There was also a click of girls attending Salve and living on campus that were from my high school.

We all knew each other well and hung out a bit. My mask — the persona that I portrayed to survive — exuded confidence. However, the real me was extremely shy and had no confidence at all.

Instead of waiting around to see Kay again and try and talk to her as any guy who has any confidence would have done, I chose to ask around — some of the girls I knew — about this goddess I had seen.

I found out her name, that she was from Rhode Island, and we knew some of the same people (on and off campus). I asked one of the girls that we both knew to introduce me to her. I finally met her a couple days later. I have never felt that way before, or since, meeting Kay. It was the proverbial "love at first sight".

Her eyes would sparkle as we talked and got to know each other. I recall smiling and feelings of joy and happiness. Those feeling were foreign to me, but a most welcome change. We started dating immediately.

She was living on campus and I was commuting that year. I would spend time with her after classes and would drive down some days or nights when I had no classes. We'd go to campus parties together and some clubs. We just enjoyed being together. She was like most in college; she liked to drink. Her drink of choice was a mudslide. I never drank but most every one of my friends in high school and college drank socially. It was — and has always been — common and widespread in college.

I cared deeply for her and would make sure she didn't drink too much when we were together. I'd always buy her a two-drink maximum when we were out. She'd sneak in another every now and again. With all the problems and trauma I'd faced in my life due to alcohol and addiction — and the disorders which were controlling and destroying my life as a result — It tore me apart every time she drank. She knew my feelings about alcohol and especially drugs. She didn't know the reason behind it — the pain and suffering beneath the mask. That pain and suffering seemed to subside a little bit every time she would tell me that she loved me and always wanted me to love her. I know she loved me. I loved her too. More than she ever knew.

She came back home from Newport most weekends. She lived in a town a short distance from my neighborhood. We'd spend time out and about when she was home. She only attended Salve for one semester. She just wasn't into the studying. She moved back home right after that first semester.

We'd continue to hang out through my second semester. During this time and through the summer of 1984 we were together.

I remember her constantly asking me to meet my mother. She knew how close I was to my mother and wanted to make that acquaintance — which impressed me greatly. I dated my share before and after Kay. I only felt a connection with and comfortable enough to introduce my first girlfriend, Lisa, to my mother, and Kay.

One day she stopped by my house unexpectedly. She came in and we sat at the kitchen table. She came by specifically to meet my mother.

My mother came home and I made the introduction. Kay said to my mother, "*Very nice to finally meet you*", as she emphasized the word *finally*, looked over at me and raised her eyebrows. I had been hesitating making the introduction as my depression and anxiety were spiraling me into a living hell and I was very confused about how to proceed with our relationship. I was living a lie by not taking off my mask and letting Kay in to see my soul — who I really was.

I remember my mother's first words when Kay left; "*She is absolutely beautiful. What a gorgeous girl.*" She certainly was. Inside and out.

Kay and I, along with a couple of my buddies, *Chichi* and *AC*, and their dates, would hang around Newport, Narragansett, Galilee, and Scarborough Beach(s) most of the summer. A few clubs here and there. Being with her and being by the ocean, especially at night — under cover of the darkness which helped to blur my suffering — were two things that soothed my soul. I never wanted it to end. However, as with everything that could have been good in my life, this, too, had to end due to the disorders which controlled my emotions to the point I could never let anyone in to see the truth of my life — that tormented soul that was slowly bleeding out. It would be less painful I believed to lose the person I cared for and loved than for me to let down that wall, take off my mask, lay down my shield, and expose that truth of my life.

Kay was highly influenced in life by her two older sisters. I would hear through the grapevine that they wanted Kay to date and marry an older, established guy who had money to burn. She was beautiful and could have had any guy she wanted, that's for sure. I never brought up to her what I had heard nor offered any resistance because I knew at this time I couldn't be completely honest with her and I could not enter into a serious relationship if I couldn't be totally truthful. This killed me inside because I knew in my heart that Kay was the one for me. The woman I wanted to be with the rest of my life.

I called her angel eyes. Eyes being the mirror to the soul, I saw her purity that first time our eyes met. My eyes, on the other hand, were always concealed behind my mask. I couldn't allow anyone — even the girl of my dreams — to peer through that window to my bleeding, tormented soul.

There was no anger when we did go our separate ways. Sadness, yes. We never argued. We got along great. We enjoyed being with each other. It was just the wrong time in my life. Looking back, it was then and would always be the wrong time in my life due to the disorders that imprisoned me. They destroyed a relationship with a woman that could very well have been my soul mate for life. My living, breathing savior. The wind in my stagnant sails.

It devastated me knowing that I could not open up and be *me* with someone who was so special in my life. Kay could have been the happiness that has eluded me my entire life but for the strangle-hold these disorders had on that very life.

We'd keep in touch for a year or so post our parting ways. I sent her a birthday card and every now and again a "just thinking of you" card. She'd call now and then to say hi or just talk.

I heard she married a few years down the road. I don't need to know him to say he's the luckiest guy in the world.

We had a special connection, chemistry and attraction to each other. She was the only girl I ever dated that I felt I could have married. We had discussed marriage a couple of times and I told her I just wasn't ready in my life or she would be the one. Kay was also the only girl I ever dated that made me wish I had been *normal* and where I needed to be in life emotionally — to be able to share my soul and the secrets of my life — and career-wise, in order to take care of her. My life was always dangling and being controlled by the strings of these disorders.

Honesty, loyalty, respect, and honor have been of utmost importance to me in every aspect of my life, throughout my life, and to this day. This is the core of who I am, what I am made of, what I am about. One of the most important facets to me in any relationship is honesty. With hindsight, and knowing more about my disorders and my life as it played out, this was the problem: I was badly and repeatedly traumatized since the age of five, suffering terribly emotionally, and hiding behind this public persona to protect myself throughout my entire life. As a consequence, I couldn't be honest with Kay about the real man behind that facade. If I couldn't let her in and be honest, I had to let her go. It was the only respectable, fair thing to do. It took a toll on me then and it still hurts to this day, some thirty years later.

I can say with relative certainty that letting Kay get away from me was one of the biggest mistakes and regrets of my life. If I had not been at the mercy of these disorders, I never would have let her go. Ever. I've never stopped thinking about her or what could have been.

I was not able to let down that wall and let her in to see my pain. My reality. The grief oozing from my soul and contaminating my mind.

After all, she was with and loved the persona I took on — she knew all of the mask, not all of the man behind it. She saw a confidence and air of cockiness, a tough exterior, not the person on the inside. He was the polar opposite of what his mask outwardly portrayed.

The man on the inside was too kind and caring for his own good, very emotional, traumatized badly, suffering deeply, and in hellacious emotional pain.

Where I come from, kindness and being emotional is often taken as weakness. On the streets, you have to be a *hard ass*. You can't be "*soft*" or you will be chewed up and spit out. If I took off my mask and dropped my shield — unveiled my true self to her — would she still be *interested* in the *real* me? *Attracted to* the real me? *Love* the real me? *Be there for* the real me? Would she leave me broken hearted after revealing myself?

I couldn't submerge completely if I wasn't being honest. I didn't realize this at the time, but it tore me apart. A disappointment and pain I feel every time my mind wanders and then settles on her captivating brown eyes and beautiful, smiling face. A regret I live with. A remorse I will die with.

These disorders destroyed any and all relationships and happiness that *could have been* in my life.

I didn't know — I never knew — how to deal with the pain and suffering I was feeling. It has been repressed — buried — for decades. My training temporarily quelled the pain and kept my keel even from day to day so I was able, though barely, to put one foot in front of the other. My mask kept all prying eyes at a distance and unaware of what I was going through emotionally. Kay didn't have a clue, either.

There have been relationships before and after K. Not one did I feel as I did when with her. It was special to me. To her, too, I know. I have never stopped thinking about her over the many years and all that I most likely lost due to this curse I've lived with my entire life.

I know she had no idea how much I truly loved and cherished her. The girl of my dreams was not possible either due solely to these disorders which controlled my every move throughout my life.

It has taken me many decades and the past few years of a painful yet eye-opening and cathartic psychotherapy to begin peeling off that mask and body armor. I was unable to take it off and reveal my true self even for the one girl that I could have married and perhaps could have saved my soul from the cruelest and darkest depths of the hell it was banished to.

I spend as much time as possible by the ocean these days. It still comforts my soul today as it did during my childhood and throughout my earlier years. There has been a void in my heart as I've walked the shoreline the past thirty years. I think of Kay often and *still* miss her.

Letting her go was one of the toughest decisions I've ever had to make. This was another devastating blow and loss in my life.

Another *normal* piece of the puzzle that wasn't meant to fit or be.

Another one-sided battle with these disorders where my chances were zero and none.

I had been contemplating taking time off from college at the conclusion of my sophomore year. That time rolled around soon enough and I was now suffering with even more devastating anxiety than was the case in high school and through my first two years of college.

Moving on and away from Kay at the end of the summer following my sophomore year catapulted me into my deepest and darkest depression to that point in my life.

My life — that tiniest bit of well-being that remained — was now crumbling at an extreme pace. It felt like a disease was ravishing my mind — and in a sense it was — and I was getting closer and closer to the end.

Once again, my training was the medicine, the primary outlet that kept my keel even and allowed me that connection to sanity. My training was what provided me the ability to blend in and function as normal as possible, day to day, in most capacities.

It was around this time that an all-out war between the disorders which controlled me into emotional imprisonment from the age of five and my escape route — my training — was taking place. As with any addiction, my daily, multiple doses of training were losing a bit of its' endorphin effect.

I needed another outlet — another escape — to occupy my mind and keep the full effects of these disorders from totally consuming me.

Depression was now beginning to take a much more forceful grip on me and propelling me into a life of solitary confinement. A life of indescribable desolation that would grow more barren and painful each year for the next two and a half decades.

I was being molded a recluse. Isolating more and more at the hands of disorders that would stop at nothing to completely destroy me.

I could no longer focus or concentrate on much of anything. I figured this was a good time to pursue my songwriting interests since I was trapped — both emotionally and physically — behind prison walls and needed to find an escape as fast as possible.

11

I began writing up to sixteen hours a day at times, trying desperately to clear the pain and sorrow from my mind and soul and splatter it all on paper, one song, one story at a time.

The cathartic nature of deep, trance-like writing was both painful and rewarding at the same time. It became an outlet to bear my soul. A sidekick addiction with my training.

I always had a burning desire to be a professional songwriter. It had been a dream of mine as far back as I can remember. I had no faith in my ability nor was I optimistic that any good would come from it. However, I also knew that it was now or never to make that move and try as best I could to make that dream a reality. If I had a shot at all, it would be at this time in my life. A time when I needed to convey my pain, suffering, and despair more than ever before. I had no one to talk to. My songs became my support and validation.

This is a song I wrote towards the end of 1984 — as I came to that fork in the road — about following your heart and never giving up on your dreams. If I'd only been able to heed my own advice at the time and keep that promise I made to myself, I may have found that pot of gold; my peace of mind and happiness:

"Dreams in The Wind"

V1	*Night-time falls and[1] voices from within[2]*
	Widen my eyes and[3] thicken my skin[4]
	Remindin' me of a dream I'd taken hold[6]
	Made a promise to myself ... never to let go[8]
CL 1	*(And) each day I fight[1] to keep the dream alive[2]*
	The road is long and hard[3] (and) it's a million miles wide[4]
CL 2	*Nobody knows the pain[5], been the places I've been[6]*
	Time and time again[7] chasin' dreams in the wind[8]
Chorus:	*When dreams in the wind[1] blow away like dust[2]*
	(Then) the blood in your veins[3] (it) can only turn to rust[4]

Got a dream in your soul[5] (and) you hold on tight[6]
Full speed ahead[7] mornin', noon, and night[8]

V2

Daylight breaks (and) the day has arrived
made it through the night, again, I survived
One more scene, played the cards I was dealt
(And) now twenty-four more hours ... under my belt

CL 3

Tested the water, saw the hungry sharks
I live and I learn from the school of hard knocks

CL 4

Nobody knows the pain, been the places I've been
(Yeah) when all faith is lost chasin' dreams in the wind

...Chorus 2...

...Add 8-16 bars music before lower bridge...

Bridge:

The wind is seldom upon your back
Dreams too often fall through the cracks
Your love, your passion, your peace of mind
Never let go of what you feel inside ... (solo)

...CL 2...

...Chorus 3... (add new last line):
Full speed ahead[7]...never losin' sight[8]...(x2)

© Steve DiGrossi

The next five years can be summed up with five words; songwriting, training, anxiety, suffering, isolating.

My hiatus from college began in September of 1984. I threw myself into writing, consistently, day in and day out, building my song portfolio while hopelessly trying to escape the emotional pain. This, along with my training, got me through the days and nights.

Each and every line of lyric created and arranged was a very painful, but emotionally purging process. For some songwriters, the process might be less stressful, less painful, and the story — the song — comes rather easy. I've dreamed, literally, of certain lines while others came to me in strange ways and places. However, I don't recall any of the couple hundred song drafts I would compose over time coming easy. Perhaps my PTSD weighing heavy on the songwriting process and creating more stress and thicker walls to break through. Some songs might get a solid first draft in a couple days to a week. Others could take months. Still others have never been finished. Sitting on the back burner much the same as my life has been.

This is a song I wrote during the beginning of this five-year hiatus that speaks to my growing despair and constant confusion about my life and the world around me:

"Don't Know Where I'm Goin' But I'm Almost There"

A

Don't know what I'm doin'[1]..in this place ..I[2]
Can't make heads or tails of[3] ..this rat race[4]
With two steps backwards[5]..year after year ..I[6]
Don't know where I'm goin'[7] ..but I'm almost there[8]

A

I can't tell 'ya what it's[1] ..all about[2]
My world is upside-down[3] and it's.. inside-out[4]
This search for meaning[5] ..it ain't really clear and ..I[6]
Don't know where I'm goin'[7] but I'm almost there[8]

B

I don't know where I'm goin'[1] but I'm almost there[2]
Day after day[3] on a wing and a prayer[4]
The clock keeps tickin'[5]..(the) dreams disappear and ..I[6]
Don't know where I'm goin'[7] but I'm almost there[8]

B extension

...16 bars music...

A

I can't tell 'ya what[1] tomorrow.. will bring[2]
I'm feeling' out of touch[3].. with everything[4]

Life hangs in the balance[5].. peace up in the air and ..I[6]
Don't know where I'm goin'[7] but I'm almost there[8]

B   *I don't know where I'm goin' but I'm almost there*
Day after day on a wing and a prayer
The clock keeps tickin'.. (the) dust never clears and ..I
Don't know where I'm goin' but I'm almost there

A   *Don't know what I'm doin'.. in this place ..I*
Can't make heads or tales of.. this rat race
Look to the future.. it ain't really clear and ..I
Don't know where I'm goin' but I'm almost there..

© Steve DiGrossi

Lost, confused, without the least bit of hope, and suffering in isolation, only *my* life could keep on getting worse, never missing a torturous beat.

After six years of living in California and continuing his addiction, problems, and heartbreak for my mother from afar, my brother finally hit rock bottom and asked his mother to get him into treatment. She did. She got him into and paid for one of the most renowned rehabilitation facilities in the country at the time.

During the summer of 1984, after several months of in-patient treatment, he moved back in with my parents and myself for the next year and a half to just shy of two years. I was twenty-years-old at this time, just finished my second year of college, and desperately struggling with depression and anxiety.

This arrangement — my brother's living under the same roof with me once again — sunk me deeper into that depression. Many of the bottled up early life incidents, feelings, and anger began boiling to the surface. The nightmare that played over and over in my mind from childhood was closer now to suffocating me than ever before.

There was no pause or stop button to rid my mind and soul of reliving trauma.

More scar tissue from years of that trauma was being ripped open and flooding my mind with additional and relentless, self-destructive pain, suffering, and anger. The timing couldn't have been worse for me emotionally.

It was, once again, a situation I didn't quite understand, had no control over, and further damaged an already crippled soul.

I had mixed feelings at this time about a lot of things, including his living with us again. I never approved of my brother's actions and attitude, regardless of any addictions. He was very unappreciative and always had an attitude of entitlement, prior and post his recovery, and to this day. I respected him as he was still my older brother, but I would tell him — and anyone else — when I thought he was wrong or being disrespectful. And that was much too often.

In retrospect, I can see that his returning to Rhode Island during this most difficult to date time and phase in my life added tremendously to my anxiety and depression.

My brother began working in carpentry while in Rhode Island post his recovery. My father secured jobs for him renovating and remodeling homes and businesses in Rhode Island to get him going. I actually worked with him the first year he was in Rhode Island. Severely depressed and unable to keep my mind on my studies, I had already decided to take a hiatus from college during this time and throw myself into my passion; songwriting. The renovation work was just one job that helped pay the bills while I focused the remainder of my time on creating songs and the training that was my only escape from the hell that was my every breath.

Aside from falling into a deeper and much darker place during this time in my life, I was also isolating more than ever before — staying far away from everyone and everything.

My parents eventually allowed my brother to stay in their Florida condo so he could begin a *new* life. A fresh start away from where all the chaos began. They had an understanding between them that he would be a guest in the condo and an agreement that he would care for the property when they weren't there and pay a portion of the maintenance costs. This would allow him to get back on his feet while taking on some responsibility, paying a few bills, and earning his credit (rating) back.

He continued in carpentry when he arrived in Florida and, to the best of my knowledge, has been a self-employed carpenter, and sober, since.

I've heard that he became a "born again Christian". However, part of that equation is, at the very least, the fifth commandment to "Honor thy father and thy mother". As I see it, you must practice what you preach or hypocrisy is what you teach.

Apart from a selfish and cold nature, I believe the years of addiction had taken some toll on my brother's mind, leaving a few screws loose up there. I say this based on my own observations and experiences with him over the many years — from childhood throughout adulthood. He has outright disrespected and dishonored his mother and father time and again since I was a child and to this very day. He has maintained an attitude of entitlement, never once thanking his mother for her standing by and helping him, always, in every way. For saving his life and sacrificing her own in the process.

His attempt to kill me (in the years to come) — his blood, his own brother — is a pretty good indication of a twisted mind.

I would come to learn an exceptionally sad truth in the years ahead; sanctimony and treachery were alive and kicking, shamelessly running through the veins of most within my immediate family.

With all that I would endure through decades of battling PTSD, depression, anxiety, and isolation, this — these people, this *immediate family*, this portion of the curse — would become one of the most painful realities I've had to accept in my life.

I knew a lot of my brother's friends when I was a child. Some were cool and others complete nut-jobs. A few that have always stood out to me; neighborhood guys, *Ace Z*, a friend of my brothers, and his brother, *Marco Z*, who was a professional boxer and protégé of Richard "Dickie" Callei, a Rhode Island mobster who was shot five times and killed back in 1975. Word on the street was, while Callei was given control of some rackets, he was skimming and stealing from New England Mob boss, Raymond Patriarca Sr., who was serving time in prison. For this he was killed. Word also had it that Marco wound up with an awful lot of cash and properties that Callei entrusted to him prior to his killing.

I spent some time with Marco during the mid-2000's when I lived in Las Vegas. He had been living there for the past couple decades and was big into real estate. When my parents came to visit me in Vegas, I'd take Marco and my father out to dinner. Marco was a generation younger than my father, and I a generation or so younger than Marco. However, it was good for the soul reliving some of the good old days (and the stories). Days when the neighborhood was a family. Good people and the best of times. I always wished I was born twenty-five years or more earlier than I was.

I remember Marco's brother Ace would always give me tons of cool fireworks near the fourth of July. Not much is better than fireworks and the fourth of July when you're a kid! Full-blown PTSD or not, the fourth was a magical time during my childhood. A time when my spirit would escape from my imprisoned mind and delight in all the beautiful colors exploding in the unbounded, excited sky above.

Then there was *Slick*. He was a character! He used to drive this cool, black, early 1960's Cadillac back in the day. I recall sitting on the stoop in front of my father's North End store and just waiting for him and other riveting characters to drive or stop by the store to say hi. Slick looked a lot like the very Popular mid-1960's singer/songwriter Johnny Rivers. He was a cool cat!

My brother had a good friend, *Tommy F ("T")*, that he grew up with during his childhood and up through his adulthood while in Rhode Island. Tommy was a cool guy too. A rare breed. He was a respectful and kind person. He wasn't a troublemaker. He wasn't an addict. He wasn't a "tough guy" or trying to be one, but an easy-going, genuinely nice person. He reminded me a lot — physical appearance and personality — of my friend, Jimmy G.

Tommy had been living in Florida and was in Rhode Island at this time. He heard my brother was back in town and wanted to come over and see him, my parents and myself. He hadn't seen my brother in some ten years.

Tommy came over one afternoon. First thing he did was give my mother a big hug and kiss and told her how much he'd missed her. My mother returning an even bigger kiss and pinching his cheeks. It was close to Christmas time. Always thoughtful and with a big heart, T took over a nicely wrapped Christmas gift for my mother.

He said hello to my father and shook his hand. He looked over at me and said, "*Damn, you got big. Look at those muscles! I remember when you were this small*', holding his hand waist-high showing my height back in the day. We shook hands. Everyone talked and caught up a bit.

It was great to see him. I always liked T. He was a good person. A bit naive, but a good soul. He was always happy. Always smiling.

T talked with my brother for some time then went to speak with my father. As T was leaving, he told my brother he'd call him soon and see him in Florida when he got down there. My brother was planning on moving down to south Florida over the next year or so and staying in our parents' condo until he was able to get his feet back on the ground.

My family and I found out about a month or so later that T had been killed. He'd been chopped to pieces and thrown into a dumpster.

We learned of this through a connection my family had in the AG's office. The report on T's murder suggested that he had transported drugs from Florida to Rhode Island. He was then robbed of the drugs, killed, chopped into pieces, and thrown like a piece of trash into a dumpster.

When I heard this, my heart sank and my eyes welled up with tears that didn't stop flowing for days. I've been mad in my life, but I was beside myself with a fierce anger this time.

If there is one thing that has sickened me throughout my life, it's drugs, those that deal in drugs, and the evil that comes of it.

From a very early age, my goal in life was to be a DEA agent. I had always planned on dedicating my life to doing my part in stopping this cancer and the savages that control this trade. My hand was on the doorknob to DEA when my line of duty accident ended my dream, goal, and life as I knew it.

I knew that T should have known better. But he didn't deserve what happened to him. No human being does.

I found myself once again looking to the infinite sky, having to believe that if there is a God up there, T's end came quickly and without being tortured. That the killer(s) barbaric method of disposing of a human being was carried out after his soul had left his body and was safe and at peace with his Maker.

During this hiatus time and throughout most of my teenage years and adult life, I would always buy, sell, and invest in everything from antiques and vintage collectibles to silver and gold commodities. I would answer and place newspaper and magazine ads throughout New

England as well as other areas throughout the country. I would purchase jewelry, time pieces, precious metals, collectibles, and anything in distress. I reveled in the diversity of items and the hunt for them. It offered my life a small bit of excitement as well as paid some of the bills.

I hadn't read a comic book since I was ten-years-old, but I always loved searching for and collecting vintage comics and magazines above all else, and do to this day.

I also had a strong interest and fascination with real estate from an early age. Shortly after my hiatus from college began, I would also, with a bit of urging from my mother, go to real estate school for the required 45 hours of real estate courses, pass the real estate exam, and become a licensed real estate agent in the state of Rhode Island.

I began working part time as an independent real estate contractor with a local real estate company. I learned about the business of real estate from the ground up while making my own schedule and hours and a buck in the process.

I worked in a new office that was being managed by two guys; *Cream Puff,* the son of the owner, and his sidekick, *Schlemiel.* Two of the very few guys I've ever met who lacked every bit of common sense and then some. I'd have referred to them here as Curly and Moe but that would have been an undeserved compliment to them and an insult to the Stooges.

Cream Puff was a few years older than me and the type of guy that never worked a day in his life but had everything handed to him on a silver platter.

Schlemiel was at least ten years older than me.

Neither had an ounce of class. Each was very disrespectful, inconsiderate, and had "better than thou" attitudes towards everyone. I didn't know if I was in a real estate office or a used car lot half the time!

One of my closings through this office I remember quite vividly;

I trained intensely for a couple hours prior to the closing. This was necessary any time I would have to be "in the spotlight" so to speak — parties, meetings, interviews, crowds. Intense training was the medicine that quelled my depression and anxiety for a brief while, mostly by way of an endorphin kick which would get my serotonin and norepinephrine levels back up, resetting that chemical imbalance in my brain responsible for depression and many of my anxiety attacks.

All parties to the closing — eight people including myself — were sitting at the conference table. There had been a couple interruptions in the proceeding. It was now moving forward but this closing had been going on way too long. I began to have an anxiety attack as I sat there in the middle of the proceeding.

I tried desperately to wipe the pouring sweat from my face and head without anyone noticing my meltdown.

All the while I am focusing my mind on my body freezing on a block of ice in the middle of an Alaskan winter! Anything — any thought — that might bring my body temperature and heart rate down and stop this attack.

Then I hear, very loudly, verbatim, "*He's sweating like a Pig!*"

I look up, and Cream Puff, this classless, tactless buffoon, is pointing directly at me from across the table.

I did and said what I had learned to do over the years when "caught" in this situation — in the midst of an anxiety attack; I quickly rattled off, "*I just finished with an intense two-hour workout plus a five mile run prior to coming here. My blood pressure is through the roof. I'm dehydrated.*"

I didn't want to excuse myself in the middle of this closing, that's why I stuck it out and stayed put. I might have gotten through it unscathed if not for the unprofessional, childish outburst of this dimwit.

However, at this point, I was not only in the middle of an anxiety attack with all eyes on me, I was enraged and wanted desperately to reach across the table and pull Cream Puff's eyeballs out of his head! I excused myself before I exploded, went to the bathroom and attempted to dry off and cool down. This was nearly impossible thanks to this moron spiking my anxiety to several times greater than what would have been if not for his pointing out my profuse sweating to everyone in the room.

I stuck it out at that particular office a bit longer but would eventually leave.

Cream Puff and Schlemiel were two simpleminded peas in a pod. Neither belonged in a management position. Each of them had no clue how to effectively communicate. Neither could lead two nuns in a minute of silent prayer! Both, however, needed a good old-fashioned ass-kicking to knock some common sense and respect into them. Before it came to that, I decided it was in my best interest to avoid being around and dealing with either of them.

Cream Puff's ignorant outburst that day confirmed my long-held belief that The Wizard of Oz's Scarecrow was alive and well, a licensed Rhode Island real estate agent, and still in search of a brain! And Schlemiel — speaking of The Wizard of Oz, one of my all-time favorite classic movies — he would be right at home and in character as one of the wicked witch's flying monkeys!

Aside from any work to make some money, I spent the first couple years of my hiatus writing intensely and building my song portfolio. About two years in, I began placing ads in music oriented papers and magazines. I was trying to find a (compatible) musical composer. As a lyricist, I needed an *Elton John* so to speak. I was looking for a songwriting partner to complete my work by breathing musical life into the lyrical content. This was needed in order to secure vocalists to demo the songs and take it to the next level.

It is very difficult (for someone else) to feel and understand the song — the lyrical creation — without the components of musical composition and vocals to complete the birth of that *song*.

I already had the arrangement of the lyrics, music, and vocals done. It was all alive and playing perfectly in my head. I knew finding the vocalists wouldn't be too tough. There are plenty of great singers out there to hire for demo work.

But, first, I needed what would prove to be impossible to find; the right collaboration with a musical composer.

As I placed ads, I would routinely get unsolicited calls or run upon ads offering to write the music to my songs for a fee. This sales pitch has been around forever. Bottom line, if you have talent and someone is in a position who knows it, sees it, and can benefit from it, they are going to pay you, not you pay them.

I helped out some local musicians here and there throughout the duration of my five-year hiatus and this time frame of placing ads. I would assist them in creating some original lyrical compositions/songs. One instance working with a local garage band stands out above all others; I was contacted by the guitarist/lead vocalist who read one of my ads. He had nothing to offer me as I was looking for a songwriting partner/musical composer. However, he asked if I could help create some original songs for his band. He was a nice kid, around my age. Awesome guitarist, though he didn't read or write music. He played by ear. He didn't understand the (lyrical) structure of songs, either. However, he left that to me and I was able to take some of his ideas and a few of his lines and build a couple of solid, structured songs he could call his own. He loved the songs I created for him and couldn't thank me enough. However, his band's drummer wasn't too happy (or musically inclined for that matter). After reading one of the songs I wrote for the band, he rattled off, rather angrily, "*what's with all the rhyme? I don't like this at all. There's too much rhyme.*"

And with that bone-headedness I realized that in addition to bona fide and talented musicians, there will always be some out there *playing* in garage bands that really don't understand (or want to understand) the basics of a song or what is required to create it and then structure it to be commercially appealing. It takes a little more than looking cool behind a drum set to find some success with a song, a band, and within the music industry.

One of my ads placed in a local Providence musician's magazine was actually answered by *Jimmie Zane*. Jimmie was a well-known songwriter from Providence, Rhode Island. He was born Loreto Franchi on Federal Hill in Providence in 1910.

Jimmie was a struggling songwriter who finally caught a break when he learned that Eddie Fisher was recording a new album in New York city in 1952. Jimmie took it upon himself to head up to the recording studio where Eddie Fisher was recording and introduce himself and a song, "If I Ever Needed You, I Need You Now."

Eddie Fisher loved the song. He recorded it and it went to number one on the charts. Jimmie had made it! This was his first commercial success. The rest is music history.

Jimmie went on to become a very successful songwriter, writing and co-writing hundreds of songs along the path of his career for the likes of Elvis Presley, Nat King Cole, Al Martino, Doris Day, Eydie Gorme, Bobby Vinton, and many others. He also wrote the soundtrack for the Elvis Presley movie *Kissing Cousins*.

Jimmie called me in response to one of my ads. I couldn't believe who was on the other end of the line! We spoke a bit and he asked me to meet him at his Jewelry business in Providence. He had a reputation of being a very generous and kind man. He would employ people at his business even if he didn't need the help — just to help them out to make a buck.

Jimmie was in his mid-seventies when we first met.

I took a diverse bunch of songs consisting of some country, R&B, and my forte, rock/hard rock, from my growing portfolio for him to look over and critique.

I liked him as soon as I met him. Very down to earth, very helpful, and we both loved the craft of songwriting. If we weren't separated by several generations of musical styles and current trends within the music industry, we might have started writing some hits that very day!

However, in the songwriting world, such a match is rarer than hen's teeth. Like trying to find that proverbial needle in a haystack. There are very few songwriting teams that have that special creative power and magic. Just to name a few of the greatest songwriting teams and gods of song creation; Paul McCartney and John Lennon, Rodgers and Hammerstein, Elton John and Bernie Taupin, Jimmy Jam and Terry Lewis.

Jimmie Zane and his regular writing partner, *Al Jones*, made an historical mark on the music industry as well. Kudos, Jimmie!

As we discussed many things related to music over the hours we spent together that (first) day, I couldn't help but notice the numerous royalty checks strewn about his desk that had just come in the mail. Jimmie showed me a few of them and noted that the amount of money he received annually from the royalties on his numerous hit songs over the years was enough to retire several times over and take care of generations to come. He was very proud of one that he held up; it was a royalty check for a song he wrote for Elvis, my musical Idol!

Jimmie then began to look over my songs (lyric sheets). A couple comments he reiterated that stuck with me: First comment; he thought some of the songs might be a bit too long. Going into four to five minute songs. He mentioned I should shorten the length to no more than three minutes.

I understood where he was coming from, but, we were writing from two different musical styles, generations, and trends. In his day, most of the songs were short and sweet. Fast forward several decades to my writing style. We are now being heavily influenced by 1980's hair bands such as Bon Jovi, Cinderella, Def Leppard, Guns n Roses, Van Halen, Dokken, Scorpions, Poison, Warrant, Skid Row, and many others. Skid Row's front man, Sebastian Bach, as well as Warrant's lead vocalist, Jani Lane, is the typical hard rock vocal and style that was present and common throughout a number of my songs. Many of my songs were written and arranged for this very type of vocal and sound.

In addition to being an incredible vocalist, Jani Lane was also a fantastic lyricist and songwriter. He died in 2011 of Acute

Alcohol Poisoning.

Once again, an addiction to try and drown pain and suffering had taken another musical talent. Another human life snuffed out by what more often than not lies at the core of the addiction — emotional and/or physical pain, suffering, or shame — which is depression in a nutshell.

Addiction — any addiction — is almost always an attempt to control feelings by ignoring or repressing them, escaping from the painful reality.

It has been my experience, through decades of battling pain and depression, that until we understand, feel, accept, and deal with these emotions, those of us suffering with depression can never truly be "healthy."

🦋 🦋 🦋 🦋

Though I was a fan of and influenced by many great vocalists, songwriters, and musicians from all genres of music throughout the 20th century and into the 21st, the 80's hair bands' rock was my style of song and writing. It was a country mile and then some from the days of Eddie Fisher. The styles, structures, and content were worlds apart. While my emotion and strength has always been in this area of hard(er) rock, I did write R&B and country when I was fortunate enough to have "the feeling" or some lines or theme come to me.

The second comment that really stuck with me; Jimmie would also say time and again as he perused my lyric sheets that I had an incredible and beautiful way of composing and arranging my lyrics and telling the story. He said I was a fantastic lyricist. Jimmie Zane telling me that he was impressed with my songwriting! Doesn't get much better than that!! I was floating on a cloud — I was in seventh heaven. I was honored.

Then, I saw Jimmie's eyes light up. I wasn't sure what song he was looking at until he raised the lyric sheet up and said,

"I really like this one. This is very unique. Can a have a copy for myself?"

It was a country song I wrote titled, *"A Dozen Roses Too Late".*

I was flattered as it was a copyrighted first draft — it still isn't complete to this day! He was in awe of the title of the song and where the content was going. He had his secretary make a photocopy.

This lead us into a discussion about country music. He told me that he still had some connections in the music industry but they were limited to country music and in the Nashville area. He said he would be more than happy to make some introductions for me if I was interested. I wasn't very knowledgeable about the music industry and, as I told him, my songwriting strength was definitely not within the country realm, though I wished then as I do today that it was! I love country music — as well as R&B/Motown which has soothed my soul for the many decades of pain and misery I've had to endure — but didn't know if I would be/could be very prolific in that genre as my soul and strength was in the rock/hard rock style.

🦋 🦋 🦋 🦋

My mother is eighty-seven-years-old as of this writing. She loves country music and her favorite is Rascal Flatts!

🦋 🦋 🦋 🦋

He told me to think about it and just let him know when I was ready and the calls would be made on my behalf. It was truly an honor but, as with everything and everyone else in my life, I would not follow up. I would never ask him to make those calls. Crazy, I know! This is Jimmie Zane offering to make introductions for me because he believed in my songwriting. I was so deep in darkness and isolation I had no clue what an opportunity I had in front of me. My mind always clouded by PTSD, depression, and anxiety, I could neither see that opportunity nor grasp it if I had.

Truth be told, those disorders have kept my life from progressing in every way possible for as long as I can remember.

The invisible chains of these conditions kept me permanently shackled within a cold and dingy dungeon hell I'd been crawling in since I was a child. Unable to break free of those restraints that held me down and held be back my entire life.

I've never believed in myself, regardless of what others may have said or may have seen in me. I was always uncomfortable in my own skin and feared others seeing — knowing — the pain and suffering, the tormented soul behind my mask.

Whenever I attempted to come out of the darkness for a glimpse of the sunshine — a peak at the real world — those invisible chains that forever bound me would immediately reel me back into the murk and isolation. Isolation became my life. I was safe in my cocoon.

I learned that Jimmie had passed in 1998. I am grateful that I had the opportunity to spend some time with him back in the mid-80's. He was an old school, class act. If not for the disorders which had controlled my life during that time — and ever since — I am sure I would have taken Jimmie up on the help and introductions he offered.

A couple generations removed, but we had a lot in common. Most importantly, we were both passionate songwriters and we both knew and felt that when in each other's presence.

Part of this curse I've lived since childhood has been its unyielding grip on and its complete control of my life. Emotionally imprisoning me. Keeping me from anyone and anything that has been important to me and in my life. Always constrained by those imperceptible disorders that restrict my ability to communicate and function normally with those around me. Those disorders constantly echoing doubt and negativity in my mind; convincing me not to even bother, don't call the person back, don't follow up, don't show up. No one is interested in me or what I have to say or may be able to do. Without fail, controlling me back into isolation.

It has always been less stressful and less anxiety producing to just keep believing that I wasn't worth much and had no chance of success at all — in anything — from relationships to a career choice. I had no chance at happiness. Even when I made attempts to move forward, I was already defeated in my mind and would pull away, retreating back into isolation where I was safe. I've done this my entire life. It is part of the cycle of these disorders that control the mind. That kept me moving two steps backwards and further into that darkness, year after year. Never an ounce of ambition, drive, or belief in myself. Always tormented and crippled by pain, fear, doubt, and despair.

As time progressed onward post my high school days, I began isolating more and more with every new year that rolled in. I would avoid any type of social gathering as my PTSD, depression, and, worst of all, my anxiety, was intensifying each year. Anxiety and panic attacks becoming more frequent and my sweating as a result more profuse, regardless of my training prior to any social events. Needless to say, beginning in my early twenties — around this "five-year college hiatus time" in my life — I started avoiding any and all get-togethers, including all family functions.

I clearly remember the last family function I ever attended. It was a graduation party for my cousin Gio combined with a birthday party for his brother, my cousin Rico. It was mid-1980's and the get-together was held at the Classic Restaurant on Charles St. in North Providence, Rhode Island.

I was in a very deep depression, writing songs up to sixteen hours a day, and isolating like never before. I didn't plan on going to the party as my anxiety was ridiculously high at this point in my life. I had been avoiding all social gatherings the past few years. However, I decided to go as I thought I might be able to get through it and really did miss being around and with my family.

I worked out intensely for a few hours prior and leading up to the event. I would always do this (an intense workout) prior to any get-together where there would be lots of people or any spotlight possibly on me. It produced the needed sense of calmness and evened my keel by releasing endorphins and getting my serotonin and norepinephrine levels back up. It chemically re-balanced me.

My intense workouts — my medication — worked in much the same way as an alcoholic's bottle, a drug addict's needle or pill, or someone taking script anti-depressant or anti-anxiety meds; It was the fix needed in order to chemically re-balance and function "normally". Training quelled my anxiety and alleviated some of the overbearing darkness of depression. The workout itself was my drug of choice. The positive effects of which could last for hours, sometimes the whole day and evening. It was needed to offset and combat the PTSD, depression, and anxiety that otherwise controlled my thoughts and life.

I remember arriving at the party. The place was packed! First thing I did, as always, was to locate the bathroom and exits. I always tried to stay as close to the bathroom as possible. The closer, the less likely anyone would notice my getting up so often.

I said hi and talked to some family. I remember the anxiety beginning much sooner than in the past. I remember thinking that all good things come to an end — my *medication* was beginning to lose its effectiveness. That terrified me and increased my anxiety level even more.

I began getting up every 15 minutes or so and going to the bathroom to wipe off the sweat pouring from my face and head and from my body as it was beginning to soak through my clothing. I was trying desperately to calm down, my heart pounding as if it would soon and certainly burst through my chest. I was having a combination of major anxiety and panic attacks during this entire function. I was getting dizzy and everything started to spin in slow motion. I came closer than ever to passing out this time. I looked like a drug addict going through withdrawal, I'm sure. It always bothered me that anyone who might have noticed one of my anxiety or panic attacks — my meltdown — would probably think I was on drugs or withdrawing from them. Me of all people! The symptoms being very similar to that of an anxiety or panic attack.

I stuck it out for a couple hours or so and, after this incident, I realized that even my training — my primary outlet and medication — wasn't going to quell the anxiety at large gatherings any longer. I vowed that this was the last of any social events that I would attend, family or otherwise.

I pulled away from any and all social events and family get-togethers from that day on. I would not attend any social gatherings of friends or family ever again, including the weddings of my niece, nephews, and cousins in the years to come.

I've stayed away from large groups of people since this turning point day and social event and for the past 25 years.

Not one friend or family member knows the truth behind my falling off the face of the earth and not showing at any of the cherished events that took place the past two and a half decades.

Hopefully, they will know the truth with this book and my story and understand my lifelong, daily demon battles. What my life truly was behind that mask. The reality behind the facade.

The underlying theme of many of my songs is *dreams* and *keeping the faith*. Not giving up on either. I clung to each throughout most of my life as I desperately struggled to function — to survive — while battling disorders that were ripping my life to shreds, tearing apart both my mind and soul. I strived to maintain and achieve both — dreams and faith — in light of the hell that I was forced to live day in and day out, throughout my life.

Around the fourth year into my hiatus and constant writing, I began to get very frustrated, doubting myself more than ever before. My songs were my way of keeping the faith, my belief alive. The lyrical creation was my innermost feelings — my heart and soul — speaking to my mind. My songs were my cheering section, my constant support.

This is a song I wrote about this time in my life:

"Runnin' Out of Time"

V1   *(I'm) Walkin' down this road[1]*

No warnin' signs[2]
So many distractions[3]
Creep up from behind[4]
Gotta keep the faith[5]
Gotta follow my heart[6]
Livin' for the dream[7]
'Cause it's all I've got[8]

CL
(musical climb[1])
Someway[2]... Gotta stay the course[3]...
Never lose control[4]
(musical climb to vocal[5])
'Cause every day[6]... Get one step closer[7]...
To the end of the road ... and I'm[8]

Chorus:
Runnin' out of time[1]
Runnin[2] out of[3] time[4] ("time" echoed 2x/ bars 4,8)
Runnin' out of time[5]
Runnin[6] out of [7]time[8] (bars 2,3 & 6,7 vocal
stretch)

V2
Lookin' over my shoulder[1]
Into the past[2]
I can see the future[3]
And it's comin' fast[4]
Gotta move ahead[5]
Gotta keep in time[6]
Seize every moment[7]
While I reach for the sky[8]

...Climb 2...

...Chorus 2...

Bridge:
...Add Musical Bridge...

...Climb 3...

...Chorus 3... +

... Runnin' out of time
Runnin' out of time...

© 1988 Steve DiGrossi

Unfortunately, and rather cruelly, the disorders that controlled my life would in time steal from me both my dreams and my faith.

Looking back, I didn't see that sometimes a dream may not arrive or be attainable when I truly wanted or needed it to be, even at the eleventh hour — with deleterious disorders controlling my every move or not. Sometimes the dream — and life's meaning — may be a few hours, or a few decades, further down the road.

I feel this is now my time; a rebirth and a new dream, meaning, and faith is being born through these pages. This being my thirteenth hour.

Going into my fifth year of writing and building my portfolio, I decided to start contacting music publishing companies. Some in New York. Most in California. It was going to be a bit difficult to completely showcase my songwriting ability as I didn't have any of my songs on demo. I would have to submit my songs by way of lyric sheets only. A song isn't complete — isn't brought to life — until arranged with musical composition and vocals. My greatest challenge in songwriting has always been finding a musical composer to collaborate with and create the *finished product*.

I had contacted (by mail) a number of music publishing companies and several executives within these companies. Some requested *demos only* of my songs, others agreed to look at my lyric sheets. All this taking place now during my fifth year of intense, trancelike writing and an ever deepening isolation. PTSD, depression, and anxiety in complete control of my every move.

Over the following months, I received a fair share of *form letter* responses ("*Thank you, but we're not hiring at this time*") but did get a number of personal responses, offers, and some great feedback as well. Most importantly, in response to the offers I received, I was able to speak with several executive-level people within the music industry who personally offered me a job as a staff writer with their companies.

I should have been ecstatic, but, in addition to being completely spent and deeper in the darkness than ever before, I was having a difficult time wrapping my head around accepting the *work for hire* offers. That arrangement meant I would have to accept a weekly pay check and give up all copyrights to the art I would create and breathe life into while working for any of these companies. I'd never get a royalty check — and that financial security — like Jimmie Z.

In retrospect, this may have been the break I had always hoped for and needed in my life. Though, as usual, I couldn't see it through the eyes of and a mind controlled by PTSD, depression, and anxiety. Once again, I found myself second-guessing my ability and worth. I had no faith or belief in myself at this time or at any other time in my life. I was totally lost and confused. I had no one knowledgeable in this area — no one in my life — to bounce questions or ideas off. I had no one to speak with for an informed opinion or to help me see through the confusion in my head, the pain and fear that was the hundred foot wall and always present in my life and confining me from any real progress. On reflection, I probably should have spoken to Jimmie Z about the offers and opportunity. He was the only one I knew that understood the industry and how it worked. However, again, my mind was completely controlled by these disorders and reaching out to *anyone* was just not possible at that particular time and while in that paralyzing death grip.

It had been five years of continuously pouring my heart and soul into this love, this pursuit, this dream of mine, and I felt it all coming to an end just as it may very well have been beginning. An end that was controlled every step of the way by the disorders that tormented my mind and soul from the age of five and for every minute of every day of the next forty years.

Whenever I look back at my life — whether through pictures or recalling events — it is always clear as day to me that I didn't have one happy bone in my body due to these disorders. Healthy and happy is all I ever wanted to be and feel. It is what I prayed for to my Higher Power since childhood. For myself and those I loved and cared for. Peace for the world around me. I longed for happiness since I was a kid. I just wanted to be able to smile, to feel joy and a sense of peacefulness, and to be — to quote from a Commodores song written by Lionel Richie — "*Easy like Sunday morning.*"

I never had an ounce of confidence in anything I did my entire life. I never felt I was worth very much. I had a very traumatizing, very sad and lonely childhood. Always unable to feel like a child, act and live like a child.

The disorders I suffered with carried this curse into my adulthood. I pulled away and isolated from everything and everyone — groups, clubs, people, opportunities — from life itself.

This is what PTSD and these other disorders have done to me and do to too many others in the same predicament. Suffering with the same disorders. This is a war within. Those around you cannot see — they cannot understand — what is going on on the inside. The daily battles, every minute of every day. Vicious emotional beatings that lead you to isolation, where you are safe.

These disorders destroyed my childhood as well as my adulthood. I had no control over the power that convinced me I was worthless and incapable and confined me to isolation throughout most of my adulthood.

I have been courted my entire life by the darkness and pain that comes of these disorders. Disorders that have completely derailed my life. As Ozzy Osbourne's "Crazy Train" lyrics put it; *Mental wounds still screaming, driving me insane, I'm going off the rails on a crazy train.*

My life has been a constant state of bone-chilling, gloomy winter days and nights.

My life's scale always fully tilted to the left. No Normal. No balance. Ever-bound by invisible chains emotionally imprisoning me into isolation.

I have been near death emotionally since childhood. There is some life lying half-frozen beneath the armored surface. Everything above frozen solid. My outlets — my training, my songwriting, motorcycles — provided some emotional balance, harmony, sunshine, and warmth to my life. A brief defrosting of my soul. A tantalizing peek at possibility.

I had one more idea, one final card to play in securing my dream of working and creating — without being a *work for hire* — within the music industry.

The idea was not something I have ever been comfortable with but it was my last option. I would play this card a year or so post college graduation and give my lifelong dream and heart's desire one last shot.

However, right now, I needed to finish my last two years of

college to fulfill my mother's dream and the promise I made to her that I would go back and graduate from college if things didn't pan out in five years.

I also needed that "college graduate" feather in my cap to fall back on my second dream of becoming a DEA agent.

12

I reapplied to Salve Regina College, declared Administration of Justice as my major, and would begin my junior year in September of 1989. I'd be attending full time and commuting from Providence, as I did my sophomore year five years earlier.

While I was sinking deeper and deeper into a depression with each passing year, and my ability to focus and concentrate always dwindling, my five-year hiatus from college somehow proved beneficial in recharging my batteries with regards to studying. It was also the first time in my life I had some clarity and a clear game plan in effect. I knew exactly what courses I needed to take for my declared major as well as my double-minor in psychology and philosophy. I had everything written down, step by step, month by month, for the next two years.

I knew how important my graduating college was to my mother. I made her a promise I would graduate and I would never — could never — let her down. I kept as focused as possible on the task ahead while battling these disorders 24/7 as I'd done my entire life.

I continued to write songs and bear my soul on paper. The fire forever burning inside for this love of mine I now had simmering on the back burner.

I also continued to train like my life depended on it. Which, strange as it may sound, it truly did.

Returning to college at the age of twenty-five was a bit unsettling to say the least. However, it was not going to be my fifth culture shock up to this point. That would come nearly six years to the day down the road. I felt like an old man attending classes with children. Yet the age difference was a mere five to six years. It felt like decades between myself and the majority of students back then. I was, as usual, full of anxiety and deeply depressed but also had a sense of purpose and focus like never before.

Surprisingly, I was somehow able to stay focused and concentrate on the task at hand — the game plan for the next two years. I was also now "unknown". I didn't know anyone in the college with the exception of a few instructors from my previous years. I didn't have that reputation to live up to. I didn't have a spotlight on me. My mask and armor was still in place and weighing heavy on me as always, but was needed to survive, attention focused on me or not.

It would stay in place until I began to strip it off, little by little, some twenty years later — through therapy and a recovery process — as I began to understand, accept, surrender to and heal from the decades of never-ending trauma that had been my life.

I met one of my dearest friends, *Honey D (HD)*, my junior year. She had graduated from a community college with an associate's degree seven years earlier and, like me, decided to take a hiatus from college and pursue another direction.

She was accepted into the ADJ program at Salve and began full time in January of 1989. One semester before I would begin.

We met in one of our ADJ classes my first semester back at Salve. Two anxiety-ridden students who were trying their best to remain invisible in the classroom and out of the spotlight. However, we noticed each other, connected, and hit it off immediately.

HD was very quiet and shy, but always had a big smile on her face. She was a year older than me and, I would find out soon, suffered with social anxiety. She had an extreme fear of speaking in public and within the classrooms. She didn't learn of my anxiety or other disorders for nearly twenty-five years post our initial meeting and friendship.

HD also commuted to Salve. She would make the commute, as I did, two to three times per week to attend full-time semesters junior and senior year.

We would become very close friends and remain such to this day. HD is one of those very few blessings in my life. She is an extremely special person. A wonderful and true friend. She is family and I love her very much. She is also one of the smartest people I've ever known. Incredibly intelligent! During our time together at Salve, I was always impressed at how much she knew and understood within our field of study. She knew the law like nobody's business!

I also met a good friend, *Pete R (PR)*, during a 1989 summer class I took at Salve Regina to "get back into the swing of things" prior to the beginning of my junior year in Sept of 1989. I would take a summer class or two both the summer of 1989 and summer of 1990 in order to keep my full time semesters manageable. I did, however, take six classes/eighteen credits a couple semesters, in addition to my summer classes.

PR was also a year older than me and had been taking some classes here and there at Salve over the years, beginning in 1983. We never ran into each other and hadn't been in any classes together prior to the summer class of 1989. He began attending full time at Salve in 1990, one semester after I began my full time junior year.

PR lived in Middletown, Rhode Island, just a few miles from Salve, and commuted to classes. He was also majoring in ADJ and we had several classes together over the semesters. He, HD, and I would be the "three old amigos" in class! PR, however, was just the opposite of HD and myself. He was extremely outgoing and loved the spotlight. He didn't have an ounce of anxiety when it came to social activity, class discussions, or oral presentations. He was always answering questions, asking questions, and participating in discussion. All while HD and I were trying desperately to remain out of any discussions or spotlight.

PR was a good-natured, family-loving guy with a good heart who I considered a friend. He would be in the same category as my good high school buddies, Rocco F and Jimmy G.

However, like most everyone and everything else in my life, I would pull away, not keep in contact, and disappear from the face of the earth. PR would contact my mother every now and again in Rhode Island to see how I was doing and where I vanished to. I gave very few, if any, people my forwarding addresses and I changed phone numbers several times in order to completely disappear.

It's simply incredible what PTSD and these other disorders do to your mind — controlling you into isolation. Making you firmly believe that no one really wants to know you, be around you, care for you.

Another of the greatest regrets of my life was having to turn down PR's request to be best man at his wedding in 1993. This wasn't too long after our graduation from Salve. I tried desperately to explain to him at that time why I couldn't do it. My mask always in place and hiding the complete truth of my life. I couldn't get beyond explaining my anxiety in social settings and asked him to remember how I sank in my chair in our college classrooms, hoping to bypass any attention that might come my way. Hoping to avoid any spotlight.

I told him to remember that I was the only person to graduate from the ADJ department at Salve Regina with a BA in the Administration of Justice who did not do one single, required, oral presentation.

I think he understood about the anxiety but there was no way at that time to explain the depth and severity of the disorders that were in control of my life and consuming me, piece by piece, each and every year of my life from childhood.

I have felt guilty and ashamed of myself — living with regret — ever since for not being able to fulfill his request to be best man at his wedding. A very special day and time in his life. It was an honor and, like every other opportunity and honor that came my way during my life, I was not able to accept it, participate in and share the special occasion, and live my life as any other normal person should and would.

PR's request wasn't the first and wouldn't be the last honor bestowed upon me that I would have to decline. However, it was the most difficult and has bothered me the most over the years. PR was a genuinely good person and friend and I couldn't tell him the truth of my life and why I couldn't be at his side during his wedding and special day.

These are the things that these disorder destroy. They take away your ability to be *normal*. They take your life away, literally, by way of emotional imprisonment, and leave you with nothing but regret and pain.

I hope with my story that PR, as well as other family members and friends, may see the truth and understand where I have been in my life and the reason(s) behind my actions then and now.

There were some truly wonderful, dedicated, and gifted instructors at Salve during my freshman and sophomore years as well as when I returned for my junior and senior years. Many of whom were current or former law enforcement officers, FBI agents, career military, and attorneys that had been teaching there for decades.

If not for my disorders, as had been the case my entire life, I would have had some truly incredible connections and friendships both with staff and students.

I connected with many of my instructors but not one was ever aware of the disorders which were controlling and destroying my life. I must say, my mask may have been the most effective and deceptive tool I had incorporated into my life in order to survive. Creating that persona that kept everyone from knowing and seeing my pain and suffering. My weakness as I believed most of my life.

As was the situation during my high school years, I would have to speak with most of my college instructors whose classes required oral presentations. I would have to explain my severe social anxiety, panic attacks, and inability to function in any capacity should I be required to speak in front of a group of people or the class itself.

I was unable to do oral presentations and there were many required within my major field of study.

There was a vast difference in the caliber of my college instructors compared to my high school teachers. Most of the college instructors were much more professional, knowledgeable, and compassionate and were teaching because they wanted to make a difference in the students' lives. Most all were very understanding of my severe anxiety and fear of oral presentations.

Being a bit older than most, it was obvious I wasn't trying to get out of required work within the classes but had a serious anxiety problem. And, with mask in place, my instructors didn't know the half of it!

I was allowed to do lengthy and detailed term-type papers in place of my oral presentations. I remember some of the students looking at me at the end of the classes' oral presentations — I knew what they were thinking. Some outright asked; "*How did you get out of that oral?*" I'd tell them a partial truth; I had very bad anxiety in front of large groups and the instructor was very understanding and allowed me to do an in depth paper in place of the oral presentation. Well, most of the Instructors, that is. I did have one instructor during my last two years at Salve, a philosophy instructor, *J. Dumaz*. He lacked any and all forms of professionalism, compassion, and, quite frankly, common sense. He was a mayor of Dummyville, right along with Cream Puff and Schlemiel! He would cause me a lot of grief regarding my inability to participate in the oral presentations required in his class. A required class for my philosophy minor and only this instructor taught the class.

I almost came to blows with this guy but for one of my ADJ instructors, *V. Andolina*, coming out of a classroom when he heard raised voices in the hallway.

I was in a heated discussion with this philosophy instructor regarding his lack of compassion and condescending attitude towards me. Andolina came out of his classroom, politely interjected, pulled me aside, and told me the guy was a complete asshole and lacked every semblance of common sense and professionalism. My thoughts exactly. He told me to file a complaint with the college based on the instructor's unprofessional attitude. He said I wouldn't be the first to do so. I was from the streets. That would be ratting on the guy. I let it go, but, truthfully, would have liked to have had an "in the alley, man to man" with Dumaz!

I took his failing grade for the oral presentation I didn't deliver, but still passed his class — with the lowest grade I'd receive in all of my four years of college.

A real piece of work this instructor Dumaz was. Part of his philosophy teaching was that of Buddhism. What better lesson than karma having its way with him in the years to come. What goes around will usually come around.

I began working part-time in retail security in 1990, during my junior year of college. It was a well-known, twelve chain, New England based department store.

My mother happened to see an ad in the local paper for the position and thought it might be good experience for me considering my studies and the direction I was going towards with a career in law enforcement. She somehow convinced me to go and fill out the application even though I was taking six classes/eighteen credits this particular semester.

I applied for the position and, surprisingly, I was called within a few days for an interview. I was, as usual, full of anxiety just thinking about the interview and didn't believe for a second that anyone would be interested in hiring me for this position — or any other. As was common, I would train like an animal for a few hours leading up to the interview. It always helped calm my nerves, evened my keel, and provided a sense of euphoria for a time being. When I arrived for the interview, I noticed a half dozen others waiting for the same interview and position. A couple people went in and came out before me. I was called in and, to my greatest surprise, I was hired on the spot. The others in the waiting area weren't even given a shot at the interview. The human resources manager said she was highly impressed with my interview and I was "perfect" for the job.

The security department was actually separate from the retail stores. Meaning, there was a corporate security department with a security director that handled all security issues for the twelve stores. The individual managers of the retail stores had nothing to do with the security department. We would follow security department rules and procedures, not the store or store manager's employee policies. This human resources manager was actually doing a favor interviewing for the security manager who was out of town. I would meet with the security manager within a couple days to confirm my hiring and position. She felt as though I was perfect for the job also.

The security department was very accommodating in working around my full-time college schedule. I began a few days later. As with everything else to date, I was very nervous and anxious but my training and my mask always kept my keel even and me looking *normal*. No one ever had a clue of the emotional catastrophe that lay beneath that protective armor.

Post a five-year hiatus and intense isolation, lightning would strike twice as I became rather popular in my life once again — both within the security department(s) of the store(s) and within the retail section, which consisted of the retail management team and the retail associates within the various departments.

It was like high school all over again. The strange, but welcome feeling of being popular as well as the added pressure of keeping up the game face needed to survive — needed to keep my tortured and bleeding soul a secret.

I quickly became the number one store detective in the twelve store chain, earning praise from the security director as well as the team of store managers.

My first year, I was awarded "Detective of the Year" within the security departments of all twelve stores. This came with some monetary bonuses and offers to move up the security management ladder. Management was aware of my intentions of moving on and within law enforcement at some point post my graduation from college. However, they would tell me time and again that they would like me to consider a career within the security department of the chain.

I did accept the first offer of becoming security supervisor for my store as I still had another semester to go and nothing material in the workings as of yet. All this happening while I was commuting to college full time (with plenty of studying this time around), training multiple hours each day, still writing music, beginning the application and written exam process for federal law enforcement agencies, and working a minimum of twenty hours per week — some weeks to thirty hours — within the security department.

I would have my dear friend, HD, hired when I became security supervisor. HD wasn't too excited about or comfortable with theft apprehensions. However, her strength was in writing reports and representing the department in court with shoplifting cases. She excelled at both and was an integral part of the team.

As part of my compensation for being awarded detective of the year, I was given a blank check from the security director for dinner for four at any place of my choosing. I chose a steakhouse known for their "caveman cut steaks" and took along a couple friends, *Linda M*, who was also the security manager, her husband to be, *Dan*, a local police officer, and my date, *MM*, a young lady I had been seeing a little bit of the past month or so.

It was the middle of the winter, lots of snow and it was arctic cold outside.

My date and I met Linda and Dan at the steakhouse. We were all having a decent conversation while eating when, as my (bad) luck would have it, I began to have an anxiety attack. Not only was I starting to sweat profusely, I had a very heavy sweater on due to the extreme cold that evening. I was beginning to boil over! I had trained myself into and through an intense workout earlier in the evening to stave off any possibility of this happening. My medication had been losing a bit of its effect the past couple years and this happened to be one of those times it didn't serve its purpose.

This was going to be bad! I excused myself from the table and went to the men's room. I couldn't stop sweating and the consequential stress caused me to start shaking, almost uncontrollably. The anxiety attack quickly moved to a full-blown panic attack. I took my sweater off in the men's room and tried desperately to cool off with cold water from the faucet splashed all over my face, head, and upper body.

I just couldn't get this attack under control no matter what I did (or didn't do). All kinds of things were going through my mind as I was beginning to panic times ten. I thought of running out of the bathroom and into the parking lot where I could dive head-first into the snow. That should cool me off! I thought of running out of the bathroom directly to my car and driving off so I wouldn't have to be seen in this condition. That wasn't going to be an option, I had a date back in the restaurant. If I didn't, I probably would have made a run for it, it was that bad!

I was in that men's room for at least twenty minutes and could have stayed another twenty hours to no avail. I returned to the table and everyone just looked at me as if they had just seen a ghost. Dan said, "*We were getting worried about you. I was just about to come in there and make sure you didn't fall into the toilet.*"

Linda and my date said, pretty much at the same time, "*You look real sick. Are you okay?*" I wasn't about to let anyone peek beneath my mask and know my true pain and suffering. I said, "*Not sure how it happened so quickly, but I just got a case of food poisoning. I'm sick to my stomach. I've been vomiting in the men's room and can't stop sweating. I've never felt so sick in my life.*" Except, that is, for every other time I've had the same anxiety and/or panic attack in social settings! Luckily (if that is possible), we were just finishing up with dinner when I had gone to the men's room. Everyone else was done when I finally returned to the table. I told them I couldn't eat another bite; I was much too sick. Needless to say, the evening was cut short and, as usual, it wasn't possible for me to enjoy the occasion or the company due to disorders which had controlled my life from childhood and saw to it that there was no socializing, no *normal* in my life. No attempt at that normal ever went unpunished and without complete embarrassment.

About a year or so into my employment with the security department, I would receive a letter of commendation from the director of security for a jewelry company that leased a space within the department store. I had stopped a theft of one of their high end jewelry display cases from a counter-top. It was mounted down but a strung-out shoplifter had somehow cut the cable — which sounded an alarm — grabbed the case and started running. I had to tackle him and, in the process of his fighting back and wrestling him into submission, I smashed into a display table and tore a hole in my knee that required a half dozen stitches to close. After getting the shoplifter subdued and under control, I found the knife he used to cut the cable along with a used syringe and needle in his pocket. I said a quick prayer and thanked God I wasn't stuck with that needle.

I remember the store's retail manager as well as several of the department employees coming over to me once I had the guy restrained. They all commended me on being so professional, kind to and as gentle as possible in handling the shoplifter in light of the circumstances.

I remember telling the guy as I had him pinned beneath me that it would be alright and I didn't want to hurt him but I needed to get the merchandise back, it was my job.

He was heavily under the influence of drugs — possibly jonesing and needing another fix quickly — frothing at the mouth and shaking violently. I understood completely and felt for the guy. I knew he needed some professional help, someone to talk to, someone who cared, someone who truly gave a shit about him and his life. I knew he needed another "medicine" to take the place of the drugs. Another "outlet" to cope with his pain and demons. I knew all too well what he was feeling.

Of the many hundreds of apprehensions and security cases/incidents I was involved with during my time with the security department, there is one in particular that stands out in my mind and, for some reason, resonates with me to this day; there was a young lady (late 20's) that was apprehended one afternoon for shoplifting in the store. She was with a little boy — a child around the age of five. When she was taken to the security office to be processed, prior to arrested, the child first caught my attention. He looked very familiar. As I looked at her identification and began asking a few questions, I realized this was the child of a neighborhood kid, *Tony P*, that I hung around with pre my high school years. The boy's mother, Tony's wife, was hardly recognizable. I hadn't seen her — or Tony — in some ten years. It wasn't only the years that had changed the mother's appearance, she was now an addict. I remember her from my teenage years. She was a neighborhood girl and simply gorgeous back in the day. All the guys were hot for her. Tony was always considered by all the girls as a heartthrob. A handsome kid who the girls swooned over. They were a good looking couple and together from the early days. This young boy was their son.

I remember my eyes starting to well up as I looked at him. Tony, the boy's father, was doing an insurance job — aka: arson — for a guy one night in a local, vacant multifamily home. Something went wrong. Tony ran out of the home completely engulfed in flames. Screaming and in shock, he ran back to his nearby home — on fire, literally. He was taken to the hospital where he would lay, in a coma, with third degree burns to his entire body. He would suffer terribly for a time and soon after die from his wounds.

When I looked at this handsome little guy — the spitting image of my childhood friend — and knowing what happened to his father, I couldn't help but to be overcome with emotion. I looked at his mother, *Tori R* — who is now breaking the law with a child in tow. I asked her why she was jeopardizing the well-being of her son by shoplifting in his presence. She remembered me from the neighborhood and began to cry. She explained her addiction and that it was the result of her not being able to cope with what Tony had gone through and how he died. I had a heart-to-heart talk with her for some thirty minutes, in the presence of other security personnel, as was customary and procedure within our department regarding apprehensions and investigations within the security office. I knew that if she was arrested she would also be charged with child endangerment and I wasn't going to be the one to come between that boy and his mother, regardless of her crime and addiction. I gave her the number to the security department and told her that I would do whatever I could to help her get over her addiction — for the sake of her son and my old friend, Tony.

I cut her a break and told her she owed it to her son to get clean and give him a shot at a decent life. He already had a couple strikes against him and deserved better. She thanked me. I never heard from or of her again.

Hopefully she was able to get it together and the little guy beat the odds that seemed to be getting stacked against him. I knew *that* feeling intimately as well.

In 1990, during the first semester of my senior year, I took the Federal Law Enforcement and Investigation (FLEI) Exam. This written exam took place at the federal building in Providence, Rhode Island. I drove down and took the exam with Honey D and Pete R.

I ran into my good friend, Rocco F, at the federal building. He was an attorney and working for a judge within this particular building at this time in 1990. We chatted for a few minutes and he said he'd give me a call, he wanted to get together. He mentioned he had gone to our fifth year high school reunion a few years back and reminded me that we had planned on getting a few of the guys together for that reunion but I didn't return any calls and didn't show. He wanted me to go to our tenth year high school reunion coming up in 1992. I told him we'd talk when we got together.

He gave me a call a few days later and we talked about getting together for lunch the following week. I told him I'd give him a call to make a plan. I never did. As had been the case now for some time, I was falling deeper and deeper into a depression with each passing year and, aside from school and work, was isolating more and more.

I always wished I was able to explain my life to Rocco. He was a good friend and had no idea. I always wanted him to know my truth and the reasons I never kept in touch, showed up at reunions, and just fell off the face of the earth.

I've said it before, but can't emphasize enough; this is what these disorders did to me; they pulled me away — isolated me — from everything and everyone that meant anything to me from childhood and throughout my entire adult life.

I couldn't stand myself. Always feeling like I was never good enough. Worthless. I was sick and tired of having to hide behind a mask and persona when it came to people who were important to me and in my life. I just didn't know how to shield myself and survive the emotional torment that ruled my world without that protective armor.

The FLEI exam had several parts to it and lasted approximately five hours. There were forty thousand applicants that took this particular entrance exam this year.

It was the first step and necessary to pass and score highly to be able to move on to the next step within federal law enforcement agencies such as the U.S. Secret Service (Uniform Division), which was part of the Department of the Treasury in 1990 (in 2003 became part of the Department of Homeland Security), U.S. Border Patrol, which is now also part of the Department of Homeland Security, and ATF (Bureau of Alcohol, Tobacco and Firearms), which is part of the U.S. Department of Justice.

The Drug Enforcement Administration (DEA), which was and still is part of the U.S. Department of Justice, required a college degree and was looking for extensive law enforcement experience during this time. DEA didn't draw from this hire list and I didn't have that experience yet. My goal was to become a federal law enforcement officer with another of the agencies and, within a reasonable time, laterally move over to the DEA. I had been told that a lateral transfer from one federal agency to another is quicker and smoother than transferring up from a local or state law enforcement agency. Of course, I would still have to attend and pass their 18-week basic agent training program at the DEA Training Academy in Quantico, VA, before becoming a DEA agent. I was actually looking forward to attending the DEA Training Academy whether I had been to another training academy previously or not. I wanted to earn my way from the ground up with DEA.

In retrospect, and knowing more now about my life-long disorders and the causes, being a DEA agent was my way of saving another person — the world — from what I had to endure as a child and throughout my life. I didn't want anyone else to be traumatized by the effects of alcohol or illegal drugs. I wanted to do my part to protect society from these evils. I would have given my life to do so. It would have been less painful than the destructive aftermath of my line of duty accident as a state trooper — which was all for naught. Or was it?

🦋 🦋 🦋 🦋

Nearly two decades removed and through therapy and a recovery process, I have found a sense of peace in my soul as I learn more about the disorders that have controlled my life since childhood as well as the circumstances that have been my life. I have a feeling that I am exactly where I need to be at this time — reaching out through my words, sharing my experiences and my story, and helping others not to suffer as I have suffered, not to go where I have gone. Very similar to what I would have accomplished if I had become a DEA agent. Only difference being, my life is not in danger on the front lines and I firmly believe I can reach and help many more people via my story and establishing countrywide, life-saving support groups post-publication of this book than I ever could have as a DEA agent. The end may justify the means after all. Meaning and purpose found and fulfilled.

🦋 🦋 🦋 🦋

I earned a score of 96% on the FLEI exam. This ranked in the top 1% of applicants that took the exam that year and put me at the top of the hiring list — or so I thought.

Most of my ADJ instructors (several of whom were retired FBI agents) were amazed and delighted at the same time at the score I achieved.

Little did I know, I would soon get a firsthand introduction into (reverse) discrimination, top 1% or not.

I began receiving notices that I was being considered for Border Patrol agent positions — many of those positions in Laredo, TX. I wasn't crazy about this but was willing to do and go where I needed to in order to get my foot in the door and move on to a career with the DEA. I *always* responded, as required, and immediately, that I was still interested and willing to accept the job offer, wherever (the location) it was being offered.

I would also get notices that I was being considered for a position with the Secret Service Uniform Division as well as other positions being filled within various federal law enforcement agencies that drew from this hiring list. It never went beyond that notice in the mail. I couldn't understand what was going on. I scored top 1% in the country and it seemed like I was being looked over. This went on for over two years! Letter after letter saying I was being considered for one position or another with different federal agencies and would be contacted for an interview. That never happened. Frustrated, I eventually called a few of the agencies and spoke with different people about my situation. Each would tell me that the position had been "filled internally". The position was always *filled internally* every time I inquired!

I hadn't applied to any other departments — local or state — as I was convinced that I would be hired by one of the federal law enforcement agencies based on my qualifications and high standing on the hiring list. It was a wasted two-plus years of my life but another valuable lesson learned.

As my senior year of college wound down and graduation approached, my mother asked me if it would be okay for my brother to come in from Florida and attend the graduation ceremony. I agreed, but insisted that she not make a big deal about it with family as I didn't want to be in the spotlight and uneasy during what should be a joyous day.

My mother never knew until some 20-plus years later the severity and depth of my PTSD, depression, and anxiety. However, she did know that I had been uncomfortable around crowds, even if that crowd was family.

I wanted my graduation to be low-key, and the smaller the crowd, the better.

My brother did come in from Florida and did attend my graduation. He told me he was proud of me. However, I knew better. I always felt a sense of resentment and jealousy from him and never believed anything he said. I saw right through him. He was full of shit.

He (and the rest of this immediate family) would prove in the years to come that my intuition was right all along. It was a sad day when I realized, beyond a shadow of a doubt, that members of my immediate family loved and cared for me — and my mother — less than the few enemies I'm sure I made during my lifetime.

Everything I was taught from childhood and believed about *family* would prove to be false as it applied to my immediate family, with the exception of my mother and, for the most part, my father.

As I look back at this special time — among others — that should have been a happy, celebratory occasion in my life, it is clear that I was always a very unhappy person. A person controlled by and suffering with disorders that tore my life to shreds, refusing to allow any sunshine into that darkness that was my life since early childhood.

Every picture of myself I reflect on, I seldom see even a hint of a smile. I can see in my own eyes the pain and suffering. It's incredible how no one else ever noticed this. At least no one ever brought it to my attention.

Never an ounce of joy, even during these "dues have been paid", "feather-in-my-cap" moments.

I remember my mother telling me how proud she was of me that graduation day. She would always tell me that she was proud of me for the simplest things I may have done or, to her, the greatest.

My mother has told me many times over the years that the three highlights of her life were my high school graduation, college graduation, and FHP academy graduation.

If it brought a smile to my mother's face, if it made my mother happy — even for a moment — it was worth whatever pain, suffering, and sacrifice I needed to make to accomplish the goal.

13

I had never concentrated so intently on studying and doing well in school as I did those final two years of college. I graduated with a 3.4 GPA (combined for my junior and senior years) and was named to the Dean's List three semesters of my final four semesters. Would have been four semesters if not for the ignorance of Dumaz! All things considered, not too shabby. I was exhausted and completely burnt out upon graduation. Not sure If I could have gone another semester. Graduation came just in time!

Post college graduation — spring 1991 — the depression and isolation began to spiral out of control like no time prior, all while applying and testing with various law enforcement agencies for employment.

It was also during this time that I began working full-time within the security department. I stayed on, full-time, until leaving the security department towards the end of summer 1993.

Several times over my final year with the company, I was offered a management position within the security department. At this time, our retail store had merged with another retail store. I sat down with our security director and the security director from the retail chain we had merged with. Both knew that I was currently applying and testing with various law enforcement agencies and of my intentions of going on to a career in law enforcement.

Each of the directors told me that they didn't want to lose me and wanted to know what it would take to keep me within the security department of the merging stores. We discussed pay raises and a move up to district manager a year or so post my accepting a manager's position within the department. I told them I would think about it but couldn't commit at that time as I was already on a federal law enforcement waiting/hiring list and that had been my goal for many years. Each said they respected my honesty as well as my dedication and desire to become a federal LEO agent but were willing to do what they could to keep me in the security department and moving up that management ladder.

If becoming a DEA agent wasn't my second most important goal and dream in life, I wouldn't have hesitated in accepting the position(s) and guarantees they were offering me. I truly enjoyed working with these people and within this department. In retrospect (and once again), if I had gone that way I might have been spared the crippling physical pain and nightmare that was some four years down the road ahead of me.

Within a year of the two retail stores merging, I had a run-in with the new human resources manager. I had been frustrated the past few months since the merger as this new manager was interfering with the security department and becoming a serious and disrespectful pain in the ass. I mentioned this to the new security director months prior and he told me that she had no authority within the security department and I should, in his words, "*put her in her place.*"

I tried to explain to her, on numerous occasions, and always politely and respectfully, our security department policies and procedures. How it was prior to the merger — and presently — and that according to *my boss*, the new director of security, she was out of line and overstepping her boundaries.

One day she intentionally spewed a few nasty comments my way while speaking to me in a very condescending manner. I never disrespected anyone and have never been able to remain cool and calm — the gloves come off quickly — when being outright disrespected, regardless by whom or where I am. She really pushed my buttons this day and, luckily for her, she was a *she*. I was working with HD when this happened. HD actually had to physically pull me away as I became very heated, very quickly.

I told this human resources a-hole exactly what I thought of her and told her to explain to the security director why they just lost me — and HD — as an employee.

Both HD and I then quit and walked away. It just wasn't the same after the merger and, regardless of what the security director would say, the atmosphere was not conducive to doing the incredible work we had done the past several years.

I'm sure I would have handled the situation a bit differently if not for horrid disorders always controlling my emotions and the ever-intense pain and anger that was always brewing just beneath the surface, waiting to boil over.

I had met an incredible bunch of genuinely nice people from within the security department as well as from within the retail end of the store during my few years of employment with this company. When I finally left the store, my disorders would, once again, keep me from contacting anyone that I had become friendly with. As always, the invisible chains of PTSD and depression would hold me down and hold me back. That controlling power always echoing doubt and negativity in my head.

Yet again, I lost out on some relationships that should have been special and lifelong.

It was right around this time in my life, during a winter's morning while taking a shower at my house, I heard the side doorbell ring. No one else was home. First thought; what timing! I figured it was probably one of my uncles and they would either hang around a few minutes or come back later on. Then I thought; my car was not there and no other cars were in the driveway or in front of the house. Whoever it is should know that no one is home — why ring the bell?

Less than a minute after that doorbell rang, I heard a very hard, very loud pounding on that side door. I knew this was no one I knew. Whoever it was, was banging loudly on that door for a reason; If there is a dog in the house or anyone sleeping or hard-of-hearing, they wanted to know who was in there. I realized immediately what was about to happen. I jumped out of the shower and as I was heading to the closet where guns were kept, I heard the glass shattering. I grabbed a loaded .38 revolver and headed for the kitchen. The side door lead into the small doorway, off the kitchen area. As I came around the corner of the kitchen, still dripping wet, my heart pounding fiercely, I saw a large figure draped in dark clothing with a black hoody pulled over his head. He was coming up the three steps to the kitchen from the side door, an object in his hand that resembled a gun.

The second he hit the middle step of that small stairway, he noticed me coming around the corner. I saw him pull the hand up that was holding the object. By his reaction, I knew he was startled. I raised the gun and said, "*you picked the wrong house, asshole!*" Before he could fire off a shot, I unloaded one first. However, dripping wet and buck naked, I slipped at that very second. The bullet missed him and went through the door. I'm pretty sure he shit his pants. As he ducked, I got off another shot falling to the floor. This made him turn and run like hell back through the door he just broke through. I got up from the floor and ran down the three steps to the side door. As I ran through the door, I saw him jump into a car that was backed into my yard. Obviously, a driver waiting in that car for him. The car whipped out of my driveway, tires screeching and rubber burning. I was unable to get the plate on the vehicle or notice if it even had one.

The neighborhood had begun deteriorating years before with outsiders moving in and, now, it was common to see people you had never seen before lurking in the neighborhood. Shady looking characters everywhere you turned. There were still a few families living in the area that had been there for generations. We still looked out for one another. It only took a few minutes before the local police department cruisers were swarming the area and looking in yards.

I learned later that several neighbors had called the police when they heard the gunshots. I threw on a pair of pants and a shirt and went back to the door to find a couple local police officers looking around. I told them what happened and they came in to take a report. They were local officers and had had enough of the break-ins and seeing the neighborhood go to shit. As the one officer was taking the report, he said to me, "*You should have killed the fuckin' dirt-bag.*" I thought to myself; It's probably a good thing I slipped on the wet floor or he certainly would have been dead and I would have been caught up in a legal nightmare. All while I was sitting atop a federal law enforcement hiring list and waiting to move on with a career in law enforcement. Maybe this turned out for the better? I had every right to defend myself and use deadly force in this instance, but, no doubt this would have put a damper on or, even worse, an ending to my law enforcement goals. Then I realized what truly could have been; what if my mother was home alone when this scumbag piece of garbage broke in? What might he have done to my mother? My blood began to boil and in that split second I wished I had put him in his grave so he had no chance to do this again, perhaps killing someone in the process. Someone's mother, child, or grandparents.

It would be another ten or so years before I convinced my parents that it was time to move. When that time finally came, my parents were in their late seventies. They would move to a very nice, family owned, fifty-five and older complex in a beautiful area of North Providence. However, my mother would never be the same again. She was forced to give up her home — her pride and joy, her security. She loved her home, as every woman does. She would no longer be able to tend her garden or decorate her yard and porch. She was broken hearted. It hurt me deeply knowing how badly she felt. Seeing her so torn apart by the loss. Having to give up her home because of what the neighborhood — and society in general — had become. It was a necessary move at that time and a move for the better. It wasn't their neighborhood any longer. They weren't safe in that neighborhood any longer.

I had a contact that was able to get me an almost impossible one-on-one interview with a high ranking official, will refer to as *MJ*, with the Secret Service at their downtown Providence headquarters. PTSD, severe depression, high anxiety and all, I jumped on the opportunity as I knew the importance of this interview.

I trained like an animal days leading up to the meeting and a couple hours before the interview to keep my keel even and get my endorphins kicking in order to alleviate some of my depression and anxiety.

I arrived at the Secret Service's downtown Providence headquarters and met with MJ, who was a close friend of my contact that set up the interview. MJ was very up front and honest about what was going on at this time during the early 1990's. After we chatted a bit and I explained the letters/offers of employment I had been receiving from being atop the FLEI exam's hire list — several offers of which regarding employment with the Secret Service Uniform Division — he began to explain things beginning with, "*Off the record, here's the story.*" He went on to tell me that I had everything that his (Secret Service) agency — or any other federal agency — would want in a new recruit. He said I was smart, sharp, articulate, enthusiastic, and in great shape among other compliments.

Imagine the impression I might have made if I had actually been "normal"?!

He said that the main problem was that all the federal law enforcement agencies had to fill their openings/available positions with 50% minority candidates (female, black, Hispanic) from the FLEI exam hire list. Basically, what this means, is that even though I scored the higher test grade and placed at the top of the hire list, I was being looked over/passed on for minority candidates who were not as qualified as I was. This is reverse discrimination. This is complete bullshit! I don't care what color or gender you are, or if you are green with purple antenna, the most qualified for a position should get the job. Period!

He went on to say that 25% would have to come from those who have prior law enforcement experience with other law enforcement agencies and the remaining 25% from within the respective law enforcement agency (aka; positions filled internally).

I jokingly said to him after he explained this, "*I'm a short Italian guy, does that qualify me for minority candidacy? Come on, how many short Italian guys do you have working for the Secret Service?*" He laughed and then replied, "*we actually have many Italian agents within the department.*" He then mentioned to me that since we shared a mutual friend, he wanted to be up front with me, off the record. He then said, "*even though you have everything this particular agency would look for in a new recruit, we wouldn't be able to hire you due to your father's background*". My heart sank. I felt both extreme disappointment and anger at the same time. I responded, "*I appreciate your honesty. I have always throughout my life been accountable for anything and everything I've said or done — and will take the praise or the punishment for my words or actions. However, regardless of what my father may have done or been involved with in his lifetime, I won't allow anyone to hold his or anyone else's actions against me. I have never been in trouble or arrested in my life. I am my own man and responsible for my own actions — no one else's — and shouldn't be excluded from consideration or held accountable for someone else's choices in life.*" He agreed with me and recommended that I get law enforcement experience with a local or state agency and then reapply to federal agencies, specifically the DEA, which I explained to him was my primary goal and interest. However, employment with the Secret Service wasn't going to be possible due to family background. I would also have a much better chance being in the 25% mandatory hiring group with prior law enforcement experience.

Needless to say, I learned a couple valuable lessons that day. The first about (reverse) discrimination — which had just slapped me square across my face. I also learned that day that regardless of who you are and what you do in life, you will always be associated with and judged by the actions and lifestyle of those in your family, for better or for worse.

I am my father's son regardless of his lifestyle and whether I approved or not of what he may or may not have done during his lifetime. I am who I am. My father who he is. However, my loyalty has always been and will always be to my *true* family and friends first and foremost — always, regardless of what others may think or say of the family member or friend.

In that respect, I certainly understand what MJ meant and where the Secret Service was coming from with its unwritten hiring policy based on a person's family history.

Over the next month or so I would discuss this meeting with my contact and a few other active and retired state and federal law enforcement agents that I had been introduced to by a mutual friend. I wanted to get the opinions of those in the know regarding what I should do, all things considered. The consensus was for me to apply to the Florida Highway Patrol (FHP) and become a state trooper to gain the experience needed not only to qualify for the 25% mandatory hiring group that most federal agencies were filling positions with/hiring from, but, most importantly, to be able to then apply directly to and move on specifically with DEA from my position as a state trooper.

FHP was at the top of the list because I preferred state law enforcement to a local department and I had been familiar with south Florida since my childhood and was comfortable there. I also loved the year-round warm summer weather.

However, I still had one last bit of unfinished business I needed to take care of before going all-in with the application process for FHP.

I had completed my college education and earned a BA in Administration of Justice. It was now towards the end of 1992 and well over a year since graduation. I was still working full time in retail security and would continue there until the end of summer 1993. I had been sitting on top of a federal law enforcement hiring list for nearly two years with no luck at all.

Songwriting was still alive and flowing through my veins like a bouncing river. It was now time to play my last card regarding my dream of working within the music industry. I needed to give this one last shot before I moved forward with the plan and my second dream of a career in law enforcement as a DEA agent.

It was time to have a conversation with my father about my songwriting and connections I know were in the palm of his hand in years past.

I never asked my father for anything. I had a difficult time my entire life asking anyone for anything — be it help, a favor, directions if I was lost! I can count on one hand the times I may have asked for a favor during my lifetime. I knew my father had strong connections with certain people who, along with their families, controlled much of the entertainment business in the not so distant past.

A bit of history as to how it all began:

My father's Mentor growing up was Vito R. Vito was twenty years older than my father and the father my dad never had. Vito came up in the North End of Providence as my father did. He was a Charles Street guy with strong ties, connections, and power spread across the United States from the 1920's prohibition days up through the early 1970's. Vito was a close friend and in tight with *CR*, who was a major smuggler and bootlegger of alcohol during prohibition. The main operation out of New Jersey and New York. CR was also a close friend and partner of Al Capone. Al Capone was originally from Brooklyn, NY, and moved to Chicago in his twenties to take advantage of smuggling alcohol during prohibition. Through CR, Vito, at an early age, would be introduced to Capone, Charles "Lucky" Luciano, and Frank Costello. Lucky Luciano, a Sicilian, was the original "Godfather" and head of the Genovese crime family, formerly known as the Luciano crime family. He is the mastermind behind splitting New York City into five different Mafia families and establishing the first commission in the early 1930's.

Luciano and Frank Costello met on the streets of New York in the early 1920's. They became good friends and business partners. Some of the very old school members of Luciano's family didn't approve of Luciano and Costello's partnership because Costello wasn't Sicilian. Costello was from my father's *paese* of Calabria, Italy. Back in the day, the very old school Mafiosi were not willing to work with anyone who wasn't from Sicily. They didn't trust anyone — even other Italians — that wasn't from their paese of Sicily.

Frank Costello would be appointed as the new acting boss of the Genovese crime family during the mid-1930's by Luciano, who was serving a lengthy prison sentence but still running things behind the scenes and from behind bars. Vito Genovese had been the acting boss but fled to Naples, Italy, to avoid a murder indictment in New York. Costello became one of the most influential and powerful mob bosses that ever lived.

Costello was a close friend and partner of Vito R, my father's goombah and mentor. Vito was also close with another of Luciano and Costello's close friends and associates, Albert "The Mad Hatter" Anastasia. Anastasia was also born in my father's paese of Calabria, Italy. Anastasia was the boss of the Gambino crime family through most of the 1950's. He became one of the most ruthless and feared Mafia bosses in the history of the Mob. He would be gunned down while he sat in a barber chair in a Manhattan barber shop in 1957.

My father as a young man was connected with each of these powerful Mob bosses. These men — Luciano, Costello, Anastasia, Vito R — were the Gods of the Italian Mafia in the day.

I've been privy to information and heard some incredible stories from my father, and others, throughout my life. A conversation my father had with Anastasia one Christmas eve always stands out in my mind. As does a meeting with Costello.

Then there are the stories, information, and facts that can only be taken to the grave for obvious reasons.

Many are not aware of the low-key meetings that took place at the Chalet restaurant on Mineral Spring Ave. in North Providence, Rhode Island. My father part of and sitting in on many of those meetings. This was one of the main gathering spots for top mobsters back in the day. One story that I am comfortable sharing and that not many are probably aware of; Vito R was a made member of the Genovese Crime Family. His connections and alliance with Costello, Luciano, Anastasia, and others was not well known to many, but to those who truly ruled the roost. During the 1940's, Vito established strong relationships and bonds for Raymond Patriarca Sr. of Rhode Island with the Genovese Crime Family of New York. Through Vito R, Raymond Patriarca Sr. would be put in place and become head of the New England Mob/Patriarca Crime Family in the early 1950's.

Vito, however, called the shots from behind the scenes for many years of Patriarca's rule of the New England Crime Family.

There was a shifting in power and areas of operation from New York throughout New England with the death of Anastasia in 1957. However, Vito was and remained one of the most powerful and low-key mobster in New England for decades. Most didn't know this as he was an old school, old-timer who kept a low profile. These are facts not known to many, including law enforcement and many low-level mobsters that were operating in Rhode Island. This is how the old school mobsters operated. Low-key, off the radar as much as possible, calling the shots and pulling the strings from behind the scenes.

Vito was very ill and hooked up to a dialysis machine, his kidneys failing the last couple years of his life. My father was rather despondent during Vito's sickness and was beside himself with grief for some time when Vito finally passed in 1976. My father loved him as a father and, I know, would have taken his place and died for him in a second if that was possible. They were both old school. Both from a time and place when loyalty, honor, respect, and your word meant something. My father still speaks of him often. He was the last of the Mohicans. He was *family*. He was loved. He is missed.

Most of my father's era friends had passed on when I had spoken to him in 1992 about the entertainment connections. There were still a couple old-timer, close friends living who still had these strong connections and pull within the entertainment business. One of the two was an old school mobster, *Silvio S.* Unfortunately for me, he was currently serving a lengthy prison term. My father said to me, *"Everybody's gone. Dead or in jail. If this was twenty years ago, Silvio would pick up the phone and in five minutes you'd be taken care of. You'd be the new executive in there."*

The other was *Adamo C*, a close friend of Silvio's and a lifelong family friend of ours. Adamo had one of the most powerful positions in any North American Union. He was considered the "*Godfather*" of that particular union. He headed the organization and had strong and wide connections and influence on both sides of the fence.

Adamo came a long way from the streets of the North End. Like my father, he dropped out of school in the ninth grade and came up on Charles St.

Adamo's son, *Tino*, was a partner in the law firm of one of my father's closest and dearest friends, *Aldo L.*

Aldo was a generation younger than my father. My father grew up in the North End with Aldo, Aldo's father and uncles, Adamo, and many other connected and made guys who came up from the streets of the North End.

My father would later help Aldo, and others, get elected to political office in Rhode Island and other states.

Aldo passed in 2010. My father, who is not an emotional man, was distraught. I've only seen him this way a few times during his lifetime. When his mother — my grandma M — passed, and when Vito R passed. He speaks of Aldo and the good old days often. A time when men were men and friendship, honor, respect, and loyalty truly meant something.

My father contacted Adamo and explained my situation; I was a lyricist/songwriter and was looking for a connection within the music industry in California. I made it clear I wasn't looking for a job as a lyricist or songwriting — I had already passed on that work for hire opportunity a few years back — but was more interested in getting my foot in the door and perhaps working for a music industry executive as a gofer to learn the business from the ground up, rub elbows with music industry people, and make my own connections and way from there.

My father and I went to speak with Adamo at his office (in Providence). He had retired from his union position a few years earlier but still maintained an office within his son's law firm. I told him what I was looking for. He said to give him a couple weeks and come back to his office. We did. He was making progress but wanted to make sure I got something solid with someone he knew personally and trusted.

Trust was very important — especially during the time frame of the late 1980's through the mid-1990's. One of the problems during this period of time was that everyone was being watched, wiretapped, and/or under indictment(s) for various "criminal activity", much of which to do with labor racketeering. The Mob and its associates controlling and/or having a major influence in the labor unions as well as the music industry. Lots of people were "flipping" — wearing wires and ratting out others to save themselves from prison time. No one wanted to talk on phones, making progress a bit more time consuming and difficult.

Go back in time some six decades to the 1940's. There was a guy named Frank Sinatra. Much of Sinatra's success — his being signed to record labels, getting parts in movies, headlining Vegas shows — was directly related to his connections with the Mob and top mobsters. Without those connections, regardless of his talent, he may never have been as popular as he was. He may never have been one of the best-selling artists of all time!

Connections are needed sometimes in life. If you have them, most will use them to open a door. Once the door is opened and the introduction is made, it is up to the person to perform. Frank Sinatra did just that. I could have, too. But, once again, a break wasn't in the deck of cursed cards I'd been dealt during my life.

Adamo was ailing and had been suffering with the beginning stages of dementia. He took a turn for the worse and died shortly after he began to make some calls and moves on my behalf.

Tino contacted my father to let us know that Adamo has passed.

He told us that when he went to Adamo's office, all of Adamo's notes about me and the contacts and progress he was making was sitting front row, top of his desk. It had been his number one priority.

Adamo was another last of the Mohicans, old schooler. Classy, kind, and caring. From a generation and time long gone.

This would have been a once-in-a-lifetime game-changer for me. For my life. Once again, as my luck would have it, as soon as I got to the threshold, crawling on my hands and knees as always, the door was slammed shut in my face. Another cruel tease, another slap in the face that would become common in my life.

My entire life, I couldn't catch a break if it landed in my lap.

This could have been — would have been — *the break*, the chance I needed to find that peace in my soul, that meaning in my life, that happiness in my heart.

Yet again, normal wasn't in the cards for me. A day late and a dollar short all over again. And, this time, bad luck — this *curse* as I've seen it and lived with my entire life — would rip my heart from my chest and incinerate my dream.

In addition to the never-ending depression and anxiety, I was now completely frustrated with following this dream — my heart — and truly and deeply disgusted with life itself.

Why could I never catch a break? I would think over and over in my mind, *just once in my life I'd like to catch a break ...a real break. If only I'd been born back in the day.*

It was time to finally throw in the towel. My last card didn't pay off. I wasn't getting any younger and I wasn't getting anywhere chasing my heart's desire — my true love — working and creating within the music industry.

Being on top of the FLEI hire list got me nowhere. Time to throw in that towel, too, and focus on the (new) game plan of getting to my second dream of becoming a DEA agent. I would now dedicate my total but divided and mutilated attention to this endeavor. It was time to make my move towards that goal. I would first become a state trooper with the Florida Highway Patrol as I'd discussed with some law enforcement contacts prior and had thought through for some time.

As was the case when returning for my final two years of college, I had the game-plan in order, all moves written down, step by step.

14

It was 1993 as I began to execute the plan of becoming a state trooper with the Florida Highway Patrol. My depression was at its highest level ever as I had to leave another love behind. First being K at the end of my sophomore year of college and now having to give up a part of my soul — my songwriting and the dream of working and creating within the music industry.

Seems there is no possibility of light entering this darkness.

Granted, I have my second dream coming into play now, the game-plan in order and, ready or not, I'm moving forward. However, I am not completely focused as I'm grieving the loss of everything that could have finally made my soul feel alive.

All this additional darkness and pain while I am now beginning the application process with the Florida Highway Patrol. That process began with my contacting FHP and requesting a State of Florida employment application. This was the summer of 1993. I was shooting to be included in the next FHP academy taking place in the fall of 1994, well over a year down the road and plenty of time to complete the testing process.

Once the application was received, filled out, and returned, this first step in that process — and the waiting game — had now begun.

I had been told by several different people affiliated with the Florida Highway Patrol that the entire testing process would take between six months to one year. During the process, I wouldn't know if I was moving on to the next phase of testing until I was contacted (in the beginning by mail) and advised of the next step.

I found myself even more anxious than usual and frequenting the mailbox all too often! The waiting — not knowing — between the phases of the application process was tough.

I received a letter a month or so later congratulating me on successfully completing the first step in the process. I was given a time and date for the next phase of testing; the written exam. It would take place within the next two months in south Florida. There was also a lengthy supplemental application I received that needed to be completed and taken with me to the next phase of testing along with copies of various documents including my birth certificate and social security information.

I would fly down and stay at my parent's south Florida condo —

where my brother just so happened to *still* be living — for the next phase of testing. My parents would also go down for a few months during the winter. My father would usually stay a bit longer. My mother never cared too much for Florida or the hot weather and looked forward to returning to Rhode Island sooner rather than later.

I arrived a week prior to the exam. I hung out with my brother a bit while awaiting the testing day. We mostly got along but my guard was up at all times. I always felt a very disturbing, cold bitterness from him. I don't know if he was jealous that I accomplished a few things in my life or maybe the fact that I never drank alcohol or took drugs. Possibly he thought that I felt I was better than him. I really don't know. What I do know is when I'm getting bad vibes from someone. That was *always* the case. Sometimes he said things — other times he did things — that proved my intuition was correct. Either way, I had business to take care of. That is the only reason I was there, and temporarily.

I completed this phase of the testing process and headed back to Rhode Island — and waited.

I received a letter a couple months later congratulating me on successfully completing the testing to date. There was a time and date for the next phase of testing; the polygraph test. It would take place in one of the FHP substations in Miami over the next couple of months. Once again, I would fly down to Florida and stay in my parents' condo. My brother was always told in advance whenever I was going down. He knew the reason and, instead of being happy for me and supportive, I always felt that sense of ill will and his not wanting me there. This from the very person who pretty much single-handedly destroyed my emotional well-being beginning at the age of five and ruined any chance of a normal life I would ever have. To this day, unless he reads this book someday, he really has no idea that his choices in life, his actions and his lifestyle, are what caused the bulk of the trauma that triggered the disorders which shattered over forty years of his younger brother's life. And the worst from him was yet to come.

I arrived again about a week in advance of this testing phase. Showed up for the exam and flew back to Rhode Island — and waited.

I received a letter a month or so later congratulating me on passing the polygraph exam. There was a time and date for the next phase of testing; the psychological and physical exams.

As was the routine now, I flew down to south Florida about a week in advance, would show up for the scheduled testing, fly back to Rhode Island, and wait.

This time I got a call from an FHP background investigator who congratulated me on successfully passing all phases of the testing to that point. He asked me lots of questions and sent more forms and applications to fill out for the next phase of testing; the background investigation.

He would be handling my application from this point forward.

The background investigation in Rhode Island would be done by the Rhode Island State Police.

Over the next several months, I would hear from many people — former employers, friends, relatives, neighbors — who would tell me that they were contacted, by phone or in person, by the Rhode Island State Police who were asking a lot of questions about me. The local portion of the background investigation was in full swing. This portion of the application process would go on for several months.

I had spoken to the FHP background investigator who was handling my background investigation and application in general. He assured me that I would be in the fall 1994 academy if I passed the background investigation portion of the application process. There was still nearly half a year remaining before the academy, so I felt pretty confident.

Couple months go by and I hear nothing. I called the FHP background investigator. He noted that everything was going fine and he would be in touch shortly. Couple more months go by and I call the background investigator again.

He notes that I passed the background investigation portion of the testing process but he missed the deadline to submit my application for the final interview, which was taking place that week. I was not on the list to be interviewed for the upcoming FHP academy.

This was my first encounter with incompetence within FHP. It wouldn't be my last.

This is a recruiter who bungled and botched his sole responsibility. He actually admitted this to me! He said, verbatim, "*I dropped the ball on this one.*"

He missed the deadline with my application for the final interview and the previous phase had been completed months ago! I had passed the background investigation portion and my application sat in limbo when my name was supposed to be added to the list for the final interview and list for the upcoming 2004 academy.

Because of this recruiter's incompetence, I wasn't included in the final interview portion of the testing phase and missed my shot at the 2004 FHP academy.

I would now have to wait another year for the next FHP Academy of fall 1995.

In the meantime, I would have to re-test certain portions of the application process all over again. Those particular test results were only valid for one year.

Here we go again! More waiting, more anxiety, more bad luck.

It is now closing in on the end of 2004. I had started the FHP application process well over a year ago. the 2004 academy is in progress. I would now have to retake the polygraph, psychological, and medical portions of the exam. I was going through the testing process once again with the same background investigator that flubbed my application the first time around. Just great!

I was scheduled to take the polygraph several months down the road, the spring of 1995. My mother suggested that I might be better off staying in Florida at their condo (with my brother) the six months or so leading up to the next academy I was hoping to be a part of — and not having to fly back and forth several more times. It was getting quite costly for me with all the trips back and forth to Florida. I decided at this time it probably would be best that I move down to south Florida for the last portion of my *retesting* leading up to the Fall 2005 academy.

My parents and I spoke to my brother and let him know that I had a few more phases of the testing to retake and I would be staying at the condo until the beginning of the Fall 2005 academy. He said that was fine.

He had been living in my parents' condo for the past eight years or so. My parent's way of helping him to get back on his feet. They — especially my mother — had been helping him to get back on his feet for the past thirty years! And my mother being emotionally battered every step of that three-decades-long ordeal.

If for some reason I wasn't included in that 2005 academy, I didn't plan on sticking around any longer. I would probably apply to another department, but definitely wouldn't be staying in the condo with my brother.

I moved down to the condo a few weeks prior to my polygraph

exam. From the get-go, the tension could be cut with a knife. My brother's bitter attitude towards me was more obvious than ever before. From the minute I got there, I would begin hearing, "*How long are you staying?*" It was clear that he didn't want me there.

I told him before I got there and again and again, very clearly, the exact date of the fall 2005 academy and I that had a few more phases of the testing process over the next few months. However, regardless of what happened, I would not be there beyond that point.

I hadn't been there a week when one night he started again with the *how long are you going to be here* crap. I was eating at the kitchen table. He was sitting in the living room watching TV. I told him we needed to have a serious talk. I began to explain to him my plans once again. He chimed in and said, "*I don't want you here that long.*" I started to get rather aggravated and told him that first of all this was already discussed and agreed to before I came down to the condo. Secondly, he didn't own the condo, he and I were guests of our parents. He turned beet red and the veins in his forehead began to bulge. He started screaming at the top of his lungs, "*This is my fuckin' condo, I want you out!*" I told him again, the condo belonged to his mother and father. If anything happened to our parents, he owned one third of it, his brother and sister the remaining portion. He started shouting about the fact that his name was on the title with our father. I told him what he already knew and agreed to at the time he moved in to the condo; our mother wanted his name on the condo title with my father so he could establish his credit back by showing he "owned" property. He knew the arrangement. No one gave him a condo or fifty percent of the condo. Once again, my mother was trying to help him get established and on his feet. He had been taking advantage of our parents — especially our mother — ever since I could remember. Worst off, they allowed it to continue every day of every year for decades on end. Our parents owned the condo. Not him, not me, not our sister.

He jumped up from the chair he was sitting in while I sat eating at the kitchen table. He was now yelling so loudly, he was spitting all over the place. A soulless animal chanting over and over, "*I want you out of here. This is my fuckin' condo!*"

He then quickly picked up a chair from the kitchen table and, while screaming, *I'll fuckin' kill you!,* slammed the chair full force over my head.

A million things went through my mind in a split second. Each one went back to my mother. Blood pouring down my face from a gashed-open head wound, I thought; *I can break this motherfucker's neck in two seconds — and he deserves it. My mother gave up half her sanity saving this piece of shit's life while losing focus on her needs and her life in the process. If I hurt or kill this animal, it will destroy my mother, regardless of the situation here.*

A surreal feeling came over me like I've never had before. I felt like I was in some kind of a wicked and crazy dream — a nightmare of the worst kind. This couldn't have just happened! My mind just couldn't compute the betrayal. This goes against everything I believed and was taught from childhood — from my (real) family, my culture, the old schoolers of my parents' day and Father's life, and the streets I grew up on.

It took everything I had to remain calm. As I got up, turned around and looked at him, he was holding the chair above his head and kept screaming, *"I'll fuckin' kill you! Come on, come at me, I'll fuckin' kill you!"*

In addition to knowing what this would do to my mother if I acted on my first instinct to break his neck and shove the chair and his head up his ass, I also knew I was bleeding profusely and my blood pressure could plummet, causing me to pass out — with this nut-bag hovering above me with a chair!

Within a few minutes or so of his trying to kill me and telling me he was going to do just that, he began saying, *"I'm sorry... I'm sorry... I didn't mean it."*

I had both blood and tears pouring down my face. I simply could not believe that my own flesh and blood would betray me — try and kill me!

I have never in my life to that point been so deeply hurt emotionally, so disappointed, so damn angry.

This was the first of five betrayals during my adult life that were truly incomprehensible and devastated me.

I walked out the door to get some distance so I didn't snap and kill this animal. Within a few minutes, two police cruisers pulled up and two officers walked over to me. Someone in the small condo complex called the police when they heard yelling and whatever else they may have heard. One of the officers, looking at the blood pouring from my head, asked me what happened. I told him everything was okay, I tripped and hit my head on the edge of the kitchen counter.

The police officer knew better. He asked if I wanted to press charges. I said nothing.

However, in my head, I was seething. I knew right then I would never trust, respect, or love this "brother" ever again. I couldn't. He didn't deserve my friendship, my respect, my love, my loyalty. He was no longer family to me. In retrospect, he never was. Yet, his betraying me and trying to kill me would be a joke compared to his betraying his own mother and father in the years to come. Until that day, I had never felt such pain, anger, and hatred in my life.

He and the majority of this "immediate family" have been, as I've said before, a greater curse in my life than the hell I've endured since childhood.

I would not agree to do a police report and I refused medical attention, even though the paramedics — EMS arrived about the same time as the police — said I should go to the hospital with them as I needed some stitches to close up the head wound.

The officer said he had to take a report because he showed up at the scene and my injuries were obvious. Regardless of my explanation as to what happened, he said he needed to enter the home and speak with anyone else who may be in there. He went into the house and did just that. The *other person* in the house stated it was an accident and he was sorry. He basically ratted himself out. The officer came back out and asked me once again if I was sure I didn't want to press charges. I reiterated that everything was okay, I tripped and hit my head. He said a report would be filed based on his observations even though I didn't want to press charges or say what really happened.

I packed my car and left that evening. I drove twenty hours straight through to Rhode Island, stopping only a few times to gas up and go to the bathroom. I was dizzy, my head still oozing with blood, and I was severely crushed emotionally from the betrayal.

All this happening and I have a scheduled polygraph re-test coming up in less than two weeks in Miami.

I spoke with my parents when I got back to Rhode Island. They were as shocked as I was regarding what this piece of garbage had done. However, being the most dysfunctional family on the planet, there would be no penalty to pay for his actions other than they would now take his name off the condo's title and sell it within the next couple of years. Instead of punishing him — making him accountable for his actions, which he has never been throughout his life — my mother gave him the cash to purchase his own place. What?!

Adding insult to injury, my sister and everyone else in this deranged immediate family continued to communicate with him as if nothing at all had happened.

I recall overhearing phone conversations with laughter and joking between my brother and sister, niece and nephews within a week of his trying to kill me.

This was absurd! I lost all respect for most within my family at this time. He should have been banished from the family as punishment. Period.

This has always been the problem within my family — there was no hierarchical system or structure. There was no patriarch leading the "family" and calling the shots, making sure everyone was accountable for their actions. There was no setting and enforcing of boundaries. Making sure that no one disrespected another family member and, if so, consequences resulting.

My father's life was the streets and that life was his other family. However, he had no idea how to manage and control his own biological family.

I can say with one hundred percent certainty and beyond any reasonable doubt that if I had a son who did to his brother what this animal did to me, he would have been in a body cast for the next six months, and when released from the hospital, tossed out in the street to fend for himself.

The greatest damage you can do to any unit — a family, an organization, a military unit, a system, a country — is to allow betrayal and disrespect to go unpunished, to forgo accountability and consequences for a member's unacceptable actions or breaking of the rules. It weakens and eventually will destroy that unit.

My mother would say now and again over the years in trying to make sense of this situation that my brother has always been jealous of me because I got all the attention. Again, I say, *what*?! His addiction sucked every bit of oxygen from within our home during my childhood. All the attention was on him and saving his life by enabling him. I was gasping for air throughout my childhood. Trying desperately to survive the emotional devastation that began at the age of five and later became the master that pulled the strings of and controlled my entire life right into hell. No one even knew I existed — or what his addictions were doing and did to me and my life. His selfish, ruthless, and violent behavior — and being allowed to continue year after year with no consequences or punishment — were a major contributing factor that destroyed my childhood. His actions and addictions were the primary catalyst that caused the trauma and disorders that stole the *normal* from my entire life.

Twist the knife yet again, years later, with this chair incident. He physically — and literally — tried to kill me. There is no greater betrayal. The Latin phrase *"Et tu, Brute?"* from William Shakespeare's play, *Julius Caesar,* says it best.

I returned to south Florida within a week and rented a place. My parents owned a condo and I was forced to find a place to live and pay rent for several months while completing the re-testing process with FHP.

Once again, my father — in particular, being the head of the household, the patriarch — overlooking and covering up a serious problem within our family that needed to be addressed and dealt with; there were never consequences for my brother's opprobrious conduct and destructive behavior, just more enabling and looking the other way.

🦋 🦋 🦋 🦋

My mother forfeited her entire life babysitting her oldest son
as well as her husband. Crying and praying... crying and praying.
From the sidelines, I watched, endured, and suffered with
her, from childhood and consistently throughout my entire life.

🦋 🦋 🦋 🦋

My brother was never made to accept an ounce of responsibility for his actions. In retrospect, neither was his daughter, my sister or her children.

As had been the case within my family as far back as I can remember, dysfunction at its finest along with codependent ways of thinking, feeling, and behaving would prevail. My mother and I always trapped in this unreal and sickening atmosphere surrounded by what always seemed to be the enemy — and later in life proved to be just that.

My mother and I were cut from a whole different cloth than these people. I've asked myself for years, *where did these others come from*?!

Needless to say, in addition to the disorders that had controlled and destroyed my life up until this point, this newly added trauma — blood-betrayal — weighed heavy on my mind and created a different kind of pain and anger I could never begin to explain. This not only ramping up my PTSD, depression, and anxiety to horrendous new levels, but also causing a new and additional round of trauma (PTSD) I certainly didn't need in my life. All this while awaiting the re-test of the polygraph in less than a week and looking to attend a state law enforcement training academy in less than six months.

I arrived at my re-test for the polygraph in south Miami. Same Lieutenant (Lt.) that administered the test the first time around would be re-testing me again this day. Prior to the poly, I had to fill out a few forms and answer some questions. Then I was hooked up to the machine.

The Lt. asked me if anything had changed since my last polygraph of a year-plus ago. I may not have said anything, as I don't believe the incident with my brother was what he meant by "any changes since the last polygraph", but I knew there was a report taken and this may have gotten back to FHP somehow. There's no avoiding or lying on a polygraph test. I had to lay it all on the table and let him decide. I told him my brother tried to kill me a couple weeks earlier by hitting me over the head with a chair. The look on the Lt.'s face has stayed with me to this day. It was a combination of pure shock and deep sympathy rolled into one. I wasn't sure which of us was going to shed a tear first, but it was me.

The additional pain I had to endure from the outright betrayal of my brother had increased my PTSD and depression tenfold. He was pretty much single-handedly responsible for destroying my emotional well-being from childhood and creating the PTSD and other disorders that decimated my adulthood.

His betrayal — trying to kill me — is one of the worst blows and some of the deepest pain and sorrow I've ever had to endure in my life to that point in time. It seems as if this person won't stop trying to destroy me until I am no longer breathing. What did I ever do to deserve this in my life? What did my mother ever do to deserve this type of son and immediate family in her life?

The Lt. giving the polygraph was a compassionate guy. He looked me deep in the eyes and said, "*You need to stay away from him. What he did is far from a normal reaction. It seems to me he's psychologically defective and can't control his rage. Don't give him another chance to hurt you or pull you down to his level. You don't need that or him in your life.*"

Words of wisdom from someone I knew all of a few hours.

I received a call about a month later from my FHP background investigator. I passed the polygraph for a second time. I was scheduled to take the psychological and medical portions once again.

I re-took both the psychological and medical exam a couple months later.

I was soon thereafter contacted by the background investigator who notified me that I had passed both exams once again. So far, so good.

The completed background investigation by the Rhode Island State Police was still valid so there was no need to redo that portion of the process. My background investigator mentioned that he would just do a quick background check to make sure there were no changes since his last background investigation into certain areas such as my credit standing, driving record, or any possible arrests since the last investigation.

I was contacted once this was completed and, finally, had a date and time for the final step; the oral interview. This would take place towards the end of the summer, a month or so before the start of the fall 1995 recruit class in Tallahassee, FL.

As always, I had been training very intensely. About one month prior to the oral interview, I was doing fifty-yard wind sprints in a vacant, tarred lot. I tore my right hamstring about halfway through one of my sprints, falling face first onto the hard surface. I've had many injuries during my day training and fighting; broken bones, deep gashes and cuts, tears, dislocations, herniations, and just about every other injury possible. This was one painful injury! My hamstring area inflamed and turned a deep black and blue. I couldn't stand or put any pressure on the one leg. What timing! If I get into the academy, I've got a month to recuperate to 100%. It goes without saying, I couldn't put pressure on the one leg for several weeks. I hobbled with crutches to get wherever I needed to go. A doctor visit being one stop a few days post the injury.

As with most injuries I've had during my day, I have found that many surgeons will tell you that surgery is needed when, in fact, you may not need surgery and may have other options. I've been told I needed surgery several times in my life. I have always stayed away from any type of operation. Once again, I was going to do it — heal — my way. Unless and until I cannot move, I truly don't trust anyone cutting me open and rearranging anything inside of me.

Knowing my body, I decided to work on the tear and try and heal it myself as I've done with most all injuries I've had in my lifetime. First and foremost, I needed to stay off the leg for a couple weeks, keeping all pressure off the hamstring.

I had already iced the area pretty much around the clock the first few days, trying to get the swelling down as much as possible. I would use some heat therapy in the weeks that followed. I had the hamstring wrapped tightly with ace bandages for a couple weeks. In between bandaging, I would use my own brand of physical therapy, including low-impact stretching and exercising of the injured area to keep a good blood-flow working, strengthening and healing the injury. The doctor who recommended surgery also prescribed pain and anti-inflammatory meds. I didn't fill either script. I was going to heal this injury as I've done others in the past. It took a good month of consistent therapy on my part, but it all worked out in the end.

I was a bit nervous for some time (including my time at the upcoming academy) whenever I pushed myself with any exercise — running, sprinting, squatting — or training regimen that forced my hamstring to work at capacity. It eventually healed completely and without surgery.

I trained, as always, the evening before and several hours leading up to the oral interview on that day, which took place at a hotel in south Florida. I showed up on my scheduled interview morning to a sea of hundreds of applicants, all of whom had passed the previous portions of the testing process and had an equal chance of getting into the academy — for which there were approx. 120 spots. It would all come down to the oral interview before a panel of FHP top brass. This was the portion of the testing process that created the most anxiety and fear for me. Waiting around for hours on end before I was called for my interview didn't help, either. Everyone in attendance was told it would be a five to ten-minute interview per applicant. I was anxiety-ridden but, strangely enough, when I got in front of the interview panel and began answering my first question, I felt much more comfortable than I ever thought I would be. No doubt, my "medication" was doing its job this time around as it had done the majority of the time across my adult life.

A formal interview became somewhat informal towards the end, as I asked and answered questions outside the scope of the interview. There were smiles, laughter, and a few compliments came my way from panel members. As the interview wrapped up, I was told by one of the FHP majors on the panel, with a friendly grin on his face, "*That was the longest interview I've sat through at this phase of testing.*"

I replied, "*My apologies, I was a bit nervous.*" To which he then replied, "*You'd have never known it. Great job.*" I said thank you to him and everyone else on the panel for their time and the opportunity. The interview lasted nearly thirty minutes!

Most times throughout my life I have felt as though what I was feeling inside was being broadcast across my forehead in neon lights. While others may have seen something in me and believed in me, I never believed in myself. Irrespective of any emotional disorders or physical disabilities, progress in life is very difficult — stymied or completely halted — when you possess no self-confidence and don't believe in yourself. No one ever did know the despair and ever-present feelings of worthlessness, the pain and suffering, fear and anxiety that was consuming me from childhood and throughout my life. My mask — along with my outlets — kept it all hidden and me appearing as normal and confident as possible. Necessity being the mother of invention, I created one hell of a mask and persona during my lifetime. That mask, along with my intense training — my primary outlet and medication — allowed me to function and to survive.

I've heard many times during my recovery process and my "coming out" if you will, that I had put on an incredible game face over the decades. No one could fathom what I was telling them about my lifelong pain and suffering — the bleeding, tormented soul and stifled life behind that mask. Those that caught a glimpse of the outside saw a facade. An illusion. I quite often wonder just where I would have gone — what I would have accomplished and the good I could have done in life — if I'd had the opportunity to be normal from childhood.

I received a call about a month later from my FHP background investigator. He said, "*Congratulations. You've been invited to attend the XXth recruit class.*"

I had been waiting a few years to hear those very words. There was an awful lot of stress and pressure to this point. A large portion of that due to the background investigator's dropping the ball the first time around, causing me to miss the '94 academy, forcing re-testing of certain portions of the exam phase all over again, and having to wait around another year and a half for this fall '95 academy.

It would get much more intense once the upcoming academy began in less than a couple of months' time.

It was time to start purchasing the required necessities for the academy.

I ran into a few other recruits at a uniform store in Miami. We talked a bit, exchanged phone numbers, and made a plan to meet up and travel the four hundred-plus mile drive north to the academy in Tallahassee. That day came soon enough.

We all met at a rest area on the turnpike in WPB. There were five cars in this group making the six hour-plus drive up to the academy. Ten of us total. One of the other guys drove up with me.

Half a day later, we would arrive at the hotel we'd made reservations with several weeks prior. We had two rooms and five guys in each room. I, along with a couple other guys, had already paid in advance for the two rooms. The other guys who didn't chip in for the rooms got a free night's stay, but slept on the floor.

Next day arrived and we were only a few miles from the academy with a mandatory morning arrival time. Everyone got ready, dressed in suits and ties, and we were off.

15

I arrived at the academy in the middle of a storm; thunder and a heavy down-pouring outside and a deluge of pain and uneasiness going on inside my head.

From all around me and every angle, from the inside to the outside, I felt as though I was being crushed. Smothered. Drowned.

It should have been a special day in my life. I had accomplished so much to get to this point. However, I was in the absolute deepest of depressions and heightened anxiety ever to this date. My brother's betrayal a few months earlier no doubt a catalyst that exacerbated my egg-shelled emotional state and ever-controlling disorders. And, for some reason, the gates to the academy made it feel as though I was about to enter a prison. I had been emotionally imprisoned for the past couple of decades and now, perhaps, my physical being would be confined as well.

This day would be the fifth and, to this date nearly twenty years later, the last culture shock of my life.

There were FHP brass, staff, and drill instructors standing in the rain and others under a canopy already yelling out commands at the one hundred twenty or so recruits running to enter the academy gates before they were locked. If you didn't get through those gates on time, you would be sent home. The intense pressure and stress was on from the second the recruits arrived.

This is how it began. Dozens upon dozens of recruits dressed in suits and dresses — now on the academy side of that gate — standing in the rain, in formation and at attention, hanging on every word of the instructions being yelled out, often nose to nose, right in your face.

Needless to say, the breaking of the weak links began immediately as we lost a half dozen recruits within the first couple hours of the verbal assault and extended natural shower. One of which, a guy from Miami that drove up with us. He had just completed four years in the army. I remember thinking to myself as he walked off the academy grounds; *I guess he isn't willing to go through this again or at this intensity.*

After a couple hours of the initial introduction to academy life, a command rang out from *Lt. Ace*, primary academy drill instructor and a rather large, intimidating figure. The brim of his trooper hat pulled down tightly and partially hiding his eyes, ordering all recruits to return to their vehicles, get the necessary and required materials, and return back to formation in ten minutes to be instructed on where and with whom you would be living for the next six months.

Of course, as my luck would have it, I had locked my keys in the car during the rush to get into the academy gates a couple hours earlier. Everything I had and needed as well as the guy's that drove up that morning with me were in the car.

We both tried punching and kicking out the windows. No luck. We tried smashing the car windows with whatever we could find laying on the ground, including rocks and tree branches. Still no luck.

I'm the one person who needs to be "invisible", needs to stay out of the spotlight and remain low key. Now, before the academy even begins — the first hours of a six-month academy — I have to stick out like a sore thumb, my tail between my legs, and approach the drill instructor with the news that I cannot get into my vehicle because I accidentally locked the keys in there during the rush to the academy gates a couple hours earlier.

All the while, the other hundred-plus recruits are now being assigned their dorm rooms and roommates and I am in a main office explaining my situation to *Chief Keeno*. I was allowed to call AAA to have someone come out to get my door opened. This is something that could only happen to me! AAA arrived about an hour later — which was the longest hour of my life! I retrieved my items, as well as the other guy's items, from my car, parked it where it was assigned, and returned to join my recruit class, already in progress.

I was having a massive anxiety attack at this time. Luckily it had been raining and I had been standing in it for the past several hours. The sweat pouring from my head and face blended seamlessly into my rain-soaked body and the thoroughly drenched suit I was wearing.

My roommate was recruit *Stretch*. A tall (6'2"-ish), very thin guy around my age. He was a college graduate and a former insurance salesperson prior to applying to FHP. What made this academy a bit different was that FHP was most interested in and actively recruiting college graduates to eventually fill their ranks and, in doing so, was waiving certain physical standards requirements if you possessed a college degree. There was also no age limit. We had several recruits — male and female — in our class in their fifties. Many in this recruit class had college degrees and, while intellectual, lacked the physical conditioning that is usually required within military (units) and law enforcement agencies.

I found it a bit disturbing that certain requirements to get in — and stay in — the academy were waived and/or overlooked for many with college degrees. i.e.: the physical agility exam/testing. We had both men and women in my academy that couldn't complete one pull-up. Bottom line, when you are seriously out of shape, and in a law enforcement/state trooper uniform, it sends a psychological message to the criminal (or anyone else that sizes someone up) that you are not in control and not to be respected. That is a fact on the streets and among criminals in general. I am, and always have been, a firm believer that a person should be in — and be required to remain in — excellent physical condition, weight proportionate to height, and able to perform physically at a certain level if going into a law enforcement training academy, graduating from that academy, and becoming a law enforcement officer. These standards should not be lowered or waived because someone has a college degree. These standards were lowered to allow many recruits with college degrees the ability to get into and to graduate from my FHP training academy. There were plenty of recruits that were, and quite obviously, extremely overweight and out of shape and would not — should not — have gotten as far as the academy to begin with. This was proven from the minute the academy began — literally from the moment we walked through those gates — and all recruits were doing (many attempting) hundreds of pushups, sit-ups, jumping jacks and much more, being pushed to the edge emotionally and physically.

This intense physical portion of the academy throughout the six months was paradise to me. It was a small and quick fix of medication handed to me on a silver platter. Unbeknownst to anyone else, of course. For many, it was their breaking point. We would begin losing recruits within the first hours and throughout the six-month training academy due to the vigorous physical activity as well as the higher level that needed to be maintained by each recruit with regards to the academic portion of the academy. There was always at least eight hours per day of classroom teaching — in addition to hands-on training — and constant written exams and physical tests. All recruits had to maintain a passing score of 80% on each test/exam (some exams required 100% in order to pass) or the recruit was shown the door and had to leave the academy. We lost recruits due to failing scores on exams beginning with the first test on the day following our arrival up until a couple weeks before graduation. We started off the academy with well over one hundred recruits and graduated with seventy-plus.

The first day continued non-stop into the early morning hours of the next day. Hours upon hours of being subjected to the paramilitary style of the training academy; yelling in your face, learning formation, hours of standing at attention and learning to "make way" for superiors. Pushups, pushups, and more pushups. Recruits puking, some passing out, others being broken and shown the door.

Just when you thought you'd get an hour of sleep, into your room come drill instructors pulling you out of bed, having you re-make your bed properly and, yes, more pushups.

The rooms were inspected daily and should that bed not be made properly, there was hell to pay. Your appearance and uniform was inspected and studied each morning at formation and throughout the day. There had better be no wrinkles. The creases in your uniform needed to be sharp enough to cut your finger. Your shoes polished to perfection. Any brass on your uniform had better see a clear reflection as if it were a mirror or it wasn't going to be pretty for the recruit or the rest of the unit — as everyone payed, each and every day, for the slacking of the weaker link(s).

The first month was the absolute worst for me of the entire six-month academy. During this time, recruits had no privileges — hadn't paid their dues — and we had to stay at the academy during weekends. We hadn't earned the privilege to use the academy gym or do anything else during this time. It was a 24/7 lockdown that month.

Every day of the academy for the next six months would begin at 5:00 a.m. and the days usually didn't end until around 7:00 p.m. It was lights out by 10:00 p.m., no exceptions. Twelve hour days of non-stop classroom teachings, training, drilling, and stress for six months.

I was unable to escape and train when and how I needed. That first month I wasn't able to get my hands on nutritious, quality food and supplements to store in my room's locker so that I could avoid the mostly disgusting, usually greasy, safe-bet to say "unhealthy slop" that was the cafeteria's breakfast, lunch, and dinner. I felt like a drug addict that was sentenced to prison and forced to go through withdrawal — cold turkey — as I had no "medication" as I'd known it the past twenty years prior to this lockdown phase of the academy.

I was unable to engage in my own routine and system of intense training to get my serotonin and norepinephrine levels up and even my keel.

Aside from the less than adequate (as it pertained to my personal needs) and behind the times PT portion of the academy, and my own one-hour training regimen in my room every morning at 3:00 a.m. and prior to the 5:00 a.m. recruit class PT, I was unable to do my thing, so to speak.

The academy staff strongly emphasized teamwork, attention to detail, and discipline. The latter two a way of life for me. Discipline I had in abundance. Each day was a process of building a recruit's character, maturity, self-confidence, and leadership skills while weeding out and breaking the weak links. If I hadn't been emotionally imprisoned and under the control of PTSD, depression, and anxiety my entire life, perhaps I would have been able to find and build my self-confidence through the experiences of this academy. That wasn't the case. I was too far gone to feel confidence about any part of me or my life, regardless of what I would accomplish, was told or by whom. The other qualities this academy was building in recruits I have always possessed. However, I was unable to put to use as PTSD, depression, anxiety, and isolation kept me from normal interactions most of my life. The academy would not be able to free me of the twenty-year death-grip of these disorders.

We had an academy staff member, *Lt. Rugops*, that drew a picture on the chalkboard the first day of our academy. He wasn't much of an artist, but as he described his drawing, the picture became quite clear; It was a large whale swimming in the ocean. the whale was releasing excrement which landed at the bottom of the ocean. There were objects below the whale excrement. He would tell us many times throughout the academy, "*You are all lower than whale shit right now. You have to earn everything beginning here. You have to earn the right to wear this uniform and to be called a Florida state trooper.*" Everything had to be earned. I'm on board and all about this. That's how it should be in every organization. In life. Pay your dues. Earn your stripes. However, not everyone here was paying their dues. There was favoritism and looking the other way for some recruits.

Lt. Rugops also said, loud and clear, just prior to our graduation in the fifth month of the academy and during our recruit class graduation photo, "*The entire first two rows wouldn't be here years ago. You were all too short. You're lucky.*" I thought to myself; *that's a hell of a thing to say to two rows of recruits who had busted their asses to get to that point in the academy. That was a bit ignorant and disrespectful.* But what do I know. Lt. Rugops was an older, big and tall guy — an easy 6'3". He was a good old boy with the southern drawl and a dinosaur mentality; opposed to change, whether for the good of the department or the citizens for whom we were being employed to protect and serve. I'd find out soon enough he had plenty of company in this department.

There was a "wall of shame", as I called it, where each recruit that was broken, forced or flunked out of the academy, would have their recruit name badge affixed. The caption above the wall read, "*If you can't run with the big dogs, stay on the porch.*" No recruit ever wanted to know that their name was being affixed to this wall. Nearly half those that showed up that very first day would have their name badge tacked to that wall before the academy graduated six months later.

There were some recruits that should not, in my opinion, have made it through that academy. Some were carried — treated with kid gloves — because of their college degrees. There was also favoritism with some who had family members already employed by or retired from FHP. One recruit — though he was a really nice guy and I liked him — should not have been able to continue through the academy. As others in his very situation — injuries that would sideline them for more than a couple of weeks — were shown the door. He injured his foot the first few weeks of PT and did not participate from that day forward in any morning PT that took place. That PT beginning each morning at 5:00 a.m. Cardio and endurance training including miles upon miles of running mixed with various stretching, strength, and overall conditioning exercises. We'd run and train in the rain, snow, and below freezing temperatures. I never knew it got that cold or even snowed in Tallahassee, Florida!

There was the natural, testosterone-laced competition between some of the guys, myself included. I was a target for some of the younger guys (early twenties) who didn't seem to like the fact that I was older than they were and beating them at every physical challenge. The only challenge during the entire academy that I didn't stand out and shine was achieving the best time in the distance run (several miles). I've never been a distance runner — having short, stocky legs — but was a strong sprinter. Sprinting was my thing when it came to the running phase of the academy and no one could touch me there. One of my favorite parts of the morning miles was the very last quarter mile. Recruits were allowed to break away from the pack and sprint this final quarter mile back to the academy dorm. The advantage of getting there first was getting a shower before everyone else — no waiting in long shower lines — and having a bit more time getting dressed and ready for morning formation and inspection prior to breakfast. I was always the first of a usual three-pack of us back to the dorm, sprinting full-force up three flights of stairs and first into the showers. You had only one minute to shower, as there would be a line of dozens of recruits yelling for you to hurry up so each could get in and get out and prepare for inspection at formation.

The academy was a typhoon of never-ending, 24/7 stress and worry — from the shower to passing daily physical and academic exams to trying to sleep a couple hours each night.

There were many former and active military in the academy. recruit *Zip* was one, and a really nice guy. A big guy who served eight years with the marines. He would say often throughout the academy that it was much tougher than his boot camp. Most others said the same. With this academy, unlike military boot camp, there was the added academic studies and never-ending pressure that was draining. Everyone knew the drill — should you score below 80% on any written exam or fail any test, you were shown the door. That ever-lingering worry is very stressful when added to the paramilitary drilling 24/7 for some six months.

There were also those in the academy who, while showing courage, could not keep up with the majority of the recruit class in running and other cardiovascular and strength training exercises. They would hold the entire class/unit back and, as with any paramilitary based training, the unit would pay for the mistakes or weaknesses of the individual(s) falling behind.

The entire unit would be forced to do additional pushups, sit-ups, extra miles and everything else under the sun until the weak link caught up or broke and left the academy. Some didn't break but should have been shown the door. If any of these recruits — both male and female — were in a fight with a hardened criminal, or any man who could handle himself, on the streets, each would have certainly been overpowered and hurt badly, if not killed. If any of these recruits had to back me up — come to my aid/assist me on the road — I would be in serious trouble if I had to rely on that person's physical ability, endurance, and strength to help me out of a bad situation. And, that did happen as FHP graduated — carried — some recruits who were far from physically fit enough to be called a state trooper and wear the uniform most of us had to earn each and every day with blood, sweat, and tears.

When I finally earned that state trooper uniform and title and hit the road to protect and serve, most times if I needed a routine backup I would ask for the local police department or a deputy from the sheriff's office to back me up. I found that most of the local officers I came in contact with and/or knew in my patrol areas were more on the ball and in better physical condition than most I was working with at FHP. As unfortunate as that was for me and for FHP, if my health or life depended on my backup, I needed to feel comfortable and certain that my backup could handle the situation. I always felt more at ease with the local police department backup as I knew most of those local officers within my patrol area were on top of their game and had my back.

Our morning PT portion of the academy was flawed, to say the least. Many of the stretching and conditioning exercises were antiquated and did more harm than good in my opinion. To make matters worse, soon after the academy began, staff would call on individual recruits to "lead" the exercise program (portion that morning) as well as lead the class in other areas throughout the day. This was, in my opinion, a mistake with regards to the recruit's leading the exercise program. Many of these recruits who were called upon to lead the class during our morning PT knew very little — if anything — about proper exercise form and exercise grouping (putting exercises together, performed one after another, without resting, to create a cardio and conditioning program). The class more often than not was doing exercises back to back (grouped) that were doing more harm than good to the body — twisting and putting the body in unnatural positions while putting undue pressure on joints instead of strengthening the muscles. I know when an exercise and/or grouping does more harm than good. I may not have had any confidence in myself throughout my life or gave myself any credit (when credit was due), but fact being fact, truth being told, I was also, without doubt, more knowledgeable of proper exercise, form, and training, and in better shape physically, than any of the recruits (and staff) in my class. Don't get me wrong, there were some male and female recruits and staff in the academy that were in excellent shape, just not at my level of fitness and training. Proper and intense cardio, flexibility, and strength training had been my life for some 20-plus years. It was necessary for my very survival. I knew the movements and placing of them in the grouping were wrong. I felt it, literally, all along. Exercises forcing improper range of motion and improper stress on joints — and then grouped together — did more harm than good for and to my body (and most likely everyone else's). However, I was in a paramilitary training academy and could not say anything, stop exercising, or slack regardless.

I would eventually suffer the consequences of these antiquated exercises being unsoundly grouped together by inexperienced, deer-in-the-headlights recruits leading the class.

The academy staff would constantly say to us, "*when you leave here you will be in the best shape of your life.*" That may have been so for some who never exercised at all prior to the academy. I left that academy in the worst physical shape and condition of my life! However, even at my lowest point of physical fitness during this six months, I was able to accomplish the academy record for pushups, sit-ups, and the stretch and reach for men. I performed one hundred twenty strict pushups in sixty seconds. Sixty-seven strict sit-ups in sixty seconds. I also had the greatest distance for stretch and reach for male recruits.

It's not possible — whether properly exercising or not — to be in "the best shape of your life" and healthy if you're not eating nutritious, quality food. The food being served in the academy was not conducive to a healthy lifestyle. It was mostly fried, greasy, and very unhealthy. I had no choice the first month. Once we earned "privileges" to move about and I was able to get to the market, I purchased cans upon cans of albacore tuna and sockeye salmon that I stocked in my room's locker. Not something I would normally focus on as the core of my daily diet, but it was leaps and bounds healthier than the crap being served in the cafeteria. My mother would also send me care packages every couple of weeks and I had quality protein supplements and vitamins shipped to me monthly. I also had my own, homemade variety of MRE's (Meal, Ready-to-Eat).

After that first month when I was able to get my hands on halfway decent food, I very seldom would eat anything from the cafeteria — especially after the food poisoning incident; nearly everyone in the academy — including staff — was affected. The common denominator was traced backed to the cafeteria and its food that day. Most everyone began vomiting and had diarrhea beginning that night and lasting for several days. Many recruits and some staff wound up at the hospital, dehydrated and sick as dogs. Some had to be hooked up to IV's. It was that bad. I vomited my brains out that evening and was totally drained. I flooded my body with fresh water to rehydrate and swore I'd never eat in that cafeteria again if I could avoid it. The kitchen was truly filthy and the food was just as bad. How no one died from food poisoning during that incident was a miracle itself.

Thanksgiving was the first time recruits were allowed to leave the academy aside from the couple weekends we had finally earned prior. We had strict instructions that we needed to be back at the academy — in uniform and at formation — at 8:00 p.m. that coming Sunday evening. Anyone who arrived after that deadline would be locked out and expelled from the academy.

The one portion of this academy that was most grueling to me was the constant pressure of knowing you would be shown the door if you fell below the minimum required 80% score on written exams or other daily tests as well as the added stress and pressure of leaving the academy and something possibly happening that would prevent you from returning at the required deadline time. I watched dozens of recruits throughout the academy miss the minimum required score on written and other exams as well as missing other deadlines and failing to follow directions. Each was shown the door. That is an awful lot of stress and pressure, every minute of every day, for some six months. Needless to say, knowing how bad my luck had been most of my life, I wasn't about to take a chance on flying back to Rhode Island during the winter for a couple days to celebrate Thanksgiving and getting my return flight delayed or postponed due to a snow storm. Not to mention, my depression was at its deepest and worst ever during this academy. I didn't need anything else to go wrong.

I decided to stay at the academy during the few days of Thanksgiving break. I told many of the recruits my plans and the reasons for my decision. They thought I was crazy not to get out of that place when I could.

Several of the recruits invited me to join their families — within Florida — for Thanksgiving dinner. I thanked them, but declined.

I spoke with the chief and explained my reasons for staying at the academy during this short break; I didn't want to miss the return deadline should a plane be delayed or postponed by a snow storm in New England. The chief and the rest of the staff were surprised that I was going to remain at the academy — alone — during this time.

However, they respected my decision not to take that chance. They knew that graduating from this academy was too important to me. No one knew that I had been in isolation and alone most of my life. I was used to it. It was my "normal".

I did remain at the academy — completely alone — for about four days. I trained like an animal day and night, ate properly and, as my life had been going for too many years, sunk deeper into that depression. I was truly at my lowest point emotionally to date. Of all places to be in this condition. My PTSD, depression, and anxiety pretty much off the charts. My luck couldn't have been worse — or could it?

Once we earned the privilege of using the academy gym after that first month, I would train every chance I got through the weekends and whenever we had down time and I was permitted to use the gym. Being in the deepest and darkest of depressions to date, I would go for broke whenever training. I would train very heavy with the weights and get into a zone to temporarily quell the pain that never left my mind. I was holding firm at a very muscular 150 lbs. and was routinely benching to 300 lbs., 100 lb. dumbbell presses, and squatting as heavy as possible while avoiding going overboard so I didn't hinder my distance running each morning. I was shadow boxing intensely and hitting striking pads — Muay Thai style, fists, elbows, knees, feet — for hours on end. It was balls to the wall and then some whenever training. I was looking to add extra endorphins to a mind and soul begging for its medicine. This was the only way I could ever subdue the pain and anxiety and keep my mask and body armor impenetrable. I needed that more than ever before during these most intense six months. Being in the worst physical shape of my life due to the antiquated and improper PT exercise regimen, and the greasy cafeteria slop I had been eating several times a day that first month or so, didn't help the situation any.

We were able to leave the academy for a few more days come Christmas. Once again, I decided to remain at the academy and not chance having my plane delayed or postponed and not making it back to the academy by the deadline time.

There was no way I was going to take that chance and jeopardize my short range goal of graduating this academy and becoming a state trooper — my stepping-stone to moving towards my ultimate goal of DEA a year or so out.

This time around, there were a few of us that remained at the academy during the Christmas break. We all volunteered a couple days

— along with some marines — at a food shelter and also handed out toys to some of the kids in the area. It was a good feeling helping out in this way during Christmastime and seeing the smiles on the kids' faces. It brought a little joy to my soul, which was always becoming more burdened by my disorders and weighing heavier with pain with each passing day.

The academy was definitely less dreary — less prison-like — during this break compared to the Thanksgiving break as I had some company this time around. It kept my mind a bit occupied and off the constant thinking and worrying that was all too common in my world.

There were a bunch of guys in the academy — mostly on my floor of the dorm — that hung out together. During weekends, we'd all try to relax a bit; go to dinner, hit the mall, training and studying together was common. Most of these guys were younger than me. A few in their very early twenties. A couple my age and older.

I was closest throughout the academy with *Dante*. He was a few years older than me, a husband, father, and an EMT from the Bronx, NY. A real nice guy. He would get very homesick about three-plus months in and decide he was going to leave. I tried to convince him to at least take the Florida Officer Certification Exam which was coming up for our recruit class in a few weeks. If he passed this exam and still decided to leave the academy and FHP, he could get on another department in the future with the certification.

Word got around that he was planning on leaving. Lt. Ace, *Captain Corki*, and Chief Keeno himself, knowing that Dante and I were close, approached me and asked me to talk some sense into him. I had already tried that but would try again, to no avail. Dante was hell-bent on leaving the next day and did just that. I guess he was broken in another way — homesick — and gave up. He swore up and down that it was the right decision, that he had thought it through and wanted to leave and be with his family back home.

I remember watching his car leaving the academy grounds. It was a sad day. He was a class act guy.

I gathered together some academy pictures from Christmas and other events (when they became available) that he never got the chance to see and sent them to him a month or so after graduation.

He called to thank me and tell me his leaving the academy was the biggest mistake of his life. I told him that he had to do what he had to do at the time, for whatever reason made sense to him. I tried in every way I could at the academy to make him see the situation from other angles — especially the fact that he had come so far and there was just the state certification test remaining and less than two months until graduation. He told me that he called academy chief Keeno and asked if he could re-apply to the academy and do it all over again, that he made a serious mistake leaving. Chief Keeno told him that FHP would not allow him to enter the academy again or consider employing him as he "gave up" and left of his own free will.

Like everyone else in my life, I wouldn't keep in touch with Dante. I never saw him again after that day I watched his car roll off the academy grounds and head back to his family in the Bronx. My phone number changed a couple times after this phone conversation and I lost his contact info along the way.

My parents left Rhode Island for their south Florida condo after the new year. I hadn't seen them since the prior summer. We'd talk on the academy pay phone whenever I could on weekends. I missed my mother desperately. I always felt if I wasn't around — within a reasonable driving distance — I couldn't protect her. She had been taken advantage of by everyone in her immediate family as far back as I can remember. More so when I wasn't around. She never wavered, though. Always remained a loyal wife, mother, and grandmother. Always putting everyone else before herself. Always there first and foremost for her family and friends. Always giving and giving of herself. Never asking anyone for anything and never receiving much, either, other than pure grief and being shit on from her immediate family.

My parents would make the long drive from south Florida to Tallahassee to see me towards the end of January. They stayed in a hotel in Tallahassee that weekend. I spent as much time with them as possible over the two days.

As soon as I looked at my mother, I noticed immediately the stress and pain heavily embedded on her face. I had only seen that kind of drawn-out, deeply stressed and worried look affixed to my mother's face a few other times during my life. That moment — that image — Pops into my mind every now and again and it still bothers me a great deal to this very day. She has always had her own health issues burdening her and has been under severe stress most of her adult life at the hands of my brother and father and, most recently — the past five-plus years as of this writing — the rest of this demonic, immediate family. Lots of pain and suffering that no mother — no wife — should have had to endure. This time, though, I knew that my brother's betrayal of me and trying to kill me almost a year earlier really affected her in a very bad way. He had once again dug that knife into his mother's soul and twisted it. My mother and father knew how I felt about him — the anger, hurt, and, yes, hatred I had felt for what he had done. I made no bones about it, no attempt to hide it. Maybe I should have, but that's not who I am. I always say what I mean and mean what I say. I never sugarcoat and never lie about my feelings towards someone. My father would always tell me when I was growing up, "*Hug your enemy.*" He knew how I was. I knew what he meant. I guess if I wound up a part of that life, I would have had to do a lot of hugging to survive. I wasn't part of that life and it just wasn't my nature to bullshit anyone, for any reason whatsoever.

My mother would try and bury the hatchet between me and my brother by asking me if it was okay for my brother to attend my upcoming academy graduation. Absolutely not I told her. She understood completely. However, I knew as a mother the last two things that she ever wanted to see in her lifetime were; one of her children die before her — and that is the main reason I didn't break his neck when he tried to kill me — or her own children not speaking to each other. I would, in time, forgive him, and speak to him once again, for my mother's sake. However, I would never love or trust him again — or forget.

When he finally betrayed his parents some years down the line — along with their daughter and grandchildren — I vowed to never speak to him or the rest of these vermin again. I cut the cord. I disowned him and the rest of this parasitic immediate family. True colors had been shown. Money-worshipping, cold-hearted, ungrateful, unconscientious, disrespectful animals they proved to be.

My mother — an angel on this earth — has been crucified by her own immediate family. She has had to endure the pain and suffering of her own children and grandchildren turning their backs on and betraying her. Treating her worse than a case of leprosy. She lived every day knowing and feeling the lack of respect and love from her own blood.

I've said it before and I will say it again and again; having these people as my immediate family has been a greater curse in my life than living each and every minute of the past 40-plus years with the pain and suffering I've had to endure both mentally and physically.

It has always tormented me that my mother has had to put up with and live through such disrespect and pain at the hands of her own immediately family. A curse, no doubt, in both of our lives.

My mother's birthday was around the corner when my parents came up to see me. While I was severely depressed and at my lowest point ever emotionally, and knowing I wouldn't be able to spend time with her on the most important day of the year to me — my mother's birthday — I made sure she enjoyed at least the couple days we had together until my graduation a couple months down the road. Regardless of the circumstances, any time my mother and I spent together was special for the both of us. We always made each other smile and laugh and brought a small piece of joy to each other's heavy hearts.

Defensive Tactics (DT) training began and that was a welcome treat for me. However, there were parts of the training that weren't so enjoyable. Being sprayed in the face with OC (pepper spray) wasn't much fun. It was painful. It felt like my eyes were going to pop out of my head while my face was slowly burning off.

To me, the absolute worst was the forced exposure to CS gas. I remember that night in the open field like it was yesterday. It was like living a nightmare. You can try and hold your breath, but when you finally breathe this crap in, it suffocates you. It creates an immediate panic attack as you feel like you are being crushed alive from the inside with every breath.

I was very familiar with anxiety and panic attacks as I had walked hand in hand with that evil for the past twenty-five years to this point. It was panic on top of panic attack while trying desperately to breathe. Of all the training and exposures within the academy, this is the one required exposure I regret not dodging somehow. And some recruits did just that. I didn't want this stuff in my lungs, seeping into my organs. This stuff is poison and can cause all kinds of long term health problems. The effects of this toxic gas can be horrible. I don't believe we should have been forced into exposure with this particular chemical agent. There were a few recruits who did pull their shirts over their heads and faces and, against direct orders, in the dark of the night, while stepping on and over those who had fallen in front of them as a result of the CS gas exposure, went around the CS cloud we were told to walk directly through.

I was always uncomfortable if the spotlight was on me and I was now getting an awful lot of attention during DT training, especially the physical contact portions of the academy. Being closely watched or not, DT training was the most enjoyable — if that was even possible — part of the academy to me. During this phase, recruits had to wrestle each other and practice and perform moves on one another as well as on striking pads.

There was one instructor, *Tasman (Taz)* — A trooper from Miami — that came up during this phase, as well as the vehicle operations phase, as a volunteer instructor. He was a cool guy and big into martial arts. We hit it off immediately. He would call me *Kickboxer* in front of the entire recruit class and academy staff throughout the whole time he was there as a volunteer instructor. He even invited me to watch a kickboxing match one night on TV with him and a couple other troopers volunteering that week. I accepted, hung out with them and talked martial arts for a couple hours. They kept asking me to demonstrate some moves and flexibility exercises.

Finally, and reluctantly, I did. They said that they were astounded at my speed, control and flexibility. I never had confidence or belief in myself throughout my life. These complimenting words I had heard many times before regarding my abilities and it always gave me a little but much needed boost for my ego and the self-esteem that was on life-support since childhood.

Word got out to the academy staff about my demonstration that evening.

Lt. Ace came to my room one night soon after and asked me what exercise I would recommend he do to get his heartrate up to burn more fat. This was incredible! Lt. Ace having enough confidence in my abilities and knowledge of training to ask me my opinion regarding exercises he could do to get into better shape! Obviously, I was on cloud nine and totally flattered. I showed him a very simple, very low impact way to get the heart rate up while working the upper body at the same time. Quite simply, correct shadow boxing, in front of a mirror for twenty to thirty consistent minutes. I demonstrated both in slow motion and full speed ahead! I showed him a shortened, five-minute shadow boxing workout that I recommended he do to begin with. His first words to me were, "*I could hardly see your hands moving. That was fast. You're damn good!*". I then showed him how to incorporate the lower body into the mix with some simple kicks and flexibility exercises. Lt. Ace just shook his head in amazement. He said, "*Thank you, I'm going to give it a try.*"

I replied, "*You're very welcome, Sir. I hope it does the trick for you.*"

I vividly remember the next day; in the middle of our classroom teachings, Lt. Ace came into the room, as usual, in full trooper uniform and drill Instructor mode, hat tipped low over his eyes, looked at the class from the podium and said, "*DiGrossi*". A bit stunned, I replied, "*Sir, Yes, Sir.*" He then proceeded, "*that exercise routine you showed me the other night (several second pause) ...I tried it last night and I can hardly move today. It got my heart rate way up and got me sweating buckets. That's a great workout. It did the trick.*"

Everyone in the recruit class — including other staff members — just turned around and looked at me. I'm sure I looked like a deer in headlights — stunned and uncomfortable — but this was a rare moment. I was being singled-out and recognized by *the* Lt. Ace, primary drill instructor! I felt both very nervous and very proud at the same time. The latter emotion near extinct in my world.

Lt. Ace was an incredible guy. I had the utmost of respect for him from the moment we met that first day in the rain. We would have a significant, man to man, off the record discussion about FHP, the staff, volunteer instructors, and the academy itself one Sunday afternoon a couple weeks prior to my graduating.

I clearly understood the psychological game of trying to break the recruits. It went on from the moment we arrived at the academy until the very last week, some six months later. I knew this before I entered the academy. Not sure what others were expecting — especially those that broke and left — but this paramilitary training is necessary to weed out weak links that can destroy an organization or entire unit.

Primary drill instructor, Lt. Ace, and *Sgt. Wright*, a short, female drill instructor, did their job — and did it well — and took no pleasure in breaking recruits. They didn't get off on watching recruits squirm. They didn't go outside of the realm of their job — professionalism — and abuse their authority.

There were some incredible, respectable, professional and sincere academy staff members as well as instructors who volunteered for a period of time during certain phases of the academy. Some I admired wholeheartedly, such as Lt. Ace. And then there were some, as in every profession, who were there for the wrong reasons.

There were two troopers in particular who came up to the academy at different times to volunteer. I can only speak for myself regarding my experience(s) and what I had encountered with each of them; one of the troopers, *Nonutz*, was a volunteer from Miami. May have been about my age, give or take a few years. Not sure if I reminded him of someone he didn't like or if maybe he just didn't like the fact that I got a lot of attention for my physical abilities. Either way, he overstepped his boundaries and went too far with his verbal abuse and outright disrespecting me on two different occasions. As a man and someone who grew up on the streets, I can usually read people like a newspaper. This trooper would try desperately to provoke me on two different occasions. For no reason whatsoever, he came up to me, pressed his nose to mine while gritting his teeth, and said, "*You really think you're pretty bad, don't you? You're nothing!*" Normally, a recruit would answer, beginning with *sir*. I chose not to answer him at all. We were alone in the corridor both times he intentionally disrespected me. He waited until I was free of my unit before he approached and confronted me. However, there were a few other recruits in the area who I know saw him do this and probably heard his uncalled for, unprofessional comments. I knew damn well he wasn't trying to push my buttons to see if he could get me to snap or break. This was personal to him for some reason. I also knew that he knew I wouldn't risk being thrown out of the academy by engaging in a back-and-forth or knocking his head off his shoulders, which I no doubt would have done if I wasn't in that academy.

You don't outright disrespect another man — another person — without the possibility of a war breaking out. How I grew up and where I came from, the biggest insult you can bestow on another man is to outright disrespect him. On the streets, a man has only one option when this happens; to avenge his honor and go to war.

I stayed calm, but if he was a mind reader during the two occasions when he intentionally disrespected me, he would have known he picked the wrong person to pick on — training academy or not — and, for no reason whatsoever other than he was a coward and a bully.

I asked around my recruit class about this trooper Nonutz from Miami. I specifically asked a buddy of mine from Miami, Viz, that I drove up to the academy with from south Florida. Viz was from Miami and he had a lot of friends and connections in that city. I also trusted

Viz more than I would anyone else in the academy as I knew he was a bit streetwise and we connected on that level from the get-go. I asked Viz to make a few calls to some of his friends in Miami — both civilians and troopers he knew — and get some information about this trooper who was intentionally busting my balls and outright disrespecting me. Viz knew I was not happy and if I wasn't in that academy, I would have shoved that trooper's head up his ass.

Viz got back to me and let me know that a few of his friends knew this particular trooper. All said he was a good guy. Really?! Obviously, I had met the other side they didn't know.

I told Viz to tell his friends that knew this trooper personally that I didn't appreciate the disrespect and would see him when I was out of the academy and wearing the same uniform.

Strangely enough, word traveled awfully fast and must have gotten back to him as he called me aside a few days later and apologized for being an *asshole*, as he put it.

I replied, without the "sir" as was proper and routine, "*No problem, trooper. We all have bad days.*" I had seen his true colors. I knew looking into his eyes that he knew once I wore the same uniform *he* was going to be the "nothing" and there wasn't much he could do about it — except apologize. He was a coward and bully wearing an LEO uniform.

The second trooper, *Donutz,* that showed those cowardly true colors appeared younger than me, was visibly out of shape, sloppy, his stomach hanging over his belt, had a southern drawl, and would constantly try and provoke me throughout the week he was volunteering at the academy. I would hear, "*Where did you get that accent? You're a New York greaseball, aren't you?*" He would also laugh at me and say, "*Where did you get that haircut? You look like a retard.*" All the while, making sure that no one else was listening or paying attention. It wasn't done in the presence of others or around staff. It wasn't said and done for any reason other than this trooper was a bully and a punk. He most likely was bullied himself throughout his life before the metal trinity — the gun, badge, and handcuffs — artificially bolstered a sense of security and feeling of manhood. He was now going to abuse his authority, push his weight around, and feel like the tough-guy he could never be without that trooper badge adorning the FHP uniform on his back.

He knew I couldn't stick my foot up his ass — as he certainly needed — and he was going to treat me the way that bully in high school treated him. He was nothing more than a weak-minded, bully punk who lacked any and all qualities of a real man and lived and breathed now for the metal-fabricated manhood (MFM) provided by the trooper uniform he wore.

These are the types of LEO's that give the uniform — and the law enforcement profession in general — a bad name. This type of bully and coward wearing an LEO uniform is the primary reason too many people — especially the younger generations — don't like or respect cops (in general).

If he was speaking to me and treating me this way in a law enforcement training academy, you can only imagine how he was abusing his authority on the road. One bad apple *can* ruin the whole bunch — and too often does. This is the kind of LEO you see on the news beating a handcuffed person, shooting someone in the back, and outright abusing their authority like the cowards that they are. I've seen it both as a civilian and as a state trooper. I've witnessed it firsthand from both sides of the fence.

This type of LEO is the weak link that was never removed — or somehow got through — during the law enforcement testing process, the training academy, or while employed as an LEO.

The metal trinity — that symbol of authority — goes to the heads of some in law enforcement. More often than not, those that are weak minded, cowards, and bullies to the core, and, clearly, never had and never will have a real man's bone in their bodies.

They need this metal-fabricated manhood — the authority — to *feel* like a man. However, they will never be real men. Real men have strong minds, compassion, understanding, respect, honor and discipline.

Those that were there for the wrong reasons didn't know (not unlike most during my life) the man behind that mask. No amount of psychological torment or paramilitary training doled out by staff — or cowardly bullying by the few — could compare to the emotional pain and suffering I had lived with each day of my life for the past twenty-five years.

Some of this psychological warfare and the couple instances of outright disrespect and bullying may have irritated me, but this was bagatelle compared to the never-ending pain and suffering I had to endure from childhood as a result of PTSD, depression, anxiety, and bullying. Keeping cool in this fire was a walk in the park compared to hell's inferno I had been crawling through since childhood.

About one month prior to our academy graduation, I heard a Pop and felt a very sharp, severe pain in my neck/cervical spinal area during one of our 5:00 a.m. recruit-lead PT classes. The recruit was blindly leading the class through a grouping of unnatural, antiquated exercises — as had been the case for months.

I had known and felt the negative effects of these unnatural movements and exercises for some time. Now, this method had taken its' toll and had caused a herniation to one of my cervical discs. I didn't say anything, as I have had some rather severe injuries during my day and have always been able to heal rather quickly with proper exercise, nutrition, resting the injured area a bit, and flooding that area with a constant blood flow (by way of massage and light exercise to the injured area). I figured I could do this without saying anything as there was only about a month of the academy remaining.

Next day was a Saturday and our day off. My neck felt much worse this next morning. I hit the academy gym late morning to try and get some blood flow in the area. I was having a very difficult time now moving my neck at all. The pain was one thing I could deal with and get through, not being able to move my neck at all was going to cause a serious problem for me in this academy. I began to do some light shoulder movements to get some blood in the neck/cervical area. I felt the pain increase quickly. I realized immediately that this injury — a spinal injury — was unlike any other injury I had sustained during my life. And I've had and suffered most of them. It was much different than the broken bones, severe gashes, concussions, torn hamstring, ACL injuries, rotator cuff injuries, dislocations, all the sprains, strains and tears I had suffered with in the past and recovered from on my own.

The pain would get worse as the day went on. I would have to go to the hospital that day as I couldn't move my neck or put any pressure on it at all. Forget sleeping for the next few weeks!

I had an MRI done that afternoon at an orthopedic doctor's office that was provided by workers' compensation. My first encounter with the State of Florida's Workers' Compensation System. This disgusting, filthy, rotten and corrupt system would become a nightmare for me in the years to come and part of the second major betrayal of my life. It was determined via MRI that I had herniated a disc in my neck.

I filled out the proper paperwork within the academy as was

required anytime a recruit was injured. My anxiety now multiplied many times over. I began sweating profusely — the combination of fear knowing the severity of the injury and the added and elevated stress was making me dizzy.

My first thought and concern was that I wasn't going to be able to do my thing and train intensely — medicate — for a couple of weeks to quell my never-ending (and ever-growing) depression and now severely heightened anxiety. I would still go through my 3:00 a.m., one hour long, morning training regimen in my room that I wouldn't — couldn't — miss unless I literally could not move my entire body. Next thought, I was worried sick that I was going to be shown the door as I was now injured with a month to go.

However, one by one that following Sunday evening, Lt. Ace came to my room, Capt. Corki, and even chief Keeno. Each telling me not to even think of leaving because of my injury. They assured me that I could take a week off from physical activity to heal as I had already proven myself in that phase of the academy. I remember the serious look on the captain's face as he began speaking with me. He said that the department needed guys like me in its ranks. He said, precisely, *"Don't even think about leaving. We need guys like you in the patrol. You're conscientious, strong in mind and body, and a leader."* I was shocked that he thought so much of me and wanted to make sure I didn't walk.

The staff knew I was close with Dante, who had left a few weeks earlier. Perhaps they thought I would walk too. As much pain as I was in both mentally and physically, I wouldn't have done that. I have had a difficult time my entire life even thinking of quitting — giving up. The one positive thing I came into this life with — I'd been born with — was a fighter's heart. It's something that can't be bought. It's something that can't be taught. You have it or you don't. For me, it would be easier to die than to quit. I'd never be able to look in the mirror again. I couldn't live with myself if I gave up — on anything.

I continued with everything my recruit class had scheduled over the next few weeks remaining until graduation. I took about a week off from PT and physical contact (drills), during which time I wore a doctor prescribed neck brace to keep the spine stable in that area. It healed but was obviously weakened badly.

Moral of the story; If you are going to exercise — or, specifically, any law enforcement training academy incorporating and promoting exercise and health — and are looking to reap the benefits of such, you *need* to be doing tried-and-true, modern variations of exercises and grouping routines, properly performed, while eating nutritious, quality food.

I would come to know personally in the months and years ahead that FHP and the state of Florida were decades behind the times in LEO technology. And, quite honestly, I found that many who wore the FHP uniform, including those that had stars and stripes adorning that uniform, lacked common sense. Many in the ranks and calling the shots were dinosaurs within the department and change wasn't happening — for the good of the recruits or the department — on their watch.

I believe that some of the up-and-coming bright lights in the ranks knew this and were hoping to add intelligent "new blood" to the ranks to change things for the better. To help FHP catch up with the times.

If I hadn't had a dream of becoming a DEA agent, I wouldn't have thought twice about climbing that ladder and helping to change the organization for the better — starting at the FHP academy.

We had representatives from various companies and organizations, ranging from insurance to the NRA, come into our academy to speak to the recruits about what benefits these enterprises could provide to us as state troopers.

Immediately after a speech from an insurance salesperson with a major insurance company, we had several of our academy staff members tell us that should we as state troopers ever get injured, FHP as well as the state of Florida and its' workers' compensation system would take care of our every need. They would be right there every step of the way making sure we were taken care of. We had nothing to worry about.

I believed this. I had no reason to doubt this. I also had no one to tell me differently.

I remember as a child and throughout my teenage years, my father and many of his friends and associates telling me to never trust anyone in government and law enforcement. I would hear that same sentiment before I left for the academy — that they (FHP) would sell me down the river in a second. I would find out a couple years down the road when I was seriously injured during a line of duty accident that my father and those of his life were correct. There was no honor within this department or the state (of Florida) government. No one had my back. What they told me (us) in the academy about taking care of me if I was injured was all a lie. A complete crock of shit!

When I needed the help of FHP, the state of Florida and its' workers' compensation system most, I was outright betrayed, swept under the rug, and treated worse than the criminals I had put my life on the line to protect society from.

It would become one of the top five most hurtful and damaging betrayals of my adult life — all at the hands of FHP and the state of Florida.

When I entered the academy, I had an outline of the entire six-month curriculum. I knew what was going to be taught and during what phase of the academy. I was well prepared and ready for what was coming; the academic training (classroom teachings, lectures, and written exams), physical training, practical exercises, law enforcement scenarios, firearms training, defensive tactics training, DUI and crash investigations, crime scene and criminal investigations, first aid, vehicle operations and so much more that would be covered in depth by the staff and mastered by the recruits. However, the one small, fifteen-minute portion of the entire six-month academy curriculum that created the most anxiety for me — which began long before I even entered the academy — along with sleepless nights and downright fear, was the mandatory oral presentation. It was going to be required towards the end of the academy, creating even more stress and anxiety as I would have preferred to get it over with as quickly as possible. I almost convinced myself not to show up and attend the academy because of the fear I had of doing this one and only oral presentation. That's how terrified I have always been of "the spotlight" or having to speak in front of crowds — my lifelong disorders ramping up that fear and anxiety many, many times over.

I did attend the academy and that oral presentation came soon enough. The format for this presentation; the recruit was to go to the front of the class and pick a piece of paper from a canister. That piece of paper would reveal a topic that you had to discuss in detail while fielding questions from the recruit class and academy staff. The oral presentations would proceed in alphabetical order, so I knew about when I would have to take the podium.

My knees shaking and, yes, sweating profusely and wiping that sweat from my face and head continuously, I sat there watching the recruits before me doing their thing. Some were very comfortable speaking and performing in front of the class and academy staff, others were nervous as could clearly be seen. At least I knew I wouldn't be the only one deathly uncomfortable and squirming around up there! What topic would I pull from that canister? How the hell can I talk about something I know nothing about?!

Then I heard, "*DiGrossi, you're up.*"

I made sure my mask was in place and affixed very tightly — game face is on — as this was going to be a very bumpy ride! I walked up to the podium, anxiety-ridden, and my wobbly, jello legs barely holding me up. I reached into the canister and pulled out my topic; SKYDIVING. I now had to speak in detail about skydiving for the next ten to fifteen minutes while answering questions about my topic of discussion. Truthfully, I only remember the one last question from a fellow recruit, *Simmons*, during the entire ten to fifteen minute "speech" of mine. He asked what the minimum height was that you could jump from the plane to have a safe and successful skydiving jump. I remember blurting out that you needed to be at a minimum of two thousand feet for a safe jump. I had no idea what the hell I was talking about or talked about for the past ten to fifteen minutes! He started to ask a follow up question and I remember getting a little aggravated as I wanted to be done with this presentation. In the middle of his follow up question, I remember interrupting him and saying, "*Your time is up recruit Simmons. I won't be taking any further questions.*" Everyone in the room, including staff, began laughing.

I remember cracking a smile through my tough-as-nails mask and feeling like this was almost over. That mask and body armor on autopilot, protection mode. I then said, "*thank you all for your time. Skydive safe.*" Don't know where that came from, but it got a few more chuckles and it was over.

I had lived with the fear and building anxiety of this moment for well over one year! There was more fear and anxiety produced from worrying about this ten to fifteen minute presentation than any other time during the six-month academy, including my neck injury. It was now over and I was one step closer to my short range goal of graduating this academy and another step closer to my long range goal of becoming a DEA agent.

🦋 🦋 🦋 🦋

About a year down the road, the recruit that asked that final question during my oral presentation would pull over a friend of mine from Rhode Island, Rose G, for speeding in Orlando, Fl. She was a local police officer in Rhode Island and dropped my name to trooper Simmons. He laughed and brought up the academy. He told her to say hi to me and that she wasn't getting a ticket that day because he had pissed me off once before in the academy and didn't want to piss me off again. I remember when she called to tell me. I don't laugh often, but I did this time.

He was a nice guy in the academy and, obviously, remained a nice guy and became one of the professional, quality troopers wearing the FHP badge and uniform.

🦋 🦋 🦋 🦋

As stressful as each and every minute of this academy was — primary trigger being the constant fear of not passing the almost daily exams and tests and being shown the door — the granddaddy of all the written exams, the Florida Officer Certification Examination (FOCE), was the one that drew the most sweat from the brows of the recruits. It would come up approximately one month prior to our academy graduation and, should you not pass any of the five separate tests of this written exam, you were gone. Not only were you tossed from the academy after nearly five months of blood, sweat, and tears, you weren't even able to get your foot in the door of another law enforcement agency without holding title to a passing grade on this Florida Officer Certification Exam.

Everyone knew that regardless of their (academic) standing in the academy, there was only one shot to pass this multi-hour, five portion written exam covering all facets of the law and law enforcement that is the curriculum within this academy and any law enforcement training academy.

The five separate tests for the law enforcement required courses covered the following; (1.) Legal (2.) Interpersonal Skills and Communications (3.) LE Investigations (4.) LE Patrol (5.) Defensive Tactics, Weapons, Vehicle Operations, LE Traffic, Medical First Responder.

It was extremely nerve-racking every minute of every day of the many months just thinking about and leading up to this exam. It was pure agony the couple weeks following the exam while awaiting the results.

If you passed this state certification exam, you could literally leave the FHP training academy and were almost guaranteed to get a job with one of the numerous law enforcement agencies throughout the state of Florida. Many of those agencies actively recruiting FHP academy recruits who would consider leaving the academy post passing this Florida Officer Certification Exam.

It was of paramount importance to pass this exam.

I breathed a sigh of relief that seemed to last for an hour when I received notification — both via Lt. Ace, who broke the news to the recruits, and a letter in the mail stating the results — a couple weeks post this examination. I had passed all five tests within the examination with the following scores; (1.) 85% (2.) 92% (3.) 90% (4.) 98% (5.) 90%.

There were many from within our academy who failed the exam and had to leave with only a few weeks remaining until graduation. They had come so far and passed all exams and tests — academic and physical — to this point, over many months, and now it was over for them.

Our recruit class had been whittled down the previous months — attrition by way of breaking or flunking — but this exam delivered the most punishing blow to those who fell below the passing mark on any of the five separate sections/tests.

This particular training academy, which put a very high priority on recruiting college graduates, allowed the recruits who passed the FOCE exam and would now be graduating the academy to pick the county and troop area they wanted to go to/work within based on their academic standing at the time of graduation. The recruit with the highest academic GPA in the academy would have first shot at where he/she wanted to go, as long as a position was open in that county/troop.

There was a list of available trooper positions within each county and troop area on the blackboard. We would begin the process with the number one highest academic standing within the academy and go down the line picking from there. I had graduated in the top 10% (academic standing) and was pretty much at the front of the line to pick from the list. Once a position in a particular county/troop area was gone, it was gone and you'd have to pick whatever county/troop area was second on your list and so forth.

My area of choice was south Florida. I was intent on going back to this area as I knew it rather well. My parents lived in south Florida and I was comfortable there. I was able to secure that position but it would turn out to be just another mistake I would make in my life that would come back to haunt me. Part of that being, and according to the

National Highway Traffic Safety Administration, I-95 in Florida has been the most congested, dangerous, and deadliest stretch of highway in the country (for traffic and accidents) for decades. The southernmost counties being the worst part of the I-95 highway stretch through Florida for accidents and traffic fatalities. It would prove to be the area that ended my career and life as I knew it. If I had known better, as others did regarding patrol areas, I would have picked a nice, laid back area on the west coast, northern or central Florida, to do a year or so with FHP peacefully, without all the extra work, risk, and pressure, and then move on to DEA fresh and in one piece. It didn't work out that way. Luck has never been on my side.

There were actually recruits — mostly female — that began bitching and crying because they didn't get their county/troop area of choice. *Damn*, I was thinking to myself, *a little weak and wimpy for a state trooper to be complaining and crying over something we all knew going in to the academy was to be assigned in the first place.* FHP could send you to any of the sixty-seven counties where troopers were needed. No recruit had ever been given the opportunity *to choose* the troop and county they wanted to work.

We just made it — succeeded where many had failed — through a six-month paramilitary training academy with no guarantee which troop or what area (county) you were going to be sent and now a few recruits are literally crying over this?!

I had been wanting to speak with Lt. Ace, one-on-one, off the record, at some point before I graduated. I respected Lt. Ace above all else in the academy and wanted him to know my feelings about that as well as my feelings regarding the academy, staff, and what I thought of some of the instructors who volunteered throughout the six-month academy.

It was a Sunday a couple weeks prior to graduation. I spotted Lt. Ace alone, in plain clothes, shredding some papers in the back of the academy. I approached him and asked if he had a couple minutes to speak *off the record.* He said, "*What's on your mind, DiGrossi.*" We spoke for nearly an hour about a few different things. Most important to me, I wanted him to know that if it hadn't been for the respect and admiration I had for him and Sgt. Wright, I may not have stayed throughout the academy as I had become very discouraged regarding the less than acceptable professionalism and overall quality of some staff and volunteer troopers during the course of this academy. Lt. Ace and Sgt. Wright's professional attitude and genuine concern — along with a few others from the academy staff and volunteer troopers — for the recruits and the betterment of FHP gave me hope. I didn't — wouldn't — mention names. Lt. Ace respected that but had an idea of whom I was speaking as at least one incident was common knowledge within the academy. I let him know I had a difficult time respecting any trooper who concealed his metal-fabricated manhood beneath the FHP uniform I had busted my butt to earn the right to wear. Lt. Ace replied to this, "*I'm FHP through and through, till the end. I want to be here one day as chief of this academy. You can change things, too, by moving up the chain of command.*" He would go on to say what I have always known — that there is good and bad in every organization and it takes leaders with vision to make change(s) for the better. He said I had what it takes to do that.

I knew that he understood and agreed with what I was saying.

I also knew that his heart, complete dedication, and loyalty was to and with FHP. I respected that. I couldn't tell him that the academy and FHP were a stepping-stone in my game plan to become a DEA agent. That I had no intention of sticking around too long or moving up the FHP chain of command/ladder at all, especially after seeing with my own eyes some of the unprofessional, disgusting attitudes of staff and volunteer troopers and living with and through it for the past six months.

I accomplished what I had set out to do.

I let Lt. Ace know that he had had a positive influence on my life and my decisions during the academy, that I was grateful for his leadership, fairness, and professionalism, but I also had real concerns and doubts about the competency and overall quality of others within the department. Those troopers who I had witnessed firsthand that lacked the essential ingredients — courtesy, respect, fairness, professionalism, and high ethical conduct — necessary to be a respected law enforcement officer and representative of the Florida Highway Patrol.

I was about to join a team and some of the players I had no confidence in or respect for. It made me question the competency and effectiveness of the leadership of this organization. That bothered me. My first instincts would hold true in the years to come.

At last, the day has come! Here I am, about to graduate from a six-month state law enforcement training academy that broke many. I have now earned the right to be called a state trooper and wear that prized FHP badge and uniform. I was now finally a step above that whale shit! However, I felt no happiness. I don't recall even smiling. I do recall the strange feeling that came over me that last night I would be sleeping in the training academy. The same feeling I had when I took the very last step from the academy grounds post-graduation and hit the highway heading towards south Florida, as a Florida Highway Patrol state trooper.

Another feather in my cap, yet I'm numb. Empty inside.

What would it take in life for me to find happiness? To finally believe in myself and my abilities?

I wondered then as I do to this day, and as I've stated before throughout these pages, just how far I could have gone in life — how much better I could have done and been — how much I could have accomplished, how much good I could have done if I had lived a "normal" life and wasn't controlled — emotionally imprisoned — my entire life by PTSD, depression, and anxiety?

A day hasn't gone by in decades when I don't think about just how much I could have accomplished in life ...If only.

Fast forward to the present and, now, the past eighteen years a horrendous, debilitating physical disability churning out never-ending, mind-bending pain 24/7 without reprieve. Was it ever even possible to be happy with the curse I've lived?

My mother and father, my sister, brother-in-law, two nephews and best buddy, Honey D, would come to Tallahassee for my graduation. I knew this would be a little tough for HD as she suffers from social anxiety. She had no idea — no one did — that my anxiety and other disorders even existed. My mask always in place and protecting me. When I invited HD, I told her that I would understand if she couldn't make it. She said she wouldn't miss it for the world.

The night everyone arrived, we all got together and went to dinner to celebrate. It was great to see them all after six months of a paramilitary training academy.

There was a graduation banquet the next evening and the graduation ceremony the following day. It was very uncomfortable for me as these two events were crawling with people, including all the top brass from FHP, politicians, and the media covering the event.

Once again, I tried to feel joy and happiness for my

accomplishment and the beginnings of what I had planned for my career move to the DEA. However, the disorders that controlled me and destroyed my emotional well-being always had me feeling like a fish out of water in large crowds or if in the spotlight. And, more often than not, anxiety would strike whenever or wherever. Instead of enjoying the special time and event(s), I couldn't wait until it was finally over and I could be free of any and all the peering eyes and escalated anxiety.

The graduation banquet and ceremony were semi-formal events. It was the first time in six months I — or any recruit — would attend an academy or other event and not be wearing a recruit uniform. I wore a suit to the graduation dinner. It was the same one that was completely soaked that very first day standing in the rain for hours at the academy gates. It was the only suit I had with me. It had been thoroughly cleaned, of course, but still had some remnants of the torrential rains it was subjected to. It would be the last time I ever wore that suit.

Everyone looked very sharp, dressed to the nines and ready to celebrate the moment. Everyone had a great time. I remember looking around and seeing everyone smiling, laughing, enjoying the special occasion. Everyone but me.

I tried as best I could to put on a happy face, but I was dying inside. No matter what good had been done or what I may have accomplished in my life, I could never find that elusive happiness — it just wasn't in there. Even at this point in my life, I was unlike all the others. I still couldn't find any joy or be that *normal* I had always dreamed of being.

The graduation was the next morning. It was time to leave the academy for the very last time as a recruit. The recruit class — all of us dressed to perfection in our FHP trooper uniforms for the very first time — would board the bus taking us to the graduation ceremony taking place at the Tallahassee-Leon County Civic Center.

Upon arrival, there was our class drill formations prior to the graduation ceremony and an opportunity for family members, press, and others to take pictures of the entire class before we moved inside for the ceremony. It was a totally different feeling standing in formation with my class this time, all of us now in full trooper uniform. We had slowly and painstakingly swapped out that recruit uniform for the earned-only FHP uniform.

The graduation ceremony had its share of guest speakers and some awards were handed out as we moved closer to the actual graduation. Once it began, pictures were taken of each recruit as he/she was presented his or her badge by Colonel Wadel, director of the Florida Highway Patrol. I remember taking that picture, walking off stage, and my mother wrapping her arms around me, kissing my cheek and saying, "*I'm so proud of you. Congratulations.*" One by one, my family, some academy staff and some members of my graduating class would congratulate me on my accomplishment. I had just completed a grueling six-month training academy, graduated, and had finally earned the right to wear the badge and uniform of the Florida Highway Patrol. I was with my family and was about to be pinned by the most important person in my life; my mother. And I felt no happiness. The years of living with PTSD, depression, and anxiety wouldn't allow such an emotion to enter my soul. The grip of these disorders forbid joy in my life. I had been emotionally imprisoned for far too many years. Peace in my soul was alien to me. If someone could have seen beyond that mask and body armor, they would have seen an intense suffering, a burning pain that forever brewed in my soul that could not be suppressed, overcome, or extinguished by any compliment, deed or accomplishment this day or throughout my life.

All these years later, I still see all the smiles and laughter of that day in slow motion. Everyone was so happy for me. I only wished I could feel the same — some of that joy and happiness to balance out my dreary, lifeless existence.

It was time for my mother to pin me (be the first to affix my state trooper badge to my uniform). She did so with gleaming pride. I was most relieved and found that ever so tiny bit of happiness in my soul knowing that I made my mother happy and proud of me. To me, that was more important than the accomplishment itself.

After my mother pinned me, she kissed my cheek again, and this time said, "*You are so intelligent. You can do anything in life you want. You've always made me so proud.*" She then said, verbatim, "*Your Father doesn't deserve a son like you.*"

Those words have lingered in my head to this very day. I knew what she meant. I know how she hurt. She was always terribly disappointed and angry that he wasn't the father she wanted him to be for me or my siblings. He wasn't the husband she so deserved. I understood and felt her joy and happiness that day as well as her pain and disappointment in many areas throughout her life. However, she was ecstatic this day. I was able to bring joy to her soul and dissipate her sorrows, if only for a short while. The intense exhilaration I know she felt I carry with me to this day. It gives me the strength to get through some days I may not otherwise get through.

That moment my mother pinned me was the most peace I had felt over the past six months and one of the very few instances of contentment I've ever experienced. One of the few times in my life I felt my heart beating and knew I was alive. I may not have been normal, but I was certainly alive at that moment.

We all went back to the academy to move me out. I gave my family a complete tour of the entire academy and told a few stories in the process. Last stop was my dorm room to gather up my things and head out for the last time. I was finally leaving the academy as a state trooper. It was bittersweet to say the least. I couldn't wait to get out of there and start my kind of training again and be able to eat some decent food. On the other hand, I had a very strange feeling taking my last steps from the academy. It felt like I was leaving a piece of myself behind somehow.

I knew I'd never return to reconnect with that piece of me that would be forever housed at the FHP training academy. A very, very strange feeling it was, indeed.

My sister and her family drove back to Rhode Island from there.

My parents followed behind me in their car as I hit the highway, Honey D in the passenger's seat, co-piloting, heading towards south Florida and never looking back.

That unsettling feeling I had leaving the academy that very last time some eighteen-plus years ago has always remained a part of and mystery to me.

16

We had stopped about halfway back to south Florida to stay in a hotel for the evening. However, I was having a major anxiety attack and still reeling from that strange feeling I had as I took my last step from the training academy. I decided I would rather keep driving the few more hours, wind in my face and mind focused on the road. My parents were tired from the drive and following me the past few hours, but realized I needed to keep moving. No one ever knew throughout my entire life the real reasons why I felt and acted as I did — until this story.

While I was nearing the end of the academy and knew I would be graduating and working in south Florida, my mother had been searching for a place I could rent when I returned from Tallahassee. She found me a place and, as was common with my mother, had the entire place furnished for me while I was still at the academy.

She's always thought of me, her family, and everyone else in her life before herself. Always wanting — needing — to make everyone else comfortable and happy, all while her pain and suffering throughout her life was bottled up pretty much the same as mine. She lived and breathed for her family. That is what kept her going. She gave every bit of herself — selflessly — to each of her children and grandchildren and would later in life, when she needed them the most, be betrayed by every last one of them.

Just the thought of how my mother has been taken advantage of and treated, disrespected and betrayed by her very own children and grandchildren sickens me to this day. I've said it many times before and I can't emphasize it enough; regardless of the devastating emotional and physical pain I have had to consistently endure throughout my days on this earth, that immediate family has been the number one greatest curse of my life.

I'm sure there is some form of dysfunctionality within many, perhaps most, families. However, this immediate family takes the cake as it relates to self-absorbed and unappreciative, cold-hearted and wicked.

HD and I stayed at my place when we arrived back in south Florida and my parents returned to their condo just a few miles down the road. HD hung out with us for a couple of days before heading back to Rhode Island. It was an extra special occasion having her there. She's always been able to make me smile and laugh. She has always been family and, as tough as the event was for me — *always* unbeknownst to anyone — I felt more comfortable having her there, however much pain and suffering was taking place within my mind and soul. We may not share a bloodline, but we most certainly are family.

I had a week to get things together before I was to report to my troop for a brief orientation, meet my two primary Field Training Officers (FTO's) and to pick up my take-home patrol vehicle.

Post the academy, there was a three month FTO training period that would begin a couple weeks after graduation. New troopers ride and work with an FTO who critiques your knowledge of procedures, the law, and everything else in between to make sure, in their opinion, you are ready for solo patrol.

Nice thing about being a state trooper, besides the take-home patrol vehicle, you don't have to show up at the station for roll call. You go 108 (in service) right from your patrol vehicle at home or wherever you are at the time your shift begins and 142 (out of service, duty completed) from your patrol vehicle or wherever you are at the completion of your shift. Very little time is spent at the patrol station. That worked just fine for me. The less I was in the spotlight or around large groups of people, the less anxiety and the better.

I should have been on cloud nine during this time in my life. I had paid my dues and earned my right to wear the FHP uniform and to be called a state trooper. However, as was the case throughout my life, I would fall deeper and deeper into that depression, suffering more and more with anxiety and isolating with each passing year, regardless of any accomplishments. Of all times in my life not to be able to celebrate, to feel good about myself, be happy and enjoy my accomplishment, this was the worst to date.

I kept going each and every day — fighting the demons — with one goal on my mind; I was moving forward to become a DEA agent where I could make a difference in people's lives — save the world so I thought. Perhaps even save that child inside of me whose life had been turned upside down by others' addictions to alcohol and drugs.

During the several month FTO phase, new troopers are mostly learning codes, procedures, laws, and getting to know the environment; areas, other troopers and officers from the various local departments.

That first day "on the job" — FTO phase — had arrived. I would meet my first FTO at his house, leave my patrol vehicle there and drive with him. We did this for the first couple of weeks before he began driving with me in my patrol vehicle. I worked the morning shift (6:00 a.m. to 2:00 p.m.) the first couple months as most of the FTO's had seniority and this shift was prized. It was the shift most senior troopers wanted to work. Most being married and having children, they wanted to be home with their families in the evening.

My first FTO, *FTO #1*, was a few years older than me, had a wife and a small child. Nothing out of the ordinary happened during this portion of my FTO training. You spend a lot of time with other troopers and law enforcement officers and learn things about them. FTO #1 told me a story a couple weeks in about how he met and married his wife. She was his best friend's girlfriend and, as he put it, he wanted her. Rick Springfield might have been proud of him (*Jessie's Girl* song reference here), but I wasn't. I lost quite a bit of respect for him with that story. To me, that's betrayal of your best friend. It goes against everything I believe. How I've lived my entire life. My world has been — and always will be — about honor, respect, loyalty, and trust. Aside from that, only thing I remember vividly about him during FTO training is that he was adamant I do things his way. He'd of given Frank Sinatra a run for his money with how many times I'd hear him say it's going to be "*My way!*"

I told him, man to man, I would do things "his way" during my FTO training but I didn't agree with *his way* of doing most things and *his way* of communicating with the public. Case in point; this FTO was gung-ho about Saturday and Sunday morning position-playing for drunk drivers. There were a few local spots and bars where he liked to play-position around 6:30 a.m. and wait for patrons to come out, get in their cars and drive away. If there was the slightest of swaying, speeding, or any indication of the driver being inebriated, he would pull them over for suspicion of drunk driving. I remember one instance in particular where he shadowed (follow closely behind, listening and observing) me to see how I would handle the situation. As with anyone I would stop during FTO training or when I was on solo patrol post that initial training period, I gave everyone the benefit of the doubt and treated everyone with respect and expected the same in return. As we pulled the vehicle over for slightly swaying over the center line of the roadway, I approached the vehicle from the passenger's side while the FTO shadowed me — observing and critiquing my every move and communication with the driver. I told the driver why he was being stopped and asked for his license, registration, and proof of insurance. He didn't have his insurance card with him. I confirmed via dispatch the vehicle was insured. When I returned to his vehicle, I asked him to step out so I could perform a field sobriety test as I had suspicion he may be under the influence. The driver complied and passed the test. He never offered any resistance, never showed any sign of being intoxicated, was coherent and respectful throughout the traffic stop. I decided to give him a warning for the ever-so-brief swaying and not having his insurance card in the vehicle. He thanked me, extended his hand to shake my hand, to which I reciprocated and shook his hand. My last words to him were, "*Drive safely, chief.*" Where I come from, calling someone *chief* is common and respectful. Same as calling someone *buddy* or *partner*. True, however, that calling someone chief, buddy, partner, or pal can also have sarcastic overtones — it's all in the way you say it. Many civilians that I would come in contact with during my time with FHP as a state trooper would call me — and most male troopers and police officers — "*Boss*". It was most common with convicted felons and street guys. A simple term of good will when someone doesn't know your name. Also a polite way of bullshitting the trooper with some respect. Stroking your ego. Nothing more, nothing less. However, again, it's all in the way you say it. When we returned to the patrol vehicle at the conclusion of the traffic stop, FTO #1 said to me, "*You need to walk up to the driver's side of the door.*" I replied, somewhat amazed, "*What? Approaching on the passenger's side is a personal preference and matter of my safety. I have more control of the situation and oncoming traffic from that position and angle.*" He reiterated his comment. I told him I would do it that way — *his way* — during his phase of FTO. I didn't agree with him and wasn't about to argue the point. His next comment, "*You needed to give him two tickets instead of two warnings.*" I told him it was my discretion. In that instance, the driver was entitled to warnings for the minor infractions. He was a gentleman from beginning to end and not everyone needs to get hit in the pocket to learn a lesson. FTO #1 then said, "*He deserved two tickets. You should have given him two tickets.*" I told him that he should have told me that when I returned to the patrol vehicle to run his license and see if he had any outstanding warrants. Otherwise, I was under the impression it was my call and that is the way I would have done it whether during FTO phase or on solo patrol. His last comment irritated the crap out of me; "*was that guy an Indian?*" Once again, I replied in total amazement, "*What?!*" "*You called him chief*", he said. I explained it was common and courteous to call someone chief where I came from. It was a way of being respectful and broke the ice. FTO #1 then said, "*You can't call someone chief if they're not a legitimate chief.*" He was dead-serious. This was simply ridiculous. Once again, I told him I certainly would remember that during FTO with him but I had every intention of treating people with courtesy, respect, and a firm but polite attitude.

Needless to say, we butt heads a little bit for a month or so. He was the type of guy that would have given his own mother a ticket for five mph over the speed limit.

FTO #2 came along during the second half of the FTO phase about six weeks in. This would mostly be a night shift (2:00 p.m. to 10:00 p.m.). FTO #2 was a nice guy. Also a couple years older than me. Married, no children. He was always polite and courteous when dealing with the public. However, he was a wild man — full speed ahead — to say the least. He liked driving fast — very fast! I was a speed demon myself on motorcycles most of my life. I had never driven with someone — my being in the passenger's seat — where I got a bit nervous ...until now! Every time I rode with him, I knew I was in for a day/night of NASCAR! I remember him doing in excess of 120 mph on several different occasions on a major expressway a bit more rural than I-95. The bug splatter at night was intense at these speeds! It wasn't the speed that worried me but the fact I was at the mercy of someone else's driving ability — I had no control of the vehicle. Aside from that, it was a decent learning experience during this phase of FTO and with FTO #2.

My first introduction to a major disaster was during my FTO training with FTO #2. It was May 1996. ValuJet Flight 592 had crashed into the deep-water swamp of the Everglades. Familiar faces from news and media around the country — the world — were present for weeks on end during the initial phases of search and recovery.

We didn't know it at the time, but this crash would result in the death of 110 people — everyone aboard. A surreal situation with devastation at an unreal level. No intact bodies, and very few large pieces of the plane, were ever recovered.

I also rode with several other troopers during my FTO phase. They would "fill-in" on days/evenings when my two primary FTO's were off-duty or had other obligations to fulfill during this time. Some were very knowledgeable and sharp and meant well in their critiquing and teachings. I got along with and connected on one level or another with most. Others lacked every bit of common sense and had no idea how to constructively critique a new trooper's performance. They were fill-ins for the FTO's, but a few could do more harm than good in this position — both as a temporary FTO and a state trooper.

There was one trooper, *Biffy*, who filled in for my FTO one day. I was driving one afternoon and he was sitting in the passenger's seat. We were heading southbound on I-95, outside lane at 70 mph. Out of nowhere, a vehicle on the first inside lane flew past us as if we were standing still. The vehicle was easily traveling in excess of 100 mph. I remember picking up my speed and hitting the emergency lights and siren at the same time. Trooper Biffy actually said to me, "*What are you doing?*" I replied, "*That vehicle is traveling in excess of 100 mph and endangering the lives of everyone on this highway. We need to stop him. Make sure he isn't under the influence or just robbed a bank. Maybe find out what the rush is.*" Trooper Biffy actually said to me, in all seriousness, "*He's going too fast, you can't catch him in this traffic without going even faster.*" "*Are you kidding me?*", I replied. "*No, you can't drive over 100 mph with the lights on or not*", was his response. I truly couldn't believe what I was hearing. This had nothing to do with me being in FTO phase or not. He was dead-serious. This was a trooper who turned his blinders on years ago and forgot what his job was; protecting and serving the general public. Whether you consider driving over 100 mph on a major highway with moderate traffic flow driving without due care and attention or reckless driving, it is, nevertheless, a major moving traffic violation that endangers the lives of innocent people. As a state trooper, part of your training is vehicle operations; knowing how to drive at high rates of speed and controlling a vehicle! Part of your job is to stop anyone driving a vehicle recklessly with a wanton disregard for others on that road. I began increasing speed and moving over to the inside lane. Biffy said again, "*What are you doing?*" My reply, "*We're catching up to and stopping that car.*" As my speed increased to near 100 mph, my lights and siren blaring, I was just about to pull into the inside lane as I could see the vehicle a short distance ahead. As I began to cut over into the inside lane, a vehicle a short distance in front of me in my present lane, I noticed through my peripheral vision that trooper Biffy pulled his legs up onto the seat, knees tucked in, put his hands over his head and began to scream. No, I'm *not* joking! He truly believed I was going to hit the car in front of me before moving into the inside lane. Don't get me wrong, I can relate to being uncomfortable driving with someone else — especially when that person may be speeding (case in point, FTO #2) and you have no control of that vehicle whatsoever. However, this reaction shocked and concerned me. Is this the type of back-up I am going to have to rely on out here if my life depends on it? Biffy then insisted I terminate the pursuit. I could not believe this. However, I decided to comply rather than have to take trooper Biffy home to change his undies.

I ran this scenario by numerous other troopers and LEO's the following day — including my shift Sgt. at the time — to see what they would have done. Each and every one said it was my job to make sure that vehicle was stopped from further endangering the public.

During the FTO phase and for a time thereafter, I would get together with other troopers and LEO's from other departments either during our shift or off-duty to grab a bite to eat. On one instance, a few of us were off-duty — and in plain clothes — and got together at a local restaurant. One of the other troopers had invited trooper Biffy. I remember upon leaving the restaurant, a (civilian) guy said to Biffy, who was also in plain clothes, "*who the fuck are you staring at?*" Trooper Biffy was a prime example of an LEO with metal-fabricated manhood (MFM). Biffy, without hesitation, whipped out his badge and said, "*I'm a state trooper, you still have a problem?*" I shook my head and kept walking. Totally embarrassed, I'd have nothing to do with such cowardice.

I would soon find out that trooper Biffy had plenty of company in this category. I would also learn firsthand in the months to come that my particular troop had more incompetence than competence flowing through its leadership (ranks). More MFM's beneath the supervisory uniforms here than could be believed. Many of the supervisors from Sgt.'s right up to the district commander — the captain — were the blind leading the blind. It was both embarrassing and disgraceful, really. I'd often take a bit of friendly razzing by LEO's from other agencies about it. Once again I realized that, as my luck would have it, I came up with the shit end of the stick picking this troop as my number one choice during the academy. If I'd only known about this particular troop beforehand ...

Summer of 1996 rolled around and FTO training was over. I was now on the job solo. It was a good feeling to be out on my own. I had learned a few things leading up to this day — both directly and indirectly — about the job, FHP and, specifically, my troop. I found in general what I had heard along the way was true; 99% of the job is routine day in and day out. However, it's that 1% of the time when the shit hits the fan and things can take that turn for the worse that keeps you on edge. However, even that 99% daily "routine" can be very stressful. Dealing with criminals and drunks, the angry and the injured and everything in between. Nothing much is really different from day to day relating to your duties; enforcing laws, court time, dealing with and helping people, and working crash after crash after crash in this district!

There was also the other stressful side of the job — having to deal with the incompetence of the command structure within my troop.

The majority of a morning or afternoon shift consisted mostly of working traffic accidents. Accidents and doing their respective reports never ended. However, I found coming in contact with and dealing with drunks was the worst for me. I had to relive the trauma of my childhood with each and every drunk I had to deal with — and there were way too many. Accident upon accident the result of a drunk driver. Mothers, children, elderly injured and killed due to those who drink and drive. The punishment for those driving drunk — injuring and killing innocent people — was far from serious enough. I understand addiction rather well. However, addiction or not, if you want to consume alcohol (or any other intoxicating substance for that matter), you have to understand beforehand that you cannot get behind the wheel and drive, endangering innocent people. If you do, you should be held accountable and punished accordingly. Unfortunately, more often than not, the punishment amounts to a mere slap on the wrist at best.

However, not all traffic crashes were alcohol related, and many were just as devastating; I had just completed my several month FTO phase just one week earlier. I was now working the evening shift (2:00 p.m. to 10:00 p.m.). It was late afternoon during the daily, weekday traffic rush (4:00 p.m. to 6:00 p.m.) when I received notice from dispatch of a signal 4 (vehicle crash), possible signal 7 (dead person) just south of the XX road on-ramp to I-95 southbound. Upon arrival, approximately ten minutes post that accident, I noticed an overturned vehicle off the right shoulder breakdown lane, at the bottom of a grass embankment. There were several other local law enforcement officers at the scene. FTO #2 had pulled up at the same time as I did. The vehicle had overturned at the on-ramp merge point and rolled several times, across the breakdown lane (right shoulder) and down the grass embankment.

It was later determined through eyewitness accounts and accident reconstruction that the driver was speaking on her cell phone and didn't notice that traffic was stopped just ahead on I-95 southbound. At the very last second, in an attempt to avoid colliding with the stopped traffic, the driver oversteered to the right while traveling at approximately 45 to 55 mph, tried to correct the right oversteer by oversteering to the left which caused the vehicle to flip on its right side and roll several times, moving across the breakdown lane and down the grass embankment.

This was my patrol area and would be my crash — and death — investigation.

As a state trooper in south Florida, highway crashes are non-stop throughout your morning and afternoon shifts. In my district, we also got stuck working all unincorporated area crashes off the highway. This would be *the one* of all crashes I had ever worked that would stay with me, haunting me to this very day.

As I approached the two other officers who were on the scene, and before the paramedics had arrived, I noticed a young girl (later determined to be seventeen-years-old) laying perpendicular to the side of the overturned vehicle. The vehicle had come to a rest overturned on its' left side. The young girl's head was partially trapped beneath the left door panel area of the overturned vehicle. Her head and face, completely blue and purple, was swollen to twice the normal size. As soon as I looked at her, I had a sick feeling in my stomach. One of the two officers at the scene looked at me and said, "*I already checked vitals, she's gone.*"

FTO #2 walked over to me at that very second, knowing this was going to be my first signal 7, and asked if I was okay and could handle it. He noticed (could see) in my face how I was feeling inside. I couldn't believe that this girl was dead. I couldn't believe the reason this girl was dead; solely due to the fact that she wasn't wearing a seat belt. I had never been a proponent of seat belts. I believed it was a person's right to decide whether or not he/she wanted to wear that belt or not. My entire outlook about seat belts changed that very day. Not a day went by I didn't tell people — especially family and friends — to please wear that seat belt. This girl should have been — would have been — alive if she had only had that seat belt on. She was ejected from the open driver's side window as the vehicle began rolling. The vehicle rolled over her and landed on its' side, and on her head, killing her instantly.

I told FTO #2 I was going to need help with this one. I was not going to be able to gather her belongings without some assistance. It was my job to collect her belongings — the jewelry she was wearing, her cell phone, anything and everything in the vehicle and on her person. As a courtesy, we as state troopers would clean the blood from the items, inventory each of the items, and return the items in a package when we made the death notification to the family. FTO #2 removed the jewelry from her body for me and removed all items from her pockets before she was taken away. He walked me through the entire process as I was half in shock. He actually did most of the crash investigation and items recovery at the scene for me. I remember FTO #2 saying, "*you have to get used to it. It gets easier as you experience it more and more, and you will.*" He then handed me her driver's license so I could begin to accumulate the information necessary to return the young girl's belongings and make the death notification to the family. I looked at the picture on the license and then looked over at this young girl laying lifeless, beneath an overturned car, on the side of a congested, noisy and filthy highway.

The paramedics showed up moments later. Checked vitals again and put a white sheet over her. I was truly beside myself with grief and I didn't even know this person. This was the first of many signal 7's I would work. It also happened to be the most painful, intensely sorrowful.

It took a couple hours to investigate and clear the scene. It was now time to go to this young girl's home, approximately twenty miles southwest, and make the notification. FTO #2 followed me to the home and would stick with me through the entire process.

I still couldn't believe how such innocence was lost in a split second. She could have survived this accident with nothing more than a story to tell if she had only been wearing that damn seat belt!

The entire way to her home I was anxiety stricken. I couldn't get the picture of her lifeless body just lying there out of my mind. Her head and face half beneath that vehicle, purpled and severely swollen. She was gone... forever. Her family would never see her again. They would never speak with her again. And I now had to deliver that news. It has been some eighteen years and I still cannot get that picture —

that grief — or the screams and images that were to come during the notification out of my mind.

When I arrived at the home of the deceased, I rang the front doorbell. FTO #2 was behind me. A woman came to the door holding a cordless phone. The second she saw that I was a state trooper, the phone released from her hand, she dropped to her knees and began screaming and crying, shaking and flailing about the floor. A mother's instinct; she knew her daughter was never coming home again. She knew why I was there. I almost couldn't speak. I was half-paralyzed seeing and actually feeling this mother's intense pain. This was something that I truly wasn't expecting. I wasn't ready for this.

I had my sunglasses on — and they would remain on throughout the evening. My eyes filled with tears and my heartrate began to elevate. As I leaned over to try and comfort the mother, two young girls, around the same age as the deceased, came from behind the mother and began to pick her up and console her.

FTO #2 headed off to neighbors' homes to gather more information about the family and also to see if there were friends close by that could come to comfort this family.

Within minutes, one of the girls ran upstairs and I heard glass breaking. Then I heard a neighbor scream, "*she's going to jump!*" I ran outside to see the young girl crawling on the roof. I asked her to go back inside so we could talk. She assured me she wasn't going to jump but needed to get into her sister's room, which was locked. She broke the outside window from the rooftop and was going in that way. At this time, we now had paramedics and local police officers at the scene. The neighbor called 911 after seeing the young girl on the roof.

During all the commotion and heartbreak, FTO #2 and myself were speaking with a number of neighbors to try and get more information so we could be of some assistance here. We learned that the father was a federal LEO. We secured the weapons we found in the home as we didn't know how he would react when learning his daughter had died in a car crash. He could very likely be suicidal when he arrived home to such news.

We needed to do everything possible to avoid more tragedy. We had a neighbor/friend call to tell him that there was an emergency and he should come home as soon as possible. A couple of the neighbors who knew him well were waiting for him along with myself, FTO #2, and a couple other local officers. When he arrived home, the plan was for his friend to get his car keys before he found out exactly what had happened. We would then access his vehicle and secure all weapons for the safety of the father. That is exactly how it played out. When the father pulled up to the house, the friend got his car keys and the father continued up to his front door. FTO #2 asked him for his duty weapon and any other weapons on his person due to the volatility of the situation. He complied as he asked several times, "*what's going on?*" As soon as he saw his wife and daughter crying, he began screaming. He ran to his left, inside the foyer area of his home, and began smashing his head and face, full force, into a brick wall. There was blood everywhere. We immediately — with the help of his friends and neighbors — restrained him so he wouldn't harm himself further. With the help of this family's friends and neighbors, we were able to get as much control of this heartbreaking situation as possible.

I remember feeling a need to get away from all the commotion for a bit once it was somewhat under control. I walked to an area in the front of the house that was away from everyone and all that was still going on. I needed to try to compose myself, if that was possible. Hours of this was starting to take its' toll. I was having another very bad anxiety attack. I was beginning to sweat profusely from my head and it was pouring down and mixing with the tears rolling down my face from beneath the sunglasses I would not remove. I couldn't believe the pain and suffering I was witnessing. I kept thinking to myself; *why did it have to be my face the mother saw at the front door that intuitively told her that her little girl was gone forever?*

The vision of the mother collapsing in anguish and knowing it was my face that brought the news of her daughter's death weighs heavily on me to this day.

One of the girls that was in the home (a family friend) when we first arrived walked over to me. She noticed the tears rolling down my face from beneath my sunglasses. As much as I tried and fought through this with everything I had, I was truly feeling overwhelmed with grief. Knowing and feeling the pain that this family was now suffering. She said, "*I can see this is very difficult for you.*" Trying to keep composed, I replied, "*It is. But it's nothing compared to the pain and suffering you are all going through. I only wish there was something more I could have done.*" She touched my hand and said "*thank you.*" She turned and walked back to the family.

Not many days have gone by over the past eighteen years where I haven't thought of the young girl that died that afternoon *or* her family. The images — specifically three of them — have remained in my mind's eye for nearly two decades;

-An innocent young girl laying half under that vehicle — her head crushed — dead.

-A mother opening her front door, seeing my face, dropping to the floor, screaming, crying. My knowing that this mother equates my face with her worst nightmare.

-The father in a split second of realizing what had happened, nearly losing his mind, slamming his head and face full force into a brick wall, having to be restrained so he didn't kill himself.

The deepest of pain, the worst of nightmares had come to be for this family.

I had done a fair share of death notifications after this day. Not one affected me the way this one did. I found it bothersome that some notifications were just "matter of fact" from the next of kin. I've heard everything from "*it's about time*" to "*hope the will wasn't changed.*"

This incident would be the most intense, most emotionally painful notification and single day I had been part of as a state trooper. FTO #2, a veteran at that time with dozens upon dozens of death notifications, would concur that it was the toughest notification he'd been a part of in his six years as a state trooper.

I actually had to tweak and adjust my mask when I became a trooper and hit the road. I had to notch down a bit the tough exterior part. The last thing I wanted was for anyone to think I was like these others I had known of my entire life and had the displeasure of meeting and being mistreated by firsthand during the academy; the metal-fabricated manhood (MFM) troopers/law enforcement officers.

I actually bit my tongue and swallowed my pride quite often as a state trooper. With the public, that is. I didn't react to disrespect from civilians while in uniform. Disrespect is something I'd never let slide outside of wearing that uniform. I was probably the easiest going trooper on the road. I cut more breaks than anyone and gave out more warnings in place of actual tickets than any other trooper in my troop. I was told to ramp up the tickets on more than one occasion by superiors. I believed in talking to people. Communicating and reaching people with compassion and understanding and offering help and advice when I could — that's why I was there. I kept my pain and suffering behind the mask as always but adjusted my outward attitude to be approachable given my position. I was always very polite, firm when I had to be. I wasn't there to take advantage of people or abuse my authority like some. I never wanted anyone to think I was *that type* of person, *that type* of LEO. The kind that I, and many other LEO's and civilians, had no respect for. Nothing is worse than working among those in uniform who are cowards and bullies, abusing their authority — and there were a number of them. The majority of them filling the supervisory ranks within my particular troop.

There was one Sgt. (of several), *McCluskey,* in my troop who was the epitome of metal-fabricated manhood. A coward. A bully. A punk with a badge who abused his authority.

I remember pulling up one night behind a traffic stop that he was on. Routine back up. It wasn't required or requested — it was a professional courtesy on my part. I was just getting off my shift and decided to check it out, make sure everything was okay. I didn't realize it was McCluskey or, quite honestly, I wouldn't have stopped. I realized it was him as I began walking up to the stopped vehicle. He was on the passenger's side of that vehicle and didn't see me or hear me pull up. As I walked up to the passenger's side of the stopped vehicle, I heard him loudly scolding the occupants. The way he was speaking, I figured the occupants were wise-ass kids. I then heard him berating the driver for driving too slowly on the interstate. I was now right behind him and said, "*everything okay, Sarge?*" His reply, "*Yeah, you can leave.*" A real piece of work this guy was. I was close enough to see the faces in the vehicle very clearly. The driver was an elderly gentleman and the passenger was an elderly woman.

The woman looked directly at me. She was crying and had a look of fear on her face that bothered me. She was quite obviously intimidated. This asshole coward with three stripes on his sleeve was senior bullying and verbally abusing these people for driving too slowly on the highway! I had no doubt from what I heard and seen; his tone, his posture, his response to me when I approached.

I knew this Sgt. was a bully and a coward the day I met him. He proved me right time and again. My blood was now boiling. I had no respect for this guy as a trooper, as a Sgt., as a man. Where I come from, you earn respect in life. I don't care how many stripes or stars you are wearing on your uniform, you earn those and the respect of those around you. He was a coward and bully who happened to have a gun, a badge, and the authority to terrorize the innocent, elderly, and whomever else he so chose. I wanted to break his face but was bound by the structure of this paramilitary organization to obey superiors. Unless, and until, he disrespected me as a man, I would have to let it slide. I would, in time, and not much later, ask this coward to meet me at some point when we weren't working to discuss a few things. I wanted to speak with him off the record, out of uniform. He knew what I meant.

Not having an ounce of manhood, his method of dealing with someone in uniform like me — on that same law enforcement level — who he couldn't bully in the way he wanted to was to put pen to paper and write you up for insubordination or some other bullshit written reprimand. A real wussy. This is the type of person that gives all of law enforcement a bad name. This type of person doesn't belong in that position of power. The authority trip is the only reason this type of person got into a career in law enforcement to begin with. McCluskey — and those MFM's like him — needed that authority, that power to bully people he otherwise would crap his pants if he encountered. That badge was his protection from the rest of the world.

On the flip side, I encountered many in law enforcement — real men and real women from within FHP and surrounding agencies — who were there for the right reasons. Decent people and professional LEO's who wanted to help and protect others from the bad guys and the evil in society.

I had many encounters, mostly during traffic stops, with hardened criminals. Many just released from prison. During my conversations with these men, I would almost always hear the same question and comment; "*what are you doin' here? You're not like the rest of them.*" I would always tell these guys that there are good and bad in every profession, but I know what you mean.

I had a BA from college but I earned a Ph.D. growing up on the streets. I knew and understood what made people tick. I knew how to effectively communicate with all kinds of people from all walks of life, PTSD and depression consuming me or not. I also made sure that my kindness wasn't taken for weakness, especially among the hardened criminals.

I'd cut breaks for many people where possible. Some just down on their luck and in need of that break. Some others were in law enforcement and within the fire department, which was actually quite common. I'd routinely get calls through my troop's dispatch from guys thanking me for being so fair and professional. I always believed in helping people out when they are in a less than serious jam and it was possible — showing them that *there are* good cops out there with a heart, some compassion and understanding.

Maybe in return these people would do someone else a favor or offer some assistance or help to someone else down the road that could use a hand. Pay it forward with a smile, some compassion and kindness.

Sometimes, my hands were tied and an arrest was warranted. I would often do my arrest (signal 15) paperwork at one of the Sheriff's office sub-stations in my patrol district before transporting the arrestee to the county jail.

Tony Amato was a captain with the *XX* Sheriff's Office and was at this sub-station often. He would always ask me to move over to a career with the Sheriff's Office and leave all the bullshit and blind leadership that was FHP — particularly my troop — far behind. Capt. Amato wasn't the only one who would ask me to jump ship. I was asked, and quite often, by other brass and deputies with the Sheriff's Office and officers from various local departments to move over and be a part of their team. Each reiterating the same sentiment; there was no leadership or morale within FHP in this county. It was seen as a dead-end agency. I was wasting my career and being paid peanuts compared to other agencies. This was all true and certainly the case within my particular troop. If I hadn't been planning on moving to DEA, I would no doubt have taken Capt. Amato or one of the others up on that offer.

There were a number of troopers that graduated from my academy — as well as one of my Shift Sgts., *Nuzzy*, who was a class-act, top-notch trooper and supervisor that I respected — that left FHP rather quickly due to these very reasons. Some went with the Sheriff's Office, others to local agencies. I would have followed suit if I wasn't planning on leaving shortly and going with DEA. In retrospect, if I'd only left FHP early on as others did, things may have turned out for the better; I may have avoided a life-altering line of duty accident and my life may not have been flushed down the shitter physically, emotionally and in every other way possible.

During my time with FHP, my troop was drastically understaffed and very poorly managed. The incompetence of the leadership in my troop was astounding. Most of the supervisors — Sgts. right up to the captain — were a joke. The morale couldn't have been worse. It was a horrible environment to be in if you were an LEO. There was no confidence in the leadership whatsoever.

I recall on more than one occasion working the midnight shift (10:00 p.m. to 6:00 a.m.) and being *the only* road trooper on patrol that evening in the entire county. That is correct — *the only* road trooper on patrol that shift in the entire county. This was insane! This wasn't Alaska where one trooper will routinely patrol a couple hundred square miles of nothing-ness. Florida is the fourth largest of all states and XX county is one of the largest — most populous — counties in the state of Florida. There is also an extraordinary volume of traffic and people here on vacation. I-95 in Florida had been deemed, year after year, the most dangerous and deadly stretch of interstate highway in the United States by the National Highway Traffic Safety Administration. I-95 in XX County being the absolute worst stretch in the entire state. There were non-stop accidents throughout my morning and afternoon shifts. One after another, day in and day out. Injury upon injury, death upon death.

To make matters even worse, we had a captain, *Blart*, who controlled our troop into the ground. Word had it that Captain Blart made a deal with the then Sheriff of XX County to have his understaffed troop handle all accidents which occurred in unincorporated areas of that county. What?!

One may ask why the leader of an FHP district troop would do such a thing when his very own troop was drastically understaffed, his troopers overworked, underpaid, and operating with a morale level lower than any other law enforcement agency in the state. Word was that he sold his own men (and women) down the river in order to build brownie points for a family member who was employed by the Sheriff's Office. While kissing the ass of the county Sheriff to earn a favor or two for the family member, and at the expense of his own troops and department, this "leader" guided his troops and department into a perilous working environment and beyond. This was a captain whose leadership and decisions were sinking his own ship. However, he was part of the good ole boy network. His nose also firmly buried up the right upper-echelon brass' asses as he was promoted to major immediately prior to announcing his retirement. Yet another promotion and rank not earned. A promotion which ramped up his retirement pay, bonuses, and rewards at the expense of taxpayers. A promotion immediately pre-retirement for blind leadership and a *job well done*. Blart was handed FHP's and the state of Florida's revised version of a golden-parachute. He wasn't being terminated for blind leadership and partially sinking his own ship, he was being rewarded!

🦋 🦋 🦋 🦋

There was such a plainly visible problem during this time frame with sections of the state's government and, specifically, FHP, being controlled and manipulated by good ole boy (GOB) insiders, that some powers that be demanded the Patrol be taken over and run by an "outsider". That eventually did happen, one time and not for very long, beginning two years prior to my employment with FHP. A new FHP Director was appointed and took over from 1993 to 1998. FHP had a new Colonel — Wadel — that wasn't part of and controlled by the GOB network. He was a law enforcement outsider from Illinois.

Wadel would be the first and only Director of the FHP who never attended the FHP academy and wasn't promoted from within the agency. No one had ever worn the FHP uniform as a state trooper or FHP brass without paying their dues at the academy.

Needless to say, this didn't go over well with the deeply embedded GOB insiders.

No outsider was going to be able to infiltrate and change this old guard network and their control. Not sure if the FBI could have accomplished that goal.

🦋 🦋 🦋 🦋

Making matters even worse in this county, some troopers and supervisors from my troop were giving moving violation tickets to off-duty, local officers and sheriff's deputies. Some even gave tickets to fellow off-duty troopers! I worked with local police officers who were on the receiving end of this lunacy and literally hated some of our troopers and supervisors. That's not the way to go in law enforcement. You have to take care of and look out for one another. This is your back-up, the men and women who assist you in your time of need and can save your life. You don't want bad blood among agencies. There were several troopers and FHP brass — Mostly MFM's — who created a lot of bad blood by being ignoramuses.

I'm in no way saying that if another law enforcement officer commits a crime, you look the other way. However, troopers (LEO's in general) have a tremendous amount of discretionary power and there is no need — no reason — to be giving fellow LEO's tickets for minor traffic violations.

I was working the midnight shift and patrolling an area of I-95 in south Florida. It was about 2:00 a.m. I noticed a car traveling at a high rate of speed and swaying a bit from lane to lane. I followed (shadowed) at a distance, pace clocking the vehicle's speed and continuing to watch the lane swaying for another mile. Speed was 15 mph over the speed limit but I was most concerned with the swaying. I needed to pull the driver over to see what the story was and make sure he didn't cause an accident — hurt or kill someone should he be under the influence. I got behind the vehicle and called in the tag prior to the stop, as was routine and required per midnight shift policy. As I put on my emergency lights, I noticed the driver look in his back seat a couple times. I initiated the stop in the right hand shoulder breakdown lane. I kept my spotlight glaring in his rearview mirror so he wouldn't see me approaching.

Something just didn't seem right with this person or this stop. I walked around the back of my vehicle and came up on the passenger's side of his vehicle, my flashlight and eyes probing the interior. I noticed a male driver with both hands on the steering wheel and what appeared to be two small children seated beneath a blanket in the back seat, only the tops of the two small heads showing from beneath the blanket. The driver never took his hands off the steering wheel or looked my way even though my flashlight was streaming through the windows. I knocked on his passenger side window, he looked over and powered his window down.

I told him I had pulled him over for speeding and swaying between the lanes of travel. He apologized, his hands still gripping the steering wheel. I asked him to turn the ignition off and to see his driver's license, registration, and proof of insurance. He took his hands off the steering wheel to gather the requested items and handed them to me, including the keys, through the passenger's window. He then placed both his hands back on the steering wheel and looked straight ahead. I had a weird feeling about this stop. Something didn't seem right, but I didn't feel as though it was sinister, just strange. I wanted him to be as calm as possible. I didn't want him to think I even noticed

the two little heads peeking from the blanket in the back seat until I ran
a check on him. I asked him to keep his hands on the steering wheel
and stay in the vehicle while I went back to my cruiser and ran his DL.
I could have had him get out of the car, checked immediately for
weapons on his person and in the vehicle or even had him stand in
front of my car or sit to the side of the road where I could see him
more clearly and control the situation most effectively. Again, my gut
said something was strange, not sinister, so I went with my intuition,
which has seldom, if ever, let me down.

Everything came back clean. No record, no warrants, valid DL,
registration and insurance. I returned to his vehicle, thanked him for
his patience, and returned his DL, registration and insurance card while
holding on to his keys while I investigated a bit further. I didn't give
him any tickets but told him I was cutting him a break, just be a bit
more careful in the future — especially with kids in the car. I asked him
why he was speeding and where he was going. He apologized once
again for speeding and said he was taking his kids for a ride, turning to
the back seat occasionally to speak to them and that may be what
caused him to sway a bit. I asked him the kids' names and told him I
thought it was a bit late to take the two children for a ride. He told me
their names and said that he takes them for a ride whenever he goes
out for a ride.

He mentioned that he drives often with his kids and that it helped
him with his depression and anxiety. I knew all too well about doing
what is necessary to quell anxiety and depression, but some pieces of
the puzzle here were still not fitting. I asked him if it was okay if I
opened the back door and checked on the kids sitting beneath the
blanket. There had been no movement from them since the initial stop
some ten minutes ago. He said they were "sleeping" but it would be
okay for me to check on them. I still felt that something wasn't right
with these kids, but couldn't put my finger on it. I didn't request
backup during this stop as, again, I didn't feel the situation was
anything but a bit odd.

My heart was beating rather quickly as I leaned into the back seat,
one eye on the driver, the other on the kids, flashlight in my right hand
and my other hand on my sidearm should these kids be injured or
worse. As I peeled back the blanket from the kids' bodies, one of the
strangest feelings I'd ever felt came over me. It was a combination of
pure relief and, strangely enough, complete understanding of the

situation. During this time, the driver never once took his hands off the steering wheel or turned around to look. The two "kids" were two life-like, children-sized dolls. I put the blanket back over the kids as I found it, the two little heads peeking out from the top. I closed the back door, went back to the passenger's side window and handed the driver his keys. I said to him, "*the kids look peaceful and happy this evening.*" He smiled for the first time.

I then said, "*you feelin' a little better this evening?*" He replied, "*I lost both my children in a car accident not too long ago. This helps me.*" My eyes began to tear up a bit and I said to him, "*you're a good Father and a good man.*" He said, "*thank you.*"

I knew his pain. I felt his pain. I lived with my own pain and suffering from depression and anxiety every day of my life. This guy no doubt had lost his two children and this was his way of coping with that loss, quelling some of the pain and suffering. However strange his behavior may have seemed ten minutes earlier, I now completely understood the situation, his pain and suffering, and his outlet to cope with that pain. I then said to him, "*you have to buckle up the kids in the back seat.*" He looked at me as if I had two heads, but I knew that he knew someone actually got it. Someone actually understood. He said, "*I will, thank you again, trooper.*" He did just that and we both went our separate ways.

Of all the encounters I had during my routine shifts, I think of that early morning chance meeting often. I hope that I somehow offered validation to his situation that day and maybe, just maybe, helped him in getting to the next phase of recovery from his loss and trauma.

17

November *XX*, 1996. One of the absolute worst days of my entire life. A day that would begin a spiraling even further downward of my fractured life that I could never have imagined in my wildest dreams.

This was the beginning of the end of everything that I had clung to my entire life in order to function and survive.

I had been with FHP just over one year. I was working the afternoon shift. I received a call regarding a signal 4 (crash) in an unincorporated section of the county. An area that should have been serviced by either the local PD or sheriff's office, no thanks to our troop's captain.

I arrived on the scene shortly after the accident occurred. It was a several car pileup caused by a drunk driver who plowed into the rear end of a vehicle that was stopped at a red light. That car then launching forward and hitting the vehicle in front of it and so on. As usual, I was the only trooper in that area and would be handling the scene solo. A couple local officers were there when I got there. I remember one of the officers saying to me, "*how did you get stuck with all of these unincorporated area wrecks?*" I told him it was absolutely ridiculous and I shouldn't be there to begin with. He then said, "*this one has multiple injuries. I took the keys from the drunk that caused it and told him to stay in his car. He's totally trashed, fell asleep.*"

Paramedics were on the scene, tending to the injured and getting ready to transport a few of them to various hospitals. Without getting into the boring details, accidents with injuries are a very long, detailed process of written and diagramed reports. Add a DUI to the accident and the fact that I was working this crash solo and this is now multiple hours of taking a state trooper from where and what his job truly was. I should not have been working this wreck in this unincorporated area and outside of my I-95 patrol area. That blind leadership of captain Blart was just about to cause me my lifelong dream of a career with the DEA and, most importantly, my physical health and a portion of my sanity.

Once I was able to gather all the information from those involved in the accident and being transported to the various hospitals, I was able to head over to the vehicle and person that caused this accident. His vehicle was the last at the scene, all others had been towed. He had been sleeping in the vehicle since my arrival and since the local police officer told him to remain in the vehicle. As I began to approach this vehicle, I could not see anyone inside of it. All of its windows were darkly tinted. As soon as I got to within touching distance of the driver's side door, flashlight in my right hand to try and see inside the vehicle, out of nowhere that door was flung open very forcefully and impacted me like I have never been struck before. I have been in multiple accidents in my life and more fights than I can count. I have had my body banged up pretty badly from head to toe over the years. This impact threw me back and, being off balance to begin with and unable to break my fall, I landed full force directly on the back of my head.

This made it different from any impact or accident of the past. I knew it the second my head hit the pavement. Probably due to the circumstances surrounding this accident, I wasn't totally clear-headed and wasn't paying attention to detail as I should have been. In retrospect, I should have made sure that I could see the occupant before approaching that driver's side door.

I remember the instant sharp, shooting pain I felt throughout my neck, both arms and into my hands. I knew immediately I was in trouble. I've had just about every injury during my day but this was different. The feeling — the electrocution-type, intense and sharp pain — and the strange sensation itself that came over my body. It was slightly reminiscent of the academy injury. I knew my spine was damaged once again. Only this time, it was very serious.

Another instance where a million things raced through my mind in all of a few seconds. However, the one thing that I couldn't get out of my head was the feeling that this was the end. I knew my body. My entire life was dedicated to bringing my mind and body together as one. For me, this had been necessary for survival since childhood. I usually knew exactly what every pain and discomfort was and what caused it, how serious it might be and what I needed to do to recover. I had a strong feeling that very moment that my body was seriously damaged and in the worst possible place — the spine.

There is no injury worse than a spinal injury. It affects each and every part of the body and mind.

I knew it was bad, but had no idea of what I was truly in for physically and emotionally — and the battle for help and fight for justice during the months and years that were ahead.

This was the most freakish of accidents that caused an incredible amount of physical damage from my cervical spine right down through the lumbar portion of my spine and into my hips. However, the major problem and pain at this time was my cervical spine and the damage that was done which seriously affected my arms and hands. I suffered from migraine headaches since childhood. However, in addition to that blinding occasional migraine headache, I would now have constant pain and pressure in my head. Dizziness and loss of vision became common.

This accident and injury also brought about another round of PTSD while further deepening the disorders which existed for decades prior to this incident. A double-whammy of the worst kind. The kind of accident and damage that could only happen to someone with the worst of luck in the history of mankind.

I believed my entire life I was indestructible — invincible — physically. I was in such incredible shape. I trained since childhood, hours upon hours, day in and day out for years on end. How could such an incident cause so much damage? I know for sure the academy accident was the catalyst here. That injury sustained during the academy seriously weakened my spine. I also know for sure that if it wasn't for bad luck my entire life, I'd have had no luck at all.

I had felt that this incident was the ultimate slap in the face from my Higher Power — the God I grew up believing in. My emotional well-being from the age of five was mostly destroyed by alcoholism and addiction.

Now, ironically and cruelly, the most important and needed part of my life — my physical well-being, my ability to train, my medication — is about to be flushed down the toilet, in a split second, at the hands of a drunk. Alcoholism once again impacting and destroying my life. This time inching closer to finishing what it started some twenty-five-plus years earlier. Siphoning the remaining blood from my veins. Sucking out the last breath of oxygen from my lungs. About to take my primary outlet — my means of escape — along with my hopes and dreams that I'd hung onto by the skin of my teeth since childhood. About to create a matching physical pain to compliment and compete with the never-ending emotional pain I've lived with since the age of five. Could there be a worse curse for someone? Especially someone like me whose health and training was the sole medication that maintained — sustained — my sanity? Someone who has survived solely through his outlet? That ability to train quelled the emotional pain and allowed me to move forward and blend in enough to survive while hiding those disorders which crucified me every minute of every day throughout my entire life.

This day was certainly the beginning of the end for me. And it had only just begun. What was to come over the next months and years would make my previously tortured existence look like child's play. It would be evil multiplied many times over as only this cursed being's luck would have it.

Every step of this life, if it could go wrong, it would and it did go wrong. Never able to catch a break even if it landed square in my lap.

Knowing that I could hardly move my arms and neck, I called for another trooper from outside the area to come to the scene and take over and complete the remaining investigation. I wasn't going to be able to so much as move my fingers, let alone wrap up this crash investigation.

The driver — the drunk — later tested .275 BAC. That's three and a half times the legal limit of .08.

This driver had a suspended license, was driving someone else's vehicle without permission, the vehicle was not registered and it was uninsured.

I had refused to be transported to the hospital that evening. I had hoped, though I had felt and known it wasn't going to be possible, that I could "sleep it off" and feel better the next day.

Instead of concern for my injuries, the superiors on duty were more perturbed about my having to leave before my shift was over. I went 142 (off duty/home) and the nightmare that began earlier that day would continue for the next eighteen years.

I had no additional health coverage outside of the Florida State Workers' Compensation System (WCS), which I believed would help me get the necessary diagnosis and treatment for a full recovery. After all, we were told in the academy that if we were ever injured in the line of duty, FHP and the state of Florida had our backs. We had nothing to worry about.

Everything my father and those of his life had told me was about to come true. There would be no honor, no loyalty, not an ounce of genuine concern shown to me from this department or this state government.

FHP and the state of Florida would now see me as no more than a number that would cost them money for a debilitating injury that could not be corrected.

They would sell me down the river and treat me for the next three-plus years worse than an Al-Qaeda terrorist.

I was about to live the second most painful betrayal of my life; FHP and the state of Florida treating me worse than a hardened criminal as I was caught up in this corrupt, dirty, filthy, disgusting web of injustice called Florida State Workers' Compensation System. A horrid network of bought and paid for puppets from doctors to the unscrupulous Judge of Compensation Claims (JCC), *D. Lucifer*, who oversaw my case. His strings pulled by the ruthless cruds who call the shots within this unjust system. Each one on the payroll of the state of Florida. Their job, in the words of the very first WCS doctor I saw the next day regarding my injuries, "*I've got thirty minutes to make you better and get you back to work.*"

This is exactly what many of our military troops face when returning from overseas battles with life-altering injuries. Most times, they are swept under the rug and dragged along, month after month, year after year, caught up in red tape and a disgusting and unjust system that treats its very own worse than criminals — worse than our very own enemies. Unless and until light is cast upon the case and problem — media attention specifically — no one does a thing about the injustice and shameless, deceitful actions of our own government officials and agencies. If not for the media attention surrounding many cases of our injured military troops returning home to this very same predicament and treatment, not a thing would have been done about it and for these troops.

For me, I would now be stuck in this web of outright abuse for over three years. Fighting tooth and nail for one thing; Justice.

FHP failed and betrayed me.

The state of Florida failed and betrayed me.

The justice system itself failed and betrayed me.

There is no loyalty, no honor with these agencies and among these types of people unless you are part of their bloodsucking network of hypocrisy. This system — portions of our government — and those controlling it are more criminal in their ways than those spending time behind bars, and they get away with it, time and again, destroying peoples' lives in the process.

Post my accident, and knowing how severe the spinal injury and newly amped up PTSD, depression, and anxiety was, I tried desperately to get the help I needed to get well and get a clean bill of health. That wasn't going to be possible as every doctor I was sent to was a puppet being controlled by the state of Florida's WCS. They needed to play down my injuries — outright lie — and get me back to work as soon as possible. Not one doctor listened to my cries for help but insisted I would be fine if I took prescription pain (narcotic) medication. That was their remedy and duty to their master in order to return me to work — falling apart as I clearly was — and continue to get referrals from and make money off the state of Florida's WCS.

After several months of getting nowhere in this system — my new physical injuries getting worse and my existing emotional disorders totally out of control — and getting no help from FHP or my troop's brass, I decided to try and reach out to a government official to cut through some of this red tape bullshit and outright abuse and get the help I needed.

I wrote a three-page letter to then Florida senator *T. Jenson.*

I explained how I, a state trooper, was injured in the line of duty and how I was now experiencing, firsthand, for over four months, the unfair and abusive Workers' Compensation Law and the implications of the 1994 revisions — the changes that have adversely affected the injured worker.

I explained that I — or any injured worker in this state — had no say with regards to whom I receive medical treatment from or the kind of treatment, if any, I may receive. I was at the mercy of an insurance carrier and the physicians whose strings they pull. The "managed care" portion of the Workers' Compensation Law states that you <u>must</u> be treated by physicians provided by the WCS only, and, in my opinion, those physicians are motivated more to satisfy the insurance carrier who has hired them, and so continue to get referrals, than in fairly evaluating the injuries and/or disability of the injured worker.

One example I included in this letter to the senator was those very first words out of the mouth of the first workers' compensation physician with whom I met to evaluate and treat my injuries, "*I've got 30 minutes to make you better and get you back to work.*" The nightmare began here with this first greased-palm puppet.

I explained to the senator that over the past four months I was quickly and unprofessionally moved in and out of offices by physicians who rarely looked up at me from the in-hand clipboard which held the prescription pad and the physician's complete attention. I'd explain my pain and problems to each physician. Not one physician paid any attention to what I was saying — each busy as a bee writing prescriptions for pain medication. I would then be handed the script and hear the same line time and again, "*see you in two weeks.*"

Next visit arrives and my injuries are still there and the symptoms much worse. Physician number one now sends me to physician number two. It takes another two weeks to get an appointment with physician number two. All the while, suffering, and a worsening condition with no proper medical attention, just scripts for pain meds being thrown at me.

Physician number two repeats the same process; not looking at me and not paying attention to a thing I'm saying, just writing prescriptions for medication and then the all too common, end-of-appointment phrase, "*see you in two weeks.*"

I did hear a few (contradicting) comments by physicians along the way, such as; "*You'll probably need surgery*" to "*The pain is all in your mind.*" All in my mind?! Really? Is this a physician bound by a Hippocratic oath or a minion schmuck wearing a white lab coat and calling himself a doctor? This "pain is all in your mind" physician, after finally reviewing my MRI (it took ten weeks to finally get the MRI scheduled and done. This should have been done the first few days of my injury) and nerve conduction test results, determined that I had two (more) herniated discs, a compression fracture at C-7, extensive nerve damage, and blackouts possibly being epileptiform.

He wasn't sure about the blackouts, but arranged no further tests to determine the cause. There were more intelligent and compassionate *healers* back in the days when we all lived in caves!

Neither of the five WCS appointed physicians I had seen over the four months leading up to my writing this letter listened to a thing I had to say about the severity of my condition. Not one showed an ounce of concern for the pain and suffering I was enduring.

Each one had the magic remedy; prescription pain medication. A Band-Aid over a gunshot wound to appease their master — the unfair and corrupt Florida Workers' Compensation System.

My condition, of course, continuing to worsen as I was unable to get any legitimate medical attention or treatment for my injuries.

I asked the senator if not able to help me personally, at the very least, any influence the senator may have in affecting a revision of the

1994 Workers' Compensation Law would be deeply appreciated not only within the law enforcement community but with the majority of the electorate — the working public — who, time and again, under this new law, are having their benefits terminated by the insurance carrier (WCS) for invalid reasons. Instead of protecting the working public, this current law — and this WCS — is abusing people and destroying lives and families both financially and health wise.

Several weeks later I received a mostly "form letter" thanking me for taking the time to bring this matter to the senator's attention. The senator would be looking into it. Yeah, right! Our politicians hard at work for the people! What a joke.

Unless and until media attention is brought upon such injustice, it will continue on, uninterrupted, destroying the lives of hard-working people and their families along the way.

I never heard anything else from the senator or anyone that was willing to get involved and help me to get proper medical attention and some justice here.

Workers' Compensation Law — Florida statutes chapter 440 — notes that workers' compensation is designed to "*assure the quick and efficient delivery of disability and medical benefits to an injured worker and to facilitate the worker's return to gainful reemployment at a reasonable cost to the employer.*"

Holy Christ, what bullshit!!

I may have had the slightest shot at justice in the state of Florida if not for my employer actually being FHP/the state of Florida and their puppet Judge of Compensation Claims, D. Lucifer, being a personal friend of the MFM captain who had it in for me and would stop at nothing in achieving his goal of revenge for my putting him in his place, man to man, outside of FHP.

I was told by the WCS's primary doctor and my FHP superiors I couldn't go back to full patrol duty with my documented injuries unless I actually said to the WCS's primary doctor, "*I'm fine. I'd like to return to full duty.*" This certainly wasn't the case, but necessary as I was getting nowhere — absolutely no medical help and any possible shot remaining with DEA was slowly slipping away. Finally, against my better judgement, I said what they all wanted to hear; "*I'm fine. I'd like to return to full duty.*"

I hadn't slept for more than a couple hours on any given day in months. I was constantly dizzy with numbing headaches that just wouldn't quit, was in severe physical and emotional pain, anxiety-ridden and angry as hell after being treated like a piece of crap — a disposable number — by FHP and the state of Florida's WCS. There was absolutely no concern from FHP or the state of Florida for my well-being or getting me the help I needed. I was part of the *team* and I was betrayed.

It wasn't the first time in my life I'd been betrayed but it was one of the five times I've been betrayed in my life that truly hurt, scarred me deeply, and created an anger like no other. And, that knife they stuck in my back would soon be twisted and dug deeper with each passing month. Over three years of a tormenting injustice I would have to endure at the hands of those calling the shots within this corrupt and broken system.

I returned to full duty in the spring of 2007. I was losing my vision quite often while patrolling and on duty. I couldn't think straight or see straight. Every day was intense physical and emotional pain that would not subside, coupled with the inability to sleep.

I remember during midnight shifts constantly stopping at gas stations to pick up ice to cover my head and face with. An attempt to try and stop myself from drifting off while driving. I was a zombie.

I returned to full duty as an FHP state trooper against my better judgement. I knew I was in no condition physically or emotionally to be there. No one else in the department really cared. I was able to see quite clearly during this time everything I had painfully come to know to be true over the past five months since my injury; I was expendable. I was a mere number to this agency and, specifically, my troop's brass. I was that warm body that was needed to fill the position behind the wheel of the FHP trooper vehicle. The captain of my troop and most of the supervisors would have put a mannequin in a trooper uniform, propped it up behind the wheel, and sent if off on patrol if they could have.

There was no honor, no respect, no loyalty within this troop's leadership. Not one had my back. Not one gave a rat's ass about me or my condition. All that mattered to most of the supervisors/brass was that there was a trooper behind the wheel and visible out there on the highway, regardless of whether that trooper was healthy or not.

From my first week as a member of this particular troop, it became clearer and much easier to see why the morale here was minus zero; this good ole boy network — my troop in particular — was being run at every level by a slew of incompetent, unprofessional, self-serving buffoons.

Knowing and speaking with LEO's and brass from other law enforcement agencies, I am confident that most other agencies — especially outside of the state of Florida — and their leadership would have had my back. However, as my luck always had it, I wound up with the shit end of the stick once again.

My return to full duty in the condition I was in was a last resort solely to try and salvage my dream of a career with the DEA.

While trying desperately to keep my physical and emotional condition under wraps from DEA, I reached out and tried to pick up where I had left off a few months earlier. I still had a bit of hope that maybe, just maybe, I would be able to continue my progress forward with DEA.

My line of duty accident happened a little over a year into my employment with FHP. I had begun the process of moving forward with DEA just weeks prior to this accident. Making some calls, talking to various people, getting all my ducks in a row so I could move forward and on to what had been my dream and goal since childhood. This very accident would change all that.

I was eventually told by one of my contacts within DEA that I would not be able to move up the ladder to a career with that agency as I wouldn't be able to attend the DEA training academy due to my spinal injury. I was now considered "damaged goods" having such a serious and documented injury. I was now a liability that no agency could take a chance with, whether sending me to a federal law enforcement academy or hiring me via a lateral transfer to another local or state agency. I was trapped. Not only was my health on the line and deteriorating rapidly, it would be near-impossible to move on to *any* other law enforcement agency.

My childhood dream of becoming a DEA agent was over. Once again, as was common throughout my life, this door too would slam shut as soon as I reached the threshold, crawling every step of that way on my hands and knees.

After losing my vision yet again while patrolling during one of my midnight shifts, I finally realized that not only was my LEO career over but I was going to most likely become an LEO death statistic if I continued on full duty in this condition. I was going to die in the line of duty as I was in no condition physically or emotionally to be there. I had finally had enough of continually being denied the proper medical attention I needed and by doctors of my choice.

I had been swept under the rug and had been waiting around for someone to help me, to rescue me. That wasn't going to happen. If I didn't seek out legal representation regarding this situation and begin seeing doctors who were not on the payroll of and being controlled by the state of Florida's WCS system, I wasn't going to get any honest help with my situation and injuries.

I decided to get an attorney and fight for the proper medical attention I was entitled to and deserved. It was time to stop dillydallying and to fight for Justice.

I had been treated worse than that academy "whale shit" and I had earned my position and I was part of the team! I was in this battle alone with no support from my own agency or immediate superiors. If I had to make waves and file a lawsuit against FHP and the state of Florida, so be it.

I would endure a three-plus year war with FHP and the state of Florida's WCS that was nothing less than pure injustice at all levels. I learned from personal experience that not only some MFM troopers and supervisors within my troop abused their authority and had no fear of consequences, but so did those within the state of Florida's WCS and, specifically, their bought and paid for JCC puppet that oversaw and ruled very partially on my case.

I had been going through hell for months since my line of duty accident. Not only did I have to deal and live with disorders that emotionally had devastated me since childhood, I now had a physical disability creating a never-ending physical pain that equaled and rivaled my lifelong emotional pain and that I could not quell. My ability to train — my medication — was drastically reduced from this injury. Mobility problems began from the waist up. Headaches like I'd never had prior. Dizziness was common for quite some time. I could hardly move my neck for nearly a year. Shooting pain up and down my spine and arms. Hands and fingers haven't stopped tingling to this day. They go numb any time there is pressure on my head and neck.

I could not sleep in a horizontal position during this time and for the next couple of years! Sleep would now become something of the past. Any sleep I was able to get was done sitting in a reclining chair with my neck positioned vertically — without bending in the slightest — so there was no pressure on the cervical spine. I have yet to sleep more than several hours in one night since this accident and spinal injury. I still, to this very day, cannot put direct pressure on my cervical spine when sleeping, making it very difficult to sleep at all. I wake within a couple hours in terrible cervical pain and with numb hands almost on a nightly basis even though I sleep with special pillows and in crazy, uncomfortable positions to keep my spine straight and from curving. It's been a no-win situation.

My lower spine during this first year post the accident was painful and bothersome but nothing compared to my cervical spine and pain. My lower spinal vertebrae would, however, in years to come, collapse like dominos. This line of duty accident being the catalyst for that catastrophe.

Training was difficult but absolutely necessary for my survival, more so now with the physical disability and pain. I could no longer lift anything over my head (and to this very day). I could no longer hit a punching bag, spar, roll, or do anything that would jolt my spine or cause pressure in and around my cervical area. I spent the majority of my time trying desperately to create an endorphin kick to quell not only my lifelong emotional pain that had now multiplied many times over but now this new, consistent, horrible physical pain.

Could my luck truly get any worse in life?

The answer to that question was yes. And much worse in the months and years that followed.

Most of my training would be concentrated below the waist — leg work. I still did whatever training I could, whenever I could, but my health and training was seriously and majorly compromised by this spinal injury.

Now, in addition to a lifelong battle against disorders causing emotionally crippling pain, I was plagued by a physical disability with consistent, intense physical pain that I could not suppress. I felt my lifelong, primary medication — my ability to train — beginning to slip away from me. My emotional state was near total collapse and the outright evil and injustice I was dealing with by way of FHP, the state of Florida's WCS and a most despicable, dishonest JCC would push me to my absolute limit and near-breaking point.

With everything I had been through and endured during my life beginning at the age of five, the injustice and malicious treatment I was subjected to by these people and this system proved to be one of the worst and most emotionally damaging incidents ever to occur in my

lifetime. It created a hatred and anger like I had never felt before —
and it took nearly twenty years, therapy, writing this book, and
beginning a recovery process to begin to let the pain and hatred for
these evil people and their injustice leave my soul.

It was the most painful betrayal I had ever felt to this point in my
life next to my brother trying to kill me a couple years earlier.

I had been in a major depression for years and isolating as a result.
This injury and the injustice I was subjected to every day for the next
several years once again deepened my depression and pushed me even
further into isolation.

It was the worst isolation of my life to this point. I seldom left my
home. Sure, there were some friends, neighbors, family, and fellow
troopers who would call to see how I was doing, stop by to see me
every now and again, but, like I had done my entire life, I would push
all away, never return calls and disappear more and more into an
isolation where I was safe from additional stress, pain, and anxiety.
Eventually, people stop trying to contact and connect with you. The
mission of the disorders accomplished.

At one point during this time when I went out again from full day
— and for the last time — May 2007, Capt. Blart came to my home.
Not to see how I was doing or if there was anything he or FHP could
do to help me get the medical treatment I was due and entitled to (or
the disability pay and other financial benefits that were being withheld
by FHP and the WCS system), but to try and push his weight around
— put the screws on me — and get me back to full duty. Get that
warm body behind the wheel of the FHP vehicle and back on the road
busting ass to clear the unincorporated wrecks he burdened his very
own understaffed troop with. The same troop, due mostly in part to
this Capt.'s blind leadership, that had the worst morale of any LEO
agency in the county and, perhaps, any other FHP troop in all of
Florida.

He gave me an ultimatum; he rudely ordered me to return to full
duty or resign.

I thought to myself that very second, "*this ignorant, arrogant, self-
serving asshole is a captain?*" A security guard at Disney World is more
qualified to run this troop than this guy!

He was out of line. First off, only the WCS's puppet doctor could
return me to full duty and he wouldn't do so — couldn't do so with my
documented spinal injury — unless and until I *lied* directly to this *Dr. N*

about my condition and said, "*I am fine*", which I had no choice but to do the first time around in April of 2007 in order to try and salvage my career and move forward with DEA. I was furious and highly insulted. He came to my home in full uniform — I was not on duty and not in uniform — and he outright disrespected me not so much with what he said but how he said it. In my world, there isn't anything worse than straight up disrespecting another person. Between men, it can be deadly where I come from. Hotter than a branding iron and without hesitation, I took my badge from my wallet, handed it to him, told him to stick it up his ass and to get the fuck out of my house before I broke his face. He flat out and intentionally disrespected me and was disrespected in return.

He quickly exited my home.

Instead of this captain talking to me in the days to come (or on this very day) and settling any differences like a man, he would, like the MFM coward that he was, put pen to paper and his lies to the ear of his close, personal buddy, Lucifer, the JCC.

Not having a man's bone in his body, he would fabricate reports to the JCC noting I said certain things I had never said. i.e.: he wrote a report claiming I said that I didn't like midnight shift because I couldn't sleep. I loved midnight shift! It was made for me, all things considered. I couldn't function because of lack of sleep due to my line of duty injuries and condition. It had nothing whatsoever to do with the shift and this POS Capt. knew it.

I had also heard via other troopers that this unprofessional and vindictive Capt. Blart would also make some calls to people heading the WCS — in addition to his conversations with the JCC — and say and do anything possible to get his revenge.

My father and those of his life would always say, "hug your enemy." It was their version of "keep your friends close and your enemies closer." I understood this perfectly and, if I had been involved in "that life", I most certainly would have had to adjust my attitude — bite my tongue and swallow my pride in the face of disrespect — and become a good bullshitter. Your very life depended on it. In retrospect, perhaps I should have begun that very day with this asshole Capt. instead of allowing him to push my buttons. I have always said what I felt — spoke the truth —

regardless of consequences. No one ever had to wonder what I was thinking or what I thought of them.

Once again, my honesty and straightforwardness in life would come back to haunt me. This Capt. made sure he supplied the JCC, his "close, personal buddy", with bullcrap reports about me that he completely fabricated. He made sure the judge, Lucifer, knew he didn't like me and wanted me screwed. Lucifer certainly complied.

🦋 🦋 🦋 🦋

I did resign a couple weeks later as I had been betrayed several times over by FHP/my superiors and the state of Florida's WCS.

My career in law enforcement ended with the spinal injury I sustained from that line of duty accident. The only place — agency — I could have remained as damaged goods was FHP.

I couldn't possibly continue on as a state trooper — or an LEO — with my injuries and I wouldn't in a million years work side-by-side with these back-stabbing, self-serving, incompetent cowards that made up the chain of command in my district's troop.

This agency — my very troop and most of its supervisory brass — was truly the bottom of the barrel when it came to honor, trust, respect, loyalty, competency, professionalism and class. Everything I had heard about my troop's leadership by other LEO's and LEO brass in south Florida was now clear as day and proven to be true as the sky was blue.

I've never swallowed my pride or bit my tongue in my life — except on a few occasions, always remaining professional, when dealing with the public when I was on duty as a state trooper. I've never kissed or stuck my nose up anyone's ass to appease them or get ahead at my job or in life in general. I could never look at myself in the mirror and live with myself if I did. Part of growing up on the streets is learning how to "con" and do just this with an ulterior motive. It's the one lesson of the streets and growing up as I did that I could never bring myself to do. It's a wonderful psychological tool to get ahead in life and keep your enemy off-guard if you can do it. I was never able to sugarcoat or keep my true feelings about anything or anyone concealed. Never able to bullshit and con someone into thinking — believing — that I was happy if I wasn't, if I liked them if I didn't. I paid the price many times over throughout my life by not conning some asshole who held the reigns into thinking I liked or respected him. So be it. I've never compromised who I truly am and that is something that I will always be proud of. I will always be able to look in the mirror and know I didn't sell out who I was for anyone or anything. I stayed true to myself always, regardless of the consequences.

I remember once during the beginning of my recovery process in 2012, my therapist asked me if perhaps I had a chip on my shoulder. "Chip?", I replied. "I have so many chips accumulated throughout my life that I have no shoulders left!"

A lifetime of trauma, betrayal, pain and anger molded a very particular feeling and attitude necessary for my very survival.

I went through more than a handful of attorneys before I was fortunate enough to find one that was willing to take on FHP and the state of Florida's WCS.

The first few attorneys that were representing me were recommended by LEO organizations of which I was a member. The few after that were referrals from previous attorneys unable to help me, as well as from research I had done.

With each of the attorneys that I would go through within that first year, the routine and outcome was always the same; meet with the attorney, take all of my doctor reports and supporting documentation for my injuries, and discuss my intentions — which were to finally get the proper medical attention that I deserved and was entitled to and to sue FHP and the state of Florida's WCC for the benefits that were being withheld and denied and that I rightly deserved and was entitled to.

Some attorneys would refer me to qualified physicians for proper medical attention and some it was quite clear to me were more interested in having their friends and family make some extra cash repeating medical exams and the such.

I refused to play that game. I wasn't looking to make other people extra money at my expense and off of my suffering. If the attorney wasn't sincere, honest, and upfront, I moved on to the next one. It was extremely frustrating trying to find not only an honest and sincere attorney to represent me that didn't fear FHP and the state of Florida's WCS, but finding qualified and sincere physicians in the state of Florida concerned with helping me as opposed to lining their pockets with money from unnecessary exams and procedures.

With each attorney I would see during this first year of desperately trying to find proper legal representation, I would hear the same few statements from each attorney within a few weeks of representing me;

"My hands are tied."

"It's a no-win situation with FHP and the State of Florida's Workers' Compensation System."

"It's going to be nearly impossible to get you the benefits that you are entitled to here in Florida. This is the worst state in the country to get hurt in and be fairly compensated, especially your case against a state agency."

The last attorney I heard this from, *M. Savitz*, a partner in a smaller south Florida law firm, was also the most sincere. He said he had a friend who was an attorney that he'd like for me to call and meet. His friend might be willing to take on the difficult and nearly impossible-to-win battle against FHP and the state of Florida.

I met with his friend, attorney *S. Brosco (SB)*, who was at the time working for a very large law firm in south Florida. I knew from our first conversation that SB was an upfront and honest person and he truly wanted to see justice served in this instance. He knew I was being screwed. So did every other attorney I spoke with.

However, each one realized that they wouldn't be paid if we didn't win — and winning even a clear-cut case of a documented line of duty disability such as mine was a long shot with FHP and this state of Florida's WCS.

SB took on the challenge and injustice and, in time, it seemed to me it became a very personal battle for him too. He would get so deeply involved and upset with the blatant injustice we were facing that his law firm would tell him he needed to back off from spending so much time on my case. There was very little to no attorney money/compensation involved for his law firm in this no-win situation. Again, a no-win situation not because the evidence didn't support my entitlement to benefits and total disability due to my line of duty accident — it clearly did — but for the simple reason we were fighting a state agency — FHP — and the all-mighty, make and break your own rules, do whatever you want and get away with it, state of Florida's WCS.

Little did we know at the time, that was only part of it. And the lesser of the evil parts. The other unjust part was the puppet on the strings of the state of Florida's WCS and personal friend of my troop's captain. A manipulative and dishonest Judge of Compensation Claims,

D. Lucifer, who oversaw and had complete control of my case — and sole discretion of its outcome.

I remember SB telling me one day, maybe a year into representing me, that he was going to be leaving his present law firm and start his own law office. He said that it was a bit premature, but the time had come. I got the feeling that my case may have had something to do with his leaving the law firm. I asked him if my instinct was correct. He said that his representing me and the time he was spending on my case did have a role in his timing. His law firm told him to back off, he was spending too much time on my case and it wasn't going to be worth it.

Obtaining justice, my benefits, and the ever-mounting attorney fees was a very long shot with this case against FHP and the Florida state WCS.

SB was a straight-forward, sincere, and honorable person and attorney. A rare breed all-around. I gained an awful lot of respect and admiration for him during the time he was representing me. There aren't many people that I have come across in my life that I can honestly say is a class act and an honorable person that I truly admire and look up to. SB is one of the few. I made sure he knew how I felt and told him that I did consider him family and was forever grateful and always loyal as a true friend for all that he had done for me.

SB was also the only male figure that had ever seen a tear in my eye during my adult life. He was part of an extremely trying, painful time and chapter in my life that lasted over three years and took a hefty toll on me emotionally as well as physically.

Another of the greatest regrets of my life was not keeping in touch with SB once the case had finally ended. I was in total seclusion and the worst emotional state of my life to that point. Anxiety and panic attacks as common and expected as a sunrise. I would soon change — once again — my email address and phone number and move on to Las Vegas where my isolation, physical and emotional pain, and ever-constraining disorders peaked and nearly took my sanity and life in the worst of ways.

SB did leave the law firm he had been working for when he took on my case. He started his own law office while still representing me. My case occupying a lot of his time and energy. He believed in me and the case. The injustice that I was made to endure was bothering him I believe as much as it was me. I think we were both learning an awful lot — about the law, the system, injustice, corruption, people — during the couple of years he was representing me and until the very ending of this nightmare.

18

I had left Florida in 1999 and moved back to Rhode Island. Reason being twofold: I needed to remove myself from the area as my anger levels and the hatred I had been feeling was brewing at an extremely high temperature and ready to boil over. I wanted to rip a few heads off, actually. I needed to get out of there before my emotions really took over and I put myself in an even worse situation. I also needed to see physicians that I trusted would accurately diagnose my injuries and provide options for some kind of relief and recovery. I would learn in the months and years ahead that was not going to be possible with my injuries. I was told time and again by doctors and surgeons that the only thing I would be able to do is find a way to live with the pain. I knew all too well about living with pain — and now it was going to be many times worse than I had experienced and endured the past twenty-five years.

I lived with my parents when I returned to Rhode Island. This was made even more difficult as it was my deepest of depressions to date. Year after year, for decades on end, I continually sank deeper and deeper into that darkness. I needed to be alone. I never wanted anyone, especially my mother, to know my true pain and condition. I needed to keep the severity of my emotional and physical pain from everyone around me. This was going to be extremely difficult living with my parents at this time in my life. It was tough through my younger years hiding my emotional pain and despair and this was many times more severe now.

I lived in seclusion — isolation — throughout the battle with FHP and the state of Florida's WCS and for the next four years in Rhode Island until I moved to the southwestern part of the country — Las Vegas specifically — at the advice of my doctors. The dry climate in this area being best for the painful arthritic condition throughout my spine.

This was, to date, the worst time ever in my life emotionally and physically. I never believed I could be in such a position *physically* — chronic, intense physical pain — on top of the emotional pain, imprisonment, and torture that had been my life for some twenty-five years.

I had never contemplated suicide in my life but I had begun thinking of it often the past couple years and over the years to come. My physical and emotional pain progressively worsening with each passing year right up until I began writing this book, sixteen years to the day of my line of duty accident.

I was existing, every minute of every day, with inconceivable physical and emotional pain and was extremely angry at my Higher Power for allowing this pain and loss in my life to continue. I would experience the third greatest betrayal of my life to date — mere months after the second most painful betrayal by FHP and the state of Florida: I would stop praying and lose all faith in the Higher Power I once so strongly believed in. That faith and belief that my mother instilled in me as a child was gone. I could no longer believe in a God that would allow this kind of pain and loss in my life, year after year, continually worsening in every possible way. I considered this at the time total betrayal by my Higher Power. I stopped my daily prayers of the past thirty years and cursed this God daily for what my life had been and how it continued to worsen.

I had questioned my Higher Power's light in my life for a very long time. Now, just when I needed my God the most, I was totally abandoned.

I felt as though my Higher Power had taken away my entire childhood and, now, my lifelong dream (of DEA), slamming shut yet another door as I crawled to its threshold.

My God had snatched away in one fell swoop the majority of my medication — my primary outlet — needed to quell the emotional pain and survive the emotional imprisonment I had endured since the age of five. Replacing this with a physical disability producing a consistent, intense pain which now rivaled my emotional pain.

As if this wasn't enough torture, all within this very same time frame, I had been betrayed by FHP and was being persecuted, bullied, and victimized by a dishonest JCC and his master, the state of Florida's WCS.

Though, worse yet, was the pain and anger I had felt and was living with feeling betrayed by my Higher Power. A pain and anger that I could never convey in writing.

What kind of God allows this never-ending pain, misery, and torment?

Emotional, and now physical, crucifixion on a daily basis, year in and year out, my entire life?

What kind of God allows not an ounce of positive balance, not a ray of sunshine to pierce the persistent darkness in someone's life?

A life completely unbalanced and overtaken by never-ending pain, loss, and misery.

Death would have been less cruel than the torment I'd lived with the past twenty-five-plus years and was about to endure — multiplied many times over — for the next fourteen years to come.

To hell with God! There is no God in *my* life. There never has been I would feel now. That faith and love for my Higher Power was turning to a very deep anger I never thought I could feel for a God I once believed in and prayed to daily.

In the years to come, as my emotional and physical well-being had once again made a turn for the worse, the pure anger I felt for my Higher Power became pure hatred.

Some nine years down the road from my line of duty accident I would endure the most damaging accident in my life. It decimated what remained of my lower spine and near crippled me. I found nothing but hatred for that Higher Power at that time. He wasn't protecting me now or ever, he wasn't carrying me — he dropped me square on my head and left me to be devoured by wolves. It was total betrayal to me.

I remember SB coming up to Rhode Island a few months after I moved back there. He was going to depose not only my doctors but the doctors in Rhode Island that the state of Florida's WCS had hired and sent me to for their Independent Medical Exam (IME) to counter and diminish my doctors' diagnosis and professional opinions.

We met for lunch on Federal Hill when he flew into town. He had been wanting to try some authentic Italian cuisine. The Hill was the place in the day for that!

He did the depositions the next day and he was back off to Florida.

If anyone is familiar with the injustice and added emotional stress and anger I had to endure during the several years of this unjust horror, it was SB. He had witnessed it and lived it firsthand too. No one knows the injustice and torment I had to endure due to this corrupt system and dishonorable JCC better than SB — as no one knows that torment, pain, and heartache I had lived with, consistently, for over forty years better than my first and second therapist.

Fighting the state of Florida was the same as trying to stand up to and fight any other bully. And that is precisely what this state of Florida's WCS and all of its' puppets were; bullies. I had endured years of bullying during my childhood. This was just another form disguised as a state agency with a JCC — the sole "trier of fact" — giving the appearance of impartiality and fairness. Both this state agency and this judge pushed their weight around, doing whatever they wanted, with no fear of consequences for their unjust actions.

There is no impartiality here. A claimant has no "rights" to an impartial jury of his peers. There is no jury looking over the evidence without bias and deciding based on fact. There is a member of the state of Florida's WCS — the Judge of Compensation Claims — put into his position by a governor of the state which employs and pays him. The decision this JCC hands down, however biased and fallacious, is final. What this JCC says and rules goes. Your only recourse is an appeal to the First District Court of Appeal — which we did. This was a joke too. Just another spoke in this wheel of injustice.

I liken this all-controlling state WCS system to someone who seriously hurts or kills a member of your family. Then you — the victim's family member — are the one deciding what happens to the perpetrator. It isn't going to be fair.

This entire fiasco called the State of Florida's Workers' Compensation System was pure madness and injustice — and they got away with it. Most likely, still continue to get away with it. Crushing injured workers — emotionally, physically, and financially — and their families in the process.

I had been followed and videotaped while in Florida by private investigators that this WCS had hired. They did the same thing when I moved back to Rhode Island. They would stop at nothing to try and bury me. Try and dig up *anything* — at any cost — that might help them negate the truth, the facts of the case; that I was seriously and permanently injured as a result of my line of duty accident and was entitled to and deserved benefits — just compensation — to that effect.

Their own doctors — bought and paid for puppets — couldn't refute the evidence and the facts of my line of duty accident and the disability which resulted. However, they could — and did — downplay my injuries and manipulated the MMI (Maximum Medical Improvement) system by which benefits and the extent of the disability are determined. These puppets on the payroll of the state of Florida's

WCS would consistently say that I was not at MMI and could possibly get better. Though my condition worsened every year, as documented by tests, reports, MRI's, and testimony from my doctors, the puppet doctors' evaluations remained the same; not at MMI.

This MMI and IME (Independent Medical Examination) gibberish is how this bully — this state WCS — keeps control and manipulates the truth and facts of a disability case.

The three-plus year battle with this bully agency was similar to what one might see and come to expect during a criminal prosecution; the prosecutor (the bully here) in a criminal case would pay his "experts" to say one thing while the defense would pay their "experts" to say the exact opposite. You have two "experts" — doctors in my case — contradicting each other; totally disabled vs not totally disabled. Serious injury vs not serious injury. At MMI vs not at MMI.

How is that possible, right? It's not. It all comes down to money. Only difference with my situation, I had now been thoroughly examined by legitimate doctors and the only money they received from me was the same as they would receive from any other patient — the cost of the visit and examinations. Those examinations — nerve conduction tests, MRI's, X-rays, comparisons to previous MRI's and X-rays, and a host of other necessary tests and examinations — proved my injuries were a direct result of my line of duty accident and that my injuries were not going to get any better, any time soon — they were permanent.

The state of Florida's WCS (the bully) would now send me to the doctors (puppets) on their payroll whose job it was to downplay — minimize — my injuries and say I was not at MMI and could fully recover. There is no fully recovering from bulging, herniated, compression fractured discs in the spine causing bi-lateral radiculopathy, extensive nerve damage and spasms throughout the spine, both arms and hands, or the emotional trauma (PTSD) I had endured as a result of that line of duty accident and was continually being subjected to by the bully.

This is what they would do, time and again, for years. This, in addition to their puppet JCC causing delays, stalling, and outright being dishonest and bias with his overseeing and controlling my case. Their non-stop bullying tactics and continual injustice wear you down and emotionally beat you senseless.

My attorney knew that I was permanently disabled and the facts supported this. He wanted me to apply for Social Security Disability around 1999. I was against this at first. My reasoning was that I didn't think the federal government was responsible for my disability benefits. The state of Florida was responsible and should be held accountable.

However, as we discussed, I had a claim against FHP and the state of Florida and the entire WCS system was run by the state of Florida. It was going to be a very long shot getting justice here.

I went ahead and applied for SS disability. I was found to be totally disabled both from a physical as well as emotional standpoint. I began receiving disability benefits rather quickly.

The majority of people who are injured and/or disabled and apply for SS disability benefits are refused, especially the first time applying. Many have to reapply over and over. My medical records and the facts of my disability were so clearly evident, I was awarded SS disability benefits the very first time I had applied.

What does that say of the Judge of Compensation Claims — "The trier of fact" — and the state of Florida's WCS who claimed there was no evidence to support total disability and denied every claim based on the judge's opinion of my/the claimant's "credibility" and that claimant's refusal to follow doctors' recommendations — which was, solely, to take prescription pain medication/narcotics?

Worse yet was the fact that, aside from the First District Court of Appeal, I had no recourse for justice. The state of Florida's WCS controlled the doctors to the JCC and everything in between.

This judge, Lucifer, at the beginning of the case, asked me, through my attorney, SB, if I would like him to recuse himself in place of another JCC. Reason being; he acknowledged that he was a close, personal friend of my former FHP Capt., Blart, and there was bad blood between the Capt. and me. Same Capt. I told to stick my badge up his ass. I didn't know at this particular time, but the Capt. had been in this Judge's ear ever since about me.

Being in such an emotionally fragile state not only due to the disorders I had suffered with my entire life but from the emotional and physical results of that line of duty accident and, most importantly at this time, how these people and this system had treated me and what they had put me through, I was unable to think clearly. I should have had him recuse himself. It was a very big mistake on my part. One of the biggest mistakes I've ever made.

I remember asking SB what he thought about the judge recusing himself. He left it up to me but said he thought that the judge would be fair and base his ruling on the evidence and facts of the case. I guess in my heart at that time I still truly believed that a *Judge* would be honorable, fair, and impartial and rule based on the evidence and facts. I was naive, as his ruling was most definitely swayed by a personal friendship with the Capt. who disliked me and made that known to his friend, the JCC overseeing my case. What a system!

I received no pay or financial benefits from FHP or the state of Florida during this three-plus year battle and injustice.

This judge would go on to deny me my benefits time and again over the years leading up to his "Final Order" in 2000. Each time, including his final judgement, his reasoning was that I was "not credible" and that I refused to follow my doctors' instructions — which was, exclusively, to take medication for pain.

I certainly could have lied and said I will take — am taking — pain medication. However, again, no doctor or judge has the right to demand I take medication — especially narcotic pain meds — when I don't believe in putting that medication into my body. It's putting a Band-Aid over a six-inch-long, straight-to-the-bone stab wound, so to speak.

Bottom line, pain medication was not about to make me "better". The facts were the facts; I had a permanent and severe spinal injury as a result of a line of duty accident that was not going to get better any time soon — it was going to progressively worsen, as it did over the next decade and a half.

The ultimate slap in the face, after living this nightmare, this injustice for over three years, was receiving and reading the puppet JCC's twenty-four page "Final Order" in January of 2000. The "final *blow*", the "final *injustice*" handed down and ever-so-craftily written in an attempt to hide the truth — the facts of this case — and to justify his unsound, unethical, and bias decision.

He makes note that the claimant's attainment of MMI was left as an issue for his determination. Really? He's not a doctor! MMI — again, this is one of the insurance industry's tools and ways of controlling an injured and disabled person's benefits, limits of such, or any at all. This, along with their IME's.

Doctors who provide these MMI's and IME's — bought and paid for by the insurance company/WCS — keep the ball always in their court, regardless of the truth and facts of the case/claim.

As with the entire proceeding, I had no say and no choice whatsoever. Might as well have been living in China or old time Russia.

No rights, no justice, no recourse — at the mercy of a dishonest system and JCC.

The entire twenty-four pages, this "judge" continually points to the "fact" that I refused to take medication for my physical as well as emotional pain.

This is the only "fact" that is correct and honest within his entire "Final Order" ruling.

He notes, verbatim, "*Claimant had refused to comply with the treatment regimens prescribed by his doctors.*" Other statements to this effect throughout his slyly written tirade of a ruling, "*I do not believe that the claimant is as disabled physically as he claims. The claimant complains of severe and unrelenting pain, blackouts, and severe headaches which cause loss of vision, radiating neck pain, dizziness, and an inability to putting pressure whatsoever on his head or neck. Yet he consistently refuses to take any prescription medication for his physical or his emotional condition which might improve or relieve his symptoms*" ... "*The claimant continues to refuse offered treatment in the form of medications*".

A blind person could see — without even reviewing the true facts of the case — where this judge was going regardless of the medical facts before him and those medical reports that were conveniently left out of the mix. During his six pages of "*briefly summarizing this claimant's medical history*", he either conveniently left out or was not provided a complete medical history during the time line he had introduced into his final order.

There were multiple doctors (visits) and their reports and opinions not included in that "brief summary". Each portion of the medical history that was left out was from a doctor and/or report supporting my claim of permanent disability and to rightfully owed benefits as a result of such. Coincidence?

He would rule against me, denying *all* claims. He noted, "*I agree with the employer/carrier that this claimant lacks credibility. The Judge of Compensation Claims, as the trier of fact, has the right to determine the credibility of witnesses, including the claimant. There are many inconsistencies and discrepancies in the claimant's testimony. As example of this, the claimant told Dr. N that he had no pain, only an occasional stiff neck .... consequently, Dr. N released the claimant to return to work.*"

Dr. N was the primary physician I was made to see and a bought and paid for puppet of the State's WCS. The JCC's example above refers to the time that this Dr. N told me — face to face in his office — I needed to say that I was fine and wanted to return to work for him to release me to full duty. That is what I had to do and did at the time. However, I never said I had no pain and only a stiff neck. Quite obviously, the puppets put whatever made up comments they want — and wanted me to say — into their reports.

This judge goes on to say, "*Thereafter, the claimant did, in fact, return to work for the employer herein, The Florida Highway Patrol, but he then began to complain about working the midnight shift.*" I never complained about working the midnight shift. I told Capt. Blart that I was having difficulty remaining awake and alert due to my condition and not being able to sleep because of said condition. My lack of sleep and overall physical and emotional condition had absolutely nothing to do with the midnight shift. I preferred the midnight shift. There were hardly any signal 4's to work compared to nothing but signal 4's (and mostly in unincorporated areas of the county) to work during the morning and afternoon shifts. There were other troopers on the midnight shift that would actually catch some z's at home, or at their girlfriend's house, while on duty. That's how great the midnight shift was! It didn't matter what shift I was working; I couldn't sleep at any time throughout the day or night due to my injuries. This portion of his report came directly from MFM Blart, without doubt. This Capt. twisted my words around and did — said and wrote in reports — whatever he had to do to turn the screws on me due to my telling him to stick my badge up his ass. That's what a coward does. Blart's weapon was a pen and paper and having the judge presiding over my WC case, D. Lucifer, as his close, personal friend and avenger.

This judge goes on to write, "*The claimant's supervisor told the claimant he must adjust to the hours. Shortly thereafter, the claimant alleged experiencing a blackout while driving a Florida Highway Patrol vehicle. In May 1997, the claimant stopped working all together. The claimant then returned to Dr. N in June of 1997, and told the Dr. that he, the claimant, had lied because he had wanted to return to work. The claimant then told Dr. N that he really never had been pain free and he was also having episodes of loss of vision.*" Once again, absolutely ridiculous how these puppets have manipulated the facts and my words. I was having loss of vision episodes all along due to my condition and lack of sleep. I never lost consciousness and never said that I lost consciousness. I also didn't "return" to Dr. N of my own free will. I was told by the state of

Florida's WCS coordinator that I must go back to him. I told this Dr. N very clearly when I was forced back to see him in June of 1997 that the only reason I told him I was fine and wanted to return to full duty was because he made it quite clear during our April 1997 visit that if I didn't say *those very words*, he could not — would not — release me to full duty.

Again, each of these puppets will say and write in these reports what benefits and protects them, not what was actually said or transpired during these exams and visits.

This judge, at no time, ever spoke with me in person regarding anything; any written reports he had before him, questions regarding what he claimed to be discrepancies and inconsistencies, or reasons for my refusing to take medication.

I had no opportunity to be heard. Regardless of whether the reports were accurate, inaccurate, or altered — and most were inaccurate and altered with regards to statements I had made — there was no opportunity to clarify or correct what he considered "inaccuracies".

In retrospect, it wouldn't have mattered anyway. This judge's mind had been made up long before any facts were presented him.

Throughout this final order, he continually noted that I "lacked credibility."

Credibility? The doctors — both my own and the puppets controlled by the State of Florida's WCS system — provided the medical facts in this case. Not my credibility. Here we have a dishonest, bias, puppet on the strings of the state government that employs him calling into question my credibility. If I was anything throughout, I was too honest. Brutally honest as I've been my entire life. I told each and every doctor that I had seen during this unjust nightmare that I did not take medication, regardless of my condition. I never took medication prior to this three-plus years of hell I was put through, I haven't taken medication in the nearly twenty years that followed. It is my body, it is my mind, it is my choice. The medication itself was not going to correct my damaged-beyond-repair spine or alleviate the emotional pain that was exacerbated by this corrupt system and all of its' dishonest puppets.

I had even heard these very words from others, "*flush it down the toilet.*" Meaning, don't be honest, say you are taking the medication. Probably what I should have done. What most would do. It's not my style. It's not who I am. I don't compromise who I am or what I believe for anyone. Never have, I never will.

However, I learned the hard way that honesty and honor within a truly corrupt system controlled by less than scrupulous players was not rewarded, but punished. Unfortunately, and contrary to my beliefs and how I'd lived my life, honesty was not the best policy. My honesty about not taking medication turned out to be a major factor that this JCC skewed and used to craft a twenty-four page deceitful, unjust, final order ruling.

As U2's lead singer, Bono, sings in the first line of the song *Who's Gonna Ride Your Wild Horses*; "*you're dangerous, 'cause you're honest.*" Since I was a kid, that honesty more often than not had been harmful to no one but me, advantageous to others.

Here's the kicker; the employer/carrier/state of Florida's WCS asserted defense that; "*the claimant is not permanently and totally disabled*". Yet they also claimed within the pages of this final order ruling entitlement to an offset for social security disability benefits I was currently receiving.

I had been found to be permanently and totally disabled many months prior to this judge's "Final Order" by the federal government's Social Security Disability Division and was receiving SS disability benefits for the injuries and disability sustained during my line of duty accident.

MMI had clearly been attained and the facts of my disability reviewed and ruled on by the federal government — awarding me a form of justice and the disability benefits that were denied me by this puppet judge and due me by the state of Florida, not the federal government.

However, I was grateful to have the federal government/SS Disability Division basically contradict everything this judge was saying and his unjust ruling — which noted "denied" for nearly every claim set forth by my attorney. His primary reasoning for denying me anything and everything throughout his ruling that was requested by my attorney and rightfully due me was; "*compensation can be denied where an injured employee refuses reasonable treatment that can remove or modify a disability.*" He was referring to my refusal to take medication/narcotics. However, even invasive treatments such as surgery have no guarantees that a person will not be worse off post the operation or procedure. Medication/narcotics to quell my pain is far from "reasonable" treatment when (the primary cause behind) my childhood PTSD, way of life and beliefs, and my extensive history of health and fitness are taken into consideration and respected — which was certainly not the case here.

Pain medication certainly could not "remove or modify my disability."

Bottom line, this judge, Lucifer, biasly ruled against me basing his entire decision on the fact that I would not take medication and he found, in his opinion, that I had a "credibility" problem and "lack of candor". This, in addition to his avenging duty for his close, personal friend, Capt. Blart.

These are this judge's very own words in determining the outcome of my case;

"*I have spent a considerable amount of time deliberating and deciding this case in light of all of these facts .... He has consistently refused reasonable medical treatment modalities .... Based upon the totality of the evidence, and when considered in conjunction with the issues concerning this claimant's credibility and lack of candor, it cannot be said that such refusal is reasonable.*"

Judge Lucifer's entire ruling was based not on the facts, but on the *sole fact* that I refused to take narcotic pain medication and his concocted notion that I had a "credibility" issue and lack of candor. Me, of all people! I've been honest to a fault my entire life.

This ruling was not only insulting to me but was a travesty of justice that forever tarnished my belief that justice always prevails.

This ruling and this judge, Lucifer, completely changed my opinion of judges in general. Nothing — absolutely nothing — is worse than a judge who has complete authority, answers to no one, and has no fear of consequences for dishonest actions and rulings. Nothing — absolutely nothing — is worse than injustice imposed by the very person who is supposed to be impartial, rendering a decision based on facts, uninfluenced by his personal friendships or other outside influences.

Judge Lucifer — the entire state of Florida's WCS — was a roadblock to due process. This was, for me, a complete breakdown of our system of justice — of which I lost all faith and trust.

Nothing is more damaging to our justice system than those working within this system — from LEO's to judges — who abuse their power and authority, resulting in society's loss of faith (confidence) and trust in that very system. This rings true of our elected government officials as well.

This corruption — abuse of power and authority — has reached epidemic proportions in our country. Is there any wonder why so many no longer have faith or trust in our justice system or our government?

The judge was supposed to be "honorable" and "impartial". This judge was neither. It doesn't matter if the judge likes me/the claimant or not, believes me/the claimant or not. The evidence in this case were the facts and clearly pointed to total disability as a result of my line of duty accident. My credibility wasn't on trial.

I wasn't testifying for or against anyone where my "credibility" would bolster or negate the facts of the case. I wasn't given an opportunity to refute any so-called "inconsistencies" and "discrepancies" which this judge considered to be the facts of the case, burying the truth with his discretionary power and deviously crafted Final Order.

This judge, Lucifer, lacked all honor, impartiality, and professionalism. If there is anything in this life that I have been sure of with absolute certainty, it is that this judge had his mind made up regarding me and the facts of this case prior to any evidence and facts supporting my claim were even presented to him — which he clearly and intentionally discarded in favor of the bullcrap that his "close, personal friend", Capt. Blart, had been whispering in his ear for the sole purpose of destroying my credibility and influencing this judge's opinion and ruling against me.

Lucifer wasn't going to award me anything. He denied each claim. He was not only a puppet to his master — put into his position by the governor of the state of Florida and employed by that very state — but was going to see to it that his "close, personal friend" got his revenge. And he did just that.

I remember one evening during the writing of this rather difficult section of the book and very agonizing chapter in my life, I became very angry reliving the injustice that I had to endure for several years. Reliving the hatred I had felt and that had taken over my soul. That had been repressed — buried, yet forever brewing — for nearly twenty years. Through therapy and a recovery process over the past couple of years, I was learning positivity, among other lessons necessary to heal. I was finally beginning to accept and process the consistent traumatic events throughout my life, feeling and dealing with them, and letting them go. Letting the anger, pain and negativity leave my soul. A final grieving and cleansing if you will.

I was also in the process of trying to reconnect with my Higher Power.

I remember saying to my Higher Power, "*It's incredible the pain, torture, and injustice I have gone through my entire life only to be treated like a criminal and then stabbed in the back by my employer, the state of Florida's WCS, and a most corrupt Judge of Compensation Claims. I have never been compensated for anything in my life and losing my health and career in the line of duty and the injustice that ensued is something I should very well have been compensated for. Florida still owes me compensation for the faith and that portion of my life that they destroyed.*"

It was a Friday, January 31, 2014. I went to bed that evening and had a very strange, prophetic dream: I was alone, seated in a completely darkened classroom. I could see a blackboard on the wall in front of me, but nothing else. As I sat there, words were appearing on the blackboard — in neon, no less! First words — question — on that blackboard; "*Search your soul. Do you need financial compensation or your soul to be fulfilled with meaning?*"

Before I could speak, a number appeared on the blackboard; 11. Strangely enough, I had been seeing the number 11 for the past fifteen years. Not sure why, but everywhere I seemed to look, there it was, the number eleven. It had become a favorite number of sorts. I didn't think anything of it. Next question that appeared on the blackboard; "*Will you choose a lottery win over your soul's meaning?*"

Still confused, I remember thinking, and thinking hard; *Good question at this very time in my life*. Before I knew it, there was a second number on the blackboard; 12.

I now had a number 11 and a number 12 glowing in neon on the blackboard. Next question came; "*You will receive one more number and then must decide — financial compensation or your soul fulfilled with meaning.*" A third number then Popped up on the blackboard; 20. There were now three numbers glowing in neon on the blackboard; 11-12-20. Final question written on the blackboard; "*Your decision?*"

At this time in my life — at this place in which I had arrived — I chose my soul's fulfillment over the financial compensation, regardless of the fact that I didn't have two nickels to rub together and my life's savings that paid the bills each month was dwindling very quickly.

I remember waking that next morning — only a few hours sleep as was my normal. The REM sleep and dream was a rarity that night.

Between the neck and lower back pain, it has been very difficult to sleep for nearly twenty years. However, I felt refreshed emotionally alongside the ever-common physical pain.

I had played the Florida lottery on and off for years. Never once winning more than the dollar it cost to play. I could rip my tickets up before the drawing knowing for certain I wasn't going to win! Luck wasn't in the deck of cards I'd been dealt in life. The Florida Lotto's next drawing was Saturday evening, Feb 01, 2014. I didn't play. I had no desire for some reason. I remember checking the number on Sunday, Feb 02, 2014 — my mother's birthday. No one had hit the six-digit number drawn that Saturday evening Feb. 1, 2014. The jackpot rose to six million dollars. The numbers drawn that Saturday evening were: 11-12-20-23-33-44. I was both amazed and at ease. I often wonder if I had chosen the financial compensation in my dream, if the final three numbers would have been 23-33-44 that showed up, glowing in neon, on that blackboard. It didn't matter either way. I had something much more valuable at this time. I had a feeling of rebirth and new meaning in my life that was going to come to fruition and help not only the healing of my soul but the healing of the many I will be able to reach with my story. That is something no amount of money could ever buy.

Most ironic of all, this dream occurred during reliving this trauma and a near-meltdown writing about the line of duty injury that began the decimation of my spine and the loss of my only escape — my only bona fide medication — my training.

This, coupled with the extreme injustice and added stress and emotional pain I had to endure at the hands of FHP, the state of Florida's WCS, and their dishonorable JCC puppet. This twofold occurrence at that time in my life was one of the main reasons in the months to come I would stop praying and lose all faith in my Higher Power.

🦋 🦋 🦋 🦋

It is very important to note that my greatest fear going into the writing of this book was that I would not be able to complete it. I would not be able to focus and concentrate and finish what had become my new outlet, my new meaning. This, coupled with a growing sense of urgency to complete the book as quickly as possible as my mother was in her late eighties with mounting health issues. I desperately wanted — needed — to share the finished story with her. However, writing this story was something that I just couldn't rush — it was an entity that flowed of its own free will. I relived the trauma, processed it, and documented it when my mind was ready and allowed me to move forward. It was a grueling but cathartic task.

I had been shut out of every opportunity to find meaning throughout my life. I feared this would be no different. The anxiety produced and forever idling in the background from this fear was incredibly exhausting during the years it took to write my story — each word of which written lying flat on my back on a hard surface.

However, little by little, that anxiety and fear would slightly diminish as I came closer and closer to completing the story and began to feel, for once in my life, that perhaps I was being guided along towards my truth, my meaning in this life. I was where I needed to be and doing what needed to be done.

The book — my story — would be completed in due time. This was my window and, as I'd written in the Introduction section to this story;

"My story a candle on the sill of this window. A pinch of possibility illuminated. The sharing of my story .... is not only for the purpose of soul purging catharsis, but also, and most importantly, to offer solace and hope to those whose existence has been turned upside-down as a direct result of any emotional and/ or physical disorder."

🦋 🦋 🦋 🦋

My only option to possibly receive the justice I deserved was to go to the media. I wanted desperately to go to Geraldo Rivera or one of the news magazine TV shows such as 60 minutes or 20/20. I know this could have brought attention to the injustice and, if not for me, could have possibly spared the next person seriously injured and disabled while working in the state of Florida from going through the torture and outright injustice I had to endure for over three years.

I spoke to my attorney, SB, about this move I wanted to make. I trusted SB completely. He had proven time and again over the course of a couple years representing me that he was a most honest, sincere attorney and person and had my best interest at heart. He knew I was being screwed by this judge and the Florida State WCS and that this was an injustice that was truly sickening and should be exposed.

As I've previously stated, SB is one of the few people I've met in my life that I truly admired and will always consider "family". He is honorable, respectful, and believes in fighting for justice. He is also one of those special people that I've lost contact with over the years due to the disorders that have controlled me into isolation.

I hope to reconnect with him someday and share my life story with him. A three-plus year portion of which he is fully aware and can attest to the emotional pain I had been subjected to at the hands of this unjust Florida WCS and a disgraceful JCC.

I would not go forward with any type of media contact and potential exposure of my case unless SB agreed. He thought about it, we discussed it, and SB did say that it was a good idea and may just bring the injustice to light to prevent it from happening to others, and possibly getting me justice in the process.

However, after thinking about the consequences that may befall him for shedding a national spotlight on this Florida WCS and injustice, SB said to me, "*If I do this, I am going to be black-balled here in Florida. I have a wife and kids that I have to take care of. I won't be able to work here any longer. I don't think it's a good idea for me. If you want to get another attorney to represent you in that area, I understand your position and reasoning and support you one hundred percent.*"

While it was something I truly wanted to do — and believe would have brought light to the injustice and situation — I knew what I had been through the past three-plus years and wanted this to be over. Once and for all be away from this place and these vile people that I grew to hate so much. Another attorney would also have to be familiar with the case as intimately as I and SB were. That would be very time consuming and take another attorney who was made of the same cloth as SB, and that was a very long shot. SB was unique and truly a caring and honest person and attorney.

We discussed the case and where we stood; the state of Florida's WCS lawyers were trying all along to get me to accept a petty lump sum settlement to get me out of the system and off the radar. They knew damn well I was totally and permanently disabled in the line of duty and the evidence and facts supported that — including the Social Security Administrations ruling of totally disabled and entitled to disability benefits. It was their (WCS's attorneys) duty and job to win, however they could, at all costs. The settlement amounts that were being offered were an insult. Those settlement amounts did go up after the First District Court of Appeal sent the case back to the JCC several months post receiving the appeal. It is my opinion that instead of ruling against the JCC — overturning his ruling and calling him out for his dishonesty and his overlooking the plain-as-day facts of this case proving my disability and right to benefits — which they should have done, the appeals court was letting him know he needed to look over the facts and evidence again, more closely.

As SB and I discussed, if we continued ahead with additional appeals and the like, it was going to take years and much more of the emotional stress of their games and injustice. Even if I was to finally get justice and win my disability claim with the state of Florida, SB noted that they would be calling me back to Florida every six months for an IME. I would have to continue playing their game of going to their doctors for a re-evaluation. Of course, each time I would be told I was still not at MMI. Meaning I could still get better and go back to full duty. Any benefits previously awarded would be terminated and the insanity and injustice would start all over again.

No matter what any other doctor would say about my MMI and disability — including the federal government's Social Security Disability Division — the state of Florida's WCS had the final say, sending you to their doctors, their bought and paid for puppets, who were on the payroll of the state of Florida's WCS. And that is the game that they controlled unscrupulously and corruptly.

I would most likely never be given a final and maximum MMI by any of the state's doctors, thus a game of injustice that would never end.

I was basically forced to accept an insulting lump sum settlement and agree to drop all claims and further charges against FHP and the state of Florida's WCS.

I had already applied and qualified — first time out — for SS Disability. The federal government had found me to be totally and permanently disabled based on the doctor's reports and MRI's from my line of duty accident.

The federal government's SS Disability Division finding me totally and permanently disabled — ruling in my favor — while the state of Florida continued to deny my benefits or find any disability due to the line of duty accident that occurred while I was employed as a state trooper by the state of Florida. Sounds a bit crazy, doesn't it? That is injustice and corruption within a (state) agency where those calling the shots do so without any fear of consequences for breaking rules and laws, lying, cheating, and outright abusing their power and authority.

After consulting long and hard with my attorney, I accepted their petty offer so I could finally be done with the injustice and torture they had put me through for over three years. Adding insult to injury, I hadn't been paid anything — absolutely no benefits or duty pay — over the several years of this unjust fiasco. What I had no choice but to settle for was not "compensation" in the least. The paltry settlement offer I was basically forced to take didn't even amount to the disability back pay FHP owed me that was wrongfully withheld from day one and throughout this entire multi-year case by an unethical Judge of Compensation Claims, Lucifer, who, in my eyes, is the worst kind of criminal and the most damaging to society.

There was going to be no justice possible for me in this situation — within this state and this corrupt system. I was totally screwed over by a dishonest judge and this Florida state WCS.

I received no retro or future benefits due me for a fact-proven, permanent, life-altering disability resulting from a line of duty accident as a state trooper with the Florida Highway Patrol.

I had consulted with other attorneys I had known in New England regarding my case. I was told, without doubt, if I had been disabled in the state of Rhode Island as I had been in Florida, I would have received disability benefits and been taken care of financially for the rest of my life (as I very well should have been). Or, I could have negotiated for a lump sum settlement just shy of one million dollars, which was what resolving the case was worth considering the severity of my injuries and my age upon my total disability.

I have friends and family members who were injured in the line of duty — outside of Florida — both in law enforcement positions and correctional (officer) positions and were found to be totally disabled having injuries ranging from a broken finger to PTSD as a result of gunfire. Each was awarded total disability benefits and taken care of financially — as well as their children — for the rest of their lives.

On average, each receiving, tax free, approximately $1,000 per week for the duration of their lives (with cost of living adjustments). My social security disability benefits aren't that much per month! However, I am thankful that the federal government followed the letter of the law and my application for disability through that channel was not splattered with corruption and injustice as it was through the state of Florida's WCS — where I strongly believe certain individuals should have been brought up on criminal charges and sentenced to time behind bars for their abuse of power and the injustice that resulted.

Forever present is that egg on the face of our justice system and all three levels of our government due to these very type of people and agencies. Lose the majority of the people's faith in that system and government and society is doomed — and that doesn't seem too far off to me. We're crumbling from within at a very high rate of speed. The decline in morals, ethics, and values will always take a toll in due time. Incompetence and political corruption being high on the (contributing) factor list. What's going on today in our justice system and with our elected and appointed officials has never been worse or more damaging to society and our country.

19

The four years I spent back in Rhode Island were eerily similar to my five-year college hiatus some fifteen years earlier. The years of hibernating in Rhode Island during this time could be summed up with the same four of the five words I used to describe my multi-year college breather; training (what I was still able to do and as much as possible.), anxiety, suffering, isolating. That fifth word, songwriting, was replaced by *anger*. An anger that was seething and as ever-present as the steady flow of emotional and now physical pain that completely occupied and ruled my dark, godforsaken existence.

My predicament was still unfathomable to me. I had a permanent physical disability and the injuries from which were causing unreal, consistent and intense physical pain. A physical pain I had been enduring for years since the line of duty accident. I never thought in my wildest dreams that my life could get worse. Even though, year after year, one way or another, it always did. For years, I always thought I just might wake up from this nightmare. That never happened. Instead, as only my luck would have it, the nightmare became darker, much more desolate and anxiety-ridden.

Post that line of duty accident, my emotional pain catapulted skyward at an astronomical rate. This mostly attributed to the spinal damage sustained during the accident as well as the injustice that ensued and was endured for years at the hands of FHP, the state of Florida's WCS, and an appallingly unscrupulous JCC, Lucifer.

I was living back in Rhode Island and experiencing hellacious physical pain throughout my spine. Primarily cervical and base of skull area that would not subside but only worsen and spread to other areas of my body for the next eighteen years as of this writing. That life decimated by pain and misery I had known and lived for decades was, once again, morphing for the worse. My emotional agony now had tormenting, physically debilitating company. The mobility issues and severe physical pain that began a few years earlier was intensifying with each passing year. My training — my medication — was drastically reduced by that accident and resulting injuries. However, training was my medicine. As long as I was still drawing air into my lungs, I needed whatever dosage remained of that medication — that addiction — in order to maintain my sanity and get through the day(s) at hand. I would have to sacrifice by body to save my mind.

I had lost all faith in my Higher Power. I had actually renounced the God of my childhood. That God was a complete sham. My faith and love had turned to pure anger — rage — for what I considered the ultimate betrayal. That betrayal of the highest level truly devastated me, further crushing a soul that had very little vitality remaining to begin with.

My entire life, there has been no balance but for the artificial stability I was able to create through my outlet(s) — specifically, and most importantly, my training. My ability to exercise and turn the negative energy ever so temporarily to positive energy.

There had been no sunshine to off-set the continuous gloom.

No stars to brighten the blackened canvas veiling my life. Those flickering glimmers of hope fell from my sky so very long ago.

No healthy, positive energy flow from within or around me to be found.

Only negativity spewing out from mind controlling disorders and now a life-changing physical disability.

There had actually been nothing but trauma beginning at the age of five and throughout my entire life.

There can be no *life* without balance. Life requires balance — an even flow — of both good and bad experiences. Happy and sad. Black and white. Day and night. Roses and weeds.

Without proportion on the scale of life, there is no living but a mere existence.

Imagine a life of total darkness — absolutely no sunshine and a consistent, bone-chilling wind forcing you into a fetal ball and battering you senseless. That is where I have existed — have been crawling — for some 40-plus years.

I recall medicating with music one day around this time in my life. One of the songs I was listening to was a Stevie Nicks song, *Sometimes it's a Bitch*. It reminded me of everything I had been feeling and knew to be true regarding a major ingredient I lacked in my life; *balance* — that very element being absolutely necessary for life.

I remember the first time I ever heard this song in the early 1990's. I had just graduated college and I was about to play my last card in trying to secure an opportunity within the music industry. This last move before having to put my love for music and songwriting on the back burner and completely focusing and moving on to my lifelong dream of a career with the DEA.

To me, the song speaks of the good and the bad — the dark and light — within a life. Specifically, the extremes of both ends, and the effects of such. The entire song speaks of taking life as it comes, with no regrets and a strong will to overcome and survive.

There *was* balance in *that* life, however extreme on both ends.

As for the life I've endured for some 40-plus years, I can relate completely with the dark side of the song. That portion of life's scale — the unfortunate, the pain, the *bad* in life, nothing but weeds — and its effects.

I often wish I had that balance, the "normal" during my life. The *good*, the *pleasure* portion — the light side of life's scale being active and occupied to even out and create harmony in my life.

The dark side of my life's scale was forever at full tilt. My life had absolutely no balance, no harmony.

Below is the first verse and chorus and the first two bars of music/first line of lyric of the second verse of *Sometimes It's a Bitch*, sung by the incomparable Stevie Nicks and co-written by the equally incomparable Jon Bon Jovi:

Well I've run through rainbows and castles of candy
I cried a river of tears from the pain
I try to dance with what life has to hand me
My partner's been pleasure my partner's been pain

There are days when I swear I could fly like an eagle
And dark desperate hours that nobody sees
My arms stretched triumphant on top of the mountain
My head in my hands down on my knees

Sometimes it's a bitch sometimes it's a breeze
Sometimes love's blind and sometimes it sees
Sometimes it's roses and, sometimes it's weeds
Sometimes it's a bitch sometimes it's a breeze

...I've reached in darkness and come out with treasure ...

My partner was forever pain.

Emotional battering and imprisonment my entire life which was then — and the worst of all blows — compounded by chronic, crippling physical pain and mobility issues consistently for nearly twenty of the past years.

Pain was the shadow that never left my side. That I was never able to outrun.

Pleasure was non-existent.

There was seldom breeze and mostly bitch during my life.

No roses, but a garden overrun by weeds.

No healthy, positive energy. Only negativity. One-sided misery. An extremely dark, viciously cold, very lonely life.

I truly envy those that had the opportunity in life to experience a "normal". To have harmony — *balance* — in that life. To experience both sides of life's scale without prejudice to one side or the other. Regardless how extreme the sides may have been (in Stevie's case/song) at times, without balance and harmony — (equal) activity from each side of the scale — there is only a body with a slightest of pulse, a spirit gone limp. There is no *life*.

I believe that my story — the light it sheds and the possibility it lends to helping some understand and others to overcome emotional and physical imprisonment — is the sole treasure I've come out with after some 40-plus years of this life's scale forever being tilted — completely unbalanced — to the extreme by a life of pain, despair, and darkness.

I remember an incident one evening while eating dinner with my mother and father. I had only been back in Rhode Island a very short while. My father was, at this time, in his mid-seventies. His relationship with alcohol had never faltered nor did the resulting dysfunction within my immediate family due in large part to this disease. That, along with the never-ending tension, anger, and inability to communicate between my parents made my stay at "home" during these few years that much more uncomfortable and anxiety producing. As the three of us sat around the dinner table and ate, my father dropped his fork into his plate. As I looked over at him, I could see that he was in distress. His face was red and slightly panicked as he reached for and pushed on his throat, trying to cough at the same time. Within a second or two, he got up, stumbled to the kitchen sink and leaned over. At the same time, I realized that he was choking. Whatever he just swallowed was lodged in his throat. I jumped up and dashed over to the kitchen sink. I immediately placed my arms around his waist as he was leaning over into the sink. I left palmed my right fisted hand around his bellybutton area and began forcefully squeeze-thrusting upward into his abdomen. Around the third thrust, he coughed up a piece of steak into the kitchen sink.

I learned the Heimlich Maneuver in the FHP academy. I had never had to perform this maneuver "in real life". Surprisingly, I was extremely calm during the entire episode, which lasted all of 15 seconds. It was almost as if I was in autopilot. I immediately reacted without thinking, and luckily.

I remember saying to my father, "*Are you alright?*" "*Yeah*", he replied. That was it. No "*thank you*" or acknowledgement that day or ever. That type of reaction was my normal from childhood. Validation of any sort was non-existent throughout my life but for the support of my mother as I grew older and there was enough air in the room — my brother had moved to California — for me to breathe and be noticed. Through thick and thin, my immediate family was always dysfunction at its finest.

I think my mother was more surprised that I had just saved my father's life than she was shocked that he was seconds away from death. She looked at me and said, "*You just saved your father's life.*" "*Sure looks that way*", I replied. She then said, "*If you weren't here, he would have died. I wouldn't have known what to do.*"

I've been involved with helping people and even saving a few lives over the years. It always felt good to know I helped someone and spared their families and loved ones the heartbreak. As difficult as it was to be living there with what I was going through — the absolute worst of depressions and isolation at this time and to date coupled with a viciously brutal, consistent physical pain — I was thankful I was in the right place at the right time for my father, and mother, that day.

I hadn't been paid by FHP or the Florida WCS during the several years post my line of duty disability and the entire time I was fighting for justice. I was able to keep my head above water by liquidating some assets and investments I had accumulated and tucked away over the years.

When I got back to Rhode Island, I picked up with a love I had left behind for some time. I began placing ads locally and nationally once again to buy collections, estates, and anything I could buy, flip and turn a quick profit to pay the bills or hang on to as a long term investment as I'd done years prior.

Many of those purchases/investments along the way helped me to survive financially when the going got very tough during my life. This type of investing and flipping was something I enjoyed — it occupied my mind and it kept my head above water.

My nephews would occasionally tag along with me for some backup. Answering ads — and those responding to my ads — I would deal with all kinds from the upstanding legitimate to strung out junkies looking to rob someone. An extra set of eyes came in handy every now and again.

I remember putting a deal together for a vintage collectibles collection that was stored in a warehouse in Las Vegas. I was going to fly down for a couple days, complete the purchase, have the majority of the items shipped back to Rhode Island, and fly back home. I asked my mother if she'd like to come for a few days and do some casino hopping while I took care of my business. She of course was excited. Mom loved the one-armed bandits!

I had planned to stay a week so my mother could enjoy herself and we could spend some quality time together during the trip. As my luck would have it, within a couple days of being in Vegas, I began having major anxiety and panic attacks. This wouldn't have been anything out of the ordinary but for the fact that my mother was with me. My mother had never seen me in the midst of an actual anxiety attack and emotional meltdown. No one had. That's one of the necessities of isolation — living behind closed doors, away from prying eyes and questions. Keeping your truth — your painful and shameful reality — a secret.

She would tell me years later during a conversation regarding this book, our trip, and this very incident, that she was petrified seeing me during the anxiety attacks. She didn't know what was happening or what to do. This is the main reason isolation is so prevalent with those suffering with PTSD, depression, and anxiety. It was always best — safer — to be hidden behind a mask and in seclusion rather than let anyone — especially my family and specifically my mother — see the pain, embarrassment, and suffering I had to endure during my lifetime.

At this time in my life, I was not only dealing with severe emotional pain but also the consistent and intense physical pain of a spinal injury and disability which further worsened my overall emotional condition and outlook on life.

It severely diminished — pretty much wiped out — any hope that I had been hanging on to. But this was nothing compared to what was to come.

We did leave Las Vegas the next day and my mother was now partly aware of my lifelong emotional struggle and a worsening physical pain of the past six years.

I had kept my emotional disorders pretty much a secret for some thirty years. Some felt there was a problem with me — as my cousin Bruno would tell me via email when I began writing this story — but no one knew exactly what it was or just how severe it was.

Little did I know, this deeper depth of pain and torture — this lower-level tier of hell — was small change compared to the devastation that was awaiting me around the corner in 2005 and would catapult my life into the darkest of depressions and angers and the most vicious of anxiety and panic attacks. It would be the worst of the worst times of my life and the closest to death I'd come to date.

It just wouldn't be my luck if there was some light, some positive balance on my life's scale.

Everything — physically, emotionally, and financially — would continue on its course of deterioration and decimation. Continuing rung by rung downward to the most evil depths of this hell that was my life.

During this time when I was back in Rhode Island and living with my parents, there were very few people, with the exception of my immediate family, who were aware I was even there. Though my parents never really knew what it was that kept me isolated — as I didn't know myself the exact reasons until therapy and a recovery process began some ten years later and a few months prior to the beginning of writing this book — they did know my physical disability, saw a small piece of my pain, and respected the fact that I needed space — to be alone — to deal with what was ailing me without others observing and asking questions. Needless to say, it was very difficult living with my parents — particularly my mother — during this time. I never wanted to share any portion of my emotional or physical pain — for anyone to know of or see it — especially with my mother.

As my ability to train diminished — my ability to counteract some of the depression and anxiety — isolation was more and more becoming my sole means of survival at this time in my life and in the years to come.

I would see my immediate family when they would come to my parents' home. Try and spend as much quality time as possible with them, all things considered. That was nearly impossible most times.

I did the best I could with what I had to work with throughout my life.

Isolation was the invisible cell where I spent most of my time for crimes unknown. However, I never wavered in my loyalty and my love for my family and friends. Nothing could pull me from the cocoon — isolation — but that loyalty to friends and family. Should someone ask me to do something for them, I could never refuse, regardless of my deep depression, paralyzing anxiety, and the consequences to my well-being. However, with one exception; I had no choice but to refuse any time my presence was requested at a social function or gathering. If I could, I would try to explain about my anxiety — as I did with my friend Pete when he asked me to be best man at his wedding — and why I could not be present at large social functions. It would have been easier and less stressful playing Russian Roulette than knowing the inevitable meltdown that was coming from anxiety and panic attacks in large social settings.

Like chronic physical pain, emotional pain and imprisonment — PTSD, depression and anxiety — is difficult to explain and for others to truly understand. Unless you have lived it — walked in those shoes — a complete understanding isn't possible. It's like an astronaut telling us what it was like to walk on the moon; leaving the earth's atmosphere, weightlessness, infinite space, the feeling of first stepping onto another planet's surface. We will never know the true feeling and sense without actually having been there — walking in those very shoes.

Though there are varying degrees — depth and duration — of depression and anxiety, I would offer the following analogies for anyone who has never experienced either in their lives:

1.) Phobias produce anxiety and panic attacks. If a person has a fear of spiders or snakes, heights, or confined spaces, he knows the consequences of coming into contact with such a trigger and will avoid at all costs. Just the thought of that trigger will produce immediate anxiety. This will lead to full blown panic if the particular stimulant is introduced to the person.

For anyone who has no phobias and has never suffered with anxiety or panic attacks; In my opinion, the best way to simulate a major, crippling component of what I experience during anxiety and panic attacks is to, quite simply, restrict or eliminate one's ability to breathe.

If a person cannot breathe, he *will* panic.

If a person begins to go under water, flailing about, struggling to breathe while taking water into the lungs, the body and mind reacts with pure fear. That feeling of fear — beginning with anxiety and moving to absolute panic — is what those of us living with anxiety and panic attacks feel on a regular basis, sometimes throughout our entire lives.

If a person is aware of what will cause this anxiety and/or panic attack, he will do whatever is necessary to avoid the trigger. If that trigger is people or crowds, the person will isolate and become reclusive to avoid "drowning".

During an attack the person believes — knows — that the walls are closing in very quickly, he cannot breathe, he is trapped, suffocating, and about to die. The person has no control whatsoever over the anxiety and panic but to avoid any known triggers to begin with. Unfortunately, many times these attacks will hit you out of the blue — no known trigger — when you least expect it.

These attacks are fear in its purest form.

This feeling of panic and doom will build up and can last for minutes, for hours, or consistently for days on end. Blood pressure goes through the roof, heartrate is off the charts, you are sweating and can be shaking and trembling. You can begin to get dizzy, your surroundings spinning out of control.

I have never experienced such fear and evil as long-lasting anxiety and panic attacks. The couple times in my life I was at death's door were due to anxiety and panic attacks lasting days on end. Those attacks were, in my case, a result of PTSD, severe depression, uncontrolled worry, isolation, sleep deprivation, chronic physical pain, and stress simply beyond comprehension, and all peaking at the same time.

Symptoms and intensity of anxiety and panic attacks will vary from person to person. In my world, anxiety has often lead to panic. Starting off with a constant worry and uneasiness, shortness of breath and light-headedness which manifests into uncontrollable, overwhelming, pure fear — panic; profuse sweating, heart pounding through the chest, derealization, feelings of imminent death. I am drowning. Suffocating.

Dying. And the mind and body reacts as such.

2.) For anyone who has never suffered with depression and can't begin to comprehend the symptoms, but who has had and suffered with the flu, I would offer the following analogy; A physical equivalent of depression is the flu. Flip side of that comparison, depression being the emotional version of the flu. Unlike the flu, however, depression usually lasts much longer than a week, symptoms don't start to improve but get worse with time, and can last for years to a lifetime.

The emotional imprisonment of depression and PTSD is equivalent to having the flu indefinitely.

The flu becomes the rain on the parade of the once *normal* person. That person will now have to endure several dark and gloomy days and nights with a steady and cold, heavy down pouring of rain that leaves you shivering violently. You are very limited in what — if anything — you can do with any amount of ease. You are completely worn down and feeling trapped while everyone else around you is operating normally; laughing, playing, working, interacting. Your body is battling a physical invader — a bug, a virus — that has altered, and temporarily (hopefully), taken control of your physical being; you are very weak, aches and pains in every muscle, joint and bone, sneezing, coughing, congested and your head is pounding. This bug has crept up on you and hit you like a ton of bricks. You feel like you've been hit by a bus and left for dead.

Suffering with emotional disorders is the same but for the physical bug or virus invading your body. It is replaced by emotional bugs and viruses — disorders such as PTSD, depression, and anxiety. Nonetheless, the results are the same. And too often can be fatal.

As with the flu, so goes depression. There are degrees — depth and duration — to the grip of this bug; you can suffer for a few days, you may land in the hospital, and you can also die. However, with depression, and I *am* a case in point, unlike the flu, it can last for decades — a lifetime — wreaking havoc on you physically while completely destroying your emotional well-being and your entire life unless and until the bug is brought under control.

Someone suffering with depression feels this horrendous beat down 24/7, day after day without reprieve, sometimes lasting a lifetime.

Can you imagine living week in and week out, month to month, year after year, your entire life with the flu? Those of us suffering with PTSD and depression do just that. There is no balance, no sunshine, no laughter, no joy. There is just that steady and cold, heavy downpouring of rain chilling us to the bone. One dark and gloomy day and night of nothingness after the other. It is a constant state of grieving. Pure misery.

If you have ever lost someone you love, that feeling of angst, helplessness, and desolation is what continues for those of us suffering ceaseless emotional pain. It continues every minute of every day, day in and day out, for months or years on end. It is torture. It is, for some, in many ways, much more difficult to endure and live through than any amount of consistent physical pain.

If this persistent emotional persecution could be recreated — and I'm sure someone or some government somewhere has found a way — and imposed on another, it would rank up there with the most evil methods of torture known to man.

I had lived with and endured this madness for nearly thirty years before my body would be affected with a physical invader — a crippling spinal injury — that would also, as my emotional disorders did, continue to progressively worsen with each passing year.

I now had to battle two separate wars from within; emotional and physical. Not only did I lose one engine, I had now lost both engines.

My arsenal — my medicine, my outlet — had always been exercise and training to combat the emotional battle. Now, this physical invader would make it near impossible for my body to continue on with its medicine of the past thirty years. Though I struggled desperately — and do to this day — to keep as much of that arsenal working as possible, I was now left with not only an emotional invader but a physical invader attacking and destroying my body and I had very few, if any, weapons remaining to protect myself from being destroyed.

My life has been a ceaseless emotional war since childhood. Now, for nearly twenty of the past years, it has also been a daily physical war. I truly don't know which is worse — the everyday emotional or physical battle — but having to endure two wars of this nature simultaneously, having had both engines taken out, I have felt is simply the cruelest of tortures. A curse if ever there was one. That is, unless and until my lifelong, unrelenting agony can help others to overcome, or prevent, the forceful, mind-warping grip of hellacious disorders such as PTSD and depression.

It has been my experience throughout this journey that the undenying common denominator of most all addiction is unbearable emotional and/or physical pain. More often than not, the trauma that caused that emotional and/or physical pain is being repressed. That pain, often buried deep inside, leads to depression and addiction.

Depression is perhaps the most serious and misunderstood of all disorders. It is the commonality of an awful lot of addiction, destruction, and death.

I believe that support — from individuals and groups of individuals who walk in the same shoes — is essential in understanding, coping with, and getting through PTSD, depression, anxiety, and chronic physical pain.

My mission post writing this book is to establish and bring support groups for those suffering with emotional disorders such as PTSD and depression, as well as chronic physical pain, to the forefront.

My goal is to do for those suffering with PTSD, depression, anxiety, and chronic physical pain what Bill Wilson and Dr. Bob Smith did for alcoholics beginning in 1935 with Alcoholics Anonymous (AA).

As support groups and meetings for recovering alcoholics offer necessary and life-saving support in that area of recovery, I believe wholeheartedly in the need of these very type of support groups and meetings for those of us suffering with emotional disorders and chronic physical pain.

The time has come to bring those of us suffering with these emotional disorders, as well as chronic physical pain, together, in a readily available and safe environment, to help and save ourselves as well as others suffering with the same disorder(s).

My nephew, Carlo, was beginning to apply to various police agencies in Rhode Island during the brief time I was living there post my FHP disability battle. However, he really wanted to move to south Florida and become a deputy sheriff there. He had begun the application process with the Sheriff's Office and, as an out-of-state applicant, was scheduled for a couple upcoming tests on a single day.

Carlo and I were always very close in his younger years. He asked me to go with him to south Florida for a few days while he went through the scheduled tests.

My brother had asked him to stay at his place the few days he would be in south Florida. Carlo had accepted the invitation before asking me to go with him. I wasn't comfortable with this arrangement, but I couldn't refuse. This really put me in a pickle. An extremely tough spot to be in.

Everyone in my immediate family knew that my brother had tried to kill me some years earlier. I had buried the hatchet with my brother entirely for the sake of my mother. I spoke with him every now and again but would never trust, love, or respect him — as a man, a brother, or a son — ever again. I kept the peace for my mother's sake.

I decided I needed to go to provide moral support for Carlo and to walk him through some of the testing and show him around the areas. He was fully aware of the situation and my feelings. I didn't like this arrangement but couldn't refuse his request to accompany him.

As soon as we arrived at my brother's place, the tension could be cut with a knife. Immediately, I felt his anger and resentment all over again. I was in the Devil's den and, needless to say, sleeping with one eye open for a couple nights.

Carlo would tell me within hours of our arriving that he couldn't believe the uneasy and vile-filled atmosphere. He could feel it too. It was very uncomfortable, to say the least. However, I did what I had to do for my nephew — for family. I showed him around and took him to the testing sites. We stayed a few days and neither of us could wait to get the hell out of that environment.

The last social gathering I would ever attend was the Rhode Island Police Academy graduation of my nephew, Carlo. I was still living in Rhode Island and, being as close as we were at the time, and my presence meaning so much to him, I had to make an appearance at such a cherished event in his honor. It would have been more difficult taking my mask off and explaining to him the disorders that ruled my world since childhood.

I attended, anxiety-ridden as expected. I was able to stand at the entrance of the commencement ceremony and then sit in the back row during the actual graduation — my escape route within steps. I was sweating buckets and very uneasy.

However, I was happy to see him graduate the academy — as I had done some nine years earlier, Carlo in attendance and supporting me. If not for the strong family bond with Carlo at that time and a most special occasion for him, I would never have given this a second thought. I would not have attended and put my mind and body through such trauma.

My father once said of someone who needed a beating; "*Break his legs just a little.*" As serious as the matter may have been, I can't help but laugh every time I think of this statement — and I seldom laugh. My father has always operated on another frequency. I often said that if aliens landed on this planet and their first encounter with our civilization was my father, we wouldn't have to worry about them ever coming back! He is unique in every way, be it good, bad, or indifferent.

If I had to describe my father, it would be a three-way cross between the TV character Archie Bunker, the movie actor Joe Pesci, and the comedian Rodney Dangerfield. Like Archie, he would chop up the English language and serve it to you on a platter of his own design. He wasn't a comedian by any stretch of the imagination, but as he butchered the English language and gave it back to you in his own unique story-telling, you couldn't help but laugh. Every now and again he would chuckle at his own expense, realizing why and how hard others were laughing. He knew he wasn't a book smart guy and made no excuses for his lack of higher education.

As for the comparison to Joe Pesci and Rodney Dangerfield, their TV and movie characters — both comedic and volatile — always reminded me of my father in a strange way. Again, my father is something that needs to be experienced, he truly can't be explained. However, let me try and paint a small picture of one of those characters:

Pop the corn, dim the lights, it's story time;

It was a Sunday evening dinner and family get-together at my parents' home.

Present was my mother, father, sister, brother-in-law and two nephews.

We had just finished eating dinner. Everyone was sitting around the kitchen table talking while my father sat in his favorite chair in the living room watching TV.

Both the kitchen and living room areas flowed into one large room of the finished in-law apartment. Nothing dividing the rooms — everyone could see each other whether in the kitchen or the TV room. My father's back was towards everyone else as he sat watching TV.

My father was "feeling good" (as was usual) — not fall-off-the-chair drunk, but not clearheaded either.

The phone rang. My father picked it up in the TV room at the same time I had picked it up in the kitchen. My father said "*Hello*" with an aggravated growl.

I heard the phone click on the other end — possibly wrong number or whatever, but the person on the other end hung up. My father obviously didn't catch this being half-hammered. I went ahead and baited him with a "*Hello*". My father then said "*Hello*" once again, but louder and getting even more aggravated. I decided to play along to what soon had everyone there peeing their pants and suffering with stomach cramps from laughing so hard. I said, "*Who's this?*" My father replied, "*What? ...who's this?*"

Again, his tone very loud and getting angrier. He is still sitting in his chair, beginning to move around a bit with a sense of growing irritation, back still towards us. I said again, "*Who's this?*", my voice raising and sounding angry.

My father responded, "*Who the fuck is this?*" I quickly replied, "*What? You talkin' to me?*" All the while, tears running down my face I was laughing so hard, but keeping it inside. And laughter was rare — very rare — in my world! My father was fuming at the person on the other end of the phone. He wanted to kill him! He still didn't catch on and we were only feet apart, in the same room! He then said, screamingly enraged, "*You mother fucker, come over here, I'll rip your balls off and stick them down your fuckin' throat!*"

Everyone was now on the floor laughing hysterically.

My mother said to my father, "*Who are you talking to?*" My father replied, "*Some fuckin' asshole — I can hear him laughing in the background.*"

I couldn't take it any longer. I walked up to him with the phone to my ear and told him to listen closely. I said again, "*you talkin' to me?*" He just shook his head with a shitty grin on his face.

Even within this most dysfunctional family and my suffering greatly with PTSD, depression, anxiety and isolation, there were occasional laughs. They were few and far between and far outweighed by the trauma and bad luck in my life, but there were certainly some classic events and fits of hysterics thanks to that other frequency that my father operated on.

Excluding that infrequent cackle at my father's expense, there was no laughter and smiles in my world. Aside from training, and the tranquilizing affects of music, the only other true escape I had from my cursed life and emotional imprisonment was motorcycles. Riding motorcycles had been a primary outlet and one of the few joys of my life since childhood. The spinal injury now made it difficult — and dangerous — to ride. I couldn't turn my neck completely to either the left or the right making it impossible to look to my sides and behind me when changing lanes. Last thing anyone who rides a motorcycle wants to do is rely solely on the bike's side view mirrors. This, and the fact that I couldn't bend my spine (cervical or lumbar) forward — lean over as I rode — for more than 20-30 minutes at a time took away from the joy of the ride.

I would have to pull over constantly and stop, get up and off the bike to stretch my spine, or actually lay down flat on the road/pavement to alleviate some of the added pain created by leaning into the bike (I rode sport bikes — aka; rice rockets, crotch rockets — not a Harley). Regardless, I spent as much time as possible riding during the warm months. Down in Middletown and Newport — mostly at Sachuest Point — alone by the ocean and with nature where my soul has always felt less burdened and free.

Little did I know, a few years down the road, I would no longer be able to ride at all. Yet another complete loss in my life. One of my very few outlets, loves and true joys snuffed out just as every other small bit of bliss and medication in my life had been unsympathetically flushed down the toilet by an unknown curse.

As had been the case throughout my life, this decade beginning in 2000 would be the worst of all previous decades. If I'd known what was in store for me in the years ahead, I may very well have succumbed to the constant bombardment of suicidal thoughts that plagued me during this time.

These haunting thoughts would become much too common and almost impossible to suppress during the absolute worst — in all possible ways — time of my entire life; my 40's. Fortunately, I survived — this book was written, my story told and my life's meaning of helping others begun.

I survived by virtue of a true angel in my life; my mother.

I remember, in vivid detail, every heartfelt and loving conversation with my mother from my early years and to this very day. We talked about almost everything — and I respected and trusted her opinions and wisdom above all else. However, I could never share the one thing that had been slowly destroying my mind and soul from childhood; the secret torment and hopelessness I hid behind a mask that even my mother could not see beyond. Always holding back that pain and despair I was feeling — wanting desperately to confide in her as she was always the *only* person I could ever truly trust and who *always* had my back. But I could never let her know or try and explain the true pain and suffering that was with me every minute of every day of my life. My agony would then become her agony — and she had suffered far too much in her lifetime. For this reason, and this reason alone, I needed desperately at this particular time in my life to get away from the one person — my mother — that I loved and cherished more than anything or anyone I've ever known or would know in this world. It was my way of protecting her.

Nothing bothered me more than being around *real* family, people I loved and cared for more than life itself, and not being able to fully enjoy their company and the quality moments together. That was the case 99% of the time throughout my life, but never so punishing as during this particular time and place in my life.

Emotional and/or physical pain robs you of any ability to focus and enjoy the moment. It snatches your life away like a thief in the night. It pushes you far away from everyone and everything that matters in your life.

There was, however, one thing that my mother always noticed about me and that we spoke about often when together; I was never happy. Especially during my adult years. She brought this to my attention many times over the years and always told me that all she wanted was for me to find some joy and happiness in life. She knew nothing of the disorders that gave birth to the misery that *was* my life and, at this moment in time, had only a peek at the relentless physical pain now a permanent part of my inescapable world of sheer gloom.

My mother always felt my sadness, but, luckily, never knew of the deeper and darker issues of pain and despair — that is until my therapy and recovery process began, some 40-plus years after first walking through those gates of hell.

I remember one day during this time frame in Rhode Island having a heart-to-heart talk with my mother about my being unhappy most of my life. My having absolutely no balance — no happiness, no light, no good fortune, no peace of mind in my life. We discussed my need for a change in a very big way — geographically and my very life.

I definitely couldn't remain in Rhode Island and living with my parents much longer. For the obvious reasons, as previously noted, as well as the fact that my physical pain was now worsening due to the climate in this region of the country.

My doctors had been saying that there wasn't much I could do for my consistent, intense physical pain but to take pain meds the rest of my life or learn to live with it.

Surgery was no guarantee that the pain would be alleviated or removed. Actually, chances were that it wouldn't take the edge off the pain at all and perhaps might just make the pain and condition worse.

One culprit to my pain was cold and dampness. And, the East Coast, where I'd lived my entire life, was just that. Several of my doctors had mentioned that the dry, warm climate of the Southwest might be an area that would work in alleviating some of the pain that was caused by the severe arthritis I now had throughout my spine and body. It wasn't going to get rid of all the pain but even if it eased a smidgen of the arthritic pain, that notches down the pain level a bit and it would be worth it.

I looked into this area of the country and I was going to give it a shot. It would be well worth it if I could reduce my pain levels by *any* degree. It was a toss-up between Arizona and Nevada. After speaking with some doctors and doing a little research, I decided on Las Vegas, NV. I had been there before and was a bit familiar with the areas.

I had always loved real estate and this place was on fire in the early to mid-2000's. I could go out there and try and focus on real estate and feeling better. I didn't know anyone but for a few people in Vegas. And, suffering in a deep depression and isolation, that worked for me and my situation. Only other choice was to go back to Florida — the only really warm place (but damp) year-round on the East Coast. Unfortunately, (as it relates to depression and isolation), seems everyone I ever knew and their entire families either have a summer place or now live in some part of south Florida. I was going to run into people I knew at almost every turn. Everyone North of the Carolinas — especially from New England and New York — has made south Florida their new home, especially during the winter months in order to escape the brutal Northeast winters.

Las Vegas seemed like a decent fit for a few good reason; the dry weather, I didn't know anyone, and real estate was the best opportunity in the country at the time.

I decided for my 40th birthday that I'd go west to Las Vegas and check it out for the purpose of moving there. My mother wanted to come and I'd have it no other way, though I feared another anxiety attack or emotional meltdown in her presence.

We headed to Vegas for a couple weeks. I looked around, familiarized, and Mom enjoyed the Vegas strip and all the casinos. We got to spend some quality time together away from the dysfunction of the immediate family and all that ever-present tension and anger between my mother and father.

Strangely enough during this trip, I was somehow able to keep the anxiety attacks and battle rounds of deep depression from my mother having to witness it all over again.

I rented a place in Summerlin and returned to Vegas a month later.

I'd live in Vegas for the next five years which, as only my luck would have it, turned out to be the most devastating five years in my life physically, emotionally and, now, financially.

Every move I'd ever made in my life — emotional disorders pulling the strings in the background — lead down a dead end road and directly to a cliff I had no choice but to jump off and accept the damage to my mind and body that awaited below.

Las Vegas would become a suffocating, dust bowl bottom where my scourged mind and broken body plummeted, shattering into a million pieces on impact.

20

Aside from the severe and dizzying sinus infections that would begin almost immediately upon my arrival in Las Vegas, there was actually a slight improvement for me emotionally. Surprisingly, it felt as though a new door was opening and a fresh beginning was taking place.

A carrot of attainable happiness dangled before me — a cruel tease of possible parole from a life sentence of emotional imprisonment.

The first of three phases of my Las Vegas life sentence was now set in motion.

I began searching for real estate to invest in as well as a home to purchase. I truly believed — I had every intention — I would be calling this place my new home. I had been in isolation most of my life and that seclusion here might actually be a bit less difficult. I only knew a few people in Vegas. I didn't have to worry about running into anyone I knew or being invited to social functions that have caused anxiety and panic attacks my entire life. I could breathe a bit easier and loosen the mask so to speak. Breathe a bit easier in that respect. However, the chronic sinus infections, in large part due to the extreme dry climate and desert dust, would soon become one more of many contributing factors heavily influencing my anxiety and panic attacks.

I began studying the real estate market in Vegas and nearby Pahrump. Many of my days were occupied researching and looking for properties to invest in. I worked with many different real estate agents over the coming months. Many of the agents in Vegas during this time got their real estate license for the sole purpose of cashing in on the quick and easy money pouring into Vegas from buyers and investors around the country and from outside the U.S. It was a buying frenzy like no other time in history and Vegas was the number one place to be buying and selling during this real estate boom.

There were an awful lot of females from the adult entertainment industry working as real estate agents for the fast and effortless big bucks. Most that I encountered had no knowledge of real estate or the market other than it was a cash cow they wanted a piece of. They were there to flash some skin and make easy money off many of the male investors. It was Vegas and it was interesting to say the least.

However, I was looking — as I always have — to work with knowledgeable people who put in the time and effort to be successful at what they did. I came across one such agent, *Andrea*, during this time. I admired her work ethic. She put 110% in, was knowledgeable, and worked very hard for her clients.

I assured her that I would only purchase and sell through her with regards to my individual purchases and sales in real estate in and around Las Vegas. And I did just that. My word was my bond, as always.

Andrea had just gone through a divorce and, like me, seemed to be suffering with depression. We were also both at our lowest points in life. Aside from that, we actually had nothing in common. We came from different worlds with different values and beliefs. Regardless, over the coming months we started spending some time together outside of our real estate interests.

Aside from studying and investing in the Vegas real estate market, part of my daily routine (since the line of duty accident eight years earlier) was spending a significant amount of time icing and heating my spine. This included occasionally soaking in a hot bathtub (often with Epsom salt) up to the base of my skull. It was necessary to reduce some of the ever-present inflammation and relieve some of the constant pain and muscle spasms. It also kept me going with regards to the little that was remaining of my primary and secondary outlets; training and motorcycle riding.

I joined a gym where many local MMA fighters and pro bodybuilders were training. It was a bit disheartening as I knew in my day — prior to the spinal injury that derailed my life — I was leaps and bounds ahead of most of these guys when it came to physical abilities in mixed martial arts and intense training in general. It was extremely difficult psychologically not being able to train as I had done in the past. Especially watching others doing things I could no longer do. I guess I should have been grateful for what I still had at that time because little did I know how much more loss, pain, and suffering was just months ahead of me. You truly don't know what you've got until it's gone.

However, impaired by the cervical damage, agony, and mobility issues, I was still able to ride a motorcycle, be it very carefully and with much pain.

Riding was always one of my very few outlets — medications — that quelled my emotional pain and offered my mind and soul a brief escape from my everyday suffering. And, like my training, I was going to hang on for dear life until it was absolutely impossible to continue. That, too, would be right around the corner.

During the first six months I was in Las Vegas, I spent a lot of time alone in the desert and surrounding mountains trying to find myself and reconnect with my Higher Power. I did this "religiously", until the accident that completed the decimation of my spine and life.

Most times I would ride my motorcycle — other times drive — to Red Rock Canyon, Valley of Fire, Mt Charleston, or to Lake Mead to be near some of the only real water to be found in this desert. I would also now and then drive the three hundred-plus miles across the desert to San Diego to be near the ocean. Then trekking from San Diego up through Monterey — a four hundred-plus mile stretch of pure beauty along California's Pacific Coast Highway (PCH). It was the peace my soul craved. The Pacific Ocean and all of its natural beauty along this drive is simply enchanting.

Within a few months of this time, I would no longer be able to sit and/or drive these distances any longer, ending yet another of the very few outlets that offered a bit of peace and joy to my soul and mind.

The aesthetic places of nature in and around Vegas — the canyons, valleys and mountains — offered a piece of what my life has always lacked; serenity. These were places where I could meditate, soul-search, and try to find some peace in my soul, in my mind, in my life. It wasn't the ocean where my mind and soul have always felt most at ease and at home but the incredibly alluring and monstrous Mt Charleston, the breathtaking beauty of Red Rock Canyon, and the tranquility found amid the ever-present ancient Indian spirits that lingered within the Valley of Fire would have to suffice.

Just me and my bike most times in the middle of nowhere. Far, far away from not only the life and home I'd ever known some three thousand miles away on the East Coast but also even further now — literally and figuratively — from anyone I knew.

Growing up and being highly influenced by my mother, her virtuousness and her strong faith in God, I believed what I had been taught as a child; God's will for us — for me — is harmony, joy and peace. I had prayed and searched for this my entire life. It had eluded me just as long.

As I meditated and tried desperately to reconnect with my Higher Power in the various mountains and valleys of Vegas, I had a few questions for my God that had nagged at me for the past eight years since my line of duty accident and my giving up all faith in that Higher Power;

Why have I been plagued throughout my life by consistent, crippling trauma, pain, loss, and isolation?

Why has my life's scale been overwhelmed and weighed down, forever unbalanced and tilted to the extreme by darkness, pain, and suffering?

Why has no light — not an ounce of that harmony, joy and peace — entered my life?

I was actually feeling a bit better emotionally these first months in Vegas and I was hoping for once — finally — to find that light that had been forever void in my life; peace of mind, harmony, and joy within my soul. That balance I never had an ounce of during my lifetime.

I was trying desperately to reconnect, re-route and re-birth my spirit through my Higher Power. Feeling betrayed with an anger unwaveringly festering in me, it had been eight long years that I had not prayed to or attempted to connect with my Higher Power but consistently cursed that God of my childhood.

As I began to feel that slight improvement emotionally at this particular time in my life, I also began to write (songs) again. I hadn't been able to focus and write songs the entire past decade. *Fly* would be the first song I had written over the past ten years and the last song I ever wrote before the lights flickered one last time and gave way to the most intense darkness I have ever known.

Fly was conceived at the end of 2004 and completed the beginning of 2005, a few months before the accident that completely decimated my lower spine and my life, making my line of duty accident and injuries some eight years earlier look and feel like a cakewalk.

Fly was a song of encouragement inspired by and written for my nephew, Carlo. He was in his early twenties when I wrote this song and was going through some tough times, trying to find himself. He was struggling a bit, feeling lost, depressed, hopeless. Searching for what it was he really wanted to do and be in life. I couldn't help but see the similarity to my own path. Knowing and feeling that very pain and despair throughout my entire life. Only difference, I didn't drink or rely on any other substance — prescribed or not — to take the edge off of my emotional or physical pain. In the years to come, I would realize that most in my immediate family relied heavily on both alcohol and script medication to deal with life in general.

I would talk to Carlo often and try and give him the best advice I could. Most importantly, I always told him to follow his heart, be true to himself, and stay away from the alcohol, which seemed to be influencing his behavior and actions, causing some problems in his life.

Outside of those within the music industry some fifteen years earlier, I had never let anyone in to see my work — my songs. I did email Carlo a copy of the first draft of *Fly* in hopes that it would pick him up and help him to find himself, and to soar — fly — like that eagle. It is my proudest song to date.

I dedicate this song to my audience; to each of you out there that has had to endure emotionally scarring trauma. That is suffering with any emotional and/or physical disorder which has laid waste to your life. That has caused you immeasurable pain and sorrow and that may have hurled you into a life of unending darkness:

"FLY"

V 1

So many TIMES in my life[1], my back was pinned to the wall[2]
(&) Too many TIMES in my life[3], I lost my dreams, my soul[4]
The mistakes I've made[5] ...Can't tell you how I've lived[6]
...Only God Knows[7] just where I've been[8]

(back vocals: ...time and again...)
I played the hand I was dealt[1]
I paid for all that I know[2]
Where others walked I crawled[3]
Each step takin' its' toll[4] ...

...(Now) Lookin' back through the years[5]
I see I lost my place[6]...Somewhere between
"to hell with it all"[7] and biting off my nose[8]
...Just to spite my face... (Sung Solo/No Music)

CL

Now Don't you do like I do[1]
Just DO like I say[2]
Don't you live like I live[3]
Just LEARN from my way[4]...

Chorus: *Keep your head on straight[1]*
                   And your head held high[2]
                   Keep the dream in your soul[3]
                   And Fly ...((Fly ...Fly))[4]   *((= vocal and music*
                   echo/reverb))

                   Don't you ever give up[5]
                   You reach for the sky[6]
                   Ain't no one like YOU[7]
                   Now Fly ...((Fly ...Fly))[8]

V2   *So many YEARS of my life, I don't know where*
                   they've gone
                   (&) too many YEARS of my life, flash back to
                   what I've done
                   The mistakes I've made ...The darkness, pain, and
                   the sin
                   ...Only God knows just where I've been

                   (back vocals: ...time and again...)

                   I crawled through the fire
                   I resisted the flow
                   The daily demon battles
                   Survivin' blow after blow ...

                   ...(Now) Lookin' back at my life[5]
                   At the whole rat race[6] ...The twisted
                   Fork in the road[7] .... The path that no one knows[8]
                   ...That led (me) to this place... (Sung Solo/No
                   Music)

CL   *Now Don't you do like I do*
                   Just do like I say
                   Don't you live like I live
                   Just learn from my way...

Chorus: *Keep your head on straight*
                   And your head held high

Keep the dream in your soul
And Fly ...((Fly ...Fly))

Don't you ever give up
keep reachin' for the sky
Ain't no one like YOU
Now Fly ...((Fly ...Fly))

Bridge: *(4 – 8 bars music ...)*

Ch3   *>>> lead into Fade <<<*

Fade: *...don't put off tomorrow[1], what you can do today[2]*
'cause tomorrow never comes[3] ...now make your way[4]
...
....and Fly ...((Fly ...Fly)) .... ((echo))[5]...Fly ...((Fly ...Fly))[6]
.... You Fly ...((Fly ...Fly)) ... ((echo))[7] ...Fly ...((Fly ...Fly))[8]

...It's dog eat dog ...gotta fight to survive
You fight the good fight ...and Fly ...((Fly ...Fly)) ... ((echo))
...YOU'RE THE EAGLE, IT'S YOUR SKY
...now Fly ...((Fly ...Fly)) ... ((echo))

© Steve DiGrossi

I purchased my home and was investing in real estate and some other areas of interest by the end of 2004. My parents had entrusted me with a large portion of their retirement money to invest in Vegas real estate. Prior to this, going back a year or so, my parents and I, along with my sister, sat and discussed our parents' retirement fund and who would oversee the money. I made it clear, If I oversaw the fund, my brother would never see a dime of that money if any was left when my parents passed. He had betrayed and disrespected his parents for years. I had disowned him, wanted nothing to do with him, and would not allow him a penny of my parents' money. Period.

My sister agreed that I would oversee the fund and any investment(s). She said she was comfortable with that and trusted my judgement. She also insisted that none of our parent's money be put in her name. Her reasoning was that if something happened to her husband, she believed that some of his kids (from his first wife) might come after anything she owned and any money in her name.

It was agreed that I would oversee and invest the money in real estate once in Vegas.

I explained to my parents and sister, very clearly, that investing in real estate did have its risks but I was pretty certain the worst that could happen was to break even a few years after the initial investments.

Of course, many are familiar with the catastrophe that took place once the credit and real estate bubble finally burst in the mid-2000's. And, as only my luck would have it, I had an extremely large amount of my own and my parents' cash invested at that exact time. Most all of our money was lost when that bubble burst.

If I had known — If I'd had a crystal ball — that bubble was about to explode, I would have sold everything in a heartbeat, while buyers could still get a mortgage and I could make a quick profit or break even at the very least. However, I didn't know — no one did — what was coming and I held off on flipping the investments too quickly as prices were continually rising, month after month. Most every investor believed the prices would keep rising. Not many — including myself — saw the writing on the wall.

I had also planned on flipping my home within a few years. Coming up short once again in my life, the market collapsed within a year or so of my initial investments in Vegas.

I went to Las Vegas, rolled the dice in a non-traditional Vegas way and came up losing everything there; what remained of my physical and emotional health and pretty much the shirt off not only my back, but my parents' as well.

I probably should have known what was coming. After all, as it has always applied to my life, the best indicator of my future luck has always been my past luck — and that, like everything else, was predictably going to be *bad*.

The absolute worst blow to me of all with regards to the financial slaughter I encountered was the large sum of money that was entrusted to me to invest on behalf of my parents that was lost. *That I lost.* It is something I've had a very difficult time accepting and living with — continually battering myself over and over. The ever-present thought tormentingly rubbing salt in the wound daily, for years on end.

However, and thankfully, through my present-day therapy and recovery process, I am learning to accept and then release such thoughts, cleansing the mind of things I cannot change and have no control over. Finding a smidgeon of peace in my soul.

In addition to this financial disaster and continued, lifelong streak of bad luck, the worst day of my life physically, to that point, was closer than the hair on my head.

Not having that crystal ball and not knowing what lay ahead for me financially or physically, I was still feeling ever so slightly better emotionally than I had for many years. I had a new home and investments were going well (or so I thought).

I felt a two-fold sense of change happening;

On one hand, perhaps a new door finally opening? I seemed to have stumbled upon a glimmer of sunshine — a tiny bit of peace in my soul. This was a foreign but welcome feeling I had felt very few times and ever so briefly in my life. I was, however, cautiously optimistic as nothing had ever seemed to go right or pan out for me since childhood.

On the other hand, and at the same time, I was also beginning to experience an elevation in anxiety. I was alone most of my life but never felt lonely. My first introduction to loneliness came several months after moving to Las Vegas.

I now understood and could actually feel the difference between being alone and being lonely. And I was both now. It was a horrible and anxiety producing combination. One that has remained with me through the years.

Having been in isolation and out of the social loop for a very long time, I needed a buddy desperately. What better than man's best friend to help with the loneliness and hopefully alleviate some of the added anxiety I was now experiencing. If ever the time was right to get that puppy I had always thought about, it was now.

I had always been drawn to the Labrador retriever breed of dogs so I decided to search for a male yellow Lab retriever puppy with a coat as white as winter snow.

Few things can bring a smile to my face and joy to my soul quicker than an animal — especially a puppy! I started doing research locally and online for the best Labrador retriever breeders around the country and with the best customer reviews before I committed.

I looked around locally first. One stop of many was a breeder about an hour northwest in the Pahrump, NV area. I took a ride up that way with Andrea one afternoon, taking the beautiful and scenic route through NV-159 W/W Charleston Blvd. that goes directly through the heart of Red Rock Canyon and leads into NV-160 W/Blue Diamond Rd. A peaceful drive I had taken often when riding my motorcycle. We headed "over the hump to Pahrump" and arrived at the local Lab breeder's kennel just northwest of Las Vegas.

There was an awful lot of commotion as we turned into the breeder's driveway. There were a dozen or so people playing with these cute little puppies, just weeks old. Andrea and I went over and within seconds a big smile had taken over my otherwise frowned face. My soul was happy and dancing along with the little critters bobbing all around, falling all over themselves and each other, clumsy and cute as could be!

Within a couple of minutes, I noticed out of the corner of my eye an old boy — a yellow Lab easily north of twelve-years-old — standing off to the side, alone, tennis ball in his mouth and just looking on at all the attention the little guys were getting. My heart sank for some reason. I walked over to him. He dropped his drool-soaked tennis ball and a bit of life came into his frail body as his rusty tail began to wag. He hobbled a bit backwards, signaling to me he was ready to go and fetch that ball. I picked it up, my hand full of his saliva goo, and tossed it down the driveway. He slowly but happily began a trot to fetch that ball. A bit winded when he came back, but I could feel the joy emanating from his old and tired body. He was proud he could still fetch that ball! I spent a bit of time with him — a few more tosses and lots of petting and talking to him. I was happy inside that I could give to him a bit of the joy he had and remembered from his younger days, when everyone would pay attention to and play with him like the little guys a few feet away today.

Strange, but I think of that old boy often. Especially when I look at my Max and realize he isn't too far away now from that old boy's age that day. It chokes me up every now and again. I don't know why. I have always felt pain and sorrow as both humans and animals come closer to the inevitable. I see my boy, Max, getting older every day. He's nine-plus as of this writing. When I look at him, I see a bit of that old boy that day up in Pahrump. Only difference, I will be there for and play with my boy until his very last breath. He will never be alone as long as I am breathing. I know all too well that sick feeling in the pit of the stomach when you are alone and lonely.

I'm pretty sure I made the old boy's day that Sunday afternoon in Pahrump. I could see it in his weary eyes. My guess is he's playing fetch beyond the dog gates of heaven today. His eyes bright, tail wagging, full of energy and love and bringing joy to all around him.

In the midst of searching for that perfect Lab pup, my parents came down just after the 2005 New Year for a couple of weeks to spend some time with me and to see the new house.

My nephew, Carlo, would also come down for a week around this time.

As always, with my mask on and firmly in place, I did my very best to hide my pain and suffering so no one — especially my mother — would ever know my truth.

I had my own space here, was still able to train a bit and ride my motorcycle — albeit, with some difficulty — to quell and hide the emotional pain.

There was never much I could do, besides constant icing and heating, for the consistent physical pain throughout my spine, most specifically my cervical area during this time and the previous eight years.

Since I had arrived in Vegas, I had been in contact with *Marco Z*, a neighborhood guy from back in the day. We'd get together now and then for lunch and to discuss real estate among other things. I'd get Marco and my dad together whenever my parents came to Vegas. We'd go to dinner and shoot the shit about the old days and everything in between. My very early days and those that came before me are a piece of my past that I cherish. I often wish I had been born much earlier to fully appreciate and enjoy the close-knit neighborhood life and family culture of those days. I may very well have taken a different course in life. Whether that would have turned out for the better or worse, I'll never know.

It was a joy — vicariously as it may have been — reliving the memories of the old-timers' past any time I got the chance. I was certainly born in the wrong era.

Prior to my parents arriving in Jan of 2005, I found a top lab breeder online and out of Oklahoma. We emailed and spoke on the phone. I was very comfortable with this breeder. Best of all, I would also have first pick of the upcoming litter.

I would, in the weeks to come, pick my boy, Max. He was one of twelve puppies — polar whites to creams — eight females and four boys. He was born on January 28, 2005.

I began receiving pictures of the litter/pups at three weeks old. I picked the one that caught my eye and captured my heart first. He also happened to be the biggest and whitest in the litter. A puppy the breeder had named *Blizzard*.

The Breeder's comments to me about Blizzard were, "*He's one of the largest pups, one of the whitest. Big boy and outgoing. He is a beautiful puppy, gentle, playful, and smart.*" He is all of the above and so much more to this very day.

The breeder wouldn't allow Blizzard to leave his mother's side until the day he turned eight weeks old. On that very day he was put on a plane and flown to Las Vegas where I picked him up at the airport. Andrea took the ride with me so I could hold him on the way home. He sat in my lap the whole way. He was a joy and a very special, very loving puppy from day one. He's been by my side, in my heart and soul, and my best friend ever since.

Everyone who saw him as a puppy said the same thing, "*He's pure white and so beautiful. His paws are huge!*" His paws were a sign of the size to come!

I had a special area made in the backyard for Max to play while he was a puppy and also an area for him to do his doody. He knew exactly where to go within a couple of days.

I was teaching him tricks and commands the very first week we were together. He learned to sit, stay, and lay on command within days! From day one, however, it was very clear that his favorite activity was going to be playing fetch. While this is common with most retrievers, Max took it to another level. His love for his "ball" and playing fetch rivaled my addiction to training during my lifetime. It would become his obsession, his love, his outlet, his life. Max was — and is to this day — seldom seen without a ball in his mouth. We call it his *"bone"*. All of his toys are his "bones".

That ball served two purposes as the months and years came and went;

First, it was his security blanket, his pride and joy, and he just loved it.

Secondly, it kept him from picking up and eating bugs and other things on the ground if I wasn't watching his every move. He wouldn't put that ball down for anything!

Max and I had gone through dozens of balls over the months before I came across one that he wouldn't destroy while carrying it between those big, powerful jaws and hard-as-nails teeth. I went ahead and purchased five dozen of them at the time!

We have been playing with that specific brand of ball — a Jugs 9" yellow dimple baseball — for the past nine years.

From the day I got Max, I spent most of my time with him. Quality time. The type of time, attention, and love a dad should spend with his child. And Max *was* my child. The *son* I never had. I would give him everything I would have given the biological son I didn't have; Joy, happiness, love, a sense of security, constant hugs, kisses, encouragement, and reassurance.

I was to Max what my mother was to me in my life; everything.

Over the months to come, I taught my buddy lots of tricks; he would learn to spin on command, catch his tail, jump up and over, go to the left and to the right, back-up, come forward, sit, stay, lay, speak, roll over, through the tunnel, lick his lips, and much more. What is *through the tunnel* you might ask? I would point to someone (who knew what was coming) — or stand still myself — and say, "*through the tunnel, Max.*" He would run over and glide through the legs. Every now and then, being such a big boy, he would knock someone over doing this!

Max was addicted to exercise. Like father like son! We'd play fetch and tug-of-war for hours. I had to throw underhand playing fetch with Max and our tug-of-war, even though he was only a few months old, was a bit difficult and painful due to the bilateral radiculopathy and extensive nerve damage in both arms/hands, a result of my cervical damage. However, this was nothing compared to the additional and extensive, crippling lower spinal damage that was about to come.

Max and I would take long, scenic hikes up through the canyon and mountain trails. I didn't have any problems from the waist down — yet. But, again, that was now mere weeks around the corner. I wouldn't be able to walk much in the coming months, never mind hike ever again.

Everywhere and anywhere I went, Max was by my side.

I would sell my car as soon as I got Max and, to this day, drive an

SUV so that he could have his own roomy space when we traveled, went to the park, or the Vet.

He lives to go for rides and to the park! "People" parks, however. He never enjoyed the dog park and being around a lot of other dogs. He prefers and delights in being around people. The more people, the merrier he is. Max had no signs of any of the disorders that kept his daddy in darkness and isolation throughout his life, that is for sure. And that was a beautiful thing. Throughout the years, he taught me many lessons about finding contentment in the simple things and not sweating the rest. I began to understand those lessons much more clearly as I began a therapy process years later.

He craves attention and loves giving big, wet kisses to all. It's incredible the amount of smiles and joy he brings to everyone he encounters.

Max and I would get out of the dust bowl and head towards the west coast when possible. Through the desert to San Diego, CA and travel up PCH so he could be introduced to the ocean and all of its beauty. Unlike most Labs, Max was never crazy about the water. He does, however, love playing on the beach!

I would learn in 2009 when I briefly moved back to Rhode Island that playing in the deep, cold snow was Max's all-time favorite activity — where he visibly exuded the most joy — next to playing fetch. Fetch in the snow was a dream come true for him!

At first, he wouldn't step into the snow. He didn't like getting his feet wet and really didn't know what he was missing! His first introduction to snow was actually as a puppy and during the spring of 2005 up on Mt Charleston, located about thirty minutes outside of Las Vegas. He didn't seem to care for the snow at that time. However, once he got into that snow in Rhode Island in 2009, there was no getting him out!

He was nose-diving, jumping all around, running through the snow like an Elk! He couldn't wait to get into that snow every day. And, back in the winter of 2009, there was plenty of it in Rhode Island! I've never seen him enjoy himself so much. Like his "Nana" — my mother — Max loves the cold weather and doesn't care for the heat. If it wasn't for my spinal injury and the resulting immobility issues as well as the arthritic and bone pain exacerbated by cold weather, I'd no doubt be living closer to my parents and Max would be in heaven during the winter months with his Nana and Pop and playing in that cold, winter snow.

Max is a very large-boned boy. Most of his weight is from those big bones. As an adult, Max topped out at 110 lbs. and is far from overweight considering his size. There is no fat on those bones! As he gets older and has had a couple of injuries and slowed down a bit, muscle will usually atrophy, turn soft and a little extra fat takes its place, not unlike humans.

As for his diet, in addition to his "dry doggy food", he has eaten only the healthy stuff I would eat. I've always fed Max two to three times a day, keeping his meals proportioned and his metabolism a bit higher rather than having one big meal, once a day and starving until the next day. His diet is very similar to mine; lots of grilled chicken, fresh fish, steamed vegetables, brown rice, fresh fruit, lots of fresh water and even a daily, late morning bowl of oatmeal with soy milk and his favorite fruit — apples! He loves it! He has his favorite doggy snacks daily and every now and then — and always on special occasions, holidays, and birthdays — gets to indulge in steak, hamburgers, hotdogs, vanilla ice cream and pizza cheese!

The past couple of months felt like that wind of change had caught up with me and was finally blowing some normal into my life after decades of an unbalanced existence, my life's scale fully tilted by pain, suffering, and despair.

Perhaps the many months I spent alone in the mountains and desert attempting to reconnect with my Higher Power was taking place?

Could I finally be granted parole from my life sentence of emotional imprisonment?

Could some healthy, positive balance finally be seeping into my desiccated soul?

Could that meaning — *my* meaning — finally be coming into view?

Or, could it be, as had been the case throughout the past thirty-five years, these were, once again, winds of change-for-the-worse?

It had been a couple of rather joyful months since I had gotten Max. Max made me smile and feel needed even as that dark cloud relentlessly continued to follow and rain down on me.

We had bonded immediately and I now had a new friend and family member that loved me regardless of the disorders and physical disability that controlled and devastated my life.

However, as was the case throughout my life, the very few times a door seemed to open and a speck of sunshine entered my darkness, it would immediately slam shut in my face, collapsing my world back into the eternal damnation I was sentenced to since childhood. This time would be no different.

The one thing I could always count on and expect, the one thing that was for certain throughout my life; Murphy's Law was the blueprint of that life — If it could go wrong, it would go wrong.

Always a day late and a dollar short. And If it wasn't for that bad luck, I'd have had no luck at all.

My chances were always zero and none when it came to finding joy, happiness, and balance in my life.

That constant feeling of unwarranted defeat kept me forever angry. That anger fueled the fight in me and, along with my mother, kept me moving forward my entire life. Refusing to quit or give up, I always, somehow and someway, maintained a tiny bit of faith that I would someday reverse that curse.

I can't stress enough that while writing this book, what I feared most of all is the curse continuing and my not being able to complete this story and having the positive impact on others' lives I know can and will come of it.

Why should this time be any different than the past forty-five years?

All I know is it feels right this time around. For once, I feel I am right where I am supposed to be in my life, doing what I am supposed to be doing. Writing my story, shedding light on these horrendous disorders, helping others — directly and indirectly — out of and from falling into the many depths of hell where I have crawled, alone, for over four decades.

I feel my life's meaning and its truth at long last coming to fruition.

Little did I know that this was the calm before the ultimate storm.

The final plunge to the very bottom of the hellhole that had been my life was lurking just around the corner.

I would never have gotten my buddy and taken on such a responsibility if I'd known what was coming a mere couple months post picking him up at the airport that day in March 2005. If I had been in that worst-ever condition emotionally and physically, there is no way I would have wanted or been able to accept the role of caregiver when it was almost impossible to care for myself. It wasn't easy prior to the May 2005 accident that is now approaching at this time in my life — it was nearly impossible post that accident.

Aside from the emotional struggle I have endured and constantly beating myself up for taking on such a responsibility to begin with, the toughest part over the years — especially post that May 2005 accident — has been Max's constant and very heavy shedding. It contributes tremendously to my breathing problems and allergies.

I brush Max with a furminator each and every day. It does a decent job in removing excess hair but not nearly enough to keep that heavy shedding from taking place and covering everything in sight.

Keeping Max shaved doesn't help much, either. I have him shaved — a very short, #10 blade, nearly down to the bone haircut — every couple of months. I have had his hair everywhere imaginable. I do to this day. It covers the floors and carpets of the house, the entire inside of my car, every stitch of my clothing, it gets in the food, on the tables, in the bed, and I'm sure there is more than a trace amount in my lungs.

I've gone through numerous vacuum cleaners that seize up with the incredible amounts of (shedded) hair. Time and again, Max's hair has totally blocked tubing for two central vacuum cleaners. Picking it up — bending over for anything as well as vacuuming itself — is extremely difficult and painful and can, and often does, leave me near paralyzed.

Max also doesn't poop in one spot. He'll sniff and circle, sniff and circle for what seems like a lifetime to find the perfect spot and then, finally, he slightly bends his hind legs, creeping forward in his rather comical poop position while releasing ground-shaking bombs all along the course of his poop trail. Some of these *gifts* left behind are large enough to have their own zip codes! Logs big enough to build a cabin! Always a half a dozen or so gifts at a time spread across the distance he's traveled. This is routine approximately four times a day. That's a couple dozen gifts to bend over and pick up each day! I can barely tie my shoes and wipe my butt most mornings! My cervical and lumbar areas are susceptible to the minutest of pressure, bending, or twisting and must remain erect and still as much as possible.

Bending is the arch-enemy of my spine, creating more inflammation, pain, and mobility issues than would be the case otherwise.

I've been bending at the knees for years to try and take added pressure off of the neck and lower back but it's just not possible to get certain jobs done without bending at the cervical and/or lumbar spine.

I've tried several of those poop scoop gadgets, too, so I wouldn't have to bend. Each proved to be more trouble and more aggravation than it was worth to spare me the additional pain and possibility of not being able to straighten out afterwards — which has happened on many occasions — keeping my anxiety levels forever elevated, always in fear of the possible outcome every time I have to bend or twist my spine for whatever reason.

I've had to deal with very intense, mixed emotions over the years. Feelings of guilt and shame for the days I wished I'd never gotten my boy. Bitching and moaning to myself, feeling overburdened and overwhelmed, my back to the wall with a responsibility to care for my friend when I could barely care for myself.

However, as difficult as it has been emotionally and often punishing physically through the years caring for him, Max is one of the very few blessings I've had in my life.

In retrospect, and having more clarity in my life these days, I indubitably can see that he's helped me to survive in many ways. He's seen the man behind the mask. He's been there through my most painful, darkest days and nights for the past nine-plus years.

He's seen me on my hands and knees in dire pain, physically unable to move and near death. The all-too-real torment that has been my life. Through it all, he's been a source of strength to me. Licking the tears from my face and always reminding me how much he loves and needs me. As difficult and as painful as my life has been, as close as I have come to the end of my days, my thoughts were always with my mother and my boy. I could never hurt or betray either of them regardless of the living hell I was enduring.

I have come close — very close — but each of these two blessings in my life gave me the strength to pull back from that ledge at my very darkest of hours.

I would be put to the ultimate test post my accident of May 2005 and during the next four years in that desert that had become the bottom of the hellhole I existed in.

A place where I would, in March of 2008, come within minutes — closer than any other time prior — of finally ending the existence of chronic pain and suffering that worsened every year of my life for the past thirty-five years, culminating here as I dangled on the edge of sanity.

21

I had an ever so brief glimpse — a sadistic tease — of sunshine for a few months upon my arrival in Las Vegas and with my boy, Max. Then, in accordance with my lifelong streak of bad luck, that world of complete darkness — the only life I had known for the past thirty-plus years — would not only quickly return but make its grandest entrance to date. One that marked the worst day in my life with regards to my spinal injury, physical condition, and overall well-being:

It was Monday, May 30, 2005. Memorial day of all days! This proved to be the single worst day of my life to this point. A life-changing day and incident for the very worst. This was the day I fell in the shower and collapsed into the abyss.

I would hit the very bottom of that hellhole three years later in March of 2008.

In the interim, this particular freak accident would become the foremost catalyst which would spiral my wretched existence downward to the deepest and darkest depths of depression, anxiety, and isolation I have ever experienced and endured in all my years battling the disorders that were pulling the strings of my life from the age of five.

I was at death's door several times during the four years I remained in Vegas post the incident in 2005 that decimated what remained of my lower spine and any bit of hope I had been clinging to.

I had been soaking in a hot bathtub up to the base of my skull to relieve some of the chronic, severe cervical area pain of my spine and surrounding muscle tissue and nerves. I was already a bit dizzy from a recurring and intense sinus infection I had at this time. I was hydrating with water while soaking. However, when I got out of the tub, I jumped into a cold shower to cool off.

This sudden and drastic change in temperature, in addition to the vertiginous sinus infection I had at the time, caused my blood pressure to plummet and I passed out. My entire body weight crumpled — without the advantage of breaking the fall — directly onto my coccyx bone. My hips, coccyx and sacral sections of my spine right up through my entire lumbar section was blown out. It collapsed like a house of cards. My lower spine now decimated by yet another freak accident. This one, however, snuffed out what little life had remained.

🦋 🦋 🦋 🦋

I've had the last eighteen years to think and be tormented about my line of duty accident as well as the past nine years reflecting upon this freak shower fall accident which proved to be, to date, the worst day of my entire life with regards to my physical well-being.

I could never quite understand how such minor, freak accidents could cause so much and such devastating damage to my body — a body that was the epitome of top physical conditioning.

Taking into consideration my inherited DDD and Scoliosis coupled with the decades of intense, addictive training and constant pressure on my entire body, I believe it could be possible that my spine may have been inherently weakening, as well as from outside forces, and what happened was just a matter of time. Not if, but when it would happen.

While my muscles were becoming stronger, my spine was weakening year after year. My spine becoming as fragile as that house of cards — just about any jolt, quick or improper twisting movement would cause some type of damage or collapse.

In retrospect, having many years to analyze my life and injuries, it seems whatever impact or improper movement came first, beginning in my thirties, would begin the buckling of my spine. It just so happened to be antiquated exercises and an outdated and blindly implemented physical fitness regimen in the FHP academy that started the downfall. This, followed by the line of duty accident and then, the granddaddy of them all, a fall in the shower that finished the decimation of my spine, totally wiped out any hope I may have been hanging on to, and whirled my mind and soul — my life — into a cataclysmic hell at the very bottom of the darkest and most vile abyss imaginable.

My training was vastly different from many athletes who trained in any sport. Addicts — and I certainly was addicted to training/exercising and health — don't do anything in moderation. It is always excessive. My training was non-stop, consistently grueling, and always balls to the wall. So, perhaps my addiction to ceaseless, vigorous training coupled with my inherited degenerative spine diseases did more damage than good as time went on, and it finally caught up to me on these worst of all, life-changing days of my existence. I can't say for sure. However, these were minor accident that in years past — prior to my thirties —

I would have shrugged off with nothing more than a story to tell and a scratch or two from the incident.

What I do know for sure is that regardless of my theory or the emotionally tormented life I'd lived for decades prior to each of these "physical" incidents, these freak accidents spiraled my life into a hell I never thought could be possible. Most specifically this catastrophic accident of 2005 which totally obliterated my lower spine. It was the sole worst accident of my life. It caused the absolute most damage — emotionally and physically — that I've ever experienced.

A nightmare that lingers — rewinding and replaying over and over — to this very day.

🦋 🦋 🦋 🦋

I already had very severe, intensely painful cervical damage affecting my upper body; arms, hands, neck, and head. This accident would be much more damage-producing, painful, and immobilizing to this very day.

While the damage to my cervical section of my spine is far more serious with regards to possible paralysis, the damage sustained in the lower spinal area would prove to be mind-warpingly painful and a great deal more disabling both physically and emotionally.

My entire lower spine was now in worse shape than my cervical and resulted in my losing the ability to do just about everything, including the majority of any type of training; the medication I relied on my entire life to keep the keel even, get through the days, and to survive, in every sense of the word.

Anything I might want to try in the future such as climbing a mountain again, river rafting, or perhaps riding one of those bumper cars I never had the chance to indulge in as a child was now going to be a very risky proposition which could easily result in permanent immobility.

Since the line of duty accident nine years earlier, I had been focusing much of my training below the waist; running, hiking, flexibility, and leg work. That was over now too. I could no longer sit, stand, lay, or walk for any prolonged period of time.

I couldn't sit for six weeks after the initial fall. It took me two weeks to be able to stand on my feet and take a few steps. My mother had to come to Vegas to help me out.

I was now dealing with a chronic and vicious physical pain I never in the furthest reaches of my imagination believed possible.

The lower back area pain and mobility issues made my cervical damage and torment feel almost insignificant. It near-crippled me and, some days, did just that. It does to this day. I have days when I cannot move at all.

I learned early on how to crawl as best I could when possible. Sometimes the pain and spasms are so merciless I am curled up on the floor, unable to move even an inch for hours on end. It takes half a day to be able to move on all fours, and I still cannot stand.

I always keep a bucket close by. I've spent many days peeing in that bucket because I was unable to move or stand to get to the bathroom. Most times, there is no warning — I just can't move. The pain so horrible, my mind just spins in a whirlwind of shock, fear, anger, and confusion.

The emotional pain and savage fury now building and building month after month, year after year, bringing me closer and closer to losing my mind — mere steps from sheer madness over the next four years.

Of all the years of emotional and physical trauma and suffering I have endured during my lifetime, this period in my life from 2005 (post this fall) through 2009 in Las Vegas marked the absolute worst, most execrable chapter of my life to date.

I walked that line between lucidity and insanity every minute of every day before the never-ending, excruciating pain, suffering, and boundless stress peaked in March of 2008 and pushed me to within a step of my final breath. Closer than I had ever come before or since.

My mother came to Vegas a couple days after my fall to help me out. Andrea helped out a bit until my mother arrived. There wasn't much at all I could do for a couple of weeks.

As only my luck would have it, approximately two weeks post that fall, Max got very sick late one night and was vomiting and had diarrhea.

Words can't describe what the entire area looked like that next morning. The flooring, the walls, appliances, electronics, Max along with his bedding, pillows, blankets, and everything else within a ten-foot radius of his sleeping area was totally covered with vomit and diarrhea. The smell was atrocious.

Luckily, most of the flooring where the mess occurred was tile. A portion did flow onto and seep into the carpeting in the adjoining room. I couldn't believe what I was seeing.

Worse yet, it had to happen during a time immediately post the worst day and injuries of my life, when I was still unable to even walk! I was just starting to take a couple very painful steps.

I remember my mother gagging — as I was — as we both looked at the disaster that lay before us. She volunteered to clean it but I wasn't having it regardless of my condition. Though I was in tremendous pain and barely able to move, there was no way I would even ask my mother to help clean this.

I remember my mother saying, *"Only something like this can happen to you at a time like this."*

Never one to quit or give up, I fought through the pain and, finally, after five punishing hours on my hands and knees, got the mess — and Max — all cleaned up.

I went through dozens of rags and towels and gallons of cleaning solution(s). I'm not sure how I got through this without vomiting from the smell or passing out from the pain.

I fixed the garage up that evening with fresh blankets and pillows so Max would be comfortable sleeping in there — just in case he got sick again it wouldn't be in the house.

Sure enough, he did get sick one more time! Same thing all over again, only it was contained within the garage. Diarrhea and vomit all over the blankets and pillows I had laid out for him. The mess covered a portion of the concrete garage floor also. Second day in a row, second time around on my hands and knees in hellacious pain. This time it only took me three hours — and I set a world record for most cursing over a two-day period!

My mother stayed with me in Vegas for over a month and helped me get back on my feet, literally — and in more ways than she'll ever know. She had seen only glimpses into my emotional imprisonment and torment over the years and during this visit. Those glimpses more than any other person had ever seen or would see until I began therapy and a recovery process in September of 2012.

If only Max could speak, the story he could tell!

I do believe that if I had been able to open up and had someone to talk to early on in my life — if I had support — I may not have been chained so tightly to the tree in the backyard by the disorders that controlled my every move.

If I didn't have to hide behind a mask my entire life to survive —

if I'd only known better — I may never have fallen so deeply into the darkness that became my life.

It is vitally important for anyone who feels and lives with any symptoms of these disorders — PTSD, depression, anxiety, chronic physical pain, or is living in isolation — to reach out to someone you are comfortable with and can talk to.

I wouldn't wish upon my worst enemy for one minute what I have gone through — alone — battling these disorder every second of every day of my life.

Support — whether a friend, family member, support group, or a professional — is crucial. Anyone suffering with any of these disorders needs to talk to someone and have that person(s) in their corner to offer help and support. We cannot do this alone. We need compassionate understanding and support to move forward.

In all the years of my torment post my line of duty accident, I had seen many psychiatrists. I can confidently say from years of personal experience that psychiatrists are not there to talk and offer support. Their job is to diagnose your emotional problem and prescribe medication. That is what they do — psychiatrists prescribe medication to manage emotional problems.

If medication is a preferred method of treatment, a quality psychiatrist is needed. Personally, talking is my preferred method to relieve some of the emotional pain and pressure and to begin a recovery process. Finding a quality psychotherapist — support — made a world of difference in my life.

If I'd known prior to 2009 when I was first blessed with finding my first LCSW, *Nina R*, the difference between a licensed clinical social worker (LCSW) and psychiatrist, I would have been on the right path to recovery much sooner in my life.

After my mother had finally left, the gravity of the situation hit me like a ton of bricks. I was in trouble. Very serious trouble. Both emotionally *and* physically. My temple was now nearly completely demolished. The instrument — my body — through which I channeled the ability to maintain my sanity for the past thirty-five years was all but totally destroyed. My lifelong escape route was severely compromised. That path had caved in and washed down stream.

95% of what I once did physically — training — would not be possible any longer. This was comparable to someone who had been taking 1,000 mg of needed medication per day reduced to 50 mg per day. And, it would continue to worsen — the pain and mobility issues — with each passing month to the present day. I had been hit with a devastating blow from my line of duty accident nine years earlier. This fall of 2005 was the final nail in the coffin.

That most unpleasant experience of trying desperately to find quality doctors who were more concerned with my well-being than the dollars for last-option operations and unnecessary visits and referrals would now begin all over again.

It was misery during my line of duty accident and injuries and, now, here in Las Vegas, not only was I hardly able to move physically, I was emotionally immobilized like never before. The absolute worse shape of my life in every way possible. If ever I needed to find doctors I could trust, it was now. My mobility and sanity depended on it.

I would go on to see dozens of different doctors over the next few years in Vegas, mostly for my lower spinal injury, my breathing problems, and the emotional pain that this debilitating spinal injury had ramped up to barbaric levels.

Once again in my life, there was more spinal damage, more immobility, more pain and suffering, and more tests; EMG's, EEG's, CT scans and MRI's among others. Lengthy and numerous physical therapies of every kind that didn't alleviate any pain or mobility issues.

In addition to the five discs blown out in my cervical spinal area (there are only seven movable/articulating discs/vertebrae in the cervical area) as a result of the academy accident and line of duty accident years earlier, this latest shower fall catastrophe blew out everything from my coccyx (tail bone) and sacrum sections right up through L1. My entire lumbar section, L1 - L5, was pretty much shattered. The only section remaining intact was my twelve thoracic vertebrae section. That section would also take a hit and begin to crumble in the years ahead.

At this time, of the twenty-four articulating discs that comprise the spine, I now had a total of ten that were blown out. That's nearly half of my (movable) spine and this is not including the nine total fused, and now compromised, vertebrae of my sacrum section (total of five fused = S1 through S5) and coccyx section (total of 4 fused).

In addition to bi-lateral cervical radiculopathy, the constant and severe neck and head pain, tingling and numbness affecting both arms and hands, and a slew of other problems and pains from my cervical disability, I now had lumbar radiculopathy affecting my hips, legs, and feet with a chronic lumbar area pain that can only be described as the work of the Devil. It was — and still is — that severe and evil.

With nearly fifty percent of the articulating discs of my spine herniated and/or prolapsed and totally compromised (as my luck would have it, it would soon be fifty percent), I had to endure the chronic physical pain, mobility issues, and non-stop misery of this disability as well as the collateral damage that came with it and all existing defects of my spine; bulging discs with multi-level foraminal and cord encroachment, spinal stenosis, vertebral spurring, bulging discs pressing into the spinal cord, cervical and lumbar radiculopathy, neuropathy, cervical and lumbar displaced disc disease, narrowing of the disc space with dehydration, lumbar facet disease, degenerative disc disease, scoliosis, compression fractures, bone spurs, extensive nerve damage and impingement, myofascial pain syndrome, piriformis syndrome, arthritis and the list truly does go on.

I didn't trust most doctors I had seen. Frankly, I've had a hard time trusting anyone most of my life. Being lied to and betrayed time and again — doctors included — it's been difficult having faith in and trusting others. And, when it came to doctors — especially surgeons — the majority I had encountered appeared to me to be more concerned with the amount of money they could make with a surgery or two rather than that surgery being a last means.

It was a nightmare. From psychiatrists — not paying attention to a thing I was saying and constantly looking at their watches or clocks — telling me time and again I wouldn't make it if I didn't begin to take medication, to one surgeon after another contradicting each other; one would tell me that I needed cervical as well as lumbar disc removals and spinal fusions to prevent any further motion and damage of the spine while alleviating the pain. Another — usually a surgeon that I had a bit of faith and trust in — would tell me that the damage to my spine was so extensive and severe that even the surgical removal of discs and fusions wouldn't alleviate the pain.

I had pain emanating from many different affected and damaged areas, including the surrounding nerves, muscles, bones, tendons and just about every other defected and injured area of my spine.

Many doctors told me that it wasn't going to be possible to eliminate the pain. My options were stated as; *"Take pain medication or learn to live with it."* I chose the latter of the two.

One consensus among all surgeons I had seen; *"You have some of the most extensive and complicated spinal damage I've seen. Don't slip or fall, you could be paralyzed."*

I had enough problems and pain in my life. Knowing that the next minor slip, fall, or accident jarring my spine could cause paralysis — my worst of fears — amped up my already too high anxiety to another level of acute and chronic stress that, in and of itself, has taken its toll on my mind and body over the many years.

🦋 🦋 🦋 🦋

It has been my experience that most surgeons wanted to operate whether I had other options to exhaust or not. Rare that one told me otherwise. After all, a surgeon makes his living operating.

I've had every serious injury during my decades of training. I've been told twice — on two separate occasions by two different surgeons — that I needed knee surgery for a torn meniscus. I had one egomaniac surgeon look me square in the eyes and, very arrogantly, say, "I've been doing this over twenty years, I assure you that you need surgery or your knee will never be the same again. You won't be able to do what you've been doing without surgery."

I've always known my body. That mind and body connection was like no other during my 20-plus years of intense training. I decided to do my own rehabilitation both times, two different knees, and recovered fully and was back to intense training with no pain, mobility issues, or noticeable difference. Never any further problems with either knee.

I was told once by a surgeon that I needed surgery for a torn hamstring. Once again, I decided to try to rehab first without surgery. As was my usual, I did it my way with my own physical therapy regimen. I never had a problem with that hamstring ever again.

One thing I knew my entire life — that I was in touch with — was my body and how to mend an injury that was fixable without surgery.

As difficult as it may be to believe, many (serious) injuries can heal properly without surgery.

Some people panic and run into surgery without exhausting other options, usually believing that surgery is the only possibility of eliminating intense pain. However, fact is, surgery — especially spinal surgery — too often not only doesn't eliminate the dreaded pain but causes more of it and further problems.

I've heard many horror stories about botched surgeries — those that did nothing for the pain or made the condition worse. Of course, surgery does work and is needed in some instances and for some conditions. Just as medication is. Personally, I never had "good luck" and I wasn't about to undergo any (spinal) surgery unless I couldn't walk or was bound to a wheel chair and the only possibility of standing again was surgery.

Also, no doctor or surgeon can guarantee that any operation is going to be successful and/or relieve or eliminate a person's pain. There are no guarantees with surgery.

Moral of the story; listen to your body, trust your instincts, do your homework for other options and doctors and always get second and third opinions before jumping into an irreversible surgery that may cause more pain and problems down the road.

🦋 🦋 🦋 🦋

As I'd done previously for my cervical injury, I'd go the whole nine yards and then some — with the exception of surgery and script pain meds — to try and reduce my lower spinal pain and mobility issue over the years and to this day; everything from physical therapy, shiatsu, massage, pain management, chiropractic care, epidural, trigger point and facet joint injections, OTC's Ibuprofen and Aleve for inflammation, acupuncture, inversion therapy, egoscue and the remainder of the caboodle.

Heating and icing has been — and is to this day — an integral and large part of my daily regimen necessary to keep the out-of-control inflammation throughout my spine (and body) in check and my overall pain levels from rising through the roof. Without heat and ice therapy throughout the days and nights — each and every day and night — I can barely move and my pain levels skyrocket. It is helpful in decreasing some inflammation and alleviating some pain for a short while most times.

However, nothing I have tried over the many years — including most every natural and homeopathic remedy known to man — or continue to incorporate into my daily physical therapy to ease my spinal pain and inflammation, muscle spasms, nerve irritation, and compression, does the trick all the time or lasts beyond a couple of hours.

As this dire predicament began to settle in, that anger I had been harboring over the past nine years for the God of my childhood was slowly but surely turning to hatred. A hatred that would begin eating away at my soul and taint every thought that Popped into my head.

I found myself cursing that Higher Power on a daily basis for years on end. I blamed my Higher Power for all of my never-ending pain, suffering, misfortune, and loss.

I was now at war, day and night, with the God I had grown up praying to and believing so strongly in. A God, I believed, that had allowed everything that meant anything to me to be cruelly stripped away. Most importantly — the worst of blows — my body was now severely compromised and my ability to train was all but totally gone. The medicine — my training — that allowed me to function through decades of crippling emotional pain and trauma was wiped out in a mere second's fall.

My life had been emotional pain and darkness, total misery since childhood. I didn't realize until my spine was nearly completely decimated post the freak accident of 2005 and I began living not only with the emotional torment that had been my life for the past 30 years, but now was also living with significant mobility issues and a hellacious physical pain — every minute of every day, day in and day out, for the next two decades — that there are depths to this hell.

There are depths to the darkness that was my life and I had now been banished to the most horrendous and suffocating of caverns at the very bottom of that hellhole.

I now had consistent physical pain that truly rivaled the emotional pain I had endured since childhood and throughout my life.

I thought my cervical pain was a curse — this was now complete madness. A nightmare come true. This, I thought, was beyond cruel, beyond humane, beyond torture.

If this type of pain and suffering could possibly be imposed on any human being by our government, it would certainly be a violation of the eighth amendment to the United States Constitution, which prohibits the government from imposing cruel and unusual punishments, including torture — which is exactly what these disorders and disabilities have proven to be over the entire course of my life.

There is no physical injury, in my opinion, worse than a spine injury of this nature. Especially for an athlete or for someone whose training is their medication — their escape. Combine that with my undeviating emotional imprisonment, pain, and suffering of the past thirty years, now multiplied ten times over, and this is the revised, deepest and darkest hell I would now crawl in for the next ten years.

I've asked myself over the past twenty years, what is worse, consistent physical pain or constant emotional pain? I'd suffered the immobilizing emotional pain for the past thirty years, without reprieve. Now, I would get to know, up close and very personally, chronic, disabling physical pain and how this can — as emotional pain certainly does — push you to the edge of sanity and keep you forever walking along that ledge, always weighing the options of ending the misery.

Both my emotional and physical pain were at extreme ends of the spectrum. Each a reason alone to medicate or end the suffering some way, anyway.

Being my own worst enemy in many ways throughout my life — and the biggest thick-headed Italian male on the planet — I refused to give up and to give in to a life dependent on medication, and would continue, for years on end, suffering immeasurable, paralyzing emotional and physical pain ...alone, in isolation.

Perhaps, also, in some way, I'd been cutting off my nose to spite my face. I'd been hurting and very angry as far back as I can remember. I had been traumatized and scarred from childhood witnessing alcohol and drug abuse. I've had a very strong aversion to both my entire life and have never been inclined — whether to my benefit or not — to put either into my body. I plan on going out the same way I came into this world — *pure*, as my father would say.

It's another battle in my life I won't allow to break me. It's how I fight emotionally. Deep down inside, reason being, I don't want to ever feel I have anything in common — most specifically the alcohol and drugs — with either of the two male figures and their addictions that tormented my childhood and haunted each of my days throughout my entire life.

It's a very sad day for a young boy when instead of being able to look up to and respect an older brother and father he only feels disgust and a necessity to distance himself from both.

Growing up as I did, and throughout my life, everything has been a battle — a fight for emotional survival each and every day.

I've always been a fighter. Emotionally and physically, from childhood. I refused to be beaten. However, battling the steady flow of *both* emotional *and* physical pain has been a mind-bending battle like no other and nearly took its final toll on more than one occasion post the 2005 accident.

Emotional pain increased and forever elevated my anxiety levels, creating a sense of fear and panic like nothing else. It was extremely exhausting and exceptionally difficult battling the emotional enemy.

On the other hand, the chronic physical pain created a ferocious anger that made me want to fight, quite literally. Though I could barely move most days, I remained tense, stressed to the max, and ready to explode at the drop of a hat. This constant stress made both my physical and emotional condition(s) that much worse. One pain exacerbating the other. I was trapped in a no-win situation.

Never-ending physical and/or emotional pain makes most methods of torture known to man look somewhat tame. I've said it many times before, but it can only be described as the work of the Devil.

Throughout my life, and never more so than post my 2005 accident, I kept asking myself why my Higher Power would allow such vile persecution to ceaselessly enter my fully unbalanced and extraordinarily dark existence.

Why has my life been a continuous battle through the endless fires of hell?

Why am I being tortured with every step I take, making my life more difficult and painful with each passing year?

What is the meaning of such consistent suffering, such an unbalanced and dark life?

Where does this fit into any orderly pattern of normal, of meaning?

When and where, if ever, will the clarity come?

I had been asking these questions and more for over six months as I attempted to reconnect with my Higher Power in the desert and mountains of Las Vegas prior to my 2005 accident. I had resumed praying again — asking for clarity and meaning. For serenity. For peace in my soul. Asking for light to enter my darkness.

Instead, I was made to endure the most damaging accident of my life.

I can't stress enough, it was the absolute single worst day of my life to that point. The day my life went from the frying pan into the frenzied and grinning flames of Satan's hellhole.

It was the ultimate slap in the face coupled with a vicious kick to the groin.

Yet another door slammed shut as I crawled on my knees looking for light, for meaning. This time, however, it affected me very deeply and that anger I had felt for my higher power turned to a rage I had never felt before in all of my pain and struggles.

All of those questions I had for my Higher Power, the renewed prayer for peace in my soul, a bit of light, joy and happiness, meaning and balance in my life, seemed to have been for naught once again.

I truly felt as though I was being tortured. Why would my God allow this? It isn't fair. It's been over thirty years of going from bad to worse, every year, in every way. I've been paralyzed emotionally and now mutilated both physically and financially. I've lost everything along the way and now the little that remained has been incinerated here in this scorching desert dust bowl.

Post that 2005 fall, I now saw the Higher Power of my childhood as a sham. I saw that Higher Power as the enemy and the cause of all my pain and suffering. All the never-ending loss, despair, and isolation in my life.

If my Higher Power had been a physical being, I may very well have written this story from a prison cell.

I've only felt that kind of anger and hatred a few times in my life. However, the worst was still yet to come; the fourth and what would be the fifth and final, worst-of-the-worst betrayals of my adult life were awaiting me back in Rhode Island over the summer of 2009.

There has been an ember of hope forever smoldering in the back of my mind that keeps the plea — the prayer — alive. A hope to someday reconnect with my Higher Power and have those questions I've been asking for decades finally answered. At last, understanding why I've had to crawl on my hands and knees through hell's inferno — a journey of unmitigated misery my entire life. What is the meaning?

The greatest battle of my life has been with the Higher Power of my childhood.

A part of me has always clung to, believed in, and trusted that Higher Power while the other part felt extraordinary anger, thoroughly betrayed, thrown to the wolves and left for dead.

It is a war that rages inside of me to this day, though I am slowly, through my recovery process, beginning to have some clarity regarding my life's circumstances and my purpose — my truth — in this world. It

4 Green Butterflies | 366

hasn't been easy. Far from it.

I'm moving forward, one step at a time, one day at a time. Learning to accept and to surrender. Relieving my soul of the years of anger and hatred that has eaten me alive for far too long.

🦋 🦋 🦋 🦋

Until recently, I never thought that quite possibly I had been throughout my life where I was supposed to be. Doing what I was supposed to be doing. Going through what I needed to go through in order to find my truth and meaning and emerge here — where I am now — learning to trust my inner self while reaching out to help others.

Transformed, a green butterfly takes flight. A healing midnight odyssey of sharing my life's experiences — this inequitable journey — and, in return, helping to guide others away from going where I have gone at the hands of emotional disorders, a physical disability, and chronic pain.

I will say it several times throughout this story and over and over again until my last breath; the greatest gift I can be given in this lifetime is to help someone from or from going to that infernal darkness that is any and all of these disorders. Hell, in every sense of the word.

🦋 🦋 🦋 🦋

I continued to sink deeper and deeper into depression and isolation post the shower fall. My parents and immediate family were aware of my physical condition; the cervical and upper body disability resulting from my line of duty accident and, most recently, the shower fall that finished off in my lower spine what the line of duty accident started.

However, my mask was always in place and, aside from a few instances of anger and emotional and physical pain that my mother had unfortunately witnessed on a few occasions, no one knew a thing about my emotional disability and the pain and suffering that was not only my life from the age of five, but that now, with this physical disability and hellacious physical pain, had totally destroyed my life.

I was a dead man walking.

Aside perhaps from a couple of psychiatrists, not one person knew how close I was to losing my mind — two steps from insanity — and life.

That mask I wore the past twenty-five-plus years and the isolation that became my life kept my truth hidden from everyone. I couldn't bear the thought of anyone knowing — or seeing — the depth of my pain and suffering, my *weakness* as I felt it to be most of my life.

I had to keep that shame I had felt for decades hidden.

I had to remain that *rock*, that *island* to survive.

Max kept me going. I had a responsibility to make sure my buddy lived life to the fullest. Regardless of my condition, I always tried to get him out every day — to the park, playing fetch, walking with him if I could move, taking him for rides if I could sit.

Actually, if it wasn't for Max, I may never have left the house. Post that shower fall, my depression, anxiety, and isolation was the worst it had ever been and was getting worse with each passing day. It would have peaked much sooner than it did in March of 2008 — and perhaps taken its final toll — if not for Max occupying my mind a bit and keeping me focused on caring for him.

Seeing his joy and happiness gave me a sense of accomplishment and purpose. After thirty-plus years of feeling hollow and worthless, I actually felt needed. I couldn't let my boy down even though I could hardly think straight due to the consistent and unforgiving pain and mobility issues.

22

Holidays and any type of get-together for a special occasion were always very difficult for me during my life. Now, post the obliteration of my spine, just the thought of such a gathering of people became a major trigger for anxiety and panic attacks like never before. Reason being, I had no outlets remaining now; no escape, no medication to curb the pain and even the keel — to help me fit in — as I had over the course of the past thirty years.

My nephew, Carlo, had his first child, *JJ*, during the summer of 2005. He asked me the beginning of 2006 if I would be godfather to JJ and come to Rhode Island for the christening the summer of 2006. Couldn't have been worse timing, all things considered.

Not sure how I did it emotionally or physically, but I arranged for a flight summer of 2006 and headed to Rhode Island to be godfather to JJ.

Andrea watched Max for me for a few days.

I had explained to Carlo beforehand that I wasn't comfortable in crowds and wouldn't be able to make any kind of speech in church. I didn't want or need any spotlight on me — especially at this worst of the worst times in my life.

I'm sure Carlo — along with most in my family — figured there had to be something wrong somewhere as I never attended weddings and large numbered special occasions over the past twenty-five years. However, no one ever came out and asked me why I never showed at these events.

I arrived in Rhode Island and a family get-together was arranged the following evening at Carlo's house. I hadn't seen anyone in a couple of years. I bought take-out dinner from a favorite neighborhood restaurant for the entire immediate family.

Everyone was on time, with the exception of my niece, *Strega*. We waited around a bit and then started eating as the food was getting cold. She finally walked in after we all had begun eating. I hadn't seen or heard from her in a couple years. As she walked through the door, I said hello and made a joke about her being late and her food getting cold. I told her it was good to see her. She muttered a general *hello*, came around the table to me without making eye contact and gave me a very cold, meaningless kiss on the cheek. Never asked at that time or any other time how I was doing since the fall that nearly crippled me.

Never said *"good to see you"* or struck up any type of conversation. I asked a few questions and the answers were short and evasive.

Strega, along with every other member of this immediate family, with the exception of my mother, father, and myself, has always been rather cold, snobbish and aloof. However, this was an intentional snub.

Carlo noticed the cold shoulder immediately and would mention this to me a bit later.

I've always been there for Strega and the rest of my family — regardless of, and though not one of them ever knew, the pain and suffering I was going through since childhood. Nor did they know the extent of chronic pain and depression I was now being suffocated by due to the fall of 2005.

My mask always kept my pain and suffering from others. I was that *rock* as everyone believed and as my persona portrayed. However, each member of my family knew that my life revolved around honor, trust, respect, and loyalty to family and friends — and I expected the same in return.

Needless to say, I was a bit hurt and also concerned as Strega was never this cold towards *me*. After all, I was given father's day cards and considered by her a father figure when she was growing up. I was always there for her, no matter what my predicament was emotionally or physically.

Perhaps the fact that I no longer talked to her father influenced her negative attitude towards me at this time in our lives. If I didn't know better (and I actually didn't at the time), I'd have thought she was under the influence of drugs.

In retrospect, and knowing more now about her and this entire immediate family, my intuition was on the mark; there was, and would continue to be, widespread alcohol abuse and script med (possibly illicit as well) dependency going on within this immediate family. Add that to the ice that flowed through their veins and the conscience that none of them ever had, and the atmosphere becomes rather fiendish. My mother, myself, and even my father for the most part, had nothing in common with these people. To this day, I'm still not sure where the hell any of them came from.

Strega — along with my sister — has always believed that the world revolved around her. Rules didn't apply to either of them. Both — as well as others in this family — needed to be put in their place during their lifetimes and that never happened.

The result is a weak link(s) that will eventually cause the demise of any chain — any structure, any family — if it isn't fixed. And, I would learn in time, there wasn't just one weak link in this immediate family, they were all weak links!

Always a firm believer in communication, I approached her a bit later that evening and said, *"Pretty icy reception, are you okay? What's the problem?"*

With that cold and cocky attitude, which she has had most of her life, but, again, never towards me, said *"I have no problem"*, and she walked away from me.

Strike one in the world I grew up in. And in my world, there are only two strikes — not three — allowed when it comes to disrespecting someone.

A cocky attitude is disrespectful alone. Walking away when a family member — your uncle — is speaking to you and trying to communicate and resolve an issue is akin to spitting in my face.

Strega was the Godmother-to-be of JJ. We — Carlo, his wife, JJ, myself, and Strega — were supposed to drive to church together in the same vehicle the following day, as a family.

I explained to everyone in the family what had happened and that I was hurt and angry by the disrespect. Some had noticed the cold shoulder and Strega's attitude towards me, including my nephew, Carlo.

I made it known I wasn't driving up in the same vehicle with her and, post the christening, I would not be in the same room with her unless and until I received a heartfelt apology for the disrespect.

Strega has always believed that she could do and say whatever she liked and there would be no repercussions. The apple doesn't fall too far from the tree. However, she was brought up — as we all were — knowing the importance of family and never hurting or disrespecting your family, as dysfunctional as it was.

She was told by all the family members she needed to apologize. She refused.

I'm okay with that as I never want anyone to say *I'm sorry* to me if they genuinely are not.

Words mean very little to me, actions mean everything.

I drove in a separate car to the christening and church.

Getting through that day was very difficult. I was sitting in the front pew and I could feel the hundreds of eyes on me from behind. I was having anxiety attacks in church, sweat pouring from my face and body, and I couldn't get up to go to the bathroom to try and pull it together as I'd done whenever I'd been in this type of situation in the past.

This was just another form of torture I had been cursed with throughout my lifetime. I could never enjoy the company of friends or family and cherished events as the disorders that controlled my life wouldn't allow it. Any attempt at normal was met with anxiety and panic attacks that kept my life of isolation — solitary confinement — alive and kicking.

It was easier and much less stressful to be alone than to have to endure this madness.

It was difficult enough when I had my medication — my training — to keep the keel even and get me through the rough spots. I no longer had that escape but had to rely solely on my mask and getting away — or keeping away — as quickly as possible from the trigger(s).

There was a family get-together — a party — post the christening. I decided to take the high road and, against my better judgement, approach Strega again and let her know we needed to talk. We walked over to a more private area to have that talk. I told her I loved her and was there for her as I'd been her entire life. I explained that her attitude towards me was hurtful and disrespectful and she had been raised to know better. It was unacceptable behavior and I needed an explanation if there was a problem and an apology for the disrespect and all would be forgiven as if nothing ever happened.

She said, *"I have no problem and nothing to talk about."*

"How about an apology for disrespecting me?", I said.

She replied, *"I'm not apologizing to you for anything."*

I calmly explained to her that if she didn't see fit to apologize, I'd have nothing to do with her from that point on. I would not allow her — or anyone else — to outright disrespect me and remain part of my family.

From the beginning of this conversation, her attitude was the same; cocky, rude and disrespectful.

She then said, with an impudent look and exasperating exhale, *"I don't give a shit what you think or do"*, as she began to walk away mid-sentence.

I told her to never contact me. I'd have nothing to do with her ever again.

I disowned her that day.

There is a line that a person cannot cross over or there is just no going back.

She is dead to me — as the rest of this immediate family would be considered and disowned with their complete betrayal of my mother several years down the road.

A man can disrespect his wife by cheating on her. She can forgive him if it's in her heart and try again. If that man punches her in the face — crosses that line — there is no forgiving, no turning back or you are an imbecile.

In my world, only a fool allows another to cross that line without severe consequences. If you love someone to begin with — truly love and care for someone — there is never a valid reason or legitimate excuse to disrespect or betray that person, to cross that line, ever.

I realized many years later as I began therapy and a recovery process just how uber dysfunctional my family really was. Though there were many cracks in the foundation of my family, it really started falling apart rather quickly beginning around the time of my godson's christening with this Strega incident.

In addition to this situation with Strega, there was another incident that opened my eyes to the truth of another family member; my sister was livid that Carlo asked me instead of his brother, Stronzo, to be the godfather to JJ.

My sister was (is) a control freak and insisted that everyone do what she wanted them to do or she made everyone's life miserable. Ever since that day I became Godfather to JJ, I saw and felt the anger my sister now had towards me. Truly a devious, manipulative nutcase.

I never really noticed the serious and extreme dysfunction — and didn't know what it was or why until I began a recovery process — until this christening and then, in addition to cold hearts, feeble minds, and their reliance on script meds and other mood and behavior-altering substances, it became much more apparent and destructive in the years thereafter, leading to a complete breakdown and ruination of the entire immediate family.

Before I returned to Vegas, I made sure everyone knew what had transpired and my feelings and intentions from that day forward regarding Strega. Aside from my parents conveying their feelings and thoughts about and directly to this ungrateful and disrespectful niece, that ever-dysfunctional and disgraceful immediate family of mine carried on as if nothing had happened, once again.

I learned years earlier — an eye opening lesson after my brother tried to kill me — there was no leadership or structure in this family, regardless of what we were taught growing up. There has to be a true leader — a patriarch — and clear-cut rules — boundaries — in every family or organization. There has to be enforcement of those rules and penalties for breaking those rules. There has to be accountability for one's actions. Bottom line, if there are no consequences for breaking rules or for a person's negative actions within a family, there is no structure. If there is no structure, there is no real organization, team, unit, or family possible.

There was no structure and too many in this immediate family considered themselves an Indian chief, though not one of them could so much as lead a dog on a leash!

🦋 🦋 🦋 🦋

Strangely enough, the way we were brought up — the way of our culture — nothing is more important than family and the love, respect, trust, and honor among all members of that family. The reason for the Sunday dinners going back generations and to the homeland of Italy — It kept the family together. It ensured that everyone was "at the table" at the very least one day per week to keep the family bond strong and intact.

I watched the traditions — our culture — in our immediate family deteriorate and crumble, followed by the family itself, all due to the fact that there were too many Indian chiefs and no real patriarch who made sure the way of life stayed intact and family rules followed.

The younger generations decided — called the shots — and the older generations (their parent and grandparents) sat by and allowed the culture — our family — to disintegrate. All respect was lost, all honor and trust among family members gone.

It was clear to me come the mid 2000's that my immediate family was no longer a true family but a nomadic band of gypsies with no discipline, respect, honor, love, or culture any longer embedded in their bloodline. To this day, I'm not sure it ever really was a real family — at any time — but for the never-ending caring and love, sacrifices, and the life my mother gave selflessly to each of them.

🦋 🦋 🦋 🦋

Prior to my fall of May 2005 and falling into the deepest of hellholes I'd ever had to endure to that point, I came out of my comfort zone and from my protective cocoon and got to know some of my Vegas neighbors.

One of which, *MN*, was a vibrant and friendly woman in her sixties. She was full of life, always had a smile on her face, and something kind and positive to say.

We would talk occasionally in front of the houses when we ran into each other. Chatting about everything from the neighborhood to how too many from the younger generations no longer had any respect or morals.

She was aware of my line of duty cervical disability and its physical pain but had no idea — like everyone else — about my lifelong battle with PTSD, depression, anxiety, and isolation.

Though I was feeling a bit better emotionally my first eight or so months in Vegas, I still wore my mask and kept my guard up to protect myself from anyone knowing about the deeply pained, bleeding soul beneath that protective disguise.

I remember seeing her a bit after I had fallen in 2005, my emotional and physical pain never worse to that point. She could see I was in pain and having some difficulty walking. She asked me what happened. I told her about the fall and how it totally decimated what remained of my spine, creating tons more pain and mobility issues now affecting me from the waist down.

She was a very kind, compassionate, caring woman. She would tell me then, and every other time we would see each other and talk, to stay positive. To focus on the good I had in my life (she meant well, but little did she know of *my* life!). She reminded me a lot of my aunts.

Post that 2005 shower fall, I was falling deeper and deeper into an emotional inferno, my second phase of imprisonment; The 24/7 lockdown, solitary confinement portion — *"The Hole"* — of my life sentence.

When I had returned from the christening in Rhode Island nearing the end of 2006, my isolation would resume and intensify month by month — and until this very day. I barely saw my neighbors — or anyone else — as I would seldom venture outside. I was now not only in excruciating emotional and physical pain but was at war with my Higher Power. That anger for my God I carried from my line of duty accident had turned to hatred and was eating me from the inside out.

I happened to see MN's daughter one afternoon as I came back from the store and was pulling into my garage. Normally, I would shut the garage door quickly upon pulling in so I wouldn't have any contact and have to engage in conversation with anyone during this time in my life. However, we saw each other, we both waved, and she began walking over to me. She came up to the garage and said hello and mentioned that she hadn't seen me in a while. I told her I'd been a bit out of it, lots of pain and mobility issues had me down. I asked how MN was doing as I hadn't seen her in some time. She told me that MN had been rushed to the hospital recently.

She had surgery for an aneurysm and had severe complications. The doctors weren't sure if she would be able to walk again.

I couldn't believe what I was hearing.

I told her to say hello to MN and let her know that I was thinking of her and would see her soon. I knew I wouldn't be able to go see her in that condition in the hospital. I could never bare to see people I cared for suffering or dying. A hospital setting was no different for me than a wake or funeral.

I saw MN a few weeks later. She was now confined to a wheelchair — a paraplegic for life — post her aneurysm operation. She had a colostomy while in the hospital and a colostomy bag was now attached to her and part of the nightmare that took place in the blink of an eye.

MN was still learning how to operate her electric wheelchair the first time I had seen and spoken to her since she had returned home. Her family had also purchased a wheelchair accessible van to take MN to her therapy, doctor appointments, and to now get around in general. Her home had some necessary, accessibility alterations as well.

The first thing I noticed when MN rolled up to me in her wheelchair were the tears in her eyes. It broke my heart. To this day I can't help but get choked up every time I think of her that day. The halo of joy that once surrounded her was now replaced by a radiating sadness. I could feel her pain. I knew it well.

I really couldn't believe what I was seeing. One day this compassionate, beautiful soul of a person was smiling and full of life. The next day, her entire world was flushed down the toilet into a cesspool of emotional pain, suffering, and misery.

The happiness that was always present in her eyes and the joy that always emanated from her spirit had been quickly sucked through her lungs and from her life in a very cruel way.

I gave her a hug and kiss and we began talking. My mask loosely in place but she no doubt saw the tears in my eyes, heard the sorrow in my words, and cracking in my voice.

She spoke of how difficult it was being confined to a wheelchair and how depression was now a daily battle.

MN knew of my spinal injury and physical pain but had no idea of my childhood PTSD and decades of never-ending, deep depression and despair, anxiety and isolation. She also didn't know that my ultimate fear was paralysis — being confined to a wheelchair — and is to this day. That this was a very real possibility due to the severity of my spinal injury. That if I jolted or impacted my spine too harshly or twisted at the wrong angle I may never walk again. She didn't know that my consistently worrying about this, every minute of every single day, created additional and very severe stress and anxiety for the past ten years, negatively impacting my emotional as well as physical well-being.

I can't move many days and the excruciating pain both emotionally and physically can only be described as I've described it many times before — pure evil.

MN may not have been in severe pain physically, but I knew what she may be in for emotionally unless she had people by her side that understood and cared — support — and that kept her from the deeper depths of darkness that is often much more debilitating than any physical disability.

Tears rolled down her cheeks as she described to me how she now felt and now had to live. Little did she know, I understood perfectly the deep depression, pain, and anger like no other. She also didn't know that I was now at war with my Higher Power and angry as hell. That an anger that was brewing for over ten years since my line of duty accident had turned to hatred post my shower fall of 2005 and was eating me alive.

She may not have had any of the physical pain I was suffering with, but no doubt was in very deep emotional distress. I could also still walk, be it very painfully at times. She was in a place — paralyzed — where I don't believe I would be able to survive. Her reality was indeed my greatest fear.

My heart sunk seeing this once vibrant woman in this condition both physically and emotionally. This was a woman who, post my 2005 shower fall, would try to pick me up emotionally and turn my attention away from the pain and anger that was consuming me. She would always try and make me smile — and succeeded often. It was her attempt at helping me to crawl out of the little bit of darkness she knew I existed in post my fall of 2005. Again, she had no idea of my lifelong battles with PTSD, depression, anxiety and isolation. She only knew the person that came to Vegas and had that brief glimpse of sunshine before the devastation that decimated my lower spine and created my own life-altering mobility issues and an inconceivable amount of pain and anger. She knew that person who for a moment believed that the winds of change were finally blowing in a positive direction after thirty-plus years of suffering and misery. She knew only a minuscule portion of my daily battles over the past year or so. She had no idea of the life — the hell — I'd endured since childhood.

I told her I was there for her for anything I could possibly do to help — in any way. She knew I couldn't do much bending or lift heavy objects and could barely move some days. However, if she wanted — needed — to talk, I was always there and available for her, regardless of my own battles.

Luckily, she had a very close, loving family that was there for her. One of her daughters and a granddaughter would move from out of state to live with her. She was in good hands, so to speak. I was happy for her in that respect. No one knows just how important that support is unless and until you don't have it.

MN and I did have many talks over the next couple years until I left Vegas. She was adjusting but that twinkle in her eyes never did return and I could always feel the deep sadness and depression as we talked. I think of her quite often.

MN's situation cast even more doubt on my belief in my Higher Power and amped up my anger towards and ongoing war with that Higher Power.

Maybe what I believed since childhood — what I was taught — about my God was incorrect?

Perhaps my belief was based on misunderstanding — a distorted notion — of my relationship with my Higher Power?

I came up believing that good always triumphed over evil. That my Higher Power walked with and protected the good among us from evil and undue suffering. That the unscrupulous, corrupt, and heartless among us would pay the price for their actions here on earth and thereafter. However, just the opposite had been my experience.

There were people all around me in Las Vegas — a place where billions upon billions of dollars a year pour into casino and government hands — living under the city, in the sewer system.

There were elderly being victimized by conniving scammers who would take all of their money, abuse or beat them.

Children — entire families — in our country and around the world with no shelter, insufficient food, and in dire need of clean water.

It seemed to me that bad things always happened to good people.

Why is it that the good and the poor always suffer while those that should be behind bars or six feet under are smiling, healthy, and living high on the hog?

Life may not be fair, but It seemed to me during this time in my life — this phase of my existence — that happiness and good fortune was mostly in favor of those that didn't deserve that in life.

I knew people throughout my life who would just as soon kill you as look at you. I've witnessed a fair amount of the greedy, disrespectful, conniving, and ruthless get ahead in life with no scars, no pain, no accountability.

The good and less fortunate of this world always seem to carry the load, pay the price and, worst of all, seem to be the "classes of people" that are plagued by misfortune, pain, and suffering.

I was having a difficult time understanding the Higher Power justice in this — or lack thereof — and it created even more anger and confusion surrounding my understanding of my Higher Power and God's role in not only my life but the lives of the truly good and less fortunate that unquestionably needed some divine intervention.

23

It had now been nearly two years since I had been cast into this furnace, existing in this infernal region, wallowing in pain and sorrow, anger occupying my every thought. I had been longing for the ocean — the last remaining outlet that could provide some needed relaxation and calming of my mind and soul.

That destination was over three hundred miles west in California.

Since the 2005 accident, I could only sit briefly before having to stand or lay down to take the added pressure off of the spine and alleviate a bit of the pain. Driving more than thirty minutes was very painful and wasn't possible without stopping, getting out, and standing or laying for a while.

I had been spending a bit more time with Andrea. In retrospect, I would say, primarily due to my fear that if something happened to me she would take care of Max. I worried day and night about my boy as I could hardly move or help myself many days and there was no one else around to take care of him if something did happen to me. I had a responsibility to Max. I would never betray him. I could never give him up though the thought had crossed my mind more than once during this most noxious time in my life. I'd never be able to live with myself if I did.

As my condition worsened, I had to feel comfortable that he would be taken care of if I was no longer around — and I truly believed I wouldn't make it too much longer.

Truth be told, I never did feel comfortable or confident with this Andrea scenario, "*what if*" arrangement, but I had no other options.

Andrea was like a *mommy* to Max. She was there the day I picked him up and Max did love her. Aside from my mother, father, and nephew Carlo that visited a couple of times over the years, Andrea was the only other family that Max had besides me — and *the only one* in Vegas.

Though I always made sure that Max had as full and joyful a life as possible, that didn't include being around many people — if any at all — post my 2005 fall. I had been submerging deeper and deeper into that second of three phases of imprisonment in Vegas — solitary confinement, aka; "The Hole" — and became more reclusive with each passing month, eventually leading to my third phase of imprisonment — "Death Row" — in 2008.

Like many in Vegas and around the country during this time, Andrea was in the process of losing her home. The real estate market had crashed, she had no money coming in, and she was in deep debt. I had been letting her borrow money for some time for mortgage payments and other bills. She eventually let her home fall into foreclosure, realizing she would not be able to afford it any longer. She would move in with a couple of friends for the next year and half or so while working in retail to keep her head above water.

We had talked about taking a drive to the California coast for a couple of days.

I had been spending most of my time imprisoned both emotionally and behind the walls of my home, avoiding all contact more than any other time in my life. I had no escapes remaining from this worse-than-ever emotional and physical pain. My sanity-saving arsenal had been systematically and cruelly snatched away over the past years.

My soul was longing for the ocean and the aesthetics of nature that surround the coastline. Andrea and I decided to take Max and head for Pacific Coast Highway (PCH) for a couple of days. I could sit reclined in the passenger's seat when needed to relieve the added stress and pain in my neck and lower spine from the long drive.

It was worth a shot. The ocean and nature always curbed my emotional pain and filled my soul with peace and joy for a brief time. Let's see if it could have the same effect on my physical pain.

We headed out to San Diego with a plan to drive up PCH after spending some time on the beaches — including a dog beach — in Coronado. I'd done that trip before and it was a small piece of paradise for my mind and soul to absorb and delight in.

The driving — constant sitting — proved to be more damaging and painful than I had suspected. Reclining in the passenger's seat helped a bit, but defeated the purpose as I couldn't see and enjoy the trip, most especially that beautiful coastline.

I learned during this trip that it was going to be impossible to ever focus again, relax, and enjoy *anything* with such severe chronic physical pain and mobility issues.

I found myself even more angry during the couple days on the coast than I was in Vegas. I was constantly cursing (internally) my Higher Power for the condition I was in and the hell I had been banished to. It wasn't enough to have my entire childhood and adulthood stripped of any normal — any happiness and joy. I was now relegated to a life of even more misery — chronic physical pain and mobility issues with very little, if anything, I could do to try and maintain my sanity.

The couple trips to the coast with Max prior to my 2005 fall were joyful and relaxing — something I hadn't felt in decades and, but for those few months of partial sunshine, would not feel again to this day. I had cervical pain at that time, but that was a walk in the park compared to this lower spinal disability and pain. It was now simply impossible to focus on the beauty around me and along the coastline drive with such physical pain. Making matters worse, I had to care for Max on the road for two days while in excruciating pain and hardly able to move. Like a mother who spends every minute of every day with her children, when a "vacation" comes along, it is most relaxing if you can leave the stress, kids, and chores behind for a few days.

Andrea and I talked about perhaps trying the trip again at some point in the near future and leaving Max for a couple days kenneled. I wasn't crazy about leaving him kenneled for any reason but would consider it just once down the road for a couple days of possible sanity.

On the second and last day of this trip, the added stress put on my lower spine from far too many hours of sitting began to cause my back to spasm out of control. My pain levels went through the roof and I just couldn't wait to get back to Vegas — to "The Hole" — to lay down and be miserable, by myself, once again.

I needed to be alone — wallow in my own pain and sorrow as I'd done most of my life. Away from prying eyes.

The trip caused my back to go completely out upon our return. No sooner did I walk through the front door to my home and I couldn't move at all.

At this stage of spinal irritation and pain, spasms cause compression of the sciatic nerve through my back and into my leg(s) as well as the multiple nerves trapped between herniated and prolapsed discs to inflame well beyond my daily "normal" inflammation and pain. This, along with bone on bone spinal pain from the (disc) compression, bulging discs now — due to that additional irritation, inflammation and spasms — pressing harder against and further into the spinal cord, and a host of other damaged areas of my spine adding to the malevolent mix, produces an unmerciful pain level that is simply off the charts, a mere half notch from losing consciousness.

In addition to not being able to move an inch for hours on end, the pain is so intense, I can't see straight and struggle to catch my breath. Panic attacks begin and that anger that had turned to hatred for my Higher Power actually is what keeps me fighting. Otherwise, without the *heart* that fuels that fight mode — and always thinking of my mother and my boy — death was always a welcome alternative to the torture that had been my life and had worsened with each passing year since childhood, and never more so than post the 2005 accident that decimated my spine.

My parents came down for a couple weeks the beginning of 2007. It was always good for my soul whenever I could see and spend time with my mother. It was never — since childhood — a joyful or peaceful experience with both of my parents together.

The constant bickering between my parents and the toxic atmosphere that was ever-present when both of them were in the same room and around each other was something I had lived with my entire life but was too much to handle at this most dismal stage of my existence.

However, I knew it was a short vacation for them and I could keep up the game face for a couple weeks, regardless of my pain and irritability.

I know both my mother and father could see my physical pain but truly had no idea as to the depth of my emotional pain, suffering, and despair either at this time or at any other time during my life. I did everything I possibly could during my lifetime to keep everyone, especially my mother, from knowing my truth — my reality. The true state of my heart and soul.

I always tried to spend quality time with my family any time I got the chance to see them. However, being in so much pain throughout my life, that was difficult.

With the obliteration of my spine, it was beyond the realm of possibility.

The searing pain and growing mobility issues made it impossible to focus and concentrate on anything, even quality time with those that meant the world to me — my mother in particular.

I did my very best to get my mother out to a Vegas casino or two here and there during the short time she was visiting. She always enjoyed playing the slot machines. I took pleasure in knowing she found some happiness in something — anything — throughout our lives. God knows, her emotional pain and suffering during her lifetime rivaled — and may have surpassed — my very own living hell.

Secondhand as it may be, my only happiness throughout my life was found in the joy of others, most specifically my mother.

My aunt Bella and uncle Rio (my father's first cousin and her husband) were living in Las Vegas around this time. Their children — my cousins from my father's side — were living in California.

We made arrangements one afternoon to go see aunt Bella and uncle Rio at their apartment in Vegas. As always, my mask in place so no one knew the truth of my life.

I hadn't seen them in many years. It was always a good feeling for me to see family. To see people who I loved dearly and knew loved me in that same way.

It was difficult — as it had been my entire life — trying to act *normal* and communicate effectively with so much intense pain both emotionally and now physically. They were aware of a portion of my physical struggles from my line of duty accident years earlier but, like everyone else, had no idea of what was — and had been since childhood — going on inside of me and transpiring since.

Everyone enjoyed each other's company for the short time we spent together. Aunt Bella would ask me to keep in touch and, of course, I said that I would — much as I'd done my entire life with family and friends. Always unable to keep in contact — unable to deal with the overpowering emotional, and now physical, pain and despair I lived with throughout my life. Always feeling worthless and ashamed of the disorders that were hidden behind that mask — keeping me away from all that meant anything to me for decades on end.

Now, with this immobilizing physical disability and purely satanic physical pain, I was in the worst emotional and physical state of my entire life. I was not only unable to keep in contact with an aunt I loved dearly, but I would also begin pulling away from even routine phone calls to my parents as I slipped further into my *Solitary Confinement* stage — The Hole — of my Vegas life sentence and edged closer to the third and final stage, *Death Row*.

Adding to my misery, my breathing had been compromised almost immediately upon my arrival in Las Vegas. As with everything else in my life, I accepted it as part of the curse that plagued my existence and simply added it to the list of afflictions affecting my life in a negative way and lived with it.

However, towards the end of 2007, I began having a noticeable increase in anxiety and panic attacks that I could directly attribute to my inability to breathe.

With each breath I would take, it felt like I was breathing fire through my unblocked nostril.

It had always been difficult to breathe to begin with, but I now actually feared breathing because of the intense burning sensation. This alone produced a steady flow of anxiety and episodes of severe panic.

I sought out an ear, nose and throat (ENT) doctor and, one of the few times in my life, got lucky and found a very competent, compassionate doctor — *Doctor T, MD* — who was more concerned with me, the patient, than the almighty dollar.

Dr. T would also serve as my primary physician over the next year-plus.

I was very impressed the first time I met Dr. T. We discussed many things in order for him to gather some insight into my overall health and breathing difficulties.

When I mentioned my spinal disability and the resulting and quite vicious emotional and physical pain, torment, and mobility issues, he really began to tune in and listen very closely. I believe he knew what was coming next. One of the only times in my life to this point, aside from a psychiatrist or two, I slightly lowered my guard and briefly spoke a bit of my truth; I then mentioned that I had been very depressed, isolating, and suffering with anxiety and panic attacks. I had breathing problems since childhood but since moving to Vegas I found myself all too often gasping for air — as if I was suffocating.

Dr. T then told me a story about how he suffered with severe anxiety attacks during his medical school days. He couldn't breathe during his attacks and would go outside, away from people, and just keep walking. It didn't matter if it was day or night, raining or snowing, he would just keep walking until the attack dissipated. He noted that others thought he was strange, especially if walking in the elements.

He didn't talk to anyone about it but it did scare him. He said he felt "different" and "out of place". When the attacks began, he just took to the outdoors and kept walking. This was his outlet to contend with the anxiety.

A very personal story that he certainly didn't have to share but that, as an empathetic human being and mindful doctor, made a difference in my life.

I understood for the first time that I was not alone. I was not unique in my suffering. I was not a freak having these attacks. I realized this day that others, such as this accomplished and successful doctor, have suffered — and continue to suffer — with this very disorder that has controlled and destroyed much of my life.

Dr. T ran some tests, including a nasal endoscopy, and noted the obvious; I had a pretty bad deviated septum, which was obstructing the air flow through that particular nostril, and a severe sinus infection/chronic sinusitis. I also had nasal polyps. He gave me an injection (in my nostril) to temporarily open up the airway a bit. He mentioned that I might want to take an anxiety medication to reduce some of my stress and calm my nerves.

Stress itself causes inflammation and contractions within the bronchi, causing air passages to narrow and reducing air flow.

Stress has been wreaking havoc on my mind and body for several decades.

I explained to him that a psychiatrist I had been seeing for depression had also recommended anxiety medication — among others — but that I was not inclined to take any type of meds.

He made several recommendations to help me breathe a bit more freely; nasal strips to open the airway a bit, especially when trying to sleep (which had been almost impossible for too many years), a humidifier to provide breathable warm, moist air to alleviate the sinus congestion or inhaling steam from boiling water, warm compresses, saline nasal spray, and a few other remedies to alleviate some of the congestion. All of which I tried. Several of which I use to this day.

He also prescribed an antibiotic for the bacterial infection. Unlike addictive or long-term medication, I had no problem with taking a ten day, necessary supply of antibiotics to fight off an infection.

He noted that steroid injections directly into the nasal passage(s) may provide some relief in the future if the symptoms didn't subside and I was still having substantial difficulty breathing.

He also mentioned that I may very well be allergic to the dry and dusty conditions of Las Vegas — as many people were. He suggested getting out of Vegas for a couple weeks and going to California to see if there was a change in my breathing after a few days in a different, less dry and dusty climate.

A couple months had gone by since my ENT visit. I had been

incorporating into my daily routine most all of Dr. T's suggestions to get some relief with the chronic breathing problems. However, my breathing troubles were only worsening — amplifying my anxiety and panic attacks.

I had been thinking about what Dr. T said about getting out of the dusty Vegas climate for a bit to see if there was any change in my breathing.

Strange I thought; I went to Vegas primarily on the advice of my doctors to get some *relief* from the arthritic pain that added additional suffering and misery to my spinal damage and life and wound up one hundred times worse off for it.

Now, this dust bowl hell is choking the life out of me and I need to get away from *here* to be able to breathe again.

I remember thinking; Is there anywhere on this planet where that Higher Power will allow me to hang my hat and find some peace in my soul? If not, why doesn't that Higher Power that I am at war with now — hating that God every minute of every day — just end my misery?

Why must I continue to suffer every step of this evil journey, in every possible way?

Has this Higher Power no mercy?

I spoke with Andrea and we planned a trip to the California coast — PCH — for a few days. This time, I was going to board Max at a reputable kennel for a couple nights. It was a very difficult decision but I needed as less stress as possible this time around. Maybe I could find some relief from my breathing problems — and the cause — and possibly happen upon a bit of needed peace for my mind and soul in the process.

The day of the trip came around and we dropped Max off at the kennel early that morning with written instructions regarding his feeding times and to call me if there was *any* kind of problem at all. I would also be calling a couple times throughout the day(s) to check on his progress. I opted to take Max's own food to the kennel for him to eat rather than have him gobbling their food. Changing a dog's routine food can irritate the stomach, causing diarrhea and vomiting. Clearly, I was already stressed and I hadn't even begun the trip yet. He was my boy and my responsibility and I felt awful leaving him behind for a few days — even though he was in good hands and it might do me good.

We hit the road and before I knew it my pain levels from sitting began elevating quickly. I was going from driving to stopping every 30 minutes or so to stretch my spine and briefly alleviate some of the compression and pain to reclining in the passenger's seat while Andrea drove. However, again, I couldn't see anything outside the car while reclining and it defeated the purpose. Most of the trip to and from California was through the desert. Not missing too much once you've seen it along that route. However, the trip was about the beautiful and peaceful drive along PCH in California and, not sure what I was thinking, that wasn't going to be possible this time around either.

As had been the case throughout my life, I should have known my chances were zero and none — bad luck being the only luck I've ever had. Finding some peace and joy on this trip or at any other time during my life was highly unlikely.

Sunshine entering my darkness was never possible. I'm the guy that might as well just rip up his lottery ticket or betting slip before the number is even drawn or the horse race begins. I have no shot at all of winning — of being "lucky".

I tried everything to keep my physical pain in check — standing and stretching often, reclining and lying flat just as often. I had purchased a few different cervical and lumbar support seats and gadgets for driving prior to this second road trip. No luck there either. I tried some Ibuprofen to keep the inflammation down. Lower inflammation equates to lower pain levels most times. No luck. Only option remaining at this point was to try desperately to focus through the intense physical pain that was eating away at me and destroying my life, quite literally. I might have had a shot at that if I'd had only severe emotional pain at this time. However, it is pretty much impossible to focus and concentrate on anything when a body — and mind — is being tortured by an intense and chronic physical pain. The work of the Devil it is indeed.

We ate lunch and rested a bit in San Diego before heading north up along PCH. Regardless of my attempt at keeping my back pain in check, I was doomed before we even began. We'd drive a bit and pull over and try and enjoy the ocean and other sites along the way. The trip was mapped out and we knew where we wanted to stop and spend time taking in and appreciating an area. Problem for me was it was absolutely impossible to focus and enjoy anything at all while my body was being consumed by vicious, mind-altering pain.

Andrea, like everyone else, never knew the internal battle I was having and had since childhood — with PTSD, depression, anxiety, despair, and, most recently, my Higher Power. She was, however, becoming well aware of the intense physical pain, sadness, and anger that was my reality post that 2005 accident.

We continued up PCH, making routine stops along the way and trying to enjoy the serenity of this coastline and must-see destinations along the route.

I called to check on Max a couple times, including when we stopped for the evening around Santa Barbara.

I hadn't spent enough time outside of Vegas and in California to really notice much difference in my breathing. However, I did notice my breathing was a bit less labored during the trip and outside of the dust bowl.

I was hoping that my back would be feeling a bit better the next morning as we headed up to Carmel-by-the-Sea and Monterey, where we had planned on staying this second night before heading back to Vegas the next day. However, no sooner than we began traveling up the coast, my back began to slowly but surely spasm. Shooting pain throughout my spine and into my leg. Squirming in my seat and wincing with pain was all I could do.

I was so damn angry with that Higher Power. I was fighting with everything I had to keep going — trying to squeeze even an ounce of joy out of this no-win situation.

This evil concoction of pain, despair, and misery I had been cursed with had worsened each and every year of my life since the age of five.

We made a few stops that we had planned and then decided to head back home halfway through the second day rather than stay over that second night. We had a good eight-hour drive back to Vegas and I could barely move — again. Spasms were now coming faster and pain levels moving up the chart to the blindingly unbearable range come mid-afternoon that second day.

Andrea drove most of the way back to Vegas while I reclined in the passenger's seat, trying to fend off the ruthless muscle and nerve contractions of my lower spine and the state of total immobility I knew was coming — and was dreading.

To this day, I can still feel the violent and demonic pain of every minute and every mile of that eight-hour trip back to Vegas like it was yesterday.

I called ahead to the kennel and let them know I'd be picking up Max that evening. He wouldn't be staying that second night and third day.

After what seemed like an eternity, we finally arrived back in Vegas, picked Max up and, as with the first trip we had taken together some months earlier, no sooner did I hobble through the front door to my home than my back went completely out. I was unable to move even an inch for several hours, my back spasming out of control, my pain levels so intensely wicked that I would bounce between consciousness and unconsciousness the next few days.

Any time my spinal condition reaches this point, I cannot walk for several days. I begin by crawling. Then, I learn to walk all over again. It takes a day or so to just be able to stand. With each and every move, the pain continually intensifies for days. Immobility beyond being able to stand and take a few steps has lasted for ten days at a time.

I learned a couple of things during this trip;

Max had separation anxiety very badly. To this day, Max gets very anxious if I merely go to the bathroom and he can't see me. Not only was he depressed for a couple days because I left him for one night in a kennel, he was also angry and showed that to me by peeing on the floor as soon as he got back home. He actually waited until he walked through the door!

Max had never done this before — he was well trained — and knew better. I truly believe it was his way of telling me he was pissed off (pun intended) and didn't appreciate my leaving him.

He also smelled horrible from laying around in the kennel. Andrea volunteered to wash him the next day as I could barely move for several days following that trip.

I also learned during that trip that I was not going to be able to drive long distances, sit or stand for any extended period of time, without creating crippling back spasms and an inhumanly intense pain level.

I may not have looked the part, but I was seriously disabled both emotionally and physically with very little, if any, medication — escape — remaining to offset any of that pain and suffering.

I had known most of my life that emotional pain can and will ruin a life. I was the poster child for that curse. I now understood completely that physical pain can and will ruin a life as well.

Both emotional and physical pain festering within the same body and mind is the most evil of curses — a recipe for complete disaster, total destruction.

It is not possible to focus and concentrate, relax and enjoy *anything* when pain is consuming you. There is no life but merely a shell of an existence.

Every year of my life since the age of five had progressively worsened and I was now wallowing in the deepest of depressions I had ever experienced during my lifetime.

May sound like a broken record, but I consistently sank into deeper and deeper depths of depression and hell, year after year, throughout my entire life until I crashed into the absolute bottom of that abyss.

It was now 2008. It had been nearly three years since my fall of 2005 and the disorders which ruled my world since childhood had amplified tenfold since that most calamitous day of my life.

I never felt closer to losing my mind than the years in Vegas post that accident.

My anxiety and anger levels were charting a new course of extreme.

Anxiety exacerbated not only by my mind-bending emotional and crippling physical pain, but also by chronic sinus infections that left me gasping for air most days, unable to breathe.

I was now walking the finest of lines between lucidity and insanity I had ever walked.

Isolation became both salvation and damnation.

Much of the previous three years and the next couple of years — the remaining years of the 2000 decade — were an agonizing blur, an intensely painful stupor.

Day in and day out, through unobserved and meaningless holidays and New Year's Eves to my own birthdays which meant nothing to me but another year of pain, suffering, and loss to notch on the mile-long, serpentine-like belt forever tightening around my neck with each passing year, I fought a fierce battle to keep breathing one more day — every minute of every day — for the sake of my mother and my boy.

I continued to do whatever I possibly could physically to create an escape emotionally.

With the fall of 2005, I had lost the ability to engage in 95% of the training I once did. I now had only that 50 mg dose of a needed 1,000 mg's of medication remaining to work with. Nonetheless, I pushed my body — sacrificed my body — and fought through inconceivable pain and stifling mobility issues in order to preserve what little remained of my sanity.

I was not only trapped within my broken body at this time, I was shut in and alone in Vegas. The loneliness I began feeling some years earlier was now overwhelming, even with the company of my boy, Max. Worst of all, as had been the case throughout my life, I had no one to talk to. No one I trusted or was comfortable talking to about my pain, suffering, and despair. No one who knew the depth of my daily struggles now or throughout my life.

I was completely alone at the very worst time in my life.

I had no support, no way out of the imprisonment or from being crushed by the illusory prison walls that were closing in faster and faster now than any other time during my journey through this hellhole.

I had always worried about my mother as far back as I can remember. It always weighed heavy on my mind that she had no one there for her. She gave and gave of herself her entire life and never received what really mattered from her immediate family; gratitude and genuine love in return.

However, at this time in my life and being some three thousand miles away, emotionally imprisoned, and in a lockdown phase of solitary confinement, mere months from an unknown but pending death row phase of this sentence, my worries and fears added immensely to my ever-increasing anxiety and panic attacks.

There was no consolation in knowing her daughter and grandchildren were all living at the time within minutes of her. As for my father, unfortunately, his only contribution from day one was financial. He was capable of nothing further.

I never felt in my heart that my sister, brother, or my mother's grandchildren ever truly loved and cared for either my mother or father. Fact is, I don't believe any of them knew how to love or care for anyone but themselves.

I remember too many comments and incidents from childhood and throughout my life that lead me to believe these "immediate family members" had ice in their veins. They were apathetic with regards to what family truly is and meant and the love and respect that comes of that bond and relationship. The same love and respect each of them was given by my mother.

In my world, a person's words carry little weight, if any at all. A person's actions — and many times lack thereof — speak volumes and clearly show that person's true colors.

I didn't trust that if I wasn't around any of them would care for my mother in her time of need.

My gut feeling was proven correct in 2009 with the final two of the five most devastating betrayals of my adult life to date that further ravaged me emotionally and created an anger and hatred for immediate family members that goes a million miles beyond any feelings of detestation I had ever felt until that time. The fury was deeper and more intense than I harbored for the Higher Power I was still at war with and blamed for my unwavering pain, loss, and suffering of the past 40-plus years.

To this day, I have never felt such deep-seated anger and hatred as I did for these five immediate family members who would betray myself, my mother, and father in the years to come.

I became preoccupied and overwhelmed with worry about my mother, Max, and my own well-being.

Who would be there for my mother if something happened to me?

How will I be able to care for my mother — and father — as she grows older and needs some assistance when I can hardly function emotionally and physically and care for myself?

How was I going to survive in this condition?

These thoughts tormented me — playing over and over in my mind, every minute of every day, day after day, and never more amplified than the days leading up to my face to face encounter with the Devil himself in March of 2008.

I have been in a state of chronic stress and anxiety since childhood. My body producing exorbitant amounts of cortisol as a result. This has a host of negative effects within the body. One of which is producing inflammation.

Prolonged stress within a body alters the effectiveness of cortisol to regulate the inflammatory response by decreasing tissue sensitivity to the hormone (cortisol). Thus, inflammation gets out of control.

My body's only outlets for relaxation — for clarity of my mind — have slowly and painfully been eliminated due to my physical disability/spinal injury. My primary escape was always training. Aside from exercise, I have yet to find a way to truly relax my body and get the cortisol and inflammation levels under control for any significant amount of time. My addiction to training worked magic in reducing these negative effects of chronic stress. I have found it to be very difficult — if not impossible — to completely relax the mind and body when living with chronic emotional and/or, specifically, physical pain. As a result, my body continues to produce large amounts of cortisol which, in return, produces tremendous amounts of inflammation in my body, causing much more pressure, pain, and misery. Another vicious cycle I have been swirling in my entire life.

Bottom line; stress wreaks havoc on the mind and body. Chronic high levels of cortisol lowers your immunity and inflammatory responses. A body under constant stress cannot effectively regulate inflammation within the body, which promotes the development and progression of disorders and diseases such as depression, osteoporosis, heart disease, dementia, and Alzheimer's among many others.

Everyone — and most especially those of us suffering with such disorders as depression, chronic pain, and anxiety — needs an outlet to channel the stress from the mind and body.

🦋 🦋 🦋 🦋

Post the fall of 2005, I lost most all ability to train — to escape — and clear my mind, soul, and body of the vicious pain, stress, and anxiety that controlled my every move since childhood. I could no longer ride (motorcycles) either. Another of the very few loves and outlets I would lose due to the spinal injury.

I helplessly watched the nightmare unfold — cursing my Higher Power with every breath — my soul withering as each of the medicines that provided a brief escape from the insanity that was my life was plucked away from me one by one.

I remember sitting on my bike, knowing I would never again be able to roll that throttle and feel the sunshine and the warm summer wind canvassing and painting my soul with pure joy as it had done in years past. I no longer had this escape, either, to free my mind and soul for a brief time from not only the horrendous disorders that otherwise consumed and controlled my every thought and action since childhood, but now the chronic physical pain of an incapacitating spinal disability that had mercilessly snatched away and taken the place of my medication — my sanity.

I was left like a junkie jonesing for a fix. There would be nothing left to clear my mind of all that pain and murkiness that had since multiplied many times over.

There would be no more day passes to leave the invisible prison walls behind for a glimpse of freedom.

I would soon sell my motorcycle. It had been sitting in the garage collecting dust, much like my life. I hadn't been able to ride in some time but just looking at the bike or sitting on it brought back some of the very few good memories — joyful times — of my life.

It was time to lose forever — finally let go — yet another of my loves. It was another of those days I can't soon forget. Only this time the memory would be filed away with a rooted and enduring pain and anger, rage and hatred for my Higher Power like no other memory.

My stress and anxiety levels — my life — were now completely out of control.

I had moved forward pretty much cold turkey the past several years since my 2005 accident.

My thoughts of ending this misery and madness once and for all were non-stop for some four years post that 2005 fall. I never felt closer to insanity than during this time in my life. I never came closer to the end of my days during this time in Vegas.

One particular, consistent comment I had heard on different occasions from doctors and psychiatrists had been echoing in my head; *"If you don't take medication for the (emotional and physical) pain, you aren't going to make it."*

I didn't want to make it.

I struggled every day to keep breathing for the sake of my mother and Max.

After what I'd seen my mother endure during my lifetime, I could never do anything that would hurt her. As much pain as I was in emotionally and physically — and truly needed the never-ending misery to just go away, to all end — I knew even in my darkest hour that would completely destroy my mother. And I was about to be put to the ultimate test.

The inferno within this hell was about to get ramped up a hundred notches in March of 2008 when I finally came face to face with that Devil himself.

This encounter would now cast my already paralyzed life to the most horrendous and evil depths of Satan's hellhole I have ever encountered, endured, and lived through.

24

I called my parents every day when I moved to Vegas. No matter where I was (geographically) or what I was doing, I always called to check on them and touch base at least once per day.

Post that fall of 2005, with my descent further into the abyss, I began pulling back and away from even a phone call. I was in the worst shape of my life physically and emotionally. I worried and stressed myself in oblivion. Anxiety and panic attacks were torturous and now as ordinary as the nightly news.

I didn't want to talk to anyone.

I didn't want to see anyone.

I didn't want to exist any longer.

I went from calling my parents every day to a couple times per week to once a week, on a Saturday.

No one knew what I going through or how close I was to my end. Not my mother, not Andrea — who was really the only person I spent a little time with on a regular basis.

As had been the case throughout my life, no matter how much pain and suffering I was enduring, I kept it hidden behind the mask and beneath the protective armor, and I suffered alone.

I could never let anyone know my truth — that chronic pain, misery, and despair that lingered within my soul since childhood and had since multiplied many times over upon finding bad company with excruciating, persistent, crippling physical pain and mobility issues.

I went to Vegas emotionally imprisoned with a possibility of parole — the first phase of my life sentence in Vegas.

Within months, I was thrown into solitary confinement — The Hole — lockdown 24/7, the second phase of my life sentence in Vegas. Emotionally and, now, physically incapacitated post that May 2005 fall.

Soon thereafter, I was sent to Death Row. The third and final phase of my life sentence in Vegas, where I crawled all but the last twelve inches of that five thousand two hundred and eighty-foot final trek to the chair.

It was a Sunday afternoon, March 16, 2008, that began a five-day non-stop panic attack fused together with the vile disorders that controlled my life since childhood and a horrendous, debilitating physical pain and condition that would rank at the top of the list of any form of brutal, inhuman, purely evil torture known to man.

It was a face-to-face with the Devil himself.

Beginning that very moment, everything in my life went from bad to horrific.

I was falling rapidly and would soon hit the very bottom of Satan's hellhole.

I don't recall everything about those five days in the darkest and deepest chasm of evil my body, soul, and mind has ever seen and endured. Strangely, some things I remember quite vividly while others are just a blur.

I do remember my heart was still beating — I could literally hear it and feel it trying to push through my chest — and it was telling me to soldier on as I had managed to do so many times before over the years.

Now, however, I knew I would have to dig deeper than ever before to make it through what would become five days and nights of pure madness.

I truly didn't know if I'd be able to hang on this time. This time was different. Very different. My condition was much more severe all-around and in every aspect.

Everything that could go wrong with my mind and body — emotionally and physically — did go wrong.

Murphy — the Law, the blueprint of my life — would have it no other way.

A culmination of emotional and physical pain and every disorder that had been controlling and consuming my mind and body since childhood peaking in unison.

I had felt it growing more sinister from day one and by the hour, yet this massacre in the making still hit me like a hammer out of the blue.

I'd never had anxiety and panic attacks this severe and, along with my constant worrying, stress and pain, snowballing around the clock for one hundred and twenty hours straight without a wink of sleep or a bite to eat.

I had been constantly pacing — back and forth — for five days and nights straight. My feet shuffling and my body bent half over as I couldn't stand straight up and could barely move from the spinal damage, spasms, and barbarous physical pain.

The only things missing from this horror scene were the rubber room and straitjacket.

Completely exhausted, I would put my head down (my head would also slump to the front or either side on its own), begin to fall asleep and immediately jump back up shaking uncontrollably and, once again, begin pacing — shuffling — back and forth.

My entire body was trembling and twitching. Whenever I tried to sit or lay, I couldn't stay still as my body would continuously shake, my legs literally bending, extending, and jerking out of control.

I was sweating profusely and gasping for air — I couldn't breathe.

I was suffocating — going under and about to drown — over and over again for five days of unimaginable horror. The small amount of air I was able to take in through my one and only open but half-obstructed nostril felt like I was breathing in fire. A horrifying sensation by itself. It burned so intensely that I feared even inhaling, forcing me to take in air through my mouth, which felt like I was gulping down blazing shards of glass — my throat severely parched and contracted.

Dizziness gave way to lightheadedness and unsteadiness after a few days and, finally, a sense of vertigo set in and my surroundings were spinning out of control.

I thought several times over the first couple days of this barbarity that just maybe I had been bitten and poisoned by one of the many toxic insects common to Las Vegas; perhaps a Black Widow, a Scorpion or Brown Recluse Spider. Could I have poison flowing through my blood?

Or, maybe I inhaled something noxious in that horribly dry and dirty desert air?

There are Airforce bases nearby and plenty of high flying aircraft leaving their chemtrails behind to fall to the ground. Maybe these chemicals got into my lungs and blood?

I could barely move and probably couldn't get there of my own free will, still I never once considered going to the hospital. I truly wanted — needed — it to end this time around. I had had enough of the pain and suffering in my life. The course of continuous bad luck — the curse — had to end. I was fighting with myself through days of near-insanity. My inner battle kept echoing in my head;

"*Just end it!*"

"*No, you have to hang on for your mother and your boy. Don't be selfish. Ending your own misery will create a living hell for the two who need you here and love you deeply.*"

I kept thinking to myself; Why can't I be at peace? I'm on that ledge where I've been before — all I have to do is step over and I'm finally free. I've suffered my entire life emotionally and physically with absolutely no reprieve — no balance whatsoever.

There has been no sunshine, no happiness, no joy, no hope — there has been no *life*.

This time, I deserve to be free and step over that ledge. Finally, closure for this tortured, imprisoned existence.

Over those first few days I knew I wasn't going to make it this time.

I began to prepare for my final exit.

My mind teetering between lucidity and madness, my vision blurred, and my hands and body shaking, I wrote three letters;

One to my mother, one to my sister asking her to care for our parents — specifically our mother — in my place, and the third letter to Andrea.

I wanted desperately to believe that my sister would do that, but in my heart I didn't believe it and that caused an awful lot more stress and anxiety during what I felt were my last hours of pain and suffering. I couldn't even find comfort in knowing that my mother would be in good hands and well cared for if I was no longer around. My sister was the only option I had regarding that request.

Looking back at this and knowing now what I know to be true about my sister and those within my immediate family, I would have been turning over in my grave.

My father and my beloved mother would have been alone and on their own. Their very own blood disgracefully betraying them to the very end.

I asked SR in that letter to care for Max. I knew she was in a bad place emotionally and financially so I left a substantial amount of money in a large envelope attached to her letter. There was enough to make sure that Max lived a full, happy life (with her) and enough remaining to help her get back on her feet.

Once again, I had to believe in my heart that she would care for Max. She was my only chance of knowing he would be loved and cared for when I was gone.

I knew they both had a strong bond and it was my only option — my only shot — at this point. He had no other family that could or would care for him.

Many times over the last couple of days I was observing what felt to be my imminent demise by way of an out-of-body experience. I was looking down from above and witnessing this nightmare and its' devastation. My spirit seemed to have left the temple for a safe place above as my body below headed for an implosion. Looking down from above I could see myself — my body — pacing, sweating, shaking, suffocating. One debilitating symptom feeding off of and into the other, over and over again for days on end.

I believed I was losing my mind. I *knew* I was losing my mind.

Coming upon the fifth day, I was rapidly closing in on the last few steps of that final mile. Crawling through this valley of death with no sleep whatsoever, semi-comatose, and half-delusional. However, I felt no (real) break from the reality of the situation. There was a spiritual detachment from the body but my mind was aware of the "here and now" and the dire condition I was in as well as the final, much needed peace thereafter that awaited in the near distance.

I was now mere hours from hitting the proverbial rock bottom. The deepest and darkest region of this hellhole I'd ever crawled in.

My etheric body had left my physical body. That silver cord was still attached but mere minutes from its severing, allowing the passage into the long-awaited tranquility of the other side. A final and full pardon from a life of imprisonment. I would be free at last.

With mere feet remaining of the last mile, and just before the final breath, it was requisite to first pass through the door of insanity before the final exit;

As I dangled on that ledge, the inferno — dancing wildly and creeping forward in a crazed saunter behind me — begins its final engulfment of the body, seconds from incinerating the mind. I began to turn that doorknob ... It was time to pass through ...

I remember at this very second I began vehemently cursing my Higher Power for everything I've had to go through in my life — since the age of five and with no reprieve for the next 40-plus years; the line of duty accident and the freak fall of 2005 in Las Vegas that physically disabled me, leaving me with chronic, crippling pain and mobility issues. The loss of all of my outlets — my meds — my escapes needed to quell my pain, help me to fit in, function, and keep my keel even. For not hearing my pleas for help throughout my life but most importantly during the many months I spent alone in the desert and in those mountains of Vegas — prior to the May 2005 fall that decimated my lower spine — trying to reconnect with my Higher Power. For once again abandoning and betraying me when I needed my God the most.

Five days in and inches from the chair — minutes from execution — my only thought was (with) my mother and what this would do to her, and my boy who would become an orphan.

My best friend laying by my side, a look of sheer fear and helplessness in his eyes that I will never forget. He was watching me — his protector, his dad — slowly slip away.

I can say with certainty — even with the fighter's *heart* I've had beating inside my chest since childhood — if it wasn't for the deep love and respect I had for my mother and for the sake of my boy, I would not be here today.

I made two phone calls around 7:00 a.m. that fifth day of this total madness.

The first call was to Andrea. She was the only person I really knew in Vegas that could — and might be willing to — take care of Max.

When she picked up the phone, I remember mumbling the question I had on my mind for the past few days, "*Can you do me a favor and take care of Max?*" I remember her first response, "*It's seven in the morning, where are you going?*"

I remember saying, "*I don't feel well, I'm going to go to the hospital. I need you to take care of Max. Come over when you can, key in the back.*"

Though we were from two different worlds and didn't have much in common, in retrospect, it bothered me a bit that someone who had spent a fair amount of time with me wasn't a bit more concerned. I could barely speak and was half-delirious from not sleeping a wink over the past five days of pure hell I was enduring. I think anyone — a child — could have sensed the grave situation I was in and heard the desperation in my voice that day.

The second phone call I made that morning remanded my death penalty sentence back to solitary confinement — *The Hole.*

I called my sister. She picked up and I remember muttering, "*Please take care of Mom, I have to go to the hospital.*" I remember my sister saying my name and then, "*What's the matter? What's the matter?*" I was having none of that. I had nothing else to say and was getting ready to hang up when my nephew, Carlo, picked up the phone. He was crying. He said, "*Unc, please don't do anything. Hang on. Mom will be there today. Promise me you won't do anything; you'll wait for Mom to get there?*"

I had hung on the line a bit too long. I remember saying, "*I promise, Carlo. I'll hang on.*"

That vow to my nephew was my stay of execution.

Even in such a dire situation — I've been there many times over the years, none more severe or closer to the other side than this time around — it forced me to keep my fingers firmly gripped on that ledge, my legs still dangling uncontrollably — literally — for the next nine hours (and a couple days thereafter) until my sister arrived in Las Vegas. My vow forced me to honor my word to my nephew.

🦋 🦋 🦋 🦋

Carlo and I had a very close relationship during his younger years. Of all the immediate family members, he was the only one that had half a heart. A portion of him was conscientious and caring — the other half was like the rest of them; self-centered, money-worshipping, ungrateful, and incapable of caring for and loving anyone but themselves.

He could have gone either way in life. I had hoped I influenced him for the better. Unfortunately, and, as I'd see it firsthand, with the help of alcohol and script meds (and who knows what else), he eventually lost that warm side and became one of the heartless vultures in this immediate family and a part of my life's curse.

🦋 🦋 🦋 🦋

I was certainly cut from a different cloth — and in many ways. Even at death's door I could never break a promise, go back on my word, or betray someone. Carlo knew me pretty well when it came to the code I lived by.

What he didn't know is that his heartfelt plea and making me promise to hang on kept me from crawling the final twelve inches to that chair — finally going over that ledge — on the worst of days ever spent in the deepest regions of that hellhole I've existed in my entire life.

🦋 🦋 🦋 🦋

Regardless of the depth and duration of my suffering, I know in my heart that I have my worst days — my most difficult and most painful days emotionally — ahead of me.

My mother is in her late eighties and battling some serious health problems and my boy has a few more dog years remaining.

Through therapy and my recovery process the past couple years, I am learning — trying desperately — not to dwell on the inevitable. That constant worrying and stressing about the things I cannot change or control have contributed heavily to my severe depression, anxiety, and panic attacks throughout my life. An evil and torture that truly can't be understood unless it has been lived.

Though I've been to the very bottom and each corner of Satan's hellhole during my lifetime, there are still a couple depths of pain and suffering down there that I've yet to be acquainted with and have had to endure. One most specifically that I can only hope, for the sake of my mother and someday finding that peace and joy in my soul that has always been her wish for me, I am able to weather when that day arrives. And, in a time to come, move on and forward, making my mother proud by finding and fulfilling my life's meaning in helping others suffering debilitating emotional and/or physical pain from or from going where I have gone — the diabolical darkness — and existed my entire life.

🦋 🦋 🦋 🦋

I had never reached out to anyone (for help) during my lifetime, regardless of my emotional or physical situation or need. If it wasn't for my obsessive concern and deep love for my mother and my boy, I wouldn't have made either of those calls that Friday morning and my story would never have been told.

As for my lifelong battle with these disorders; PTSD, depression, anxiety, isolation, chronic pain, despair — as I've stated time and again, and as difficult as it may be to understand how it was possible, no one ever knew. Post my line of duty accident (and fall in 2005), all anyone knew was a portion my physical disability and physical pain. No one ever knew or realized the depth and duration of my emotional disorders and what that perpetual darkness and complete imbalance was doing — and had done — to my body, mind, and soul since childhood.

The total decimation of my lower spine in May of 2005 with that freak fall in the shower pushed me to the very edge.

Andrea came by my house that Friday afternoon, some six hours after that first call. I hadn't seen or heard from her in over a week. She and my sister would be the only two people to see me in that near-death condition — to see a portion of my tormented and bleeding soul that I had concealed behind a mask and protective armor my entire life.

I could barely stand and was still in full-blown panic attack, shaking and twitching uncontrollably, my surroundings spinning in circles like a carousel at a carnival.

However, I didn't discuss with Andrea the torment I had been enduring for the past five days — nor was she ever aware of my emotional misery and disorders then or over the course of my life.

As far as she knew, and aside from what had to be obvious in my physical appearance, I had a very bad day or two with pain and was unable to sleep.

I asked Andrea to pick my sister up at the airport in a few hours when her plane landed. She did and both returned to my home approximately twelve hours from that first call I made earlier that day.

Andrea left within an hour of their return to my home and my sister and I began to talk a bit. Nothing in depth, as my family was never able to communicate too effectively with one another and I, even in this grim condition, wasn't about to discuss my emotionally imprisoned life since childhood and everything I had been going through emotionally and physically since my line of duty accident and the fall of 2005.

It's sometimes difficult for even me to believe, as I reiterate throughout these pages, but not one person ever knew the extent of my pain and suffering and the torment I lived with every day of my life since the age of five. Unless and until this story — this book — is published, no one will ever know the truth behind my life. And these pages barely scratch that surface.

I remember my sister taking a couple pictures of me when she finally arrived. Peculiar I though. I didn't ask why, but I was pretty sure she needed something to remind her of what she had witnessed.

When I looked at the pictures a few days later, I could not believe what I was seeing; my face was completely sunken in, my eyes were barely open, but the ghastly emptiness told the story — I looked the proverbial picture of death.

Strange as it may seem, these pictures immediately brought to mind what I'd seen when studying (in high school) the Holocaust of the 1940's and the concentration/death camps. The inhumanity and torment that could be seen in the eyes and from the physical appearance of those that were imprisoned and tortured in these camps.

I thought; *Where is God in this world?*
Why?

What is the purpose and the meaning of this? of life?

I immediately deleted the pictures from her phone. There was no way anyone was going to see me in that condition. I wore a mask my entire life to keep my pain, suffering, and despair hidden from everyone. These were pictures of frailty — of weakness some might consider — of a person completely beaten down and going out for the count. A tortured body and mind awaiting its final exit.

Ironically, however, this time the door that slammed shut in my face as I was mere inches from its threshold was none other than death's door. Surprisingly, it seemed no matter where a door may lead on this journey, I was never allowed to enter.

My sister knew just from looking at me and listening to my distorted murmurings that I was in grave condition. She may not have known the reasons — the disorders, despair, and extent of the pain and disability — behind what got me to that stage, but she knew not only from my first utterance that morning on the phone but also from the deathly physical appearance that slouched before her. I told her I hadn't slept in five days and was having severe panic attacks as a result. I never went into further details of my past or present pain and suffering.

My sister had spent many years as a medical transcriptionist. She was rather knowledgeable of medications and their uses. She had with her some trazodone she wanted me to take to get some sleep that evening. She knew my feelings about medication — especially addictive medication.

Trazodone is one of the longer standing, tried-and-true, safer meds on the market for depression, anxiety, and sleep. I knew that I wouldn't make it going another night with absolutely no sleep. I took the trazodone and, finally, was able to get a few hours sleep. The trazodone did seem to calm down my racing heart, anxiousness, and inability to stay still. I did wake often as I was still having difficulty breathing but was able to fall back asleep without the shaking and trembling keeping me awake.

Sleep deprivation alone is deadly. Combine that with everything else I was experiencing and I still, to this very day, don't know how I was able to get through five days of that pure torture and insanity and remember any portion of the nightmare at all.

I spoke with my parents the day after my sister arrived — Saturday. I was still very much out of it and they could no doubt hear it in my voice. Luckily, I had finally slept a few hours. They also knew something had to be very wrong if my sister came to Vegas unexpectedly as she did. However, as was common in my dysfunctional family, we never discussed anything. Especially emotions. My sister told them everything was fine, she just wanted to see me and needed a vacation.

I could hear the deep concern and fear in both my mother and father's voices as they kept asking me if I was okay. I told them not to worry about anything, that I was fine. I could never tell them — especially my mother — what I'd been going through during my lifetime and what had happened to me the past week. I never wanted my mother to worry about me. She spent her entire life worrying and caring for everyone but herself. If she ever knew the extent of my lifelong pain and suffering and what I had gone through that past week in Vegas, it may fully shatter her already broken heart. It was best no one ever know my story. I wanted it that way. I needed it that way.

My sister and Carlo had a peek into the horror that I lived for a few days but there was never any further discussion of the depth and duration of the madness I lived with every minute of every day, uninterrupted for the past 40-plus years.

During the following week my sister stayed in Vegas and accompanied me to a few doctor appointments. She would tell me a time or two, "*You should come home and be with family. You need your family now.*" It sounded right but it didn't feel right. I heard what she said, but knew in my heart there was no sincerity or compassion behind her words.

Since childhood, the only sincerity and compassion from words or actions within this family was from my mother. the others sometimes talked the talk, but never walked the walk. This day was no different.

I would soon hear how much the last-second flight cost and who paid for it ... who said who should go to Vegas ... and who this and who that. I sensed certain family members wanted me to reimburse the cost of the flight to and from Vegas and come up with an award for the all but genuine attempt at being truly concerned, being "family", and doing what real family does for one another.

I had forgotten about the cash and exit letters in the envelopes on the dining room table. I didn't even realize that they were there until I was able to sleep a bit and started coming around a few days after my sister arrived. I don't know if my sister or Andrea ever noticed the letters with their names on it. No one ever mentioned anything to me. We had spent most of our time in the living room, thankfully.

One of my appointments that week was to see a psychiatrist, *Dr. D*, that I had seen several times since living in Vegas. I explained what happened and he said what I'd heard many times before, "*Of all the patients I've ever seen, you would benefit the most from medication. It can save your life.*" He wasn't the first psychiatrist or doctor to convey that sentiment and he wouldn't be the last.

The emotional and physical pain had been taking its toll for decades. It was too little too late as far as I was concerned and, most importantly, I didn't want to be under the control of any drug — then or at any time in my life. It's how I've chosen to live and to suffer — primarily due to my feelings of repulsion towards drugs/medication. This a direct result of the trauma — PTSD — I'd endured during my childhood at the hands of those addicted to drugs (and alcohol).

He recommended several medications ranging from addictive antidepressant meds to anxiety meds. I explained that I didn't want to take anything addictive and have to wean off the medication at some point down the road. He assured me that if I was feeling better in a few months and wanted to terminate the use of the medication, he would reduce the dosage(s) and slowly wean me off the medication without any side effects. He insisted I needed medication or I might not make it next time. I told him that considering the condition I was currently in, I would try the one antidepressant medication in order to pull me from the deepest and darkest region of hell I'd ever endured and get me back to my "normal" pain and suffering — a hella couple rungs up the ladder.

Along with that medication, I requested a script for trazodone as I felt comfortable with its track record as one of the safer and less addictive of the medications recommended for my anxiety and inability to sleep.

Needless to say, I took the antidepressant medication all of two days and decided it wasn't for me. I wasn't willing to become addicted to any medication under any circumstances. I called the doc to let him know. I didn't have to wean off the medication as I hadn't taken it long enough.

As for the trazodone, I still have the original script from March 2008. There were thirty pills dispensed for that script — there are still twenty-two pills in the bottle some six-plus years later and as of this writing. I keep it around as a constant reminder of the time I spent crawling in the valley of death.

I also had an appointment to see my ENT, Dr. T, that week. I didn't have a primary care physician and Dr. T had been serving that purpose for me. I had multiple tests done including a CT scan of my brain and sinuses and blood tests for everything under the sun. I also had more injections directly into the nostrils to decrease the inflammation and open the nasal passage a bit so I could breathe a bit easier.

My blood tests came back the following week with very high elevations in certain areas that concerned Dr. T. I discussed this with him and we decided to redo the blood tests since the first time around was in very close proximity — within a week — to the five days I'd gone without sleep and food and my mind and body were stressed to extremes.

Second round of blood tests a couple weeks later were mostly normal with a stress-related area or two borderline.

I took my sister to the airport a week after she arrived. My legs were still wobbly and I was still very uneasy, fatigued, and more emotionally and physically fragile than I'd ever been before. With what I'd been through, I guess I was fortunate to even be walking and talking.

I returned home and fell back into the only life I'd ever really known — an existence of isolation, wallowing in physical and emotional pain, despair, and misery.

Once again, constantly worrying about my mother, if and when I was going to be unable to move from the spinal disability and, now, making my anxiety and stress that much worse, if I would ever go again to that depth — the absolute bottom of hell I had just endured for five days.

It was now summer of 2008 and a couple months post the worst five days of my life. Andrea had broken with the friends she was living with, was in a worsening financial situation, and had nowhere to really go. I had an extra room and told her she could stay at my home if she wanted.

I was most definitely at my lowest point ever during this time in my life and, with the continued and constant worrying about my mother and Max should something happen to me, I figured — perhaps a bit selfishly — that having Andrea closer to Max might be in my (and

Max's) best interest.

On the flip side, she had relied on me financially to keep her head above water on many occasions over the years. One hand washes the other so to speak.

Neither of us had anyone else to rely on in Vegas. She did have parents who lived in Florida but they were estranged during this time.

Both of us were in emotionally fragile states and perhaps there for each other in the wrong ways, for the wrong reasons. We really didn't have much in common, if anything at all, and were worlds apart when it came to our culture — our ways of life, beliefs, and the moral code we lived by. It was never more evident than when we were both living under the same roof. It wasn't easy, but it seemed to work for each of us during this time in our lives and with our predicaments.

Andrea was still working full time in retail so I had my space to wallow in my pain and misery without being under a magnifying glass. She knew — and saw — my physical pain and mobility issues. However, I never spoke of or showed any emotional pain or despair in her presence. She probably assumed I didn't venture much beyond the walls of my home due to my physical pain and mobility issues. Again, she had no idea of the emotional imprisonment, anxiety, and isolation that I'd lived with my entire life and that had worsened drastically since my fall of 2005 in Las Vegas.

All in all, it was actually a bit of a relief having someone around who could help a bit, mostly with Max, when my back went out and completely immobilized me, which happened all too often.

My breathing problems continued to escalate. I'd had breathing difficulties my entire life but nothing like what I'd been experiencing since moving to Las Vegas.

There are very few things in life — if any — that can create greater anxiety and panic than not being able to breathe. Anyone who has experienced an airway obstruction, for whatever reason, understands the pure fear that comes as a result.

Of the most essential components of human survival — oxygen, water, food, shelter, sleep — oxygen is the most basic human need. The one we — our brains — need the most consistently, without delay, or we will die. Within several minutes of oxygen deprivation, the brain will be severely damaged. There is virtually no chance of survival — even in a vegetative state that will result from too many minutes of oxygen deprivation — beyond fifteen minutes without oxygen.

Needless to say, and aside from all other miseries that were my life, not being able to breathe — having to gasp for oxygen — was another form of torture I certainly didn't need. It significantly compounded my existing anxiety, pain, despair, and overall daily struggle to survive.

I went in to see my ENT once again. I had been trying all recommendations by him to alleviate my breathing problem. Nothing was working and the problem was worsening. We discussed surgery for my deviated septum and nasal polyps that may be helpful in opening up the nasal passage(s) and breathing easier. Surgery has always been an absolute last option for me. He also noted (again) that perhaps the dry, dusty climate of the desert just didn't agree with me. Maybe I needed a climate with some moisture in the air. Pretty much the story of my life; bad luck. The blueprint of my life; Murphy's Law. I moved to Vegas on the advice of doctors who believed there would be fewer arthritic flare ups in the warm, dry climate of the southwest. Thus, a bit less pain caused by the arthritis I had throughout my spine and body. That arthritic pain triggered (and increased) by moisture and high humidity common of the climate on the east coast where I had lived my entire life prior to moving to Vegas. Now, I was being told that I needed the very moisture in the air that causes additional physical pain within my spine and body in order to open up and lubricate my nasal passages so I could breathe more freely.

I had come to Vegas most specifically to decrease my pain levels by reducing the additional arthritic pain caused by the damp, moisture-laden air of the east coast. That made perfect sense to me. And, for anyone else, it may have worked and may have even been sealed with a happy ending to the story. But this was *my* life — my curse. Nothing in my life ever flowed smoothly or to my benefit.

Now, after coming to Vegas and losing everything — emotionally, physically, and financially — the very climate of this area was suffocating me.

Even journeying to the very bottom of Satan's abyss here in this desert dust bowl wasn't enough bad luck and torture, there was still so much more awaiting me with every step I would now take to leave this naturally barren, stifling chamber of horror behind me.

I've said it before and will say it again; I couldn't catch a break if it landed in my lap! And if it wasn't for bad luck, I'd have no luck at all!

I was now ready to seriously consider and begin planning my departure from Las Vegas. So much had gone wrong here. Too much had been lost here.

I was still suffering terribly emotionally and physically and not being able to breathe was the straw that broke the camel's back. Whatever the cause(s) may have been for my breathing difficulties in Vegas, I am certain to this day that there was also something in the air there — natural or chemical — that was toxic to my body.

My nephew, Carlo, had been trying to convince me to move back to Rhode Island since the incident of March 2008. He would reiterate that I should be with family and we should look into starting a business together in Rhode Island. Spend more time together — as family should. I would find out soon enough, much to my dismay, that Carlo was now a master of talking the talk without being able to walk the walk. He had crossed over to the other side.

It was now closing in on the end of 2008 and some eight months since the worst week of my life. The holidays were upon us and I had never felt more anxious, lonely, and despondent. I pledged to myself that this would be the last holiday season — the last year — I would ever spend in Vegas. No matter how bad it could be or get elsewhere, it couldn't compare to what I'd lost and lived through here. Or could it?

I spoke to Carlo and we made a tentative plan to drive back to Rhode Island towards the summer of 2009. He would fly out to Vegas when I was ready and help drive the five day, nearly three thousand cross country miles back to Rhode Island.

There was no way I would be able to do the drive alone. I couldn't sit for more than thirty minutes at a time and that was on a good day. I'd have to recline in the passenger's seat most of the drive and still get out of the car every hour or so to stand or lay flat. And, most importantly, if my back went out, it would be impossible to move — or drive — at all. If I was alone, I'd be stuck on the road somewhere unable to move an inch — and I had Max to care for.

Carlo offered Max and I stay with him, his wife, and my godson, JJ, until I found a place to rent in Rhode Island. I felt — I knew — the offer wasn't sincere but my back was to the wall. I wasn't comfortable with that arrangement at all, mostly due to my gut feeling, but didn't have any other option at this time.

I also needed my space for obvious reasons.

In addition to this, Carlo had two dogs and I didn't know how Max and his dogs would interact with each other.

However, I didn't think it would take too long to find a place for me and Max and we'd be out of there quickly.

As difficult as it was, I was going to try "something different" for once in my life.

Something that took me way out of my comfort zone.

Still, my gut feeling was telling me that aside from being close to my mother and father, staying at Carlo's home, however briefly, and being around this immediate family was a very bad move.

Carlo was the only immediate family member that ever displayed any sense of family, however little it may have been. From his youngest days, I tried to instill in him (as I did my other nephew and niece) the old school and cultural values. In his earlier days, he seemed to understand, appreciate, and incorporate these principles into his life. We always connected on that level and were very close at one time.

However, it was right around this time — the trip back to Rhode Island from Vegas and the days and months that followed — that I noticed he was beginning to exhibit behaviors I had never seen in him before. Behaviors the others in this immediate family were all about; disrespect, indifference, ignorance, selfishness, lack of discipline, money worshipping, hypocrisy and deceitfulness to name a few.

He seemed now to be like the rest of them in this immediate family; no concern for or real sense of the honor, loyalty, and respect required and necessary within the family, though each had been brought up to understand the importance of this code of behavior — this way of life — and incorporate it not only within the immediate family, but life in general.

As I've said before, they could talk the talk but *never* walked the walk.

Carlo may have taken a few steps along that old school, principled road earlier in his life, but he was no longer walking that path.

I didn't feel right about the whole thing from the very beginning — going back to Rhode Island to be with these people who are supposed to be my "family". Nevertheless, I was leaving the asphyxiating dust bowl sooner rather than later and I was going to give this a shot.

I spoke with my mother about this many months prior to the actual move back to Rhode Island. She was simply elated I was going back "home" and would be closer to her — which made it easier for me to feel like it was the right decision.

My emotionally imprisoned life and isolation had gotten me

nowhere over the course of my lifetime but deeper and deeper into that hellhole that I existed in. If something isn't working after a reasonable amount of time, it's time to make a change and look to progress a bit. I've always felt that way, but it was easier said than done when my world had been controlled by emotional disorders from childhood. It had always been very difficult just putting one foot in front of the other and never more so than when I lost most of my ability to train — my medication — post the accidents.

I let the thought of moving back to Rhode Island to be with "family" stew a bit — a good six months — and then, against my better judgement and gut feeling, I decided I needed change and to try something different for once. Especially at this time in my life and with my current predicament.

Maybe my instincts were wrong and this was just what I needed to rise from the ashes of the funeral pyre that had half-incinerated my mind and soul during those five days spent with the Devil himself. Maybe I should give this a try; go back to the cold weather that increases my pain levels but, perhaps, being with "family" will lessen the emotional pain that I've endured my entire life.

Regardless of the pain trade off, and most importantly, I needed to see and be around my mother at this time in my life.

A couple months prior to the planned move back to Rhode Island — approximately one year to the day that began my five days of near-insanity — I developed a lump under my right armpit. It started off as a nagging pain that felt and looked like a small pimple. It slowly grew to the size of a pea and then ballooned to a size a bit larger than a golf ball, with the surrounding area of my armpit severely inflamed. At its peak, and for a few weeks, I wasn't able to completely put down my right arm.

It was quite painful and irritating to say the least. I was also once again plagued by added worry and anxiety thinking of what it could be and mean this time around;

Tumor? Cancer?

I've always believed that I had some kind of poison in my blood during the time I spent in Vegas. Whether I was breathing in some allergen that didn't agree with me or there was some kind of toxin in the air I was breathing and accumulating in my system.

There was also the possibility that I'd been bitten by a poisonous insect that caused an infection and toxins to spread throughout my system.

What I did know for sure is that I had a very difficult, almost impossible time breathing in Vegas and that worsened the longer I remained there.

In addition to my emotional and physical pain and misery intensifying, I also felt quite ill during my years in Vegas like I'd never felt any time prior. To this day, I firmly believe I had something foreign making its way through my blood.

Whatever this poison was under my armpit it had no doubt been caught and trapped by a lymph node.

I went to see my ENT regarding the lump and asked him to recommend a primary care physician who dealt a bit more with this kind of situation. In addition to prescribing an antibiotic, he did recommend a primary physician, *Dr. J*, who I went to see a couple days later.

Dr. J was everything Dr. T said he was; compassionate, understanding, and a wonderful person and doctor. We talked for quite a while. He happened to be a former police officer from the Midwest turned MD. Go figure! I wish I would have been fortunate enough to have Dr. J in my corner earlier on in Vegas. He was up there at the top of the class with Dr. T. I trusted and respected both of them.

Dr. J examined me, ran some tests, and ordered more blood tests. He looked at the lump and said what I had been thinking; A lymph node caught some bacteria or toxin in my blood and expanded into the lump that was now beneath my armpit.

I was concerned it may be cancerous and wanted to do a biopsy to hopefully rule this out and lessen my elevated anxiety a bit. Dr. J said that he didn't think it was cancer but that couldn't be ruled out without the biopsy. He suggested and prescribed another antibiotic to begin taking that day along with the one I had been taking the past few days. He said to give it a bit more time to see if the lump started to decrease in size. If not, we could move ahead with the biopsy. He noted that the biopsy would require a surgical incision and I should just go ahead and remove the lump if going to go that route at all.

I have always felt queasy whenever thinking about surgery for any reason. It's not something I've ever considered — not even at this point in my life when I could be dealing with cancer.

Over the next month, the inflammation and the lump was slowly decreasing in size. It leveled off at pea size but was still very tender to the touch.

I was leaving Vegas with a scheduled trip back to Rhode Island planned in a few weeks.

My nephew, Carlo, was flying down to Vegas in a couple weeks to drive back to Rhode Island with me and Max.

I decided to put off any further doctor visits or biopsy until I returned to Rhode Island.

I didn't need any more bad news or problems delaying my exit from Vegas.

I had talked to Andrea about my leaving Vegas and that it was necessary due to my breathing problems. I just couldn't breathe any longer in the dry, dusty climate.

She was still working in retail and was still a licensed real estate agent in a collapsed market and economy. She would list and sell properties when the opportunity arose.

Most of the opportunity and incentive around this time in Vegas for real estate agents was in rentals. No one was buying and everyone was looking to rent. I had her handle the rental of my home and oversee and take care of a few other things for me — for which I paid her much more generously than the going rates for a real estate agent or property manager.

I cleaned out my home and sold the majority of the furniture and electronics. I told Andrea that she could have whatever she wanted that was remaining, sell the rest and keep the proceeds.

I donated most of my clothes to charity. I told her to donate whatever she didn't want when she was finished going through everything, which ranged from kitchenware to outdoor furniture.

Andrea would move out of my home and in with another friend about a month prior to my leaving. She was no longer happy in Vegas and we talked about possibly getting together at some point down the road. I told her I was always there for her even though I could no longer stay in Vegas. While we truly didn't have much in common and we were complete opposites in many ways, we did develop an atypical bond during the time we had spent together. We agreed to keep in touch.

Carlo flew down to Vegas the third week of May 2009, a few days prior to our drive back to Rhode Island.

Before we left, I wanted — I needed — to climb Lone Mountain one last time.

I hadn't done the climb since my accident of May 2005. It had always been a joyful, peaceful, short climb to the top. The 360-degree views of the entire valley and Las Vegas strip from atop the mountain was simply breathtaking.

Since the fall of 2005, I was unable to bend my spine from the cervical down through my lumbar sections without severe pain and a hefty, crippling price paid if I did. However, I wanted Carlo to reach the top and I needed to see the view one last time before I left Vegas and what had been the worst five years of my entire life far behind.

Carlo had asthma when he was younger and was a bit weary of the climb. It's a short (one hour or so), but moderate incline with some loose terrain along the several beaten paths to the top where the elevation reaches approximately 3,300 feet.

I remember beginning the short trek with Carlo. From the first steps leading up the trail, the pain and pressure in my spine was growing but I pushed forward. If at any time my spine went completely out, I was in serious trouble — but at least Carlo was there to call for help.

When this does happen — my back goes totally out — there is absolutely no way I can move. I am completely immobilized with the absolute worst pain one can imagine; every muscle and nerve along my lower spine — including the sciatic nerve — into my hips and buttock spasms.

The degenerated and mangled bones and discs along this area of my spinal lock, sending me to the ground, curled into a ball, unable to move an inch if my life depended on it. Movement at this point is simply impossible.

This has happened in my home on many occasions. If there was a fire in my home while in this condition, I would not be able to move. Not being able to so much as budge due to this condition is a fear I have lived with constantly for the past nine years and to this very day. Never knowing when this will happen causes anxiety around the clock, every minute of every day of my life.

🦋 🦋 🦋 🦋

Flexeril is the only script medication I will take (occasionally) as of this writing. It eases the muscle spasms when this occurs, but still takes half a day to get me up off the floor and several days to help me walk a few steps.

It was a medication that had been recommended for years

since my spinal injury(s) and I completely disregarded it, as I have done most all medications throughout my life.

However, it was recommended once again in 2010 when I moved back to Florida.

After doing some research, and realizing my condition (and mobility issues) was progressively worsening with each passing year, I decided to give it a shot if and when my back goes out or I know it is about to go completely out.

Sometimes when I feel the spasms and crippling episode coming on, I will take a 10 mg Flexeril to "nip it in the bud". I am still very hesitant in taking this medication — any medication — and do so very sparingly and only if I am certain that my back is going completely out or is already completely out.

Over the past four years as of this writing, I have taken Flexeril, on average, once — one 10 mg tab — every few months. Even if my back is half out and I can barely move — as long as I am able to get from point A to point B — I will not take the medication. I can handle — and have handled for decades — the unbearable pain levels. I cannot handle being in a position where I simply cannot move.

I have been alone my entire life. There has been no one there for me or my boy, Max. I have to be able to move to take care of us. There isn't much that is more anxiety producing than knowing at any minute, at any time, I may be totally immobilized and not be able to move even if my very own life depended on it.

🦋 🦋 🦋 🦋

The constant stress and anxiety produced from the ever-present fear of permanent paralysis that I live with on a daily basis is exhausting and, in and of itself, wreaks havoc on my entire body — emotionally and physically.

All that said, I was going to the top of Lone Mountain one last time — and Carlo was going to see that incredible 360-degree view from the mountain's peak.

Half way up, Carlo wanted to head back down. He was getting a bit nervous and was having some difficulty breathing. I've never had asthma, but I could relate because not only did I have difficulty breathing my entire life, I had been gasping for air the entire five years I had been in this arid dust bowl environment.

He was feeling a bit anxious and down at this point. He didn't think he'd be able to make it to the top. I convinced him that he could do it. If I could do it in my condition, he could do it.

We trekked forward and up and before long reached the very top. It was as beautiful a view as I had remembered during the many times I had hiked to the top prior to my fall of 2005.

We hung out for an hour or so and took in the beauty of the valley from the apex of Lone Mountain. We took a few pictures, created an awesome memory together, and then we headed back down much more carefully than we ascended. It was far more dangerous and it would be much more likely to fall going back down due the moderate incline and the loose terrain along the trails.

Regardless of the severe pain and half-crippling effect of the climb and descent, it was a wonderful feeling in my soul being able to get up to the top and see the view one last time. It was that much more special having encouraged Carlo to make it to the top and being able to share the experience and view with him.

It was the last good memory of any time Carlo and I would spend together.

The next morning, May 27th, 2009, was the last day I'd see Las Vegas.

Could my life get any more unlucky and miserable after leaving the worst five years of my entire life behind?

As only my luck would have it, the final two of the top five most painful, worst betrayals of my adult life were waiting for me back in Rhode Island.

25

Five-plus years removed as of this writing — the day I left Vegas and the worst chapter to date of my life behind — I still ask myself; was everything I've gone through and everything I've lost part of my Higher Power's plan?

Will the end justify the means — the 40-plus years of nonstop, absolute torment?

Will my story — a life of uninterrupted pain, suffering, and despair — shed light on these disorders and help others from or from going where I have gone?

I feel in my soul that the answer to these questions is yes.

If my story — this infernal journey — can help one person from or from entering the depths of hell I've endured since childhood and consistently for over 40-plus years, then, after all is said and done, I beat the house.

I left my shirt and half my sanity in Sin City. Still, however, I may very well have left Las Vegas the greatest winner ever. Time will certainly tell.

Carlo, Max and I hit the road early that morning of May 27th, 2009, for a five day, nearly three thousand miles, cross-country road trip back to Rhode Island.

I felt my lower spinal pain increasing with each mile of road traveled. As per my normal now, I'd have to recline in the passenger's seat most of the drive and still get out of the car every hour or so to stand or lay flat in order to temporarily alleviate a bit of the ever-increasing lumbar pressure and pain. My cervical pain not faring much better.

There was some absolutely incredible, wide-open, and beautiful scenery along the way. I wish I'd have been able to enjoy each state's backdrop during this — what would be my last ever — coast to coast road trip. However, I was fortunate in that I'd done this road trip a couple times in the past via other routes and prior to my lower spinal decimation.

Another sentiment and fact I can't stress enough; It is extremely difficult — impossible actually — to focus and enjoy anything in life when forced to endure chronic, mind-bending pain.

I found myself trance-like for most of the five-day journey and, as always, at the mercy of emotionally and physically debilitating pain and depression.

We arrived back in Rhode Island on May 31, 2009. I would be staying at Carlo's house with him, his wife, and my godson until I found a place for me and Max. I was hoping to be able to spend some quality time with Carlo as well as my godson. However, as the living situation, as well as my gut feeling about the entire move back to Rhode Island to be with "family" for "support", didn't feel right from the get-go, that would be wishful thinking on my part.

Aside from the mutual love and loyalty I always felt and had with my mother — love and loyalty to some degree I felt from my father — my intuition would prove to be correct once again in the weeks to come with regards to everything I felt — knew to be true — about this situation and each member of this incredibly dysfunctional, self-absorbed, cold-blooded immediate family.

Max would now be living with two other dogs in the same house, sharing most of the same space; a young male German Shepard and the matriarch of the pack — the boss — a loving but dominant bulldog.

I could see that it was very uncomfortable and stressful for Max and I tried to keep him with me wherever I went. We were now two fish out of water it seemed.

Max slept in the spare room with me. I had no plans on staying any longer than it would take to find a place for me and Max. I figured that wouldn't take more than a couple of weeks at most. However, as I started looking for rentals beginning the first couple of days I was in Rhode Island, it was obvious that this was going to be very difficult. Most places had a firm policy; no dogs allowed. A few would accept a small dog — if less than 25 lbs. These days, even dogs are discriminated against!

Within a few days of living there, Carlo's wife began complaining to me one morning that Carlo didn't spend any time with her and his son. She would say time and again, "*He goes out all night, every night. He never spends time with us.*"

This complaining — soon coupled with her crying — became a morning ritual I had to endure. However, I never responded to her comments or engaged in the conversation discussing my nephew or his behavior.

I was not only now witnessing firsthand the behavior that she was describing and that I didn't know existed but was also temporarily trapped — once again — living under the roof of what appeared yet another dysfunctional family with alcohol, among other things, fueling the fire.

I did, however, on several occasions while living there, speak to my nephew (in private) about her crying to me regarding his not spending time at home with his family. I guess I was hoping he'd get her to stop the morning drama. No such luck.

My birthday was coming up within a couple weeks of my arrival back in Rhode Island. My mother wanted to have a small family get-together to celebrate. Something I had never been comfortable with but decided — as I was here to do — to try something different and, perhaps, I could begin to emerge from the cocoon; the isolation and depths of pain and depression that had been my entire life.

I asked everyone in my immediate family (sister, brother-in-law, nephews and their wives) to meet at my mother and father's place a few days prior to the party so we could discuss a family matter; Strega.

I hadn't spoken to Strega in some three years nor had she made any attempt during that time to contact me, apologize, or reconcile. I was okay with that. As far as I was concerned, she was dead to me. I had disowned her years ago, wanted nothing to do with her, and refused to be in the same room with her under any circumstances.

I made it clear during the family sit-down to discuss this matter that I was a little upset and a bit hurt that everyone nonchalantly accepted her disrespecting me — another family member and her uncle — with no consequences for her actions.

We all sat around and discussed this family matter in detail. Every single member of the family that was there looked me square in the eyes and agreed with me that what she had done was disrespectful and she needed to not only apologize but understand should it happen again, she'd be ostracized from the family and all family functions. Everyone agreed that this would be the consequences for her actions if she didn't acknowledge the disrespect and apologize.

Everyone was on the same page — *talking the talk.*

There was total agreement within the family — there would be unity of the family and enforcement of boundaries here. She would be held accountable for her actions past, present and future.

Everyone wanted her to come to the party that was planned at my parents' place for my birthday. It would be just the immediate family, of course. I was against her being there — at "my party" — but agreed that if she apologized I'd forgive her, for the sake of the family, and we could all move forward. However, I wanted everyone to know that I firmly believed she would not apologize but would come to the get-together for the sole purpose of proving she can do what she wants and there is going to be no penalty for her actions — most importantly, for her outright disrespecting family.

Everyone agreed that they would talk to her and let her know she needed to apologize and, if she didn't, she was no longer welcome at family get-togethers.

In the days to come, she promised her grandfather, my nephew, my sister, and my mother that she would apologize.

My birthday arrived and, as I predicted, she made her grand entrance and made no attempt to apologize. She did exactly as I said she would. My intuition has always been spot-on. I was truly hoping I was wrong this time around.

Everyone told her (and she agreed with them) prior to the get-together — and again as she walked through the door — to apologize. She said to each of them this very day — my birthday — verbatim, "*I'm not apologizing.*"

She spit in the face of every member of this family by lying to and disrespecting each one of them. If she had been a man that day, I would have put her head through a wall — especially for making my mother cry by lying through her teeth and, once again, disrespecting her family.

The fast-paced crumbling within my immediate family had begun due to one weak link that no other member of this family, with the exception of my parents, had the backbone to stand up to and call out and punish for her pernicious and flippant attitude and actions towards her own family.

My mother was extremely disappointed and deeply hurt not only because her granddaughter did what she had done but that she had blatantly lied to her and everyone else in this family about the apology and did so for the sole purpose of conning her way into getting an invitation to a family get-together where she could once again turn her nose up and be disrespectful to family with absolutely no consequences.

She did exactly what I told everyone she was going to do.

Making matters worse, not one member of this family, with the exception of my mother and father, kept their word regarding this matter and what had been discussed and agreed to.

It was all downhill in this family from that very day - *my* birthday. What should have been a special day and time. If that was even possible in my life and within such a screwed-up and weak family and structure.

I would come to realize in the years ahead that these people most certainly shared a severe personality disorder with a behavioral pattern bordering on sociopathic.

I had been back "home" and staying at Carlo's house for a couple of weeks. Max had his routine down and knew where and where not to go both indoors and outdoors.

I would walk him in the rather large, grassy yard in the morning so he could do his thing. The yard was wide open. There was no fencing between the abutting properties. Max knew to stay within a small area of the yard, and he did.

Sometimes I'd let him lay outside in the yard by the home's rear door to get some sun while I was getting ready for the day ahead.

One neighbor's property line was approximately 50 yards to the rear of Carlo's house. That neighbor had a large German Shepard chained to a tree in his back yard. The dog barked an awful lot and appeared to me to be aggressive and mean. Gee, I wonder why?

I brought this up to Carlo once as I was concerned not only for the dog always being chained to a tree but if the dog got loose and came after Max. Max is a big baby. A love dog. He's not a fighter in any sense of the word.

I knew Max would never go near that property line or dog but was very concerned should that Shepard get loose and come after Max. My nephew said there was nothing to worry about. He mentioned that the Shepard was loose often but never came onto his property or came after his dogs. He mentioned that the Shepard was afraid of his bulldog. He also mentioned that the owner of the Shepard — the neighbor to the rear — was a younger, cocky guy he didn't particularly care for.

One morning a couple weeks into staying at Carlo's house, I was getting ready while Max was laying outside the rear door getting some sun and waiting for me.

I jumped three feet in the air when I heard Max yelping in panic. I had never heard my boy cry with such fear before. I ran to the back yard and saw the neighbor's Shepard on top of Max biting him. As soon as that Shepard saw me running at him he got off Max and ran back to his yard. Max was shaking like a leaf with some blood coming from his neck area. I was furious!

I spoke to my nephew about this that evening and he, reluctantly, talked to the neighbor about it the next day. I was assured it wouldn't happen again. I told my nephew If it did happen again — that neighbor's Shepard attacked Max on my nephew's property — it wasn't going to be pretty. He knew what I meant and asked me to keep calm. He said he didn't want me to get into trouble. His words at this time in his life said one thing and actions another.

I realize dogs fight and it's not our place to intervene. If Max instigated, he would get no protection from me. He would learn his lesson the hard way — taking a doggie beating. However, this was a bit different. Max was minding his own business, not straying from his property, and this Shepard came onto that private property, chased after him and attacked him for no reason. I wasn't about to let that happen again.

If Max was my son, I'd teach him how to stand up for himself and fight back. Not to be bullied. I had plenty of experience as a kid with bullying, being picked on, and attacked for no good reason. I couldn't teach Max to stand up for himself and I don't think there's a canine kickboxing school where timid dogs can go to learn how to protect and defend themselves from other bully dogs. Since getting him some training in "doggie MMA" isn't possible, I protect him as any dad would his child. There is no difference to me in the relationship I have with my dog than any man has as a father with his son — my nephew included. I would go to the ends of the earth to protect my boy.

A few days later, as only my luck would have it, it happened a second time. I heard Max yelping for his life. I ran out the door — a bat in hand this time — to see Max being mauled once again by the neighbor's Shepard. I ran at that dog full force and chased him like there was no tomorrow. I could see the look of fear on that Shepard's face when it finally got back to its property, turned, and stared at me.

At that same time, the Shepard's owner came out of his house. I was so angry at this time there was probably steam coming from my ears. The guy was actually laughing ... as if my dog's being attacked and bitten was some kind of joke. I told this classless punk neighbor, among other things, that should it happen a third time on my nephew's property, he wouldn't need the chain for the tree any longer and he'd be answering for his dog. We had a few more words and, luckily for him that day, he didn't approach me and get in my face. I was done — finished — with his dog attacking Max and this guy's cocky, irresponsible attitude.

I spoke to my nephew that night about this most recent attack and problem. This incident actually opened my eyes to many things. Particularly, my nephew's new- found apathy towards our relationship. I found this to be very peculiar as we were always very close.

Since I'd come back to Rhode Island and been living under the same roof, I'd noticed an even more significant change in his attitude and behavior towards me, and family in general, than I had sensed prior to my arrival in Rhode Island this summer.

He definitely wasn't thinking straight — as he once did. I was pretty sure he was getting deeper into the (alcohol) drinking, at the very least, and it was affecting his attitude and judgement. Whatever the reason, he was not the person I had known, spent quality time with, and taught family values to since his early childhood.

He was more aggravated with our — Max and I — being there than concerned for Max's well-being. This, in addition to the situation with my niece a few days earlier, was the beginning of what would become the demise of our relationship and strong family bond. He just wasn't himself. He was inconsistent and off-kiltered with his loyalty and respect. It was a bit disheartening, but I was beginning to realize that I didn't know this person any longer.

I remember explaining to him my feelings and position with regards to Max being attacked and hurt — twice — on his property by the neighbor's dog. He knew my relationship with Max and how I would protect him the same as I would my very own son — or his son, my godson. He acknowledged the same feelings, relationship, and bond with his dogs. However, he wasn't backing me and siding with me regarding this situation — he was creating a divide between us. He didn't have my back — twice in two weeks. He said he wouldn't have reacted the way I did. What?!

I was protecting my boy. This made no sense. Who was I talking to here? Knowing him and his temper, if the tables were turned, he would have exploded and escalated it to a much more serious level than I did. I offered this analogy to him; he visits me at my home in Vegas. His son — or his dog — is in my backyard. A neighbor's dog crosses into my yard and viciously attacks his son or his dog — both minding their own business. He sees this. What do you do? He knew exactly what he'd do in that situation and mumbled, "I'd fuckin' kill it." I'd never known him to be a hypocrite before this day.

True colors had been shown. He was now no different than the rest of this despicable immediate family.

As much as I love animals and especially dogs, I know exactly what I'd do if that happened to his son — my godson — or his dog in my yard in Vegas, or anywhere else for that matter.

He should have had my back no matter what. As family, you always have the other's back whether right or wrong. If wrong, and after the fact, and sticking together as family, have a discussion about it — but never turn your back on family, especially when the family member is in the right to begin with.

For the next week or so that I lived there, I had to be with Max every time he was in the yard. I carried a bat while walking Max to make sure he wasn't attacked again. That Shepard would just stare and bark at me and Max from the tree he was chained to in the next yard. I knew what would happen if I wasn't with Max each and every time he went into the yard to do his doody or just lay in the sun. I also knew what would happen if that dog attacked Max again.

Everything I had been feeling in my gut about this move and these people was coming true. I was only a few weeks into my return to Rhode Island and had never in my life felt more uncomfortable around "family" — especially this living situation with my nephew.

The sob stories continued from Carlo's wife each morning and, while I never responded to her comments about Carlo or engaged in conversation with her about him, this one particular morning I was extremely aggravated as I realized I was being continuously baited with each passing day.

She was just itching for me to say something so she could confront her husband and let him know how I felt. Hopefully, my comment(s) in agreement with her sentiment to possibly sway his night-time activity and get him to spend more time with his wife and son.

She knew the close relationship and mutual respect that Carlo and I had between us — at least we did prior to my arriving back in Rhode Island. If anyone could sway his behavior, it would probably be me, and she knew that. However, I wasn't about to get involved in this. I was already extremely uneasy with this living situation and was trying desperately day and night to find a place so Max and I could get the hell out of there asap.

She then mentioned once again that he is never home at night spending any time with her or JJ. I began feeling extremely irritated and started to think of the reason I came back to Rhode Island, against my better judgement; Carlo convinced me that I should be with family. That we'd spend time together and start a business. I hadn't seen him, either, in several weeks but for a few days and nights since I'd been there. And, during those few times, things had been said and done on his part that made me feel ill at ease and unwanted in his home.

He was living a different life than I had believed and his attitude was out of character and a mystery to me now. My only thought was that he was getting deeper into alcohol — and, most likely, something worse. It does run in the family. It does change behaviors and lives.

After several weeks of her prodding and my growing more uncomfortable, irritated, and feeling let down and betrayed, I walked away as she was complaining this particular time and said, under my breath and with my face turned completely away from her, "*He forgets he has family.*" I had no idea she had bionic ears! I also didn't see any harm or disrespect in the murmured, undirected blurt. I was actually talking to myself and letting off some steam and releasing the frustration of the entire situation.

She had taken my under-the-breath mutter and ran with it. Decided to pit me against Carlo as she knew we had a strong bond and that, I believe, if she could convince him that I thought he should be home with his family more often and said such a thing, it would impact his behavior to her advantage. Not a chance, it created an even wider divide between us.

We began to drift apart after he, very disrespectfully, approached me about the "comment" a few days later and took the entire situation out of context. There was a blowing out on his part. My first impression was that he was under the influence of something during this time, as he began throwing and breaking household items and yelling things I'd never have believed he was capable of saying.

I decided at that very moment it was time to leave this home and situation.

He did apologize the next morning and said it would never happen again. However, the rather disrespectful and thoroughly uncharacteristic, aloof attitude did continue and I knew I would soon have to cut the cord between us. This was completely inappropriate behavior within our relationship. It was unacceptable between family members. Family never does and says the things that were done and said during this time by him.

I'm all about a second chance when someone makes a mistake. However, two strikes and you're out in the world of disrespect.

Where I come from, with two strikes for the same offense something is no longer a mistake but a lifestyle characteristic that isn't going to change with another chance and without that person being aware of and correcting the behavior.

He was always a little different from the rest of the completely heartless immediate family. He wasn't any longer.

He once understood the importance of family, the bond and respect within that family. He didn't care any longer.

Again, I could only attribute his behavior to being under the influence of something. I knew he drank — and perhaps a lot. I knew he took script meds — and perhaps a lot. Whether this, or some other mood altering substance was part of the attitude change, I can't say for sure but believe it certainly had something to do with it.

On the flip side, unfortunately, a tiger can't change its stripes. I always thought he had at least half a heart. I was wrong. Under the influence or not, he proved to me during this time — his truth revealed — that he was just like the others in this immediate family. He was just a better schmoozer when "himself" and not under any influence. He certainly wasn't *anything* like me, my mother, father, or my real family; my uncles, aunts and cousins.

I Moved myself and Max into a hotel over the following couple of days. This is how and where I would spend the next seven months until I moved back down to south Florida.

I had an awful lot of my belongings packed in Carlo's garage that I had to now move into a rented storage unit. It took me several times as long to move as it would someone without my spinal injuries and mobility issues. I could hardly move to begin with and all the bending and picking up left me immobilized with an extremely elevated pain level for more than a week after the move.

As for Carlo, our relationship was severely strained from the incident that took place days earlier. We drifted completely apart a few weeks after I moved into the hotel — which happened to be immediately post my godson's birthday — and for the next four years, with no contact whatsoever.

Speaking of my godson's birthday, another incident occurred that very day that, once again, opened my eyes to just how warped these people were — my sister in particular; I was sitting on the front porch with my four-year-old godson (he turned four this very day) and my boy, Max. The three of us were doing some bonding; talking, playing with a couple of JJ's toys, and having Max perform some "tricks for treats" for us.

My sister had just arrived. She pulled in to the driveway, got out of the car, walked up to the front porch where we were sitting and playing and, without even acknowledging me, said immediately to JJ, "*You gonna give nana a kiss?*" JJ didn't get up and didn't give her a kiss. She then said to JJ, with a very angry look on her face and a very loud, harsh tone, "*because uncle Steve is here you don't get up and kiss your nana? You get up right now and give me kiss!*" He still didn't move. He pretty much didn't acknowledge her in the same way she didn't acknowledge me — and I wasn't yelling like a madman at her like she was yelling at this four-year-old child — and on his birthday!

To me, this was borderline emotional abuse. She was way out of line. And it didn't end there. She continued yelling at him and threatening not to buy him any more toys if he didn't get up and kiss her immediately. I truly couldn't believe what I was seeing and hearing. Is everyone in this immediate family completely fucking nuts?!

I don't think my sister was under the influence of alcohol, but I do know she took script meds. Again, I can't say if that influenced her appalling behavior but can say with certainty that she was definitely not the sister I knew growing up. She was *always* on the cold and cocky side — just like Strega — but never towards her immediate family. She was also a control freak — as her son, Carlo, certainly was. Never more evident than this very day — and in the worst of ways. It was going to be her way or no way. What she wanted and how and when she wanted it or she'd make your life miserable.

I didn't know this person. I didn't like being around this person.

I couldn't wait to get far away from this atmosphere and all of these people who just weren't right in the head.

No sooner did I move Max and myself into the hotel and he was actually attacked — bitten — and hurt by another dog. Again! What the hell is going on?!

My bad luck now seemed to be rubbing off on my boy.

We were in a large grass area in the rear of the hotel where I would play fetch with Max. It was close by to another area where dogs would do their doody. There was a young lady walking her dog. It was a pit-bull mix, about 50 pounds — half the size of Max. She asked if Max was friendly as she wanted to approach with her dog. I told her he was very friendly but I was more concerned with her dog. He didn't look too friendly to me. She assured me that he was. Her dog was already on a leash. I put max on his leash and she walked up to us with her dog. I'm no Dog Whisperer, but I could clearly see this dog was not wagging his tail and appeared to be uneasy and aggravated. Of course, Max began wagging his tail and immediately began his sniffing routine. Within seconds, the other dog snapped and took a chunk out of Max's face. Max let out a very loud, piercing cry and immediately backed up to me. I had pulled him back at the same time I heard the cry. The other dog was pulled away also. Max had blood dripping from his face and was shaking terribly. I couldn't believe this! I was seething that this "friendly" dog just took a chunk out of boy's face! I was also a little disappointed that Max *still* didn't defend himself. It just wasn't part of his good-natured, big baby, canine character.

I took Max to the vet where he was cleaned up and received a few stitches to close the gash. The dog's owner did offer to pay the vet bill — and I accepted.

One thing is for sure, my boy certainly didn't have my blood flowing through his canine body. He would have fought to the death if he did. Either way, I felt his anxiety and pain of the past several traumatic events. The emotions brought me right back to my childhood days and years of being bullied.

Both Max and I desperately needed some open, breathing space to try and relax from all this added trauma that seemed to follow me — and now him — everywhere without fail.

Before Max was introduced to his first winter playland a few months down the road, I took him to my favorite go-to place for serenity since my early teen years — Sachuest Point and connecting second and third beaches of Middletown, Rhode Island.

We would spend many days there at summer's end and through the fall months just walking the beach and taking in the abundance of surrounding beauty.

As the weather began cooling with a New England chill in the air, the visitors began to disappear and Max and I had the entire piece of paradise to ourselves.

I took my father with us a couple times so he could get out a bit in the fresh air. He was beginning to have trouble walking at this time in his life and would sit in a beach chair as Max and I walked the shoreline and played fetch.

This is the one place I have always been able to connect with my inner self and for a brief while soothe my soul's pain. It has always been and always will be a very, very special place to me. A place I long to be physically whenever in Rhode Island. A place I often go to in my mind as an escape and meditation tool.

My mother has never been one to sit idly around — whether that be in the midst of nature or watching TV. She needs to keep moving and occupying her mind.

Whether that be in the form of her constantly cooking and cleaning or store to store shopping to a couple of the very few things that require sitting still that she delights in, such as quality time conversing with friends and family or spending some time at the casino slot machines. This keeps her away from the aggravation and anger of being around my father and it allows her to function each day without her thoughts continually dwelling on a lifetime of pain and sorrow that she has had to endure at the hands of her husband and immediate family. Thoughts that would no doubt otherwise overwhelm and destroy her sanity.

This is what works for her — her outlets, her escapes, her meds — and keeps her mind sharp and her soul content.

Whenever and wherever my mother and I were together, I'd take her as often as I could to do some shopping at her favorite stores and for a little slot action at any nearby casinos — the one-armed bandits one of her favorite of all pastimes!

In Rhode Island, the two big casinos are in nearby Connecticut — Foxwoods and Mohegan Sun. She also had the smaller, local casino, Twin River Casino, literally around the corner in nearby Lincoln, Rhode Island. This one almost within walking distance so she frequented more often, most times alone, occasionally with a friend or one of my aunts. It always made me feel good to see her smile and happy. Both shopping and the slots offered her a brief escape from the deep emotional pain she'd lived with most of her life — again, much of that heartbreak at the hands of her own immediate family; most specifically her children and grandchildren.

God knows, I can count on one hand the times her adult children and grandchildren — combined — may have taken her out for a cup of coffee or to go shopping. And her husband — well, that has always been her number one cause of stress. It is a very sad, often angering, always frustrating-to-watch, codependent relationship that has crushed and imprisoned my mother throughout most of her life.

She's told me often throughout my life that I have made her happy and kept her going during her darkest times. She's done the same for me.

Her happiness has always been my happiness.

Her pain has always been my pain.

Her love has always been the only light in my darkness.

I had spoken with my sister a few times over the couple weeks since the blowout with my nephew — her son. She was now even more dysfunctional, inconsistent, and hypocritical during our conversations.

During one phone conversation, as we were somehow speaking about depression, she became very angry and insisted I needed to take medication.

I made a statement that I don't take drugs of any kind. To me, whether you have a script or not, the meds are still drugs and they're just not for me. I don't want them in my body or affecting my thought-process or attitude — as it appeared quite clearly to have done with her and other members of this immediate family.

For me, it's a very, very strong aversion to drugs of any kind — script or illicit — that I've had painfully and deeply etched into my mind by alcohol and drug-related traumatic experiences of my childhood.

I remember the phone call ending just fine. However, some ten minutes later she called me back and left a very angry and rude message about my "disrespecting her" and calling her a "drug addict".

I'd say (again) I couldn't believe what I was hearing but, by this time, after what I'd seen and heard from her and the rest of these people since coming back to Rhode Island, I was more disgusted than surprised.

I was, as always with family, very polite and respectful during our conversation and I never said to her — or implied — that anyone taking script medication was a drug addict. However, I also knew all too well that she needed some excuse to drive a wedge between us as I was no longer speaking to her son. Being the control freak that she was, this was her way to control a situation and person (me) she knew very well she could never control. She had no chance of that bullshit with me, and she knew it. So, she created a divide and distance by concocting a lunatic excuse and story about my "disrespecting" her and calling her a "junkie" to try and justify her actions.

That was the last day I ever spoke to my sister.

I had had enough of the dysfunctional behavior and lunacy from her and from within this immediate family. It was a form of trauma that caused me great pain from childhood and throughout my life.

After the past month or so of being in the middle of these people, I realized just how warped and impaired their minds were. However, I still didn't fit the final piece of that puzzle until some five years later.

I came back to Rhode Island for support and found a truth about my immediate family that was dispiriting and impossible to ignore; these were self-absorbed liars, hypocrites, and heartless individuals.

I never knew just how dysfunctional, broken, and twisted they were until I threw myself into the middle of this clan and watched what felt like a mad feeding frenzy among unconscientious, savage cannibals.

I needed to detach from these vicious, stony-hearted people I had lost all respect for and get far away from a "family" — from individuals — I am, to this day, ashamed to say I share the same blood with.

I had been betrayed many times in my life. To this particular point in my life, only three other betrayals had caused such pain and anger.

This was the fourth major betrayal of my adult life; my entire immediate family, with the exception of my mother and father, lied to, disrespected, and turned their backs on me. They created even more stress, depression, and anxiety in my life that I certainly didn't need and that further damaged my body, mind, and soul.

All this after convincing me to return to Rhode Island to "be with family".

I always knew from childhood to stick with my gut instincts. I never had anyone to rely on then — with the exception of my mother — and that was the case now.

However, I also needed to try something different — trust someone — and attempt to recover from a life of trauma and the absolute worst five years of my life; those years I spent in Vegas at the absolute bottom of that hellhole.

I let my guard down, trusted, and returned to the most wicked, disconnected, and fractured of families. If ever there was a clan of heartless, blind leading the blind, it was these people. This family put the *dys* in dysfunction.

I knew since childhood the entire structure of this family was not normal — I just never realized how rotten and cold these people were until this time and, most specifically, the fifth and most damaging betrayal of my life that was just around the corner.

I truly didn't know these people whose bloodline I shared. In retrospect, I guess I never really knew them. Being emotionally imprisoned my entire life and remaining mostly in isolation, I didn't spend a lot of time around anyone, including my immediate family.

I always felt it in my bones and in my gut, but, If I'd actually known the real truth of their souls, I'd never have gone back to Rhode Island or spent a minute with any of them then or at any other time during my life.

I still had a small lump under my right armpit that I needed to have checked out a bit further. I went to see two different doctors — one specializing in cancer — for their opinions. Both doctors told me that I would need an open surgical biopsy for this particular lump. A needle biopsy wasn't an option in this area for some reason. Not surprisingly, each said that If I was going to go ahead and do the open biopsy, I might as well just have the entire lump surgically removed while in there.

I had seen the doctor specializing in cancer for the second opinion. Though he reiterated what the first doctor said regarding the surgical incision biopsy and removal of the lump, he did tell me that aside from never seeing anything quite like what was growing under my armpit — he said it was "*very unique in shape and feel*"

— he believed it was non-cancerous and an infection that had settled in the lymph node. However, there would be no way of knowing for sure without the open surgical biopsy or removal. He said to give it a bit more time and if it didn't completely go away, we could remove it.

I have always felt queasy whenever thinking about surgery. It's not something I've ever considered — not even at this point in my life when I could be dealing with cancer. I decided to give it more time to see if it would finally clear up. It did after nearly a year.

A few years later, I would develop a lump of sorts in my inner right bicep area — just inches from where the lump developed under my armpit. I've yet to have it checked out.

26

I returned to Rhode Island to try and crawl out of the hell I'd been banished to since childhood. I knew in my heart that any help and support (as was offered) from my "family" was a long shot that would probably lead straight down another dead end road. It turned out even worse than I could have imagined.

I was now falling back into that deepest and darkest of depressions that nearly consumed me in Vegas. My physical pain was through the roof — due in part to the (additional) arthritic pain that was compounded by the cold and damp New England weather. On the other hand, with everything that had happened with this immediate family since I had returned, my anger, stress, and anxiety levels were off the charts once again.

I needed to talk to someone. In the past, I'd talk to a psychiatrist now and then to let off some steam and relieve a bit of stress. There was a psychiatrist, *Dr. S*, I'd seen years ago in Rhode Island post my line of duty accident. A really nice guy, but a psychiatrist.

I made an appointment to see Dr. S. He was familiar with the extent of my depression as it related to my physical disability and pain. I never discussed with him the emotional trauma I sustained beginning at the age of five, my dysfunctional family environment, or the abundance of other traumatic experiences that plagued me throughout my life.

I never completely opened up to anyone about the pain I'd been suffering with since childhood and throughout my life until I saw my second LCSW in 2012 in Florida.

About five minutes into our conversation, Dr. S said to me, "*You're not going to take medication, are you?*" I replied, "*Absolutely not. I just need to talk about it to alleviate some of the stress.*" He then said to me, "*I've got the perfect person for you to talk to. She's wonderful and I think she can really help you in that way.*"

He made an appointment for me to see *Nina R*, a Licensed Clinical Social Worker (LCSW). The first LCSW I ever saw on a regular basis.

The timing was right as I was quickly descending once again into the depths of that hellacious inferno I'd nearly perished in back in that desert dust bowl several thousand miles west.

Nina would have a positive impact on and make a difference in my life with her understanding, compassion, and willingness to help.

She helped not only me, but most importantly, a mere few months down the road, she would help my mother through debilitating anxiety and a very deep and horrid depression — a direct result of her children and grandchildren turning their backs on and betraying her.

Nina would become one of the very few blessings in my life as a result.

I am forever indebted to her for what she has done — and continues to do — for my mother. I consider her today the sister I never had. The daughter my mother never had.

I never knew the benefit of finding someone — having someone in my corner — who truly understood, cared, and wanted to help me. I didn't know what an LCSW was.

When a person suffers, day in and day out, with emotionally and/or physically debilitating disorders or conditions, it is difficult to do even the everyday basics such as eating and just moving. There is not an ounce of motivation or desire to be found in our bodies and minds. We need someone to literally take us by the hand and show us the way — from helping us to make appointments to keeping us on our toes and seeing different possibilities. We will otherwise keep to ourselves, and often isolate, when suffering with chronic physical pain and/or emotional disorders such as PTSD, depression, and anxiety.

Nina was the first angel that ever came into my life and helped me by communicating understanding, compassion, and validation of my pain and suffering.

It is very important for anyone who is suffering with PTSD, depression, anxiety, isolation, and other impairing emotional and/or physical disorders to have someone to speak with regarding their pain. A friend, a priest, a family member, but, most importantly (and especially in the very beginning of addressing the disorder), a qualified, professional LCSW who understands the pain and suffering associated with these disorders and offers compassionate support and hope to those of us living this nightmare.

There is a Buddhist proverb; "When the student is ready, the teacher will appear." Whether I may have been ready or not, I consider having met and connected with each of my LCSW's, both in 2009 and

2012, one of the few times in my life when luck may have finally found me. One of the few times in my life when Murphy was caught sleeping. Murphy's law being the blueprint of my life and the adage; "Anything that can go wrong, will go wrong." And it most certainly did in my life, time and again, in every way possible, for some four decades.

Nina was most certainly the blessing in my life that had always eluded me. She, along with my second LCSW, *Jill B (JB)*, helped me to find a fragment of peace within my soul and a glimmer of light within my life to build upon and guide me away from a life of complete darkness.

I would see Nina on a weekly basis for approximately five months until I left for south Florida. Our conversations helped relieve some of the anxiety and ever-growing emotional pain I was going through during this time not only from unresolved past trauma in my life but the most recent elevation of anger, stress, and physical pain associated with all aspects of the move back to Rhode Island. The betrayal I felt by my immediate family and the cold, damp weather ramped up my emotional and physical pain once again to near catastrophic levels.

Talking about that anger and pain — especially the anger I felt regarding the way this family had been treating and disrespecting my mother — relieved a bit of the emotional agony but there was very little, if anything, that anyone could say or do to alleviate my mounting physical pain.

We discussed my getting with a pain management doctor and, with her help and guidance, a couple weeks later, I did just that.

With a little bit of encouragement and a gentle push by Nina, I went in to see a pain management doctor that was highly recommended by an orthopedic surgeon I had recently seen.

During the initial visit, we discussed my pain, injuries, and the most recent MRI's I'd gotten a few days earlier that he requested and were needed for assessment.

He strongly recommended I get a facet joint injection.

A facet joint injection is primarily a diagnostic injection. It is usually used to determine the cause of back pain. However, it was his opinion that a great deal of my pain was originating directly from that particular lumbar facet joint. I knew that wasn't the case. I know my body better than anyone — any doctor or any study or exam that can be done of it. I knew from past experience, prior MRI's, and speaking with dozens of doctors over the years that my spinal damage was so severe and extensive it would be nearly impossible to get rid of any significant amount of pain — especially focusing on one particular area such as a facet joint that may or may not be contributing to my pain levels.

There were just too many seriously damaged and diseased areas in and around the spine associated with and causing the intense pain for any one specific treatment in any one specific area to have a significant effect on my overall pain level.

Perhaps this doctor knew that as well but truly believed what he was saying about a substantial amount of my pain originating from this particular facet joint.

To me, it was pretty obvious, actually, from the MRI's alone that he was incorrect. Not to mention what I was telling him of the pain and areas affected.

However, I made this move (to Rhode Island) to try and do things — and think — a bit differently since the ways of the past hadn't worked in decades. I needed to try and trust others' judgement, especially professionals specializing in spinal damage and pain management.

So, once again, against my better judgement and a strong gut feeling, I went along with his recommendation and the FJ injection and, as only my luck would have it, suffered the consequences not only immediately post the procedure but to this day as I have more pain and problems in that particular area of the lower spine than I had prior to the facet joint injection.

I don't know exactly what happened or what may have gone wrong. The procedure is performed using fluoroscopy for guidance to properly target and place the needle — and to avoid nerve injury or other injury or damage. What I do know is that instead of getting any relief from the lower back pain, the intensity of the pain actually increased and pretty much immobilized me for the next couple months immediately post that procedure. I could hardly move for many weeks after this injection. I could barely move my back and left leg during this time.

I also sustained a permanent muscle collapse in my lower back around the injection site. Go figure, right?!

The intense physical pain and mobility issues worsened post that procedure and the colder, damp New England weather continued to make matters even worse.

I had started taking much more OTC Ibuprofen post that procedure and that I'd ever taken in the past. My physical and emotional pain levels were once again rising through the roof as was the inflammation that my body was turning out in abundance.

Inflammation is an underlying cause of many diseases and my body was now producing it much more than in the past. The inflammation and the pain was simply out of control. The Ibuprofen did seem to — sometimes, but not always — reduce a bit of the inflammation and added pain associated with it.

It has been simply incredible — almost impossible to believe — the amount of consistent and intense pain from multiple areas I have had to endure for decades not only emotionally but physically as well due to this spinal injury and disability.

As I look back at my life, I truly don't know how I survived but for the sake of my mother and, hopefully, as is my heart's desire, to help others enduring similar, crippling emotional and/or physical pain and misery.

It seemed to me now that I most certainly jumped from the frying pan into the fire — in more ways than one — with this move back to Rhode Island. I came back to Rhode Island for support from my family — at their request — something I didn't ask for and had never sought out at any point in my life from any of them. Instead of receiving any familial emotional support, I was betrayed and learned the hard truth — the reality — of my immediate and most dysfunctional family.

I was still dangling on the ledge and leaping from the never-ending, crippling pain was a constant thought I couldn't shake. I continued to push my body to the max, sacrificing my physical well-being in order to preserve that tiny bit of sanity that remained. I exercised as much as I could but my body — my spine — wouldn't allow any real training and endorphin kicks were few and far between. Getting my serotonin and norepinephrine levels back up — chemically rebalancing — was nearly impossible without the ability to train intensely.

I needed to somehow reduce my emotional and physical pain levels and keep the keel even for the sake of my mother and my boy, Max.

I tried every natural remedy known to man over the years — nothing worked for me then and to this day. I was pretty much out of options. I couldn't help but to think — believe — I was put on this earth to suffer. A life of complete darkness without so much as a hint of light — or luck — ever entering. A world with no smiles. No happiness. My life's scale always fully tilted by pain, misery, and despair. Completely unbalanced. Emotionally imprisoned. Physically disabled — a term and condition it took me nearly twenty years to say and accept the reality of.

As bleak and disheartening as the move back to Rhode Island became — all the additional torment and the daily *agita* from the day I arrived until the day I left — there were a few positives that came of it; I got to hang out with and get to know my godson as well as spend his birthday with him this year. I hadn't seen him since his christening several years earlier.

I got to witness my boy, Max, find and enjoy a love second only to his playing fetch and walking in the park with his favorite ball — his pride and joy — hanging out of his mouth; romping in the deep snow!

I was introduced to Nina, my first LCSW. She helped immensely with the added emotional pain, anxiety, and deepening depression that resulted from my being in Rhode Island with this family.

I was also able to see and spend a little time with a couple aunts, uncles, and cousins I hadn't seen in over twenty-five years. It was still far from easy being around anyone — especially at this time in my life — but I got through it somehow and it felt good afterwards.

And, most importantly, I got to see and spend quality time with my mother each and every day I was there. It soothed my soul a bit during this very difficult, emotionally and physically painful transition of sorts — from bad to worse as had been common throughout my life.

Max's favorite holiday — Thanksgiving — was now upon us. He might have been afraid of his own shadow and might very well have been the biggest "chicken" around, but, to me, he was a turkey. A turkey with a tail! Anyone who may have seen Max relaxing in his favorite position — laying stretched out on his back, legs reaching for the sky, and that big belly of his sticking out and resembling a very large turkey — would concur. It wouldn't have surprised me if he began to "gobble" instead of "bark" as he got older! Chicken or turkey-boy, my best friend had the warmest of hearts and on birthdays and holidays he'd feast right alongside of me. This day was no different but for the fact that we weren't alone today. This was the first

Thanksgiving I had spent with my parents in some years. It was also the first holiday that I realized — that I knew in my heart — aside from my mother, father, and Max, I was pretty much alone in this world. I had no immediate family. The family I knew growing up may have been dysfunctional but I had always believed there was a strong familial love and we had each other's backs. I was wrong. I was very wrong. The truth of their souls was being revealed with each passing week. It angered and disgusted me. It was beginning to fill me with a hatred that would grow and grow until I began therapy and a recovery process a few years down the line. Subconsciously, I believe I knew the reality of it all along — from a very early age — and was in denial until that recovery process began.

That notorious New England winter was beginning to settle in. It was getting colder by the week and my pain was increasing right along with it. The smell of snow was in the air and flakes of all sizes and shapes were making their way down, blanketing everything that didn't move — and some that did.

I've always loved the snow — especially watching it fall against a black sky in the middle of a frosty and silent night. It truly is beautiful. There would be plenty of it this particular winter.

Max wanted nothing to do with the snow at first. He wouldn't even step in it. However, before I knew it, I couldn't get him out of it! He would run and jump and dive in it! He's never liked the heat and this newfound, cold, fluffy white stuff kept him cool and as happy as could be as he frolicked aimlessly in it. Most Labs love the water and swimming. Max was a cross-country skier and snow diver!

Unlike the years prior to my spinal injury and physical disability when this winter wonderland was truly refreshing and welcomed, it now created a more painful, elevated misery and the ice and snow that came with it the possibility of falling and accidents. Not to mention the bending I would have to do to clean and remove ice and snow from and around the car. All of this increasing my chances of further damage and pain or, worse yet, finally having that accident or sudden movement that permanently lands me in a wheelchair. My ultimate fear. The one thought — and possible outcome — that has created instant and increased anxiety and panic attacks for nearly twenty years. I don't believe I could handle complete immobility — or would even attempt to.

It's very difficult to avoid *an accident*. That's why they're called "accidents". It's something that isn't planned but happens unexpectedly and unintentionally. However, certain conditions that may lead to an increased possibility of a particular incident or catastrophe can be avoided — thus reducing the chance of an unfortunate outcome. With my disability, I just couldn't stay in an area with such weather conditions. As much as I wanted to remain as close as possible to my mother, I couldn't live here with these frigid, wet and icy winters increasing my pain and mobility issues as well as my chances of falling or having an accident that would further damage my spine and more than likely land me permanently in a wheelchair.

It tore me apart inside just thinking that I'd have to leave my mother soon. Especially now, at this time in her life, in her eighties and when she needed family by her side the most — and had no one. She could never count on her husband for anything and now could add her children and grandchildren to that sad but true list of good-for-nothings.

Damp, cold, slippery conditions were the enemy. This is the reason I moved out to Vegas in the first place. The only option I had remaining to find a warm climate year-round was to return to Florida. I couldn't escape the dampness of the East Coast, but could escape the brutally cold winters, snow, and ice by moving as far south as possible.

Still having a very bitter taste in my mouth from everything I had lost and all the injustice I had endured in Florida, it was my only real option regarding year-round warm weather if I was to stay on the east coast and try and remain as close as possible to my mother at this time in her life.

Andrea and I had kept in contact since my move from Vegas. She was handling and keeping an eye on some of my real estate interests in Las Vegas and Pahrump. She was still working in retail but in a dire financial predicament.

We had spoken about moving to Florida together. She had been estranged from her parents for some time and they were living within driving distance of where we decided to move in south Florida.

We never discussed it, but she'd make comments here and there and her actions would indicate that she was very depressed and angry inside. In retrospect, I believe she had some serious problems with her marriage and divorce as well as her family growing up. Another product of a dysfunctional family with the emotional scars buried deep inside and the pain and anger coming through in spurts here and there.

We decided to move to Florida after the New Year.

Andrea came to Rhode Island a few weeks before Christmas. Regardless of the start of the immediate family's demise during this holiday season, the five of us — my mother, father, Andrea, Max, and I — all enjoyed each other's company and the time together.

I was still hiding — and suffering terribly — behind my mask and a few years from beginning psychotherapy and a recovery process with an incredible LCSW that would help me to further understand what had gone on and what had gone wrong in my life and the reasons for my feelings and behavior throughout the past four decades.

Regardless, we spent Christmas and New Years with my parents. Just the five of us. Being with and around my mother always produced a peaceful feeling in my soul — however, it was bittersweet during this holiday season as I was also feeling a great amount of anxiety and sadness knowing I would have to leave shortly.

It bothered me an awful lot that even on this most cherished holiday and season within our culture — Christmas — there had been no visits to my parents, no calls or cards, no attempts at apologizing or making amends from any of my mother's children or grandchildren. There had been no sign of love or respect from any of them throughout this holiday season and for all the birthdays, holidays and years that would follow.

This wasn't family. Hyena don't treat each other in such a cold and vicious way. These people were sick, heartless, and rotten to the core.

Through it all — what was to come and to this very day — I've yet to meet a person who has suffered so much pain and disappointment in life and still had such a positive outlook and had maintained such an incredible sense of humor as my mother. She is truly a very special person. She deserved so much better in her life.

I was brought up believing that the most important people in my life were my family. Everyone in my immediate family came up of the same culture and with the same beliefs and values — honor, trust, respect, and loyalty within family. Those days seem to have ended with my parents' generation. I was on my own now — no one else believed in and lived by the *code* any longer.

I knew in my heart that this immediate family was more than merely dysfunctional — they were at the extreme ends of selfish and cold-blooded. They were mindless traitors that I was ashamed to share the same bloodline with. I had disowned them all at this point for what they had done to my parents — my mother particularly.

As was the case when I lived in Vegas, only multiplied several times over now, I worried constantly about leaving my mother behind with these no-good vultures hovering around. Knowing the deep pain and heartbreak these people caused my mother, I would try to make light of the situation by joking, "*When you hit the lottery, make sure they don't find out. You won't be able to get rid of them!*"

It is said in my culture that "family always has your back." These people would just as soon stick a knife in mine. Actually, they did just that to myself and my mother. I've also heard throughout my life that "blood is thicker than water." Whoever said these things didn't know these people and the ice that ran through their veins.

The pain I've felt over the years with regards to this family is for my mother and her having to live with the truth of her own children and grandchildren.

Slowly but surely, it all became crystal clear to me. I realized that these people were more of a curse to me and in my life than the hell I'd endured consistently for nearly forty-five years. The straw that broke the camel's back — that opened my eyes to a reality I could never have believed otherwise — was the intentional, constant and outright, cold-hearted disrespecting and betraying of their own parents and grandparents. Specifically, the angel that is my mother.

This would become the fifth, and final as it relates to this story's timeline, most distressing and painful, major betrayal of my adult life; my mother's very own children and grandchildren turning their backs on and betraying their mother and father, their grandparents.

With everything I've been through in my life, nothing has hurt me more than the pain I know my mother has suffered at the hands of her very own children and grandchildren.

There is no excuse — no reasoning — that could *ever* justify the blatant and vicious disrespecting and betraying of their parents and grandparents.

I have been consumed by anger most of my life. Very few times, if any, have I felt such overpowering anger and hatred as I have felt for this immediate family for what they have done to my mother.

There is a Mark Twain quote; "*Anger is an acid that can do more harm to the vessel in which it is stored than to anything on which it is poured.*" I can tell you with absolute certainty that this is true. It did a serious number on my mind and body throughout the years — and never more than during this fifth most hurtful betrayal of my life. Luckily, through therapy and my recovery process, I've learned how to accept and let go of such persistent and harmful negative feelings.

I came back to Rhode Island with promises of family support and hopes of climbing a few rungs up from the absolute bottom I'd hit a year-plus earlier in Vegas. Hoping to leave behind a world of isolation and darkness I'd endured my entire life.

Instead of love and support, instead of holding the ladder for me as I struggled upward, it was kicked out from under me by my very own blood.

I left Rhode Island having suffered two of the five most painful, worst betrayals of my entire life — both at the hands of my immediate family.

I dragged my beaten body and seared mind from this damned place reeling now with even more pain and anger than I had when I arrived.

27

A few days after the New Year, Andrea, Max and I hit the road and headed down to south Florida where we would settle and try and begin anew. As usual, the trip — many hours of sitting — would prove to be excruciatingly painful.

We arrived in Florida and stayed in a hotel while searching for a place to rent in the area we had decided on. It took a couple of weeks, but we finally found a place to rent where the owner would allow a dog. It was a nice, laid back, predominantly retiree area. I knew no one there and, once again, I could disappear into obscurity.

I left Rhode Island extremely angry and hurt and with more pain, anxiety, and depression added to my already overwhelmed existence. With what these heartless monsters had done and would continue to do to my mother, my emotional condition was regressing right back to the absolute bottom of that hellhole I'd endured in Vegas some years earlier.

There have only been a few other betrayals in my life that have caused such intense anger and hatred — this one was the worst of the worst for me. Because of the pain it caused and toll it took on my mother, this one betrayal alone did as much damage to my mind and body as the others combined.

The increased anxiety, deepening depression, anger, and hatred — along with that always looming black cloud — would continue for the next two-plus years, plunging me back down to the darkest of places I had been trying desperately to escape since Vegas.

Thoughts of the ledge — ending the pain and misery — were playing over and over in my mind during this time. It was a daily battle once again to keep breathing. I had a few very close calls and I nearly hit that very bottom but for finding an LCSW towards the end of 2012 that would, through therapy, finally guide me on the road to recovery.

Within a few weeks of my moving back to Florida, my uncle *Nico* died. It was one of those few times in my mother's life that she nearly lost it and came very close to having a nervous breakdown. What contributed heavily to this emotional devastation was the fact that she had no one there — no children or grandchildren — to console her, to lean on, to pick her up. It all hit her at once.

I had left her Nina's phone number, my therapist in Rhode Island, just in case she needed to talk to someone at any point. Nina had always told me to make sure my mother had her number and to call her if she needed to talk or needed any help with anything at all.

My mother hadn't slept in several days, was suffering with anxiety attacks and was very close to a nervous breakdown. She did call Nina and they met at my mother's home. From that day forward, my mother has called Nina her angel.

Nina may very well have saved my mother's life during this time. At the very least, she kept her from a severe nervous breakdown.

Nina has been a blessing in both my mother's life and my own. My mother and I consider her family — real family. She has shown more compassion, love, and genuine concern for my mother than her own children and grandchildren.

They have been seeing each other every two weeks now for nearly five years. In addition to this, Nina has truly been the daughter my mother never had. Nina takes her to doctor appointments, brings her flowers, calls to check on her, and genuinely loves her. The feeling is mutual. She has brought joy and hope — life — back to my mother's life. Again — and I can't convey this sentiment enough — I am forever grateful and indebted to Nina for what she has done for my mother and the genuinely kind and loving person she is.

As if this all wasn't enough, my brother-in-law stopped by my parents' house a few days after my uncle died with some news; he was divorcing my sister after thirty-plus years of marriage.

He had always respected my parents and loved my mother dearly — more than her own children and grandchildren. His actions have always proven that fact.

He wanted to tell my parents the news personally and say goodbye as he was moving out of state.

They talked about the disrespect, vile attitudes and behavior, the betrayal, and the collapse that had taken place within the family. He told my mother that he loved her very much and could not believe how she and my father were being treated by her own family. He said it was disgusting and didn't know what was wrong with these people.

He told my mother that my sister was taking the pending divorce very badly and would probably need her mother's support. *Really?!* Here's a daughter that has shown through her venomous words and actions that she could give two shits about her own mother. However, as was common with my mother, always thinking of everyone else — especially her "family" — before herself, she contacted her daughter and told her that she was there for her.

Her self-centered daughter did come by and her mother did console her. They cried together and her daughter told her, verbatim, "*You and Dad are the only family I ever had.*" Once again, I have to say, *Really?*! Actions speak much louder than words. And what you do — or don't do — in life is a reflection of your true soul.

After a couple weeks of keeping in contact with her mother — "*the only family she ever had*" — it was back to the same intentional and despicable, cold-hearted attitude, disrespect, and neglect. And it would only get worse over the coming months and years.

I could never understand how my sister or the rest of this "immediate family" looked in the mirror and lived with themselves. I realized in the years to come — through therapy and a recovery process — these people all lacked a conscience, among other things.

Within several months of my moving back to Florida, one of my greatest fears (with regards to my own physical well-being) came to be; I was rear-ended by another vehicle as I was stopped at a traffic light. The driver of that vehicle was too busy texting to be paying any attention to driving.

Knowing what could result from any sudden jolt to my spine, I had been holding my breath every time I drove for the past fourteen years since the line of duty accident and initial spinal injury.

No sooner did I come back to this place where I had lost everything but a faint pulse, and the bad luck picked up right where it had ended well over a decade ago.

Max was in the back of my SUV with his head hanging out the window. Upon impact, he was nearly thrown out the window but somehow half of his 110 lb. body wound up in the front seat. He was shook up, and his mouth was bleeding.

I felt the impact and pain throughout my spine but it was immediately evident by the intense and sharp pain within the cervical area that this section took the brunt of the damage. I knew immediately there was now more spinal damage and the coming of more pain and mobility issues. My only hope was that paralysis wasn't going to be part of this accident scenario.

Police arrived, took the report, cited the other driver and yet another nightmare was on its way. Before that began, I took Max to the Vet the following day to make sure he was okay. He didn't need stitches but was a bit wobbly for a couple days from the impact to his head.

I, on the other hand, was dealing with even more pain and mobility issues than prior to the accident, and I couldn't move my neck.

I now had to find an orthopedic doctor (in south Florida) specializing in spinal damage. Within a couple days of the accident, I went to see an orthopedist who would request new MRI's of the spine and compare the new films to my most recent MRI's of less than a year ago in Rhode Island.

I had five cervical discs gone prior to this accident. The impact from this accident blew out another cervical disc. I now had six cervical discs decimated and more bone, nerve, and muscle damage in that area and throughout the lumbar area of the spine caused by this latest accident. The pain in my lumbar section also increased substantially due to the jolting from the impact.

I was now about to be caught up in more insurance bullcrap in the state of Florida. This is the last state on planet earth someone wants to get hurt. The insurance companies in this state are even more controlling and vicious than is the norm around the country. The only people who benefit from accidents in the state of Florida are attorneys, doctors, and the criminals who fraudulently file claims. The legitimately injured person is pretty much hung out to dry. I'd been there before with my line of duty accident. It's a sadistic game controlled by the insurance companies and those in their pockets who profit substantially from that industry. The little guy with real injuries and the resulting pain and suffering almost always comes out on the losing end in this state.

My insurance company (policy) paid for medical up to my PIP (personal injury protection) limit. Once again, however, the insurance company will do everything in their power to control which doctors you see and what treatment you receive for your injuries. After that (insufficient) PIP is exhausted, you are on your own regarding medical coverage.

My pain and mobility issues were now worse than ever. As I've said many times before, I couldn't catch a break if it landed in my lap. My life — the pain and suffering — only continued to worsen with each passing year from childhood up until the present. Regardless of what I tried to do or where I tried to do it — from isolating most of my life to changing my environment and outlook — that black cloud continued to follow me and the curse slowly and agonizingly consumed me.

The orthopedic spinal doctor that I was seeing regarding this most recent and additional damage to my spine recommended a four level cervical fusion to "possibly" reduce some pain.

After many questions on my part, he concurred that it was very unlikely that the fusion would reduce the pain to a bearable level considering the extensive damage spread throughout other (the cervical and lumbar) areas of the spine which were also contributing to my overall pain levels and mobility issues. He then stated what most every other doctor I had seen over the years had said to me,

"*You can live with the pain or take pain medication.*"

I wasn't willing to become reliant on — and perhaps addicted to — script pain medication nor was I willing to take a very long shot chance with a cervical spinal fusion.

He recommended a pain management facility to try some injections for the pain and inflammation.

I had had a very bad experience with my first attempt at pain management through injections not even a year earlier in Rhode Island; the facet joint injection(s) that did more harm than good that time around.

However, I was once again at a point where I needed to try something that may reduce some of this intensifying pain and inflammation as well as the increasing mobility issues.

I went to the pain management center and began a round of different types of injections — including epidural injections — over the next few months. In addition, the script medication Flexeril was once again recommended for the severe inflammation and spasms going on throughout my spine and other affected, damaged areas. This time (2010) was the first time I decided to give Flexeril a try. However, I would only take the medication on an as needed basis. That would be if I was in a predicament where I literally could not physically move or I knew for certain I was about to be in that very position. Knowing my body very well, I would take the Flexeril occasionally to "nip the immobility in the bud". On average, I've taken one 10 mg Flexeril tablet every few months since the summer 2010 rear-ending accident.

I don't take this medication for pain but to prevent my body from going into crippling spasms that keeps me incapable of moving sometimes for days. In the past when this did happen, I'd be crippled in a ball, laying on the floor, and have to pee in a bucket that was always within reach in my home. Sometimes, I'd be completely unable to move for up to two days. It would almost always take nearly two weeks to be able to move my back and legs freely once again. The pain is unimaginable when this happens as not only does everything go out along the spine, the sciatic nerve is affected into my hips and legs and adds to the crippling affect and overall misery.

Andrea would often have to help me to get up after half a day laying unable to move in excruciating pain that truly can't be described but to say one might go as far as cutting off a limb if that would get rid of this horrific and crippling, "in a category by itself" pain. It is the highest level of pain tolerable before losing consciousness. It feels as if stakes are being pushed through the body from different angles, nailing the body to the ground beneath it. It is then I am unable to so much as move an inch.

I didn't get much extended relief from the injections. Aside from a week or two of a numbing effect, the misery was always in high gear. As was common throughout my life, my problems, pain, and suffering just continued to mount. This always pushing me further and further away from hope and deeper and deeper into depression and isolation.

This accident of 2010 caused more damage, pain, and mobility issues that I didn't need. My body and mind were already overwhelmed with enough pain and suffering for a thousand lifetimes. However, that black, blighted, ominous cloud never missed a beat, remaining directly above me wherever I might be. That cloud was much larger here in Florida and hell-bent on causing more trauma and suffering in my life. The physical disability and staggering loss I sustained here some fourteen years earlier just wasn't enough. There was so much more to come.

I was quickly falling back into a depth of darkness that I needed desperately to stay away from. I was, once again, dealing with unreal pain levels and worsening mobility issues while my anxiety and panic attacks were holding the shackles of isolation firmly in place.

Andrea had a couple weeks' vacation coming up from work the end of the summer and wanted to take a trip somewhere. I was really in no condition — emotionally or physically — to drive any great distance but decided that seeing my parents and getting back to Sachuest Point would be worth the pain and discomfort of the ride and be good for my soul at this point. As usual, Andrea would have to do most of the driving while I reclined in the passenger's seat. Max could take up his favorite spot in the back, his head hanging out of the window, ears dancing in the wind. At least one of us would be in the happy zone.

I knew this would be very difficult on my spine but I needed to try this drive one last time. I'd done this drive a couple dozen times prior to my line of duty accident back in 1996 and most recently a bit over six months ago when we moved down to Florida from Rhode Island.

It's a twenty-two hour, rather boring, straight-forward, traffic congested drive along I-95. We'd stay over at the half way point in North Carolina.

We packed the car and hit the road. Not sure what I was thinking. Nothing had changed but the increase in pain and discomfort, once again from bad to worse, and especially with sitting.

There wasn't much of a rush so we stopped pretty much every hour so I could stand and/or lay to relieve the building pressure and pain and Max and Andrea could go to the bathroom or grab something to eat or drink.

It was a difficult trip mostly because of my pain and discomfort levels. However, I think both Andrea and I realized from the onset of this trip that we weren't able to give the other what was desperately needed; compassionate support and a connected, meaningful, comforting conversation with a smile and a laugh. We had nothing in common but for an emptiness inside.

Speaking for myself, I was in a very bad place and emotionally vulnerable. I felt for the next year or so that I was being taken advantage of emotionally and financially. However, what initially brought Andrea and I together in Vegas — aside from the real estate business — was loneliness. I never knew what true loneliness was until Vegas. And, it was a horrible, anxiety producing feeling. There were times during Vegas and afterwards I would have sat and talked to the Devil himself — be it Charles Manson, Osama Bin Laden, or Adolf Hitler — in order to shake the anxiety and panic attacks produced from being alone and lonely.

We arrived in Rhode Island a couple days later and stayed at the same hotel I lived in for seven months less than a year ago. Strange as it sounds, the hotel felt like "home" to me. It would have been a private hell of anxiety and loneliness during those seven months if not for Max and his company. We hung our hats here once again. This time for only a week.

Aside from seeing my parents again, a couple aunts and uncles who came over to my parents' home, my good friend Honey D, and visiting Middletown, Newport, and my favorite "special place" of all — Sachuest — It was a very stressful couple weeks with Andrea.

We hit the road and headed back to Florida a week after we arrived. The drive back was even more painful and uncomfortable both physically and emotionally than the drive up to Rhode Island.

Regardless, and in retrospect, I am glad that I did the trip. It was more than likely the last long-distance road trip I'd ever be able to take. My spine has gotten much too fragile to sit that amount of time any longer, even with hourly breaks.

I have been trying to get up to Rhode Island every summer since by way of a two-and-a-half-hour non-stop flight. I've made the arrangements and reservations to fly the past two years in a row and have had to cancel both the original flights and rescheduled flights as I wasn't able to move or sit when the departure days came along.

My parents came down the winter of 2010-2011. They stayed with me, Andrea, and Max through the holiday season and for several months of the New Year. It was always a true pleasure to spend time with my mother. It was, on the other hand, torture having to spend any amount of time with both my mother and father together.

Nothing had changed between them since my childhood, it had only gotten worse. The atmosphere was always tension filled and toxic with both of them together. However, I made the best of it and tried desperately to enjoy my mother's company and the holidays with her regardless of the ever-present, noxious aura that surrounded me.

A few weeks prior to Christmas, I was driving my mother to a store. Max was in the back seat area, his head hanging out the window as usual. We got off I-95 and were at the stop light of the off-ramp. We were impacted from behind by a vehicle whose driver never hit the brakes.

According to the police report post that accident, the vehicle was moving at approximately 45 mph when it impacted my stopped vehicle.

The front of the other vehicle went under my SUV, picked it up, and the impact pushed and folded the entire front of the other vehicle up — like an accordion — and into the windshield of that vehicle.

The first thing that went through my mind was my mother and if she'd be okay. This woman was days away from turning eighty-four-years-old and this was a very hard, metal ripping, glass shattering impact.

I had been estranged from and at war with my Higher Power for well over ten years. I hadn't prayed to or believed any longer in that Higher Power of my childhood. I found myself at that very second praying that my mother was okay and would not suffer any serious injuries from the accident.

It seemed that black cloud would envelop anyone or anything within arm's reach of me.

I remember, what seemed to be in slow motion, looking over at my mother to see if she was okay. We both had our seatbelts on. She was still in her seat. I remember the look — grimace — on her face. I asked her if she was okay. She replied, "*I think so. That was one heck of a whiplash.*" She then immediately said to me, "*Did you get hurt? How is your spine?*"

I told her to stay in the car. Don't try and stand or move her neck until the paramedics got there.

Max was, again, second time within six months, bleeding from the mouth and shaken up from a rear-ending.

I knew I was screwed once again. I felt the excruciating pain throughout my spine — from my cervical down through my lumbar and right into the sacrum section.

I could hardly move my lower back and legs. I knew immediately that the brunt of the damage was lower spine this time around.

I felt a sense of relief that my mother *seemed* to be okay but I was also outraged. I wanted to break this idiot's face who just plowed into my vehicle. I was angry as hell at that Higher Power that hadn't protected me or kept me out of harm's way since childhood. But the only thing that mattered at this point was that my mother was and would be okay. I wouldn't know until the paramedics arrived.

A police officer arrived to take the accident report at the same time the paramedics arrived. I told the paramedics to check out my mother first. I was in terrible pain and having trouble standing but I was up and out of the car.

The driver of the other car was also out of her car and, remarkably (or not), was unphased physically. However, it was obvious to me she was under the influence of something. I'd seen and dealt with this very scenario dozens of times before as a trooper.

Paramedics wanted to transport my mother to the hospital. My mother was having none of it. She told them she had some pain in her neck and was a little dizzy but that she did not want to ride in an ambulance. I told them I would take her to the hospital for further tests to make sure she had no serious injuries.

At the same time, I called Andrea to pick up Max at the accident site so I could take my mother over to the ER. My vehicle was still drivable. The other vehicle was not and had to be towed.

I spoke with the police officer. He knew I was a former state trooper and said to me, verbatim, "*She's high on something.*" "*She definitely is*", I replied.

After giving her a field sobriety test, which she barely passed, he came back and told me she was under the influence of prescription medication which, she said, made her dizzy. No kidding?! Driving dizzy, under the influence of meds that affect your ability to see and think clearly, and endangering the lives of innocent people! This type of inconsiderate asshole is usually what winds up killing someone's loved one(s) on the road eventually. And, walks away unscathed — physically and legally.

She was cited for the accident, the scene was cleared, and I took my mother over to the ER to get checked out further.

My mother had a severely strained neck from whiplash and her blood pressure was very high. Aside from the resulting trauma to an almost eighty-four-year-old woman, I was thankful that her injuries didn't seem to be worse this day.

I then prayed once again that my mother would have no residual symptoms from this accident. I felt a bit hypocritical with the two prayers but firmly believed that I was owed as much (if there was a Higher Power in my life at all) for the consistent pain and suffering I'd endured not only once again this day but for each and every one of the dark and dingy days over the entire course of my life; the past 40-plus years.

A second rear-ending accident in less than six months resulting in more spinal damage, pain, and mobility issues.

The steady flow of pure bad luck and complete imbalance in my life was so unbelievable it was almost laughable.

I come back to this damn state where the second part of my life's nightmare — a line of duty spinal injury resulting in a physical disability — began nearly fifteen years earlier and the bad luck picks up right where it left off, continuing on its path to destroy what remained of my spine and create even more pain and misery in my life.

Max was limping when I got home. I took him to the Vet the next day to get checked out. Nothing was broken, just sprained. He didn't need any stitches for the cut in his mouth and on his tongue.

Max and my mother fared rather well, all things considered. I was thankful for that but cautiously optimistic knowing my luck.

I obtained a police report a few days later and it didn't mention a thing about the driver of the other vehicle stating she was dizzy from taking prescription medication. Nor was there mention of the officer's field sobriety test or his observation regarding her condition. Unreal! It was part of her statement and what caused the accident. It should have been included in the accident report. Either incompetence or laziness — or both — once again here in Florida.

I made an appointment to see a second orthopedic doctor for my most recent injuries to my spine. Once again, I had to get new MRI's — open and seated MRI's due to extreme claustrophobia and anxiety — and they were compared to the last MRI's of six months ago.

Another disc was blown out from this most recent impact. This time, the added damage made its way (up) from my L1 disc in the lumbar section to my T12 disc in the thoracic section.

In addition to this, as with the first rear-ending some six months earlier, there was now more nerve, muscle, disc, and bone damage throughout my cervical and lumbar sections.

This most recent orthopedic doctor reiterated what several orthopedic spinal surgeons had said in the past; the severity and extent of damage to my spine was incredible.

Now, from this most recent (the second in six months) accident, that damage had progressed and worsened once again. The damage to my lumbar spine section as a result of this most recent accident had now rendered that particular area very risky for surgery. My current orthopedic spinal doctor mentioned that a four level fusion to the lumbar section might have been possible prior to the accident, but the area was so damaged and fragile now that he didn't recommend it. He did note that we could still do a four level fusion of my cervical section.

Didn't matter to me either way as I wasn't about to have surgery at any portion of my spine unless and until I couldn't move at all.

He recommended I continue with pain management and reconsider taking script medication for pain. I did on the former, still no interest regarding the latter.

The pain and mobility issues in both my cervical and my lumbar sections, through my hips and into my legs, was now far beyond anything I had experienced to date. I kept thinking to myself; this progression of pain and mobility issues due to accidents — pure bad luck — is something that could only happen to me.

On top of that, being in the state of Florida, I would have to prepare for a war with the insurance company just to get proper medical to possibly alleviate some of the pain and mobility issues. It would be a small miracle if I could get some — any — medical treatment that would get me back to the pain levels and mobility I had *prior* to these two accidents. Highly unlikely and, even if it were possible, the emotional pain and damage would be irreversible.

I continued (and occasionally do to this day) with pain management and various injections for my lumbar as well as my cervical pain and damage. I received very little pain relief from the injections. However, a little relief that lasts a week or two and nips the crippling effects in the bud was the reason for the injections in the first place and a positive any way I looked at it.

All things considered regarding what I've been through during my lifetime, there has been *nothing* physically worse than being completely unable to move accompanied by that chronic, crippling, horrific pain.

Emotionally, there is *nothing* worse than persistent anxiety and panic attacks.

Due to this most recent accident and further damage and pain, both were coming back full force to haunt me. I was once again slowly and very painfully heading back down to the Vegas death row phase of the deepest and darkest depression I'd ever endured.

Making matters even worse, the other driver's insurance had lapsed. She was uninsured. I did have uninsured motor vehicle coverage with a $25,000 bodily injury policy with my insurance company. I had paid that additional premium for over twenty years, just in case. However, as is common with insurance companies — especially in the state of Florida — regardless of the fact I had paid a premium for that coverage and it had been in place for two decades — without one claim — they would resist paying for any medical coverage beyond my PIP.

I had been with this insurance company for over twenty-five years with not one auto accident or claim. They refused to pay for my medical beyond my PIP coverage even though I had an uninsured motorist policy that provided coverage for any medical beyond that PIP amount.

Their claims adjuster — an extremely arrogant and rude, hired bully — stated that the reason for denying the medical coverage beyond the PIP was that I had a "preexisting injury." WTF!? Seriously?? And these insurance companies get away with this bullshit!

The reason for the doctor requested MRI's post these two accidents was to confirm (or not) if there was "new" and further damage. There clearly was new and further damage to my spine and surrounding muscles, nerves, and bones as a result of each of these two accidents over the past 6 months. The MRI's themselves, the technician's correlation study between the last and most recent MRI, and the doctors' reports clearly showed this fact in each instance.

Any doctor can and would attest to the fact that my spine is extremely fragile. Each has told me over the years to avoid "accidents" or I could wind up in a wheelchair. The last thing on this earth I want or need is further damage to my spine. However, any jolt or sudden movement — however that may occur — does just that to my spine; it causes more damage. Both accidents clearly caused new and further damage to my spine — no fault of my own.

The average person with a healthy spine may or may not have sustained any damage to his or her spine as a result of either accident. My spine is in a category of *fragile* by itself. It's so extensively damaged and weak that I kneel and brace when I so much as sneeze. I hold my breath every time I have to bend over. This was all explained and documents furnished to this claims adjuster. The facts once again fell upon deaf ears and injustice came back to haunt me.

The insurance company stopped paying my medical when my PIP benefits were exhausted. I wasn't notified and had no idea they had stopped paying until I got hit with nearly eight thousand dollars' worth of pain management bills. I had to call — and keep calling — the POS claims adjuster for months on end. I was stuck dealing with a complete moron! She dragged and jerked me around for over a year trying to wear me out and break me down so I would just go away. All while I was being swamped with medical bills that this insurance company was responsible for.

She actually had the nerve and stupidity to keep saying to me — over and over — that my injuries were preexisting and I wasn't entitled to my own policy coverage!!

I let her know that I was a loyal client of that insurance company for the past twenty-five years and didn't appreciate being treated like a criminal and an idiot. I had an uninsured motorist policy in effect that I had been paying for the past 20-plus years just in case this very thing ever happened.

She knew the facts and the truth. Someone with a single brain cell could clearly see it. However, and obviously, her job was to screw as many clients out of money as she could. Most likely getting a bonus for all the money she saved the insurance company by denying claims and torturing people until they gave in or gave up.

This is what these insurance companies do; they hire claims adjusters who, like car salespeople, employ their own brand of tactics to sway you one way or wear you down another. Their job is simple; try and break you so you give up the fight and the insurance company keeps your money — the majority of it or all of it.

After being treated disrespectfully and as if I were an imbecile for well over a year by this nincompoop claims adjuster, I told her what I thought of her and to kiss my ass.

I called the insurance company and told them I wouldn't deal with this person any longer. I reiterated to the "supervisor" what I'd been telling this claims adjuster all along. I had enough of the game playing and injustice. If they didn't pay my outstanding medical bills, I'd get an attorney and sue them.

I also let them know that I had an additional $17,000 left on that uninsured motorist policy for medical treatment that I was entitled to. They already screwed me out of $8,000 of a $25,000 policy. I insisted they pay the outstanding medical bills of $8,000 or I would retain an attorney and sue them for the entire portion which I was entitled to for medical purposes related to this most recent accident.

Another claims adjuster called me the very next day and we finally, after briefly enduring his own brand of bullshit tactics, worked out an agreement to have my outstanding medical bills paid.

I had been with this insurance company for twenty-five years without one accident. I was angry as hell and fed up with how I'd been treated so I decided it was time to go with another insurance company.

After everything I'd been through and adding insult to injury, not one major insurance company would insure me because I was now deemed "high risk" in the (Florida) auto insurance world for being involved in two accidents within a three-year period. And that's just *involved!*

The few companies I found that would insure me wanted a monthly mortgage payment for that service now!

Both of the accidents were 100% the fault of the other driver and I was being penalized and marked as a "high risk". Truly unreal how these insurance companies make and break their own rules and pretty much rob us all blind.

These insurance companies are a nightmare. In Florida they are the worst of the worst. Just downright ruthless. They take your money each and every month and when the time comes to insure you, they do everything in their power to screw you instead.

They literally have a license to steal — extort — your money. There is no morality or ethics in the insurance business. It's a business, like most others, that's all about profit at the end of the day. If that means screwing the legitimate, little guy, so be it. They do it each and every day to thousands upon thousands of us and get away with it.

In the state of Florida, as I've noted previously, the only ones that seem to come out ahead with these insurance companies are the attorneys, doctors, and the criminals who fraudulently file claims. The legitimately injured are too often left holding the bag (of shit) and nursing an ulcer.

For the past fourteen years since the first spinal injury, most holidays had been much more depressing and anxiety producing than had been the norm prior.

2010 had been a difficult Christmas. It would have been even more punishing — much darker — if my mother wasn't with me the couple months post that second accident.

2011 would prove to be even worse.

Once my parents returned to Rhode Island, I began to slowly slip back to a place I had hoped I'd never have to see again.

It was now even more difficult to function physically and emotionally than it had been the past year — all due to these two accidents that caused more physical damage and pain. I couldn't sit, stand, or lay half as long as I did prior to these accidents.

Needless to say, I was now much more miserable, depressed, and angry. Part of that anger was due to the fact that I didn't get to fully enjoy the company of my mother during the past few months. The other part of that anger was just a boiling over of hatred for my Higher

Power.

Every year of my life since childhood proved to be more damaging physically, emotionally, or both. I would continually curse that Higher Power, screaming questions I've asked for decades;

How much more of this unrelenting darkness do I have to endure?

When will my pain and suffering be enough?

Why is there never any balance, any light in this torturous, ill-fated existence?

Making matters worse, I was sleeping with the enemy so to speak. The relationship with Andrea had been defective and rather virulent since we crossed over from a business relationship to a personal relationship. More so, since we began living together. That was never more evident than after we arrived in Florida.

We had been living together well over a year and the situation was getting worse by the month. I was in a very fragile, emotionally vulnerable state and was putting up with never-ending emotional abuse.

We spoke several times over that first year about her moving out. The problem on her end; she was unable to support herself financially. I offered to help get a place of her own, paying a few months rent in advance for her. She said she wouldn't be able to afford the rent after that as she wasn't making enough at her retail job.

I had told her many times that this situation wasn't working and we couldn't live together much longer. We needed to figure something out.

There came a time after that first year she decided she was going to move to northern Florida and live with her parents. They had been communicating since we arrived in Florida and seemed to have buried the hatchet. One afternoon, she packed her belongings and headed to northern Florida.

After a few hours of feeling a little sad, I actually felt free and as if a weight had been lifted from my shoulders. I knew that going our separate ways was the right thing for both of us to do.

A week later, Andrea called me, sobbing like a baby. She apologized for the things she had done and said. She then asked — begged, actually — if she could "come back home to me and Max — her family."

Here we go again! Another person in my life throwing around the word "family" who truly doesn't know the first thing about family — the respect, love, and loyalty that *is* "family".

She said she had made a big mistake and should never have left.

She was masterfully crafting her words to play on my emotions. Being her deceitful self to get what she wanted.

I knew immediately from our conversation things weren't going her way at her parents' home. Her back was against the wall in the middle of nowhere and she felt trapped. Trapped and desperate enough to lie through her teeth to get back to me and Max and away from the rules and conditions she'd have to abide by while living with her parents.

Being a product of a severely dysfunctional family, I reverted back to the codependent behavioral pattern I learned as a child and told her she could come back. Just like my mother, always thinking of others before myself.

Once again, I knew in both my gut and my mind that this wasn't the right move. I knew I should have said *no* and both of us continue to go our separate ways. However, being in such a severe depression, emotionally vulnerable, and thinking with my heart and not my head, I made yet another mistake that created more stress and trauma in my life over the coming year.

Andrea returned a couple days later and within a few weeks picked up right where she had left off. Not only were we an amalgam analogous to fire and ice, water and oil, but, most importantly to me, everything that was important and meant something in my life and that I stood for — respect, loyalty, honor, trust — meant nothing to Andrea.

It was an unspoken truth; we both saw this relationship as an arrangement. Quid pro quo. She had security and someone to rely on financially. I had someone around to take the edge off some of the ever-mounting anxiety and to be there for Max if something happened to me. There had been nothing in common beyond that since the beginning.

There was no loyalty on her part. She proved otherwise time and again. Constant lies and betrayal many times over the years. I didn't trust her but it was okay, the arrangement was what mattered to me at this point in my life. I wasn't devastated by her lies or betrayal as I'd been in the past by those who I trusted and was loyal to the death.

I was, however, more angry with and ashamed of myself that I would allow someone to lie to me time and again, cheat, and steal from me with no repercussions.

Prior to Vegas, I wouldn't have spent one minute with someone who crossed any of these lines. I'd have been gone without hesitation, in a heartbeat.

Call it emotional vulnerability. These disorders will do that to you — even to us guys who are too ashamed to admit it. Regardless, I was pretty much taken advantage of as I'd have never put up with the abuse that came with this arrangement under any other circumstances.

Even as I recollect the situation and write this story, I feel embarrassed as a man to have allowed this to continue.

However, as crazy as it may sound, and I've mentioned this previously, there were two reasons — two very important, sanity-saving, life-altering reasons as far as I was concerned — I overlooked the constant lies, theft, and betrayal and allowed the abuse to continue as long as it did;

First and foremost, having someone around kept my anxiety levels a notch lower. Loneliness had finally found me and had become a rather serious problem some seven-plus years ago when I first arrived in Las Vegas. Loneliness caused much more anxiety and increased panic attacks in my life. It was easier and more appealing to surround myself with misery and emotional abuse from someone than be alone and lonely, at the mercy of anxiety and panic attacks. It was the lesser of the evils. Having someone around with whom I had nothing in common and that was taking advantage of me and a situation was worth the trade-off of lower anxiety levels.

Anxiety and panic attacks are the absolute worst, most frightening and devastating emotional disorders known to man. Pure evil.

Anxiety in complete isolation was the greater of the evils here. So, I put up with and endured a situation and someone I never would have spent five minutes with otherwise. Ironically, it made my parents' noxious relationship look rather lame.

Secondly, I truly believed that Andrea was the only one Max had a shot with if something happened to me. I needed someone to care for my boy if something did happen to me. Since I'd met her, I'd been on that ledge almost daily. Chances were 50/50 of making it another day. I couldn't leave my boy alone. He needed someone to care for him. This was the only shot I had and I did what needed to be done at that time.

About a year after Andrea returned from her parents' home, I finally had had enough. At this point, as detrimental to my health as the effects of loneliness were, this toxic arrangement was now at a level of iniquity that nearly equaled the anxiety and panic attacks produced by loneliness.

This very relationship was a major contributing factor that was sinking me deeper into depression and causing additional emotional problems.

I've always said that if I'd been lucky just once in my life, I'd have found my soul mate and I may never have fallen so deeply into PTSD and depression and been so consumed by these disorders. I know that Kay was that woman some twenty-five years earlier. Like any other possibility of light in my life, it just wasn't in the cards.

I'd think during this time and most of my adult life what a truly shitty hand I'd been dealt — every day, in every way. Darkness layered with more darkness. That may have been really sweet and wonderful if my name was Hershey and I happened to be a chocolate bar. However, that wasn't the case. There was never anything sweet in my jar of bitter blackness. No Genie in my bottle of blues.

I told Andrea that she had to find a place to live over the next few months. Whether that meant going back to her parents, living with a friend, or getting a place of her own, our arrangement was over.

She found a place a few months later and moved out.

I began therapy and a recovery process some months later.

Among other things, I was learning how to let go of the pain, anger, and shame I felt for allowing someone to take such advantage of me. For participating in an emotionally abusive relationship that went against everything I stood for and believed in.

I was learning to forgive. Especially myself — my own worst enemy.

Andrea and I would keep in touch over the next couple years, but there was nothing at all remaining. She was still a very angry person and meaningful communication was still not possible. We were on different wave lengths with totally different values and beliefs, from the day we met until the day we parted. It was almost always unpleasant any time we talked, texted, or saw each other.

I've learned many valuable lessons throughout my life and this uninterrupted battle with these disorders. One invaluable lesson; always being alone and, specifically, *lonely*, is a horrendous, anxiety producing, utterly odious and evil sentence to bear. However, being around others — as I've learned from this past relationship as well as those within my immediate family — *who make you feel alone and lonely* is the greater of the evils.

I bear no ill will towards her. It took me well over a year into therapy — a recovery process — writing this story, and reliving the traumas of my life to process and let go of the pain and anger I have felt over the many years not only regarding this Andrea chapter but all the endless days of darkness I've endured throughout my life since childhood.

Knowing even more now about myself, these disorders, and Andrea's actions and behavior than I knew during the tempestuous time we spent together, I sincerely hope that she gets the help she needs to overcome her repressed pain and denial and finds some peace in her soul as I have in mine.

28

The past couple of years since arriving back in Florida hadn't been any better emotionally or physically than my days in Vegas. It was actually a steady decline in both areas.

Physically I was in much worse shape now post the two accidents that happened within one year of my returning to Florida.

Emotionally I was inching closer to that Vegas bottom with each passing month.

Now, post the break with Andrea, I was once again having to deal with the loneliness that had become a major trigger for anxiety and panic attacks some years earlier in Vegas. My anxiety and panic attack levels were rising out of control right along with my physical pain and mobility issues.

Never has there been a lull in the pain, suffering, and consistent bad luck. And there wouldn't be one now, either.

With the arrival of the 2012 New Year and that black cloud forever hovering ominously above me, yet another dark surprise awaited me. Another "welcome back gift" from the sunshine state.

While this one incident wouldn't further damage my body physically (though it may very well have through the stress it caused), it certainly did a number on me emotionally with the tremendous amount of aggravation, stress, and anger it brought to my already painfully dismal existence.

I had become a victim of identity theft.

I had just checked my bank accounts online and noticed that there had been a withdrawal of several thousand dollars from one of my accounts. After a bit of digging and contacting the bank directly, I learned that the IRS had put a lien on my account and withdrew nearly three thousand dollars.

Let the nightmare begin; the first step was to contact the IRS. As I suspected, and the IRS quickly confirmed, someone had stolen my identity. Someone had filed income tax returns with my social security number and personal information.

I had to fill out numerous forms (including an IRS Identity Theft Affidavit) and submit copies of multiple pieces of personal documentation (social security information, driver's license, credit card and banking statements) proving who I was to the IRS.

I had to do this with other agencies as well, including the three major credit bureaus where I put a credit freeze and credit alert on all three of my credit reports.

The legwork with the IRS and credit reporting bureaus is a drop in the bucket compared to everything else that has to be done — and worried about — after your identity is stolen and you are the victim of fraud.

This nightmare — the hassle and aggravation it caused — continued for months on end adding more anxiety and rage to my already overwhelmed emotional condition.

Anyone who has been the victim of identity theft and fraud knows all too well the headache, stress, and anger this causes. It is a very long, bumpy, and unpleasant ride to say the least. One that leaves you constantly looking over your shoulder, wondering what is coming next.

I had enough problems and now I had this hassle added to the mix.

Worst part was having to deal with the incompetence along the way. Aside from the IRS, who was to the point, knowledgeable and professional, most that I had to contact and deal with created much more aggravation and anger.

Day in and day out for months on end, you become glued to a telephone. Half of the day, sometimes more, listening to the same phone game; "press this number for this ... press that number for that." After what seems like a lifetime, an actual person finally answers the call. Unfortunately, it's usually a bungler to compound an already bleak situation.

Like every other business in the USA nowadays, the employee whose job is to *help* you was almost always apathetic, reading from a script, and spoke very poor English (it seems that many major companies in the US have cheap labor and call centers outside of the US). Most times, I couldn't understand a thing that was being said!

I kept saying to myself, over and over; *What the hell is this country coming to?!*

This identity theft incident would have been just another "part of life" experience. One of those pain-in-the-ass things that we all encounter every now and again. However, it was, to me, just another part of that perpetual darkness and complete imbalance that ruled my world.

There was never any chance of anything good coming my way. Always that dark cloud hovering overhead, raining down nothing but gloom.

Ain't no sunshine .... the anthem that rang true every single day of my life since childhood.

I was totally disgusted. Totally drained. Emotionally and physically Exhausted.

It was now the summer of 2012. Another dreaded birthday had come and gone, edging me closer to the half-century mark. I felt the past seven years since my Vegas accident — and all that had transpired since that time — had done more damage emotionally and physically than any other time during my life. My mind and body had deteriorated far beyond my chronological age.

I knew — felt — exactly where I was heading and at a much more rapid and intense speed than the previous months and years.

I'd been there before and going back was a worse fate than death. I desperately needed some kind of relief from the raging fire that was beginning to consume my mind once again, pulling me back to within steps of insanity.

I spent my days with my boy, Max. My body permitting, I took him to the park as much as possible, sometimes up to three times per day. He occupied my mind, and always found a way to make me smile. Briefly sheltering me from the inferno that was closing in.

I always felt as though I was cheating Max out of life — out of living. I felt guilty because I was constantly in so much pain and so uncomfortable in my own skin, I would invariably go to a specific park that was less frequented than others. It would usually be just me, Max, and nature at this lakeside park. There were very few, if any, other people or dogs around most times.

Max was very outgoing and loved being around people. My disorders kept me very uneasy around others. I didn't want Max to have to live like I'd lived my entire life. I did the best I could while battling the pain, depression, and social anxiety to get him out and at least chase some birds and see a few people and dogs here and there.

That empty and gut-churning feeling of loneliness — a major trigger for anxiety and panic attacks — was back full-force to haunt me once again.

Max was a blessing but couldn't extinguish the advancing conflagration from within.

This time frame in Florida was eerily reminiscent of my Vegas days of consistently deepening depression, heightened anxiety, and that death row phase that lead up to the last mile.

I was slowly but surely once again falling back down to the absolute bottom, deepest and darkest corner of that hell hole I'd existed in my entire life.

In the interim, I desperately kept searching for an escape from the mounting pain, anxiety, and despair.

I'd compare my emotional well-being throughout my life to a rollercoaster ride but for the fact there were never any highs, just lows and lower.

There had been "three M's" in my life that provided a brief escape — a short-term lift — and helped quell the never-ending pain that shadowed my every move:

Martial Arts, Motorcycles, and Music;

Martial Arts and *Training* had been reduced by 95% over the years with the various injuries to my spine. I had very little training I could still do that provided any relief. However, I desperately clung to — and continue to hang on to this day — that 5% that I was still able to painfully push my body through. This little bit of training caused more physical pain but briefly alleviated a portion of the horrendous emotional pain that continued to mount rapidly. I continued to sacrifice my body to save my mind.

I am a huge MMA and fight fan. Sometimes when I'm watching pro fights, out of nowhere I'll get choked up. I still have a difficult time accepting the fact that I could have been, should have been, would have been at the top of that game if I had gone that route early on in my life.

If this spinal injury hadn't left me disabled and barely able to move most days I'd at least still be training as a middle-aged man, feeling euphoric, and in better shape than most of the young bucks out there.

Motorcycles. Riding had come to an abrupt and heartbreaking end years ago in Vegas when the lumbar portion of my spine totally collapsed.

I remember the last time I sat on my bike. I knew I'd never be able to ride again. I still feel the intensity of that anger I felt the day of that realization. That loss still stings to this very day. I always tear up whenever I think about it. Like training, another part of my soul — another outlet for my mind's stability — was cruelly ripped from my life.

Music. I still had my music. While I couldn't focus or concentrate on my own songwriting due to my emotional condition, I could escape in the notes and words of others' songs as I'd done since childhood.

I'd been drowning the pain with the music as far back as I can remember. It was the only escape that remained in its entirety. However, this escape was sometimes a double-edged sword; while much of the music soothed my soul and lifted my spirit to a better place, many of the songs from my childhood and early adult years always brought me back to a time and place that was very traumatic in my life. Waves of emotional pain evoked by the very escape that partly soothed my soul.

Some songs triggered anxiety and panic attacks. Others eliciting such a strong, painful emotion, I'd get sick to my stomach.

Looking at certain pictures (photos) or watching certain TV shows and movies from back in the day has the same nauseating, anxiety producing effect. Taking me back to a time and place that still haunts a part of my soul.

Strangely enough, there are even certain smells, sights, and sounds that have this same effect; taking me back to a horrible, traumatic time and place in my life, triggering dreaded anxiety and nausea. This being a direct result of the PTSD I've suffered with since childhood.

However, and thankfully, there are plenty of beautiful sights, delightful smells, wonderful sounds, and healing music that soothes my heavy soul and takes me to a more desirable, more peaceful place in my mind.

Music often took the edge off, relieved the anxiety and, like the few other outlets I once had, helped me to blend into the "normal" that never existed in my world. I rely on its calming effect each and every day. There's magic in the music, for sure.

There was also the big "N"; *Nature.* The great outdoors.

Animals and the ocean always did the trick. Being around either *always* soothed my soul.

However, unlike the three M's, this wasn't a "go-to" escape that I did every day, every chance I got, to stifle some of the pain. The ocean was some distance away.

I got there as often as possible but that was far from enough to help get me through my days and nights.

Nature in all its glory was outside my door but there were way too many days I could hardly move, never mind take a walk in the park or go sit on a bench and take it all in. That's very difficult, if not impossible, and even more so with people around, when overwhelmed by pain, mobility issues, misery, and despair.

However, I pushed myself far beyond my comfort zone and did start spending more time around nature and the ocean during this time in my life — much of it with my buddy, Max.

Nature — specifically animals and the ocean — has always been a reliable medicine for my soul. Though I needed it now more than ever before, it wasn't going to be enough any longer. I knew I was at a critical, emotional point of no return. If something didn't drastically change — and very quickly — I wouldn't pull through this time.

I was descending rapidly.

Everything in my life since childhood had gone from bad to worse each and every year for some 40-plus years. Never a ray of sunshine. Never the slightest break from the persistent pain and torment that existed every minute of every day.

The walls were closing in faster than ever. Everything was coming to a head as it did in Vegas four years earlier.

I was one rung — mere days — from hitting absolute bottom yet again. Gasping for air. Going under. Suffocating.

It had been nearly three years since I'd spoken to anyone about my ceaseless and ever-mounting pain and suffering. Almost three years of worsening misery and anger seething and ready to boil over. I needed to talk to someone who understood my pain and circumstances. I had to release some of the pressure, get my head back above water, and be able to catch my breath.

If I hit that absolute bottom again, I'm not sure I would make it from the ledge this time around.

I was now in much worse condition physically than I'd been when I hit that bottom four years earlier in Vegas.

Emotionally I was closing in on a complete collapse. My mind was frenetically racing. I was crumbling at an accelerated pace. Without some type of intervention, that complete collapse was inevitable.

I reached out to Nina, my first therapist, in Rhode Island. I contacted her to see if she might know or be able to recommend a trustworthy therapist close by me in south Florida.

She acknowledged that she was glad I reached out to her and that I certainly needed to talk to someone. She could hear it in my voice.

Unfortunately, neither she nor anyone in her office knew a

therapist down this way. They couldn't recommend anyone but she told me to make sure I found and saw an "LCSW", and one I was comfortable with.

I did the research and narrowed it down to three LCSW's in my area. My first choice was an LCSW, *Jill B (JB)*, whose website provided a synopsis of her experience, her counseling offerings and objectives for her clients. There was something about the wording that got my attention. Unlike the other LCSW's I'd researched, this one just felt right. There seemed to be a deep compassion and concern coming through her written words.

If this LCSW's heart is as genuine as the words felt to me, I might have found someone who can truly provide the help I needed to begin climbing out of this quicksand that has contained me for over forty-five years and that was once again coming very close to swallowing me whole.

JB was my first choice and my first call. Hopefully, I could get an appointment without having to move down the list.

I remember calling and getting voice mail. I left a message and received a call (back) a couple hours later. I was able to get an appointment within a few days.

That very first appointment was on September 13, 2012.

The day my emotional well-being would begin a change for the better.

The day I would begin a very slow, very painful but cathartic, positive life-changing ascent from the bottom of that hell hole I'd existed in for the past four and a half decades.

It was no small task as the trauma I'd endured and disorders emotionally imprisoning me began at the age of five and continued, uninterrupted and unresolved, for the next 40-plus years.

I not only had a lifetime of emotional pain and imprisonment to deal with and recover from, I also had a chronic and intensely vicious physical pain and debilitating physical disability of the past sixteen years that made my life that much more hopeless and less bearable. I saw this as a torturous double-whammy that could only have happened to this cursed soul.

These are two very different, paralyzing pains and conditions — emotional and physical — that have torn my life apart for decades.

Some say that emotional pain far outweighs any physical pain. I can tell you from over forty years of firsthand experience that each has its own distinctive elements of evil. The daily battle against the vile, crippling affliction of each is quite different but no less devastating.

Battling both of these demons at the same time throughout my life has created not only an intense pain, anger, and despair, but also a crystal clear understanding and knowledge that only those walking in those very shoes — engaged in that actual dual battle — can comprehend; living with and then attempting to recover from two broken legs is one thing. Living with and then attempting to recover from those two broken legs in addition to two broken arms is a horse of another color.

I was at my lowest point since Vegas' death row and would no doubt have been walking that last mile one more time if not for the intervention of therapy.

From my first psychotherapy session with JB, the unraveling began. Peeling back the layers of trauma that had been my life since the age of five. Each year of that life from childhood on archived one traumatic event after another. Pain, suffering, anger, and despair buried deep inside, tormenting and imprisoning me behind that facade I'd created over thirty years earlier in order to survive, in order to keep that bleeding soul — that weakness so I thought — a secret.

Every Tuesday at 2:00 p.m. — occasionally twice per week — for the past two years as of fall 2014, I've been in therapy learning how to emotionally heal. In order to accomplish that goal, I was reliving traumatic events of the past that had triggered the disorders that had crippled me emotionally and had kept me in isolation most of my life.

The process was shocking, confusing, and became overwhelming at times. I was opening up and revealing a tortured soul that I had spent my entire life concealing in order to protect myself. I was breaking down emotionally not only during therapy sessions but daily — anxiety and panic attacks abundant — grieving my pain, suffering, and losses from the past 40-plus years.

During therapy sessions, I was in a safe environment being guided by a professional and compassionate, very understanding therapist who was, for the first time in my life, aside from Nina, someone I trusted and who validated the adversity I'd endured consistently since childhood and throughout my entire life.

I soon came to realize that none of this curse — the traumatic events, the disorders, the pain, anger, despair, and bitterness I'd felt most of my life — was my fault. I didn't choose that black cloud — the trauma — that continually hovered above me, steadily raining down sorrow and misfortune, creating a completely unbalanced, dark, lifeless existence. I didn't ask for it, but I certainly got it and needed now at this time in my life to understand it, accept it, process it, grieve it all finally and, for the last time, let it go and focus on the positive.

The only way out of the darkness is through the darkness. One step at a time, one day at a time, tackling and processing one traumatic event at a time. As with any recovery, it is always a work in progress.

There are stages of recovery — healing — leading from a life of persistent, crippling pain and infinite sorrow to finding some peace, light and balance.

It takes years — sometimes decades — to fall into the deepest and darkest regions of PTSD, depression, and other disorders and addictions. The journey back up through the blackness in search of light is no different — it is no less difficult or painful — but for the reward that awaits on the other side.

I always knew I was different than others. From childhood I never fit in. I was always worried about everything and everyone, always hurting inside, always crawling in the darkness.

As the real picture and truth of my life started to unravel, it was very difficult to accept. I knew it was bad. I just never knew how bad, empty, and unbalanced until now.

I began to feel that If depth and overall duration of emotional and physical pain could accurately be measured, I no doubt would have held a couple of Guinness World Records.

At some point over the first couple of therapy sessions I had said to JB, "*If I wrote a book about my life, no one would believe it. It would probably be considered a work of fiction.*"

JB responded, "*Why don't you write that book?*"

I had said this very thing many times over the years to psychiatrists, but JB was no psychiatrist. She was a compassionate, understanding psychotherapist who knew the cathartic value of my chronicling the trauma — pain and suffering — that had consistently plagued me since the age of five.

I wanted so much to do it but, as had been the case throughout my life, had no confidence in my ability to actually tell my story in book form. I didn't believe that I'd be able to complete the story, either. I figured that door, too, would be slammed shut in my face at the very last minute.

The thought of writing my story played over and over in my mind every day until I decided two months later — exactly sixteen years to the very day of my line of duty accident — to start writing the story, regurgitating the decades of repressed pain and anger, suffering and despair onto paper.

Writing this book — sharing my story — was an integral and most crucial part of my recovery process. It allowed me to unearth and confront the repressed trauma and demons buried deep inside, process the pain and anger, and let it all go while at the same time helping me to find some peace in my soul and that meaning in my life; helping others through *my* lifetime of pain, suffering, and firsthand knowledge of these disorders. Offering a view into the hell that is every one of these disorders, the life changing and life ending effects of these disorders, and what we — those of us who walk in those very shoes — can do to overcome those effects as well as to help others around us suffering in silence.

The first year and half of therapy was the most difficult. Resurrecting the demons that have haunted my soul since childhood and throughout my entire adult life.

It was excruciatingly painful. I felt my condition — both emotionally and physically — worsening. The added, daily emotional trauma of re-experiencing horrible events and unbearable feelings fueling the physical pain, and vice versa. The stress of reliving traumatic event after traumatic event over the course of a lifetime was taking a toll. I was being emotionally smothered on a daily basis and I was more angry than ever before. Short-fused became no fuse at all. I found myself lashing out at everyone and everything at the drop of a hat. I had even less patience now than I'd had most of my life prior to this recovery process.

My anger and stress levels were through the roof for well over a year of my initial therapy. I was dealing with a new pain and rage that took on a life of its own. Ironically, birthed by the therapy process itself. It was a ferocious beast that could only be tamed by confronting and conquering one repressed, traumatic event at a time.

I'm not sure if I've ever felt more trapped. I had all this additional and most potent negative energy surfacing and swirling around in my head. That rage burning through my veins from years of buried pain and anger that was now being dug up in therapy and had to be relived all over again. This, in addition to the entire multi-year process of writing this very book.

I was being bombarded day in and day out with over forty years of suppressed anger and torment that I now had to deal with, process, accept, and let go in order to continue forward and up through the many levels of darkness in search of the light on the other side.

I kept thinking to myself; I'm supposed to be feeling better as a result of therapy and I'm feeling worse than I ever have. Nothing but more pain, anger, stress, confusion, and despair. That's where JB always kept me on track. Encouraging me and supporting me while validating the bad luck, that shitty hand I'd been dealt since childhood — an unbalanced four decades of pain and suffering — and guiding me through the darkness and uncertainty to the light, hope, and peace that awaits on that other side.

Our paths crossed at exactly the right time in my life.

29

A couple months into my therapy, winter 2012, my parents came down for the holidays. Once again, we'd all be under the same roof for the next five months.

As I've stated many times throughout this story, it was always a joy to see and spend time with my mother. It was another form of torture to endure any time both of my parents were together in the same room.

The timing truly couldn't have been worse this time around.

All of the pain and anger two months into a recovery process was multiplied tenfold and beginning to boil over from the ongoing therapy. I was on edge, consistently irritable, and fully steamed to begin with and prior to their arrival.

As much as I love my parents — my mother always and forever the most cherished and important person in my world — it was, literally, detrimental to my health being around both of them together for any extended period of time.

The tension between them produces an incredibly vile atmosphere that simply cannot be explained, only experienced.

The last thing I needed — especially at this crucial point in my healing process — was added stress and anger.

I had hoped that as both of my parents aged — being in their mid and late eighties during this time — they would perhaps learn how to communicate, to ebb and flow, and lose all the hostility between them. Not a chance of that happening.

It was, as it had been since childhood, a very unpleasant, stressful environment of dysfunctionality and codependency. Decades removed and the scene was as if no time had passed at all.

I vowed to myself I'd never do this again. Even a masochist would shy away from this type of pain and torture.

Adding fuel to the fire, my father was reaching for the bottle now more than ever.

Drinking was in his genes and also an integral part of the wise guy lifestyle he was part of since his teenage years.

All of his friends — the old schoolers of his day — had passed and his way of life as he knew it came to an end. Whether he became depressed, felt alone and out of place, I don't know, but the drinking was always what drowned whatever ailed him. And it — and he, at eighty-seven-years-old — was now even more difficult to be around than any time previously.

At this time in my life, the continual drinking in my home was bothering me more than it had in years past. It enraged me to another level I had never experienced. It had been a major factor in causing the disorders that had ruled and destroyed my world from childhood. It was now counterproductive to my healing process.

I had no patience or sympathy any longer for a drunk, no matter who it may be. I found myself losing it — talking to myself, steaming heavily, and having to leave my own home on numerous occasions so I didn't completely explode.

I had been reliving and processing a lifetime of trauma the past couple of months — this very type of situation being one of them — through therapy and needed to put the pain and anger of those damaging events to sleep for good. My very sanity depended on it.

My father's drinking, in addition to my parents' constant, sickening bickering, was driving me absolutely nuts at this time in my life. This was, out-and-out, the worst I'd ever felt under the same roof with both of them.

I couldn't take it any longer. I exploded with anger — pure raw emotion — and began yelling at the top of my lungs about his drinking in my home and the constant bullshit between him and my mother. I had never raised my voice in my parents' presence or shown this emotion — disgust and anger — in the past.

I felt like a rebellious child having a temper tantrum.

I actually felt very guilty and ashamed of my reaction afterwards but realized it had been brewing for decades and was necessary for my recovery — healing — process.

I was boiling over and the new boundaries I had set for the sake of my sanity — no drinking in my home being one of them — were being ignored.

I tried desperately to explain and make my father understand what had happened in my life and how he was partially responsible — much to do with his drinking.

I knew I could never make him understood what I'd been through in my life — what these disorders are and what they'd done to me. What it's like living with emotional and physical pain each and every day of your life — year in and year out. No balance to that life. No light in that life. No joy. Just relentless pain and misery.

However, I could see in his eyes at that very moment he did understand the (emotional) pain before him. He may not have understood what caused it, but by my words and actions that day, he knew it was there and very deep.

I remember the look on his face. He became very quiet and actually said, "*If I've ever hurt you, I'm sorry.*"

I couldn't believe what I'd just heard. That was a first for my father. A partial acknowledgement and an apology. He seemed to have gotten a portion of what I was saying but there was no getting through to him — that impenetrable, self-centered mentality — the depth of the trauma I'd suffered from childhood and throughout my entire life and exactly what it had done to me — and how he was continuing to contribute to that agony by drinking and becoming inebriated in my home.

With his next breath, he said, "*You should have a glass of wine every now and then, it will relax you.*"

I couldn't win for losing!

I began writing this book — sharing my story — sixteen years to the very day of my line of duty accident, November XX, 2012. It would take the next two years — December 2014 — before I was able to complete the first draft.

I dove into it at that very time partly as an escape from the added tension and anger of being under the same roof with both of my parents once again. I had no other escape route at my disposal.

November XX has been one of the worst days of each year for me since that fateful day in 1996. I find myself each year on this day wallowing in pain and sorrow, reliving the day and the life-altering outcome of that incident.

Not only would the therapy process be bringing all the decades of repressed trauma, anger, and suffering to the surface, but the writing of my story would amp up the pain and (final) grieving to another level.

Aside from JB's always encouraging me to continue, I don't know how I moved forward with the story as it was creating so much more additional anxiety, pain, and anger as I relived traumatic event after traumatic event, and then some, with every stroke of the keyboard — every word I'd have to write.

The upside was that I was inching forward with each therapy session and with each line of my story I was able to write, process, finally grieve, and move on and away from the deeply embedded trauma.

The picture — the mystery that was my life — was becoming clearer and clearer.

With each piece of the puzzle I was able to fit into this unbalanced and bleak existence, I could feel a slight sense of relief, a tiny bit of weight removed from my soul.

The further I was able to delve into my soul and pull out the pain and anger that had been idling there for decades, the more I could feel that very soul finding a sense of peace and purpose.

It took well over a year of writing — as well as individual therapy — before I could feel any significant and positive change. It is a slow and arduous journey from the darkness but with each traumatic event dug up, confronted, accepted, and overcome, I could feel the purge mending — slowly healing — that soul that had been ripped apart and bleeding every minute of every day since the age of five.

The 2012 holiday season had come and gone and my mother's 86th birthday was just around the corner.

Having been in therapy for the past five months, I found myself dealing with a pain and anger like never before as I tried desperately to understand and accept my life as it was unfolding through this recovery process.

Instead of feeling any better emotionally, I continued feeling much worse. Being around people — simply going to the store — had become even more difficult and anxiety producing than prior to the beginning of therapy.

And I now had family — cousins I hadn't seen in decades — living right around the corner. Less than a mile from my place.

I felt that my escape back into obscurity — untouchable isolation — was in jeopardy. I didn't need to run into anyone I knew, especially family. Or did I at this very time in my life?

This unexpected and simple shuffling of the deck — along with my therapy and writing this very story — would turn out to be the beginning of my emergence from that cocoon I'd been trapped in since childhood.

Little did I know, I was about to begin finding bits and pieces of light and truth. And, finally, understanding and acceptance of myself and my life — those cards I'd been dealt long ago.

I certainly didn't know it at the time, but my cousins moving to the area would become an integral part of my recovery process and a first step of my transformation.

My cousin, Pina, and her husband, *Renzo*, along with their son, *Franco*, had moved into my neighborhood a year earlier.

I hadn't seen my cousin Pina in several decades or ever met her husband or son — as was the case with most of my cousins and their significant others and children.

Pina's mother — my mother's sister, Paola — lived about an hour south of us with her husband, my uncle Fausto. They would be coming up to Pina's house on my mother's birthday. Pina's brother, my cousin Vio, was also in town with his partner, *Tore*, and wanted to share his birthday — which happens to be the same day as my mother's — with my mother.

The plan was for my mother, father, and myself to go over to Pina's house to celebrate the two birthdays with family.

Needless to say, I was still too far gone to be among family I hadn't seen in decades, or crowds of any kind for that matter. A very deep depression, anxiety, and panic attacks still controlling me into isolation. That, along with a physical pain that was through the roof, and mobility issues that kept me reeling with anger.

I felt horrible I wasn't able to spend the night with them, but I'd already missed decades of family get-togethers and celebrations. This would be no different but for the fact it was my mother's birthday they'd be celebrating.

My mother really wanted me to go but could clearly see I was in no condition to do so. She was just beginning at this time to have a better understanding and get a deeper glimpse into what my life truly had been since childhood and the reasons I vanished from the family and life itself.

I knew my mother would have a wonderful time with them and insisted she go and celebrate her birthday that evening and enjoy the company of family.

One afternoon, a couple weeks before my parents would be returning to Rhode Island, I asked my mother to call my cousin Pina and let her know that I wanted to see her and meet her husband and son. Normally, this would *never* be the case with my depression, pain, and anxiety. However, it was a rare occasion that day. I was somehow able to workout much more intensely than was common at this point in my life. I had quite an endorphin kick that shot my serotonin and norepinephrine levels way up, numbing my physical pain and resetting that chemical imbalance in my brain that kept me forever imprisoned. It was one of those very few and far between days that my mind was a bit free and clear of fog and pain and I wanted to make the best of it by stepping out of the isolation and taking a first step forward with my recovery.

It was important to me that we meet outside around the park or local shops as I didn't want to feel claustrophobic, confined, and panicky being stuck in someone's house or a restaurant when the artificial high of the endorphin kick wore off.

My parents and I met Pina and her husband, Renzo, by a local park. Her son, Franco, was working that day.

It was a strange but comforting feeling to see family I hadn't seen in some thirty-plus years. Lots of memories and emotions flooded my mind all at once.

My mother had told me over the years about Renzo and his back problems.

He had some serious spinal and mobility issues of his own and we hit it off immediately. We talked about the pain and suffering that only those of us walking in those shoes can truly understand. I couldn't sit this day and Renzo couldn't stand, but we all chatted and caught up a bit for an hour or so in the park.

I tried to explain a little of how my life played out over the decades — from my childhood PTSD up through my line of duty accident — and the reasons behind my not being around all those years.

I did the best I could at that time revealing a bit of my soul and the regret I felt for being out of the family loop for the past thirty-plus years. I told them about my therapy process and this very story I was writing and that it would all be much clearer in time.

I told my cousins that as much as I wanted to stay in touch, until I was in a better place emotionally, I couldn't guarantee I'd be seeing anyone again any time soon.

No one knew at the time, including myself, that this short, thirty-plus year in the making meet up was my very first step forward, away from darkness and into light and my truth.

Before my parents left during the spring of 2013, I gave my mother the first draft of the introduction section of this book to read.

Needless to say, she cried after reading it. She said she never knew how I felt, what I was going through, and just how bad it really was for me. No one ever did. I made sure of that.

I told her it wasn't her fault and to never feel guilty that she didn't know. I was surprised but grateful she made it through this life herself with the shitty cards she'd been dealt.

My mother has always been my rock — my strength to persevere through the depths of that hell I'd been banished to since childhood.

I asked her to have a few aunts, uncles, and cousins read the introduction section. It was both my next step towards peace and recovery and my way of breaking the news about my existence and the forthcoming book that would answer a lot of questions. Let them know the truth about my life — the disorders and conditions that had kept me from family and life in general. The burning regret I've felt being away from my family for several-plus decades and the agony from missing that family connection and solid bond with my aunts, uncles, and cousins.

It has been one of the greatest regrets of my life but one I truly had no control over.

April 2013. My parents had returned to Rhode Island the previous month. I was now focusing more intensely on introspection and writing my story while dealing with the mounting emotional pain of that very process.

The calm — the healing — would slowly come, a little at a time, after the cathartic storms.

A week before my parents left, I emailed a good friend, Honey D, as well as my cousin Bruno, with a brief note about what I'd been through during my life and the forthcoming book about that very life and the disorders that had controlled me into isolation and a living hell beginning at the age of five.

Part of the therapy process — the healing process — was a "coming out" if you will.

I needed to finally reveal a portion of that bleeding soul I'd concealed and protected behind a facade my entire life in order to survive. I would begin with those that I needed to know my story before anyone else.

Both my friend Honey D and my cousin Bruno were astounded by what they had read — what I had revealed to them.

I then emailed to each of them the first draft of the introduction section of this book. Neither could believe I'd been hiding such pain and sorrow for so long. Both of them were very understanding and supportive.

The one thing that really stood out the most to me and hit me in the heart was what my cousin Bruno emailed back to me after reading that introduction draft. I've mentioned this in a prior chapter, but it is so very important in understanding these life-altering disorders and how others can help a loved one from or from ever going to the depths of hell that I have gone.

He said, "*I always knew there was something wrong, I just couldn't put my finger on it. I wish I had known and could have helped.*"

Any time someone you care about is acting out of character or just doesn't seem right to you, you should dig a little deeper and have a heart-to-heart talk with that person.

Don't shrug it off. Don't let it go.

Let the person know you are there to support him/her. Let the person know he/she can talk freely and in confidence with you about whatever may be bothering him/her. Together you can work through it.

If I had someone in my life that had picked up on my out-of-the-norm childhood sadness and progressively worsening depression and isolation as time went on, I may not have had to endure the decades of endless emotional imprisonment and torment that became my life.

It was nearing the end of spring 2013 when my mother received a call from her grandson, Carlo.

It had been just shy of four years since there was any communication at all between them.

He apologized for his behavior and waiting so long to do the right thing and reconcile with his grandparents. He was the only one who came to his senses. The only one among the five of them that had half a heart to begin with.

He made an appointment to go over to my parents' place with his wife, his son, JJ, who was now going on eight-years-old, and his daughter, *Pessa*, going on three-years-old — the great-granddaughter that my parents had never met.

There was, according to my mother and father, heart-felt apologies from Carlo to his grandparents and a promise to never let something like that happen again.

My parents — most importantly to me, my mother — forgave him that day and their relationship was back on track.

As of this writing — 2014 — he's been keeping in contact with my parents and is there for them — so far — if need be.

He has been taking the kids over to see their great-grandparents. My mother and her great-granddaughter, Pessa, had developed a very special bond from their very first meeting. My mother calls her "little princess".

Carlo gave his grandmother back a sense of family, love, and appreciation that she'd been completely stripped of. He brought back a piece of joy to her soul. For that, and only that, I am thankful — regardless of what I know to be the truth.

Carlo asked my mother if it would be okay to contact me. My mother asked me to accept his reaching out and his apology. I told my mother as long as he apologized to my parents and they had forgiven him, I would bury the hatchet with him for the betrayal and nearly four years of disrespect towards his grandparents and myself.

There is nothing that I wouldn't do for my mother. As long as she is alive, I will do whatever she asks and that makes her happy and brings a smile to her face. However, I knew in my heart, and that gut feeling that has never steered me wrong, that he hadn't changed. Again, a tiger can't change its stripes, a leopard cannot change its spots. I had seen and knew his true soul, as I had the rest of this family. But, as long as my mother was genuinely happy and had someone there for her — even half there as was the reality — I would go along with his charade. He's always been very manipulative and cunning. Most are taken by that. However, I could always smell bullshit a mile away. I was ten steps ahead of him and the rest of this family. Not one of them could shine my shoes when it came to knowing and understanding a person's true soul and their intentions. I've been able to read people like a newspaper since I was a kid. It's been a sixth sense and survival tool I've had since early childhood — and it's not always a welcome sense as I see things and people as they truly are, in reality, and in their souls. A person's truth — their core — can be very unsettling, ugly and detestable.

Carlo did contact me initially via email. We then spoke on the phone to put some things into perspective. He apologized for everything that happened between us and with his grandparents. He swore it would never happen again.

I knew better.

For the sake of my mother, I forgave him. I told him we'd need to discuss things in detail, in person, at some point. I don't like talking on the phone about such personal things. I prefer to look into someone's eyes when speaking. However, being so many miles apart, we had no choice but to cover certain bases via phone.

We agreed we'd speak in more detail about things when we were able to get together.

We have kept in touch with an occasional call, but mostly via texts.

I may have been in a severe depression and controlled into isolation by PTSD and anxiety most of my life, but I was always there for my family. I spent a lot of quality time with my nephews and niece when they were children and through their growing years. I taught them right from wrong, the importance of family, and the ways of our culture.

Unfortunately, a rock will never absorb water.

It happens every now and again in many families. There is usually a black sheep of sorts — and usually just one. However, my immediate family was dysfunctional to the extreme. This "family" was destroyed not by one, but by five exceptionally disgraceful, self-centered, stony-hearts who had proven, time and again over the years, that they were incapable of loving and caring for anyone but themselves.

30

It was the beginning of Summer 2013. Max had been limping on and off for about six months. This almost always occurred later on in the evening after spending the day running and jumping when we played fetch with his favorite ball.

He would lay down afterwards and then, when he got up to get a drink of water or to go outside to do his thing, he'd begin limping.

Labs are notorious for hip dysplasia and I assumed he was having some hip problems as he was getting older. He was eight-years-old at this time.

Usually, after a good night's sleep, he'd be fine the next day — the limping was completely gone.

However, one day he was in a full sprint to fetch his ball and he turned his 110 lb. body too quickly. He fell to the ground and when he got up he couldn't put any pressure on his rear left leg.

He would whimper any time he tried to put pressure on that leg. I immediately began icing his whole left leg area to keep the inflammation down and got him to the vet the next day.

I had thought — this time and for the past six months — that Max had been having trouble with his hip. Post the vet's examination and tests, it was determined that Max injured his left knee, most likely tearing a ligament.

The vet couldn't be sure how severe unless and until surgery was performed. The vet also noted that due to his body weight and suspected injury, it would require surgery or it may never heal properly.

I'd heard those very words regarding my own injuries throughout my life.

I'm not a fan of surgery unless it's absolutely necessary for survival or to move again.

I didn't believe this was the case unless and until other options were exhausted and Max didn't improve — could not stand on that leg at all and get back to being mobile without pain.

I was worried at first because if Max didn't heal via other options, I probably wouldn't be able to care for him post-surgery. With the severity of my spinal injury, I would definitely not be able to pick his 110 lb. body up and help him to go do his doody if he was in a leg cast and/or couldn't walk or put pressure on that leg for days, weeks, or months.

I did some research and found out that most dogs as large as Max will usually blow out the other (right) knee after the first (left) knee is surgically corrected. And, even worse, the surgically repaired knee may very well tear again, especially with larger dogs.

He's a very big boy and that's a lot of pressure on his joints and knees. Surgically repaired or not, the hard and fast paced running and fetching would have to be eliminated to spare him a life of pain and misery that I knew all too well as a result of debilitating physical injuries.

I opted to try for Max what I would do for myself — and have done many times in the past — in place of surgery; prescription (canine) anti-inflammatory meds (rimadyl 100 mg) for a couple weeks, constant icing, massage to get blood in the area, and rest to see if it would heal on its own.

I also would have to keep Max on a leash at all times for a month or so to make sure he didn't run or jump around and further irritate and damage the knee.

He began walking with a faint limp after a few days of therapy and gradually his knee began healing and getting stronger. He was doing great.

After a month or so, he was walking fine with no limp at all. After a couple months of rehabbing him, I let him begin roaming and running on his own and at his own pace. All the while, he'd have his favorite yellow ball in his mouth. There was no playing fetch and I really had no intention of ever throwing that ball again as I knew what could happen now as a result. However, he would always drop that ball at my feet and look at me with those sparkling, full-of-life eyes that told me how very badly he wanted to go fetch that ball. I gave in one day about three months into his recovery and gently lobbed the ball all of ten feet. Very big mistake on my part. Not only tossing the ball but not throwing it far enough. He shot for it and stopped on a dime, twisting and reinjuring his left knee.

We were back to square one of three months earlier.

This time around was even worse than the first. This time, he would whimper whenever he tried to get up, sit down, or moved the wrong way.

His arthritis didn't help any either. He was obviously in much more pain after reinjuring the knee. I added some prescription (canine) pain medication (tramadol 50 mg) to the previous months' therapy regimen and began the process all over again.

I knew now that no matter how well Max may recover — if at all — this second time around, there would not — could not — be any further fetch games for my boy.

The absolute worst thing about this second time around injury was watching Max go into a deep "doggy depression". An emotional state I was much too familiar with. He would lay around with no movement whatsoever — not even a tail wag which had been non-stop for the eight-plus years we'd been together.

I could see the pain and sadness in his eyes, and it killed me. Whenever he'd cry out in pain, my eyes welled up with tears and I felt a sadness like I'd never felt before, right alongside of a blood boiling rage from knowing he would most likely never again be able to do what he loved and lived to do — run and play fetch.

My boy was raised with a very active lifestyle beginning the day we got together when he was eight weeks old; lots of all-out running, fetching, and playing every day. He lived to run and fetch his favorite ball. He loved fetching that ball more than he enjoyed eating! This is the one thing he looked forward to each and every day more than anything else. This was his life. His joy.

It sickened me how my bad luck and lifelong curse had now touched him. He was now going to have to live with an injury and predicament similar to my situation; I lived my entire life for training and exercising — It was my escape, my joy, my means of survival. Max lived to play fetch. To run, spin, jump, retrieve. Fetching to his heart's content. It's what most Labs are born to do. Max, however, took it to another level, as I did with training in my life — the more the merrier. Full throttle, wide open. Although it was addiction in my case.

When he'd see me get his ball, he'd know it was time! His eyes would light up, he'd spin in circles and that tail would wag non-stop. He was about to experience pure joy — and he couldn't wait, and never wanted to stop. He was in all his glory fetching that ball. Blissfully free. The essence of elation.

I knew this injury he had sustained was a game changer. He knew it too. Like me, his body wasn't going to allow the all-out physical exertion any longer.

I thought it was a very cruel fate not only for myself but now my best friend.

My boy had been stricken with this curse that followed me since childhood.

Regardless of what I've been through during my lifetime and all that I've lost — and never had — due to these disorders and physical disability, nothing compares to the pain I feel watching someone I love suffering — be it a person or animal.

Mercifully, a couple months post that re-injury, we were back at the park.

He was once again happy-go-lucky, walking and (slowly) running on his own, limp and pain-free. The tail was once again non-stop wagging and that spark of life and pure joy came back to my boy's eyes.

Though we couldn't play fetch any longer, Max always had his favorite ball in his mouth and was still chasing — at a much slower pace — those birds!

Max was, like most dogs, a "bird bully". He would see a bird and begin a slow stalking, then break out into a full speed dash (prior to his last knee injury) while letting loose a deep, mean growl and bark (with the ball still in his mouth!). As the bird flew away from the "danger", Max, for a brief moment, felt like a lion — the king of the jungle. You could see it in his short-lived swagger. However, in reality, my boy was the biggest baby on the planet! He was afraid of his own shadow, quite literally! On more than one occasion, that bird didn't take to flight quick enough and Max would stop dead in his tracks and retreat. He didn't know what to do!

He's full of love. For people that is. He's not at all comfortable in the company of other dogs. When he meets someone, it's kisses, kisses, and more kisses. Right along with his powerful tail wags, butt rubbing against you, and pushing through the legs that could — and did — knock some people over.

I've always felt a deep sense of joy any time Max was playing. His pure happiness during our walks and playing fetch emanated and was highly contagious. Seems the only joy I've found throughout my life was always vicariously. Nonetheless, it soothed my soul knowing my boy was happy and healthy. That's all we can really hope for those we love. When one of those vital elements is missing, it causes me a very deep pain and distress and that is what I began to feel after Max's knee injury(s).

Max has always been the shadow that never left my side. Through thick and thin, always there, always my true friend, always encouraging me to carry on in his own special, canine way. There's nothing I wouldn't do to make sure my best buddy is happy and healthy.

🦋 🦋 🦋 🦋

Closing in on winter 2014, just as I was completing this story, Max made a mad dash one morning to chase the birds in the backyard. He once again — for the third time — hurt his left knee. So far, this time around, he doesn't seem to be in any pain (thankfully). However, he is limping more than the previous times and doesn't seem to be able to put as much pressure on the injured knee as he once did.

Round three has begun and I am continuing with the treatment and therapy that did the trick the first two times. It's still early into the re-injury. I'm keeping my fingers crossed and hoping that this time around he is able to once again heal and get back to walking, pain-free, and without a limp. Unfortunately, Max's days of running and chasing birds must come to an end.

He's getting up there in age now, and with a recurring injury, I will have to begin keeping him on a leash so he doesn't completely and irreversibly damage that knee and have everlasting pain and mobility issues like his daddy.

🦋 🦋 🦋 🦋

Once Max's knee injury was fully mended and there were no further mobility and pain issues, I fell back into that black hole of deeper depression, anxiety, and anger.

His pain and suffering had my undivided attention for several months.

I was still in a very bad place emotionally during that time. However, once I knew Max would be okay, every bit and then some of the emotional pain, suffering, and anger came back full-force and hit me like a Mack truck. It was accompanied by a full dose of loneliness that I'd been battling since Vegas and had been worsening for the past year and a half.

I hadn't been back to Rhode Island in several years. Severe emotional and physical pain or not, I needed to try and get back to Rhode Island to see my parents and hopefully some of my aunts, uncles, and cousins.

It felt as though this is what my soul was yearning for at this time in my recovery process. With the heightened anxiety, pain, and anger levels, I'd have preferred to drive the distance if it was a few hours away. However, there would be no way I could drive that distance — flying would be my only other option.

I needed to make sure Max was well cared for and able to stay in his own home the few days I'd be gone. I did a bit of research and found a professional pet sitter that lived up the street from me that would care for Max in my home for a few days during my trip.

I knew I wouldn't be able to do all the sitting and standing beyond a few hours with the average layover flights, so, a direct, non-stop flight would be the only way I could fly. And, those flights were few and far between out of PBI to Rhode Island. It took some time and patience, but I was able to get a direct, non-stop flight at the end of summer.

However, when that day came around, I was in no condition to travel and hadn't been fully mobile for several days. I was not only in excruciating physical pain; I was barely able to stand. There would be no way I could get on that plane and take that trip.

Making matters worse, commercial airline seats are horrible for anyone with a back and/or neck problem. If you're not in pain when you first sit, you will be very shortly!

Traveling by air would now become almost impossible, primarily due to my continually worsening spinal injury and mobility issues.

I was trapped yet again.

The ticket I had purchased was non-refundable but good for one year from the date of purchase. When spring and summer 2014 rolled around, I tried once again to get back to Rhode Island. Same situation once again. I was not able to physically take that flight.

Even the simplest of tasks were now becoming almost impossible.

I had been working on my emotional imprisonment issues through therapy and was making some progress, but my physical disability and mobility issues continued to worsen and kept me doing time.

No matter what or how hard I tried, whether in my past or my present life, even the best of scenarios always felt like one step forward and two steps backwards. Once again, I couldn't win for losing.

In an attempt to quell some of the ever-increasing physical and emotional pain, I began to concentrate a bit more on my meditating. I was also looking to try something new to possibly alleviate some of the inflammation and mobility issues. As far as supplements, I'd tried all of them claiming to reduce inflammation and pain. I didn't see any change in physical pain or inflammation with any but do believe there is some benefit from a concentrated form of Curcumin with a good absorption rate.

My therapist also suggested giving Egosque a try. I thought I was familiar with most forms of exercise out there, but I'd never heard of Egosque.

Egosque is a method of gentle, corrective exercises tailed for each client based on his or her structural misalignments. It is supposed to reduce or eliminate chronic pain by getting the posture back into balance and alignment, returning the body to proper function.

I met with the Egosque instructor and was evaluated based on my posture.

Some other factors — such as my spinal disability and pain levels — were also taken into consideration. I was given a group of exercises to perform each morning to correct my structural misalignment. I did these exercises prior to beginning my regular exercise regimen each morning.

I found that the combination of Egosque exercises performed over time did have a slightly positive effect on my posture and some areas of pain, such as my hips. A little bit of something is better than a whole lot of nothing. If it doesn't involve meds or surgery, I'll try whatever might ease the pain and mobility issues.

I have been incorporating the Egosque exercises into my morning meditation and exercise regimen ever since.

31

I was now one year into therapy — recovery — and had been feeling worse emotionally and physically with each passing month.

I was becoming more angry and had a "don't give a shit" attitude for some time about everything — including my therapy.

I had mixed emotions as I progressed through psychotherapy and my recovery process. I was slowly and painfully, week by week, month by month, peeling back the layers of trauma that had been my life.

I was learning so much detail and truth about myself, my family, the life of pain, suffering, and plain ole bad luck that I didn't ask for — trying desperately to process it all, have a final grieving and, for once, just leave it all behind for good.

It didn't work quite that way. It wasn't so simple.

Most times, the pain and anger was so deeply embedded in my soul and my very being that I began rebelling against the bitter, uprooted emotions brought to the surface by the very processes of therapy and writing this book.

Strangely enough, each of these two processes worked hand-in-hand in helping me to get through much of the darkness that had been my life. For me, I don't think therapy itself would have been as effective without the process of writing the book, and vice versa.

This entire first year — and many months thereafter — I felt as though this therapy, too, wasn't working. Why was I not feeling better emotionally but actually feeling worse?

I would learn over time that is how much of the therapy and recovery process works — at least that is how it played out for me.

I had to go through even more pain and darkness before there were glimmers of light. It gets worse before it gets better. The storms here come before the calm.

As is common with most recovery, every now and then, I would fall off the wagon so to speak. It would all get to be too much and I'd fall back into the old mind-set; the negative ways of thinking and feeling. That intense anger and pain, bitterness and hatred would wash over me like a sudden and violent thunderstorm. It could last for hours or for weeks. Just a pouring down and gushing out of all the deeply entrenched and built-up pain and anger.

I would almost always stay put — in my home — when I began feeling this way. Everything and everyone would irritate me. I was truly on edge and didn't want — or need — the trouble that could arise from such a boiling over of intense pain and anger. Oddly enough, that occasional regression is a normal part of the recovery process.

This intensity would continue as the 2013 holiday season approached. I dreaded the holidays as they caused a deeper, darker depression and a major elevation in my anxiety and panic attacks.

During this particular holiday season, that ferocious beast — loneliness — wouldn't leave my mind alone. It had been ominously stalking and tormenting me once again the past year. It was now triggering unimaginable, additional and persistent anxiety and panic attacks. I felt like the days of Vegas' death row were upon me once again.

I remember telling my therapist, JB, from the very beginning of therapy — from day one — and continually over the following months and to the present day, that the two things I needed to avoid at all cost but had no control over were:

1. Anxiety and panic attacks.
2. Becoming totally immobile/wheelchair bound.

I had a shot through therapy of better understanding and controlling to a certain degree the anxiety and panic attacks. However, there was — is — nothing I can do to prevent another accident from permanently crippling me.

Ironically, just that thought is a major cause of daily anxiety and, too often, panic attacks.

It would take nearly two years of therapy and learning from and dealing with the decades of repressed trauma, pain, and anger before I was able to begin changing my thought process for the better. Consequently, decreasing the frequency and intensity of the anxiety and panic attacks.

This 2013 holiday season happened to be the first time in over four years that my parents spent a bit of the holidays (Thanksgiving and Christmas) with immediate family — their grandson, Carlo, his wife, and their two children.

It was a good feeling knowing that my parents — especially my mother — were with their grandson and great-grandchildren, enjoying at least a portion of two special days this year. It provided me a bit of peace not having to worry about my mother and how she would be handling this holiday season.

With the 2014 New Year came the beginning of a noticeable sense of change for me emotionally. I began to feel slightly less weighted down by the trauma of the past.

Through therapy, which had been going on now for sixteen months, and writing this story, which had been in motion for fourteen of the past months, I was feeling a slight sense of peace in my soul as I'd never felt in all my years.

The pieces of my life's puzzle were beginning to fit. There were still pieces missing that I would eventually find and connect, but there was now much more clarity than any time in the past. I could clearly see just how bad it had been — and still was — and why. It was none of my doing. These were the cards I had been dealt.

As painful and as devastating to my life as all those Jokers in the deck had been, it was imperative to my sanity — any possible light in the future — to let the murky water continue to flow under the bridge and out of my mind and soul.

The only control I now had over the traumatic events and emotions of the past and the debilitating painful physical disability and predicament of the present was whether I allowed myself to continue to be controlled and destroyed by the pain and anger — the negativity — or learned to change my thought process (and outlook) to positivity.

It's not an easy task. Especially having to deal with not only the emotional trauma and pain since childhood and consistently throughout my life, but having to deal and live with an excruciatingly painful spinal disability and mobility issues for the past seventeen years that have only continued to worsen. That alone is a very hard pill to swallow. One that has been stuck — even through therapy and a recovery process — in my throat for a very, very long time.

I believe I would have progressed quicker and much more effectively if I didn't have to deal with two separate — emotionally and physically — but equally crippling disorders.

One always fueling the other and creating an almost impossible-to-win situation.

As was common throughout my life, there could be no signs of light without more darkness following closely behind.

Emotionally, I was beginning to feel a weight lifted and a sense of peace in my soul but, at this very same time, I began having new physical pain and mobility issues.

I can think of no injury worse than a spinal injury. It affects *every* part of the body and mind.

I could no longer lay on my side — fetal position — or on my stomach when trying to get my *normal* few hours of sleep each night. My spine had once again taken a turn for the worse. Laying and trying to get any sleep at all was now as painful as standing and sitting had been for years on end.

I'd been trying desperately to change my outlook and attitude to one of positivity — and I had been able to make progress to some degree — for well over a year at this point. I didn't want to feel like the victim any longer. I needed to leave all that pain, rage, and negativity in the past.

However, at this moment in time, in addition to the daily physical pain that was my normal, I had to deal with the fact that I was going to actually fear — more anxiety — trying to sleep at night as I knew what I was in for now; more pain, suffering, and anger just attempting to get a few hours sleep laying down.

When does this curse end?

When does the sun finally shine through that dark cloud that has hovered above me my entire life?

Are you even up there, God?

As soon as I had accepted, processed, and let go of bits and pieces of my past emotional trauma, I was being bombarded with new trauma that was causing an extreme amount of rage and more doubt about the whole therapy process.

The little bit of peace I had recently found in my soul was being tested. I knew it was there, I could feel it. On the other hand, I knew how very disappointed and angry I was having to constantly deal with new and additional physical problems, pain, and suffering.

I was being torn in two different directions; I was feeling a genuine sense of peace in my soul and at the very same time I was still cursing that Higher Power every minute of every day for the physical pain and suffering that continued to worsen in every way possible.

The cervical pain when laying has been horrible over the past eighteen years since the line of duty accident and has also, as my lower spine has, progressively worsened to the point that it has severely impacted my ability to get even a few hours of that "normal" sleep each evening.

The cervical damage is so fragile at this point in my life that the most minuscule of pressure from brushing my teeth causes more pain and irritation in this area.

When trying to sleep, I now have to lay with a particular feather/down pillow in order to adjust the contents to make a hollow for my head and be able to bunch the edge of the pillow to form a firm support for my neck so there is no bending whatsoever. My spine must be completely horizontal at the cervical section or it is impossible to sleep with the additional pain and discomfort.

The cervical pain and problems are just half of the nightmare.

Sleep is no longer possible in either the stomach or side positions, as this now causes excruciating lumbar pain — in addition to the cervical — when laying.

I now have to lay flat on my back with a pillow under my legs in order to sleep at all. This is the same method — laying completely flat on my back — that was necessary to write this entire story — every word of it — over the two-plus years it took to complete the first draft of the book.

It is very uncomfortable for me but the only way to get a couple hours sleep. It wasn't bad enough I hadn't slept more than a few hours on any given night for the past eighteen years. Now, I consider myself "lucky" if I get an hour or two and can lay there at all!

Force of habit and being very uncomfortable trying to sleep on my back with a pillow under my knees, I constantly try to move to a fetal position or on my stomach during the night but the increase in pain makes it impossible, forcing me to either get up for a while and stand or get right back into laying on my back with the pillow beneath my knees. And, this position isn't foolproof, either — I have nights when I can't sleep one wink.

My body (and mind) has somehow adapted to two to three hours sleep — a meditative state of rest — each evening over the past two decades. I'm not sure how much more sleep deprivation either that body or mind will be able to handle going forward.

The damage and degeneration in my spine has moved forward at a ridiculously fast pace and has become so viciously painful that I now have to lay down on my back — wherever I might be — to relieve the pain and pressure from standing or walking beyond fifteen minutes or so.

If sitting too long, I have to stand. This is the only way to relieve some of the pain and pressure that consistently builds throughout my cervical and lumbar spinal areas every minute of every day from doing nothing more than standing, sitting, walking, or laying. Add just about any other type of bending or twisting and it can be — and usually is — crippling to the point I cannot move for days.

One of the spinal doctors I'd recently seen said with regards to this progressive, irreversible deterioration; "*Ninety-year-old men don't have this kind of degenerative disease. You have some of the worst damage I've ever seen in a spine.*"

Additionally, now, when I roll out of bed, I am unable to stand upright immediately. I am hunched over in severe pain and it takes a good ten to fifteen minutes to get my spine erect once again and for the severe pain to subside enough so that I can move.

Each morning, I look like one of the slouched-over apes at the beginning of the human evolutionary chart!

My spine had always been stiff and painful whenever I rolled out of bed. However, this was now another level of stiff and pain.

Bottom line; while I work feverishly on improving my emotional well-being through acceptance and positive thought, I am being forcefully pulled back into a negative thought pattern controlled by rage and pain due to an ever-worsening physical disability.

It's an emotional tug-of-war with my sanity on the line.

Consequently, I continue to sacrifice my body in order to maintain the tiny bit of sanity I have remaining. Addiction to training — regardless of the minuscule amount I am still able to force upon my broken, pain-riddled body — will always be a part of who I am and the preferred method of quelling even the slightest amount of the emotional pain that has imprisoned my mind for decades.

I've lived with consistent, deep, crippling emotional pain my entire life.

I've lived with constant, excruciating, debilitating and ever-worsening physical pain for the past eighteen years.

Each of these pains takes a different toll on the body and mind.

Each creates a unique and devastating suffering.

Both emotional and physical pain existing together, for years on end, creates an exceptionally intense negative force of energy.

Each is a raging inferno consuming everything in its path.

Together these conditions are a volcanic eruption that is nearly impossible to contain.

Bringing each of these conditions/disorders — emotional and physical pain — independent of each other, under control and manageable without the use of medication, is very difficult.

Both of these conditions/disorders — emotional and physical pain — *together*, occupying and devouring the same body and mind, is like trying to control that volcanic eruption by water bombing it from above.

If there is any possibility whatsoever of containing that eruption — the combination and coexisting, consistent emotional and physical pain — I believe the human mind can do it.

Some bring strong faith and prayer into the work that has to be done. I'm not at that point. I'm still in the process of trying to reconnect with and regain faith in that (a) Higher Power.

I realized during the first year of my therapy and recovery process that the only way I could subdue that eruption without script medication was to learn to effectively control my thoughts and actions. Mind control.

If it's gonna be, it's up to me.

Whatever the mind can conceive and believe, it can achieve. Turning the negative thought to a positive thought. Channeling the negative energy to positive energy.

This would soon become a primary and crucial task of my recovery. The goal being to someday overcome — or, at the very least, keep in check and from erupting — both the emotional and physical pain, the suffering, and anger that has been my life throughout every step of this forty-five-year hellacious journey thus far.

Most of the first year of recovery I was learning about, understanding, and accepting my past while trying to rid my mind of all the anger and negativity associated with the traumas of yesterday.

I had been working on resetting and reprogramming my way of thinking — the thought process — as it pertained to the daily digging up and forever brewing grief of my past. It took all of that first year and then some before I even began to notice the slightest of difference.

It's been one step at a time, one day at a time. Learning once again to crawl before I could walk.

As I slowly and painfully waded through the recovery process, confronting head-on the decades of buried trauma, I began to understand, accept, finally grieve, and then, little by little, let go of the demons of the past.

I have found it to be of utmost importance and for the sake of my overall health and sanity to *let go* of those things that I have no control over.

Fast forward nearly a year and half into that process, I slowly began to turn some attention to and focus on changing my attitude about *the present*, applying what I'd learned about and practiced regarding acceptance, a final grieving, and letting go of yesterday's traumas and pains. An unfamiliar sense of peace began to fill my soul during this time frame (about 18 months in) of my therapy and recovery as this process — a surrendering — played out.

I've been a fighter since childhood. Always refusing to give up or to be beaten. Always standing up for who or what I believe in and what is right no matter the consequences. Surrendering to the pain, suffering, and anger that was my life for some forty-five years was actually, for me, the only possible option to keep that true grit in me alive, my sanity intact, and move to bring a fresh airflow into my collapsed lungs. It was similar to using psychology rather than the fists to get a point across. Mind over matter to some degree.

Surrendering loosened the stranglehold of PTSD and depression that controlled my life into isolation and near-insanity.

I no longer had to fight — every minute of every day — the demons that had ruled my world since the age of five.

It's an ongoing process and not every exorcism, so to speak, leaves the soul completely.

The pain and suffering associated with some trauma(s) takes more time than others to diminish or overcome. However, the few shackles that were removed from my soul beginning around January of 2014 gave me the bit of hope I needed to continue forward. It was far from total peace, but a few steps above and from the hell I'd endured for the past forty-five years.

It was progress in the right direction and I was, for once in my life, proud of myself.

I'd been running against the wind my entire life. It was now time to stop fighting my greatest enemy — myself. I needed to go with the flow of what I was now feeling — that bit of accomplishment and small victory over the decades of trauma and the rewarding, slight sense of peace in my soul.

I felt I now needed to begin to focus even more intensely on freeing my mind and soul of the pain, suffering and anger, the negativity and chains that molded my perception of life and dictated the entire course of that very life.

It was at this point of my recovery — the beginning of 2014 — that I began focusing more directly on incorporating my very own form of Mental Calisthenics into the process.

I realized that the past year-plus of trying to slowly reprogram my thought process was not impossible, but was certainly a very difficult endeavor as consistent pain, suffering, and anger had been deeply embedded for some 40-plus years.

I knew now that regardless of where I'd been and what I'd felt my entire life, I had to rid my mind of all the negativity and its self-destructive energy that enveloped me emotionally, physically, and spiritually.

Whatever thought one affirms is the thought that is empowered.

Thinking positively about today and tomorrow and attempting to bring harmony into my life would be essential to finding any form of happiness, meaning and peace as I moved forward.

The first twenty-five years of my life was intense, consistent physical training. I now had to transfer that dedication, determination, and discipline over to mental training for my very survival.

All of that discipline that created my physical temple had to be applied to re-creating a mind that would focus on the positive of today, in spite of all the horrors of the past and the pain of the present.

My physical temple may have crumbled but that discipline and dedication that built it lived on and will always be the core of who I am. It could now be applied to changing my thought process for the better as it related to my present and future.

In much the same way I spent hours a day, every day of my life for twenty-five years building a strong body through physical training, I would now apply the basics of that physical training to alter and strengthen my mind; Mental Calisthenics.

I began to repeat positive phrases over and over to myself;

"Things *will* get better."

"Things *will* begin to fall into place."

"It could be much worse."

"Stay positive."

"Focus on the all the beauty that surrounds you."

I was slowly replacing the decades-old phrases and thought process that had been a direct result of all the trauma and misfortune over the course of my life.

I began to realize that with each new day, I had a new chance.

4 Green Butterflies | 504

Where I decided to look is where I could actually go.

What I could see — conceive — is what I could be.

The key was to stay focused on the positive — and the repetition of positive thoughts.

Each and every time a negative thought would pop into my head, I had to emotionally kick its ass — knock it out of the thought process and replace that negative thought with a healthy, positive thought.

Emotional repetitions of positive thoughts. Beginning with one a day and increasing the volume as the mind accepts and absorbs the new positivity and change.

With this change slowly comes a clarity in outlook and strengthening of attitude.

One negative vibe at a time transformed to a positive.

Like the physical training that strengthened my muscles and core, mental calisthenics would be vital to strengthening my mind and guiding me from the decades of total darkness and imbalance.

This new attitude would determine my altitude.

I had been to and lived in every region of that underworld, my soul was longing for elevation, blue skies and freedom. I saw no other way I could overcome the torment of the past, the nagging pain and resounding despair of the present.

Make no mistake about it, this has been an extremely difficult undertaking while living with consistent and debilitating physical pain. That disorder alone is a very tough barrier to overcome — making it almost impossible to focus on anything *but* anger and negativity.

It has been more difficult overcoming the consistent physical pain barrier than the emotional pain barrier thus far. That is, as long as severe anxiety and panic attacks are not a fixed part of the daily emotional equation.

PTSD, depression, and chronic physical pain are battles fought every minute of every day. It can be very difficult — some days impossible — to feel or remain positive and optimistic. There are days when I fall off the wagon, as is common and expected with any form of recovery. I'm no different than any other person trying to overcome and recover.

I accept the bad days as being a normal part of my recovery. I eventually pick myself up and continue to work on having my thought process focus on the glass being half full rather than half empty. Slowly replacing the decades of negativity and pessimism with a new positivity and optimism. Realizing that the circumstances of my life tomorrow will be molded by my mental conduct of today.

Day by day, step by step, I'm learning to feel and to live in the present and for today.

Any time a negative thought enters my mind, I try to extinguish it immediately and replace it with a positive thought. I continue to work daily on leaving any lingering negativity and anger of yesterday behind. Allowing any of it to enter and control my thoughts robs me of yet another day and of any possibility of a peaceful tomorrow.

I trained my entire life bringing my mind and body together as one. Physically, every repetition of exercise strengthened my body and indirectly my mind. I did this every single day for hours on end for some twenty-five years.

Mental Calisthenics can do for my mind — and each one of us striving to overcome and heal — what physical training once did for my body. Practicing — repetition after repetition — positive thoughts to change the mind's chemistry from negative to positive and begin healing emotionally. Begin feeling grateful for the small gifts every day and stop wasting precious time and energy crying over spilled milk. On things I — we — cannot change and have no control over.

Change is very difficult. We are creatures of habit. Changing the thought process — especially after decades of living, feeling, thinking a certain way — is far from easy but is possible and necessary for survival sometimes.

I have feasted on inner grief, pain, and anger my entire life. It consumed my soul, my spirit, my entire being.

I can't change a physical disability that produces excruciating and crippling pain on a daily basis but I can change my attitude to begin an emotional healing process. It's the one and only thing I do have some control over in my predicament.

In looking back, and having the past couple years of therapy and a recovery process under my belt, I recognize that my life-altering accidents as well as the lifetime of trauma and bad luck could very well have been even worse. I am also aware that this reel is still in motion and the ending of this journey is mostly in my hands — and my mind.

It took over forty years of falling into this hole — this darkness — this way of life. It's safe to assume climbing out isn't going to happen overnight. But with discipline, dedication, and determination on my side, little by little I'm feeling that sense of peace slowly and warmly moving through my veins, opening my eyes, and reshaping my mind.

32

My mother came down to Florida the beginning of 2014 to spend her birthday and a few weeks with me.

It was the first time in decades I actually felt a little at ease and was looking forward to perhaps seeing other family members with her this time around.

The slight boost in my optimism and positivity was the result of the Mental Calisthenics I'd been focusing on as well as being able to overcome some of the demons of my past during the preceding nearly year and a half of therapy and recovery.

I felt as though I was for once in my life beginning to see the light — literally and figuratively. I was beginning an emotional rebirth of sorts. Finally, on that road to *Shambala* ... and raising my consciousness to a higher level.

My mother and I were invited to my cousin Pina's house one evening in March 2014. My aunt, uncle, and some family friends were coming up and wanted us all to get together. I had passed on all invitations over the many years, including the last time my parents were in Florida one year earlier.

I was still a bit apprehensive about being around groups of people which always triggered anxiety and panic attacks. I spent my life in isolation to avoid those horrific attacks. However, at this time in my life, I had been focusing on changing my mind-set and thought process, concentrating on the positive, and slowly beginning to emerge from that cocoon that protected me my entire life from further anxiety and pain.

I struggled with the decision to go or not right up until the very last minute. I knew I wouldn't be able to make any progress towards light and balance remaining in that protective cocoon any longer. I told myself if I began to have anxiety attacks in the presence of family and friends, I would, for once in my life, reveal the truth and explain where I'd been — the isolation — the past thirty-plus years and why; PTSD, major depression, and anxiety/panic attacks keeping me in that seclusion.

It was time in my life to lay my cards on the table — eye to eye.

I had begun that process months earlier by contacting my good friend Honey D and cousin Bruno by email and having my mother hand out the first draft introduction section to this very book to some of my aunts, uncles, and cousins.

My mother and I did go to my cousin's house that evening.

It was the first time in almost twenty years that I had seen my aunt and uncle.

It was the first time in thirty years that I sat among family and friends in a social setting.

It was a first step towards light after decades of crawling in complete darkness.

I felt a bit anxious a few times during this family get-together but kept thinking positive — repeating positive phrases (in my mind) and staying focused on conversation.

I found myself revealing bits and pieces of my truth here and there — my life as it played out since childhood.

The more of my truth I could get out there for all to hear and see — especially the family I cared so deeply for and hadn't seen in decades — the more I began to feel those chains slowly being removed from my soul.

It all worked out in the end. I got through the socializing with minor anxiety but without an attack. I was a little uneasy with minor sweating but, thankfully, I wasn't visibly dripping buckets of water from my face and body as had been the case throughout the past forty years whenever in the spotlight or among groups of people.

I left that evening with a sense of accomplishment and a new beginning.

I did, however, in the days to come, think often of that particular night and all I'd missed in my family over the past few decades. Most importantly, that family bond that grows stronger through the years of coming up with and being a fixed part of the (family) unit.

I couldn't help but think what a friggin' number PTSD, depression, anxiety, and isolation had done to my life. I wallowed in the pain for a few days, then I immediately switched modes to positive thoughts and was thankful not only for making it through the evening relatively anxiety free and able to move physically, but for the opportunity to finally begin anew.

Outside of my therapy sessions, I'd begun to open up and reveal portions of my life-long pain and suffering more these past few months than I'd done combined the past few decades.

I felt I was on my way — finally accepting those cards I'd been dealt and moving in the right direction. I was slowly surrendering to the truth of my life. No longer feeling that overwhelming weight of shame and the additional pressure and stress of always hiding that truth.

I had started a process of peeling back that mask I'd worn and that protected me the past thirty-five years.

I began discussing my emotional and physical pain with a few people here and there. Mostly older, retired people that I came to know through the clubhouse gym in my neighborhood. Many of whom had physical pain and mobility issues of their own as well as suffered with depression. I found it to be very comforting speaking with others who walked in the same shoes — who understood the emotional and physical pain and how it negatively affects every aspect of your life.

It was another of those strange but welcome feelings knowing that many I shared my pain with really got it.

I would almost always hear the same comments when discussing my pain;

"You'd never know looking at you."

"You hide your pain very well."

Looks can be very deceiving. And practice makes perfect. I had thirty-five years to build and perfect that facade. Thirty-five years' experience in protecting myself from others seeing and knowing my pain, suffering, and despair. I had been in survival mode since childhood. No one knew the psychological fragility that lay beneath that mask I created over three decades ago.

However, this was now the beginning of a new chapter in my life. Slowly peeling off that protective layer and revealing my truth. Not only to aid in the healing of my soul — catharsis — but to eventually be able to help others heal theirs as well.

I was becoming even more convinced of the benefits *Group Therapy* and *Group Meetings* could have for those of us suffering with these disorders — most of us alone, in silence, in the shadows, stifled by the stigma attached to such disorders as PTSD, depression, and anxiety.

It doesn't help those of us struggling with these disorders that we live in a culture where emotional disorders are not discussed — they are swept under the rug and kept mum.

People are forthcoming about struggles with such conditions as heart disease and cancer, talking openly and receiving support and understanding. Disorders such as PTSD, depression, and anxiety are a dark secret.

I felt in my heart that once I completed this book and was able to get my story out there to help others, I would begin focusing on creating these very group therapy meetings — paralleling how Bill Wilson and Dr. Bob Smith began AA in 1935 — for those of us suffering with and overwhelmed by emotional and/or physical pain. Coming together to discuss our pain and compassionately supporting each other can alleviate suffering and save lives.

Socialization is one thing that PTSD, depression, and anxiety takes from those of us suffering with these disorders.

However, there is strength and healing being among and able to speak with and listen to others who suffer emotionally and physically as you do. Who walk in those very shoes. Who intimately understand the ongoing battle to get through another day.

One thing that made my life and my recovery much more difficult was the fact that these disorders controlled me into isolation and, aside from my current therapist of the past couple years, I had no one to talk to or to lean on who understood my pain and suffering. I never had. My mother was *always* there for me. During this time as well. However, as a man — especially a man whose world was controlled and being destroyed by these disorders — there are situations and feelings that cannot be shared with your mother.

I firmly believe — I know to be true — that having an understanding and compassionate significant other, a close friend, or support group to talk with, help pick you up or get you over a hump occasionally, makes a crucial difference in the lives of those of us afflicted with these disorders.

For many years I have felt there should be widespread and accessible support groups — group therapy meetings — for people suffering with PTSD, depression, anxiety and chronic physical pain. Support groups similar to and as readily available as AA meetings.

I shared my thoughts and vision about this with my therapist, JB, beginning the first week of my therapy back in Sept 2012. How I firmly believed that a group therapy setting for those of us suffering with such disorders as PTSD, depression, anxiety, and chronic physical pain would be very beneficial and a lifesaver in many ways.

I had brought this up to JB quite often throughout our one-on-one therapy sessions. She was interested and said she'd look into the possibility.

It took a year and half of my nagging her but she did come through and finally put together the very first group therapy session on March 26th, 2014. There would be six of us in this particular group with our therapist, JB, overseeing and guiding us.

For the past seven months, as of this writing, group therapy sessions have taken place every two weeks for ninety minutes per session. This particular group therapy meeting is a *closed* therapy session. Meaning, we started with six members and agreed to keep it at six — closed to any new members joining the group — so that all involved could become more comfortable and familiar with each other and the sessions could be a more intimate, open atmosphere of close-knit members.

It is of utmost importance that you are comfortable in the group setting and with all its members and have faith in the therapist that is leading that group or making any progress towards healing — recovery — is unlikely.

If after a few meetings you are not comfortable — don't feel emotionally safe — with certain members of the group or, quite frankly, don't have faith in the ability of the leader/therapist, you will not benefit from that particular group or setting.

If this is the case, you should immediately find another group (or therapist) in which all the pieces fit and you feel emotionally comfortable, ready, willing, and able to support and be supported.

You must feel in your heart and know in your gut that the group therapy setting is a safe place for you to open up and share with understanding and compassionate members or it will not be beneficial to your healing and growing — your recovery process.

My plan post publication of this book is to focus my time and energy on organizing both open group therapy meetings (where walk-ins are welcome and available to all) and closed group therapy meetings throughout the U.S.

The goal is to make open group therapy sessions available and easily accessible to any and all who suffer with emotional and/or physical pain and would like an emotionally safe place to go to give and/or to receive support and encouragement from others who walk in their very shoes. No one truly understands these disorders better than those of us who suffer in their stranglehold each and every day and live the nightmare.

I believe with all of my heart that these type group therapy sessions — bringing together those of us suffering emotionally and/or physically, who are ready, willing and able to be a part of a compassionate and supportive, healing group dynamic — can and will improve and save lives.

It is reassuring and inspiriting being among others who live firsthand your very pain and suffering. Knowing you're not alone any longer. No one is judging or criticizing. There is a genuine comprehension of and validation for the pain and suffering that each of us have in common.

Through considerate communication amongst group members, each person is able to receive and/or offer compassionate support, help to ease each other's pain, comfort and begin to heal our own aching souls.

Open and closed group therapy meetings are something I envision growing throughout the United States, in every major city, where those of us suffering can come together in a safe environment and discuss our pain and sorrow and receive unconditional support in return.

It is something that needs to happen more than ever before.

I know that if something like this existed and I was aware of it during my darkest days, I would have attended and quite possibly might have been spared from a further descent into the abyss.

Every thirteen minutes in this country someone takes their life.

Suicide — depression — is among the top ten causes of death in the U.S.

The underlying common denominator of most all addiction and suicide — from my childhood Idol, the king of rock, Elvis Presley, to one of the greatest comedic minds ever, Robin Williams, who, ironically, passed as I was writing this very chapter the summer of 2014, and the thousands upon thousands of common folk every year that we hear nothing about — is consistent, unbearable, and extreme emotional and/or physical pain.

That deep-seated anguish is severe *depression* in a nutshell.

Ultimately, it is hopelessness (about our circumstances) that drives people over that ledge to take their very lives.

Over 90% of all people who commit suicide share one or more of the emotional disorders I've discussed throughout this story.

However, the commonality and number one cause of suicide is untreated depression.

Talking about your feelings — be it via group therapy, a therapist, or a trusted friend — will usually prove very beneficial in helping a person suffering with depression and may very well get that person over a hump that otherwise could lead to leaping from that ledge.

I have believed in the power of group therapy for those of us suffering emotional disorders long before I was instrumental in putting our first group therapy session together in March of 2014.

Actually being a part of that healing support system for over six months as of this writing, I am looking forward to doing my part in bringing these groups and this opportunity to fruition for each one of us who suffers immeasurable and undeviating pain and despair each and every day of our lives. I feel it is part of my calling and my meaning on this earth.

Noticeable transformation was now taking place around this time in my life. I started coming out of that cocoon and feeling a bit more comfortable in my own skin.

I would get together with my cousins every now and again as well as a couple guys from the neighborhood. We'd grab something to eat or just shoot the shit for a while.

It was (slowly) getting a bit easier to be around people as time went on and I learned more about myself, the disorders that controlled my mind throughout my life, and my mind-set and outlook gradually became more positive through mental calisthenics.

Summer 2014 had arrived and one of my cousins, Lia, who I hadn't seen in over thirty-five years was coming down with her husband of the past few decades, *Domenic*, and her daughter, *Jenna*, as well as my cousin Pina's daughter, *Ellie* — all of whom I had never met — to spend time with my cousins in the area.

Lia wanted to see me when she came down. She had read the first draft introduction section of this book many months earlier and was now slightly familiar with my lifelong plight and why I hadn't been around family for several decades.

Once again, I found myself quite anxious leading up to the get together at my cousin Pina's house just around the corner.

After over forty years of keeping away from groups of people, family, and friends due to the disorders and anxiety attacks that kept me in isolation most of my life, I knew, once again, I had to show up for this get together in order to keep progressing in my recovery — moving away from that stranglehold of the past and moving towards additional peace in my soul and light in my life.

Through mental calisthenics throughout the week leading up to our get together, I was able to turn all the negative thoughts and fear into a positive. I did, however, struggle once again right up to the very last minute but was able to move past the lingering fear and anxiety and show up.

It was a truly warm and exhilarating feeling being able to see — and finally meet — members of the family I have loved and missed so very much over the decades of oppressive emotional imprisonment that shackled me into isolation and away from everyone that ever meant anything to me.

We all sat around the table in the way of traditional Italian culture; intimately conversating with plenty of food, drink, and Italian pastries to enjoy.

I discussed at this time in much more detail where I'd been and what I'd been through over the many decades no one had seen or heard from me. The reasons behind my disappearing act and fading into obscurity.

It was the deepest I'd gotten with anyone outside of therapy sessions discussing my pain and suffering, my anxiety, and isolation over the past four decades — the disorders and misfortunes from childhood throughout my adulthood.

There were a couple uncomfortable spots for me, but, most importantly, I didn't have an anxiety or panic attack.

I was on my way to recovering and possibly getting back a bit of the past — the family time and the "normal" — that had eluded me my entire life.

One more step in the right direction.

Once again, I was revealing my truth, overcoming the long-standing anger, pain, and shame I had felt my entire life and was moving forward with my recovery one step and one conversation at a time.

Little did anyone know, this was the beginning of a major part of my recovery process. My blending back into family — into society — and tasting a bit of that *normal* I'd never really known during a lifetime of battling demons and isolation.

33

Awareness: Recovery for me began with awareness.

I always knew from very early childhood that something just wasn't right with me emotionally. I felt different. I wasn't happy like the other kids. I didn't fit into that world.

I had no idea — there was no awareness — just how severely the traumatic events beginning in my childhood and continuing throughout my life had affected my ability to live a normal life.

Once I found my current therapist, JB, I was able to begin peeling back — digging up and becoming totally aware of — the layers of trauma that began when I was five-years-old and subjected to witnessing alcohol and drug abuse within my home.

As a child, I had seen things I didn't want to see. I had felt things I didn't want to feel. One traumatic event after another for years on end.

This is where it all began — and the trauma from all angles would only continue to pile on throughout my life, deepening the emotional disorders that controlled that existence while burying in my crushed and tormented soul years upon years — decades — of pain, anger, and despair right along with any chances of *normal* I ever had.

My training became the medicine — the escape — that was necessary for my very survival. In much the same way the alcoholic or addict reaches for the bottle, pill, or needle to get rid of the pain that is buried in the soul and just too much to bear.

Most all addiction is an escape — an outlet — from the underlying pain and despair that we are unable to *accept*, process, and let go.

Acceptance: I had to first rewind to childhood and peel back all those layers of trauma — uncover all of the demons — that had consistently tormented every fiber of my being as far back as I could remember. Trauma that kept me grieving every minute of every day, my entire life.

In order to begin a recovery process, I had to go through a once and for all, final grieving process that had been bypassed for decades.

Once I had exposed — identified — the underlying problems and became *aware* of these core issues that were causing such overpowering pain and anger, I had to *accept* and face each demon head on.

The battle had to be fought and won from the inside. No fists, only the mind.

I began accepting and addressing all the unfinished business —

this very story a major, therapeutic component in my recovery process — one traumatic event at a time, in its entirety.

One by one, one step at a time, understanding each layer, each instance of trauma, processing it, accepting it, surrendering to it, and letting go of these unresolved issues of pain and anger that had been consuming my every thought — destroying my mind — since childhood.

Some easier than others. Some I am still working on. Some I may always be working on.

Whether we are recovering from traumatic events in our lives as with PTSD and depression or recovering from addiction as with alcohol and drug abuse — the steps and process of that recovery may be a bit different for each of us — the goal is the same; *Balance*. Finding peace and harmony within our lives.

We're all broken in one way or another. Though some of us give Humpty Dumpty a run for his money!

Finally becoming aware of, understanding, and accepting all the buried trauma of my past and the reality of my present allowed me to move forward. This is the beginning of a recovery process. In my case, from a lifetime of unfluctuating trauma.

Acceptance is followed by growth.

Signs of peace and healing began to follow as I surrendered (let go), one traumatic event at a time, to the constant anguish that spanned over four decades.

I began to open my heart and allow it to breathe.

I finally accepted myself and my present circumstances and was being set free.

It is imperative to identify and accept the underlying trauma in order to change for the better. Otherwise, as had been my case for nearly forty-five consistent years, unresolved trauma slowly destroys a person from the inside out. It literally eats you alive — devouring your mind, body, and soul through these very disorders, addictions, or, ultimately, death.

Recovery is, to me, about stopping — or greatly decreasing the intensity of — our pain and feeling better emotionally. Adding light to the darkness. Balance to the scale of life.

Balance being the ultimate goal of recovery.

Through recovery, I am learning — with each step and each day — how to deal with today's pain and with over forty years of an agonizing crucifixion, an entire existence of torment and despair. Events that ripped the child from my childhood and left me completely void and lost as an adult.

Fighting, screaming, and angry as hell some days, I am learning to accept the reality of my life and present day situation — one feeling at a time, one day at a time. It often gets worse before it gets better. And, I can't stress enough, there *are* those days when I (all of us recovering) fall off the wagon and begin to think negatively, doubting everything — regressing back into the counterproductive thought process, total despair, and intense anger that ruled my life for decades.

When these days come about, more than ever I focus on mental calisthenics — positivity and what is good in my life.

Practicing an attitude of gratitude.

Letting go of the negative energy. Allowing it to leave my body and mind, replacing it with positive thought(s) and hope.

I have earned my Ph.D. several times over regarding these disorders and their complete control and decimation of *life*.

These disorders of the mind as well as chronic physical pain are a nightmare like no other.

Recovery is far from a walk in the park. But it *is* within reach.

Clarity of mind and peace within the soul is achievable for *each* of us and worth fighting through the additional pain and discomfort of confronting the buried and brewing trauma(s) that caused the emotionally paralyzing agony and despair in the first place.

The tiniest bit of light on that unfamiliar other side can be blinding at first, but it is that light that those of us recovering must continue to move towards. It is the very essence of recovery — of life — the awareness, acceptance, and peace that allows us to be balanced and free.

Light can be found in being comfortable with and able to confide in a trusting and understanding friend, family member, therapist, or within a group therapy setting among others who walk in our very shoes.

Compassionate support illuminates and makes a world of difference in the lives of those of us suffering with these disorders.

There are few things, if any, more important and beneficial in this recovery process than simply knowing that you are not alone, there is someone who understands and validates your pain and suffering, supports you, and is willing to help you navigate through the darkness and despair that is each and every one of these disorders.

🦋

Quite often throughout the years and during our conversations, from childhood to this day, my mother would always tell me that all she wanted for me — her wish and what she prayed for — was for me to find happiness.

One conversation that has always resonated with me was a call from my mother when I was living in Las Vegas during the worst years of my life. She wanted to know if I'd heard the new song, *My Wish*, by her favorite country music group, Rascal Flatts. "*Of course*", I responded. "*That's a beautiful song, I wish I'd written it*!"

She told me that she thinks of me every time she hears that song. She wanted me to know that *My Wish* was *her wish* for me.

Needless to say, every time I hear that song, I get very emotional, my eyes tear up, and I realize how very important it is for me to make that *wish* of my mother's a reality.

There is one song in particular that spoke volumes to me as a child and never more loudly than this very day — at this particular time in my life. A song that has always reminded me of my mother and her wish for me.

That song touches my soul in a deep, spiritual way, calling to mind the one person on this earth — my mother — who has inspired me through all the darkness that has blanketed my world.

She was my reason then and is my passion today for existing and moving forward to do my part in this lifetime.

That song is *Let It Be* by the Beatles. Written in 1969 by two of the most prolific and successful songwriters of all time, Paul McCartney and John Lennon.

This is a song that, today, for me, is a guiding light of hope.

Slowly, through therapy and a recovery process, I am learning to *Let it be ...*

There will be an answer ... Let it be ... Whisper words of wisdom ... Let it be.

That *answer* is this very story and my ability at this particular time in my life to help others from or from going to that diabolical darkness that is each and every one of these disorders.

The crux of my prayers from childhood was peace, health, and happiness for myself and all others. The nucleus of my wish — as well as my mother's wish for me — will be realized with my ability to bring awareness to these disorders and to help others from or from going to that infernal, intangible yet fully restraining prison cell where I've languished the past forty-five years — every minute of every day — in solitary confinement.

Somehow having been guided through this four-decades-long war with consistent pain, suffering, and despair, I have found a candle to illuminate not only my darkness but, it is my hope and goal, some of the darkness of others.

My meaning being the light I can now shed on these disorders and what needs to be done to ease and overcome our individual daily battles and, together, have a significant impact on the war against these wicked emotional conditions.

I've come to realize — the enlightenment — through my recovery process that it's not about how I started this life, it's about how I will finish it.

Where I look, I will now go. What I think upon, will now grow.

I'm learning from yesterday and leaving behind — letting go of — that traumatic past that I've come to accept, focusing on what I know I can do to make a difference in peoples' lives today, and laying the groundwork for a tomorrow where those of us suffering with these disorders are no longer alone, in the shadows, and stigmatized.

A world where those of us suffering debilitating emotional and/or physical pain can come together and support each other, heal, and recover together.

My hope is that this story and book serves as a platform — a springboard — that brings awareness to and understanding of these disorders while allowing me the opportunity to start across the U.S. — and bring to the forefront — group therapy meetings for those of us living and suffering with disorders such as PTSD, depression, anxiety, and chronic physical pain.

As the late, great Sam Cooke sang, *"It's been a long, long time coming, but I know a change gonna come."*

My mother has always felt a special affinity for butterflies. She has always surrounded herself with butterflies. Not the live butterflies, of course, but butterfly magnets on the refrigerator, butterflies affixed to mirrors and windows, butterfly pins and pendants, pictures of butterflies everywhere.

Butterflies have always made my mother smile. Brought joy to her soul.

Strangely enough, after nearly forty-five years of being trapped — emotionally imprisoned — and isolated within my cocoon, I have finally, through my recovery process, begun that *change* — my final *transformation* into that butterfly.

A green butterfly, in fact.

A change. A transformation. A rebirth. A resurrection. A transition through which I have felt profound changes within my soul and mind and now have a sense of meaning and purpose, desire and drive, as I've never experienced throughout all of my years.

From a lifetime of perpetual darkness and complete imbalance, I am emerging to a glimmer of Light — understanding, meaning, peace within my soul, freedom. Given wings to guide me to that Light and purpose for reaching and spreading that Light to others whose tunnel of complete blackness seems impassable.

34

It was the first week of July, 2014. I was feeling a bit upbeat as I was slowly nearing the completion of the first draft of this very story.

I had been dealing with a heavy load of added anxiety for nearly two years to this point battling one steady, reverberating negative thought that idled in the back of my mind; that something would happen and I would never be able to complete this story and move forward to fulfill that dream and meaning in my life of helping others from or from going to the depths of hell I have existed in my entire life.

Having that door slammed shut in my face at the very last minute is how my life played out since childhood. Any real chance of sunshine entering that darkness was always zero and none. Why should this time be any different?

My mother had gone for her annual checkup a week earlier. She underwent routine testing and additional scans of the stomach area. Her doctors — lifelong, caring, professional, and very competent doctors who care deeply for my mother — have always kept a close eye on her bowel condition as my mother has had severe intestinal problems since she was a child.

My mother, now eighty-seven-years-old, and still very independent, takes herself to her doctor appointments. She doesn't have a "daughter" or any immediate family to rely on or that are there for her, with the exception of Nina, her current therapist — or, as my mother calls her, her angel.

My mother received a call from one of her doctors who attempted to explain a concern found during this most recent checkup. She wanted her to come back the following week.

My mother has always had the attitude that she really doesn't care, good news or bad news — she feels *fine* and that's all that matters.

I asked her to have Nina go with her to the appointment the following week so I could get a better understanding of what was going on.

Nina sees my mother every couple of weeks at my mother's home, calls often to check up on her, helps her out in any way she can, and has always been there for my mother over the past four and half years. They have become very, very close during that time.

I had spoken to Nina prior to my mother's follow-up appointment and asked that she contact me to let me know exactly what the concern was regarding my mother's checkup results the prior week.

Nina did go with my mother to the follow-up appointment and did contact me immediately following that appointment.

It was this day that I learned my mother had been diagnosed with an abdominal aortic aneurysm (AAA) approximately twice the size of the normal abdominal aorta.

This hit me like a ton of bricks. There had only been a few other times in my life that I had been impacted so intensely by emotional pain, worry, and fear. I came closest to death each of those times than any other times in my life.

This time, however, my mother's mortality was staring me square in the face — and I had nowhere to run. I knew I had to face this and, somehow, try to accept it, process it, and "let it be".

However, I was completely crushed emotionally like I'd never been in all my years of darkness. My stress and anxiety levels soared out of control. I fell back into the negative thought pattern and the anger and hatred for that Higher Power of my childhood was brewing up once again. I felt an extraordinarily violent rage inside that pushed me to a very frightening place of near-breaking. I can only assume this is a place where those people who *snap* go right before they act upon that intense and overpowering anger that is boiling through their veins and readying for the explosion.

If there was *any* individual responsible for my mother's condition at this time, and I was able to get to him, I no doubt would have put an end to his days. However, there was no one to confront and not a damn thing I could do about it. I was powerless ... but for how I could wrap my mind around this reality — this truth — and deal with it.

I physically crumbled to the ground that day and for many of the days that followed.

With everything I'd been through in my life, I'd never been so shaken, so beaten emotionally.

My mother's health and well-being is my Achilles' heel. My Kryptonite.

Nothing could have prepared me for the extraordinary emotional pain and anxiety — the overwhelming feelings of despair and suffocation around the clock for weeks on end.

I've taken some hits in my life — both physically and emotionally — I'd never been hit that hard.

This was the most devastating blow of my life to date. The absolute worst news I'd ever been confronted with.

However, as only that blueprint of my life, Murphy's Law, would have it — as every past experience throughout my life regarding *luck* had proven — if it could go wrong and get worse, it would. And it certainly did once again and for the absolute worse in the few months that followed.

I spoke with my mother that evening after I did some research on her condition. I broke down several times while speaking with her. I pleaded that she cut back on her smoking, stop stressing so much, and start relaxing and taking care of herself — no one else.

She had spent her entire life worrying about and caring for everyone but herself. The enemy now was her smoking and high blood pressure from her constant worry and stress — most of the stress at this point in her life due to her own children and grandchildren betraying her as well as her having to endure the tension and anxiety of living with my father.

I asked her to stop the housework and some other activities that kept her lifting and bending — these habits and activities, as well as her constant cooking, kept her mind occupied and relieved some of the stress. A double-edged sword now. She couldn't afford to stress or strain any longer. It was now a matter of life and death.

Part of recovery is learning to forgive. It is said to be the strongest of medicines.

I'd been in therapy and recovering now for almost two years. While I'd forgiven most, there were others — immediate family members specifically — I couldn't find a place in my heart to forgive. The way they'd treated my mother was simply unforgivable in my world. I didn't dwell any longer on the pain and anger they'd caused me and the additional trauma to my life for what they'd done to my mother — I had *let it be* and *let it go*.

However, at this particular time, my mind was oscillating wildly but leaning far to the left with anger and negative thoughts no matter how desperately I tried to bring the pendulum back to the center and off to the right to focus on the positive.

This was the most intense rage I'd ever felt in my life. If these people were dead, I'd have spit on their graves. I would have taken pleasure in watching them burn in hell for what they'd done to my mother. Not one of these heartless animals was there for her.

My mother and I discussed her coming to Florida to spend the holidays. I initially didn't want my father to come but, after speaking with my mother and her explaining to me that my father was becoming more depressed with each passing month, I decided to go back on my promise to myself to never have both of my parents visit and stay together with me again.

It had been torture for me each and every time I was under the same roof with both of them — from childhood to the very last time they (both) visited and stayed with me two years earlier.

I set a boundary that last time they visited me and swore I'd never do it again.

However, with both of my parents nearing ninety-years-old and health issues mounting, I decided that I'd have my father come with my mother as it may very well be the last time I see either of them.

I spoke with my father and told him he wasn't allowed to drink (alcohol) in my home. Period.

As I told him last time he stayed with me over the 2012/2013 holiday season, I wasn't dealing with the bullshit any longer. It was bad enough without the alcohol fueling the toxic atmosphere that was created when both of them were together and under the same roof.

I went ahead and arranged to have my father's car transported to Florida as well as purchased my parents' flight tickets for the second weekend in November — the earliest they could leave Rhode Island as each had a few more doctor appointments through that first week.

No sooner than they were packed and a little over one week out from that flight — the last couple of days in October 2014 and as I was closing in on finishing this story — my mother began having severe pain in her stomach. It was a Thursday evening, October 30th, 2014.

The pain, strangely enough, was only severe any time she would lay down. She was unable to sleep for several days, even with the prescription sleep meds she had been taking for the past four and half years since her near nervous breakdown at the hands of her children and grandchildren.

She has had a lifetime of colon problems — diverticulitis, colitis, and a host of other serious bowel disorders and diseases. She had also been diagnosed several months earlier with the abdominal aortic aneurysm — and this was excruciating pain in her lower right abdomen area.

Still, my mother refused to go to the hospital and decided to wait a few days from that Thursday to see if the pain would subside.

My mother didn't tell me of this until the following Sunday, November 2nd, 2014. She never wanted me to know her pain and to worry. We are two peas in a pod, right down to keeping our pain — and subsequent worrying — from each other. I insisted she call her primary care doctor, *Dr. Floriana*, first thing the next morning, Monday the 3rd. She agreed and my worst fears and a nightmare like I hadn't lived in all my decades of darkness began that very week.

She went in to see Dr. Floriana — by herself — that first Monday of November 2014. The doctor was baffled by the lower right quadrant pain that was only present when my mother was laying down.

My mother had a physical exam, blood work, and was scheduled for an ultrasound scan the following day.

She was a nervous wreck as she hadn't been able to sleep beyond a few hours for the past several days and the stress of the health issues was taking its' toll.

The bad news began late that Monday with the results of the ultrasound;

It showed spots on her liver and the base of her lungs.

Her doctor immediately ordered a CT scan of her upper chest/lungs the very next day. My mother was still having none of it. She didn't want to continue with *any* tests.

Her doctor asked her if it would be okay to speak with me.

Doctor Floriana called me that evening and explained she was very concerned the spots may be cancer and wanted to do more evaluation — and treatment if possible — beginning with the CT scan the following morning.

Dr. Floriana explained to me that if the CT scan showed more lesions in the upper lungs, she believed it to be cancer but needed to do a biopsy of the liver to confirm — as opposed to a biopsy of the lungs which was far more dangerous, all things considered.

I explained everything to my mother and told her I would support whatever she decided to do. Whatever she felt in her heart she wanted or didn't want to do about this finding and the impact to her mind and body in possibly fighting what could be an imminently life-threatening condition and situation.

I did ask, however, for me, that she at the very least go ahead with the CT scan of the upper chest/lungs the next morning.

My mother agreed but insisted, regardless of whatever the results of that CT scan were, she was getting on that plane Saturday the 8th of November and coming to Florida to spend the holiday season and her birthday with me while she still felt good and was able. She would "deal with it" when she returned to Rhode Island.

Dr. Floriana called me back that afternoon with the results of the upper chest/lung CT scan. The news couldn't have been worse. There were large lesions in her upper lungs consistent with cancer.

Dr. Floriana suggested a liver biopsy be done immediately — the next day.

Regardless of my and the doctor's conversations with my mother regarding the test findings, scan results, and the doctor's opinion, my mother was still having none of it — she wasn't going to do any further tests.

I discussed this with her doctor. Her doctor knew my mother was hell-bent on coming to Florida but didn't want my mother to stay the four months until March.

Dr. Floriana felt it was of utmost importance for my mother to continue with the testing and treatment options, if any, sooner rather than later. Dr. Floriana told me that we should try and get my mother back to Rhode Island to continue with the tests and any possible treatments immediately post the New Year at the very latest.

Dr. Floriana explained to me that my mother's cancer had spread from her lungs to her liver, and more than likely to other areas and organs. Further tests were needed to determine those other areas and if there were any treatment options possible at this stage. The doctor then told me, not in so many words, and being as tactful as possible, that my mother didn't have very long to live. Unable to contain my grief, shaking uncontrollably in the midst of a panic attack, and barely able to put two words together as I was crying like a baby, I pushed the doctor for a time frame. Dr. Floriana said that my mother would probably not make it beyond another year at most.

I've never in my life felt such sudden and overwhelming emotional pain and emptiness, despair and helplessness. Pure anger. I could feel everything in and about me change at that very second. I would *never* be the same person again.

I passed the doctor's concern along to my mother — minus the fact that the doctor implied that she didn't have long to live, which I know my mother already knew in her heart — and continued to discuss a time frame and possible options with her. Her mind was made up. She didn't care what was going on inside of her, she wasn't undergoing further testing at this time, wasn't going to be biopsied or cut open, and wasn't undergoing any treatment — especially chemotherapy — that was going to make her even more sick at her age.

I needed to support her decision — and I did — whatever that may be, whenever that may be.

She opted to get on the plane that coming Saturday and spend the holidays with me — in what will most likely be our last Thanksgiving and Christmas together.

I tried desperately to remain strong. However, I found myself breaking down continuously throughout the days and nights awaiting her arrival. This would also continue post her arrival.

I would wake — after getting an hour of sleep (on a good evening) — sweating, shaking, and crying.

I have been beside myself with the deepest of grief I have ever felt.

The additional stress and agony thinking of the inevitable and, worst of all, the possible pain and suffering ahead for my mother is tearing through my soul in places I didn't know existed.

I would take her aneurysm and cancer from her body and place it in mine in one second if I could.

I would sell my soul to the Devil to make sure my mother doesn't see one minute of suffering from either of these evils that are dwelling within her body.

There are only two furthermost depths of pain, anxiety, and emptiness remaining in this nightmare of an existence I've endured for some forty-five years;

No torment will ever equal the intensity of that emotional pain that will surge through my mind and body should I have to watch — powerlessly — my mother suffering with a cancer that is ravaging her.

All the preparation in the world cannot ready me for the deepest of anxiety and emptiness — the emotional electrocution — that is to come the day my mother passes.

I will know no greater love in this world than that of my mother.

I could know no greater pain in this world than my mother's suffering and passing.

Any time I went to visit my mother or she came to visit me, I've always bought for her the most beautiful bouquet of flowers I could find.

From the moment she arrived on that Saturday, November 8th, 2014 — and each and every week throughout the 2014/2015 holiday season that she was with me in Florida — I had waiting for her four separate bouquets of flowers.

Four (4) being my mother's favorite number.

A couple dozen roses and the most colorful and fragrant of mixed flower bouquets.

I would find as many green flowers as I could, including green roses.

Green being my mother's favorite color.

Like butterflies, flowers have always brought a smile to my mother's face and joy to her heart.

I looked deep into my mother's beautiful, clear blue eyes upon her arrival that Saturday evening — as I do each and every day we are fortunate enough to spend together. I saw no sign of distress or disease.

She was upbeat, still looked twenty years younger than she is, and appeared more spry than ever. There was no *immediate* indication — symptoms — of the evil that was lurking inside of her body.

However, I have noticed, several weeks post her arrival, that she is, more so than any time in the past, visibly worried, getting very tired, and unable to keep up the pace she once did. Age definitely one factor, her condition — the cancer continuing to spread throughout her body — another.

Forgetfulness — issues remembering — slightly more common now.

Mom is still smoking. Perhaps not as much as in the past. However, she is coughing an awful lot.

She is now quite hard of hearing. She will not even consider hearing aids. This being the least of my worries for her.

And, as always, constant bowel problems. Either continuous diarrhea or she is unable to move her bowels at all for days on end and the intestinal pressure and major problems begin. This has been happening more often the past few years — and already several times over the few weeks she's been here with me in Florida. The constipation, backed-up bowel problem is also creating additional stress and pressure for the aneurysm condition — which is not good at all.

Add her very high blood pressure to the mix — the foremost

contributing stress factor being my father — for which she's taken script meds for years, and none of this is conducive to fighting off disease or infection.

Each condition — especially her lifelong high stress and blood pressure levels — further breaks down the immune system and body itself.

My mother came down with pneumonia several years ago and began having more severe lung problems since that time. She has been coughing more and more with each passing year.

In addition, she continues to lose weight. She is a small woman to begin with coming in at five feet and weighing 100 lbs.

Her cancer no doubt contributing to, more than likely causing, her noticeable weight loss and increase in coughing.

My mother underwent further testing when she had pneumonia and was then diagnosed with the first stages of chronic obstructive pulmonary disease (COPD). Her doctors told her to cut back on the smoking.

Smoking has always been one of the few things that, according to my mother, actually calmed her nerves. She's a nervous wreck 24/7 as a result of being around my father and — again reiterating — most recently, dealing and living with the pain of being betrayed by her own children and grandchildren. The smoking also seems to calm and relax her in the morning and usually, strangely enough, and according to my mother, helps her to move her bowels — relieve her constipation. She calls the cigarette her "physic" (an old-fashioned term for "laxative"). Another double-edged sword if ever there was one.

I am helpless but for trying my best to stay positive and strong and spend as much quality time with her as I can while she is still mentally and physically able. Easier said than done, as too often when I look at her I find myself hurrying off to another room where I break down and cry.

I have, unfortunately (or not), broken down in front of her a couple times. We have also cried together. As always — even during this most dire of circumstances — she tells me not to worry, she doesn't want me to get sick over this. She points out her age and that we all have to die.

I understand and accept the circle of life. I am not sure that I can ever accept the pain and suffering that often accompanies it at the final stages of that cycle — especially to those among us who are truly angels on this earth, as my mother most certainly is.

With or without assistance, we should all — most specifically, those among us who have been diagnosed *terminally ill* — be able to die in peace, pain-free, and with dignity as life comes full circle.

My greatest fear is the pain and suffering, emotional and physical deterioration that may lie ahead for my mother.

35

On the flip side of all this — as my heart shatters knowing that this is more than likely the last holiday season I will ever see and be able to spend time with my mother — I am once again struggling through non-stop aggravation, complete revulsion, and greatly increased stress and anxiety being around my father. My blood pressure is simply through the roof.

It is difficult enough trying to remain calm and maintain my sanity in my father's presence alone — it's 24/7 *agita* of the worst kind being under the same roof with both of my parents. It has always been this way.

There has been no change since my childhood in these departments with the exception that it has gotten worse.

No matter their age or the severity of health issues, there has been no improvement in the toxic atmosphere that is present each and every time both of them are together in the same room. And that toxicity is without even speaking to one another. Should one speak or make a comment to the other, it simply ramps up the intensity of venom already hanging heavy in the air that surrounds them.

Either way, It's a complete nuthouse — minus the bars on the windows and the tranquilizing drugs.

It is an extremely frustrating, exceptionally sad predicament to be in. Most especially that I am unable — struggling desperately — to spend one-on-one, quality time with my mother at this critical time in her life — in our lives.

My mother's around-the-clock caregiver role began to develop as a child, when she lost her mother at the age of three. She always felt a responsibility to care for her siblings and took on the role of mother from a very early age.

With her oldest son and her husband, she continued the codependent behavior — never catching a break to care for herself. Her entire life, always giving of herself and neglecting her own wants and needs to care for others.

Even at this stage of her life — eighty-seven-years-old — cancer beginning to consume her body, and with very little time remaining — she continues to cater to her fourth child — her husband — who never grew up, waiting on him hand and foot as if he were a king.

All the while, cussing under her breath, as her vehement disgust with him and for the disconsolate life spent with him swirls about the air like a seething tornado, taking out everyone and everything in its path. It is a very powerful, asphyxiating force of negative energy that rules the air.

As a child and throughout my life, I've seen with my own eyes things my father has done and I've heard with my own ears things that he has said.

Many years ago, I told him to never treat or speak to my mother in a disrespectful way in my presence ever again. I won't stand for it. If they both choose to continue to live within that textbook codependent relationship with all the unhealthy, anxiety producing, and anger eliciting negative energy that fuels the cycle, that is between the two of them.

I set a boundary some years ago and, unfortunately, due to my mother's dire health circumstances, I went back on a promise — that boundary — to myself and allowed both of them to come to Florida this 2014/2015 holiday season where we were all under the same roof, around the clock, once again.

I had truly hoped that due to their advanced age and health issues, things would be more calm — less stressful — for once. No chance of that I found out within minutes of their arrival.

I have told my mother many times over the years that if she wanted to leave my father and that dreadful situation, I was there for her always. She could live with me and I'd take care of her.

It has always hurt me deeply knowing how truly sad she has been in this cult-like, almost brain-washed circle of codependency. In my opinion, it is a no-win situation but to completely remove oneself from the relationship or set certain firm boundaries with consequences.

My mother once said of my father, "*He's an albatross wrapped around and hanging from my neck.*" A striking visual that reveals the codependent struggle of having to deal and live with something far beyond a mere thorn in the side or simple dead weight.

I have seen it, felt it, lived it my entire life. And still some of the worst, most repulsive and insulting things I have ever heard come from my father's mouth were to come just weeks ahead.

I know the whole story, the entire truth from the inside of this exceptionally dysfunctional family. As with the story of my life that I reveal in these pages, I have barely scratched the surface of my mother's abiding agony.

4 Green Butterflies | 533

Since my childhood, my father has proven, time and again, he lacks not only the intellect to understand and to change his attitude and behaviors but also any amount of desire to do his part as a husband — as a man. It wasn't there when he was thirty-nine and it's not there fifty years later. He is still quite comfortable in his position of constantly receiving and never giving.

Any guy who believes that providing financially is all that is required as a husband and father needs a bit more than just a reality check. A mere physical presence with no emotional connection and support is detrimental to the development of children and any meaningful relationship.

Though my father hasn't treated or spoken to my mother disrespectfully in my presence in many years, I know it continues in private even after I explained to him, time and again over many years, in detail, that men — real men — don't speak and treat a woman in certain ways. My words have always fallen on deaf ears and a maladaptive thought process.

As a man — as my mother's son — It is extremely frustrating, saddening, and rather enraging knowing what I know to be true of their codependent relationship and having to continue to be present in such a vile, sickening atmosphere of constant tension, revulsion, and anger.

My mother has been a slave to the grind of codependency as far back as I can remember, beginning with her oldest son's addictions as well as her husband's alcoholism, which rages to this very day.

She has been a prisoner to the wants and needs of others, and most tightly fettered by these two individuals.

Codependency is a form of addiction. It becomes a way of life.

Even though the addiction may be killing you — and it took a very high toll on my mother's health and well-being for decades and to this very day — it is very difficult to break free of the chains.

As I've stated many times throughout these pages, my mother deserved so much better in her life. Codependency did to her what PTSD and depression did to me — it kept a dark cloud forever lingering above her, raining down pain and sorrow. It imprisoned her.

However, we have always had each other. Each being the other's bit of light in our dark and sorrowful worlds that we cleverly disguised and hid from prying eyes in order to survive our own agonizing realities.

As I'm being bombarded by suffocating thoughts of my mother's mortality, adding fuel to an already out of control fire at this lowest, most emotionally painful time in my life — Murphy's Law forever in full swing in my world — I am, for the first time in my life, actually observing behavior and hearing jaw-dropping, bone-chilling comments from my father that have completely opened my eyes to another side of him.

Perhaps, and highly likely, I knew that side was always there but was in denial — until the truth finally and forcefully shook me like a 9.0 on a Richter scale.

His anger and frustration quite possibly heightened during this time because he was unable to drink in my home — or drink every day as had been his norm throughout his life.

He is, however, at a rather healthy, ignorantly bliss, ripe old age of eighty-nine, sneaking off every now and again to the bar area of a local restaurant for a drink.

I have also found a few empty, individual serving mini bottles — nips — in his car and the garbage can. A functioning alcoholic he'll be — and my mother a codependent slave to — until his last breath.

Perhaps years of repressed and pent up pain, disappointment, and anger in his own life he could never deal and live with without coddling the bottle — and blaming others — begins to boil over and is being released in bits and pieces of uncontrollable verbal rage in my home.

My mother has been the sole target of his disrespectful, bush-league emotional and verbal abuse as far back as I can remember.

Now, I was also being added to his angry, soul-revealing, soliloquy-like verbal bashings.

He is not senile, he doesn't suffer with Tourette's syndrome, and he is not drunk — but spurting out angry, atrocious, highly offensive comments about my mother and myself while in the bathroom or in the backyard — where he obviously believes no one can hear him.

His soul is showing its true colors, his awry mind revealing his truth as each shocking and hateful comment flows from his lips.

What I heard my father spewing — the essence of his soul and mind — during a one-month period in my home over the 2014/2015 holiday season I would never have believed if I hadn't heard it with my own ears. Especially, and most specifically, spurting out this insensitive, insulting verbiage at a time when he was aware — I had explained to him, one-on-one, face-to-face, my mother's dire condition in detail — of my mother's terminal illness and the short time she had remaining.

I eventually confronted and called him on it when I'd finally had enough of what, to me, amounted to treachery. Talking to himself in private or not, it is *what* was being said about me and my mother as well as the anger in his voice that revealed to me what his soul felt and his mind believed at that time.

Since my early childhood, it always appeared to me, and never more than at this very time, that my father lacked any capacity for sympathy and empathy and was totally consumed by self-centeredness.

Just when I thought I had felt all possible pain, disappointment, and betrayal associated with this family, I had yet another rude awakening by my father; a complete breach of trust as I saw it.

And with that, a light bulb went off in my head.

This is when I first realized the type of personality — of which some may consider a "disorder" — I was dealing with. This wasn't just a man with very limited intellectual capacity — which I'd known about my entire life and attributed this to his inability to reason and empathize — but a man with a seriously off-centered behavioral pattern untypical of the norm.

I've heard my father say on many occasions throughout my childhood and life,

"*I live in my own mind.*" He wasn't kidding, that is for sure!

His mindset a throwback to the Stone Age.

It became quite obvious to me at this time that these particular personality traits — the inability to reason, sympathize and empathize — combined with bits and pieces of that deviant behavioral pattern was the commonality among all within this immediate family, with the exception of my mother and myself.

I was now fully aware and finally understood much of my life — the emotional pain, suffering, and despair — as it was impacted and played out since childhood; my mother and I were surrounded and emotionally battered by this consistent, abusive madness and irrationality. However, and fortunately, scathed as our minds were, we always had each other — and only each other — to lean on and get through our days.

Still, after all is said and done, and aside from this underlying commonality, my father was nothing like the others; same ballpark, yes, but two totally different leagues. My father may not have had a halo surrounding his head, but he shared none of their depravity. That exceedingly evil quality and way of behaving is the key trait that separated my father from the others in this immediate family. He wasn't twisted in the same direction as these others. *These others* are disciples of the Devil. Evil to the core.

Interaction with my father or just being in his presence was no longer going to be possible at this particular time in my life — it wasn't an option any longer. It was a trigger that had caused a world of hurt since childhood and would now be a further detriment to my recovery as well as impede my ability to spend quality time with my mother during what is most likely our last time together.

I felt all along, but now knew in my soul and with absolute certainty, what I needed to do; accept and detach (*with love* as it applied to my father. I could never feel any form of love for the pure evil that was each of the others in this immediate family) in order to free myself of the chains that have emotionally bound me my entire life to him and a group of people with whom I — and my mother — had nothing in common but a skin color gene.

A group of people with whom compassion and intelligent communication was not possible.

A group of people who contributed heavily to the disorders that controlled and ruined most of my life.

A group of people who contributed heavily to my beloved mother's emotional pain, suffering, and health issues.

Detachment was absolutely necessary to my recovery process and for my emotional survival.

As I'd done years earlier with the others in this immediate family who have contributed tremendously to my — and my mother's — years of pain and suffering, I would have to cut all ties — at least temporarily — with my father in the weeks to come. Again, this was absolutely necessary in order to maintain what sanity remained in my life and to be able to focus completely on my mother and our time remaining together.

Only difference with this detachment being, while I lost a lot of respect for my father over the years, I still cared for and loved him, as I know somewhere in his heart and his own world of obstructed emotions he cared for and loved my mother and me. I had not an ounce of concern or love remaining for the others. And can say with certainty, I never will again.

After decades of agonizing trauma — much of it at the hands of my own immediate family — which began at the much too early age of five-years-old, I finally realized, as a result of this incident with my father and during this recovery time in my life, the truth — the reality — of this immediate family; they all certainly inherited a couple specific, negative personality traits of my father's; that inability to reason and empathize. In that respect, they were carbon copies. In my father's defense, however, he wasn't "evil" or "conniving", as the others were. These others were at the extreme end of heartless and malicious. A level unknown and inconceivable to most. A wicked, despicable attitude and abusive, destructive behavioral pattern that existed within this immediate family and that besieged and emotionally tormented both my mother and me.

I may not have wanted to believe it, but the evidence — extreme and repetitive instances of insensitive and mean-spirited actions — was much too clear and convincing at this point.

What I first began to see and feel from childhood, and then again, never so strongly, in 2009 when I returned to Rhode Island from Las Vegas, had come full circle.

That final piece of the puzzle had fit and the picture it revealed truly sickened me.

The impact of the reality before me — the newfound clarity — was like getting kicked in the nuts. However, and oddly enough, that crushing truth had liberated me.

In order to do the disrespectful and intentionally hurtful things these people have done — consistently, with no remorse whatsoever — to their mother, their grandmother, it is simply impossible to have a *conscience* or a *heart*.

This truth was the final piece of the puzzle that eluded me my entire life.

This immediate family has proven to be incapable of feeling genuine concern and love for anyone but themselves.

These people feel no shame, guilt, or remorse.

They are entirely self-serving.

Never willing or able to admit when wrong.

Never willing or able to apologize or feel compassion and empathy for others.

This has been the case, over and over again, as far back as I can remember.

They have demonstrated, time and again, a complete lack of conscience and heart.

It is impossible to reason with this type of person. It is a complete waste of time and energy to even try. After a lifetime of dealing with, learning firsthand from, and being victimized by this type of twisted personality, I can say with certainty that the only way I was able to protect myself from the continuing, destructive negative impact it — they — had on my life was to completely detach; get as far away as fast as possible, disengage and distance myself both emotionally and physically.

As far back as I can remember, and never so clearly as this very day, I've watched the majority of this immediate family walk all over my mother like a dirty door mat.

My mother has been an emotional punching bag — disrespected, used, and abused — by her very own blood.

I can forgive — and have — those that have hurt *me* personally and purposefully.

I will never forgive a family that has caused so much pain and trauma — such emotional devastation — in my mother's life.

At long last, however, through four-plus decades of unwavering, pure misery and the past two years of an eye-opening therapy and recovery process, the *silver lining* is in finally becoming aware, understanding, processing, accepting, and *letting go* of a reality — an immediate family — that had consistently tormented, traumatized, and devastated my entire existence.

Through an unmerciful pain and darkness that continues to stalk me, I am staying focused on the positive, the road and work ahead of me, and those that I truly cherish and love.

One of those upsides for me at this particular time is watching the incredible bond and genuine love between my mother and my boy, Max. Two souls on this planet I love dearly and know will always love me, always have my back, and never betray me.

Max took immediately to my mother when they first met in Vegas just weeks after I got him. Almost ten years ago! I never realized until recently just how precious time really is. It waits for no one. Before we know it, the curtain falls on yet another chapter of life and it — and those you love — is gone in the blink of an eye.

Max becomes my mother's shadow whenever they get to see each other and spend time together. More so now, as I sense he feels my pain and worry this time around. He won't let her out of his sight, tagging along wherever she might go — from the bathroom to smoking a cigarette outside. He's always right by her side.

She carries on regular conversations with him. Max understanding and responding to every word.

She's commented many times that he's smarter than some people she knows. I couldn't agree more, adding he is also loyal and has a big, loving heart unlike many people that have been in our lives.

She truly loves his company. He keeps a steady smile on her face, joy just beaming from her when they are together. Seeing their special relationship brings that same joy to my soul. It's a beautiful thing to watch and to feel. More than anything, he makes my mother laugh and feel genuine love, and that is priceless to me.

36

Thanksgiving 2014 arrived. It was a little bittersweet. I was making progress in that I was feeling a bit better emotionally than I had in years and I was looking forward to going to spend Thanksgiving with family — something I hadn't done in well over thirty years. This being another major step in the right direction. However, I was dying inside knowing this would most likely be the last Thanksgiving I was able to speak to, see, and hug my mother.

I was having some anxiety just thinking what may transpire in front of all these people should my thoughts begin to focus on my mother's condition and mortality whenever I looked at her.

I had been breaking down almost every time I looked at her over the past couple of weeks since she had arrived. I didn't want to have anxiety and panic attacks, completely breaking down in front of all these people. Again, this is one of the main reasons — anxiety and panic attacks — that I've been in isolation the past thirty-plus years.

I kept at my emotional calisthenics of repetitive, positive thoughts and prepared myself to go to Thanksgiving dinner at my cousin's house — where my aunt, uncle, cousins, and family friends would all be gathered to share the special day with my mother, father, and myself.

My going meant the world to my mother as I hadn't been to a family function or holiday gathering in well over three decades. I wasn't about to let my mother down. Being with and around her family has always been her happiness — what has kept her together and going.

We arrived at my cousin's house where I had the chance once again to see and be with family and friends. Some I hadn't seen since my early teenage years. Some I'd never met before.

The one thing that stands out to me over all else this day is the happiness that was beaming from my mother. It was for me a blessing as I was able to see my mother in her truest form; full of joy as she was surrounded by family — real family. Those that genuinely care for and love her deeply.

It was only the second time in over thirty years that I sat among family at a social function. The first in over thirty years that I sat with family at a holiday dinner.

All-in-all, it was yet another positive step in the direction of recovery; finding balance, light in the darkness, peace of mind and soul.

I did have a few incidents of minor anxiety but, thankfully, I was able to keep it in check and under control.

It turned out to be one of the most peaceful, meaningful days I have had in decades.

It had been a very, very long time since I'd seen my mother so full of life and so very happy as she was on this day.

My mother told me that evening before she went to bed that it was the best Thanksgiving she's ever had — because I was there, smiling, and appeared comfortable in my own skin for once in my life.

The day certainly was a blessing for us in many ways.

It is now two weeks from Christmas 2014 as I bring my story to a close.

I am hoping that my mother remains healthy and her Christmas this year is as joyful to her as Thanksgiving was. I will do everything in my power to make that happen.

My mother's 88th birthday is coming up in February. There are plans for us to get together with some family (in Florida) to celebrate.

I am remaining positive, hopeful, and staying as strong as possible so that we may share what has always been and will always be the most important, cherished day of the year to me and in my life: the second day of February; the day a bona fide angel — *my mother, my friend, my strength, my light* — was born into this world.

AFTERWORD

Hearing of my mother's aneurysm in July 2014 did to me emotionally and immediately what my 1996 line of duty accident did to me physically, only multiplied a hundred times over. It simply crushed me as I'd never been crushed before.

Speaking with her doctor four months later in November of 2014 and hearing the word *cancer* attached to lesions found in her lungs and liver was, in a split second, my fall of 2005 and subsequent rock bottom of 2008 all over again, combined and multiplied one thousand times over. No news could possibly be worse for me and in my life than my mother's terminal cancer diagnosis.

It ripped to milli-shreds what little was remaining of my broken, beaten heart.

It sucked but the very last breath from my body.

It created an instantaneous, viciously gut-wrenching pain and void, sorrow and suffering like I'd never felt during my entire existence crawling through those bowels of hell.

Above all else I've endured in my life, this news — this reality — shook me the hardest and most violently.

My mother's mortality sank to the core of my soul. It was an overwhelming feeling of emptiness and an agony of another depth I'd never experienced before.

I felt my anchor in this bitterly cold, deep and dark sea of disorders was slowly being raised and taken from me.

As I'd lost my ability to train — my medication — many years earlier, I was now faced with losing the linchpin that kept that final seam intact and from bursting throughout my entire life; my beloved mother — the tether that spared me, time and again, from a straight-out splattering.

I have had an extremely difficult time with the sickness or death of loved ones since childhood. This, however, is my mother. The most important and loved person in my agonizing and godforsaken world.

No amount of emotional calisthenics could keep my keel even and focused on *any* positive thought upon hearing this news. I cried uncontrollably for several weeks on end — and do to this day — dwelling on my mother's mortality and the deepest of heartaches and emptiness that will settle in and forever reside in my soul from that day she is no more until my very last breath.

A void that will reliably and tormentingly ache in complete blackness.

My deepest pain and darkest days are ahead of me.

Of all the inordinate, consistent and debilitating emotional and physical pain and suffering I've endured over the past 40-plus years, all of it combined will be nothing compared to the extreme agony that will come the day my mother passes. The fight of my life will begin that very day.

There is only one scenario that can possibly be worse — more painful and damaging to my soul — than my mother's passing; If I have to watch, helplessly, my mother suffering, her mind and body slowly and painfully being ravaged by cancer.

My only hope to continue forward from what will no doubt be the absolute worst day(s) of my entire life will be focusing on the positive, guiding light of forever nurturing love and compassion that my mother sowed in my very being beginning way back on the first of my days in the summer of 1964.

I have had no greater love, support, or inspiration to keep breathing than that of my mother. A true angel on this earth and in my life. She has been the only flicker of light to ever enter the darkness that has been my reality since childhood.

My mother taught and instilled in me compassion, kindness, and unconditional love. Strength, honor, and loyalty.

All that I ever was, all that I am today, and all I may ever be, I owe to my mother.

My mother has always been my one and only cheering section. Always offering words of wisdom and encouragement. Always telling me to keep my head up and to believe in myself. She may not have known the depth of what I was going through most of my life, but she did feel — maternal instinct — some of my pain and despair.

Later in life when I began therapy and a recovery process — started to peel off that mask and discuss the totality of my pain and suffering — my mother couldn't believe what I'd been going through and living with. What I'd been concealing since childhood. She cried and cried. I made sure that she knew she was the only reason I survived to begin with. She should be proud of the mother and person she is and always has been. I wanted her to know that her tears should be of joy. I was finally — after 40-plus years of emotional suffocation — starting to breathe freely, see clearly, and progressing in a positive direction emotionally.

I needed her to know that I was now moving towards a better place in my soul and in my mind and I could never have done that without her in my life.

Only that God I am still at war with knows how many times I've dangled from that ledge over the decades. My mother being the sole reason I never clutched the hand of insanity and took that final, fatal step.

She has always been that guiding light and motivation that kept me hanging on from childhood until this very day.

She is the force behind my moving on and towards helping others suffering as I have suffered.

Through all the trauma and heartache that has been her life, her faith has never wavered. She has always maintained her incredible, engaging sense of humor. Her smile always the magic that lights up any room. Always a way of making everyone — anyone — feel joy, love, and happiness when around her.

Those beautiful, clear blue eyes a reflection of the most loving, peaceful soul I've ever known.

A woman small in stature and dwarfed furthermore by the biggest, warmest, most loving of hearts her God ever granted to our kind.

My mother is my hero. My number one idol. She has been the lone anchor in this savage sea of mayhem that has been my world.

The only positive force and light that has ever seeped through the perennial gloom that smothered all of my days.

My mother is the inspiration that fuels my passion to help as many people as I can who suffer and exist each day with debilitating emotional and/or physical pain from or from going to that diabolical darkness I've endured without remission for over forty years.

My mother is the oxygen that keeps this shattered and heavy heart beating and this new-found meaning and fire burning.

My spirit charred but strengthened. My soul ripped open but enlightened. I hold out hope for days of warm, bright sunshine and brilliant blue, joyous skies. And one day — in my mother's name and honor — fulfilling my meaning in this life and, finally, basking in that peace and happiness that was my mother's wish and prayer for me.

My Mother

My Friend

My Strength

My Light

In Loving Memory of My Mother,

O.M.M.

2.2.27 - 6.12.15

I Love You Always and Forever.

Thank you for taking the time to read my story.
If you have any questions, suggestions, or would like to lend
a hand with my mission, you are always welcome to contact
me.

4GreenButterflies@gmail.com

Made in the USA
Middletown, DE
25 March 2016